N.P. Day

Frontispiece

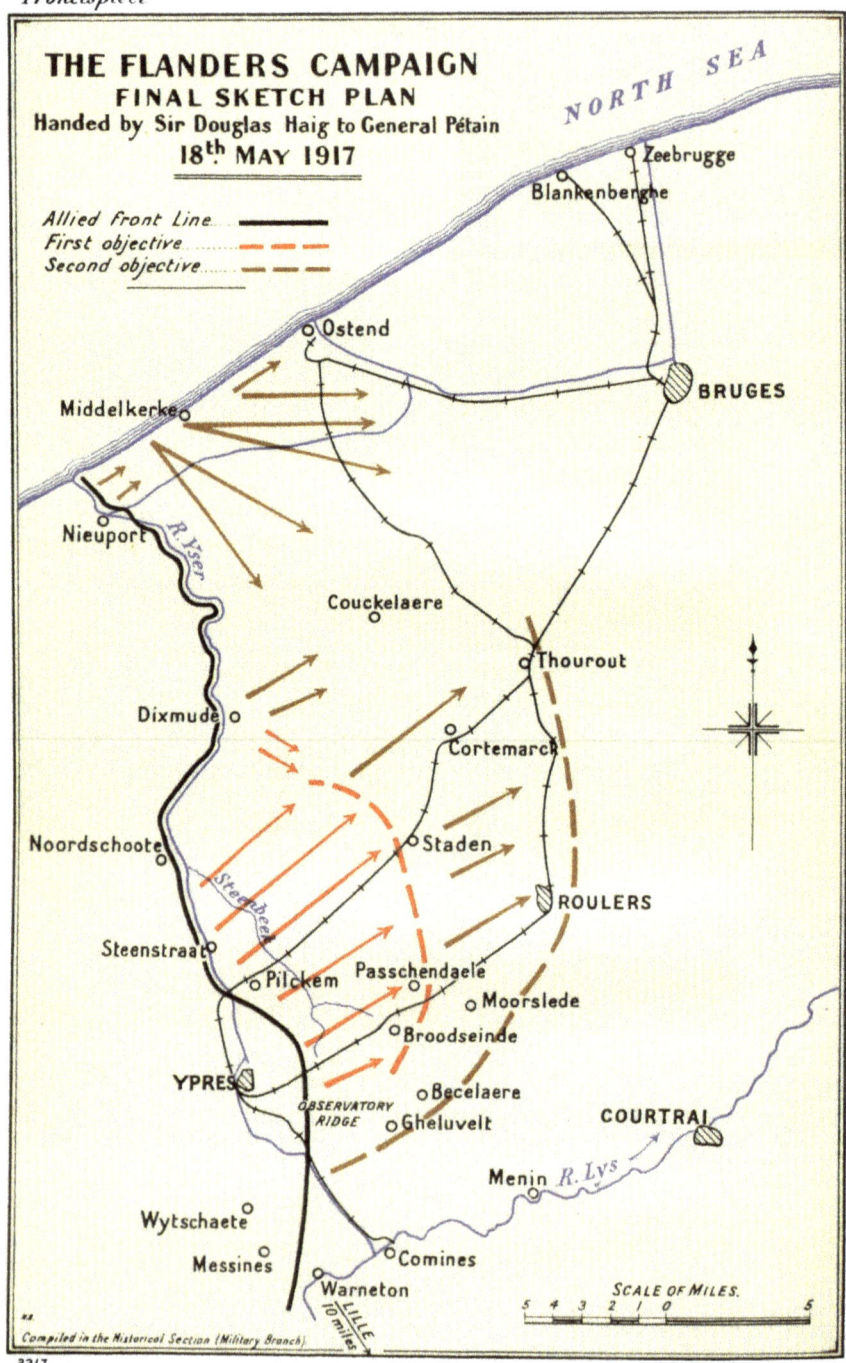

HISTORY OF THE GREAT WAR

BASED ON OFFICIAL DOCUMENTS
BY DIRECTION OF THE HISTORICAL SECTION OF THE
COMMITTEE OF IMPERIAL DEFENCE

MILITARY OPERATIONS FRANCE AND BELGIUM

1917

VOLUME II
7th JUNE — 10th NOVEMBER

MESSINES AND THIRD YPRES (PASSCHENDAELE)

Completed and Edited by
BRIGADIER-GENERAL SIR JAMES E. EDMONDS, C.B., C.M.G.,
HON. D. LITT. (*Oxon.*) R.E. (*Retired*) p.s.c.†

The Naval & Military Press Ltd

in association with

The Imperial War Museum
Department of Printed Books

Published jointly by
The Naval & Military Press Ltd
Unit 10 Ridgewood Industrial Park,
Uckfield, East Sussex,
TN22 5QE England
Tel: +44 (0) 1825 749494
Fax: +44 (0) 1825 765701

www.naval-military-press.com
www.military-genealogy.com
www.militarymaproom.com

and

The Imperial War Museum, London
Department of Printed Books

www.iwm.org.uk

In reprinting in facsimile from the original, any imperfections are inevitably reproduced and the quality may fall short of modern type and cartographic standards.

PREFACE

This volume contains the account of the two Flanders offensives of 1917 called, officially, "The Battle of Messines 1917" (7th–14th June), and "The Battles of Ypres 1917" (31st July–10th November)—the latter better known as "Third Ypres" or even as "Passchendaele". The Ypres offensive, according to the official "Battle Nomenclature", includes eight battles: Pilckem Ridge (31st July–2nd August), Langemarck (16th–18th August), Menin Road Ridge (20th–25th September), Polygon Wood (26th September–3rd October), Broodseinde (4th October), Poelcappelle (9th October), First Passchendaele (12th October) and Second Passchendaele (26th October–10th November).

The Battle of Messines, with its tremendous artillery bombardment and its record explosion of land mines containing nearly a million pounds of high explosive, was a triumph of organization and of the co-operation of the artillery and the engineers with the infantry; it was one of the very few operations of the War in which the infantry, without tanks, had scarcely more to do than go forward and take possession. The only controversial point about "Messines" is whether, to avoid the heavy casualties which ensued, the infantry should not have gone farther, or whether the main line gained should not have been withdrawn to the reverse slope of the ridge.

With the long-drawn-out fighting before Ypres it is very different. Almost every point in connection with it became in the after years a matter of controversy, or rather a reason for attacking the reputation of Field-Marshal Earl Haig. Its inception, its execution, its continuance, and the ground conditions all came under public review. The campaign was adjudged by (at the time) influential civilian critics as "purposeless", "a reckless gamble . . . with nothing to show but a ghastly casualty list", "a muddy and muddle-headed adventure". Most extraordinary legends obtained circulation and gained general credence. To distort the picture, the name of "Passchendaele", that of part, and the bad part of the battle, which rightly belongs only to the last period of four weeks after the weather had broken and conditions did become appalling, has been attached to the whole three and a half months which the Third Battle of Ypres lasted. Thus " Passchendaele " came to connote not, as it should, a wonderful Canadian success in mud and rain, but a long persistent struggle under such conditions. Essential facts were entirely overlooked : e.g., that September 1917 was a month of fine weather, that several attacks were made in clouds of dust—once through "a wall of dust and smoke"—and that the ground was so hard as late as the morning of the 4th October that pieces of shell and bullets ricochetted.[1] Ignored, too, were the very good reasons, secret at the time, for attacking in Flanders and continuing to attack in spite of adverse conditions. These reasons were the urgent demands of General Pétain for a diversion on account of the mutinies which had spread through a large part of the French army, and the demands of the British Admiralty, in consequence of huge shipping losses, for the suppression of the U-boat bases on the Flemish coast. The Intelligence reports of the very serious enemy casualties and the lasting effect of the campaign on his plans and on the morale of his troops and of his Homeland, now known to be correct, were labelled " extravagant " and " ridiculous ".

Aspersions on the military character of Field-Marshal Earl Haig should not require contradiction, and the minimizing, even complete ignoring, of the success of his troops, both British and Dominion, should not require correction ; but some refutation of the legend cannot be entirely neglected. The mis-statements continue to flourish. They crystallize in what was written in a newspaper article on Earl Haig, eighteen years after events.[2]

> " Why has not Haig been recognized as one of
> " England's greatest generals ? Why, as a national
> " figure, did he count far less than Lord Roberts, whose
> " wars were picnics by comparison ? The answer may
> " be given in one word—' Passchendaele ' ".

---

[1] The dated photographs in this volume and in the A.O.A., and the Canadian map reproduced in Sketch 28, might now be examined. The margins of the streams only were boggy.
[2] *News Chronicle* of 25th March 1935.

PREFACE

Our late enemy thought differently. The following truly represents German military opinion.[1]

"The circumstance that Haig never could act really independently, but always had to make his decisions subject to conditions imposed on him, is no reason to deny him the position of a commander-in-chief. Dependence on others was often the fate of great commanders. What is more important is whether his actions were conducted with strategic ability, firm will, strength of character, acceptance of responsibility and political insight. Haig possessed all these qualities and used them in 'harmonious combination' as Clausewitz requires of a great commander. By means of these powers he saved France in 1916 and 1917, and pre-eminently on that historic day, the 26th March, 1918.[2] Finally: if the ultimate victory over the Central Powers was not accomplished on the battlefield, but was gained on quite another plane, yet in the last three years of the war Haig contributed the most to prevent a German victory. Thus he really remained 'master of the field'".

The reputation of Earl Haig has undoubtedly suffered in England and Wales from the label "Passchendaele" being attached to him—to connote unnecessary suffering and all the horrors of winter warfare—but it stands high not only in Germany, but in France and in the U.S.A.

The principal items in the indictment against Earl Haig in legend depend on gross exaggeration of the British casualties and on the misrepresentation that the whole area of the battlefield was a morass, ignoring that really muddy conditions were confined to certain stretches and patches, and that the really bad weather extended only over the first and last periods.

---

[1] Translated from " Heerführer des Weltkrieges (Great Commanders of the World War) ", issued by the " Deutschen Gesellschaft für Wehrpolitik und Wehrwissenschaften ", the equivalent of our Royal United Service Institution. It contains excellent appreciations of ten great commanders of 1914-18 by different hands. The selected ten are the younger Moltke, Joffre, Falkenhayn, Conrad, Alexeiev, Enver, Cadorna, Haig, Foch and Hindenburg-Ludendorff. The Grand Duke Nicholas, Maréchal Pétain and General Diaz are not included and neither Sir John French nor Nivelle.

[2] This must refer to the Doullens Conference, when at Haig's suggestion Foch was appointed to co-ordinate the operations—and make Pétain fight.

As the charges have been made publicly by no less a personage than the Prime Minister at the time, the late Earl Lloyd George, they cannot be overlooked here.[1] The statement, made by him and other eminent writers, which colours the whole of the indictment of Haig is the easiest disproved. It is that the casualties at "Passchendaele" were "gigantic", "nearly 400,000", "more than at the "Somme".[2] The source of this total appears to be the German wireless; it is found in the Bavarian Official Account;[3] "An 400,000 Mann hatte der Feind auf den "Schlachtfeldern Flanders verloren (the enemy had lost about 400,000 men on the battlefields of Flanders)". The statement laid in February 1919 before the Versailles Supreme War Council, when every endeavour was made to make the total as large as possible, gave it as 244,897, including the normal wastage on the Ypres front. The "Total Battle and Trench Wastage by weeks 31st July– "10th November, 1917", compiled at the time by Armies, comes to 238,313.[4] These are contemporary figures, not "an elaborate effort to gerrymander the casualty returns".

The battlefield, it was said, was "a reclaimed swamp, which "was only prevented returning to its original condition of "a soggy morass by an elaborate system of drainage". A glance at Map I[5] will show that the scene of the struggle is the ridge on the eastern side of Ypres and the gentle slope leading up to it from the Yser canal; it has never been a morass, except, perhaps, in Mesozoic times, and was drained

---

[1] See "Lloyd George" in the Book List.
[2] The British casualties at the Somme totalled 419,654. See "1916" Vol. I, p. 497. At Arras (9th April–4th May 1917), that is in less than one month, about 150,000. See "1917", Vol. I, p. 556.
[3] Published in 1921, second edition in 1923, p. 410.
[4] This table is given at the end of Chapter XVIII. A check on the total was made by adding together the casualties given in the war diaries of the combatant units. Excluding some of the Army Troops, this gave a total of just under 200,000.

The "Statistics of the Military Effort of the British Empire during the "Great War 1914-1920", gives the total casualties for the period 31st July to 31st December—that is seven weeks longer than the battle, and including the losses sustained in the Battle of Cambrai 1917—as 380,002 with "the number of wound casualties" "not the number of individual "wounded". The difference between the total number of "wounds" for the longer period and the number of "wounded men" in the battle is considerable, the number of wounds being 284,684 as against 172,994 wounded. Similar disparities occur as regards other battles; thus for Arras the "statistics" volume gives 178,419 wounds, instead of under 150,000 wounded. See "1917" Vol. I, p. 556.

[5] A description of the ground is given in Chapter VIII.

PREFACE

by its natural slope and a number of small streams. The words quoted above apply to a district called " les Moeres ", twenty miles away, near the coast between Furnes and Dunkirk.

The Commander-in-Chief has been blamed for defying the bad weather. It is simply not true that, as asserted, " Flanders was the wettest area on the front ", and that " in Flanders the weather broke early each August with the " regularity of an Indian monsoon "—the weather there is, of course, as variable as on the English south coast.[1] It was not the fault of Sir Douglas Haig that the Flanders campaign was begun so late in the year and thus towards the end encountered the normal October bad weather. He wished to open the operations in March or April, but was prevented from doing so by the French General Nivelle insisting that the British spring offensive should be staged at Arras, nearer to his own Aisne attack.[2]

It is not, as asserted, the case that " both British ministers " and French generals were strongly opposed to the under- " taking ", and that " the leading French generals had done " their best to dissuade us, and had stated emphatically that " they condemned the project and thought it a foolish " venture which must fail ". It was the exact contrary as regards the French: General Nivelle, when Commander-in-Chief, as early as 21st December, 1916, wrote to Sir Douglas Haig:[3] " If our grand offensive succeeds it is certain that " the Belgian coast will fall into our hands as a result of the " retreat of the German Armies and without a direct attack. " If our attacks fail, it will still be possible to carry out in " fine weather the operations projected in Flanders." When the grand offensive did fail, General Pétain, Nivelle's successor, first proposed to co-operate on the left of the British with twelve divisions, and after the mutinies in the French army arose begged for the Flanders operation, and volunteered to co-operate in it with the French First Army of six divisions. The French Official History actually states[4] that on the 30th June, 1917, when General Anthoine, commander of the French First Army, visited Sir Douglas Haig, he brought a message from General Pétain: " l'offen-

---

[1] See Chapter XI, Note I, where rainfall statistics are given.
[2] His whole letter (translated) is in " 1917 " Vol. I, Appendix II.
[3] See footnote above.
[4] F.O.A. v. (ii), p. 653.

" sive des Flandres doit etre assurée d'un succès absolu,
" '*impérieusement exigé par les facteurs moraux du moment*' ".
(Italicized in original.)

As regards British ministers, the decision to make the main British effort of 1917 in Flanders had been approved by the War Committee of the Cabinet on the 26th October, 1916, confirmed on the 23rd November by Mr. Asquith, the Prime Minister, who himself handed personally to Sir Douglas Haig a letter of approval, a copy being sent to the C.I.G.S. An offensive, leaving place and time to the generals—it was well known the place would be Flanders—was sanctioned by the Paris Conference of British and French ministers on 4th–5th May, 1917. The situation was obviously changed when the Nivelle offensive had definitely failed and the French army was declared incapable for a time of further effort. The War Cabinet then had doubts about persisting in the Flanders campaign, even after Messines Ridge had been captured. There were, however, three urgent reasons for the continuance of the campaign (that there was no alternative place is shown in Chapter XIX). First, General Pétain revealed to Sir Douglas Haig, as a military secret, the mutinous state of the French army and implored him, and continued to implore him, to attack in order to prevent the Germans from taking advantage of this state. Secondly, in consequence of the terrible losses from U-boat attacks (694 merchant ships in the first six months of 1917, amounting to over two million tons), Admiral Jellicoe, the First Sea Lord, stated to the War Cabinet that "if the army cannot get the Belgian " ports, the navy cannot hold the Channel and the War is " lost. . . . It is no good making plans for next year ". The third reason was the rapid deterioration of the situation on the Russian front.

Sir Douglas Haig was confident of success. The War Cabinet, unwilling to overrule both naval and military authorities, and officially ignorant of the French mutinies, on 20th July sanctioned the Flanders campaign on the understanding that it would be called off if progress did not reach expectations. A change of attitude more favourable to the offensive then took place probably owing to news of the French mutinies reaching them; for on the 25th July, the War Cabinet, by telegram, assured Sir Douglas Haig of their approval of his plans, and their " wholehearted support ".

PREFACE

At the end of August the Prime Minister at a War Cabinet meeting spoke about closing down the Flanders campaign, and in order to gain his own way he even contemplated a change of commander-in-chief if a suitable successor could be found. He called in for professional advice, not his constitutional advisers, but two officers, Field-Marshal Lord French and Lieut.-General Sir Henry Wilson, bitter enemies of Sir Douglas Haig, and they both supported his views.[1] Later the Prime Minister received some backing from Mr. Winston Churchill, the Minister of Munitions, who though sparing no effort to supply the army's demands, urged that the available strength should not be wasted in " bloody " and indecisive siege operations ". " The power of the " defensive ", he wrote, when presenting the munitions programme in October 1917, " has produced a deadlock, and " the British army is destined to be a holding force through- " out 1918 until the Americans can become a decisive factor".

No order to stop or to go slow was, however, sent to G.H.Q. When it was learnt that the removal of Sir Douglas Haig would entail the resignation of the C.I.G.S., with, possibly, disastrous repercussions among the public and the troops, who had full belief in " Wully ", as he was affectionately called, and implicit trust that the Commander-in-Chief would do his best for them,[2] the attempt to supersede Haig was dropped. But, as will be seen,[3] on the 16th February, 1918, Robertson was superseded as C.I.G.S. by Sir Henry Wilson and given another appointment.

Much has been said—without exaggeration as regards the last four weeks—of the dreadful conditions under which the British and Dominion troops fought. No other troops would have stuck to the task asked of them in the same way : determination to defeat the enemy came foremost. It must be remembered that the Ypres Salient, exposed as it was to ground-observed artillery fire from three sides, had a bad name with the troops, and hardly a night passed in

---

[1] See Wilson ii., pp. 16–17.
At the time, French was commanding the troops in the United Kingdom having been superseded by Haig in France in December 1915. Wilson was unemployed, having been removed from his last appointment as Chief Liaison Officer with the French as " persona non grata ".
[2] See, *inter alia*, W. B. Maxwell, in " Time Gathered ", p. 243 : " We " believed firmly in Haig. We trusted him absolutely. We followed him " blindly".
[3] See " 1918 " Vol. I, p. 88.

the medium artillery zone without heavy shelling and some bombing, and sleep was impossible. Further, that there were no communication trenches, nor tunnels (as at Vimy) to the front, so that reinforcements had to go up and wounded had to be brought down over the open, a trying ordeal, all round the clock. Mud did greatly add to the misery and discomfort; it was not the mud, however, but the myriads of shell craters, often with water in them, which were the effective military obstacle, which prevented the infantry from keeping up to the barrage and the tanks from manœuvring, which interfered with the supply of ammunition, and which formed a fatal handicap to the rapid exploitation of successes.

Mud was no novelty in Flanders, as most well-read people know, if not from the history of Marlborough's campaigns (referred to in the final Chapter) at least in connection with the classic phrase, " our Armies swore terribly in Flanders ".[1]

Both the weather and state of the ground are discussed in the course of the narration. All that need be said here is that mud in war is not unusual, that conditions on the enemy's side are depicted by him as much worse, and this is borne out by the fact that the British sick list compared with other years was " comparatively slight ", that of the Germans very heavy.

According to the Australians, as will be shown, the mud conditions were worse in October 1916 on the Somme than at Passchendaele[2]—and no reflection has ever been cast on the commanders in that battle for continuing operations into November. General Joffre indeed protested against closing them down.

Neither the Canadian Corps nor the Australian Corps, both of which were employed in the last stages of Passchendaele, made complaint of the conditions at the time or have done so since; they tackled the adverse conditions as part of the war and overcame them, as Sir Douglas Haig expected they would.

The successes of General Plumer in September and October are almost unknown to the British public although three times his Army broke through the much-vaunted

---

[1] Sterne : " Tristram Shandy ".
[2] See the description of the " appalling conditions " and " steady toll " of sickness " " 1916 " Vol. II, pp. 536–7.

PREFACE

German defence systems, causing the enemy to admit his failure (*Misserfolge*) to himself, and to review and change his defensive tactics again and again.[1] Yet the Battle of Broodseinde, "which nobody has ever heard of", put the Second Army on the top of the Ypres Ridge, and was regarded by General Plumer as " the best thing done by the " Second Army, as we had so little time to prepare " ; the Germans speak of it as " the black day of the 4th October ", on which " the German losses, particularly prisoners, were " terrifyingly (*erschreckend*) great ".[2]

With the experience of the previous October on the Somme in his mind, Sir Douglas Haig might well have brought the battle to a close after Broodseinde ; but, as he wrote to Major-General Sir John Davidson after one of the periodic attacks on himself,[3]

> "the mere suggestion of *a pause* in our attacks in the north at once brought Pétain in his train to see me and beg me to put in another effort against Passchendaele without delay. Knowing as I did what the state of the French army was in 1917 (for Pétain told me more than once about his awful anxieties), I felt thankful when the winter came and the French army was still in the field."[4]

Not a voice was raised against the continuance of the battle, not even in the War Cabinet at this stage, that is after the victory of Broodseinde. Had the French, Belgian and British armies been homogeneous like those of the German kingdoms and principalities, the main operation in Flanders might have been stopped or slowed down, and, say, a dozen divisions sent to the French area to turn the Battle of Malmaison from a limited major raid into a well-exploited victory. But equipment, ammunition and rations being different, such a transfer would have taken long to prepare and could no more have been concealed than the change of

---

[1] See Note at end of Chapter XV.
[2] Flandern 1917, p. 12 and p. 124.
[3] See *The Times* newspaper of 14th November, 1934, when Major-General Davidson published the letter. The statements in the letter were never questioned by General Pétain.
[4] General Pétain, on the 10th October, was still appealing for the protection afforded by the British attacks. Charteris ii, p. 259.
It has been suggested in view of the after-events of his life, that his spirit was broken by his anxieties during the long continuance of the mutinies.

garrison on the coast at Nieuport, which only brought disaster.[1]

The Australian Official History—and the Australian Corps was engaged in the final stage—puts this question:

"Let the student, looking at the prospect as it appeared at noon on 4th October, ask himself: ' In view of three step-by-step blows [20th, 26th September and 4th October, the battles of Menin Road Ridge, Polygon Wood and Broodseinde] all successful, what will be the result of three more in the next fortnight ? ' "[2]

Yet, if Haig had brought the operations to an end on the 5th October he would undoubtedly have been blamed for not continuing the struggle, as Ludendorff has been condemned for stopping the great offensive against Hazebrouck and the coast on the 30th April, 1918, when the advancing German troops were struggling in the mud and water of the Lys valley, and he feared that a counter-attack might overwhelm them.[3]

The effect of the battles was correctly gauged at the time by the British Intelligence. Its reports "about broken German divisions, heavy German casualties and diminishing German morale", and its claim that the enemy had been "shattered in spirit and in reserves", were not "cooked" in order to mislead the War Cabinet. They have since been fully confirmed by Field-Marshal Crown Prince Rupprecht of Bavaria, in chief command opposite the British, by his Chief of the Staff, General von Kuhl, by the German official monograph on the battle, " Flandern ", and the German Official Account.

In the first case, such was the effect of the Allied onslaught that Crown Prince Rupprecht actually considered and prepared a retirement from the Flanders front. This is what General von Kuhl, his Chief of Staff, has to say on the subject :[4]

"About the middle of October, the greater part of the divisions on the rest of the front of the Group of Armies [which extended from La Fère (15 miles south of St. Quentin) to the sea] had already been engaged

---

[1] See Chapter VII.
[2] A.O.A. iv., p. 881.
[3] See " 1918 " Vol. II, pp. 453–4.
[4] Kuhl ii., p. 114.

PREFACE

"in Flanders. On the whole front outside Flanders,
"even at the most threatened places like Lens and
"St. Quentin, we had no more than the very minimum
"of defenders to meet any diversion attacks which
"might be attempted. The Supreme Command, which
"hitherto had helped as far as its reserves permitted,
"was now, in view of the general situation, hardly in
"a position to provide reinforcements from the other
"Groups of Armies on the Western Front. It was,
"amongst other things, reckoned that the French would
"proceed to partial attacks to fix German forces on
"other parts of the front. This actually happened
"on the 23rd October at Malmaison. Crown Prince
"Rupprecht found himself compelled to consider
"whether in the case of his forces proving inadequate,
"in spite of the many disadvantages involved thereby
"[including the abandonment of the Flanders coast],
"he should not withdraw the front in Flanders so far
"back that the Allies would be forced to carry out an
"entirely new deployment of their artillery. The time
"gained thereby could be used for the building of a new
"defence front, with a shortening of its length and
"consequent economy of troops. The loss of ground
"and the moral disadvantage of retirement would have
"to be accepted. Preparations were duly made for this
"operation."

On the 11th October Crown Prince Rupprecht reported to O.H.L. that,

"in order to save material and men, it may become
"necessary to withdraw the front so far from the enemy
"that he will be compelled to make a fresh deployment
"of his artillery".

Then the October rains came, "our best ally", as the Prince entered in his diary on the 12th October. It was a close call, and the German General Staff publication on the lessons of 1914–18 admits that "Germany had been brought "near to certain destruction (*sicheren Untergang*) by the "Flanders battle of 1917 "—and thereby was compelled to attack in 1918, as the last chance of victory, with inadequate forces, and so lost the War.[1]

---

[1] " Die Vorbereitung des deutschen Heeres für die Grosse Schlacht in " Frankreich im Frühjahr 1918 ". Th. I.

What the British offensive had cost the German Armies is summed up in Crown Prince Rupprecht's Order of the Day of the 5th December 1917 :[1]

> "88 divisions (22 of them twice), the mass of the artillery reserve (*Heeresartillerie*), and other arms and formations of the central reserve have taken part in this, the most prodigious (*gewaltigsten*) of all battles so far fought.[2] Divisions disappeared by dozens into the turmoil of the battle, only to emerge from the witches' cauldron after a short period, thinned and exhausted, often reduced to a miserable remnant, and the gaping spaces left by them were filled by fresh divisions."

The official explanation of the "disaster" of the 4th October is that "the divisions were no longer what they had been, as a result of nervous exhaustion, fatigue and bloody losses".[3]

Under the 11th October, Crown Prince Rupprecht records in his diary: "most perturbing is the fact that our troops are steadily deteriorating".

Accounts from the rank and file tell a dismal story. "Owing to the constant rain and the exertions of bringing up ammunition, rations and water through the mud, there was much sickness, and nearly everyone had diarrhœa"; as early as July marauding and thieving were rife, and if the field gendarmerie interfered the soldiers "made short business of the gendarmes".[4]

Major-General Sir John Headlam, who had seen many battlefields,[5] remarked of the 3rd August battlefield that it was "the only one in which he had seen a remarkably greater number of German than British casualties".[6] With this the head of the Intelligence agreed.

Kuhl tells us that even "The Hell of Verdun" was surpassed, and that in Germany the Flanders battle has been

---

[1] It is given in Flandern 1917, p. 168 and elsewhere, but not in G.O.A. xiii.

[2] The total of 88, more than half of the German divisions on the Western Front, 156, does not include 2 divisions and a cavalry division, under General von Moser (see his "Aufzeichnungen"), kept between Bruges and Ghent watching the Dutch frontier in expectation of a British landing south of the Schelde.

[3] Flandern 1917, pp. 52 and 147.

[4] "Somme, Flandern, Arras" by Alfred Hermann, a machine gunner.

[5] He was brigadier-general commanding the 5th Division artillery in 1914 and then Artillery Adviser G.H.Q.

[6] Charteris ii, p. 246.

PREFACE

called "the greatest martyrdom of the World War".[1] As regards wastage and loss of numbers, he thus depicts the state of the German army after the Flanders battle:

> "The supply of reinforcements (*Ersatzlage*) was bound to become even more difficult in the ensuing years, so that in the end the conduct of the War was definitely influenced by it. On this point Field-Marshal Haig has been quite right: if he did not actually break through the German front, the Flanders battle consumed the German strength to such a degree that the harm done could no longer be repaired. The sharp edge of the German sword had become jagged".[2]

And the morale of the German nation was broken. One of the stoutest of the German corps commanders[3] makes this point:

> "In millions of letters from the Western Front from April to November came the ever-rising bitter complaints of the almost unbearable hardships and bloody losses in the scarcely interrupted chain of battles: Arras, Aisne-Champagne [Nivelle], Flanders, Verdun and the Chemin des Dames [Malmaison]. A hundred thousand leave men told the Home Front by word of mouth the details of the ever-growing superiority of the enemy, particularly in weapons of destruction."

The campaign was fought by Sir Douglas Haig, on a front favourable on account of its strategic advantages, in order to prevent the Germans falling upon the French Armies, shaken and dispirited after three years of unceasing warfare and finally mutinous in consequence of the losses in and failure of the Nivelle offensive, upon which such great hopes had been set. The campaign was sanctioned by the War Cabinet in consequence of the demands of the Admiralty that the Flemish coast must be cleared of the enemy. Incidentally, it was designed to drive the Germans off the high ground from which they had observation over the whole Ypres Salient. In its essential purpose and its incidental purpose, the campaign was certainly successful, but the coastal operation had to be abandoned because it depended on the

---
[1] Kuhl ii., p. 113.
[2] Kuhl ii., p. 115.
[3] Moser.

previous possession of the Ypres Ridge, and the Second Army's success in obtaining possession came too late in the season. Of the efficiency of the main operation there is no doubt. The German Official History[1] tells at length the failure of the High Command to exploit the Nivelle disaster and " to settle finally with the French army ". The outstanding reason given is that all available reserves in infantry, guns and ammunition were required to meet the succession of British offensives in Flanders during the summer and autumn of 1917.

In May, and again in June, the German Crown Prince, commanding the Group of Armies which had defeated Nivelle, proposed an attack in strength across the Aisne, opposite Paris, to test the condition of the French defences. " No one ", says the German Official History, " could have " been more eager to give the order to attack than the High " Command, if this had been considered possible ; but it " was unable to do so ". An estimate was made that such an attack would require 30 divisions, but only 23 were available, of these " 8 were already (in early June) on their " way to strengthen the Northern Group of Armies in order " to meet the British offensive in Flanders which appeared " imminent ". Actually about this time, as Monsieur Painlevé, the French War Minister, has revealed, only two reliable French divisions stood between Soissons (on the Aisne) and Paris.

The campaign had done even more than achieve two of its three purposes : the Germans claim that it affected the campaign of 1918 and the issue of the War; for it had exhausted their reinforcements, so that there was nothing left but the 1899 Class (18-year-olds, just called up) and recovered sick and wounded, whilst in the United Kingdom there were at the end of the year[2] a total of 74,403 officers and 1,486,459 other ranks, more than the total of 1,097,906 of the British Forces in France and Flanders, with 607,400 trained men immediately available—why they were not sent over to France is a matter dealt with in the story of 1918.

The campaign has been called an " unjustifiable gamble ". War is a gamble. General Sir Charles Harington has written : [3] " I do not know that any operation of war can be

---

[1] G.O.A. xii, pp. 554–566.
[2] See " 1918 " Vol. I, pp. 50 and 52.
[3] " Plumer of Messines ", p. 130.

PREFACE   xvii

" anything but a gamble unless the enemy tells you what he
" has got on the other side of the hill and the state of his
" troops ". High authorities, already quoted, regarded this
particular gamble in 1917 as justifiable. The war of 1939–45
has exhibited much more desperate gambles, among them
Dieppe and Arnhem and our great landings.[1]

The writer has permission to quote from a private letter
written to him by Marshal of the Royal Air Force Viscount
Trenchard as regards " Passchendaele ". The passage runs :

    " Tactically it was a failure, but strategically it was
" a success, and a brilliant success—in fact, it saved
" the world.

    " There is not the slightest doubt, in my opinion,
" that France would have gone out of the War if Haig
" had not fought Passchendaele, like they did in 1940
" in this war, and had France gone out of the War I feel,
" as all our man-power was in France, we should have
" been bound to collapse, or, at any rate, it would have
" lengthened the War for years."

An anonymous writer in " Blackwood "[2] has summed up :

    " Had the enemy been able to take the offensive
" against the French, nothing could have saved France
" from defeat and Britain from a Dunkirk of disastrous
" proportions.[3] That the Germans were unable to reap
" their advantage is entirely due to Haig's operations
" at Passchendaele."

The opinion of Lieut.-General Hunter Liggett, commander
of the American First Army, on " Passchendaele " also
seems to deserve quotation, as that of a very great soldier
who was in France at the time.[4]

    " They [the British] paid more for it than they
" could afford, more than it was worth in itself, but
" they had no choice. They had to ding-dong away,
" for Italy was all but out of the fighting and the
" French were just returning to it."

---

[1] The day after this was written, there appeared in the *Sunday Express* (17th February, 1946) an American account of the landing in N. Africa in November 1942. It begins in leaded letters. " It was a tremendous " gamble, much more tremendous than realized at the time ".

[2] December 1945, p. 416.

[3] It was in fear and expectation of such a situation that the " BCD Line " to cover a re-embarkation, enclosing Boulogne, Calais and Dunkirk, was laid out and construction begun in November 1914. (See " 1914 " Vol. II, p. 457.)

[4] In " A.E.F. Ten Years Ago in France ".

"The failure of Nivelle's offensive left the British to bear the brunt of the War in the West for most of the year. They battled through Flanders all the summer to such effect that the Germans were unable to exploit the near débâcle of the French."

Our former enemies are of the same opinion. Their official view is:

"There remained to the Allies as their one positive gain from the Flanders battle the certainty that, by tying down the Germans under intensely severe strain, they survived the crisis which arose in the interval between, on the one side, the breakdown of Russia, the onset of the unlimited submarine campaign, and the reverse of the French in April [Nivelle offensive] and, on the other side, the hoped-for time when American help would begin to be effective. In the year 1918 it turned out that their success definitely contributed to the result that the war ended in favour of the Allies; but when the Flanders battle was broken off they had no inducement to look on it as decisive."[1]

"There can be no doubt to-day ... that in point of fact English stubbornness bridged over the crisis in France.... The help which England brought to the cause of the Entente was justified by the result".[2]

The German Official History, published in 1942 "For Official Use Only",[3] thus sums up:

"The offensive had protected the French against fresh German attacks, and thereby procured them time to re-consolidate their badly shattered troops. It compelled O.H.L. to exercise the strongest control over and limit the engagement of forces in other theatres of war; two divisions on their way from the East for Italy [Caporetto] had to be diverted from Italy to Flanders. But, above all, the battle had led to an excessive (*übergross*) expenditure of German forces. The casualties were so great that they could

---

[1] Flandern 1917, p. 142.
[2] Kuhl ii., p. 110.
[3] Volume xiii, p. 97. See Book List.

PREFACE xix

" no longer be covered, and the already reduced battle
" strength of battalions sank significantly lower ".[1]

As in previous volumes, I am deeply indebted to the
combatants to whom the draft was circulated for providing
explanations, filling gaps and generally furnishing correc-
tions, additions and suggestions. I have specially to thank
Marshal of the Royal Air Force Viscount Trenchard, Field-
Marshal Sir Claud Jacob (II Corps), General Sir Hubert
Gough (Fifth Army), Major-General Sir John Davidson
(Operations, G.H.Q.), the late General Sir Hugh Elles
(Tank Corps), the late General Sir Charles Harington (Chief
of General Staff, Second Army), Colonel W. Robertson
(Operations, Second Army), and last, but by no means least,
Colonel A. Fortescue-Duguid, D.S.O., R.C.A., the Canadian
Official Historian of 1914-18, who, as on former occasions,
furnished me with important new matter as well as correc-
tions. Dr. C. E. W. Bean, M.A., LL.D., the Australian
Official Historian, had already published the volume of the
Australian history which covers the period, and the compilers were only too glad, as will be seen, to make use of its
material and his most valuable comments.

The photographs were selected from those in the collections
of the Imperial War Museum and the Australian War
Memorial, for whose assistance in the matter I tender my
sincere thanks. Endeavour was made in the selection to
show the nature of the communications and the worst
conditions; but only one, No. 6, could be found of the
Zillebeke valley on the 15th October, giving the scene
usually associated with " Passchendaele "

For the French operations and the account of the mutiny,
the compilers have had the benefit of the French Official
History, Tome V, deuxième volume.

The published volumes of the German Official Account
available in 1939 included Messines, but not the rest of the
period dealt with in this volume; in 1946, however, a
volume marked " *Nur zum Dienstgebrauch* (For Official Use
Only) ", which covers the " Passchendaele " period, was

---

[1] In April the battle strength of battalions had been 750, by July, even,
it was down to 713 (G.O.A. xiii., p. 24) ; then it fell to 640 (See p. 362).
The fire-power of the infantry, however, had been increased by the issue
in " the second quarter of July 1917 " of the light machine gun.

obtained for me by Lieut.-General Sir Brian Robertson, Deputy Commander-in-Chief in Occupied Germany. There are available also the short Bavarian Official Account, a German General Staff monograph, Flandern 1917, the War Diary of Field-Marshal Crown Prince Rupprecht of Bavaria (who was in command of the Group of Armies engaged in the battles), the two-volume history of General von Kuhl (Rupprecht's Chief of the Staff), besides a mass of regimental histories and minor works.

This volume was begun in September 1939, immediately on the completion of " 1917 " Volume I. Owing to the war, one after another, the officers successively employed on it were transferred to employment on more important work, and it was left to me to collate and edit their unfinished drafts and complete the book. For any comments made and any opinions expressed in it I am solely responsible.

I have again received very great assistance from members of the staff of the Historical Section (Military Branch I), particularly from Mr. A. W. Tarsey, who has been responsible for all the clerical work and for the circulation of the drafts. I have again had the benefit of the invaluable criticism of Mr. C. T. Atkinson, M.A. (Oxon.), Major-General Sir Henry Thuillier and Captain Wilfred Miles. The maps and sketches have been fairdrawn for reproduction by Mr. H. Burge.

As all officers concerned may not have seen the draft or the proof sheets, or may not agree with what has been printed, I beg, as I have done in previous volumes, that corrections or additions, and any criticism thought necessary, may be sent to the Historical Section, Cabinet Office, Great George Street, Westminster, London, S.W.1.

9th April 1947   J. E. E.

NOTES

The location of troops and places is written from right to left of the front of the Allied Forces, unless otherwise stated ; in translations from the German the order is as in the original ; otherwise enemy troops are enumerated like the British. Where roads which run through both the British and German lines are described by the names of towns or villages, the place in British hands is mentioned first, thus : "Albert–Bapaume road ".

To save space and bring the nomenclature in line with " Division ", " Infantry Brigade " has in the text been abbreviated to " Brigade ", as distinguished from " Cavalry Brigade " and "Artillery Brigade " ; " Regiment " similarly means " Infantry Regiment ".

The convention observed in the British Expeditionary Force is followed as regards the distinguishing numbers of Army, Corps, Divisions, etc., of the British and Allied Armies, e.g., they are written in full for Armies, in Roman figures for corps, and in Arabic for smaller formations and units, except Artillery Brigades, which are Roman ; but for artillery brigades with numbers higher than one hundred, Arabic figures are used, as was the custom at the time ; thus : Fourth Army, IV Corps, 4th Cavalry Division, 4th Division, 4th Cavalry Brigade, 4th Brigade, IV Brigade R.F.A.

German formations and units, to distinguish them clearly from the Allies, are printed in italic characters, thus : *First Army, I Corps, 1st Division.*

The usual Army abbreviations of regimental names have been used : for example, " 2/R. West Kent" or " West Kent " for 2nd Battalion, The Queen's Own Royal West Kent Regiment ; K.O.Y.L.I. for the King's Own Yorkshire Light Infantry ; K.R.R.C. for the King's Royal Rifle Corps. To avoid constant repetition, the " Royal " in regimental titles is sometimes omitted. To economize space the 63rd (Royal Naval) Division, the 14th (Light) Division, etc., are usually described by their numbers only.[1]

First-line and Second-line Territorial Force units are distinguished by a figure in front of the battalion or other number, thus : 1/8th London, 2/8th London, 1/3rd London or 2/3rd London Field Company R.E., or, when the First-line and Second-line had been amalgamated, simply 3/London ; but in the case of First-line units, the figure in front of the battalion number is sometimes omitted. Amalgamated units are shown

---

[1] The Yorkshire Regiment is usually called in the text by its ancient name " The Green Howards ".

as 5th/6th London (sometimes by a printing error, not corrected in order to save expense, as 5/6 London).

Abbreviations employed occasionally are :
  B.E.F. for British Expeditionary Force ;
  D.A.N. for Détachment d'armée du Nord ;
  G.A.C. for Groupe d'armées du Centre ;
  G.A.E. for Groupe d'armées de l'Est ;
  G.A.N. for Groupe d'armées du Nord ;
  G.A.R. for Groupe d'armées du Réserve ;
  G.H.Q. for British General Headquarters ;
  G.Q.G. for French Grand Quartier-Général (usually spoken as " Grand Q.G.").
  O.H.L. for German *Oberste Heeresleitung* (German Supreme Command). *N.B.*—" G.H.Q. in German means Grosses Haupt-Quartier, that is the Kaiser's Headquarters, political, military and naval, as distinguished from O.H.L.
  R.I.R. (on maps) for Reserve Infantry Regiment.

The spellings of " lacrymatory " and " strongpoint " are arbitrary, and were selected as being shorter than the usual ones.

Officers are described by the rank which they held at the period under consideration. To save space the initials instead of the Christian names of knights are generally used.

The German pre-war practice of writing the plain name without " von ", when it is applicable and no rank or title is prefixed, has been adopted, e.g., " Falkenhayn " and not " von Falkenhayn ".

Both belligerents had adopted Summer Time, the Allies on the night of the 9th–10th March ; it ended for both on 30th September–1st October. So throughout the volume German time is one hour ahead of British time.

Owing to printing restrictions, map references, instead of being in the margin as in earlier volumes, are given in footnotes.

The casualty totals given in the German Official History " do " not include the wounded whose recovery was to be expected " within a reasonable time " (G.O.A. xi., p. 41). For comparison with the British 30 per cent., probably not enough, should be added to the German totals.[1]

---

[1] See " 1916 " Vol. I, pp. 496-7, on this subject.

CONTENTS

CHAPTER I

PLANS FOR A FLANDERS CAMPAIGN

	PAGE
THE 1916 PLAN	1
EFFECT OF THE BATTLES OF VERDUN AND THE SOMME	6
THE CHANTILLY CONFERENCE: 15TH NOVEMBER 1916	7

CHAPTER II

PLANS FOR A FLANDERS CAMPAIGN (*concluded*)

THE 1917 PLAN	11
SELECTION OF GENERAL GOUGH	19
NIVELLE'S FAILURE	20
THE FRANCO-BRITISH MILITARY CONFERENCE: 4TH MAY	22
THE INTER-ALLIED CONFERENCE: 4TH–5TH MAY	22
THE ARMY COMMANDERS' CONFERENCE AT DOULLENS: 7TH MAY	24
DOUBTS OF FRENCH SUPPORT	25
THE FRENCH MUTINIES	28

CHAPTER III

THE BATTLE OF MESSINES 1917 (7TH–14TH JUNE)

GENERAL PLAN	32
THE MINES AND ENGINEER PREPARATIONS ...	35
BOMBARDMENT	41
THE BARRAGES AND THE FINAL COUNTER-BATTERY CONCENTRATION	46
Notes: I. Tank Organization and the Mark IV Model	50
II. Details of the Messines Mines	52

CHAPTER IV

THE BATTLE OF MESSINES 1917 (*continued*)

ZERO HOUR	54
THE ASSAULT	55
CAPTURE OF THE RIDGE	61

xxiii

CHAPTER V

THE BATTLE OF MESSINES 1917 (*concluded*)

	PAGE
THE GERMAN COUNTER-ATTACKS	71
ADVANCE TO THE OOSTTAVERNE LINE	75
CONSOLIDATION	81
THE MESSINES VICTORY NOT EXPLOITED	88
Note: The German Defence	90

CHAPTER VI

THE NORTHERN OPERATIONS

DOUBTS AS TO THE CONTINUATION OF THE FLANDERS CAMPAIGN	96
SANCTION BY THE WAR CABINET	103
THE CONCENTRATION IN FLANDERS	106

CHAPTER VII

THE NORTHERN OPERATIONS (*concluded*)

FEINT ATTACKS TOWARDS LENS AND LILLE (26TH–30TH JUNE)	112
THE GERMAN ATTACK AT NIEUPORT (10TH–11TH JULY)	116

CHAPTER VIII

THE BATTLES OF YPRES 1917 (31ST JULY–10TH NOV.) BATTLE OF PILCKEM RIDGE (31ST JULY–2ND AUG.)

THE PRELIMINARIES:

THE GENERAL PLAN	124
THE GROUND	125
THE FIFTH ARMY SCHEME	126
ZERO DAY POSTPONED	132
THE PRELIMINARY BOMBARDMENT	133
THE YSER CANAL CROSSED NORTH OF BOESINGHE	139
Note: The German Flanders Position in 1917 ...	141

CHAPTER IX

BATTLE OF PILCKEM RIDGE (*continued*)

THE CONCENTRATION	147
THE ASSAULT:	
THE SECOND ARMY	149
THE FIFTH ARMY	150

CONTENTS

CHAPTER X

BATTLE OF PILCKEM RIDGE (*concluded*)

	PAGE
THE MAIN OFFENSIVE CONTINUED	164
THE GERMAN COUNTER-ATTACKS	168
RESULTS OF THE BATTLE	177
THE FIFTH ARMY SCHEME NOT ALTERED	180

CHAPTER XI

THE FAILURE AT GHELUVELT PLATEAU (10TH AUG.) AND THE BATTLE OF LANGEMARCK (16TH–18TH AUG.)

RAIN HOLDS UP OPERATIONS	183
FAILURE AT GHELUVELT (10TH AUGUST)	184
BATTLE OF LANGEMARCK (16TH AUGUST):	
THE MAIN ATTACK	190
THE NORTHERN FLANK	198
THE BATTLE DIES DOWN	202
PRINCIPAL RÔLE TRANSFERRED TO GENERAL PLUMER	206
CASUALTIES AND RESULTS OF THE MONTH'S FIGHTING	208
Notes: I. Rainfall	211
II. The Road and Track Communications ...	213

CHAPTER XII

THE OPERATIONS NEAR LENS

BATTLE OF HILL 70 (15TH–20TH AUGUST)	219
ALTERNATIVE OFFENSIVE FRONTS	219
CAPTURE OF HILL 70 BY THE CANADIAN CORPS (15TH AUGUST):	
THE ASSAULT	223
THE GERMAN COUNTER-ATTACKS	225
SUBSIDIARY OPERATIONS	226
FURTHER COUNTER-ATTACKS	226
SUBSEQUENT FIGHTING	228
THE CASUALTIES	230

CHAPTER XIII

THE BATTLES OF YPRES 1917 (*continued*)
BATTLE OF THE MENIN ROAD RIDGE
(20TH–25TH SEPTEMBER):

	Page
GENERAL SITUATION AT THE END OF AUGUST	231
REVIEW OF THE FLANDERS SITUATION	233
THE REVISED SCHEME	236
THE NEW ATTACK ORGANIZATION	239
PREPARATIONS	242
ZERO HOUR	250

CHAPTER XIV

BATTLE OF THE MENIN ROAD RIDGE (*concluded*)
THE SECOND ARMY MAKES THE FIRST STEP
(20TH SEPTEMBER):

THE MAIN ATTACK	253
THE SOUTHERN FLANK	261
THE FIFTH ARMY CONFORMS	263
THE GERMAN COUNTER-ATTACKS	271
FINAL OPERATIONS	277
Note: Casualties 20th–25th September	279

CHAPTER XV

BATTLE OF POLYGON WOOD (26TH SEPTEMBER)

OUTLINE FOR THE FINAL PHASE OF THE CAMPAIGN	280
THE PREPARATIONS FOR THE SECOND STEP AND ENEMY INTERFERENCE	281
THE ASSAULT	284
FAILURE OF THE GERMAN COUNTER-ATTACKS	289
RESULTS OF THE SECOND STEP	292
Note: German Change in Defensive Tactics	294

CHAPTER XVI

BATTLE OF BROODSEINDE (4TH OCTOBER)

PREPARATIONS	296
THE THIRD STEP:	
THE SECOND ARMY	303
THE FIFTH ARMY	309
THE RIGHT FLANK GUARD	312
EXPLOITATION POSTPONED	315
Note: Tank Operations (General)	319

CONTENTS xxvii

CHAPTER XVII

PAGE

BATTLE OF POELCAPPELLE
(9TH OCTOBER)

THE PLAN	323
THE CHANGE OF WEATHER	325
THE ATTACK:	
THE SECOND ARMY	330
THE FIFTH ARMY	334

CHAPTER XVIII

THE BATTLES OF YPRES 1917 (*concluded*)
THE BATTLES OF PASSCHENDAELE (12TH OCTOBER–10TH NOVEMBER)

FIRST BATTLE OF PASSCHENDAELE (12TH OCTOBER)	338
PROSPECTS AND WEATHER	338
THE ATTACK:	
THE SECOND ARMY	341
THE FIFTH ARMY	343
SECOND BATTLE OF PASSCHENDAELE (26TH OCTOBER–10TH NOVEMBER)	
PROSPECTS	345
THE ATTACK OF THE 26TH OCTOBER:	
THE SECOND ARMY	349
THE FIFTH ARMY	351
DIVISIONS SENT TO ITALY	352
THE COMMUNICATIONS	352
THE ATTACK ON THE 30TH OCTOBER	353
THE ATTACK ON THE 6TH NOVEMBER	355
THE ATTACK ON THE 10TH NOVEMBER ...	358
END OF THE BATTLES OF YPRES 1917	359
CASUALTIES OF BOTH BELLIGERENTS	360
Note: The Battles of Ypres 1917. Total Battle and Trench Wastage by Weeks in the Fifth and Second Armies, 31st July–10th November	364

CHAPTER XIX

RETROSPECT

	PAGE
THE GENERAL RESULT	366
THE DECISION TO UNDERTAKE AN OFFENSIVE AFTER THE NIVELLE DISASTER	367
THE CHOICE OF FLANDERS	368
THE FRENCH MUTINIES	370
ALTERNATIVES TO FLANDERS	371
THE NATURE OF THE GROUND AND NORMAL WEATHER CONDITIONS IN FLANDERS	373
THE MUD	375
THE CONTINUATION OF THE BATTLE IN OCTOBER AFTER THE BREAK IN THE WEATHER	377
TANKS	379
LIAISON	381
TACTICS: LIMITED OR UNLIMITED OBJECTIVES	381
RELATIONS OF HAIG AND HIS GENERALS	383
SELECTION OF GENERAL GOUGH FOR THE PRINCIPAL COMMAND	384
LOSS OF TIME BETWEEN MESSINES AND "THIRD YPRES"	385
COMPARATIVE STRENGTH OF THE TWO OPPONENTS	386

SKETCHES

	The Flanders Campaign. Final Plan, 18th May, 1917	*Frontispiece*
1.	Plan for a Flanders Campaign, 1916[1] ...	*At End*
2.	Plan for a Flanders Campaign, February 1917	,,
3.	Messines 1917 : Mines and Objectives ...	,,
4.	Second Army Area : Railways and Railheads	,,
5.	Messines 1917 : The End of the Battle ...	,,
6.	Projected Advance Through Belgium ...	,,
7.	The Concentration in Flanders, July ...	,,
8.	Attacks at Oppy and Avion, 24th–28th June	,,
9.	The Nieuport Bridgehead, 10th July ...	,,
10.	Fifth Army : Stages of the Offensive, 31st July	,,
11.	Second Army Assault, 31st July	,,
12.	The German Flanders Positions, July ...	,,
13.	Battle of Pilckem Ridge : Northern Defensive Flank, 31st July	,,
14.	Battle of Pilckem Ridge : Main Attack, II Corps, 31st July	,,
15.	Battle of Pilckem Ridge : Main Attack, XIX Corps, 31st July	,,
16.	Progress of the Fifth Army : 31st July ...	,,
17.	Capture of Westhoek, 10th August ...	,,
18.	Battle of Langemarck, 16th August ...	,,
19.	Battle of Langemarck, 16th August : The Northern Flank	,,
20.	Operations of the XIX and XVIII Corps, 19th–22nd August	,,
21.	Capture of Hill 70, 15th August	,,
22.	Battle of the Menin Road, 20th September, Second Army	,,
23.	Battle of the Menin Road, 20th September, Fifth Army	,,
24.	Battle of Polygon Wood, 26th September	,,
25.	Forecast of the Stages of the Campaign, G.H.Q., 22nd September	,,
26.	Battle of Broodseinde, 4th October ...	,,
27.	First Battle of Passchendaele, 12th October	,,
28.	Second Battle of Passchendaele, 26th October–10th November	,,

---

[1] Except for Sketch 1, all dates are in 1917.

MAP
(*In Pocket*)

The Battles of Ypres, 1917

PHOTOGRAPHS[1]

No.	Date	Title	
1.	27th September[2]	Battle of Polygon Wood. Carrying Party	*At End*
2.	30th September	The Ypres–Menin Road near Polygon Wood	,,
3.	*1st October	Pill-boxes at Nonne Boschen	
4.	*5th October	Zonnebeke: Brick-kiln and Church from near Jumping-off Place of Previous Day's Attack	,,
5.	6th October	First Battle of Passchendaele. Canadian Pioneers laying Duckboard Track	,,
6.	*15th October	Zonnebeke Valley. Plank Road on North Side of Roulers Railway	,,
7.	*25th October	Near Birr Crossroads from the Menin Road	,,
8.	*28th October	Plank Road at Idiot Corner (North-west Corner of Bellewaarde Lake)	,,

	PAGE
COMMANDS AND STAFFS	388
SKELETON ORDER OF BATTLE	391

---

[1] The photographs marked with an asterisk (*) were kindly provided by the Australian War Memorial authorities; the others by the Imperial War Museum.
[2] All dates are in 1917.

LIST OF APPENDICES

		PAGE
I.	Project for Combined Naval and Military Operations on the Belgian Coast with a view to Preventing the Enemy using Ostend as a Submarine Base. General Staff Memorandum. 12th November 1915	396
II.	Commander-in-Chief's Instructions for Preparation of Plan for Northern Operations. 7th January 1916	399
III.	General Sir Henry Rawlinson's Proposals for the Attack by the Fourth Army against the Ypres Front. 27th February 1916	399
IV.	G.H.Q. Memorandum: Project for Operations in Flanders and Belgium. 5th March 1916 ...	403
V.	G.H.Q. Letter to Second Army. 6th January 1917	406
VI.	G.H.Q. Instructions for the Formation of a Special Sub-section of the Operations Section of the General Staff. 8th January 1917 ...	407
VII.	Memorandum by Operations Section, General Staff: Summary of the Proposed Northern Operation in Chronological Order. Submitted 14th February 1917	410
VIII.	Second Army Operation Order No. 1 of 10th May 1917	416
IX.	Second Army Operation Order No. 2 of 19th May 1917	418
X.	Allotment and Employment of Tanks. Second Army Order of 18th May 1917	419
XI.	Machine Guns in the Attack: General Principles. Issued by G.H.Q. before the Battle of Messines	420
XII.	Memorandum on the Present Situation and Future Plans. Written for the War Cabinet by the Commander-in-Chief. 12th June 1917	423
XIII.	Fifth Army Instructions for the Offensive of the 31st July 1917 dated 27th June 1917. Addressed to II, VIII, XIV, XVIII and XIX Corps	431
XIV.	8th Division Operation Orders of the 22nd July 1917	433

LIST OF APPENDICES—*continued*

		PAGE
XV.	Memorandum dated 26th June 1917 by Br.-General J. H. Davidson (Operations Section O.a) on the Forthcoming Operations (31st July 1917) and Reply dated 28th June by General Sir Hubert Gough (Commanding Fifth Army)	436
XVI.	Instructions for the Recovery of Tanks Damaged in Action. Issued by the Headquarters of the Tank Corps. 20th July 1917	442
XVII.	Fifth Army Operation Order No. 11 of the 31st July 1917	445
XVIII.	G.H.Q. Instructions of the 1st August 1917 to the French First Army, Fifth Army and Second Army	446
XIX.	Memorandum on the Situation on the II Corps Front by G.H.Q. (Operations). 1st August 1917	447
XX.	G.H.Q. Order of the 28th August 1917 Limiting the Operations of the Fifth Army	449
XXI.	Second Army Operation Order No. 4 of the 1st September 1917	449
XXII.	Second Army Addendum of 10th September 1917 to Operation Order No. 4 of 1st September 1917	451
XXIII.	Second Army Instruction of the 29th August 1917: General Principles on which the Artillery Plan will be Drawn	452
XXIV.	Second Army's Remarks of 12th August 1917 on G.H.Q. Memorandum dated 7th August 1917 on Best Method of Meeting the Latest System of Defence Adopted by the Enemy	456
XXV.	Second Army's Notes on Training and Preparation for Offensive Operations. 31st August 1917	459
XXVI.	G.H.Q. Order 21st September 1917 for the Attack of the 26th September 1917, the Battle of Polygon Wood	464

LIST OF BOOKS

TO WHICH MOST FREQUENT REFERENCE IS MADE

AUSTRALIAN OFFICIAL ACCOUNT (A.O.A.) : The Official History of Australia in the War of 1914–18. Volume IV. " The Australian Imperial Force in France 1917 ". By C. E. W. Bean. (Sydney : Angus & Robertson.)

BATH : " Frankreichs schwerste Stunde. Die Meuterei der Armee 1917 ". By H. Bath. (Potsdam : Protte.)
A survey of 1917, with many suggestions of what might have been.

BAVARIAN OFFICIAL ACCOUNT (B.O.A.) : " Die Bayern im grossen Kriege, 1914–1918 ". Issued by the Bavarian Kriegsarchiv. (Munich : Verlag des bayerischen Kriegsarchivs.)
As Crown Prince Rupprecht of Bavaria was in command of the front attacked, the period June–November 1917 is dealt with at length.

CHARTERIS : " Field-Marshal Earl Haig ". By Br.-General John Charteris. (Cassell.)
A life of Earl Haig by one of his most intimate friends, who had been his A.M.S. in Aldershot, and on his staff in France, becoming head of the Intelligence when Haig became Commander-in-Chief.

CHARTERIS II : " At G.H.Q." By Br.-General John Charteris. (Cassell.)
This contains mainly extracts from the author's diary from mobilization to the 14th September 1918 when he reached St. Thomas's Hospital, London, for an operation. It contains a great deal of interest.

FLANDERN, 1917 : By W. Beumelberg. (Oldenburg : Stalling.)
An official monograph issued by the Reichsarchiv in 1928 in the series begun by the Historical Section of the (then abolished) General Staff. It covers exactly the period dealt with in this volume. It is not so much a military narrative as a series of word pictures of " this tremendous struggle ".

FRENCH OFFICIAL ACCOUNT (F.O.A.) : " Les Armées françaises dans la Grande Guerre ". Ministère de la Guerre : Etat-Major de l'Armée. Service Historique. (Paris : Imprimerie Nationale.)
Tome V, deuxième volume, of 1,365 pages, compiled by five officers, covers the period of the present volume.

GEHRE: "Die deutsche Kraftverteilung während des Weltkrieges". By L. Gehre. (Berlin: Mittler.)

A logistical examination of the War to show that O.H.L. succeeded in assembling for decisive action in time and space the highest possible number of divisions. A large coloured diagram on squared paper shows the strength in divisions on the 15th and last day of every month of the War on the various fronts and in the different Armies.

GERMAN CROWN PRINCE: "Meine Erinnerungen aus Deutschlands Heldenkampf". By the former German Crown Prince Wilhelm. (Berlin: Mittler.)

These recollections are hardly more than a précis of the operations in which the troops under his command took part, but there are some statements of interest not to be found elsewhere.

GERMAN OFFICIAL ACCOUNT (G.O.A.): "Der Weltkrieg, 1914 bis 1918: Die militärischen Operationen zu Lande". Prepared by the Military History Research Institution of the Forces. (Berlin: Mittler.)

Volume XII, published in 1939, ends in June 1917 but its closing pages give the appreciations made as the Battles of Arras, 1917, were coming to an end, Messines had been fought and an offensive in Flanders expected.

Volume XIII, published in 1942 " For Official Use Only " but not obtained until late in 1946, covers the period June to December 1917 for all theatres, and the year 1918 except for events on the Western Front.

GOUGH: "The Fifth Army". By General Sir Hubert Gough. (Hodder & Stoughton.)

This covers the story of the author's commands in France from August 1914 to the end of March 1918.

HANOTAUX: "Histoire illustrée de la Guerre". By Gabriel Hanotaux. (Paris: Gounouilhou.)

A contemporary account by the eminent French statesman.

KUHL: "Der Weltkrieg, 1914–1918". By General der Infanterie Hermann von Kuhl. (Berlin: Weller.)

Kuhl was Chief of the General Staff first to General von Kluck and then to Field-Marshal Crown Prince Rupprecht of Bavaria. His history, in two large volumes, written for the German people, is an excellent general account based on official documents and his own intimate knowledge.

LIST OF BOOKS xxxv

LLOYD GEORGE : " War Memoirs ". By Right Hon. David Lloyd George. (Ivor Nicholson & Watson.)

In six volumes, published in 1934, sixteen years after the end of the War, eight years after the death of Field-Marshal Earl Haig, who is bitterly attacked, and a year after that of Field-Marshal Sir William Robertson. Chapter LXIII, in Volume IV, entitled " The Campaign in the Mud : Passchendaele ", was simultaneously published as a pamphlet of 142 pages.

On the 28th July 1938 Mr. Lloyd George, as he then was, told Br.-General Sir James Edmonds, with whom he was on very friendly terms, being of the same age, that he felt he might have misjudged Haig and Robertson, that he had kept no diary or notes, and had relied for the material of the " Passchendaele " chapter and other technical matters on a then well-known publicist on military subjects who had assisted him.

LOSSBERG : " Meine Tätigkeit im Weltkriege, 1914–1918 ". By General der Infanterie Fritz von Lossberg. (Berlin : Mittler.)

Lossberg, an officer of the Guards, became the German expert on defence, and most of the information on the subject contained in the present volume is taken from his book. In peace he had been instructor at the Kriegsakademie. In war he held a series of General Staff appointments with troops and was called upon to advise whenever trouble occurred. He was in succession Chief of the Staff of the *XIII Corps, Fifth, Sixth* and *Ninth Armies ;* in February–September 1915 he was in the Operations Section at O.H.L., and then went as Chief of the Staff to the *Third Army* for the Champagne battle, to the *Second Army*, and later the *First* in the Somme battle, to the *Sixth Army* for the Arras battle and to the *Fourth Army* for the Flanders battle, being thus nearly continuously opposed to the British.

LUDENDORFF : " My War Memories, 1914–1918 ". By General Erich Ludendorff. (English Edition : Hutchinson & Co.)

The translation of General Ludendorff's story of the War, " Meine Kriegserinnerungen ", in two volumes.

MEDICAL HISTORY : " Medical Services, General History ". By Major-General Sir William Macpherson. (H.M. Stationery Office.)

The official history of the Medical Services.

MEDICAL STATISTICS: "Medical Services. Casualties and Medical Statistics". By Major T. J. Mitchell and Miss G. M. Smith. (H.M. Stationery Office.)
   A survey of medical statistics in all theatres.

MOSER: "Ernsthafte Plaudereien über den Weltkrieg". By Lieut.-General von Moser. (Stuttgart: Belser.)
   A critical military-political history of the War by one of our principal opponents at Cambrai, who also wrote his autobiography in "Aufzeichnungen".

NEW ZEALAND OFFICIAL ACCOUNT (N.Z.O.A.): "The Official History of New Zealand's Effort in the Great War". Volume II: "The New Zealanders in France". By Colonel H. Stewart. (Auckland: Whitcombe & Tombs.)

"REGT. NO. . . ." These are references to the war histories of German units. Most of them are in the series "Erinnerungsblätter deutscher Regimenter", published by Gerhard Stalling of Oldenburg.

RUPPRECHT: "In Treue fest. Mein Kriegstagebuch". By Field-Marshal Crown Prince Rupprecht of Bavaria. (Munich: Deutscher National Verlag.)
   Contains in three volumes extracts from the War Diary of the Crown Prince, with shrewd comments.

SANITÄTSBERICHT: Sanitätsbericht über das deutsche Heer im Weltkriege, 1914–1918". (Berlin: Mittler.)
   The official report on the German medical service in two volumes. Volume I deals with general organization; Volume II with the field forces and armies of occupation year by year and Army by Army in the different theatres. Percentages but few absolute figures are given.

WAR IN THE AIR: "Being the Story played in the Great War by the Royal Air Force". By H. A. Jones. (Oxford: Clarendon Press.)
   The Official History of the Air Operations.

WILSON: "Field-Marshal Sir Henry Wilson. His Life and Diaries". By Major-General Sir Charles Callwell. (Cassell.)
   A life in two volumes, with many extracts from diaries which indicate poor military judgment.

   Note: "1916", Vol. I and similar references signify "The Official History of the Great War, 1914–1918, Military Operations, France & Belgium" by years and volume.

xxxvii

CALENDAR OF PRINCIPAL EVENTS

Mainly extracted from "Principal Events 1914–18" compiled by the Historical Section of the Committee of Imperial Defence, London. His Majesty's Stationery Office. 10s. 6d. net.

Western Theatre	Other Theatres	Naval Warfare and General Events
	APRIL 1917	
9th Battles of Arras begin (end 24th May).		
16th Second Battle of the Aisne ("Nivelle Offensive") begins.	17th–19th *Palestine*: Second Battle of Gaza.	
20th Second Battle of the Aisne ends.	24th *Mesopotamia*: Samarra taken.	
	24th/25th *Balkans*: Battle of Doiran.	29th General Pétain appointed Chief of the French General Staff.
	MAY 1917	During this month 122 British merchant ships (gross tonnage 352,289) were lost by enemy action.
3rd Battle of Bullecourt begins.		4th/5th Anglo-French Paris Conference.
4th–9th Resumption of French Offensive on the Aisne.		10th General John Pershing appointed to command American Expeditionary Force.
	12th *Italy*: Tenth Battle of the Isonzo begins (ends 8th June).	
17th Battle of Bullecourt ends.		

Western Theatre	Other Theatres	Naval Warfare and General Events
	JUNE 1917	
7th Battle of Messines 1917 begins. 14th Battle of Messines 1917 ends.	28th *Palestine*: General Sir E. Allenby assumes command. 29th *Russia*: Kerenski offensive begins.	During this month 122 British merchant ships (gross tonnage, 417,925) were lost by enemy action. 25th First contingent of American troops arrives in France.
	JULY 1917	
31st Battles of Ypres 1917 begin. Battle of Pilckem Ridge begins (ends 2nd August).	11th *Mesopotamia*: Attack on Ramadi. 18th *Russia*: German counter-offensive begins (ends 28th). 22nd *Rumania*: Battle of Marasesti begins (first phase ends 1st August).	During this month 99 British merchant ships (gross tonnage, 364,858) were lost by enemy action.

Western Theatre	Other Theatres	Naval Warfare and General Events
	AUGUST 1917	During this month 91 British merchant ships (gross tonnage, 329,810) were lost by enemy action.
15th Battle of Hill 70 (Lens) begins. 16th Third Ypres: Battle of Langemarck begins.	6th *Rumania*: Battle of Marasesti (second phase begins; ends 3rd September).	
18th Third Ypres: Battle of Langemarck ends. 20th Verdun: Attack by French begins, continuing, with intervals, till 15th December. 25th Battle of Hill 70 (Lens) ends.	17th *Italy*: Eleventh Battle of the Isonzo begins (ends 12th September).	
	SEPTEMBER 1917	During this month 78 British merchant ships (gross tonnage, 196,212) were lost by enemy action. 15th Russia proclaimed a republic.
20th Third Ypres: Battle of Menin Road begins. 25th Third Ypres: Battle of Menin Road ends. 26th Third Ypres: Battle of Polygon Wood begins.	1st *Russia*: Battle of Riga begins (ends 5th). 28th *Mesopotamia*: Ramadi captured.	

Western Theatre	Other Theatres	Naval Warfare and General Events
	OCTOBER 1917	
3rd Third Ypres: Battle of Polygon Wood ends.		During this month 86 British merchant ships (gross tonnage, 276,132) were lost by enemy action.
4th Third Ypres: Battle of Broodseinde.		
9th Third Ypres: Battle of Poelcappelle.		
	11th *Baltic Islands*: German attack begins (capture completed 20th).	
12th Third Ypres: First Battle of Passchendaele.		
23rd Battle of Malmaison begins.		
	24th *Italy*: Twelfth Battle of the Isonzo (Caporetto) begins.	
26th Third Ypres: Second Battle of Passchendaele begins.		
26th French and British divisions ordered to Italy.		
	27th *Palestine*: Third Battle of Gaza begins (ends 7th November).	
	NOVEMBER 1917	
1st Battle of Malmaison ends.		During this month 64 British merchant ships (gross tonnage, 173,560) were lost by enemy action.
	5th *Mesopotamia*: Battle of Tikrit.	5th Allied Conference at Rapallo.
6th Third Ypres: Passchendaele captured by Canadian Corps.		
10th Third Ypres: The Battles end.	10th *Italy*: Italian forces in position on the Piave.	

CHAPTER I

PLANS FOR A FLANDERS CAMPAIGN

The 1916 Plan

(Map 1 ; Sketches 1, 2)

In May 1917, before the operations near Arras had been brought to an end, preparations were in hand to transfer the bulk of the British offensive strength to Flanders. For two years, since the epic defensive battles fought by the British Expeditionary Force in the autumn of 1914 and spring of 1915 in front of Ypres[1], although the Battle of Mount Sorrel was fought 2nd–13th June, 1916, no major action had taken place in that district ; but as a potential theatre for offensive operations it had been frequently discussed.

The narrow belt of sand dunes along the 28-mile stretch of the Belgian coast in German hands contained the ports of Ostend, Blankenberghe and Zeebrugge, connected by canal and railway with the inland town of Bruges.[2] Facing the Thames estuary and flanking the cross-Channel routes from Dover and Folkestone to Dunkirk, Calais and Boulogne, these ports had been used from the time of their occupation as German bases for destroyers, submarines and submarine minelayers. Ostend harbour was of particular importance owing to its size and the nature of its equipment, while Bruges was valuable as a refuge and as a refitting base. As early as the 7th December, 1914, Mr. Winston Churchill, the First Lord of the Admiralty, had proposed to Field-Marshal Sir John French, commanding the British Expeditionary Force, a scheme for recovering this stretch of Belgian coast-line, northwards to the Dutch frontier, by means of a combined naval and military operation. An attack along the sand dunes from the mouth of the Yser, below Nieuport, was to be combined with a landing at Ostend ; but General Joffre, the French Commander-in-Chief, who was at that time more concerned with his plans to remove the German threat to Paris, opposed the scheme.[3]

---
[1] See " 1914 " Vol. II, and " 1915 " Vol. I.
[2] See Sketch 1.
[3] See " 1915 " Vol. I, p. 15.

Nearly a year later, in November 1915, the Admiralty stated that the use of the Belgian ports by the German navy constituted " a growing danger to the transport of troops " and supplies to France ", and once more pressed for combined naval and military action to free them. At their request, a memorandum[1] was written on the subject by the General Staff at the War Office in consultation with the Admiralty War Staff and Vice-Admiral Sir Roger Bacon, commanding the Dover Patrol. The recommendation was either to make a surprise landing at Ostend with a British force embarked at Dover, Calais or Dunkirk, or to advance along the coast far enough to enable heavy artillery to make Ostend at least untenable. Sir Douglas Haig, who succeeded Sir John French as British Commander-in-Chief in December 1915, was anxious to carry out the project in preference to " a great combined Franco-British offensive " athwart the Somme " ;[2] but he took the view that it would need a land operation on a far greater scale than had been contemplated. He considered that a surprise landing from the sea would be difficult to effect and to support, and that the two miles of sand dunes between the Yser inundations and the coast was too narrow a frontage for a land attack. The Belgian authorities agreed that the inundations could be drained away,[3] but they estimated that three weeks' dry weather would be needed to make the ground south of Dixmude fit for operations, and a longer period for that north of Dixmude. The process would give the Germans ample warning of the intention, and time to make further defensive arrangements.

For this reason, Sir Douglas Haig wished to by-pass the thirteen-mile frontage of the Yser inundations by a general advance north-eastwards from Ypres. He aimed not only at the capture of Ostend, but the clearance of the whole Belgian coast-line. He planned to operate from the Ypres front with two Armies, and not to attempt the coastal advance and landing until this main offensive had made

---

[1] Appendix I.
[2] See " 1916 " Vol. I, p. 31.
[3] The inundations on the lower Yser had been formed by letting in the sea at the end of October 1914. See " 1914 " Vol. II, p. 257. It was estimated that the flooded area south of Dixmude could be drained off by the Dunkirk canal in 4 days, whilst that north of Dixmude could be drained by opening the Nieuport sluices at low tide and closing them as the tide rose.

progress. Accordingly, on the 7th January, 1916, he proposed that the Fourth Army should take over the Ypres front southwards to the Ypres–Roulers railway; and he asked its commander, General Sir H. Rawlinson, to work out a scheme for an offensive north-eastwards from the Ypres Salient towards Houthulst Forest, supported by the Second Army on his right, in co-operation with an attack along the coast to Middelkerke and a surprise landing at Ostend. The necessary adjustments were to be made with the Belgian and French divisions then holding the front of the inundations and the coastal sector; and Lieut.-General Sir A. Hunter-Weston, who had gained experience of combined operations during the Gallipoli campaign, together with Vice-Admiral Sir R. Bacon, who had already planned the framework of the naval arrangements, were to work out details for the coastal attack and the landing.[1]

The difficulties to be overcome were fully appreciated. The Germans held the crest line of the low hills which form a large semi-circle around the eastern side of Ypres, and the British front and back areas within the Salient were under their direct observation.[2] The northern part of the semi-circle was formed by the Pilckem Ridge, an underfeature, which branches out parallel to the Yser canal from Gheluvelt plateau, a flat-topped area crossed by the Ypres–Menin road near the centre of the main Ypres ridge. After capturing the German defences along the Pilckem Ridge, the Fourth Army would have to cross the Steenbeek, beyond which the ground rises gradually for three or four miles to the northern end of the main Ypres Ridge, on which lie Passchendaele, Westroosebeke and Staden.

At a meeting between the Commander-in-Chief and his Army commanders on the 13th January, 1916, special emphasis was laid on the importance of the capture of Gheluvelt plateau before the Fourth Army attempted to advance across the Steenbeek; German artillery, concealed in its woods and on its slopes, dominated the low ground on either side, and could enfilade such a movement with observed fire. General Sir H. Plumer, commanding the Second Army, in whose proposed battle sector the plateau lay, pointed out that a preliminary to its capture would have

---

[1] Appendix II.
[2] See Map 1 and Sketch 2.

to be the occupation of the Messines–Wytschaete Ridge, which formed part of the southern arc of the Ypres Salient; and he added that the preparations for this separate operation were already well advanced, including the tunnelling of nineteen mines, begun the previous July, beneath the German front trench system.[1] Sir Douglas Haig agreed to this extension of his original idea, and he asked that the capture of the Messines Ridge should now be considered in association with the larger project of clearing the Belgian coast.

On the 25th of the same month General Joffre's approval was obtained for a Flanders campaign as the main British effort for the summer of 1916, following upon a series of limited attacks on the Somme, in co-operation with the French, as already mentioned, earlier in the year.

General Rawlinson submitted his scheme on the 27th February;[2] and the various threads of these discussions and schemes were put together and issued in a G.H.Q. memorandum of the 5th March, 1916, corrected by marginal notes in Sir Douglas Haig's handwriting.[3] This memorandum is worthy of study in detail as disclosing not only the frame of mind in which the Commander-in-Chief faced the project of a Flanders offensive at this period of the War, but also the relationship between the proposed sequence of events and the course the campaign was eventually to follow.[4]

The first stage was to gain observation areas along the crest of the low hills around the Ypres Salient in order to provide observed artillery support for the general advance beyond. On the right, the capture of the Spanbroekmolen knoll was to be followed at once by an attack on a five-mile front, from Le Gheer to St. Eloi, to capture the near crest of the Messines Ridge, including Messines village. In the centre, an attack on a 1½-mile front astride the Ypres-Comines railway was to capture Hill 60, the narrowest part of the main Ypres Ridge, which would give observation into the valley of the Lys and over the southern slopes of Gheluvelt plateau towards Zandvoorde. In the northern sector, the objective would be the crest of the Pilckem Ridge, from the

---

[1] See "1916" Vol. I, p. 32. Four more mines were prepared in the Armentières sector, but not fired.
[2] Appendix III.
[3] Appendix IV.
[4] See Sketch 1.

THE 1916 PLAN

Ypres–St. Julien road to Steenstraat (including Hill 29), overlooking the Steenbeek valley.

To bridge the interval of about seven days whilst the next attack was in preparation, the so-called second stage was to be a subsidiary action to take place near Neuve Chapelle, 30 miles to the south, in order to divert the enemy's attention from the Ypres operations and to hold his reserves.

The third stage was to be the continuation of the main offensive north-eastwards from Ypres. It was to be carried out on a wide front, from Hill 60 to Steenstraat, to a distance limited to about a mile to include the German Second Line across Gheluvelt plateau and the Steenbeek.

The fourth stage was to be a general advance to include the capture of the back crest of the Messines–Wytschaete Ridge and Wytschaete village. The memorandum stressed the importance of the attack across Gheluvelt plateau, towards Gheluvelt and Zonnebeke, as the timing of the main offensive north-eastward would depend upon its progress, and General Plumer considered that no advance should be made from Pilckem Ridge before Gheluvelt plateau was in our hands. If the right flank could be secured on the plateau, the main offensive by the Fourth Army from Pilckem Ridge across the Steenbeek would be continued with four corps until the right rested on the main ridge near Passchendaele, and the left on the Yser inundations, north of Bixschoote.

In the fifth stage, by which time seven corps would be involved, the northern end of the main Ypres Ridge from Passchendaele to Staden and Zarren would be occupied, and a strong defensive right flank formed along the eastern and southern edges of Gheluvelt plateau.

The objective of the sixth stage was to be the Roulers–Thourout railway, and this advance was to synchronize with the coastal attack from Nieuport and the landing operation.[1] A mobile force was to be ready during the fifth or sixth stage to move on through Thourout to exploit the situation.

On the 10th April, 1916, by a G.H.Q. memorandum, the Second Army was informed of the plan which the

---

[1] The Rawlinson scheme recommended that the coastal operation be made simultaneously with the second stage ; but General Hunter-Weston's report on 24th February suggested that it should not take place till the main offensive had made such progress that the German defence along the coast was weakening.

Commander-in-Chief had " under consideration ", and was directed to submit early a project for the capture of Messines–Wytschaete Ridge and of Pilckem Ridge, with proposals for tunnelling, and requirements in troops, heavy artillery, trench mortars, ammunition, gas and smoke. It ended, " for the purpose of calculation, the date of the " infantry attack may be taken as the 15th July "—the actual date, after last minute postponements, was the 31st.

Effect of the Battles of Verdun and the Somme

The long drawn out German offensive at Verdun, which began on the 21st February and gradually developed into a battle to wear down the French army, continued into the summer and upset the Allied offensive plans for 1916. On the 27th March, General Joffre warned Sir Douglas Haig that the British might have to employ the whole of their available resources alongside the French in the combined operation astride the Somme, in order to relieve the continued and heavy German pressure at Verdun. General Rawlinson's Fourth Army was already in position in the Somme area, and it soon became evident that events might prevent its transfer to Flanders. As late as the 27th May, however, preparations for the Flanders project were ordered by G.H.Q. to be pressed with all speed.

By the 4th June it was evident that, whatever shape the Flanders campaign might take, General Rawlinson's Fourth Army would be too far committed on the Somme to participate; and Sir Douglas Haig ordered Second Army headquarters to be prepared to direct the Flanders operation with restricted resources. A Reserve Army, formed on the 22nd May under Lieut.-General Sir H. Gough, instead of being employed on the Somme, might, if the prospects of success there seemed poor,[1] be sent, with four corps and one in reserve, to be interpolated within the Second Army, to carry out the Messines attack; the Canadian Corps, with four divisions, would carry out the Hill 60 attack; and the XIV Corps, with five divisions, would capture Hill 29 on Pilckem Ridge.

With so limited a force, only the first stage of the plan

---

[1] See " 1916 " Vol. I, p. 265.

EFFECT OF THE SOMME BATTLES 1916

at most could be considered ; but after the opening battle of the Somme on the 1st July, and the decision to continue the campaign there, that modified task was further reduced. The Messines attack alone was proposed as a subsidiary to the Somme battles, the date for it being given provisionally as the 15th July—yet even that operation could not be undertaken. By mid-August, General Plumer knew that the shafts and tunnels of the several mines which had been dug below Messines Ridge might have to withstand the winter. The unexpected duration of the operations on the Somme, covering as they did a period of four and a half months, prevented the provision of sufficient troops, labour and material for the Messines, let alone the Flanders, project.

THE CHANTILLY CONFERENCE: 15TH NOVEMBER, 1916

The expenditure of Germany's military strength on the Verdun and Somme battlefields in 1916 was known to have been great both in quantity and quality ; the best-trained and stoutest-hearted of its junior leaders and soldiers had been lost and were irreplaceable, and the German military replacement machinery was running close up to its peak capacity. The French losses, too, had been severe. General Joffre considered that the French army was nearing exhaustion ; it had carried the major burden of the war on the Western Front for two years and its casualties had been heavier than its reserve of man-power could replace. He intended to rest it during the winter months in order to nurse it back to normal health. On the other hand, the resources of the British Empire were being rapidly developed and the limit of their expansion was not yet in sight. The British army, despite its heavy casualties during 1916, was in good order and great heart, and the experience of the Somme battles had hardened the core of it to a high state of efficiency.

The important bearing of this aspect of the campaigns of 1916 on the future conduct of the War was stressed by Sir Douglas Haig at the Chantilly Conference, called on the 15th November, 1916, under the presidency of General Joffre, to discuss the Allied plans for 1917.[1] He urged that no

---

[1] See " 1917 " Vol. I, pp. 1-11.

respite should be allowed to the German army to recover from the heavy blows it had received during 1916. The plan sanctioned by the conference was a series of offensives on the Western, Russian and Italian fronts, so timed as to make it impracticable for the Germans to weaken any one front to assist another; and the sum total of these offensives was to be of a " decisive character ". It was agreed, too, that the decision would have to be gained on the Western Front, and that forces employed in subsidiary theatres of war should be reduced to a minimum. At a further meeting of the French and British Commanders-in-Chief it was agreed to launch a spring offensive by British and French forces in the Somme and Aisne sectors respectively, after which the main effort would be transferred to Flanders where operations would be continued throughout the summer chiefly by British troops. By this series of wearing-down battles it was expected that the remaining reserves of the German army would be consumed to such an extent that a break-through by the combined British and French forces on the Western Front, with the resultant victorious end of the War, might be possible before the close of the year.

The decision to make the main effort of the year in Flanders complied with an instruction of the War Committee of the British Cabinet on the 26th October, confirmed at a meeting on the 23rd November, that there was " no measure to which " the Committee attached greater importance than the " expulsion of the enemy from the Belgian coast ". The instruction was elaborated by the Chief of the Imperial General Staff, General Sir William Robertson, in a letter to General Joffre explaining that the maintenance of sea communications between Great Britain and France was vital to the successful conduct of the War, and that in the circumstances the British Government desired that the occupation of Ostend and Zeebrugge should form one of the objectives of the campaigns in 1917.

General Joffre replied on the 8th December in complete agreement. He suggested that a powerful offensive by British-Belgian troops towards the line Roulers–Thourout be launched several weeks after the beginning of the French and British offensives farther south, already agreed upon, and be followed ten days later by a French attack along the coast, combined with a naval attack on the German coastal batteries and a landing, two or three days later, by five divisions. The proposal differed from the British plan in that it regarded the offensive towards Roulers and Thourout chiefly as a means of holding the German reserves and that, even though it might have only a partial success, the coastal attack and landing would still be attempted. The British plan provided that the coastal attack and landing should not take place unless the main offensive from Ypres succeeded. The British Admiralty considered that where General Joffre's plan differed from that of G.H.Q. the latter should be followed; and that two divisions, not five, was the maximum force that could be landed on the coast.

As a result of the decisions of the Chantilly meetings, General Plumer had again been asked, on the 17th November, to submit plans for a Flanders offensive, on the assumption that thirty to thirty-five divisions would be available for operations north of the Lys. The preparations for the Messines attack were to be so advanced that it could be delivered at a month's notice in the following spring or summer. His proposals, sent to G.H.Q. on the 12th December, followed the same lines as those submitted earlier in the year. The offensive was to begin by simultaneous attacks to capture the Messines–Wytschaete Ridge, Hill 60 and Hill 29 (Pilckem Ridge), in order to deprive the enemy of his chief observation areas over the Ypres Salient, and as an essential prelude to an advance either eastward or north-eastward. Strong resistance was expected, as " the enemy " will not lightly give up the advantage he has held so long, " and his strategic line of advance via Ypres on Calais ".[1] General Plumer assumed that the organization of command outlined in the G.H.Q. letter of the 4th June still held good : that he would control the operations and that another Army would be interpolated to capture the Messines–Wytschaete Ridge. In a personal letter to the Chief of the General Staff, G.H.Q., on the 15th December, General Plumer's chief General Staff Officer, Major-General C. H. Harington, suggested splitting the force into two Armies, as the operation, with its ulterior objectives, might become too big

---

[1] It was proposed to allot four corps, (fourteen divisions) with one corps of three divisions in reserve, to the Messines operation; and four divisions each to the Hill 60 and Hill 29 attacks. This number, together with two corps, each of four divisions, in Second Army reserve and two divisions to hold defensively the Lys front from south of the Messines attack to the junction with the First Army, north of Armentières, made up the 35 divisions offered by G.H.Q.

for one Army to control: a southern Army to carry out the Messines operation, with the Ypres–Comines canal as its northern boundary, and a northern Army, which he recommended should be the Second Army, to be responsible for the main offensive north-eastwards from the Ypres Salient.

CHAPTER II

PLANS FOR A FLANDERS CAMPAIGN (*concluded*)

THE 1917 PLAN

(Frontispiece; Sketches 1, 2)

General Plumer's scheme was presented to Sir Douglas Haig at a moment when the outlook both of British G.H.Q. and the French Government was undergoing a radical change. The Chantilly plan foreshadowed the continuation of the War for at least another year; and influential political groups in France were impatient and dissatisfied at this prospect. They preferred the more ambitious proposal which was put before them " officieusement " at this time by a French Army commander, General Nivelle. He had risen rapidly to fame during the fighting, six weeks previously in October, by which much of the ground lost in the spring in the Verdun sector had been regained. He now claimed that, on the basis of that experience, the French army could break through and defeat in detail the German forces on the Western Front in a few weeks. " The German army " he said, " will run away; they only want to be off ".

Actually, the success of the attacks at Verdun in October and again in December 1916, were due mainly to the failure by the local German commanders to carry out new defence measures prescribed.[1] The French objective had been

---

[1] See " 1917 " Vol. I, pp. 91–3. The Germans had found that, owing to the growing preponderance of the French and British artillery, it was no longer practicable to fight a defensive battle in the devastated forward zone of a battle area. They therefore decided to revert to the old open warfare idea of outpost companies, supports and counter-attack reserves. A forward zone up to 2,500 yards in depth was to be held lightly, and chequered with strongpoints and machine-gun nests to break up an assault, the defensive battle being fought by a succession of counter-attack formations held back behind the forward zone, ready to recapture any lost ground.

The first edition of the new instructions for the defensive battle (*Führung der Abwehrschlacht*) was not issued until 15th December, 1916; but the new method of an elastic and deep defence, as opposed to holding a front trench system rigidly and reinforcing it, was tried during the later

Continued at foot of next page.

strictly limited to a thinly held German forward zone up to the Second Line, an advance of 2,500 yards on a frontage of about six miles, so that the experience gained might not apply to an offensive with distant objectives. The achievement, however, influenced political circles to such an extent that by the 8th December, only three weeks after the Chantilly conference, Monsieur Briand had to form a new Cabinet. Three days later a " Comité de Guerre ", created on the lines of the Committee of the War Cabinet in London, demanded the removal of General Joffre, whose ways had long been distasteful to the Chamber, and the appointment of General Nivelle as Commander-in-Chief of the Armies of the North and North-East, in his place.

In General Nivelle's plan, the French army, instead of being nursed back to strength, was to have the lion's share of the work ; the British army was to play a subsidiary part by attacking a few days earlier in the Arras sector in order to draw away the German reserves. The main onslaught, to be launched by the French in the Soissons–Reims area, was to begin with a surprise assault by two Army Groups with powerful and scientifically directed artillery support, and a third Army group was to exploit their break-through.[1] Many of the senior French generals, including General Joffre, disapproved. The Commanders of the three Groups of Armies concerned, Generals Franchet d'Esperey, Micheler and Pétain, all expressed their preference for an objective limited to the German Second Line, an advance of about a mile, on the model of the Verdun attacks in October and

---

Continued from previous page.
Somme and Verdun battles. An enquiry by German O.H.L. into the Verdun failures in October and December showed that in both instances the two counter-attack divisions were too far (14 miles) from the battlefield to reach it before the French had time to consolidate their gains ; the Army and corps commanders concerned were dismissed for their negligence. Other reasons were that, owing to heavy losses in the Somme battles, the front divisions were still at half-strength (about 3,000 instead of 7,000 rifles), and that the French gained surprise by dispensing with the normal artillery preparation.

[1] On 16th July 1916, at Tarnopol, the Germans had tried successfully a rather similar procedure. The artillery action, controlled on that occasion by Colonel Bruchmüller, was founded on the principle that the first blow of an assault should be an overwhelming artillery bombardment, lasting only a few hours, to come as a surprise, and to consist mainly of accurately aimed fire against previously located targets. It was to be of such hurricane character against both the infantry and the artillery of the defence that the garrison would be destroyed, or so demoralized as to enable the position to be overrun by the assault.

December: the infantry would still be within supporting range of the mass of the field batteries, ready to meet the German counter-attack divisions when they arrived: captured German documents had already disclosed sufficient information of the new German defence to show that by such means both the German front and reserve (or counter-attack) divisions could be most effectively and economically destroyed. The commanders further considered that General Nivelle's estimate of the inner worth of the German army was too low, and that he was asking too much of the tired French army.

Sir Douglas Haig, too, was sceptical of the success of the project; but the enthusiastic confidence with which General Nivelle outlined the plan impressed him favourably, fitting in as it did with the hopes of his own natural optimism. He agreed that a few more great blows, such as that proposed, might indeed bring about the disintegration of Germany's armed strength on the Western Front; and for that reason he approved the contention that a change from the battle ideas of 1916 was now due. " Rapid action with a break-" through of the enemy's defences on a wide front, and the " infliction of a decisive defeat on the enemy ", wrote the Chief of the General Staff on the 6th January to General Plumer after the Commander-in-Chief's talk with General Nivelle, was to replace the tactics of attrition.[1] Although he had so recently agreed to the Chantilly plan, this vision of a return to a war of movement appealed to him so strongly that he decided there and then to speed up the Flanders plan to the Nivelle model. General Nivelle gave encouragement by an assurance that, if the proposed French offensive succeeded, the Germans on the Belgian coast, taken in flank or even in reverse, would inevitably be forced to evacuate it of their own accord; and that in any event the German reserves would be drawn away from Flanders, leaving the defence so weakened that it could be broken through at will. The tempo of the War was to be quickened from a walk to a gallop, and the Chantilly plan was scrapped in its entirety within four weeks of its adoption.

In the circumstances, it is not surprising that General Plumer's proposals, which were reminiscent of the Somme

---

[1] Appendix V.

battles, found little favour; and on the 6th January, **1917**, Sir Douglas Haig asked him to recast his scheme. Two days later a special sub-section of the Operations Branch, G.H.Q., under Lieut.-Colonel C. N. Macmullen, assisted by Major Viscount Gort, was appointed to work out details for a campaign in Flanders on the new model.

The G.H.Q. letter to General Plumer and the more detailed instructions to the sub-section defining the basis for the new plan give together a clear insight into the intentions of Sir Douglas Haig at this time.[1] He proposed to co-operate with General Nivelle's offensive by attacks on the Vimy, Arras and Ancre fronts, and he accepted General Nivelle's opinion that if the French were successful the Germans would probably abandon the Belgian coast-line, and that the proposed operations in Flanders would be unnecessary. If, on the other hand, the French offensive did not succeed and "thus failed to clear the Belgian coast, we shall switch "as rapidly as possible to carry out our operations on a "large scale north of the river Lys". For this purpose the French were to take over part of the British line nearest to them, probably to the Ancre, in order to relieve General Rawlinson's Fourth Army, which would be moved bodily to Flanders.

The instructions emphasized that "the whole essence of "the new plan is to attack with rapidity and push right "through quickly. It must not be forgotten that this "attack will be delivered subsequent to attacks by the "whole of the French Armies and a portion of the British "army, and that the Germans are likely to be disorganized "and weak". This fundamental assumption was also stressed in the G.H.Q. letter to General Plumer: "It is to "be anticipated that the enemy will have been severely "handled and his reserves drawn away from your front "before the attacks north of the Lys are launched. Under "these circumstances, it is essential that the plan should be "based on rapid action and entail the breaking through of "the enemy's defences on a wide front, and get to open "fighting with the least possible delay so as to defeat the "troops immediately available before they can be re- "inforced".

The general plan was for the main "decisive" attack to

---

[1] Appendices V and VI.

be delivered by a northern Army of six corps[1] from the approximate front Hooge–Steenstraat, with the object of securing the line Roulers–Thourout, and then to continue the advance in a north-easterly direction so as to threaten the German coast defences in rear. A southern Army was to capture the Messines–Wytschaete ridge and Zandvoorde, forming a defensive right flank for the main advance. The left flank was to be covered by Belgian divisions co-operating by an attack from Dixmude towards Clercken and Zarren, whilst either a French or British force attacked along the coast from Nieuport, in combination with a landing of British troops near Ostend.

The instructions added that the Commander-in-Chief would himself control the combined Allied force in Flanders, and conduct the campaign as a whole.

General Plumer's new proposals, presented on the 30th January,[2] were more cautious than the instructions warranted. The Messines operation was still to be carried out in three movements, as had been recommended in the 1916 plan. The preliminary occupation of the Spanbroekmolen knoll was to take place previous to the main assault. The Hill 60 attack was to be simultaneous with the Messines operation, the southern flank of the latter being shortened from Le Gheer to St. Yves (a mile north of Le Gheer), and extended a similar distance northwards from St. Eloi to the Ypres–Comines canal. In this way the assault by the southern Army would be delivered on a continuous front of over nine miles, from St. Yves to Mount Sorrel (1¼ miles south of Hooge). The objective was to be the near crest of the Messines–Wytschaete Ridge, including Messines village, and the back crest, including Wytschaete village, was to be taken on the following day. The northern Army was to attack at the same time; its frontage, an extension of the Hill 29 (Pilckem) attack, was to include the entire crest-line of the Pilckem Ridge, a frontage of six miles from Bellewaarde Lake to Steenstraat. General Plumer recommended that the artillery preparation should be extremely short—the original wording of his letter " limited to one " day ", was altered to " a limited one "— the wire-cutting

---

[1] See Sketch 1.
[2] See Sketch 2.

and counter-battery work being spread out over the previous fortnight.

Despite the demand for a rapid break-through and the expectation that the German resistance would be weak, General Plumer still insisted that the first day's objective of the northern Army should be limited to the capture of the German Second Line on the back slope of the Pilckem Ridge, an average advance of two thousand yards. He considered that, although the German resistance was expected to be weak, time should be allowed for the forward movement of artillery observers beyond the crest, so that the subsequent infantry advance past the Steenbeek might have adequate and observed artillery support.

Between these northern and southern assaults would be a gap of two thousand yards, from Mount Sorrel to Bellewaarde Lake, at the point of the Ypres Salient; but General Plumer did not believe it to be practicable to assemble enough artillery in this narrow space for a central attack simultaneous with those to south and north. He recommended that this gap should be closed by converging attacks made by the inner flanks of the two Armies immediately after the main assault, in order to obtain a substantial footing on Gheluvelt plateau. He urged the essential importance of this operation in order to cover the right flank of the northern Army which, two days after its first assault, was to resume its offensive north-eastwards across the Steenbeek to a line Broodseinde–Gravenstafel–Langemarck–Bixschoote. After the capture of Gheluvelt plateau, the southern Army was to take it over as far north as Broodseinde, to relieve the northern Army of all concern for the safety of its right flank.

The coastal attack was to begin when the main offensive had arrived level with Cortemarck, eight miles north of Passchendaele, or earlier if the enemy showed signs of great demoralization.[1] The advance from Nieuport was to be made by two divisions, and to be co-ordinated with a landing at three points at and south-west of Middelkerke by a specially trained division to be embarked at Dunkirk. Two reserve divisions advancing from Nieuport were to reinforce and extend farther the line gained by the landing force. As the landing points were only between two and four miles

---

[1] See Frontispiece.

from the Allied front at the mouth of the Yser, the landing force ran less risk of being isolated than if landed at Ostend, ten miles distant, as in the 1915 and 1916 plans.[1]

General Rawlinson, asked to comment on General Plumer's scheme, made a number of observations on the 9th February.[2] He suggested that the Messines offensive, given the mine-explosions, might be made in one day instead of three, and with fewer troops ; but his chief concern was with the northern offensive for which his own Fourth Army had been selected. He emphasized even more strongly than had General Plumer that the progress of the northern Army was " absolutely dependent " on the success of the centre attack across Gheluvelt plateau to cover its right flank. The advance beyond its first day's objective (the German Second Line) would not, he added, be practicable " until " that high ground [between Observatory Ridge and " Broodseinde] is in our possession ". He agreed with General Plumer that this centre attack could not take place simultaneously with the southern attack, " for the same " ground south and south-west of Ypres is required for the " assembly of troops and artillery for both ". The alternative he suggested was that the southern attack, on the front St. Yves–Mount Sorrel, be made first, and that it should be followed in 48–72 hours by the central and northern attacks, to be combined in a single northern operation on the front Mount Sorrel–Steenstraat. To this proposal Sir Douglas Haig replied that all three attacks could be made simultaneously " if tanks were used for a surprise attack " in the centre without artillery preparation to capture the " high ground between Observatory Ridge and Broodseinde".

General Rawlinson envisaged the campaign as predominantly a succession of infantry battles. He preferred that the northern Army should deliver the main offensive with four corps instead of three, as proposed, each corps to have two divisions in front and two in support, and that the remaining available divisions should be formed into a reserve corps, preferably two ; the duty of these reserve corps would be " to feed the four attacking corps and relieve exhausted

---

[1] Other reasons for abandoning the Ostend landing plan were that German shore batteries could sweep the harbour and that mines which could be fired electrically from the shore guarded the approaches.
[2] See Sketch 2.

"divisions in a similar manner to what was done during "the Somme fighting".[1] He also proposed that the headquarters of the northern Army should be well forward at Lovie Chateau (8 miles N.W. of Ypres), "in view of the "object of its operations being a rapid advance at any rate "as far as Roulers (12 miles distant)". Against this, Sir Douglas Haig wrote in the margin: "There must be no "halt on reaching Roulers".

The memorandum by the special sub-section under Colonel Macmullen was submitted on the 14th February. Written after consultation with Generals Plumer and Rawlinson, it summarized General Plumer's plan and the Commander-in-Chief's corrections.[2] The southern, central and northern assaults were to be delivered simultaneously. The centre assault was to be made by massed tanks, as part of the northern operation, with the first day's objective limited to the German Second Line. The memorandum agreed that the capture of Gheluvelt plateau by the centre was "the most formidable of the tasks", and "admittedly "a matter of first importance to subsequent operations". For that reason, it was urged that the postponement of this assault by even one day, as proposed by General Plumer, was unsound. The capture on the first day of the woods on the western slope would enable the assembly beyond that obstacle, on the plateau itself, of the large number of tanks required to occupy the remainder of the high ground as far as the line Becelaere–Broodseinde. The second assault was to be made two days after the first, and simultaneously with the advance of the northern Army across the Steenbeek to the Broodseinde–Passchendaele Ridge. To accord with Sir Douglas Haig's instructions, the subsequent operations beyond that ridge were denoted on an accompanying map[3] by arrows to give the idea of open warfare by pursuit troops and cavalry towards Roulers and Thourout.

The only alteration to the detail of the memorandum in the following weeks was the result of a revised scheme, sent

---

[1] Sir Douglas Haig disapproved of this reference, and in a marginal note wrote: "Our objective is to break through rapidly. As soon as corps "have captured Passchendaele Ridge manœuvre becomes possible, so "divisions in corps should be reduced to three". General Rawlinson's proposal was, however, eventually adopted.
[2] Appendix VII.
[3] See Frontispiece.

SELECTION OF GENERAL GOUGH

to G.H.Q. by General Plumer on the 18th March,[1] for the capture of the Messines Ridge. He proposed the capture of both Spanbroekmolen knoll and the second day's objective on the first day, and to carry it out with three corps, twelve divisions in all, instead of with five corps, of seventeen divisions, as previously estimated; the heavy and field artillery estimate was not changed, but that for 144 tanks was reduced by one-half, in view of a probable shortage. On the 3rd April, Sir Douglas Haig suggested that the original third day's objective, the back crest of the Ridge, might also be gained on the first day; and added that, by taking advantage of the enemy's disorganization, the advance might be continued down the eastern slope to capture as many as possible of the enemy's guns in position there. The task of capturing the Ridge was accordingly telescoped into one day, or rather into five morning hours; and in the afternoon the advance was to be continued down the eastern slope to the Oosttaverne Line.

SELECTION OF GENERAL GOUGH

The Macmullen memorandum was accepted as the official version of the plan for a Flanders campaign in 1917; but although the Commander-in-Chief had approved the wording of it, he was evidently not satisfied with the spirit in which the Army commanders whom he had selected proposed to carry it out. Both General Plumer and General Rawlinson clearly had in mind a succession of infantry battles, at least until the Roulers–Thourout line was reached, a procedure which had little in common with the G.H.Q. instruction of the 8th January. They evidently did not share the vision of a rapid break through *à la Nivelle* to the Passchendaele–Westroosebeke–Staden Ridge followed by a wide sweep with cavalry through western Belgium and a decisive defeat of the enemy; so the Commander-in-Chief now sought an Army commander for the main northern offensive who would be more sympathetic to his own changed outlook. His choice fell on General Sir Hubert Gough, commanding the Fifth Army, whose lack of knowledge of the peculiarities of Flanders and of the development of the plan was outweighed by the fact that he was young, just 47. A

---

[1] See Sketch 2.

cavalryman, endowed with that rapidity of decision, that impatience of long preparations, and that urge to push on at all costs typical of old Blücher " Marshal Vorwärts " and known to the Army as " the cavalry spirit ", he was less inclined than an older man or a foot soldier to the tactics of " wearing down " battles and trench warfare. It will be recalled that, before the Battles of the Somme in 1916, Sir Douglas Haig had selected General Gough, over the heads of the other corps commanders, to command the Reserve Army and lead the cavalry, followed by two divisions, in pursuit through the gap that the Fourth Army was to make.[1] On the 30th April Sir Douglas Haig told him that he would command the main northern operation in Flanders and the landing force. The definite order is dated 13th May.[2]

Nivelle's Failure

On the 16th April General Nivelle's plan was put to the test, and the story of its tragic failure has been told in the previous volume.[3] There was no surprise, and the Germans were ready. Within a few days the French offensive on the Chemin des Dames and in front of Reims had been brought to a standstill with very heavy losses and little gain of ground. The German Supreme Command had made sure that the miscalculation—the delay in the arrival of the counter-attack divisions—of October and December 1916 in front of Verdun was not repeated. A succession of

---

[1] See " 1916 " Vol. I, pp. 267, 304, 306, 309. General Gough had written to Sir Douglas Haig on the 10th March that " we can now beat the Germans " when and where we like if we have time for a fairly good artillery pre-" paration "; his letter added that " five of my divisions can hold the " front line east of Bapaume, and all the rest of the Fifth Army is at your " disposal for any offensive you may decide on ".

The appointment of a cavalryman, General Sir E. Allenby, to command the main offensive in the Arras battles which began on 9th April was a parallel case. There, too, cavalry was expected to play a major part in the later stages of the operations (see " 1917 " Vol. I, p. 180–1).

[2] A contributory cause of the appointment was the proposal, on 24th April, for a combined attack by the French and British, on St. Quentin and the Flesquières salient respectively, about the middle of May. As this attack was in the Fourth Army area, it was more convenient to leave General Rawlinson to plan and carry it out in co-operation with the French.

[3] See " 1917 " Vol. I, Chapter XIX.

General Joffre, even before this offensive, had told British officers that the French army had temporarily " shot its bolt " and, in the interest of the Allied cause, should be given opportunity to recuperate.

counter-attack formations had been organized back for fifteen miles to absorb the thrust of the offensive; and the capture of a French operation order ten days before the assault had given time for the withdrawal of the mass of the artillery out of range of the French counter-batteries. Even so, the course of the battle had justified the critics; the inner worth of the German army had been underrated. The French army, unfit to carry out the immense task assigned to it, was strained beyond breaking-point, and the suddenness of the collapse after such reckless promises of victory gave an added shock from which it would take a long time to recover.

Although the dire effects of the Nivelle disaster were not at once apparent, Sir Douglas Haig realized that the character of a Flanders campaign would have to be modified. On the 1st May, in a memorandum for the information of the War Cabinet, he wrote, with reference to the Arras battle then in progress, that " the enemy's fighting strength is not " yet broken, and it is essential to realize that it can only " be broken by hard and continued fighting. . . . To press " on the offensive without strong and active French co-" operation would be unwise ", particularly as, he said, " my British divisions are already some 60,000 below " establishment ". On the other hand, there was the " urgent need to clear the Belgian coast this summer ". To give these operations a reasonable chance of success, he laid down four conditions: first, that the French should take back at least as much of the front as the British had taken over since General Nivelle assumed command; secondly, the French must undertake simultaneously a limited offensive; thirdly, his divisions and heavy artillery must be brought up to establishment; and, fourthly, the Belgians should hand over a small frontage required for the British attack. In conclusion, he said that success was reasonably possible, and " even if a full measure of success is not gained, " we shall be attacking the enemy on a front where he " cannot refuse to fight, and where, therefore, our purpose " of wearing him down can be given effect to "; for the first step, he wrote, " must always be to wear down [' soften ', " as is said nowadays] the enemy's power of resistance until " he is so weakened that he will be unable to withstand a " decisive blow ".

THE FRANCO-BRITISH MILITARY CONFERENCE: 4TH MAY

At the Military Conference on the 4th May[1] in Paris, at which France was represented by General Nivelle and General Pétain, just appointed Chief of the General Staff with extended powers, and Great Britain by Sir Douglas Haig and General Robertson, it was agreed that if the enemy were given time to recover from the effects of the Allied attacks, the fruits would be lost: but the original plan of the Allies was no longer operative, the rupture of the hostile front could no longer be contemplated, the object should now be to exhaust the enemy's power of resistance, and this could be attained by attacking relentlessly with limited objectives, making the fullest possible use of artillery. It was agreed that the British should assume responsibility for the main operation, the French supporting them by vigorous attacks and taking back a portion of the British front—as far north as Havrincourt, that is about sixteen miles.

THE INTER-ALLIED CONFERENCE: 4TH–5TH MAY

In the afternoon and on the following day a general Inter-Allied Conference took place in Paris, which had before them the results of the morning Military Conference. The whole situation was discussed, but Macedonia was the chief subject.[2] As regards the Western Front, General Pétain had to report that the confidence of the army in its chiefs and in the Government was undermined. Whilst this factor dominated the considerations of the French delegates, the British representatives were equally concerned about the immense shipping losses due to Germany's unrestricted submarine campaign, the sinkings during the previous month, a total of over eight hundred thousand tons, having surpassed all records. In those darkest days of the War, cheered only by the good news that, on the 6th April, the United States of America had declared war on Germany, the decisions reached by the Conference were as courageous as they were necessary. It was unanimously agreed that offensive operations must be continued on the

---

[1] See " 1917 " Vol. I, p. 429.
[2] See " Macedonia " Vol. I, pp. 315 and 350.

VIEWS OF THE PRIME MINISTERS

Western Front, to give the enemy no respite either to recover from his losses in Champagne and about Arras in April, or to gain easy and possibly decisive successes against Russia and Italy whilst awaiting the effect of the submarine campaign against Britain.

Mr. Lloyd George told the Conference that " the enemy " must not be left in peace for one moment ", and " we must " go on hitting and hitting with all our strength until the " Germans ended, as they always do, by cracking ". He emphasized that the loss of 45,000 prisoners and seventy square miles of territory on the Aisne and at Arras must have greatly affected them and induced pessimism. The British Government, he said, were ready to put the full strength of their army into the attack, but emphasized that " it will be no good doing so unless the French do the same, " otherwise the Germans would bring their best men and " guns and all their ammunition against the British army, " and then later against the French ". Mr. Lloyd George also confirmed the unanimous agreement of the Military Conference, admitting that the time and place of the attacks, and the methods to be adopted, must be left to the military authorities responsible. He said he preferred that the generals should keep their plans of execution to themselves, as when plans, were communicated on paper to Ministers it was rare that the Ministers were the only people to know them. He added that he did not want to know the present plan of attack, nor the number of guns or divisions to be engaged ; for it was essential to keep such details secret.

The French Premier, Monsieur Ribot, expressed admiration for the resolute language of Mr. Lloyd George, and undertook to continue the offensive, provided that the French reserves were not squandered. In this connection there was common accord on the lesson of the Nivelle failure : that it could no longer be a question of breaking through the enemy's front and aiming at distant objectives, but one of wearing down and exhausting the enemy's resistance ; and should that result be achieved, to exploit it to the fullest possible extent. General Pétain repeated the opinion that he had given on this matter prior to the Nivelle offensive. He advised that as German counter-attacks, probably in superior strength, would soon have to be met, objectives should be strictly limited to a zone which could be covered by an overwhelming artillery barrage : the heaviest losses, out of all proportion to gains, had, he said, occurred when the attacking infantry passed beyond that zone. " It is important ", he added, " to grasp clearly the " distinction between action in depth and action in breadth ; " to contain and destroy the enemy's forces, action in " breadth will give the best results ".[1]

The members of the conference were unanimous as to the general policy to be pursued. A series of attacks with objectives limited to the range of the mass of the supporting artillery was to be delivered in order to " destroy the " enemy's divisions ", and so prevent a decisive German offensive during 1917. It was not believed that an Allied offensive in that year could decide the War ; but by such a method of attrition it was hoped to conserve the Allied strength and to survive with a sufficient force to launch a victorious offensive in 1918 with the help of American troops which, it was expected, would by then have arrived in considerable numbers.

The military agreement was incorporated in the concluding resolution of the Conference of Ministers to the effect that the British and French Governments undertook to continue the offensive on the Western Front in accordance with the principles agreed upon at the military conferences and " to devote the whole of their forces to this purpose ".

THE ARMY COMMANDERS' CONFERENCE AT DOULLENS : 7TH MAY

Three days after the Paris Conference, Sir Douglas Haig, at a meeting of his Army commanders at Doullens, gave effect to its decisions so far as they concerned the British army.[2] He announced that General Nivelle had achieved only a limited advance and the attack was halted, so that the plan for co-operating with him was no longer operative : " the objective of the French and British will now be to " wear down and exhaust the enemy's resistance by " systematically attacking him by surprise. When this " end has been achieved the main blow will be struck by " the British forces operating from the Ypres front, with

---

[1] F.O.A. vi. (i.), pp. 785 *et seq.* This was General Foch's policy in 1918.
[2] What he said is recorded in O.A.D. 434 of 7th May, signed by the Chief of the General Staff.

HAIG'S NEW PLAN

" the eventual object of securing the Belgian coast and
" connecting with the Dutch frontier ". The Arras battle,
he said, would be continued, in the hope of misleading the
enemy as to our intentions and with the object of wearing
him down; but the troops and material employed in it
would be gradually reduced and transferred to the north.
There the operations would be continued in two phases:

(a) the attack on Messines–Wytschaete Ridge, about 7th June.

(b) " Northern Operation ", to secure the Belgian coast, some weeks later.

The Armies not employed in these operations, he said,
were to do what they could " with a view to wearing out
" as many of the enemy troops as possible ": to bridge the
interval between the two attacks in Flanders, the French,
Italians and Russians had agreed to undertake operations
to hold and wear out the enemy: and it was possible that
the Arras battle might be continued after the Messines
attack, and before the Northern Operation.

The rest of the Commander-in-Chief's statement dealt
with the moves and re-allotment of troops, and the Army
commanders were asked to submit their proposals.

The capture of Messines Ridge by the Second Army as a
separate operation would eliminate the difficulty of the
centre attack on Gheluvelt plateau which, it will be remembered, Sir Douglas Haig had proposed to make with massed
tanks.[1] With the freeing of the southern flank, the centre
attack could be made with artillery support, and be combined
with the original Northern attack as a single " Northern
" Operation " against the front Mount Sorrel-Steenstraat.[2]

DOUBTS OF FRENCH SUPPORT

The Allied representatives at the Paris Conference had
separated in complete agreement on the 5th May, not aware

---

[1] A reconnaissance report by a tank officer (Captain G. le Q. Martel) in April stated that the sector of attack was unsuited to the employment of tanks, owing to the narrow defiles between the three woods which guarded the approaches, and to the broken surface and woods on the high ground itself. The report suggested that the majority of the tanks would have to be employed north of the woods and of Bellewaarde Lake, towards Westhoek, where they might wheel to the right, taking the German Second Line in flank, and, at a later stage, advance towards Zonnebeke.

[2] See Sketch 2.

that trouble had actually broken out in the French army. An infantry division had refused to go up to the front line, and signs of demoralization, such as wholesale absence without leave and refusal to obey orders, were spreading through a large number of French units. During the following week this state of indiscipline worsened, causing intense anxiety to the French authorities.

The French Government made every effort to conceal the facts; but on the 12th May, General Robertson, Chief of the Imperial General Staff, wrote to Sir Douglas Haig that the unsettled state of affairs in France, together with the probability of a separate peace by Russia, might have a detrimental effect on the efficient prosecution of the offensive operation agreed upon at the Paris Conference. Sir Douglas Haig, asked for his views, replied on the 16th that the opinions which he had previously expressed still held good, viz., "that the action of a wearing-down "character must be continued"; that he was dividing the Flanders plan into two phases and that it was unlikely that the Russian situation would develop with sufficient rapidity to affect the first phase; but that, if it did, he could abandon it at the last moment; the second phase, which was not to take place until several weeks later, would not be carried out unless the situation at the time was favourable.

Sir Douglas Haig's reply was crossed by a further letter from General Robertson, on the 16th May, to the effect that the printed French version of the resolutions of the Paris conference, just received, made no reference to the promise given by the French Government to continue offensive action; this omission, he wrote, might signify that the French Government, on reflection, had decided not to bind themselves definitely to that resolution. The letter was followed the same day by a telegram from the War Cabinet stating that they would only support the British offensive plans on the express condition that the French played their full part; it added that the Prime Minister wished Sir Douglas Haig to be very firm on that point in his discussions with the French general, Nivelle, Pétain or Foch, whoever it might be, who was really responsible for deciding on operations, as any suggestion of an " intention to embark "on costly operations whether the French co-operated or "not may result in our fighting practically alone ". "To "this ", the telegram concluded, " or to a plan which "contains the danger of it the War Cabinet could not "agree".

To clarify the situation, Sir Douglas Haig arranged a meeting two days later (18th May) at Amiens with General Pétain, who, on the 15th, had succeeded General Nivelle in command of the French Armies of the North and North-East. General Pétain was outspoken on the unrest within the French army, and Sir Douglas Haig liked his frank and straightfoward manner; he was business-like and brief of speech, a quality rare in Frenchmen, and seemed clear-headed and knowledgeable. Regarding the French offensive intentions, General Pétain said he had in preparation four attacks, including one at Malmaison on the 10th June, (carried out in October) and another with fifteen divisions at Verdun about the end of July (carried out 20th August). Sir Douglas Haig said that these might synchronize with the prepared British offensives in Flanders, and he explained the plan of campaign in some detail. General Pétain objected to its distant aims; they were contrary to the advice he had given to the Paris Conference to restrict operations during 1917 to attacks with strictly limited objectives: from the French standpoint, however, it was essential that the British army should attack and, as he told Sir Douglas Haig, where and how was not his business. Sir Douglas Haig pointed out that the successive attacks would have limited objectives; but that "as the wearing-"down process continues, advanced guards and cavalry "will be able to progress for much longer distances profiting "by the enemy's demoralization until a real decision is "reached".

After studying a written summary of the plan,[1] General Pétain said that he was prepared to hand over the Nieuport sector temporarily, but suggested that six French divisions, including the two already holding the coastal sector at Nieuport, should take part in the Flanders campaign; he proposed that these four additional French divisions should co-operate on the front Boesinghe–Yperlee Marshes (north of Bixschoote) with the six Belgian *divisions d'armée*[2] under the command of the King of the Belgians with a French Chief of Staff, for which post General Anthoine was named.

[1] The Frontispiece is a copy of the map attached to the summary.
[2] See Sketch 1. A Belgian *division d'armée* was equivalent in establishment to two British divisions.

This offer was made to compensate for the non-participation of the French Third Army in the St. Quentin–Cambrai attack, to which General Nivelle had agreed three weeks before and in which General Pétain was unable to acquiesce, as the capture of St. Quentin would be too difficult.[1] He also regretted that the fulfilment of the promise given at the Inter-Allied military conference on the 4th May, to take over the British front northwards to Havrincourt would not be practicable; but he offered to take over at once a frontage of eight thousand yards, that of three British divisions.

As a result of this conference, Sir Douglas Haig telegraphed the same evening to the War Cabinet that the French would carry out their part as agreed at the Paris Conference, and that their co-operation would be wholehearted. The telegram added that General Pétain was in a position to give these assurances.

In the event, the Group of Armies under the King of the Belgians was not formed; but the French First Army, which had been in reserve under General Anthoine during the Nivelle offensive, was moved to Flanders, to be on the left of the British, and placed àt the disposal of Sir Douglas Haig.

The French Mutinies

Between the 29th April and the end of September, 119 " acts of collective indiscipline ",[2] 110 of them grave, occurred in the Armies which had taken part in the Nivelle offensive; of these no less than 80 were in the period 25th May–10th June.

> They took the form of " manifestations against the " War, revolutionary songs and cries, throwing stones, " breaking windows and destruction of material; " some fires were reported, but very few acts of violence " against officers were committed. Indiscipline was

---

[1] See " 1917 " Vol. I, pp. 410, 502.
The British share in this plan, the capture of the Flesquières salient, was the seed which was eventually to grow (in November) into the Battle of Cambrai 1917.

[2] F.O.A. v. (ii.), pp. 192–4, from which these extracts are taken. The word " indiscipline ", not " insubordination " or " mutinerie ", is used throughout; but, from the British point of view, the translation is " mutiny ".

" marked by the refusal to go up to the trenches,
" especially to attack ".

At the same time, " grave incidents occurred in the
" leave trains, with a few unwedging of rails. . . .
" Red flags were waved at the windows, revolutionary
" songs were sung in passing through stations ; windows
" were broken, water tanks emptied, locomotives
" uncoupled ; soldiers on duty and railway officials
" were insulted and struck ; rifles were fired. It is
" only fair to add that 60 per cent. of the leave men
" were drunk ".

Further, at the same period, there were strikes and riots
" in the interior ", which were serious in seven large towns.[1]

Faced by this situation, General Pétain and the French Government considered they had but one task, and that was to nurse the French army back to health, and that it would involve a rigid defensive policy until the American army was ready to give practical military assistance in 1918. Behind this defensive attitude the army was to be restored to its former toughness, and an immense amount of war material accumulated ; the heavy artillery was to be doubled, the air fleet enormously increased, and 3,000 small tanks were to be built, with a vast quantity of smoke shell to mask the eventual offensive. By these means, victory in 1918 might be assured ; and to all who urged an immediate effort in co-ordination with the British, General Pétain replied, " I am waiting for the Americans and the tanks ".

In this frame of mind, General Pétain sent word to Sir Douglas Haig on the 2nd June, by his Chief of the Staff to mark its extreme secrecy, that the state of indiscipline within the French army would not permit the promised Malmaison attack to be delivered on the 10th.[2] General Debeney, who brought the message, explained that the artillery battle on the Aisne front and in Champagne would be continued, but that the earliest possible French attack would, as far as could be seen, be at Verdun in the last days of July. Sir Douglas Haig replied that he counted upon

---

[1] Some interesting details of the mutinies will be found in an article in *Blackwood's Magazine* of January 1944, entitled " The Bent Sword ", by A. M. G.

[2] Monsieur Painlévé, the French War Minister at the time, states in his book (" Comment j'ai nommé Foch et Pétain ", p. 143) that at this period there were between Soissons and Paris only two divisions upon which he could confidently rely.

30 MESSINES OPERATION DECIDED ON

General Pétain to do everything possible by offensive measures at least to hold the German divisions on his front.

The lamentable state of the French army completely altered the situation, in view of the War Cabinet's insistence of the 16th May that the French must "play their full "part"; but the need for offensive action was, in Sir Douglas Haig's opinion, of more rather than of less urgency : armies do not recover from a state of serious unrest in a few weeks, as he knew.[1] The Messines offensive was due to be launched in five days' time, on the 7th June. He had visited the three corps concerned during the previous week, and had the utmost confidence in the result. On his own responsibility, without further reference to the War Cabinet and without informing them of General Pétain's latest message, which he regarded as a military secret, he decided to allow the operation to proceed. No argument, he felt, would be so effective as a success.

The Germans, unfortunately, were not unwarned. As early as the 12th May "reports of a British attack in "Flanders began to increase, and O.H.L. saw that it must "be reckoned with", and so informed the Armies.[2] The German Crown Prince's forces were to be reduced, and he was ordered to fall back gradually if attacked. He says :[3]

"When the crisis of the fight [Nivelle's offensive] was "over, my Group of Armies had to give up considerable "forces for employment elsewhere. O.H.L. demanded "that I should hand over a large proportion of my "freshest troops for Galicia and for the Flanders battle

---

[1] It will be seen in the volumes on the operations in 1918 that even then the French divisions alongside the British had not recovered their old fighting spirit, and were very carefully nursed by their commanders.

Most German accounts state that the information about the "mutinies" in the French army was not obtained until many weeks had passed. The following, however, appears in "Eine Armee meutert", by P. C. Ettighoffer, who was in the front trenches early in June when, about 2.30 a.m., three escaped German prisoners of war came over No Man's Land. The escort detailed to take them back learnt from them—and the story ran like wildfire along the front—that they had been wandering in the French lines for nearly a fortnight, and that there was trouble there. Whole divisions had mutinied, regiments had left their positions, flying the red flag. "They want to make an end of the War, one way or another. The "French army is tired". The rumours about a mutiny in the French army ceased after a few days. "Too wild to be true. No trace of a "possibility", was the verdict. "The escaped prisoners wanted to tell "a good story and make themselves important".

[2] G.O.A. xii., p. 547.

[3] In "Meine Erinnerungen aus Deutschlands Heldenkampf", p. 279.

THE ENEMY IS READY 31

" that was preparing against Crown Prince Rupprecht's
" Group of Armies ".[1]

Crown Prince Rupprecht had asked for ten divisions, if possible, fifteen. Actually, ten divisions and much heavy artillery were hurried to him from the Aisne front,[2] and the German Crown Prince was ordered by O.H.L. to stand on the defensive.

Thus had the Flanders offensive cast its shadow before it.

---

[1] See Note at end of Chapter V.
[2] " Between 1st May and 7th June, 13 divisions were added to the " *Fourth Army*, which faced the British and Belgians between Wervicq " and the coast, also 106 batteries, 85 heavy ". G.O.A., xii., p. 445.

CHAPTER III

THE BATTLE OF MESSINES 1917

7TH–14TH JUNE

GENERAL PLAN

(Sketches 3, 4)

The plan for the Messines operation, in its final shape of the 3rd April,[1] happened to conform closely to the operational decisions of the Paris Military Conference of the 4th May. It was to be an assault on a broad front, nearly ten miles, from St. Yves to Mount Sorrel; and the final objective was strictly limited to a depth of one to two miles into the enemy's position.[1] The three subsidiary objectives marked the evolution of the plan since its inception in 1915; but, instead of the capture of each being the work of a day or more, the subsidiary objectives had become halting places at which successive waves of infantry were to leap-frog the leading lines to gain the final destination within a few hours. The high ground of Messines Ridge was to be captured during the morning of the day of assault, and in the afternoon a short advance down the eastern slope was to secure possession. The idea of capturing Spanbroekmolen knoll first, proposed on the 30th January, was abandoned.

The operation orders for the battle were issued by Second Army headquarters on the 10th and 19th May,[2] and detailed orders by corps on the 15th and following days. Three corps of the Second Army were to be employed. On the right, the II Anzac Corps (Lieut.-General Sir A. J. Godley) was to assault north-eastwards and capture the southern shoulder of the Ridge, including Messines village. The IX Corps (Lieut.-General Sir Alexander Gordon), advancing due east astride the Spanbroekmolen saddle of high ground between the heights of Kemmel[3] and Wytschaete, was to capture the central sector of the Ridge, including the village of Wytschaete. On the left the X Corps (Lieut.-General

---

[1] See Sketch 3.
[2] Appendices VIII and IX.
[3] 2 miles west of Wytschaete.

THE PREPARATIONS

Sir T. L. N. Morland) was to assault south-eastwards and gain the northern part of the Ridge between the St. Eloi–Oosttaverne road and Mount Sorrel, including the strong German defences about the Ypres–Comines canal and railway and on Hill 60. Behind these three corps was the XIV (Lieut.-General Lord Cavan) in G.H.Q. reserve, ten miles back in the Flêtre area.

The left, wing of the Second Army, from Mount Sorrel northwards to the Belgian front at Boesinghe, was formed by the II (Lieut.-General Sir C. W. Jacob) and VIII Corps (Lieut.-General Sir A. G. Hunter-Weston). The II Corps headquarters had moved up to Flanders with one division, the 30th, from Arras, and took over the Hooge sector, astride the Ypres–Menin road, on the 30th May, the Bellewaarde Lake forming its left boundary.[1]

Each of the three attacking corps was to deploy three divisions in the line, the nine divisions being about equally spaced along the 17,000-yard frontage of the battle sector. In addition, three divisions (4th Australian, 11th and 24th) were transferred from the Arras–Bullecourt front, one to each corps, as a reserve, making a total of 12 divisions directly available for the operation. They were to be supported by a strong concentration of artillery, and by the explosion of a number of mines which had long been prepared for the purpose.[2] Seventy-two of the new Mark IV model tanks, allotted to the Second Army for the battle, were also to make their first appearance in action in order to assist the infantry to capture the numerous strongpoints.[3] They assembled towards the end of May in the woods and camouflaged shelters near Ouderdom and Dranoutre, six miles south-west of Ypres. The examination of probable objectives and routes had already been made with the help of air photographs and plasticine models. The 179th Tunnelling Company R.E. then prepared forward routes, making crossings over streams, railway tracks and trenches.

The German position formed a marked salient, bulging sharply westwards from the main ridge to include the

---
[1] See Sketch 2.
[2] See p. 4.
[3] Appendix X. See Note I, at end of Chapter. The old Mark I and Mark II machines, with their armament removed, were used to carry forward petrol, oil, ammunition, food, water and other supplies from the advanced dumps.

Spanbroekmolen knoll. Consequently, the two flank corps, the II Anzac and X, had to cover only eight hundred and twelve hundred yards respectively to reach their objective along the Ridge, whereas the central corps, the IX, had over two thousand yards to go. As compensation, the assault frontage of the centre corps was to be gradually narrowed down as the advance progressed—from over five thousand yards at the start to less than two thousand yards at the objective on the Ridge. It was expected, too, that the pressure by the two flank corps against the shoulders of the salient would help the centre throughout.

Special training areas at the back of each corps sector, on ground resembling that to be crossed on the day of assault, had been marked with tapes and coloured flags to show the various farms, woods, strongpoints and objectives. The assault brigades carried out at least half a dozen rehearsals over these areas, the men, wearing full kit, practising every detail, including the methods of communication and the move forward of brigade and battalion headquarters; artillery brigades rehearsed with the infantry brigades they were to support. A large model of the Ridge, the size of two croquet lawns, was constructed near Scherpenberg for all those taking part, down to platoon commanders, to study; many of the divisions, too, made clay models of their particular sectors.

During this period of battle training the front line was only lightly held, a battalion covering each divisional sector; and a succession of raids was made into the German position to gain information and harass the garrison.[1] By night, working parties were employed digging six lines of assembly trenches about a hundred yards apart, extending into No Man's Land, the foremost being in places within a hundred and fifty yards of the German sentry posts. Opposite the mines a wider berth was given, the instructions being that dug-outs were unsafe in these sectors within four hundred yards, and trenches within three hundred yards. The assembly trenches were completed in the last few nights before the assault, with unexpectedly little opposition.

---

[1] In the IX Corps sector alone, 19 raids were carried out between 16th May and 7th June, varying in strength from 300 to 12 men, during which 171 prisoners were taken and a number of Germans killed, at a cost of 172 casualties all ranks.

The Mines and Engineer Preparations[1]

By visits to the front and by staff conferences at Second Army headquarters in Cassel, General Plumer and his chief General Staff Officer, Major-General C. H. Harington, watched over and co-ordinated every detail of the preparations. The corps schemes were based on four General Staff pamphlets, issued during the previous winter, which summarized the lessons learnt during the Somme battles in 1916 for the training of infantry, artillery and engineers for offensive action, and for forward communication in battle.[2] In addition, the schemes included several progressive features introduced for the Battle of Arras on the 9th April, such as the greater attention paid to counter-battery work, the time-table barrage throughout the operation, and the application of machine-gun barrages. Similar use of the mass of experience gained in the previous two years was made by the engineer and administrative services.

In one respect, however, the Messines operation was unique. The longest considered of the preparations, and the most incalculable in its effect, was the explosion of mines under the German front defences immediately before the infantry assault. The obstinacy and duration of the underground warfare in the preparation of these mines, the depth and length of the galleries driven, the weight of the charges laid and the length of time they remained tamped and wired, makes this mining offensive the most notable undertaken in conjunction with any battle or campaign of the War.

Mining operations in the sector had begun in a small way in the early spring of 1915 at a level of 15 feet or so below the surface; but the conception of a mining offensive may be said to date from September 1915, when the then Engineer-in-Chief, Br.-General G. H. Fowke, put forward proposals for conducting mining operations on a considerable scale by driving galleries 60 or 90 feet below the surface.

---

[1] See Sketch 3.
[2] The General Staff publications were (1) " Instructions for the Training " of Divisions for Offensive Action "; (2) " Artillery Notes "; (3) " Notes " on the Royal Engineers. Preparation for and the employment of R.E. " in Offensive Action "; and (4) " Forward Inter-Communication in " Battle ".

The idea was inspired by Major J. Norton Griffiths,[1] in civil life an engineering contractor, and the proposal was to drive galleries under the Ploegsteert–Messines, Kemmel–Wytschaete, and Vierstraat–Wytschaete roads, also two between the Douve and the south-eastern corner of Ploegsteert Wood, the objectives to be reached in from three to six months. The work subsequently undertaken followed this outline closely, though not the time-table; and the tunnels were not driven to such distances within the enemy's lines as projected.[2]

Br.-General Fowke's scheme did not receive approval until the 6th January, 1916, after General Sir Douglas Haig had been appointed Commander-in-Chief; but neither the Engineer-in-Chief nor his assistant, Colonel R. N. Harvey, had waited for this approval to make at least a start with deep mining on an organized plan, as opposed to the haphazard local undertakings of the year 1915. By January 1916 several deep shafts, sign-boarded as "deep wells", were already in existence, and half a dozen tunnels had been begun, including one at Hill 60, dating from August 1915. The intention to continue these six deep tunnels to be ready by the end of June 1916 was approved by G.H.Q., and four were ready by the time stated; but when the Second Army offensive prepared for the summer of 1916 was postponed, the mining offensive took on greater proportions.

The soil formation in the sector consists of a shallow layer of sand or sandy loam, beneath which is a layer of saturated semi-liquid sand, or sand and clay known to miners as "slurry"; under these two layers is a deep seam of blue clay, familiar on this side of the Channel as "London clay". The earlier mining had been carried out for the most part in the two upper layers, but the blue clay offered a double advantage: it gave the depth recommended by Br.-General

---

[1] Major (the late Lieut.-Colonel Sir John) Norton Griffiths had been largely responsible for the formation of the first tunnelling companies. He had also introduced the system of "clay-kicking" into military mining, a process fully described and illustrated in "Tunnellers" by Captain W. Grant Grieve and Bernard Newman, p. 32.

[2] Br.-General Fowke suggested, for example, that the galleries directed against Hollandscheschuur Farm should be continued along the Vierstraat-Wytschaete road to the middle of Grand Bois, a distance of 1,050 yards. He also suggested attacking the Bon Fermier Cabaret, on the outskirts of Messines, which was almost as far. The longest gallery actually driven, that to the farthest mine at Kruisstraat, was 720 yards.

THE MINES

Fowke, and also provided a better medium for the driving of galleries.[1]

As the Germans were on the higher ground, the position was especially favourable for the work. Long galleries driven horizontally direct into the blue clay seam from shafts 300–400 yards behind the British front line would enable the mines to be placed 80 to 120 feet below the German front trench system. At that depth they would be difficult for the enemy to discover; and surprise was more likely to be gained than at the shallower levels. For tunnelling on such a scale mechanical diggers were used experimentally, similar to those employed for the construction of the Tube railways through the London clay; but neither of the two designs supplied from home gave as good or as quick results in the existing conditions as could be achieved with relays of manual labour. Great care had to be taken in the disposal of the excavated soil, for the evidence of heaps of blue clay would at once betray the secret of the depth of the mine galleries. It had to be carried away to distant woods or buried under sandbag parapets.[2]

The mining points eventually selected were: "The Birdcage"[3] and Trench 122 (near the south-eastern and north-eastern corners of Ploegsteert Wood, respectively), Trench 127, Petite Douve Farm, Ontario Farm, Kruisstraat, Spanbroekmolen, Peckham, Maedelstede Farm, Petit Bois, Hollandscheschuur, St. Eloi, the Caterpillar and Hill 60. At some of these points more than one mine was eventually established; at both Hollandscheschuur and Kruisstraat there were three. The tunnelling companies engaged were the 171st, 175th, 250th, 1st Canadian, 3rd Canadian and

---

[1] The intervening "slurry" had presented a problem insoluble to the earlier miners with their limited equipment, and one which, even in 1917, threatened in some instances to become so. In the area south of Kruisstraat, where the light upper soils are not present, the blue clay is overlaid by a very deep layer of wet grey silt, which made the sinking of shafts even more difficult than farther north.

[2] The success with which this was accomplished is shown by the fact that, although deep mine galleries were suspected (such as that at Petite Douve, discovered in August 1916), German airmen could nowhere discover any dumps of the dark bluish Ypres clay. It was not until 9th April 1917, when a German raiding party brought back a sample of clay, that the presence of a deep-level shaft considerably below any of the German deep galleries was suspected. Even at that late date the shaft was considered an isolated instance, and the extent of the work during the previous eighteen months was not appreciated.

[3] Not on Sketch 3. It is 1,300 yards south of St. Yves.

1st Australian. Three other companies, the 183rd, 2nd Canadian and 2nd Australian, were simultaneously engaged in constructing underground shelters in the area of the Second Army. The 32 tunnelling companies on the Western Front had not been increased since June 1916,[1] but with larger infantry working parties many more men were engaged in tunnelling. The work was a struggle both against natural difficulties and against the enemy, against quicksands and against the German miner with his defensive counter-mining and his camouflets.[2] Above ground, too, the Germans used trench artillery against any suspected mine-shafts, and the bomb of a heavy trench mortar was another of the deadly weapons the tunnellers had to face. The dearly bought experiences of 1916 had, however, led to improved equipment, such as noiseless air and water pumps, more accurate survey and listening instruments, better rescue apparatus and steel " tubing " for shafts sunk in wet ground.[3] The scientific study of geological conditions, care and skill in the disposal and camouflage of spoil, and the substitution of ammonal for gunpowder and gun-cotton,[4] also eased the great task. Only two mines, one at Petite Douve Farm and one of the Kruisstraat branches were "lost", and the three mines at the Birdcage were not fired; so that of the twenty-four mines, 19 were blown on the 7th June, 1917, preliminary to the assault.[5]

Although the other work of the tunnelling companies during this period was less spectacular, it was very important; in point of fact considerably greater numbers of men were employed on the whole Second Army front in defensive

---

[1] See "1916" Vol. I, pp. 73-7.

[2] A camouflet is a small defensive charge which shakes up the sub-strata and wrecks the galleries, but does not affect the surface.

[3] Cylindrical steel tubing was used, the lowest section having a cutting edge. The superincumbent weight of the added sections or rings was sufficient to sink the whole, the spoil being evacuated from the shaft.

[4] Though ammonal was the basic explosive in the charges, gun-cotton and blasting gelatine were still employed as primers to ensure the explosion.

[5] Details of each mine are given in Note II at end of Chapter; and other information in footnotes to the text in Chapter IV.

Actually, the same number of mines was fired on 1st July 1916,, the first day of the Battles of the Somme—19 in each case; but 11 of the latter were very small, being charged with only a few hundred pounds of explosive, whereas the charges in the 19 mines at Messines averaged 48,000 lbs., about 21 tons apiece, or nearly twice the average weight of those in the eight classed as "large" in the Somme battles.

mining and the construction of protective dug-outs than in offensive mining.[1]

In addition to the mining work, the Royal Engineers, with Major-General F. M. Glubb as C.E. Second Army, were responsible for the major part of the preparations. Of these, the construction of railways and roads was the most important, as they formed the essential framework of offensive operations in the war conditions of 1917. In this respect the Second Army found itself in an unusually favourable situation.[2] It possessed the three main " feeder " railways, Dunkirk–Bergues–Proven, Calais–Hazebrouck and Boulogne –Hazebrouck ; and its area was so close to the supply-bases that intensive traffic was more easily handled here than farther south.[3] As soon as adequate labour and material became available a total of 115 miles of new broad-gauge and 58 miles of narrow-gauge lines were laid, a large proportion consisting of distributing railways constructed to relieve the strain upon the roads. Where possible, each type of traffic was allotted its own trans-shipment railheads. Ammunition was distributed either by single broad-gauge lines or by light railways, the Messines offensive being the first in which light railways carried ammunition right up to many of the heavy batteries. There were, in all, four railheads for ammunition, four for engineer stores, nine for

---

[1] Up to March 1917 the percentages were : offensive mining, 45 ; defensive mining, 25 ; dug-outs, 30. Defensive mining was carried on at Hill 60, St. Eloi, Mount Sorrel and the Bluff, and at each place German miners were outclassed.

The protective work carried out by the tunnellers during the twelve months preceding the Battle of Messines, in addition to the construction of numerous machine-gun emplacements and observation posts, included 5,000 yards of subway, 6 ft. x 3 ft., underground accommodation in which over 6,000 men could sleep and over 10,000 could shelter (the largest dug-out being that under Hill 63, constructed by the 1st Australian Tunnelling Company, with accommodation for 2 battalions), 24 deep dug-outs with an average floor space of 600 square feet for brigade headquarters, and 28 deep dug-outs with an average floor space of 400 square feet for battalion headquarters.

[2] See Sketch 4.

[3] New railway construction had been carried out over a considerable period ; the line to Ypres from the important junction of Hazebrouck had been doubled in 1915, and in 1916 a line was laid from Bergues to Proven, which also was doubled early in 1917. These additions, with the existing Hazebrouck–Steenwerck line, gave to the Second Army area three double lines, each with a maximum capacity of sixty trains a day ; and a number of extensions, advanced railheads and gun spurs had also been constructed. See " Transportation ", p. 273.

supplies, and seven for the detrainment and entrainment of troops.[1] During the month preceding the offensive, about 300,000 tons of material were cleared from the trans-shipment railheads, half by rail, half by road.

The roads in the Army area, always fairly good, had been well maintained, and certain roads and tramways in the forward areas were selected for prolongation into the enemy's lines as soon as the objectives were gained, road material, both wood and stone, being dumped as close to the front line as was safe.[2] For water supply, too, certain pipe-lines were ear-marked for rapid extension, so as to provide each corps with from 150,000 to 200,000 gallons a day in advance of the old front line. Water was also stored in tanks or barrels, either in the trenches or in shell-proof shelters.[3] R.E. parks were established at Steenwerck, Zevecoten and Busseboom, on broad-gauge railway sidings from which the stores could be distributed by light railway, while trench stores were stacked farther forward.

These preparatory measures demanded a great supply of labour and material. The operations on the Somme in January and February, and the Arras offensive in March and April, had called for all available resources, and it was not until April that the major tasks could be taken in hand. On the 1st May the labour personnel employed in railways, roads and quarries, at railheads, workshops, parks and on miscellaneous duties, numbered 13,750; by the 1st June the figure was 20,400, and on the 7th, the day of assault, 31,450.[4]

The programme of preparatory arrangements was given

---

[1] The four railheads for ammunition were : Duke of Connaught, between Steenwerck and Neuve Eglise ; Duke of York, on the outskirts of Bailleul ; Fuzeville, north-west of La Clytte ; and Pacific, east of Poperinghe. Attached to each station was a depôt, holding about 6,000 tons.

[2] The extent of the traffic organization is shown by the fact that by 7th June, the day of assault, the Second Army disposed of 7,493 lorries (including 154 mobile workshops), 270 caterpillar tractors, 1,020 cars, 3,072 motor cycles and 701 motor ambulances, which was more than double the normal establishment. In all 67 officers and 1,749 other ranks of newly raised traffic-control units were employed.

[3] As the district was unsuitable for boring wells, surface supplies were chiefly used. On the left the task was comparatively simple, for Zillebeke and Dickebusch Lakes provided unlimited quantities ; in the centre the water was trapped by means of dams to form reservoirs on the slopes of the hills, and on the right it was pumped from sterilizing barges on the Lys.

[4] As always, much of the unskilled work had in the earlier stages been performed by fighting troops, chiefly infantry, who were taken off as labour units arrived. On 1st May 7,750 fighting troops were thus employed : on 1st June, 4,100 ; and on 7th June, only 1,613.

an additional impetus after the 7th May, when the date for the offensive was fixed for approximately a month ahead. A great number of extra shelters and tunnelled dug-outs had to be constructed, and such additional necessities as shrapnel-proof emplacements for the machine-gun barrage guns and for trench mortars, advanced munition supply magazines, trench tramways, protected cable communications, bomb-proof telephone exchanges, dumps for rations and for engineer stores, dressing stations and first-aid posts had to be provided. The success of the operation largely depended on the thoroughness of this preparatory work.

Bombardment

The bulk of the reinforcing artillery from the Arras battlefields poured into the area of the Second Army in the middle fortnight of May, though some of the batteries did not come into action until the last days of the month. One half of the heavy artillery with the Fifth Army in the Bullecourt sector arrived gradually, and one-third of that with the First and Third Armies was sent in two echelons. In addition to the field artillery with the divisions which had moved north, fifteen Army field brigades were sent from the First Army, five from the Third and three from the Fifth. To conceal the arrival of these reinforcements a periodical concentration of artillery fire was made in different corps areas during the previous weeks, and up to the time of the bombardment the number of firing batteries on any one day in each corps sector was limited.

A total of 2,266 guns and howitzers was assembled for the operation. The 756 heavy and medium were organized into forty bombardment and counter-battery groups, of which twelve, four to each corps sector, were for counter-battery work.[1] The field artillery available amounted to 64 brigades, a total of 1,158 18-pdrs. and 352 4.5-inch howitzers.[2] They were grouped to suit the infantry dispositions: two groups were formed in each divisional sector

---

[1] This total included 186 60-pdrs., 316 6-inch howitzers, 20 6-inch guns, 108 8-inch howitzers, 108 9.2-inch howitzers, 2 9.2-inch guns, 12 12-inch howitzers, 1 12-inch gun and 3 15-inch howitzers.

[2] In addition to the field artillery of its four divisions each corps was allotted the artillery of one of the three divisions (Guards, 1st and 32nd Divisions) of the XIV Corps, in G.H.Q. reserve. Also, the II Anzac and

Continued at foot of next page.

to cover the front of the two assaulting brigades, each group being split into two sub-groups (each sub-group of six batteries covering the frontage of a battalion).

The dumping of ammunition was carried out in two phases, half during the latter part of March and the beginning of April, and the remainder between the 19th and 30th May. During the latter period, 166 trains, carrying 65,000 tons of ammunition, were received, and the total amount dumped for the operation was 144,000 tons. At zero hour, for the 18-pdr. field gun there was an average of 1,000 rounds of shell in the gun-pits; the quantity for pieces of larger calibre was in the following proportion: three-fourths of the 18-pdr. scale for the field howitzers, 60-pdrs. and 6-inch howitzers, and about one-half for 8-inch and 9.2-inch howitzers.

The II Brigade Royal Flying Corps (Major-General T. I. Webb-Bowen) was to give vital assistance, as the back area of the German position, including the strongly fortified Second Line along the summit of the Ridge, and most of the German batteries, were out of sight of the ground artillery observers. The 300 serviceable aeroplanes of the brigade, estimated at the time to be double the number opposing them in the battle-area, enabled the artillery observation and photographic machines to work with little hindrance. To give sufficient depth, the line of German observation balloons northwards from Perenchies, about ten thousand yards behind the front, was selected as the main offensive line for air operations, which no German machine was to be allowed to cross.[1] The German defences were photo-

---

Continued from previous page.
IX Corps each had ten, and the X Corps thirteen, Army field artillery brigades; also the right field artillery brigade of the II Corps was to be attached to the X Corps for the opening day of the battle. The total given does not tally with the regular establishment of 64 field artillery brigades, as four of the Army brigades lacked howitzer batteries, four had 4-gun howitzer batteries, and one had 4 18-pdr. batteries.

[1] The Second Army front (30,000 yards) was divided into 2 beats, each of which was patrolled from dawn to dark during the bombardment period by a formation of four to six scouts flying at a height of 15,000 feet and upwards. The central portion, from le Quesnoy (3¼ miles south of Comines) to Becelaere (17,000 yards), which contained the actual battle front, was, in addition, patrolled by a formation of six to eight machines flying 10,000 to 12,000 feet, this arrangement giving two layers of fighting machines over the more important sector of the front.

Few high-flying German machines crossed the line, but one reached and bombed Bailleul.

graphed daily during the bombardment period, and the counter-battery area every other day. Artillery observation was assisted by the six captive balloons of the 2nd Kite Balloon Wing, R.F.C., which were placed within five thousand yards of the front line; and on the night before the battle (6th–7th June) two additional balloons were brought to within three thousand yards to work from a minimum height of 5,000 feet.[1]

The Second Army Report Centre at Locre Château, four miles behind the battle front, was the central receiving station. It had dropping places for aircraft messages, and was connected with R.F.C. lines, balloon, field survey company, anti-aircraft and wireless stations. It was also in direct telephonic and telegraphic communication by deep (6 feet) buried cable with the corps report centres at Bailleul (II Anzac), Mont Noir (IX) and Reninghelst (X), with corps heavy artillery and with the headquarters of divisions, so that no delay might be incurred in passing on information to the bombardment and counter-battery groups.[2]

Co-ordination of the artillery work was the responsibility of Major-General G. McK. Franks, M.G. R.A., Second Army; but the details were left to corps artillery commanders, who worked in co-operation with divisional commanders. The Second Army artillery plan, of which the final edition was issued on the 20th May, followed in its main features that of the First Army for the Arras–Vimy battle, two months previously. Captured documents and statements of prisoners taken in raids during April and early May confirmed the belief that the enemy's defence organization on the Messines Ridge had been re-constructed on the new model.[3] The labyrinth of the front trench system and the maze of communication trenches had lost their purpose and importance. The defensive battle was now to be mobile and elastic in

---

[1] Full details of the co-operation of the Royal Flying Corps with the ground forces during the battle are given in " War in the Air " iv.

[2] For ground observation, battle observation posts for both heavy and field artillery were allotted on the rough basis of one O.P. to 3 batteries, and these observers communicated through their group headquarters to the batteries, a system which combined economy of fire with efficiency.

[3] See p. 11 footnote. The second and latest (March 1917) edition of the German Instructions for the Defensive Battle, both for the construction of a defensive position (*Allegemeines über Stellenbau*) and the tactics within it (*Führung der Abwehrschlacht*), had been captured in the Arras battle, and printed translations issued to all concerned on 2nd May.

character, to be fought within zones two thousand yards deep instead of in trench lines. The forward zone, which was expected to be devastated by the preliminary bombardment, extended back to the Second Line along the summit of the Ridge, and was only thinly held; but it was chequered with strongpoints and machine-gun nests.[1] The bulk of each front division was echeloned at the back of and behind the forward zone ready to move up to meet the invader as he struggled through the network of fire from the strongpoints and machine-gun nests. These local counter-attack formations were to drive him out of the position before he could consolidate the ground gained. Behind again were two reserve, or counter-attack (*Eingreif*), divisions, one to every two front divisions; and in the event of an attack crossing the Second Line the regiments of these *Eingreif* divisions would move up and intervene as required.[2]

The artillery plan was designed to counter this method of deep defence based upon a succession of immediate counter-attacks. The strongpoints and machine-gun nests were to be battered and destroyed by the preliminary bombardment; the front divisions were to be harassed and exhausted by artillery and machine-gun fire by day and night on their overland communication routes for supplies and reliefs, and on their repair parties;[3] the enemy's artillery was to be out-fought and silenced by the strong counter-battery concentration; and, during the assault itself, the successive counter-attack formations were to be broken up and scattered by creeping and protective barrages in front of the infantry.

The systematic bombardment and counter-battery work began on the 21st May, and became intense from the 31st May. The following eight days, up to the day of the

---

[1] In each regimental sector, averaging 1,500 yards' frontage and 3,000 yards in depth, were about thirty machine-gun nests and eight strongpoints. Each company was divided into garrison and counter-attack units; the garrison units, who wore white armbands, were to hold the strongpoints and not to leave them, even though surrounded, until relieved by a counter-attack unit.

[2] Though usually translated "counter-attacking", "*Eingreif*" means "interlocking" or "gearing into" and thus conveys the idea that the divisions sent up, as we say, to counter-attack enter into the framework of the battle, under one of the divisional generals already engaged, regardless of seniority.

[3] A key-chart, based on a study of the latest aeroplane-photographs and Intelligence summaries, was issued to machine-gun companies daily by divisional artillery commanders as part of the night-firing programme. Machine guns of each division fired an average of 80,000 rounds nightly during the bombardment period.

assault, were fine and clear, apart from occasional thunderstorms, so that both the bombardment groups and the counter-battery groups had perfect observation facilities from the ground and air. They were able to fire concentrically into the German salient from three sides, and most of the German forward zone was on the western slope of the Ridge open to ground observation either from Kemmel Hill, 3,000 yards back, or from Hill 63, south of the Douve.

Owing to the waterlogged nature of much of the district, with the water-level two or three feet below the surface, the Germans had had in some areas to build their shelters and strongpoints above, instead of below, ground-level. Circular or square-shaped, very strongly built of reinforced concrete, they stood 3–6 feet high.[1] They were covered with sods or earth as camouflage; but the constant shelling soon shook off this covering, and on those bright summer evenings, when the sun began to sink in the west behind the observer, they stood out in whitish nakedness as perfect targets. In the distance they looked like, and were called, " pillboxes ", and the loopholed strongpoints appeared as pillar-boxes.

The small shelters for the outpost groups, one to hold a few men or a machine-gun detachment every fifty yards, in the old front trench system, were dealt with by the heavy and medium trench mortars near the front line. These useful weapons, of which the Second Army had been allotted 428, fired short-range torpedo-mines, which made craters up to six feet deep and five yards in diameter. Farther back, the larger pillboxes and machine-gun nests in the forward zone, many sited among the ruins of farm buildings, and also those in the Second and Intermediate (Oosttaverne) Lines,[2] where they were about two hundred yards apart with accommodation for 25–40 men, were systematically shelled by heavy and medium artillery with air observation during the bombardment period. A special bombardment given to the villages of Wytschaete (3rd June) and Messines

---

[1] The enclosed concrete shelters for the garrison were called " Mebus " (*Mannschafts-Eisenbeton-Unterstände*). The Germans had been making use of ferro-concrete in the Ypres sector since 1915; but mainly for the protection of command posts. The concrete for all this fresh work was mixed with the finest water-worn gravel brought from the Rhine in barges through Holland, and steel rods were uniformly distributed through the entire structure to obviate the effects of vibration. The result was that the shelters would withstand a 6-inch howitzer shell, and even the 8-inch howitzer was only effective with a direct hit.

[2] See Sketch 3.

(4th June), with high explosive and gas shell, reduced to ruins these fortresses at either end of the highest part of the Ridge. Meanwhile, the field artillery concentrated on smashing the maze of wire entanglements in the forward zone, and together with the machine guns, on harassing and exhausting the garrison.[1]

Farther afield the 9.2-inch and 12-inch howitzers shelled the bridges over the Lys river and the Ypres-Comines canal, also Warneton, Comines and the road-junctions, railways and bridges in the German back areas.[2]

The artillery bombardment was supplemented by bombing from the air on more distant targets by squadrons of the II Brigade R.F.C. The principal rail-centres behind the sector, such as Comines, Wervicq and Menin, were raided; aerodromes, railway stations and trains were attacked by night at low altitudes; and the villages, camps and hutments housing the German reserves were harassed by bombs and machine-gun fire.[3]

The Barrages and the Final Counter-Battery Concentration

On the 30th May a conference was held by Sir Douglas Haig at Pernes to consider the situation which might arise

---

[1] The German casualties from the bombardment were greatly reduced by the order, on 26th May, that all shelters and strongpoints were to be evacuated daily from dawn to dark, to shell-holes 100 yards distant. The "pillboxes" served their purpose by drawing the British artillery fire more than by sheltering the garrison. More serious was the nervous exhaustion caused, so that the normal front-line relief every five days had at the end of May to be reduced to two days. Already by 31st May two of the four front divisions were reported to be no longer fit to resist an assault, and the necessary divisional reliefs upset the German defence organization. See Note at end of Chapter V.

[2] A number of ammunition dumps were exploded during these bombardments, the biggest being that at Coucou, near Menin, where a colossal explosion of high-explosive and gas shell occurred on the evening of the 6th June.

Eight Special Companies R.E. were to discharge cylinder gas and oil drums on the flanks of the battlefront, before and during the assault; but owing to adverse wind conditions the programme had to be greatly reduced.

[3] For details of the air support see "War in the Air" iv. During the period 15th May—9th June, besides constant patrolling and photographic work, hostile machines were engaged in 321 combats, in which 58 were shot down and 70 driven out of control, at a cost of 33 British machines missing.

if the Germans should evacuate their front system before the day of assault.[1] The effect of the mines would be thereby nullified, and a proposal to explode them before Zero Day, occupying the mine-craters and front trench system as a preliminary to the main assault and also to make the enemy disclose his battery positions, was discussed. General Plumer said that his corps commanders, whom he had consulted, thought it better to adhere to the plan of attack as arranged, and that a previous explosion of the mines was undesirable. To make the enemy disclose his batteries and to destroy them with counter-battery fire, he suggested one or two full-dress rehearsals of the creeping barrage to simulate an attack and, with the information gained, to devote the last two days of the artillery bombardment entirely to counter-battery work. Sir Douglas Haig agreed to this solution; the new German instructions for the "Defensive Battle" showed, he said, the value placed on artillery fire in the defence, so that the importance of making the enemy disclose his batteries could not be over-estimated.

The field artillery barrages, creeping and standing, were based on a time-table similar to that used for the Arras–Vimy assault in April.[2] The creeping barrage, immediately ahead of the infantry, was to be formed by approximately two-thirds of the 18-pdr. batteries. The remainder of the 18-pdr. batteries and the 4.5-inch howitzer batteries were to lay standing barrages on selected areas and strongpoints up to 700 yards in front of the creeping barrage, lifting on to successive pre-arranged targets when the assault was within 400 yards of the objective. At each objective the creeping barrage was to become a protective barrage, 150 to 300 yards ahead of the infantry, at half-rate of fire, sweeping and searching the area to check any local counter-attacks or enemy movement.[3] A machine-gun barrage using indirect overhead fire, such as had proved so effective in the Vimy Ridge operation in April, was to lift 400 yards ahead

---

[1] A proposal to withdraw from the salient had been discussed at German *Fourth Army* headquarters, but rejected; the number and size of the mines, and the moral effect of the explosions were under-estimated. See Note at end of Chapter V.

[2] See "1917" Vol. I, pp. 184–6.

[3] For the creeping barrage the rate of fire was 3 rounds per 18-pdr. gun and 1 round per 4.5-inch howitzer per minute; for the protective barrage it was 1 round each per minute.

of the creeping shrapnel barrage.[1] These three belts of the barrage would together form a dense protective screen, 700 yards in depth, in front of the assault; while the heavy and medium artillery were to lay standing barrages on the defences and approaches farther back.

The barrage rehearsals took place during the afternoons of the 3rd and 5th June, the full resources of the II Brigade R.F.C. being used to locate the German batteries in action against each corps front. Although the German retaliation was not as great as expected, the observations showed that the Germans were reinforcing their artillery on both flanks of the offensive front behind the shoulders of the Messines–Wytschaete salient, in the areas north-west of le Quesnoy ($3\frac{1}{2}$ miles south of Comines) and about Zandvoorde.

With these and other observations it was possible to give more than two hundred German battery positions an intense shelling during the counter-battery concentration on the last two days of the bombardment period, the 5th and 6th June. The counter-battery groups were reinforced from the bombardment groups, and every available howitzer, roughly one heavy or medium to every 75 yards of front, was employed. The effect was outstanding. At zero hour on the 7th, too, the concentration on the German batteries was continued by every howitzer which could be spared from the barrage (265 6-inch howitzers being used as against 252 for the barrage). It was maintained for 30 minutes with a large

---

[1] Appendix XI. Out of a total of over 700 machine guns, 454 (II Anzac Corps, 168; IX Corps, 162; X Corps, 124) were allotted for the barrage. The procedure varied, as divisional commanders were allowed to arrange the details of both the artillery and machine-gun barrages in their sectors within the limits of the time-table; the final arrangements for each corps were co-ordinated by the corps artillery commander.

In the II Anzac Corps the machine-gun barrage was synchronized to move forward 400 yards ahead of the artillery barrage; an enfilade barrage was directed behind Messines to bar the exits from the village, and standing barrages were to cover the low ground along the Douve to prevent counter-attack from that flank. For the IX Corps, the barrage was partly a standing one on the Ridge itself, which could be reached by machine guns 500 yards behind the British front line, and partly a creeping one up to and beyond the Ridge, for which the guns were to be taken forward. On the X Corps front, which had the shortest advance to make, the barrage took the form of 4 standing barrages, each 500 yards ahead of the 4 successive objective lines.

The estimated total ammunition requirements for the machine guns was roughly 5 million rounds per corps (1 million for harassing fire, 2 million for barrages, and 2 million for S.O.S. calls), or 15 million rounds for the three corps; for Zero Day and the day following it, it amounted to 15,000 to 20,000 rounds per gun per day.

THE BOMBARDMENT

proportion of gas shell,[1] so as to neutralize the German defensive barrage until the infantry had time to move clear of No Man's Land and enter the German position. As a result of this concentrated counter-battery action the three-fold artillery superiority (2,230 guns and howitzers against 630) with which the bombardment period had started was greatly enhanced by the morning of the assault.[2] The casualties of the Second Army, too, during the bombardment period were only slightly above normal.[3]

The expenditure of artillery ammunition for the three corps during the bombardment period from the 26th May to the 6th June amounted to over $3\frac{1}{2}$ million shells (3,561,530), the cost of which was estimated at £17,500,000, and this figure was one-third less than the estimate[4].

---

[1] Subsequent evidence showed that artillery gas shell was very effective, with a minimum of expenditure. Three kinds of gas shell were used, the lethal (C.B.R.), the lethal and lacrymatory (P.S.) and the purely lacrymatory (S.K.), both for 4.5-inch and 6-inch howitzers and 60-pdr. guns, the general method being to employ concentrated bursts of lethal shell for 3 minutes, to exploit surprise, followed by bursts of lacrymatory and of lethal at intervals.

[2] The German total was made up as follows: 236 field guns, 108 field howitzers, 54 10-cm., 12-cm. and 13-cm. guns, 24 15-cm. guns, 174 medium howitzers, 40 heavy howitzers and 4 heavy (21-cm. and 24-cm.) guns. This total includes the artillery of the *Group Wytschaete (XIX Corps)*, which held the sector between Mount Sorrel and the Douve, practically the entire front of the British offensive, and also batteries on the inner flanks of the *Groups Lille* and *Ypres*, to south and north, which took part in the battle.

G.O.A. xii., p. 454, states that by the morning of 7th June *Group Wytschaete* alone had lost almost a quarter of its field artillery and nearly a half of its heavy artillery. This loss of material would probably have been still greater but for the German central wireless warning station which, by intercepting British aeroplane wireless calls, was able to warn batteries when discovered, and sometimes enabled the gun detachments to change position in time.

[3] From gas shell on the battery positions during the ten days before the 7th June ten men were killed and 98 incapacitated. The material damage done by the German artillery retaliation was of little consequence; but the inflammable nature of the various camouflage screens used to conceal the dumps caused much loss of ammunition through fire. Painted canvas had to be used, as sufficient dyed bast was not available.

[4] The "Estimated and Actual Expenditure of Artillery Ammunition in Rounds per Gun for the ten days ended 10th June, 1917," was as under:

	Estimated	Actual	Surplus estimated over actual
18-pdr.	2,105	1,453	652
4.5-in. how.	1,565	1,431	134
60-pdr.	1,550	851	699
6-in. how.	1,550	1,115	435
6-in. gun	913	616	297
8-in. how.	1,135	839	296
9.2-in. how.	1,135	797	338
12-in. how.	540	330	210
15-in. how.	345	175	170

NOTE I

TANK ORGANIZATION AND THE MARK IV MODEL

The Heavy Branch Machine Gun Corps considerably expanded its organization during the first half of 1917. The few tank companies in France at the end of 1916 grew into battalions of three companies each of 12 tanks, and the Corps was being steadily built up towards an establishment of three brigades, each of three battalions. The headquarters moved to Bermicourt, near St. Pol; and there also the workshops tested all tanks arriving from the United Kingdom, and reconditioned those salvaged from the battlefield. The driving school was at Wailly, near Arras, and the gunnery school at Merlimont, near Etaples. The home base had been moved in 1916 from Thetford to Bovington (near Wool, Dorset), where all preliminary training was carried out.

The Mark I and II tanks had differed but little in design and equipment, and opinion was still divided as to their value; as late as July 1917 a G.H.Q. Instruction stated that the employment of tanks as an adjunct to offensive operations was still in the experimental stage. The Germans had shown no inclination to copy the new weapon, and were content to take defensive measures to limit its action. Their infantry and machine-gunners were provided with a proportion of armour-piercing bullets to penetrate the plates of the Mark I and II models; pits were dug as tank traps and trenches given more traverses; and a number of anti-tank guns were devised, such as single field guns or batteries, dug-in for the purpose in a forward position,[1] or 55-mm. guns or trench mortars, with special mountings.

The Mark III tank was experimental and was never used in action. The Mark IV arrived in France at the end of April 1917. It had no advantage in speed over its predecessor; but it was easier to control, and though its armour plates were of the same thickness (12-mm.) they were made of a special hardened steel, proof against the German armour-piercing bullet. It also had several improvements in design: easier means of entrance and exit for the crew, better and safer methods of observation and fire control, detachable spuds to give a grip on wet ground, no

---

[1] In March 1917 the Germans mounted 77-mm. field guns on low wheels (43⅜-inches) and provided them with armour-piercing shell. It was proposed to issue one of these anti-tank batteries to each division, and they were to be dug-in 500–1,500 yards behind the front line and, if used singly, about 400 yards apart.

Other infantry guns, such as an adapted Russian field gun and two types of trench "cannon" were also available for anti-tank defence.

NOTE I

tail-wheels, improved transmission, a silencer for the engine, unditching gear (improved later in France by adding a long iron-shod teak beam to fasten across the tracks), and the main petrol supply outside with a capacity of 70 gallons instead of 46 in the earlier models.

In all-over length the Mark IV was the same as the Mark I without its tail-wheels (26ft. 5in.); and, by a different design of sponson, the width was decreased in the male by three inches (from 13ft. 9in. to 13ft. 6in.), and in the female to 10ft. 6in.; it was slightly higher (8ft. 2in. against 8ft. .05in.). The weight both of the male and the female was unchanged (28 tons and 27 tons, respectively), as also was the number of crew (1 officer and 7 other ranks). The armament differed only in that Lewis guns replaced the Vickers and Hotchkiss guns; that of the male consisting of 2 six-pdrs. and 4 Lewis, and that of the female 6 Lewis guns (instead of 5 Vickers and 1 Hotchkiss gun). The engine remained the 105 h.p. Daimler, which gave the tank an average speed of 2 m.p.h., and a maximum of 3.7 m.p.h. as in the Mark I model. The radius of action was slightly greater (15 miles or 7.5 hours against 12 miles or 6.2 hours), but the spanning power of 10 feet was unaltered.

NOTE II
DETAILS OF THE MESSINES MINES

Mine	Commenced	Completed	Depth Ft.	Charge Weight lbs.	Diameter at Ground Level Ft.	Depth below Ground Level Ft.	Diameter of Complete Obliteration Ft.	Length of Gallery Ft.
HILL 60								
"A" Left	22.8.15	1.8.16	90	45,700 A 7,800 G.C. 53,500	191	33	285	Branch 240
"B" Caterpillar		18.10.16	100	70,000 A	260	51	380	1,380
ST. ELOI	16.8.16	28.5.17	125	95,600 A	176	17	330	1,340 300
HOLLANDSCHESCHUUR								
No. 1		20.6.16	60	30,000 A 4,200 B 34,200	183	29	343	825
No. 2	18.12.15	11.7.16	55	12,500 A 2,400 B 14,900	105	14	215	Branch 45
No. 3		20.8.16	55	15,000 A 3,500 B 18,500	141	25	201	Branch 395
PETIT BOIS								
No. 2 Left	16.12.15	15.8.16	57	21,000 A 9,000 B 30,000	217	46	417	Branch 210
No. 1 Right		30.7.16	70	21,000 A 9,000 B 30,000	175	49	375	2,070

THE MINES

Mine	Commenced	Completed	Depth Ft.	Charge Weight lbs.	Diameter at Ground Level Ft.	Depth below Ground Level Ft.	Diameter of Complete Obliteration Ft.	Length of Gallery Ft.
MAEDELSTEDE FARM	3.9.16	2.6.17	100	30,000 G.C. / 4,000 G.C. / 34,000	205	23	385	1,610
PECKHAM	20.12.15	19.7.16	70	65,000 A / 15,000 B / 7,000 G.C. / 87,000	240	46	330	1,145
SPANBROEKMOLEN	1.1.16	28.6.16 (recovered 6.6.17)	88	91,000 A	250	40	430	1,710
KRUISSTRAAT No. 1		5.7.16	57	30,000 A	[flooded in February, 1917]		395	—
No. 4		11.4.17	57	18,500 A / 1,000 G.C. / 19,500	235	34		
No. 2	2.1.16	12.7.16	62	30,000 A	217	40	367	Branch 170
No. 3		23.8.16	50	30,000 A	202	30	332	2,160
ONTARIO FARM	28.1.17	6.6.17	103	60,000 A	200	Nil	220	1,290
TRENCH 127 No. 7 Left	28.12.15	20.4.16	75	36,000 A	181	10	232	Branch 250
No. 8 Right		9.5.16	76	50,000 A	210	16	342	1,355
TRENCH 122 No. 5 Left	15.2.16	14.5.16	60	20,000 A	195	22	323	Branch 440
No. 6 Right		11.6.16	75	40,000 A	228	28	356	970

A = Ammonal.   B = Blastine.   G.C. = Guncotton.

CHAPTER IV

THE BATTLE OF MESSINES 1917
(*continued*)

ZERO HOUR

(Sketches 3, 5)

The forecast on the 4th June predicted a continuation of the fine weather for some days, though a morning haze might make visibility poor. Corps were notified accordingly that Zero Day would be on the 7th. At midday on the 6th, zero hour was fixed for 3.10 a.m., watches being carefully synchronized for the simultaneous explosion of the mines. It was expected that at that hour a man could be seen at a hundred yards, and that the mist would be beginning to lift.

About midnight on the 6th/7th, after a violent thunderstorm earlier in the evening, the moon, now past its full, shone in a clear sky.[1] At 2 a.m. aeroplanes cruised low over the German position to drown the noise of the tanks moving up to their starting points near the front. By 3 a.m. the assault divisions, with the exception of some of the II Anzac Corps on the right, had gathered unnoticed in their assembly trenches, and bayonets were fixed silently.

The British artillery fire had been normal during the night, but half an hour before dawn a calm set in, so marked that from the front line nightingales could be heard singing in distant woods which still gave cover. "Suddenly, at " 3.10 a.m.", to quote a British eye-witness, " great leaping " streams of orange flame shot upwards, each a huge volcano " in itself, along the front of attack, followed by terrific " explosions and dense masses of smoke and dust, which "stood like great pillars towering into the sky, all illuminated " by the fires below ".[2] The nineteen mines exploded without a single failure, and the shock for many miles back was

---

[1] The moon rose at 10.37 p.m. and set at 5.9 a.m. Sunrise was at 4.41 a.m. British Summer Time.

[2] To a German observer the spectacle appeared as " nineteen gigantic " roses with carmine petals, or as enormous mushrooms, which rose up " slowly and majestically out of the ground and then split into pieces " with a mighty roar, sending up multi-coloured columns of flame mixed " with a mass of earth and splinters high into the sky ". G.O.A. xii., p. 453.

like that of an earthquake. In Lille, 15 miles away, terrified Germans rushed panic-stricken about the streets; and the shock was felt distinctly in London and in various parts of England. The fact that, unintentionally, the explosions were not all simultaneous—the last being 19 seconds after the first—had a cumulative effect on the German garrison, and their panic was further increased by the hitherto unappreciated ventriloquial character of great explosions.[1] The demoralizing effect did, in fact, far exceed expectations, especially as widespread suspicion existed that many of the earlier-laid mines might not explode after so long a delay.

Immediately after the explosion, the whole of the artillery strength of the Second Army was let loose at its maximum rate of fire. The three belts of the barrage crashed down on the first 700 yards of the German position, and the counter-battery groups deluged all known German battery positions with gas shell. The flashes of the guns in the darkness were so close together and continuous that the whole western horizon seemed to be ablaze; and with this immense artillery support the infantry of 9 divisions, with 3 in close reserve, advanced to the assault.

It was darker than expected. The smoke and dust of the mine explosions, added to that of the barrage, hid the light of the moon sinking below the sky-line of Kemmel Hill, and visibility was less than fifty yards. The dim outline of the hillside below Messines and Wytschaete was illuminated by the white and green flares sent up by the German infantry asking for artillery support; but the deluge of gas and high-explosive shell from the counter-batteries had effectively neutralized the German guns, and their barrage was thin and late. It did not begin to fall on the British assembly trenches until five to ten minutes after zero hour, by which time the assault battalions were clear.

The Assault

The II Anzac Corps had as objective the southern shoulder of the Ridge including the buttress formed by the

---

[1] To the Germans on Hill 60, for example, the explosions at Kruisstraat and Spanbroekmolen appeared to be under Messines village, well behind their front line; and British assault units reported some of the mines to be German mines behind the British support trenches.

Messines village defences.[1] On the right, the 3rd Australian Division (Major-General J. Monash) had had a difficult 3-mile approach march. German batteries had shelled Ploegsteert Wood with gas shell about midnight, just as the assault battalions were moving through it by four routes, and the gas which lay densely in the stagnant air caused about 500 casualties.[2] The need to put on gas masks, together with the effect of occasional high-explosive and incendiary shell, led to a temporary loss of direction, and it was due to the determination of the men themselves to be in time that they reached the assembly trenches with their organization and efficiency unimpaired. The assault of the two brigades, the 9th (Br.-General A. Jobson) and the 10th (Br.-General W. R. McNicoll), between St. Yves and the Douve, was assisted by the four mines at Trenches 122 and 127. The explosions, which took place seven seconds before time, blew out craters over two hundred feet in diameter and about twenty feet deep in the German front trench system;[3] and the crimson jets of flame lit up the Australian infantry as they clambered over the parapets of the assembly trenches. Some of them had only just arrived, owing to the delays, and went straight on across No Man's Land without pause. The great mine craters split up and confused the attack organization, and in the dim light difficulty was experienced in keeping order and direction. In places the successive lines merged into one dense wave; but each unit knew its task and objective so well that they were able to sort themselves out and re-form as they advanced.

The New Zealand Division (Major-General Sir A. H. Russell), approaching across the open ground of Hill 63, had been spared the gas ordeal of the Australians, and reached the assembly trenches without difficulty. Owing to the westward bulge in the German front at Ontario Farm, to include the Spanbroekmolen crest, the New Zealanders' left

---

[1] See Sketch 3. For the Staffs and formations engaged see Order of Battle, Appendix I.

[2] The gas shells contained phosgene and chlorine gas, but were chiefly lacrymatory.

[3] The work on the two mines of Trench 122, near Factory Farm, had been uneventful except for the speed with which it was completed; the left mine, with a gallery measuring 267 yards, was charged within 3 months of the start of the sinking of the shaft. At Trench 127, on the Warneton road, the miners had to drive an inclined gallery to get below wet ground; here, too, 2 mines had been completed without enemy interference.

flank was to be protected by an enfilade barrage and a smoke cloud in addition to the explosion of the Ontario Farm mine. The leading battalions of the 3rd New Zealand (Rifle) Brigade (Br.-General H. T. Fulton) and 2nd Brigade (Br.-General W. G. Braithwaite) crossed the dried-up bed of the Steenbeek in No Man's Land, and, despite the abandonment of the mine under la Petite Douve Farm,[1] they took the front trench system and moved steadily up the rising ground towards Messines village.

The 25th Division (Major-General E. G. T. Bainbridge) soon came up level with the New Zealanders. Its assembly trenches lay 600 yards back on the higher ground ;[2] but the explosion of the mine at Ontario Farm assisted considerably the first onslaught of both brigades, the 74th (Br.-General H. K. Bethell) and 7th (Br.-General C. C. Onslow). The bed of the Steenbeek, too, presented no obstacle after the dry weather.[3]

For its assault on the Spanbroekmolen position the 36th (Ulster) Division (Major-General O. S. W. Nugent), on the right of the IX Corps sector, was assisted by four mines. In front of the 107th Brigade (Br.-General W. M. Withycombe) were the three Kruisstraat mines, and, eight hundred yards to the north, the great mine at Spanbroekmolen, while the left brigade, the 109th (Br.-General A. St. Q. Ricardo) had in its sector the mine near Peckham House.[4]

---

[1] The German miners gained their one considerable success at la Petite Douve Farm. The British mine had been successfully placed under the farm, but on 27th August 1916, the Germans blew a heavy camouflet which smashed in the main gallery for some four hundred feet, killing four men ; and the charge, already in position, had to be left.

[2] The 1916 plan for the Messines operation provided for the capture of this higher ground, the Spanbroekmolen knoll, as a preliminary operation to bring up the centre of the assault level with the flanks. (See pp. 4, 19.)

[3] The first gallery of the Ontario Farm mine was not begun until 28th January 1917. It had to pass through what appeared to be an old river bed, and after 100 feet had been lost, it was decided to break away farther back, as in the case of the mine at Trench 127, and drive an inclined gallery below wet ground. Owing to the delay, the gallery did not reach its objective ; but it was below the German front line and was completed the day before the offensive. The state of the ground may be imagined from the fact that after the explosion, though the crater was a wide one, it had virtually no depth and the wet sand flowed back almost as if the mine had been exploded in treacle.

[4] One of the Kruisstraat galleries, begun on 2nd January 1916, which extended 720 yards, was flooded by a German camouflet explosion in February 1917, and a new chamber had to be constructed and charged beside the wet mine. *Continued at foot of next page.*

The huge circular craters left by the explosions went down below the brown earth to the blue clay, large lumps of which, the size of carts, lay about in the craters. The German garrison had been ordered to hold this important outpost at all costs; but the two brigades of Royal Irish Rifle and Inniskilling Fusilier battalions crossed the devastated area without meeting resistance. The shock of the explosions had killed or completely stunned the defenders.[1]

The front of the 16th (South Irish) Division (Major-General W. B. Hickie) lay between Maedelstede Farm (inclusive) and the Vierstraat–Wytschaete road (exclusive). Here, too, the shock of the explosion of the Maedelstede mine, in front of the 47th Brigade (Br.-General G. E. Pereira), and of the two mines in the Petit Bois salient, in front of the 49th (Br.-General P. Leveson-Gower), broke the back of the defence.[2] The Petit Bois mines, on the left, were fired about

---
Continued from previous page.

The Spanbroekmolen mine, started on 1st January 1916, had a gallery 570 yards long, and the mine was completed and tamped in six months, by the end of June. A branch driven in the direction of Rag Point, a German work nearly three-quarters of a mile from the shaft, was damaged by two camouflets blown by the enemy in February 1917, and abandoned. A few weeks later, on 3rd March, the enemy blew a third camouflet which damaged the main gallery short of the mine already established and broke the leads. A new gallery had to be driven; and, as there was serious trouble with gas, the work developed into a race against time. When the chamber was reached a fresh primer was placed beside the charge, and the tamping was completed on 6th June, the day before the offensive. One of the most dramatic incidents of the Battle of Messines was the receipt by the headquarters of the 36th Division of a pencilled note from Major H. M. Hudspeth, commanding the 171st Tunnelling Company R.E., to the effect that it was "almost certain" that the Spanbroekmolen mine would go up next morning.

Work on the Peckham House mine, begun on 20th December 1915, was delayed by the swelling of the clay, which necessitated the renewal of the timber with heavier sets, and the mine was not charged till 19th July 1916. Later, owing to a breakdown of the pumps, the main gallery became flooded, and in January 1917 a new gallery was driven, steel joists being used in place of pit-props, and the charge was reconnected in March.

[1] The Kruisstraat and Spanbroekmolen mines lay beneath the sector held by the *23rd Bavarian Regiment*, the right of the *3rd Bavarian Division*.

[2] Maedelstede mine, one gallery of which, directed against the ambitious objective of Wytschaete Wood, had to be abandoned for lack of time, was charged and tamped under the farm by 2nd June 1917 without serious interference.

At Petit Bois, where work was started on 16th December 1915, a mechanical excavator was experimentally used; but, after raising high hopes, it proved a failure. On 10th June 1916 the Germans blew 2 camouflets, which smashed in 250 feet of the main gallery and entombed 12 miners. It was not reopened for $6\frac{1}{2}$ days, when one of the party, Sapper Bedson, was found to be still alive; he had remained at the face of the gallery instead of crawling to the home end. No more trouble was experienced, and the 2 mines were charged in July and August 1916.

12 seconds late, and as the 49th Brigade had already started a number of men were thrown off their feet and some casualties caused ;[1] but the lines soon closed up behind the barrage.

The 19th (Western) Division (Major-General C. D. Shute), north of the Vierstraat–Wytschaete road, faced the shattered remains of two woods, Grand Bois and Bois Quarante, about and behind the German front defences. Both brigades, the 58th (Br.-General A. E. Glasgow) and the 56th (Br.-General E. Craig-Brown) with Welsh, Cheshire and Lancashire battalions, were helped by the successful explosion of the three mines at Hollandscheschuur to overrun the difficult salient, known as "Nag's Nose", on an outlying spur of the Main Ridge.[2] The divisional diary states that " there " was little resistance from the Germans, who either ran " forward to surrender, or, if they could do so, ran away ; " very few of them put up a fight ".

The X Corps (Lieut.-General Sir T. L. N. Morland) had only to make an average advance of seven hundred yards to reach the crest of the Ridge, and another six hundred yards across the flat-topped summit would enable observers to overlook the German back area as far as Zandvoorde and the southern slope of Gheluvelt plateau, the upland bastion which the Germans were rapidly converting into the cornerstone of their Flanders Position. To prevent the capture of this observation area the German defences were correspondingly strong, and they were garrisoned by nearly double the normal man-power.[3] The proximity to the German batteries massed in the Zandvoorde area behind the northern flank of the Messines salient, made this very vulnerable to a defensive barrage ; but here, too, the concentrated fire of the counter-batteries at zero hour resulted in a ragged and late German reply. Nearly five minutes passed before the defensive barrage on the assembly trenches began, by which time the assault battalions had passed on into the position.

[1] The time officially recorded between the firing of the first and last mines was 19 seconds. Those at Trenches 122 and 127, opposite the 3rd Australian Division, were 7 seconds early.

[2] The mining of Hollandscheschuur was started on 18th December 1915, and after some delay, the 3 mines, all below average size, were charged by 20th August 1916. No further interference took place.

[3] Two divisions, the *35th* and *204th*, faced the 6,000-yard frontage of the X Corps, whereas the Messines sector of 4,800 yards, opposite the II Anzac Corps, was held by only one division.

The 41st Division (Major-General S. T. B. Lawford) assaulted with Surrey, Kentish and Royal Fusilier battalions of the 124th (Br.-General W. F. Clemson) and 123rd (Br.-General C. W. E. Gordon) Brigades. The 124th was to converge on the St. Eloi salient after the explosion of a mine at the head of the salient.[1] The crater, fifty feet deep and ninety yards in diameter, made the neighbouring mine craters of previous underground fighting in this area appear like shell-holes, and little opposition was met other than that offered by the great concrete blocks of shattered shelters and the broken ground of the crater-field.

The centre and left divisions of the X Corps, which were to cover the northern flank by capturing the high ground of the Ridge astride the Ypres–Comines canal and railway, were both helped by the great explosions of the Caterpillar and Hill 60 mines.[2] The deep cuttings by which the canal and railway passed through the Ridge were a warren of tunnels and deep dug-outs which had seemed impregnable; but the

---

[1] The dominating observation area on the St. Eloi spur, the nearest to the town of Ypres, had been the scene of mining operations throughout 1915, when a number of small mines had been exploded under the German front trench system. In April 1916 these craters were recaptured by the Germans, and German artillery fire on this area of the shafts had been so heavy that a new shaft could not be sunk till the following August. The mine was notable for the unusual depth of the shaft, 125 feet, the deepest of the whole series; also because of the charge of 95,600 lb. of ammonal being, so far as is known, the largest ever used in military mining. The charge was laid and tamped on 28th May 1917, only 10 days before it was fired.

[2] The underground battle for Hill 60 was of a severity unsurpassed of its kind on the British front throughout the War. Hill 60, a mound of spoil from the Ypres–Comines railway cutting, was an observation area of great importance. The early shallow mining operations to destroy or capture it have already been described (see " 1915 " Vol. I, p. 166–70, 304–6); but deep mining beneath the German galleries did not begin till the 22nd August 1915, when a gallery was started by the 175th Tunnelling Company R.E., from an entrance in the bank of the railway-cutting 220 yards behind the British front line, to pass 90 feet below it. The work was taken over by the 3rd Canadian Tunnelling Company in April 1916, the objectives being Hill 60 and another spoil heap, called from its shape " The Caterpillar ", on the opposite, southern, side of the railway cutting. The Hill 60 gallery was completed in July 1916 after a long underground struggle, and charged with 53,500 lb. of high explosive. The branch gallery to the Caterpillar was charged 3 months later, in October, with 70,000 lb. of high explosive, after encountering still greater difficulties, including the need to wreck two hundred feet of a main German gallery above it by firing a camouflet. In November, the 1st Australian Tunnelling Company took over from the Canadians, and maintained these 2 great mines intact throughout the winter. (A detailed account of this period of the mining operations against Hill 60 and the Caterpillar will be found in A.O.A. iv., Appendix I.)

47th (2nd London) Division (Major-General Sir G. F. Gorringe), astride the canal, was able to cross the three hundred yards of the old German front trench system in fifteen minutes, close behind the barrage. To both of its brigades, the 140th (Br.-General H. B. P. L. Kennedy) and the 142nd (Br.-General V. T. Bailey) the Germans surrendered readily.

Owing to the soft ground in the valley which runs up south of Mount Sorrel the infantry of the 23rd Division (Major-General J. M. Babington) were to move on either side of it, gaining touch at the head of this re-entrant along the near crest of the Ridge. While the earth was still quaking with the tremors of the explosions on Hill 60, Yorkshire battalions of the 69th (Br.-General T. S. Lambert) and 70th (Br.-General H. Gordon) Brigades reached the crest with little difficulty.[1]

Capture of the Ridge

The terrific shock of the explosions had completely unnerved the German garrison. Over a large area about each mine German outpost groups were found dead, wounded or stunned;[2] and through these gaps in the defence the assault penetrated easily. Farther back, too, Germans ran away panic-stricken, many being killed by the barrage while others remained cowering in derelict shelters and in shell-holes cringing like beaten animals: an Australian officer has commented that never had he seen men so demoralized.

In that rosy dawn a host of British and Dominion troops were surging forward behind the cloud of smoke and dust of the deep barrage up the great breast of the Messines–Wytschaete Ridge; over a hundred battalions, about 80,000 men, were moving up the slope, and every man among them had a pre-arranged and carefully rehearsed task. Within the smoke-screen of the barrage, creeping on at an

---

[1] The battle-report of the *204th Division*, holding this sector, states that " the ground trembled as in a natural earthquake, heavy concrete shelters " rocked, a hurricane of hot air from the explosions swept back for many " kilometres, dropping fragments of wood, iron and earth ; and gigantic " black clouds of smoke and dust spread over the country. The effect on " the troops was overpowering and crushing."

[2] Major-General Harington related that on the following morning in a concrete dug-out near the Spanbroekmolen crater he found 4 German officers seated round a table, all dead, with no mark of wound on any of them.

average rate of a 100-yard lift every two minutes, the leading assault groups rushed or outflanked the many strongpoints and machine-gun nests. Some of the German shelters were reached before the garrisons could scramble out of the low entrances at the back. Elsewhere, the loopholes of the strongpoints, and any of the garrison in shell-holes outside, were bombarded with rifle-grenades, Lewis gunfire and trench mortars ; while parties of riflemen and bombers worked their way from shell-hole to shell-hole around the flanks and surrounded the defenders.

This method of pillbox fighting, which had proved so successful in overcoming the deep dug-outs on the Vimy Ridge, had been a feature of the rehearsals for the Messines operation, and it was to become characteristic of the Flanders battles for the remainder of the year.[1] The careful training, too, given to the mopping-up parties close in rear, to clear promptly the captured dug-outs and strongpoints, was rewarded by the fact that throughout the battle there is no recorded instance of the enemy firing either with rifle or machine gun into the backs of the assault troops after they had passed.

Visibility was at first so bad that direction could only be kept by compass bearing, and in some places it was temporarily lost.[2] The leading waves of infantry, however, carried out their task as planned, and mopping-up parties

---

[1] The method resembled the system of infiltration recommended by a French infantry officer, Captain André Laffargue in May 1916. Captain Laffargue's pamphlet, " L'étude sur l'attaque ", printed in the autumn of 1915 and published in book form by the Libraire Plon, Paris, in the early summer of 1916, suggested that, instead of advancing in a succession of lines, *groupes de tirailleurs*, armed with automatic rifles, hand-grenades and gas bombs, should penetrate behind the strongpoints and machine-gun nests. The pamphlet had no influence on either the French or the British training manuals at the time ; but a copy of it was found by the Germans in a captured French trench soon after its publication, and was at once translated and issued as a German manual for tactical training at the new assault-troop (*Sturm-trupps*) schools, Laffargue's idea being made a form of battle-drill.

[2] The difficulty of visibility is exemplified in the battle-report of one of the battalion commanders (10/Queen's of the 41st Division) : " on reaching " Oaten Wood [halfway between the front line and the southern end of " the Damm Strasse] I saw to my horror a battalion in fours advancing to " our immediate rear, and some of its companies moving right across to " our left flank, having entirely lost themselves ; this was exceedingly " awkward, as it was the battalion detailed to carry on the attack in " conjunction with my right to the next objective, but we got it back " into position, and all went well ".

close behind cleared the captured dug-outs without any serious delay to the general forward movement.

The thinly held German forward zone was easily overrun. The first objective was gained in the 35 minutes allotted by the barrage time-table,[1] and the two support battalions of each assaulting brigade leap-frogged to carry on the advance to the next objective, along the near crest of the Ridge, another 500–800 yards up the slope. The accuracy and intensity of the barrage was spoken of long afterwards with admiration by the infantry. Local German counter-attacks were checked and dispersed by it; but as the infantry approached the belt of strongpoints and machine-gun nests at the back of the forward zone, covering the shelters of the German Second Line, they met stiffer resistance at many points.[2]

The village of Messines was included in the second objective of the II Anzac Corps. As the southern buttress of the Ridge defences, the village had been converted by the Germans into a fortress to be held at all costs; a strong trench system with a deep wire entanglement encircled it, and for the inner defence, based upon five concrete strongpoints, every available cellar had been converted into a shell-proof dug-out. Two machine guns in action at the edge of the village were at once rushed,[3] but on the left, machine-gun fire from Swayne's Farm, 400 yards north of the village, harassed the advance until a tank crashed through the place, forcing the thirty Germans within to surrender. The 4/Rifles and 2/Canterbury now carried on the advance through the battered wire and outer trench system into the village, the pace of the barrage being reduced here to 11 minutes for

---

[1] This first objective included the German *Sonne* Line, an old trench system about mid-way between the existing front and Second Line (see Note at end of Chapter V).

[2] On an average one German regiment (three battalions) faced the assault frontage of each British division. Of this regiment one battalion garrisoned the forward zone, another was in and about the Second Line, including the belt of strongpoints in front, and the third was in reserve a couple of miles or more behind. The companies of the front and support battalions were divided into counter-attack (*Stoss*) troops (about 75 per cent.) and garrison (*Sicherheitsbesatzung*) units for the strongpoints. See p. 44, footnote 1, for instructions to garrisons of strongpoints.

[3] Lance-Corporal S. Frickleton, 3rd New Zealand Rifle Battalion, led his section through the British barrage, rushed and bombed a machine-gun crew and also destroyed the crew of another gun near by; for this gallant action he received the V.C.

each 100-yard lift. Parties of Germans sniped from doorways and windows, or threw bombs from behind walls, and machine-gun fire opened from all sides, and in crushing this resistance a number of acts of great gallantry were performed. Five machine guns were taken when about to come into action, another five were rushed from behind, and two firing across the open square were silenced by rifle grenades. Germans hiding in the cellars were driven out by smoke-bombs or killed by bombs from light trench mortars, and the German commandant of the village and his staff were captured in a massive dug-out below a former Roman Catholic orphanage, the *Institution Royale*.[1]

South of the village the 3rd Australian Division had consolidated the southern flank of the operation by establishing itself firmly on the southern shoulder of the Ridge and astride the Douve. Its right included the new mine-craters at Factory Farm (Trench 122), which the Germans tried in vain to re-occupy; and its left was at another farm where 2 field guns and 2 machine guns were taken after a gallant action by a company of the 38th Battalion.

North of the village the 25th Division had reached the Messines–Wytschaete highway along the summit of the Ridge abreast of the left of the New Zealanders. It had met little opposition except at Hell Farm, 700 yards north-west of Messines, near the top of the slope, where fifty Germans and 8 machine guns were captured after a sharp fight.

In the IX Corps sector resistance in the shambles of two small woods, a thousand yards south of Wytschaete, was overcome by the 36th Division, and also that at Bogaert Farm, between the woods, where 150 Germans were captured. The ground about the strongpoints had been literally ploughed up by the bursts of the high-explosive

---

[1] The *3rd Bavarian Division* took over the Messines sector of 4,800 yards, between the Douve and Spanbroekmolen, approximately facing the II Anzac Corps, on the eve of the battle. It took the place of the *40th (Saxon) Division* which had requested relief on 3rd June owing to exhaustion. The Bavarian division, which had been trained to be the counter-attack division behind this sector for the battle, had not completed the relief when the assault was launched, and many of its machine guns were not yet operative. The line was held by the *18th, 17th,* and *23rd Bavarian Regiments*, from south to north, with one battalion in the front half of the forward zone, one in support, about the Second Line, and one in reserve, 5,000 yards back. Messines village was garrisoned by 2 companies of the *18th Bavarian Regiment*. The regimental histories admit that the mine explosions caused a great panic (*ungeheuere Panik*).

IX AND X CORPS. 7TH JUNE

shells during the bombardment; the barbed wire entanglements which had protected this area below the crest lay piled in twisted heaps, and everywhere was the wreckage of once solidly built dug-outs and shelters. The advance by the 16th and 19th Divisions through the shattered tree-stumps of Wytschaete Wood and Grand Bois, formerly containing the finest oak and larch in the district, was helped by the discharge into them of two thousand oil-drums on the night of the 3rd/4th June, and also by the standing barrages of heavy and field howitzers, maintained on the many known strongpoints concealed there. The garrison of L'Hospice, a ruined hostel at the northern end of Wytschaete Wood, held out till 6.48 a.m. though surrounded and by-passed. In spite of the many obstacles the objective was gained within a few minutes of the barrage, soon after 5 a.m.[1]

Farther north, in the X Corps sector, the Damm Strasse was expected to give trouble. This mile-long levelled drive, as straight as a Roman road from the St. Eloi highway to the White Château, was a warren of German dug-outs, and some bitter fighting took place here at close quarters; but the onslaught by Kentish, Surrey and Middlesex battalions of the 41st Division was irresistible.[2] The White Château itself, at the northern end of the Damm Strasse, included in the second objective of the 47th Division, and once a fine residence with lawns, shrubberies and an orangery, was not taken by the London battalions without a struggle. A smoke screen, formed by 72 smoke and 124 thermit shells, fired on the strongpoints alongside the Comines canal at zero hour had covered the initial stage of the assault from that flank; but on nearing the château machine-gun fire and showers of stick-bombs came from the high pile of stone and rubble. A lodgment in the ruins was gained after two

---

[1] The *2nd Division* had held the 4,000-yards sector from north of Spanbroekmolen to south of St. Eloi since mid-April. On 4th June its commander had requested immediate relief; it was arranged for the night of the 7th/8th, so that the garrison was preparing for relief within 24 hours.

G.O.A. (xii., p. 456) states that only one officer and 3 messengers came back from the front and support battalions of the right, *44th Regiment*, garrisoning the forward area to the Second Line on the Ridge; only a few men of those of the centre, *33rd Regiment*, and not one of those of the left, *4th Grenadier Regiment*.

[2] The *35th Division* held from St. Eloi (inclusive) to the Ypres–Hollebeke road, with its 3 regiments in line, the *176th*, *141st* and *61st*; their support battalions were along the Damm Strasse and behind it, in the Second Line. The division had held this sector since 31st May.

attacks, and it was not until 7.50 a.m., after a shelling by medium trench mortars, that the survivors of its garrison, an officer and 63 other ranks, surrendered. The short advance of 300 yards to be made by the 23rd Division to establish the northern flank near Mount Sorrel was made in twenty minutes. A party of Germans made a stand in an old trench at the head of the Zwarteleen re-entrant (a valley on the south side of Mount Sorrel), about the meeting point of the two assaulting brigades; but after being swept by volleys of rifle-grenades they surrendered.[1]

The sun had risen and it was broad daylight when, soon after 5 a.m. the second intermediate objective, which included the first trench of the German Second Line along the near crest of the Ridge, had been gained along the whole front. The crust of the defence had been broken. Captured documents had made clear the German belief that at the worst the front divisions would be able to hold on to the forward crest of the Ridge until the counter-attack divisions arrived to recapture the lost ground. The moral and material effects of the mines and the barrage on the front line troops had been undervalued and the determination of the infantry assault had turned the balance.

The next, the first main, objective lay 400–500 yards away across the flat summit, and included the rear trench of the German Second Line along the back crest of the Ridge. A pause for two hours had been allotted for the deployment of fresh battalions for this advance, and also for consolidation along the near crest and on the western slope against the expected counter-attacks.

A protective barrage, searching the area in front from 300 yards forward[2] covered the work of consolidation.

---

[1] The *204th Division* held the sector of 2,000 yards, from the Ypres–Hollebeke road to north of Mount Sorrel, with 2 regiments, the *413th* and *220th Reserve*. Its third regiment the *144th*, was in reserve behind the Third (Warneton) Line and resting in Menin. The division had been in the line since 23rd February; but its forward zone extended to an average depth of only six hundred yards, on the forward slope, and in the large concrete shelters on and behind the Ridge it had not been so seriously affected by the bombardment.

[2] The protective barrage was not stationary. Starting from 300 yards in front of the objective, it swept the ground ahead, moving forward and back, to check any enemy movement. Only the 18-pdr. guns of the creeping barrage were used for it, firing at the rate of 1 round a minute. The guns and howitzers of the standing barrages were silent during the pause, unless called by S.O.S. signal.

Strongpoints were dug and wired at once under the supervision of parties of engineers along each of the successive objectives and in the intermediate areas, and machine guns were distributed in depth throughout the captured position. Pack transport was of great assistance for carrying forward machine guns, ammunition, water and rations across the rough devastated ground,[1] as also were the Yukon packs, a Canadian device which enabled a man to carry a load of from 50–65 lbs. with the aid of a balance strap across the forehead.[2]

At 7 a.m. the guns and howitzers forming the standing barrages crashed down on their allotted targets on the summit of the Ridge and on its eastern slope. At the same time the 18-pdr. guns forming the protective barrage increased their rate of fire to 3 rounds a minute and began their forward creep by 100-yard lifts every 3 minutes. Close behind followed the fresh battalions destined for the third objective.[3] The majority of the first echelon of 48 tanks of the II Tank Brigade (Colonel A. Courage) allotted for the morning assault had been unable to keep pace with the infantry owing to the broken state of the ground, which had reduced their speed to about ten yards a minute.[4] The few that caught up gave valuable assistance.

The German garrison had been defeated in detail. The front battalions had been overrun in the first rush, and few had escaped.[5] Their support battalions had then been

---

[1] Mule pits were constructed as near as possible to the front line to enable the animals to be taken forward without delay, and 300 pack saddles were issued to each division supplementary to its establishment of 153; some divisions increased this allotment by locally made saddles. The use of tanks for carrying purposes was considered, but the idea was rejected; and where pack transport was impracticable, extra carriers (i.e. 2 men per machine gun) were allotted.

[2] Yukon packs were issued on a scale of 250 to each division, and some of the carrying parties equipped with them arrived within four minutes of the capture of an objective.

[3] Divisional commanders were free to make their own attack dispositions, which depended on the distance to, and width of, the successive objectives. The New Zealand, 25th, 19th and 41st Divisions used their third brigades to gain the final objective, the remainder continued to hold their third brigade in reserve.

[4] The allotment for the morning assault was : 20 tanks to the II Anzac Corps, 16 to the IX Corps and 12 to the X Corps. The remaining 24 were to assist the afternoon advance to the Oosttaverne Line.

[5] For example, G.O.A. xii., p. 456, states that of the front battalions of the three regiments of the *3rd Bavarian Division*, holding the Messines sector, opposite the greater part of the II Anzac Corps front, only 3 officers and 30 other ranks returned.

overwhelmed before the reserve battalions could reach them in any strength. Elements of the reserve battalions had come through and shared the fate of the support battalions; but the majority had remained lying out in shell-holes on the eastern slope of the Ridge awaiting events.

The Wellington and Auckland battalions of the 1st New Zealand Brigade (Br.-General E. H. J. Brown), leap-frogging the 3rd and 2nd New Zealand Brigades, moved to right and left of Messines village, where fighting was nearly at an end, 23 machine guns being among the booty.[1] A German artillery headquarters at Blauwen Molen, in a ruined windmill five hundred yards east of the village, was rushed, and the left of the brigade captured Fanny's Farm, 300 yards farther north, with the aid of a tank which knocked in the walls, a hundred Germans surrendering. In its short advance of seven hundred yards the brigade took 7 machine guns, 5 mortars and 200 prisoners, as well as 2 field guns which parties of Germans were trying to man-handle away. The reserve brigade of the 25th Division, the 75th (Br.-General H. B. D. Baird), carried on the line to the north, and its only obstacle was Lumm Farm, on its left flank. With the help of its neighbouring division, the 36th, the place was eventually rushed by a company of the 1/Wiltshire, and its garrison of 40 Germans killed or taken prisoner.

Wytschaete village, on the summit, was the chief problem facing the IX Corps. As the northern buttress of this high-lying part of the Ridge, it had been converted, like Messines, into a fortress with an all-round defence. An outer line of trenches followed the perimeter of the village; and an inner line of trenches enclosed the houses bordering on the main square, with the church at its centre. The chief strength of the locality lay in the machine-gun emplacements and vaulted cellars along the western side. The special bombardment of the village on the 3rd June by siege and heavy batteries, followed by gas shell from field howitzers, had so battered these defences that the two assault battalions found only crumbled heaps of bricks. With a tank leading, the 1/Munster Fusiliers (47th Brigade) stormed through the ruins, whilst the 2/Royal Irish (49th Brigade)

---

[1] See Sketch 5. For mopping-up Messines and Wytschaete villages, 50 per cent. of the assault companies concerned were allotted.

THE SECOND ADVANCE. 7TH JUNE 69

overran the northern outskirts. The German survivors were no match for these two Irish battalions, which quickly mopped up any resistance. By 8 a.m. the objective of the 16th Division beyond the St. Eloi–Messines highway was gained. The 36th Division, assisted by two tanks, had come up abreast on the right, after capturing a German battalion headquarters, including 30 officers and men, in a house near the Messines highway. On the left, too, the 57th Brigade (Br.-General T. A. Cubitt), covering the front of the 19th Division, arrived with little trouble along its objective, from north-east of Wytschaete village to Oosttaverne Wood (inclusive).

The most bitter fighting in this stage of the battle took place in the centre of the X Corps sector. The first objective of the 47th Division included a great heap of excavated earth 400 yards long, " Spoil Bank ", on the north side of the canal. A number of machine-gun emplacements had been built within it, and after several efforts costing heavy losses the 21/London had done no more than gain a footing on the western end. Another attack, supported by machine-gun fire of the 23/London from the south bank, was also checked by machine-gun fire both from Spoil Bank at close range and from Battle Wood on the left. At 9 a.m. a withdrawal was ordered preparatory to another shelling of the area.[1]

South of the canal, the capture of the White Château had broken the defence, and the objective across the park was occupied without difficulty. On the right, too, the 41st Division, using its 122nd Brigade (Br.-General F. W. Towsey) easily crossed the five hundred yards of flat ground on the summit to its objective along the back crest of the Ridge whence it overlooked the eastern slope and the Roozebeek valley. Many Germans were killed or captured near the numerous concrete shelters of the Second Line in Denys and Ravine Woods, the occasional resistance being quickly crushed. The 23rd Division, on the left, had heavy casualties in its efforts to clear Battle Wood, and its position on

---

[1] Apart from a small permanent garrison, Spoil Bank (" *Kanalkoffer* ") was occupied by the survivors of the two front companies and support company of the *61st Regiment*. They were reinforced at midday by four more machine guns with orders from the regimental commander to hold out at all costs, and were relieved at 2.30 a.m. the following morning by a company of the *26th Regiment* (*7th Division*).

the northern flank was only consolidated after a long struggle.[1]

In the centre, at 8.40 a.m., half an hour after the first objective was due to be reached, a company from each leading battalion advanced behind the barrage to the observation line a few hundred yards down the eastern slope of the Ridge. They were supported by eight tanks and by corps cavalry patrols to assist in clearing the area.[2] The Germans mostly surrendered freely; they seemed bewildered at the disappearance of the entire forward garrison. Groups of them near the large concrete shelters in Leg Copse and Oosttaverne Wood offered an ineffective resistance, and others found cowering in shell-holes and behind hedges were evidence of the demoralizing effect of the barrage. At this period, too, fast R.F.C. scouts flying at a low altitude, raked with machine-gun fire any Germans they saw in front of the advance, and added greatly to their readiness to surrender.[3] The observation line, the second objective, from Bethleem Farm, south of Messines, through Despagne Farm and along the eastern edge of Oosttaverne Wood was reached with few casualties by the foremost companies. Tapes and coloured flags were placed to mark the jumping-off line for the three divisions which were to make the afternoon assault; and strongpoints were dug to act first as observation posts and later to be the support or rallying points behind the Oosttaverne Line, that is the German line east of Oosttaverne. From daylight onwards contact aeroplanes had sent a steady flow of messages to the Second Army Report Centre at Locre giving the situation of the foremost line.

---

[1] The 11/Sherwood Foresters, on the extreme left, had some hard fighting to establish position astride the maze of German trenches east of Mount Sorrel, and one part of its objective was not gained till late in the evening.

[2] Of the 40 tanks allotted for the morning assault 25 eventually arrived along the first objective where they assisted in covering the work of consolidation.

[3] Contact patrols working at low altitudes (2,000 feet and under), dropped some of their machines lower still, with roving commissions to attack any Germans they saw.

CHAPTER V

THE BATTLE OF MESSINES 1917
(concluded)

The German Counter-Attacks

(Sketch 5)

By 9 a.m. British troops were established along the length of the Messines–Wytschaete Ridge from the Douve to east of Mount Sorrel.[1] Artillery observers with the foremost infantry had a direct view deep into the German back areas, and for the first time since October 1914 unhindered movement on the western slope of the ridge was possible.

A great crowd of men were now on the crest and summit of the Ridge. In estimating the density of the allotted frontages, casualties had been calculated at about 50 per cent. of the leading brigades for the capture of the first intermediate objective, and about 60 per cent. of the troops engaged to reach the first objective, east of Messines and Wytschaete. The actual casualties had been only a fraction of these figures, and as the unforeseen congestion was neither appreciated nor corrected, casualties now began to mount rapidly.[2]

The Second Army scheme expected that the stiffest fighting of the day would occur at this period, with two fresh German reserve divisions which, according to its Intelligence Summary of the 4th June, were waiting in the Lys valley, close behind the battle front, ready to counterattack.[3] To meet them effectively it was pre-arranged that the protective barrage should be strengthened by the masked batteries, hitherto silent in forward positions, of the three divisions of the reserve, the XIV Corps.

---

[1] See Sketch 5.
[2] " Regt. No. 104 " records that " crowds of British infantry [between " Messines and Wytschaete] were seen to take off their coats on this warm " summer morning and begin to dig in along the skyline of the Ridge ; " working in their lighter coloured shirt-sleeves, they made admirable " targets for our machine guns ".
[3] This information, obtained from statements of prisoners taken in raids, was correct. See Note at end of Chapter.

72   MESSINES

But no formed body of the enemy was anywhere to be seen; air observers reported no sign of preparations for a counter-attack in strength, and could see only scattered elements of the enemy on the eastern slope of the Ridge; the only exception was a report from an air observer at 8 a.m., that enemy detachments were crossing the Lys at Warneton; but no action developed.[1] Apart from the shell bursts of the protective barrage, the scene, to quote the words of an Australian officer, was more like a picnic than a battle. Behind was ·a ploughed-up wilderness of shell holes and battered trenches, with a litter of tangled wire, broken rifles and abandoned equipment; it reached back as far as a clean-cut line in the original No Man's Land, beyond which grass still grew. In front, however, was a green countryside, with woods of leaf-covered trees, and the gentle sloping grassland was intersected by tree-lined hedgerows. The lower half of this eastern slope, where lurked most of the German batteries, was out of sight owing to its convexity; but in the distance could be seen the towns, woods and water meadows for many miles along the Lys valley. This panorama slumbered under a bright sun which already gave promise of an exceptionally hot day.

The same unexpected absence of the German counter-attack divisions had marked the climax of the capture of the Vimy Ridge two months previously. Then, as now, they had arrived late in the battle-area.[2] About 11 a.m. men digging-in along the Ridge saw in the distance, about

---

[1] The report probably referred to the advance of the reserve regiment (*5th Bavarian Reserve*), with a field artillery brigade of the *4th Bavarian Division*, from its assembly area two miles south-east of Warneton. It had been ordered to cross the Lys and, at 7 a.m., to recapture the Ridge between the Douve and Messines. Before this attack could begin it was cancelled, as the force was required to strengthen the new line south of the Douve.

[2] Similar delays had occurred in the early German efforts to apply the new defensive battle procedure, i.e., at Verdun in October and December 1916 (see p. 11, footnote). The German army and corps commanders hesitated to engage their reserves before they knew definitely the extent of the attack and the direction of its main thrust. In this instance General von Laffert, commanding *Group Wytschaete*, believed that the front divisions would be able to hold the front crest of the Messines Ridge for at least twelve hours, till the two counter-attack divisions arrived. He miscalculated the effect of the mine explosions and 'of the artillery barrage. Compare the miscalculation of General von Falkenhausen, commanding the *German Sixth Army*, in the Vimy Ridge battle commented upon in " 1917 " Vol. I, p. 354.

two and a half miles away, German troops marching towards them along the road from Wervicq and crossing the canal. Later the convexity of the slope hid them from sight, and as the heat of the morning increased a haze settled over the low ground, making detailed observation difficult. The information gathered was summarized in two reports sent to the Second Army Report Centre: one, from the II Anzac Corps at 11.15 a.m., that a thousand German infantry were moving west across the canal from Wervicq ; and the other, from the 36th Division (IX Corps) at 11.45 a.m., that three thousand German infantry were moving up the Wambeek valley north of Garde Dieu. Information at 11.30 a.m. from aeroplane observers and from the advanced captive balloon observers confirmed these reports.[1]

At 12.15 p.m. the 25th Division, north of Messines, sent back information from its advanced patrols along the second objective (observation line) that the German infantry, previously reported assembling about Garde Dieu, were advancing up the Blauwepoortbeek (a tributary of the Wambeek) ; a later report, at 12.45 p.m., added that the head of the movement had arrived close behind the Oosttaverne Line. At 1.4 p.m. other messages stated that German batteries were in action at Delporte and Deconinck Farms, and that about eight hundred German troops were moving at the double north of Gapaard. These messages were passed on at once from Second Army Report Centre at Locre Château to the S.O.S. and counter-batteries concerned, which were able to keep the German movement under shell-fire throughout.

At 1.45 p.m. these Germans were seen to cross the Oosttaverne Line in a number of waves on a frontage of about a thousand yards from astride the Gapaard–Messines highway to the Blauwepoortbeek, preceded by an artillery barrage along the first objective from east of Messines to about Lumm Farm. The New Zealand advanced posts along the observation line, unaffected by the barrage, saw ten lines of Germans approaching them across the open fields, giving excellent targets to their machine guns ; whilst farther north, about six hundred of the enemy advancing in

---

[1] Two balloons of the 2nd Kite Balloon Wing R.F.C. had been brought up to within 3,000 yards on the night of the 6th/7th, and observed from a height of 5,000 feet.

four waves met the frontal and enfilade fire of twelve machine guns of the 25th Division sited in advanced positions during the morning by the divisional machine-gun officer: six at Despagne Farm and six in a ruined building six hundred yards north of it. Shortly afterwards, at 2.10 p.m., the British artillery barrage became intense in front of the Oosttaverne Line; it had been ordered on a report from balloon observers at 1.45 p.m. that the counter-attack was imminent, which was confirmed by Second Army observers on Kemmel who had seen through glasses the bursts of the German barrage. The combined artillery, machine-gun and rifle fire checked the counter-attack before it reached the advanced posts on the observation line, and German survivors fell back to any available cover or shell-holes. The 25th Division diary states that in its sector the attack was beaten by 2.8 p.m., before even the intense phase of the British barrage opened.[1]

About the same period of the day, German troop movements were noticed in the northern sector of the battle front. At 1.50 p.m. the X Corps reported an enemy column with motor transport on the Gheluvelt–Zandvoorde road (that is 3 miles east of Mount Sorrel) moving south-west towards the canal, and later about fifteen hundred Germans were seen near Kortewilde, and parties of fifty moving along the east

---

[1] This counter-attack was delivered by the leading regiment of the *1st Guard Reserve Division*, the southern of the two *Eingreif* divisions of *Group Wytschaete*. It had just relieved the *3rd Bavarian Division* which, though specially trained as the counter-attack division behind this sector for several weeks, had been ordered at the last moment, on 6th June, to relieve the *40th Division* in the front line. The *1st Guard Reserve Division*, as yet only partly assembled at Wervicq, was ordered at 3.30 a.m. to march to assembly areas about Garde Dieu; but some of the companies had only arrived by rail from the Arras front during the early hours, and, as they were fresh to the district, detailed instructions had to be given to each company commander, and this caused many delays. At 7.30 a.m. the division was placed under the orders of the front divisional commander of the Messines sector (*3rd Bavarian Division*), who ordered it to attack the ridge on either side of Messines village and, carrying forward all the troops it met, to recapture the forward zone and the enemy's original sortie trenches beyond. The leading regiment, the *1st Guard Reserve*, did not reach the Third Line assembly area about Garde Dieu till 11 a.m., and deployed behind the Oosttaverne Line on either side of Gapaard between 1 and 1.30 p.m. Owing to the heavy losses and failure of its leading regiment to advance, the two remaining regiments of the division were held back in and behind the Third (Warneton) Line.

There is no confirmation in British accounts for the statement in G.O.A. xii, p. 459, that this counter-attack drove the British back to the old German Second (Ridge) Line and reached the eastern houses of Messines.

GERMAN COUNTER-ATTACK. 7TH JUNE 75

side of the canal near Houthem. The X Corps heavy artillery commander ordered his 6-inch guns and 60-pdr. batteries to fire on the Kortewilde cross-roads and on the road east of the canal, and German accounts bear witness to the damaging effect of their fire. The reinforcements served only to strengthen the weak German garrison of the Oosttaverne Line in the Hollebeke and Wytschaete sectors, and the intended counter-attack through Wytschaete village which was to be in co-operation with that through Messines, did not develop.[1]

ADVANCE TO THE OOSTTAVERNE LINE

General Plumer's original intention was to press on down the eastern slope of the Ridge to the Oosttaverne Line without delay; the advance of the three reserve divisions, one of each corps, was to be supported by the six previously masked artillery brigades of the XIV Corps,[2] and the new line

---

[1] The fear of a simultaneous British attack astride the Ypres–Menin road to capture the important observation area Stirling Castle—Tower Hamlets on Gheluvelt plateau, had caused General Sixt von Arnim, the commander of the *Fourth Army*, on 3rd June, to change the assembly area for the northern *Eingreifdivision* of *Group Wytschaete* from the Houthem–Kortewilde area to east of Gheluvelt. Here it would be in a position to deliver an immediate counter-attack either westwards astride the Menin road towards Ypres, or south-west across the Ypres–Comines canal, taking in flank a possible British advance across the German Second Line about Wytschaete. The disadvantage was that in the latter event the division would have an additional march of five miles to reach the battlefield, including the crossing of the Comines canal. The *35th Division*, which had been specially trained for the task, had, on 1st June, relieved the *24th Division* in the front line, and its place as *Eingreifdivision* was taken by the *7th Division*, new to the district. It was not till 7 a.m. that the *Fourth Army* commander was assured of the security of Gheluvelt plateau and released the *7th Division* for the counter-attack in the Wytschaete sector. Ordered to march from Menin at 3.30 a.m., the division had long delays before reaching the assembly areas at Gheluwe and Gheluvelt, and with the extra 5-mile march, the morning was gone before its head reached the canal, marching under shell-fire in great heat. It did not begin to cross the canal at Houthem and Hollebeke, until about 1 p.m., and suffered considerable losses from British artillery fire. It had now been placed under the orders of the front divisional commander of the Wytschaete sector (*2nd Division*) with orders to counter-attack through Wytschaete on the right of the *1st Guard Reserve Division* : but, on urgent demands from the Hollebeke (*35th*) division for assistance, the right of the division was diverted to that sector after crossing the canal, and the left did not reach the Oosttaverne Line till nearly 5 p.m., where it reinforced the remnants of the *2nd Division*, east of Wytschaete.

[2] The Guards Division artillery supported the II Anzac Corps, that of the 1st Division the IX Corps, and that of the 32nd Division the X Corps.

reinforced at nightfall. "Risks", he wrote in a letter to his corps commanders on the 15th May, "may and should be taken in order to secure that line and to capture the guns in the intervening area". It was calculated that 180 guns were in position west of the Oosttaverne Line on the front of attack and that, allowing for the escape of one-third, 120 of them should be captured. Discussion with the corps commanders, however, led to the decision that a rapid advance in this manner was not likely to be practicable in view of expected counter-attacks. The Second Army operation order of the 19th May had therefore allowed a halt of five hours along the first objective, in order to bring up additional artillery support before continuing the advance. The long pause was not expected to hinder the capture of the German batteries on the eastern slope which, it was considered, would have no chance of escape after the Ridge had been taken.

Reports which came in early in the day as to the state of the ground and the difficulty of transport led General Plumer to allow two more hours to prepare for the final advance, and at 10 a.m. he had fixed the afternoon Zero for 3.10 p.m. By that time several heavy and forty field batteries had been advanced, some to previously prepared positions with dumps of 300 rounds per gun alongside, and others into No Man's Land, a closer approach being temporarily impracticable owing to ground conditions.[1] An overhead machine-gun barrage was to be supplied by 146 guns along the near crest of the Ridge;[2] and sixteen or more guns from each division were already in strongpoints behind the observation line on the eastern slope.[3] For the afternoon advance, too, the 24 tanks in Second Army reserve were

---

[1] These batteries were in addition to the six masked artillery brigades of the XIV Corps. In all, one 18-pdr. gun would be available for every seventeen yards of front of the creeping barrage, in addition to a number of guns and howitzers not expected to be fully registered, and to be used for standing barrages on selected points near and in the Oosttaverne Line.

[2] In the II Anzac Corps sector, 36 guns of the New Zealand Division were a few hundred yards south-east of Messines, and 24 guns of the 25th Division were immediately west of the Messines–Wytschaete road to 4 Huns Farm; 54 guns of the IX Corps were about l'Enfer Wood, Hospice and Martens Farm; and 32 guns of the X Corps were about the Damm Strasse area to the canal.

[3] Each machine-gun company was allotted two mules, each carrying six belt-boxes of ammunition and two gallons of water, returning to the forward dumps for further loads; for the men, the Yukon carrier was supplemented by sand-bags, which were slung in pairs over each shoulder and took, in all, four belt-boxes.

available (12 with the II Anzac Corps and 12 with the IX); they started from points behind the old British trenches between 10.30 a.m. and noon. The tanks in the X Corps sector, assembled in Damm and Denys Woods after the morning assault, were also to participate.

Covering the front of the II Anzac Corps, from the Douve to Wambeke (exclusive), the 4th Australian Division (Major-General W. Holmes) was to carry out the attack with two brigades, each with two battalions leading. From their camp at Neuve Eglise they arrived at the old British front line at 11 a.m., and went on at 11.30 a.m. to their assembly tapes on the Ridge. The right brigade, while crossing the shoulder of the Ridge, south of Messines, passed through a fierce barrage with surprisingly few casualties,[1] and not until it reached the tapes was the message passed along that the assault was postponed for two hours, till 3.10 p.m. The men had to lie out in the open on the eastern slope for the two extra hours, exposed to artillery and machine-gun fire, which caused considerable losses. Fortunately the message reached the left brigade in time to hold it back till 1.40 p.m., when its two assault battalions crossed the Ridge north of Messines to the jumping-off tapes, the right on the mound of the Blauwen Molen and the left a few hundred yards east of Lumm Farm.[2]

On the narrower frontage of the IX Corps only one brigade, the 33rd (Br.-General A. C. Daly) of the reserve division, the 11th (Major-General H. R. Davies), was to be used. On arrival at its night assembly area near Brulooze (3 miles west of Wytschaete) at 2 a.m., it came under 16th Division headquarters (at Scherpenberg, 3 miles W.S.W. of Wytschaete) for the battle. At 9.25 a.m. an order was sent to it to go forward to Vandamme Farm, near the old British

---

[1] A German aeroplane had reported the start of this movement to German batteries behind the Lys. General Wenniger, commanding this sector, mentions in his battle report that his guns had been so reduced by the British counter-battery fire that they could not adequately deal with the tempting targets offered by columns of British infantry crossing the Messines Ridge, and that only where these came within range of the *4th Bavarian Division* artillery, on the southern flank south of the Lys, could material damage be inflicted.

[2] The message reached the headquarters of the 4th Australian Division (Westhof Farm) at 10.30 a.m., but had to be telephoned to the New Zealand forward stations, and thence sent by runner to the assembly area near the British front line.

front line; but the message did not reach the brigade, less than a mile away, till 10.45 a.m. It was 2 p.m. before the leading battalions began to cross the difficult ground of the battle area, and they did not reach the forward assembly area near Rommens Farm on the Ridge till 3.50 p.m., half an hour after the assault was due to start. At 12.15 p.m. Lieut.-General Sir Alexander Gordon, hearing of the delay, had asked the 19th Division to send forward its reserve brigade, the 57th, which was still intact, to take six hundred yards of the Oosttaverne Line from Van Hove Farm (inclusive) to the road junction south of Bug Wood and including Oosttaverne village, leaving only the southern twelve hundred yards for the 33rd Brigade. This change of plan did not reach 57th Brigade headquarters in Grand Bois till 1.35 p.m.; and, as orders to the two front battalions had to be sent up by runners, they were not informed till 2.50 p.m. and 3.5 p.m., respectively, a few minutes before the barrage moved forward. Major-General Shute, commanding the 19th Division, foreseeing difficulties, had telephoned to corps headquarters at 1.30 p.m. to ask that the barrage might be delayed 20 minutes, till 3.30 p.m., as it was possible that both the 57th and 33rd Brigades might be late; but, on hearing that the new Zero could not now be altered, Major-General Shute ordered the 57th Brigade to advance with the barrage and not to wait for the 33rd.

The brigades of the 24th Division (Major-General L. J. Bols), in the X Corps sector, from their night assembly areas near Dickebusch Lake (2¼ miles south-west of Ypres), had reached the line of the Damm Strasse, on the Ridge, before 1 p.m. without incident. Half an hour later, the two leading battalions of each brigade moved on to the jumping-off tapes near the first objective, the right on the St. Eloi–Oosttaverne road, and the left in the park of the White Château, south of the Comines canal.

At 3.10 p.m. the barrage began its forward creep down the eastern slope with 100-yard lifts every three minutes. The two Australian brigades realized that stiff fighting was ahead. During the long wait they had watched the survivors of the German counter-attack taking up position in front of and along the Oosttaverne Line, and had also seen reinforcements arrive south of the Messines–Warneton

THE AFTERNOON ATTACK. 7TH JUNE 79

road.¹ As they moved off three of the four tanks with the right brigade came over the southern shoulder of the Ridge, south of Messines, the fourth being ditched on the way; but none of those detailed to assist the left brigade, north of Messines, arrived in time.

The 12th Australian Brigade (Br.-General J. C. Robertson), together with a battalion (37th) of the 3rd Australian Division on the right, had as objective the back trench of the Oosttaverne Line between the Douve and the Blauwepoortbeek, a frontage of two thousand yards. Moving close behind the three tanks² the 47th and 45th Battalions, mostly Queenslanders, though swept by machine-gun fire from the start and suffering heavy casualties, did not falter. With the help of the tanks, an outlying position, Oxygen Trench, was overrun and 120 Germans captured in it. The opposition was coming chiefly from the pillboxes at wide intervals along the Oosttaverne Line, now three hundred yards ahead; and the left battalion, the 45th, north of the Messines-Warneton road was held up by intense machine-gun fire and by shrapnel from field guns in concrete emplacements near Delporte Farm. South of the road the pillboxes were reached by the 37th and 47th Battalions behind the dust-screen of the barrage, and many savage and bloody encounters took place as the outflanking parties moved in, the capture of each strongpoint being usually due to individual acts of great courage.³ The Germans became panic-stricken when they saw these groups of infantry filtering through their defence organization and the barrage churning up the dust behind them; many lay on the ground crying for mercy or embracing the knees of the Australians; others

---

[1] This sector had been occupied during the morning by the three reserve battalions of the *3rd Bavarian Division*, many of whose companies had gone forward to the Second Line on the Ridge and had been overrun. After the failure of the 1.45 p.m. counter-attack, two battalions of the *1st Guard Reserve Regiment* fell back on the line of pillboxes between the Blauwepoortbeek and the Messines-Warneton road, and two more battalions from the neighbouring divisional sector to the south, one of the *18th Bavarian Regiment* and one of the *5th Bavarian Reserve Regiment*, reinforced the line between that road and the Douve.

[2] No. 5 Section of 5th Company. ("H.M.S. Lucifer" "Our Emma" and "Rumblebelly").

[3] Captain R. C. Grieve (37th Battalion), seeing his company held up by a pillbox at Hun House, two hundred yards south of the Warneton Road, approached it alone from a flank and dropped two bombs through the loophole, killing the gun-crew, when the rest of the garrison surrendered. He was awarded the V.C.

who ran away were either shot down or caught by the barrage which halted about three hundred yards beyond the objective, the second trench of the Oosttaverne Line.

In the 13th Brigade (Br.-General T. W. Glasgow) the right battalion, the 49th, moving with its right on the Blauwepoortbeek, was checked, like the left battalion of the 12th Brigade, on the south side of the brook, 500 yards short of the Oosttaverne Line, having had heavy losses, including all its company commanders. The left battalion, the 52nd finding its left unsupported by the 33rd Brigade, which unknown to it had not yet reached the deployment area about Rommens Farm, began at once to incline to the left, north of Lumm Farm, to make contact. Instead of straight down the Wambeke spur, this incline took the battalion across the spur and created a rapidly widening gap in the middle of the brigade. The Oosttaverne Line was reached with little opposition; but the right now on the Wambeek brook was a thousand yards north of its appointed place. As the 33rd Brigade was not in sight, the Oosttaverne Line was occupied from the Wambeke hamlet northwards to Polka Estaminet. About 4.30 p.m., units of the 33rd Brigade began to arrive and, with the help of four tanks of the IX Corps, Joye Farm and Van Hove Farm, from which Germans were still firing, a few hundred yards beyond the objective, were occupied by them.

The attack of the 57th Brigade, covering the remaining frontage of the IX Corps, had been so hurriedly arranged that junior commanders had no knowledge of what they were to do beyond the fact that they had to move in a certain direction and keep up with the barrage. Fortunately, the German shelling was light and inaccurate, and little opposition was met; the two battalions occupied the Oosttaverne Line in their sector, including the hamlet of Oosttaverne, within twenty minutes and with few casualties. Their right gained touch with the Australians at Polka Estaminet. The resistance would undoubtedly have been stronger, but for the closeness, fifty to sixty yards, with which the infantry followed the barrage.

The two brigades of the 24th Division in the X Corps sector also easily gained their objective, which included Bug Wood, Rose Wood and Verhaest Farm. The many pillbox shelters along the northern sector of the Oosttaverne Line, where it merged into the Second Line, were occupied without a struggle, 289 Germans, as well as six field guns, being captured. The two leading battalions of the 17th Brigade (Br.-General P. V. P. Stone) had only six casualties between them during an average advance of eight hundred yards down the slope astride the head of the Roozebeek valley and the few enemy who remained to face them readily surrendered. On the left, tanks were to have helped the 73rd Brigade (Br.-General W. J. Dugan) to clear the ravines in Ravine Wood, which were expected to contain large numbers of the enemy; but no opposition was met and the infantry occupied the ravines without assistance.[1] The left of the brigade was drawn back within the White Chateau park to join up with the right of the 47th Division, which was still held up by the German machine guns in Spoil Bank north of the canal.

The expectation that about 120 German field guns would be taken in the area between the first objective and the Oosttaverne Line was over-optimistic in view of the long pauses for consolidation along the successive intermediate objectives. During the five hours which had elapsed since the start of the assault many enemy guns had been withdrawn to back positions, and owing to the convexity of the eastern slope, which fell sharply behind the Oosttaverne Line, it was an illusion to imagine that once the Ridge was captured the guns beyond it would be unable to escape. Most of the 48 guns captured in this area had been previously damaged by counter-battery fire and abandoned.

Consolidation

On the entire battle front only two small sectors of the final objective had not been gained: Spoil Bank at the bend of the Comines canal in the X Corps objective, and the thousand yards of the Oosttaverne Line astride the

---

[1] Sixteen of the 24 tanks which were to support the advance to the Oosttaverne Line reached it, and of those which remained to cover the consolidation two, ditched near Joye Farm, gave valuable assistance with their 6-pdr. guns during the following days.
Eleven tanks were disabled during the day by German artillery fire. Many of the German anti-tank guns, in emplacements about the summit of the Ridge were found to have been smashed by the preparatory bombardment.

Blauwepoortbeek depression at the junction of the II Anzac and IX Corps boundaries.

Spoil Bank was bombarded by heavy artillery from 2.30 to 6.55 p.m., but the infantry assault, delivered by three companies of the 20/London (142nd Brigade), one south and two north of the canal, failed. The German artillery had laid a barrage on the companies as they deployed, half of the left company lost direction, and the machine guns within Spoil Bank, unaffected by the preparatory bombardment, raked the lines of attack. The flank companies were soon checked and, although the centre company succeeded in advancing half-way, astride the mound, it was forced to withdraw when it found its flanks unsupported and saw a number of German reinforcements entering the tunnels in the mound from the cover of the canal-cutting. Out of 11 officers and 290 other ranks engaged, five officers and 89 other ranks became casualties; and no further attempt was made.

The resistance in the Blauwepoortbeek valley presented a more complex problem; for, during the four hours which remained before sunset of this cloudless summer evening, the situation in the entire southern half of the Oosttaverne Line became very involved. An S.O.S. artillery barrage, called for about 5.30 p.m. to assist in checking a German counter-attack astride the Warneton road from about Steingast Farm, deluged with shrapnel the leading battalions of the 12th Australian Brigade which, owing to the difficulty of recognizing the objective, happened to be digging-in 250 yards ahead of it. The Australians stopped the attack with their own Lewis-gun and rifle fire; but, as the barrage continued and casualties from it steadily increased, a subordinate officer gave an order to withdraw. This order spread rapidly to right and left, despite senior officers' efforts to stop it, and many of the forward companies fell back through the observation line and were reorganized behind the first objective on the Ridge. About dusk, between 8 and 9 p.m., the New Zealand battalion commanders in the first objective, believing the Australians had all retired and that another German attack was imminent, asked for the barrage to be shortened to the observation line. Searching the ground between it and the Oosttaverne Line, the barrage fell upon those Australians still along the objective, including the 37th Battalion on the right, and these too, now fell back through the barrage with further considerable losses. By dusk, the whole of the southern half of the Oosttaverne Line, which had been captured a few hours before with such outstanding gallantry, was left free to the enemy, and the thousand yards' sector across the Blauwepoortbeek valley was still unconquered.

In front of the central and northern sectors of the Oosttaverne Line, too, the arrival of strong German reinforcements had been interpreted by British observers on the Ridge as an assembly for a counter-attack in strength, and at 8.30 p.m. an S.O.S. signal was given for artillery support, as the expected counter-attack was considered imminent against the IX Corps sector. The resulting barrage was effective, notably the fire-concentration of 45 machine guns on an enemy assembly in the Roozebeek valley; but many of the 18-pdr. batteries, which had come forward during the day to new positions, fired short, causing casualties all along the foremost line in the IX Corps sector. Large numbers of men fell back, including the garrison of Van Hove Farm, and the withdrawal towards and through the observation line gave rise to widespread rumours and messages that the forward brigades had been forced back on to the Ridge. The S.O.S. barrage by the original front divisions was therefore shortened to lie in front of the observation line, and it made conditions intolerable for those still holding out in the foremost area. The situation was not restored until after 10 p.m., when the artillery fire ceased, and the IX Corps sector of the Oosttaverne Line, including Van Hove Farm, was re-occupied.[1]

At 10.45 p.m. General Godley, commanding the II Anzac Corps, ordered the 3rd and 4th Australian Divisions to

---

[1] Actually, General von Laffert, commanding *Group Wytschaete*, had given up any idea of recapturing the Ridge after the failure of the 1.45 p.m. counter-attack on Messines. Hearing that the Oosttaverne Line had been taken on a wide front, he had, on the contrary, ordered a withdrawal to take place at nightfall across the Comines canal and the Lys. During the evening, when reports showed that the British had halted along the Oosttaverne Line, the order was cancelled, and only the artillery was withdrawn, the mass of it taking up new positions in and behind a line northwards from the western edge of Comines. At 11.45 p.m. the *Fourth Army* commander ordered the existing foremost line to be held; and already, before dusk, the *7th Division*, the northern counter-attack division of *Group Wytschaete*, which had been delayed in crossing the Comines canal, had arrived in front of the weakly held sector of the Oosttaverne Line, northwards from Wambeke. After vain efforts to re-occupy the Line, the 3 regiments formed a zone of defence behind it in shell-holes and about the original German battery positions.

re-occupy all the ground vacated and the barrage to be maintained east of the Oosttaverne Line; but he did not yet know that the Blauwepoortbeek sector had never been taken, nor that the left Australian battalion (52nd) was out of its place, covering the whole of the IX Corps front. The order concerned only the sector astride the Warneton road, and the attack, made at 3 a.m. the next morning, succeeded in re-occupying the Oosttaverne Line between the Douve and Warneton road, evacuated the previous evening, which the Germans had only re-entered in a few places. Shortly afterwards the southern shoulder of the Messines Ridge was heavily shelled by the German artillery concentration south of the Lys, causing considerable losses; but the Australian hold did not loosen.

The situation north of the Warneton road was not appreciated by the headquarters concerned for many hours. The 13th Australian Brigade had sent forward its reserve battalion to reinforce the 49th opposite the Blauwepoortbeek sector and to join in the 3 a.m. attack; but, owing to the heavy losses of the 49th on the previous day and ignorance of the precise situation, no attack developed. It was not until 4 a.m., when the 4th Australian Division commander, Major-General Holmes, went forward to Messines with the two brigade commanders, that the facts became known. It was decided that the 33rd Brigade should take over from the 52nd Australian Battalion at dusk that evening (8th), the 52nd to move round after relief to support the advance of the 49th Battalion into the Blauwepoortbeek gap.

The morning and afternoon of the 8th were quiet; but when the relief by the 33rd Brigade began at dusk artillery observers of the original front divisions on the Ridge believed the men of the withdrawing 52nd Battalion to be Germans attacking up the slope. S.O.S. signals were sent back for artillery support, and the area was deluged with shell for the next two hours.[1] Both relieving and relieved units suffered heavy losses, and their withdrawal through the barrage gave rise to many alarmist rumours. Owing to the confusion and delay, the attack down the Blauwepoortbeek had to be postponed till the following evening.

---

[1] The shelling was increased by the fact that the German observers also believed the advancing relief troops to be an attacking force and they, too, sent up S.O.S. signals which brought down a German barrage on the same area.

These mishaps on the eastern slope of the Ridge and the consequent heavy casualties, chiefly to II Anzac Corps, were due to the establishment of two independent defence organizations—by the reserve divisions along the Oosttaverne Line and by the original front divisions on the Ridge—one behind the other, each with its own artillery support.[1] No provision had been made by Second Army headquarters to prevent the confusion inherent in such a situation, and it persisted, despite protests, till the morning of the 9th. On that day the II Anzac Corps commander ordered the corps front to be held by the 3rd and 4th Australian Divisions and the 25th Division, each to control its sector in depth, and the New Zealand Division to move back to Neuve Eglise in corps reserve. So, too, the IX Corps sector was ordered to be held in depth by the 11th and 19th Divisions, the 11th taking over the sectors of the 36th and 16th Divisions Each corps made its own final defence arrangements to secure the captured ground; but the general idea was a front defence system on the eastern slope with the main line of resistance along the Ridge, from behind which the counter-attacks with brigade reserves would take place, if needed. The change-over took place during the night of the 9th/10th, and at the same time the corps boundaries were slightly altered, the 11th Division taking over six hundred yards from the II Anzac Corps, and the 19th Division moving its left northwards to Rose Wood.

The next evening (10th) the attack made at 10 p.m. down the Blauwepoortbeek by the 13th Australian Brigade, combined with a bombing attack northwards from the captured sector of the Oosttaverne Line, was only partially successful.[2] Farther south, the 3rd Australian Division at 11 p.m. advanced six hundred yards astride and south of the Douve, and consolidated in greater strength the advanced posts established on the previous night south of the river and on the rise of ground about the Thatched Cottage, covering the right flank of the whole operation.

[1] Australian officers have stated that the days and nights following the capture of the Messines Ridge were for them the most harassing of the War. A detailed account of this period in the II Anzac Corps sector is given in A.O.A. iv., pp. 637–82.

[2] The weakly held sector of the German front between the *1st Guard Reserve Division* and the *7th Division*, i.e., from astride the Blauwepoortbeek to Van Hove Farm, had been taken over on the 8th by the *11th Division*, a reserve division of *Group Ypres*.

Prisoners taken during this advance, when examined at 3rd Australian Division headquarters about 8 a.m. (11th), stated that a general withdrawal of German troops was to have taken place at 1.30 a.m. that morning from the Oosttaverne Line back towards the Warneton Line; but that the bombardment had caught their units in the Douve sector before they could carry out the order. This information confirmed a message at 4.53 a.m. from the 12th Australian Brigade in the Blauwepoortbeek sector, that Germans could be seen leaving the Oosttaverne Line and that Lewis gunners were firing on the retreating enemy. Half an hour later patrols found the trench and blockhouses of the Blauwepoortbeek sector of the line empty, and this gap, the last in the original final objective, except Spoil Bank, was occupied.[1]

As the observation from the final objective, the support trench of the Oosttaverne Line, was not as good as had been expected, General Plumer decided to make a further short advance on the whole front, and the Second Army order to this effect was issued at 11 p.m. on the 11th. The X Corps was to take the still uncaptured Spoil Bank and the sectors of the first objective adjacent to Battle Wood and the White Château park; the IX Corps was to advance its foremost line to include Joye Farm and Wambeke hamlet, joining the II Anzac Corps east of Delporte Farm; the II Anzac Corps was to push forward its left and centre

---

[1] The German decision to withdraw was made at a conference on the 9th between Crown Prince Rupprecht of Bavaria, commanding the *Northern Group of Armies*, and General Sixt von Arnim, commanding the *Fourth Army*. (See Map 1.) The Third (Warneton) Line was now overlooked by British observers, and could be swept by enfilade artillery fire from both flanks; further, no artillery observation facilities were available behind it and also it was a continuous trench line which, being easy to see from the air and for artillery to range on, was in German experience an obsolete pattern. For these reasons, the nearest suitable position for a permanent defence was considered to be the sector of the Flanders Line between Wervicq and Lincelles (3 miles south of Wervicq), three miles farther back; and it was to be joined up with the existing front line by the Tenbrielen Line (switch) on the north flank from Wervicq to Zandvoorde, and by the Flanders Line on the south, south-east of Armentières. Fourteen days were to be allowed to prepare a deep zone of defence in front of this line, with isolated and mutually supporting strongpoints sited chequerwise. In the meantime, a bridgehead position, the *Kanal-Lys Stellung*, was to be held between Houthem and Warneton, consisting of a chain of fieldworks, with advanced posts in front of the Third (Warneton) Line. If not attacked this line would continue to be held; but, if attacked, after 14 days the garrison would withdraw to the Flanders Position.

END OF THE BATTLE. 14TH JUNE

about a thousand yards to include Gapaard spur and Ferme de la Croix, whilst its right, to be taken over by the New Zealand Division on the 12th, moved forward from Ploegsteert Wood eastwards towards the Lys, including Trois Tilleuls Farm and Hill 20.[1] The general advance was to be made on the 14th; but already on the night of the 10th/11th the enemy had evacuated these objectives and they were for the most part occupied without difficulty before the 14th by British advanced posts.

With the establishment of this new line on the 14th June the Battle of Messines ended. A great victory had been won by General Plumer's Second Army, and with a swift completeness beyond that of any previous major operation of the British Armies in France and Flanders. The capture of Vimy Ridge, a lesser operation which the Second Army had taken as a model, alone bears comparison. After two long years of patient endurance, the ambition to remove the Germans from the dominating southern face of the Ypres Salient had been realized and the aim of months of intensive labour and preparation was achieved.

All the objectives had been taken together with prisoners and material amounting to 144 officers and 7,210 other ranks, 48 guns, 218 machine guns and 60 trench mortars. The casualties in the actual capture of the Ridge had been slight; but they had later reached an unnecessarily high figure for two main reasons: failure to rectify the crowding on the Ridge, and the establishment of two independent artillery organizations. Of the total of 24,562 casualties incurred by the Second Army during the battle period 1st–12th June, more than one-half were in the II Anzac Corps.[2] In the

---

[1] To assist the New Zealand attack, the 4 mines at The Birdcage, near Le Gheer, south-east of Ploegsteert Wood, were to be exploded at zero hour. As the enemy had by then already evacuated the position, the mines were not fired. The intention to remove the mines after the War was overlooked, so that, so far as is known, the charges still remain in position.

[2] The casualties suffered by the Second Army during the period 1st–12th June, in detail, were:

	Officers			Other Ranks			Total
	Killed	Wounded	Missing	Killed	Wounded	Missing	
II Anzac Corps	71	298	8	1,714	8,904	1,396	12,391
IX Corps	24	166	–	627	3,349	1,097	5,263
X Corps	67	228	5	972	4,787	538	6,597
II Corps	3	1	–	18	83	3	108
VIII Corps	3	11	–	39	150	—	203
	168	704	13	3,370	17,273	3,034	24,562

Continued at foot of next page.

88   MESSINES

German Official History enemy casualties are given as about 23,000, including ten thousand missing, for the period 21st May–10th June; but owing to the omission of slightly wounded comparative figures are not obtainable.[1]

THE MESSINES VICTORY NOT EXPLOITED

The intention was to exploit the capture of the Messines Ridge by gaining a foothold on the western end of Gheluvelt plateau. Both the 1916 and 1917 plans had emphasized this essential preliminary to the advance of the main offensive north-eastwards from the Ypres Salient. It was hoped to take advantage of the broken flank at the south-western corner of the plateau, about Mount Sorrel, before the defences could be repaired.[2]

On the 24th May Sir Douglas Haig had written to General Plumer making him responsible for exploiting a success on the Second Army front, and he emphasized its importance, " seeing that the capture of the Messines Ridge might be " the beginning of the capture of the Passchendaele–Staden " Ridge ". He added, " in the event of the situation " developing in our favour, reserves will be placed at the " disposal of General Gough, G.O.C. Fifth Army, in order to " enable him to co-operate in an effort to gain that Ridge ". On the 3rd June General Plumer urged that it was " essential " that the opportunity for exploiting a success should be " taken advantage of at the earliest possible moment ". He had arranged for the II and VIII Corps to attack,

---

Continued from previous page.
For comparison, the casualties incurred and the strength by arms during the period 7th–12th June are given:

	Casualties			Strength		
	Officers	Other Ranks	Total	Officers	Other Ranks	Total
R.F.A. (78 brigades)	79	667	746	3,212	86,514	89,726
R.G.A. (187 batteries)	18	454	472	1,336	34,578	35,914
Infantry (158 battalions, less Machine Gun Coys.) ...	803	17,843	18,646	5,980	148,506	154,486
Machine Gun Coys. (41)	78	689	767	407	6,558	6,965
Other Troops	12	297	309	[not available]		
	990	19,950	20,940	10,935	276,156	287,091

[1] The German figures were worked out from the corps strength returns every 10 days. The casualties for the *Groups Ypres, Wytschaete* and *Lille* for the 10 days 21st–31st May are given as 1,963 all ranks, and from the 1st–10th June as 19,923 (including 7,548 missing), and from the 11th–20th June as 5,501. G.O.A. xii states that the battle casualty returns did not include " wounded likely to return to duty within a reasonable time ". About 30 per cent. should be added. See " 1916 " Vol. I, p. 497.

[2] See Sketch 2.

VICTORY NOT EXPLOITED

respectively, north and south of Bellewaarde Lake, with the Stirling Castle (2,000 yards south of Westhoek)–Westhoek high ground as a first objective, an advance of twelve hundred yards. To give additional support to the attack, 60 heavy and medium guns and howitzers were to be transferred from the Messines battlefront; and General Plumer asked for a three days' interval for the transfer.

On the 6th June, the day before the Messines battle, Sir Douglas Haig had told General Gough that " we may be " able to exploit a success quickly and reach a position which " would materially help your operations ". General Gough, however, preferred either to follow the Doullens plan (that is to include the Gheluvelt attack in the " Northern " Operation ")[1] or to conduct the proposed attack by the II and VIII Corps himself.

Early on the 8th patrols sent out by the II and VIII Corps reported strong resistance, and at midday Sir Douglas Haig asked General Plumer if the attack planned could be carried out at once. General Plumer repeated his request for three days to transfer the necessary artillery from the Messines battlefront, and Sir Douglas Haig thereupon decided to hand the two corps over to the Fifth Army. He still wished the attack to take place, and in the G.H.Q. order on the evening of the 8th stated that " as a preliminary operation " to the main northern operation, the Fifth Army will " prepare a plan for a minor offensive designed to secure " its right flank on the Ridge east of Ypres and with the " object of gaining observation about Stirling Castle."

The scheme was sent to General Gough on the following day by General Plumer, but on the 14th, at an Army commanders' conference at Lillers, General Gough stated that after a study of the ground he had come to the conclusion that if the operation succeeded " our troops would " be in a very exposed and difficult salient ". He added that in his opinion it would be wiser to have no preliminary operation, but to attack along his whole front on the day of the main offensive The postponement was approved.[2]

---

[1] See p. 25.
[2] Actually the procedure recommended by General Plumer was that which the Germans expected and most feared. Crown Prince Rupprecht states in his diary (ii., 7th and 19th June) that he saw in the British victory of Messines only the first step to the capture of the Belgian coastal ports' by a Flanders offensive. He believed the second step would be to

Continued at foot of next page.

At this conference the Commander-in-Chief explained that the general plan of the French and British—wearing down and exhausting the enemy as defined on the 7th May—still held good, but underlying the general intention was "the "strategic objective of securing the Belgian coast and "connecting with the Dutch frontier": the next step[1] was to secure the Passchendaele–Staden–Clercken ridge as a base for farther advance, and it was hoped to make it on the 25th July, the French expecting to be ready by the 21st: meanwhile, by suitable operations, endeavour should be made, by attacks near Lens (First Army) and Frelinghien (3 miles south of Warneton) (Second Army), to create the impression that the next objective would be Lille.

NOTE

THE GERMAN DEFENCE

As early as the 25th April German air observers had reported preparations behind the Messines–Wytschaete sector indicating the imminence of a British offensive. On the 28th, German O.H.L. received information from a secret agent that if the attacks on the Scarpe failed to make progress the British would begin a new offensive on the Ypres front, and this news was passed on to Crown Prince Rupprecht of Bavaria, with the comment that the greatest attention was to be paid to events in the Ypres and Wytschaete sectors. To frustrate the British preparations, General von Kuhl, Chief of the Staff to Crown Prince Rupprecht, suggested that it would be better to evacuate the salient formed by the Messines–Wytschaete Ridge position

---

Continued from previous page.
establish a right flank firmly on the high ground about Gheluvelt and Zandvoorde and on the Lys about Comines, preliminary to an offensive north-eastwards from Ypres. During the period following the Messines victory the Gheluvelt–Zandvoorde attack was expected daily. In his diary of 9th June, Rupprecht contemplated a withdrawal on the least pressure to a line Hooge–Zandvoorde–Wervicq, and thence southwards behind the Lys along the Flanders Line and Flanders Switch. (See Note at end of Chapter VIII). He doubted if the Hooge–Zandvoorde sector of this line could be held against the superior artillery concentration at the British disposal: "an improvement in the defence situation can "only come about by moving back to the Flanders Line".

On 19th June the Crown Prince Rupprecht still believed that the British procedure would be a succession of attacks on narrow frontages supported by an overwhelming artillery concentration to use up the German reserves and mak deep wedges into the German position, to be followed finally by a great break-through offensive on a wide front (*auf breiter Basis angesetzten Durchbruchsangriff.*).

[1] See Sketch 1.

NOTE. THE GERMAN DEFENCE

before an attack. He pointed out that the existing position offered itself to attack from three sides, and that the German defences lay on a forward slope, exposed to the concentric and observed fire of the British artillery; a repetition of the recent disaster on the rather similar Vimy Ridge position was therefore possible. The heavy losses both in men and artillery which might be suffered in an attempt to hold this forward slope would, he considered use up reserves needed elsewhere, and he proposed a withdrawal either to the *Sehnen* (Oosttaverne) Line,[1] midway between the Second Line along the Ridge and the Third (Warneton) Line, or to the Third (Warneton) Line itself.

Crown Prince Rupprecht concurred in this view; but when on the 30th April General von Kuhl put it forward at a *Fourth Army* conference, assembled to discuss defensive measures in the sector, he found almost unanimous disapproval. The local commanders considered the existing position, which had been brought up-to-date, was not unfavourable for a mobile defence and the delivery of counter-attacks, and maintained that it could be held. The artillery commander of *Group Wytschaete*, too, affirmed that the artillery defence was so well organized that the British batteries could be mastered. The divisional commanders concerned agreed with these views, and they were influenced decisively by a memorandum, issued two days previously by Lieut.-Colonel Füsslein, the commander of mining operations in the Messines salient, which allayed their only fear, namely that the forward garrison might be put out of action by underground mine explosions preliminary to an offensive. According to this expert opinion, the counter-mining operations had been so successful, especially during April, that "a sub-"terranean attack by mine-explosions on a large scale beneath "the front line to precede an infantry assault against the "Messines Ridge was no longer possible (*nicht mehr möglich*) ".[2] It was also pointed out to General von Kuhl that both the *Sehnen* (Oosttaverne) and the Third (Warneton) Lines were unsuitably sited; the convexity of the back slope of the Ridge made artillery observation over the ground in front impracticable, so that the infantry defence would be without artillery support. A further objection to the Warneton Line was that the angle behind it formed by the Ypres–Comines canal and the Lys river limited the space for manoeuvre and would make almost impossible counter-attacks on any considerable scale for the relief

---

[1] See Sketch 3.
[2] Four months previously (25th December 1916) Colonel Füsslein had reported that the British deep mining operations were probably intended to support an offensive above ground, and he had been given three additional mining companies to fight both the upper and lower British mine-systems; but their success had been limited.

of the forward garrisons. The nearest back line suitable to defend was said to be the new Flanders Position, three miles farther back; but such a withdrawal would expose the left flank of *Group Ypres* on Gheluvelt plateau.

After a further examination of the Oosttaverne and Warneton Lines, Crown Prince Rupprecht reported to O.H.L. on the 3rd May that a withdrawal to a rear line previous to the expected British attack on the Wytschaete salient was not practicable (*nicht tünlich*), and that so long as the German artillery maintained the upper hand it was believed that the existing position could be held. It was decided to strengthen *Group Wytschaete* at once with another division (*24th*) in the front line, with two *Eingreif* divisions (*7th and 3rd Bavarian*), and with ten heavy batteries. Further, as the British attack was expected to extend south of the Douve river, *Group Lille* was transferred from the *Sixth* to the *Fourth Army* to ensure unity of control of the defence.

During the following days the mining expert, Lieut.-Colonel Füsslein, changed his opinion about the mine danger. In his report to the *Fourth Army* on the 10th May he stated that he suspected a number of deep mines to have been prepared by the British, and mentioned five of them (Hill 60, Caterpillar, St. Eloi, Spanbroekmolen and Kruisstraat)—" should there be a big " British attack, it may be preceded by large explosions at some " of these places in front of or in our front line." On the 19th May, however, the *Fourth Army* believed that the British artillery fire was merely to counter the increased German artillery activity, and reported that, as no reinforcements of the British artillery had been noticed, " an enemy attack was not imminent, " although preparations to meet one would continue." On the 24th Lieut.-Colonel Füsslein gave a more favourable report of the German counter-measures, and General Laffert, commanding *Group Wytschaete*, stated later that the danger of the mine explosions was not held to be very great. In any case, he added, the effect would be very local, as the front trench system was only lightly held. How little attention was paid to the mine danger is shown by the fact that from the 12th May onwards the weekly reports of the *Fourth Army* make no mention of the subject, nor is it referred to in the reports of Crown Prince Rupprecht after the end of April. To all warnings, such as those by Lieut.-Colonel Wetzell, Colonel von Lossberg and others, who wrote to German O.H.L. that a withdrawal at least out of the mine danger zone was essential, General Ludendorff replied that it was a matter for the commanders on the spot.

On the 29th May *Fourth Army* headquarters reported to O.H.L. that a strong British offensive from an approximate front Ploegsteert Wood (St. Yves)–Zillebeke (three miles north of St. Eloi) was imminent, and that the situation was very serious.

NOTE. THE GERMAN DEFENCE

Demands were made to reinforce the artillery and air support of *Group Wytschaete*. On the 4th June General Laffert reported that it was doubtful whether the front divisions would be able to hold the battered forward zone or even the Wytschaete and Messines strongholds, against a determined attack; but withdrawal was not suggested.

Throughout May O.H.L. and Crown Prince Rupprecht continued to believe that the main battle front was still astride the Scarpe, in front of Arras. No fresh arrivals and no departures of British divisions had been reported on that front; but on the 27th May the *Sixth Army* headquarters reported that another big offensive was expected there at any moment. Consequently the defensive strength of the *Sixth Army* had been maintained, and the despatch of reinforcements to *Group Wytschaete* had been strictly limited. It was not until the 30th May that the full attention of Crown Prince Rupprecht was given to the Flanders front. Statements of prisoners proved conclusively that no further big attacks were to be expected in the Arras sector, and that a big attack was to take place from the Armentières–Ypres front about the 7th June, after an eight-day bombardment. Much of the German artillery and aircraft reinforcements therefore arrived too late for the battle.

Altogether *Group Wytschaete* had at its disposal to cover its front of nine miles from Mount Sorrel to St. Yves, 344 field, 242 medium and 44 heavy guns and howitzers. This was equivalent to 3½ heavy batteries to every thousand yards, and a barrage breadth of three hundred yards to each field battery. Owing to the narrow space within the Messines salient, and in order to make use of flanking fire, six of the heavy batteries were in *Group Ypres* sector, farther north. In addition, nine heavy batteries sent from the Northern Group of Armies reserve as a reinforcement arrived too late. The losses due to the British counter-battery work on the last two days of the bombardment period, and especially on the morning of the 7th June, amounted, however, to a quarter of this total of field artillery of *Group Wytschaete* and to nearly half the heavy artillery.[1]

A large reinforcement of aeroplanes (including two reconnaissance, three protection and two fighter flights), and of anti-aircraft guns, was not ordered to move to *Group Wytschaete* sector till the 6th June, and was too late. On the morning of the battle and during the preceding fortnight the aeroplane strength of *Group Wytschaete* was five reconnaissance, two protection and one fighter flights; and these were mostly below establishment; for example, the fighter flight had only

---

[1] G.O.A. xii., gives partial losses in artillery as 22 out of 118 field guns; 20 out of 60 light field howitzers; 8 out of 18 mortars; 45 out of 92 heavy field howitzers; one out of 6 15-cm. guns; and 11 out of 24 10-cm. guns.

5 instead of 14 aeroplanes, and one of the protection flights had only 3 aeroplanes instead of 6. The Group had 27 anti-aircraft guns on its strength and in use.

Two days after the battle General von Laffert, commanding *Group Wytschaete*, was removed from his command. He was blamed especially for using the two trained *Eingreif* divisions (*3rd Bavarian* and *35th*) to relieve the two front divisions immediately before the battle, and for employing as *Eingreif* divisions the *1st Guard Reserve* and *7th*, which were new to the district and untrained for the special task.[1] The German Official History (Volume XII) gives five principal reasons for the loss of the Messines–Wytschaete Ridge : the great numerical superiority of the British in artillery, aircraft and infantry and the thorough preparatory work ; the effect of the mine explosions, both in number and size beyond any precedent ; the unfavourable infantry position on the long forward slope ; the cramped deployment area for the supporting artillery within the salient which could be enfiladed from both flanks ; and, lastly, the late arrival of the *Eingreif* divisions on the battlefield.

The question as to whether a prior withdrawal should have been made from the salient remains an open one. General von Laffert, in his report after the battle, wrote that if any suspicion had existed about the magnitude of the mine danger, the front trench system would have been abandoned before the British assault, and the *Sonne* Line (mid-way between the First and Second Lines) would have been occupied as a front line, with the ground between it and the Second Line, on the Ridge, as the forward zone of defence. The *Fourth Army* report confirms this attitude, stating that the losses in men and material inflicted upon the British by making them fight for the Ridge was sufficient justification for holding the position rather than abandoning it without a struggle. On the other hand, Kuhl (ii, p. 114) writes that it was a mistake of his chief, Crown Prince Rupprecht, that he did not " simply order the withdrawal " despite the objections made to his proposal at the *Fourth Army* " conference on the 30th April ; the German army would thereby " have been spared one of the worst tragedies of the War ". This opinion is strengthened by the fact that the main objection, namely that the rear lines on the eastern slope of the Ridge were not suitable for defence, was not justified in practice ; for the zone between the Oosttaverne and the Warneton Lines continued to be held by the Germans as a front line for the remainder of the year.

---

[1] See p. 44, footnote 2.

NOTE. THE GERMAN DEFENCE

As regards losses: " In the months April to June the Armies " on the Western Front had lost 384,000 [not including lightly " wounded], of whom 121,000 were killed and missing ".[1]

" At the beginning of the great spring battles the field troops " numbered in all 5,253,000, that is 680,000 stronger than in " the autumn of 1916; 53 new divisions had been formed in " the interval, partly of existing troops; the artillery, technical " troops and air force were vastly increased. The continuation " of this expansion was intended. . . . The Ministry of War, " however, as it had done earlier, expressed anxiety about the " organization of any more new formations, in view of the recruit " situation. . . . But in the early summer four new divisions " and the Asia Corps [really a brigade] were formed, besides " numerous units. The field Armies then numbered 238 divisions " [156 in the West] and a few independent brigades, but its " numerical strength had already begun slowly to sink ".[2]

' In the West there were only sufficient munitions for the " defensive ".[3]

---

[1] G.O.A. xiii., p. 22.
[2] G.O.A. xiii., p. 24.
[3] G.O.A. xiii., p. 22.

CHAPTER VI

THE NORTHERN OPERATIONS

Doubts as to the Continuation of the Flanders Campaign

(Sketches 7, 8)

On the 16th May the War Cabinet had, it will be remembered, told Sir Douglas Haig that his Flanders project could only be given approval on the express condition that the French co-operated by offensive action as agreed at the Paris Conference on the 4th May. On the 2nd June, on the eve of the Messines battle, General Pétain, as we have seen, had frankly admitted to Sir Douglas Haig that the French army would be unable to fulfil its commitments.

On that admission the position of the Commander-in-Chief was clear: further offensives should be stopped; but at this same time, early in June, information which was given to him by the head of the Intelligence Section G.H.Q., Br.-General J. Charteris, added strength to his conviction that the Flanders project should be carried out. He was told that the German casualties in Champagne, on the Aisne and at Arras, in the spring and early summer, had amounted to 400,000, and that out of a total of 157 German divisions on the Western Front, 105 had lost an average of 40 per cent. of their infantry in those battles; that this drain on man-power was undermining the resistance of the German nation; that a marked and unmistakable fall in the effective strength and in the morale of German divisions had set in; and that, also, even should Russia make a separate peace with Germany, it was improbable that more than 20 of the 66 German divisions in Russia could be transferred, and not at a greater rate than two divisions a week, from the Eastern to the Western Front.[1] This information, summarized in writing on the 12th June, added that Germany was within four to six months of a date at which she would be unable to

---
[1] Actually, 8 German divisions moved from the Eastern to the Western Front during July 1917, that is 2 a week; 5 moved in September; 4 in October; 10 in November; and from then onwards 40 divisions from the Eastern Front and 8 from Italy arrived in 4½ months, for the spring offensive in 1918. Kuhl, ii., p. 6.

maintain even the present reduced establishment of units in the field, and that the pressure of economic conditions had definitely extended to the army. The summary concluded with the statement that, "from all these definite "facts, it is a fair deduction that, given a continuance of "the existing circumstances and of the effort of the Allies, "Germany may well be forced to conclude a peace on our "terms before the end of the year ".[1]

The effect of this information on Sir Douglas Haig's outlook is shown in the memorandum written on the 12th June, for the information of the War Cabinet, to which this particular Summary of Intelligence was attached.[2] In contrast to the cautious advice given in his previous memorandum of the 1st May, he stressed the critical condition both of Germany and of the German army, and stated that he was averse to any delay which might allow the enemy to recover. " Given sufficient force ", he wrote, " and provided "no greater transfer of German troops is made in time from "East to West, it is probable that the Belgian coast could "be cleared this summer and the defeats on the German "troops entailed in doing so might quite probably lead to "their collapse ". He estimated that, provided the general situation did not worsen, the number of divisions at his disposal, if maintained at establishment in men and guns, would be sufficient force to carry out the full programme.[3]

---

[1] The Intelligence Section's appreciation of the German reinforcement situation had some foundation. In G.O.A. xii. (February–June 1917), p. 10, under the heading " Difficulties of the Reinforcement Situation and " its Consequences ", it is stated that demands of the technical services, especially of the Air Arm, " had brought about a definite decrease in "fighting power, particularly in the infantry". It continues, " at the "beginning of April the *Ersatz* formations still contained 900,000 men ; "but as soon as heavy fighting began, a sensible demand on them must "be expected, so that this reserve would only last a few months. Then, "except for convalescents, there was practically nothing left available "but the 1899 class (18-year olds), and this had also to provide munitions "workers, lines of communication services, ancillary services and civil "officials ". Attempts to use women had not been a success and brought about the release of less than 100,000 men. The Minister of War was opposed to calling up the 18-year olds, as they had not the moral or physical stamina for a field soldier. He proposed to reduce all battalions by one company and issue more light machine guns to them as compensation.

No less serious than the question of the number was the quality of the recruits. The complaints from the front of the poor physical performances of the reinforcements sent into the field increased, and similarly of their inadequate training.

[2] Appendix XII.

[3] They were not so maintained. The infantry alone was one-seventh short at the end of the year. See " 1918 " Vol. I, Appendix VII, p. 30.

On the same day (12th June) he wrote to the Secretary of State for War, Lord Derby, begging him to do his utmost " to prevent our Government delaying to take action until " the American army is in the field. We heard the same " argument used in 1916 regarding the advantage of waiting " till the Russians would be ready this year. There is no " time like the present. Send to France every available " man, aeroplane and gun as soon as possible. We cannot " tell how our Allies [the French] will stand another winter ".

Under Br.-General G. M. W. Macdonogh, the Intelligence Section, G.H.Q. during 1914-15 had gained a well-deserved reputation for accurate information and trustworthy appreciations. In January 1916 this officer had left G.H.Q. to become Director of Military Intelligence, General Staff, at the War Office, and now, in that higher capacity, he did not agree with the deductions drawn at G.H.Q. by his successor, either as regards the critical condition of Germany, the crippling wastage of the German army, or the effect of the probable collapse of the Russian front. The Chief of the Imperial General Staff, in a memorandum to the War Cabinet on the 9th May, had in consequence estimated that the probable secession of Russia would increase the German rifle and gun strength on the Western Front to slightly more than that of the Allies, and, on the information supplied by the D.M.I., he did not admit any decrease in the fighting power of German divisions. " It is obvious ", the memorandum added, " that offensive operations on our front " would offer no chance of success ; and our best course " would be to remain on the defensive, strengthen our " positions, economize our reserves in man-power and " material, and hope that the balance would be eventually " redressed by American assistance ".

The result of this difference of opinion was smoothed out by General Robertson's request to Sir Douglas Haig to omit the appendix of the G.H.Q. Intelligence Summary from his memorandum of the 12th June " It would " General Robertson wrote, " be very regrettable at this juncture if " different estimates of Germany's resources were presented " to the War Cabinet ", and he added : " Don't argue that " you can finish the War this year or that the German is " already beaten, but argue that your plan is the best plan ". Sir Douglas Haig agreed to the omission of the appendix. Thus the War Committee had to judge his outlook and

FUTURE CONDUCT OF THE WAR. JUNE 99

conclusions on the interpretation placed on the available information by the General Staff, War Office.[1]

Confronted by the known condition of the French and Italian armies, and by the General Staff's interpretation of the possible consequences of the Russian situation, the War Cabinet hesitated to give its approval to the second part of Sir Douglas Haig's Flanders programme, that is the Northern Operations, and considered his optimistic outlook unjustified.

The situation had been complicated by recent events in Italy and Russia. In Italy, the Tenth Battle of the Isonzo, begun on the 10th May, had resulted in local successes near the coast of the Gulf of Trieste and north of Gorizia; but General Cadorna was still clamouring for reinforcements of both infantry and artillery against an expected combined Austro-German offensive. As regards Russia, little was expected from the proposed offensive, which, like the Isonzo battle, had been intended to synchronize with the Franco-British offensive on the Western Front. Revolutionary outbreaks, which had begun on the 12th March, were increasing daily;[2] a Socialist group was taking charge of the policy of the Russian Government, and endeavouring to effect a peace with Germany on the basis of " no annexa-" tions ". As a result of the change of government the discipline and administration of the Russian army had been so impaired that it seemed unlikely it would be able to continue to fight, even if so inclined.

On the 8th June, the whole question of the future conduct of the War had been handed over to a Cabinet Committee on War Policy, consisting of the Prime Minister, Lord Curzon, Lord Milner, Mr. Bonar Law and General Smuts (like the Prime Minister a lawyer by profession). At meetings of this Committee on the 19th, 21st and 22nd June, Sir Douglas Haig, who had crossed to London to attend, outlined his Flanders project, the full details of which, with its distant

---

[1] On 15th June Sir Douglas Haig wrote privately to General Robertson, protesting against a statement in a War Office summary issued to the War Cabinet the previous day, that there was " no reason to doubt the " ability of the Central Powers to continue the War well into next year ".

[2] See " 1917 " Vol. I, pp. 483, 485.

objectives, the Cabinet Committee now heard for the first time.[1]

Sir Douglas Haig reminded the Committee that in his choice of Flanders as the main theatre of operations he had been guided by the War Cabinet resolution of the 23rd November, 1916,[2] to the effect that there was no measure to which it attached greater importance than the expulsion of the enemy from the Belgian coast, and thus end the constant threat (it was never more) by submarine raiders to the cross-Channel transport of troops and supplies to France. He pointed out that an advance of twenty-five miles along the coast[3] would suffice to capture the German submarine bases at Ostend and Zeebrugge and to close the ship-canal to Bruges; and he assured them that this operation was practicable by means of his Flanders plan. The Germans, he said, would be forced to accept battle in the most difficult sector of the Western Front to reinforce: only two lateral railways, the Courtrai–Roulers–Ostend and the Ghent–Bruges–Zeebrugge lines, served the narrowing gap between the battle front and the Dutch frontier, and a British advance of fifteen and thirty miles, respectively, would put first one and then the other out of service: the British army, on the other hand, would be fighting close to, and covering, its cross-Channel communications. He asked that all possible resources in man-power and material should be made available to carry the project through. Provided adequate reserves were available to cross the Schelde, the moment they did so would be favourable for Holland to drop her neutrality, and he foresaw the possibility of a subsequent drive eastwards, in co-operation with the Dutch army, which might be decisive in forcing the Germans out of Belgium. When the 40-mile-distant line extending through Thielt and Bruges was reached, the French would be asked to advance towards Mezières–Valenciennes; and on our gaining the 60-mile-distant line Courtrai–Deynze–Ghent, or sooner, the weakened Germans would, he considered, be falling back from the whole front Lille–Champagne.[4]

---

[1] It will be remembered that Mr. Lloyd George had stated at the Inter-Allied Conference on 4th May that Ministers did not need to learn the plan of attack nor the methods to be adopted. See p. 23.

[2] See p. 8.

[3] See Sketch 6.

[4] The first written mention of these distant objectives of the Flanders 1917 plan had been in a letter to General Sir William Robertson (C.I.G.S.), on 1st May 1917. *Continued at foot of next page.*

After hearing the statement of the Commander-in-Chief, the Prime Minister said that when, at the Inter-Allied Conference on the 4th May, he had supported the idea of offensive operations with all possible vigour by the British and French armies, he had no idea that the intention was for the British army to fight and decisively defeat the German army on the Western Front single-handed. Mr. Lloyd George saw no reason to hope for more than a small initial success, and said he now preferred either to adopt the tactics recommended by General Pétain, of " wearing down the " enemy by a punch here and a punch there ", with strictly limited objectives, or else to attack on the Austrian front, capture Trieste and gain a separate peace, for which actual overtures by Austria had already been made. A German offensive against France might thereby be prevented during 1917, and sufficient strength preserved to launch a victorious offensive in 1918.

In reply, Sir Douglas Haig complained that Mr. Lloyd George did not give enough weight to the marked and unmistakeable deterioration of the German army since the start of the Somme battles, twelve months before,[1] nor to the shortage of man-power and the serious economic condition in Germany. While admitting the danger in the Russian situation, he did not believe it would develop rapidly enough to allow the transfer of sufficient German troops to the Western Front in 1917 to influence his Flanders plan—as proved to be the case. The demoralized state of the French Armies did not discourage him, for he considered that the German counter-attacks which were being directed against the new French positions, especially along the Chemin des Dames, served almost as well to hold and wear out the enemy as offensive activity by the French themselves; and he believed that the French would eventually be able to redeem their promise of offensive action.

Continued from previous page.

To some readers the outline of the campaign may seem super-optimistic and too far-reaching, even fantastic ; but a commander-in-chief usually has some quite distant objective in mind : e.g., in the Peninsular campaign, Wellington was aiming latterly to secure Badajoz and Ciudad Rodrigo, the gates into Spain, and then to reach the neighbourhood of Vittoria, so as to cut the French line of retreat into France ; in the " D Day " campaign of 1944, Field-Marshal Viscount Montgomery's plan was to reach the line of the Seine, then that of the Rhine and then Berlin (see his lecture, with diagram, in the Journal of the Royal United Service Institution for November 1945).

[1] Since admitted by German historians. See " 1916 " Vol. I, pp. 494–5.

As regards the so-called "Pétain tactics", he said that they were, in fact, what he proposed. He had no intention of entering into a tremendous offensive involving heavy losses, but to proceed step by step, and not to push attacks without a reasonable chance of success. Referring to Mr. Lloyd George's Austrian alternative, he said he was convinced that to fail in concentrating our resources on the Western theatre, or to divert them from it, would be most dangerous. He thought it at best uncertain that we should force Austria to make a separate peace, and pointed out that the Germans could reinforce the Austrian front having railway facilities better than those of France and Italy to that sector in the proportion of 5 to 2. He considered the best check to the Austro-German offensive, feared by General Cadorna, would be to continue a vigorous offensive on the Western Front. In conclusion, he adhered to the advice he had previously given to the War Cabinet, that " if our resources are concentrated in France to the fullest " possible extent, the British Armies are capable, and can " be relied on, to effect great results this summer—results " which will make final victory more assured and which " may even bring it within reach this year ".

Admiral Jellicoe emphasized the need to occupy the Belgian coast before the winter. He stated categorically that it was useless to discuss plans for next spring, as we should be unable to continue the War into 1918, owing to lack of shipping, unless we could clear the Germans out of Zeebrugge before the end of the year. Mr. Lloyd George challenged his statement, but the First Sea Lord adhered to it. In a later conversation with General Smuts, Admiral Jellicoe said that he had, if anything understated the case ; he remarked to Sir Douglas Haig that " if the army cannot " get the Belgian ports, the Navy cannot hold the Channel " and the War is lost ".[1]

Admiral Jellicoe's statements bore great weight in the discussions which followed. Two members of the Cabinet Committee felt that Sir Douglas Haig had made out his case for at least having a good try. The Prime Minister and

---

[1] Sir Douglas Haig's diary record. In April, when the American Admiral Sims reached London, " he found something approaching despair " as the news of the sunken ships kept pouring in ", and Admiral Jellicoe said to him : " It is impossible for us to go on with the War if losses like " this continue ". " Recent Revelations of European Diplomacy ", by G. P. Gooch, p. 460. *Continued at foot of next page.*

two other members thought that the project was a mistake with none of the elements of success, that it would be very costly and should be discouraged ; but they hesitated to overrule both the naval and military authorities on a question of strategy.

Sanction by the War Cabinet

The result of these meetings was an inclination to leave the responsibility for decision to the military authorities, but on the understanding that if progress did not reach expectations the operations would be called off, and effective help would then be sent to the Italians to enable them to press an offensive against Austria. Subsequent discussions within the Committee itself showed the differences of opinion on the subject of sending reinforcements to Italy, which was primarily Mr. Lloyd George's idea. One member proposed landing 150,000 men at Alexandretta to put Turkey out of the War first ; but this involved the problem of where the men and the ships were to come from. Another member favoured an attack through the Balkans ; while a third continued to back Sir Douglas Haig's plan.

During July the critical situation of some of the Empire's Allies showed little improvement. On the 1st, Monsieur Kerenski had succeeded in inducing the more loyal units of the Russian army to make an offensive ; but after a considerable advance, chiefly against the Austrians, they were unable to withstand the German counter-attack made by the general reserve of six divisions which were later in the year to appear at Riga and Caporetto, and were routed.

Continued from previous page.
That his view had justification is proved by the losses which the British Merchant Navy had suffered and were suffering :

Month 1917	Number of Ships Sunk	Gross Tonnage
January	49	153,666
February	105	313,486
March	127	353,478
April	169	545,282
May	122	352,289
June	122	417,925
TOTAL	694	2,136,126

(Official History of the Great War. " The Merchant Navy ", Vol. III, Appendix C, p. 379.)

The defeat was the signal for the Bolshevist party to obtain control in Petrograd, and with that event Russia ceased further co-operation with the Allies in the conduct of the War. Although the French army was showing signs of recovery under General Pétain's careful handling, a small German attack upset the preparations which had been made for an offensive on a wide front at Verdun to synchronize with the opening stage of the Northern Operations in Flanders and caused its postponement (until 20th August); so that for the moment the prospect of French assistance faded out.

On the other hand, the political situation in Berlin reached a crisis during the month. Confidence both in the army and in the success of the submarine blockade of England was waning, and, in addition, discontent was widespread at the continued failure of the Government to state its peace terms. Austria seemed willing to treat for peace, and on the 5th July a demand by Herr Erzberger, the Catholic leader, who had been in touch with Austria, was made in the *Reichstag*, that the German Government should declare their readiness to make a reasonable peace without annexations or indemnities on either side; he also demanded parliamentary government for the Prussian people. This gesture in the *Reichstag* was reinforced by the separate action of the Pope, who invited both sides to consider terms; but President Wilson's reply expressed the common feeling in the United Kingdom and America, that peace could not be made with the existing autocratic government in Germany, which would merely use such a respite in order to recuperate for another war.

These events did not affect Sir Douglas Haig's determination to carry out his Flanders project with all available resources; but the War Cabinet still hesitated. On the 18th July, when the preparatory bombardment for the Northern Operations had already been in progress for two days,[1] General Robertson wrote, " up to the present no " official approval of your plan has been given by the War " Cabinet "; and he added that the War Policy Committee feared the plan might involve pressing on beyond artillery support and so incurring heavy losses. General Robertson added that he had impressed on the Committee they need

---

[1] See Chapter VIII.

have no such fear, as it was well understood that the extent of the advance must be limited to the range of the guns until such time as a break-through occurred. "The "Committee", the letter concluded, "seem to favour the "Flanders plan so long as a step-by-step advance is adhered "to".

In reply, on the 21st, Sir Douglas Haig said that it was "somewhat startling at this advanced stage of the prepara- "tions to learn that the War Cabinet have not yet "determined whether the attack is to be permitted to "proceed"; and he asked General Robertson to explain to them the serious and lengthy nature of the preparations. He added that as the operation to clear the Belgian coast had been planned in accordance with the instructions of the War Cabinet in November 1916, and approved by the Inter-Allied Conference in May 1917, he had not expected any real danger of sanction being withheld at the last moment.

This letter crossed a copy of the conclusions of a War Cabinet meeting on the 20th, forwarded on the 21st, by which the Commander-in-Chief was authorized to carry out the plan explained by him to the War Policy Committee; but if, during its execution, it appeared probable that the results would not be commensurate with the effort made and the losses incurred, the whole question would be re-examined by the War Cabinet with a view to the cessation of the offensive and the adoption of an alternative plan, i.e., General Cadorna's offensive against Austria, supported by British and possibly French heavy artillery. The War Cabinet asked the Commander-in-Chief to make arrangements to give effect forthwith to this alternative plan in the event of its adoption. In a covering letter, General Robertson said that the War Cabinet wished to know the first objective of the Flanders operation so that they might be able to judge whether the operation had, up to that stage, succeeded or not.

Sir Douglas Haig replied that his opinion on the subject of diverting any resources from the Western Front had already been so fully expressed to the War Cabinet that it was useless to repeat them. As regards the first objective of the Flanders operation,[1] he said it would be "the ridge

---

[1] See Sketch 1.

" extending from Stirling Castle (1,200 yards E.S.E. of
" Hooge) by Passchendaele, Staden and Clercken to near
" Dixmude ". He expected severe fighting, entailing a
series of advances each of limited depth, and lasting probably
for several weeks, before the enemy was driven from the
whole of it ; but he believed that by that time the strength
of the resistance would have been considerably reduced and
that further operations beyond the Ypres Ridge would
present a simpler problem, and promise more rapid results.
He resented, however, the insinuation that the War Cabinet
did not trust the judgment of the commander on the spot as
to whether the operation should be abandoned at some
future stage, " or even on the depth to which each advance
" should be pushed with due regard to the combination
" between artillery and the other arms ". In conclusion, he
wrote that he had gained from the War Cabinet statement
the general impression that the plan of operations, although
approved, had neither the confidence nor the full support of
the War Cabinet ; and, as such an impression added very
greatly to the responsibilities and anxieties of a commander
embarking on such a serious undertaking, he asked for an
assurance that his impression was not justified.

Four days later, on the 25th July, only six days before
the offensive was actually launched, the War Cabinet
assured Sir Douglas Haig by a telegram which said that,
" having approved your plans being executed, you may
" depend upon their whole-hearted support ; and that if
" and when they decide again to reconsider the situation,
" they will obtain your views before arriving at any decision
" as to the cessation of operations ". Sir Douglas's reply is
important. He wrote that " even if my attacks do not gain
" ground, as I hope and expect, we ought still to persevere
" in attacking the Germans in France. Only by this means
" can we win ; and we must encourage the French to
" continue fighting". That principle was to guide his
decisions throughout the Flanders campaign.

The Concentration in Flanders

The delay of the War Cabinet in giving their sanction to
the Flanders plan had not interfered with the execution of
the programme arranged at the Army Commanders' Conference at Doullens on the 7th May. Final instructions for

THE CONCENTRATION. JUNE–JULY

the concentration in Flanders were issued by G.H.Q. on the 22nd May: all available resources were to be employed for the campaign, and it was estimated that a total of about fifty Allied divisions could be spared, of which thirty-eight would be British.[1]

The plan for the offensive entailed a regrouping both of divisions and of the Army and corps artillery, largely a transfer from the Messines area to the Ypres area, and also a change of command. The main offensive was to be made by the Fifth Army, under General Sir Hubert Gough, at the time in the Croisilles–Havrincourt sector, 50 miles south of Ypres, from the $6\frac{1}{2}$-mile frontage Mount Sorrel (west of Gheluvelt)–Boesinghe,[2] held at the time by the II and VIII Corps, the left wing of the Second Army. What remained of the Second Army was to cover the right flank of the main offensive.

On the 30th May General Gough handed over the Croisilles–Havrincourt frontage and the troops of the Fifth Army on it to the Third Army, on its right, under General Hon. Sir Julian Byng who had taken over from General Sir Edmund Allenby (who left for Palestine on the 9th June). General Gough then moved, with his chief General Staff officer, Major-General Neil Malcolm, to his new headquarters at Lovie Château (8 miles W.N.W. of Ypres), and took over his new frontage and the command of the II and VIII Corps, with their four divisions (30th, 55th, 39th and 38th), all in front line, on the 10th June. To make up the new Fifth Army to 18 divisions, towards the end of the month, as soon as accommodation, prepared by the Second Army, was available, the 11th, 16th, 25th and 36th Divisions from the Messines front, and the XIV Corps (Guards and 8th Divisions) from G.H.Q. reserve, arrived. During July further reinforcements were transferred: from the Third Army, the 15th, 18th, 20th, 29th, 48th and 51st, 61st (for reserve) and the 56th (for G.H.Q. reserve). The XIX Corps headquarters (formed 4th February, 1917) also joined the Fifth Army from G.H.Q. reserve, and the V Corps (old Fifth Army) and VIII Corps (Second Army) headquarters were made available to command reserves.

The frontage was allotted between the four corps, the II, XIX, XVIII and XIV, in sectors, apart from small

---
[1] See Sketch 7.
[2] See Sketch.

108 THE NORTHERN OPERATIONS

adjustments, corresponding to those held by the four divisions of the II and VIII Corps already in position, which remained there so that reliefs, which might have aroused suspicion, were avoided. The final allotment was:

II Corps : 8th, 18th, 25th, 30th Divisions
   XIX ,,   15th, 16th, 36th, 55th Divisions
  XVIII ,,   11th, 39th, 48th, 51st Divisions
   XIV ,,   Guards, 20th, 29th, 38th Divisions
  VIII ,,   (reserve) : 61st Division
    V ,,   (G.H.Q. reserve) : 56th Division

Each of the four fighting corps was to use two divisions in the opening phase of the campaign up to the capture of the Passchendaele–Staden ridge, and keep two in support for subsequent operations.[1]

The Second Army, which was to cover the right flank, was reduced to 12 divisions (II Anzac, IX and X Corps). In return for the eight divisions transferred to the new Fifth Army, it received the 14th and 37th from the Third and First Armies, respectively, and during the latter part of July, as reserve, the I Anzac Corps (1st, 2nd and 5th Australian Divisions).

More than half of the artillery of the Second Army—60 per cent. in the case of the heavy howitzers—was transferred to the Fifth Army. Of the 243 heavy howitzers and 546 field guns and howitzers left with the Second Army, 112 heavy howitzers and 210 field pieces were concentrated in its left (X) corps sector to support and cover the right of the main offensive.

The remainder of the British front was combed for artillery. When the Fifth Army took over on the 10th June, 203 heavy howitzers and 444 field pieces were in position; within the next three weeks these numbers were increased at the expense of the First, Third and Second Armies, to 752 and 1,422, respectively; but some batteries retained by the First Army to support the feint attack towards Lens[2] did not arrive until a few days before the infantry assault.

Three tank brigades, each of 72 tanks, were put at the disposal of the Fifth Army : the II Brigade was already in the II Corps area, having gone there after the Messines

---

[1] In March 1918 the Germans had 43 divisions on the 25-mile front of the Fifth Army attacked, that is 1.72 divisions per mile, as against Gough's 2.46 (1.23, if only two divisions per corps are counted) in 1917. (See " 1918 " Vol. I, p. 152.)

[2] See Chapter VII.

THE CONCENTRATION. JUNE–JULY 109

battle; the III Brigade was attached to the XIX Corps; and the I Brigade was in Fifth Army reserve in Oesthoek Wood (3 miles east of Lovie Château), with 24 of its tanks forward to support the XVIII Corps.[1]

The combined air strength at the disposal of the Second and Fifth Armies totalled 406 aircraft and 18 kite balloon sections. It comprised the II and V Brigades R.F.C. and the Ninth (Headquarters) Wing, together with a squadron sent from the IV Brigade in the coastal sector.

The northern flank of the main offensive was to be covered by French and Belgian troops as a result of the agreement made with General Pétain on the 18th May. The French First Army, under General Anthoine, consisting of the I Corps (1st, 2nd, 51st and 162nd Divisions), joined later by the XXXVI Corps (29th and 133rd Divisions), from the coastal sector,[2] relieved the Belgian 4th and 5th Divisions on the front Boesinghe–Nordschoote between the 5th and 10th July; the main concentration of the four French divisions was in the southern sector Boesinghe–Steenstraat, from which the proposed attack towards Bixschoote was to be launched, with the left on the Yser inundations. Its supporting artillery comprised 300 heavy and medium guns and howitzers, and 240 (75-mm.) field guns; and for air support it had two hundred aeroplanes. The six Belgian divisions, under King Albert, holding the thirteen miles of the Yser from Nordschoote to St. Georges, near Nieuport, were to advance immediately an opportunity offered in the Dixmude sector, where a gap existed in the inundations.

The decision to give to Fifth Army headquarters control of both the main offensive and the coastal operation had been modified on the 18th May when General Pétain rejected the scheme for a French and British attack towards St. Quentin and Cambrai. Fourth Army headquarters being available, on the 22nd, Sir Douglas Haig gave General Sir H. Rawlinson command of the coastal sector of the operations, with headquarters at Malo les Bains, near Dunkirk, and the XV Corps from the Somme area under

---

[1] The XIV Corps had no tank support, as the crossing over the Yser canal, which lay close to the German front line in its sector, was not practicable.
[2] See p. 27

him.[1] On the 20th June the 32nd Division, transferred from the Second Army, took over from the two divisions of the French XXXVI Corps the bridgehead on the northern bank of the Yser, a 3-mile frontage between St. Georges and the coast, the relieved divisions joining General Anthoine's Army. During the next few weeks four more divisions joined the XV Corps, the concentration area of which extended back along the coast to Gravelines, 12 miles west of Dunkirk.[2] The heavy artillery to support the coastal operation was drawn from the Second and Third Armies—in all, 189 heavy guns and howitzers; and its quota of field artillery amounted to 306 guns and 88 howitzers. For air support the allotment was 102 aircraft of the IV Brigade R.F.C., and about a similar number of R.N.A.S. machines working over the coastal area from Dunkirk.

On the 13th June, at a conference between British, French and Belgian representatives, the delimitation of zones and back areas for the various Armies participating in the Northern Operations was discussed and settled; subsequent meetings decided questions of detail such as the use of railways, roads and water supplies. The steady development of the railway network by the Second Army behind the Ypres front during the two previous years, and the well-equipped camps at halting places and traffic-control points, facilitated the concentration.[3]

Within the Fifth Army area, which extended back for forty miles, motor transport had to be stopped during daylight west of a north-south line through Steenvoorde (5 miles east of Cassel), owing to the dominating ground observation held by the Germans over the Ypres district.

The movement to Flanders left the rest of the British

---

[1] The Fourth Army front in the Somme area was gradually taken over by the Third Army during the latter part of June.

[2] The 1st Division from the Second Army and the 66th from the First Army arrived before the end of June; the 49th from the First Army came on 14th July, and the 33rd, from the Third Army, on 31st July.

[3] See p. 29 and Sketch 4. The Dunkirk–Nieuport line was doubled very rapidly during June by two Canadian battalions. (See " Transporta-" tion on the Western Front 1914–18 "). Strategic trains carried all troops coming from a distance, and tactical trains were used for the shorter distances, the divisional artillery following by road. (For note on strategic and tactical trains see " 1916 " Vol. I, p. 19.)

DISTRIBUTION

front weakly held. The First Army had 12 divisions in all to hold the 34 miles from the Lys (north of Armentières) to east of Arras, and the Third Army was left with 15 divisions, including two in G.H.Q. reserve, to hold the southern sector of 37 miles to the Omignon river; but for the moment this did not constitute a danger, as the Germans opposite were not in strength.

CHAPTER VII

THE NORTHERN OPERATIONS
(concluded)

Feint Attacks towards Lens and Lille
26th–30th June

(Sketches 8, 9)

Although Second Army headquarters had been asked early in the year to prepare for a Flanders campaign, little progress had been made except in the Messines sector owing to the shortage of labour. It was not until June and early July, at the close of the Arras and Messines battles, that this shortage was made good. Sixty-four labour companies were then moved to the Ypres front, including two Canadian and three West Indian battalions and 28 companies of the Labour Corps, in addition to six Chinese labour companies. Chinese labour companies had begun to reach the Western Front in April 1917, and by October 50,000 Chinese were at work there. During July the Army Troops companies R.E. with the Fifth Army were increased from 16 to 19, in addition to six Special companies R.E. The area handed over to the Fifth Army on the 10th June was well organized and well provided with shelters, water and communications for the small force which held it; but G.H.Q. had estimated that at least six weeks would be required to convert it, bring up reinforcements, and prepare for the offensive which Sir Douglas Haig and General Gough had in mind.[1] To bridge this interval and to keep German attention away from the French front, the attacks mentioned by Sir Douglas Haig at the Doullens Conference on the 7th May, to threaten Lens and Lille, were to be made about the end of June.

For the threat to Lens, General Sir Henry Horne, commanding the First Army, proposed to operate on a frontage of three corps.[2] The XIII Corps (Lieut.-General Sir W. F. N. McCracken) was to improve its position between

---

[1] Corps commanders, asked at a Fifth Army conference on 6th June how long they would require to complete their preparations, replied: 45 days (XIV and XIX Corps), and two months (XVIII Corps).

[2] See Sketch 8.

Gavrelle and Oppy by an advance of two to five hundred yards over a frontage of 2,300 yards; and the inner divisions of the Canadian Corps (Lieut.-General Sir A. W. Currie) and I Corps (Lieut.-General Sir A. E. A. Holland) were to attack on a frontage of 4,800 yards astride the Souchez river to cut out the German salient between Avion and the western suburbs of Lens, and to capture Reservoir Hill (Hill 65), overlooking the town. The I Corps, too, was to prepare an attack with its left division for the capture of Hill 70, north of Lens. General Horne hoped to carry out these operations during the first half of July; but when told on the 15th June that a quantity of his siege and heavy artillery would have to be transferred to Flanders early in July, he decided to begin them earlier, on the 28th June, and to reduce their scope. The Gavrelle–Oppy attack was to take place as arranged, but the operation astride the Souchez would be limited to the capture of the German front defences west of Avion and of Reservoir Hill, while the attack on Hill 70 was to be postponed.

The 28th was dull and close, and in the late afternoon, black thunderclouds piled up on the southern horizon. At 7 p.m. an intense bombardment opened from the whole 14-mile front of the three corps from Gavrelle to Hulluch, to give the Germans the impression of a large-scale offensive against Lens; artillery on the way north from the Third Army to Flanders had been side-tracked to participate and increase the intensity of the bombardment. Whilst it was in progress, a violent thunderstorm broke over the battle area; forked lightning and claps of thunder joined with the flashes and roar of the guns, and the rain came down in torrents when, at 7.10 p.m., the infantry moved forward to the assault.

On the XIII Corps front, the 94th Brigade (Br.-General G. T. C. Carter-Campbell) of the 31st Division, north of Gavrelle, and the 15th Brigade (Br.-General M. N. Turner) of the 5th Division, opposite Oppy, assaulted on a frontage of a thousand and thirteen hundred yards respectively. The Germans were expecting attack, and at 5.30 p.m., when the jumping-off trenches were full of troops, laid a barrage on them for ten minutes. It speaks well for the discipline of the two brigades that, despite two hundred casualties during this shelling, the order and drive of the assault was in no way affected. So rapid was the advance that when the German barrage fell on No Man's Land, three minutes after the start, it was already clear of troops. In the actual assault, few casualties were incurred, and, besides two hundred prisoners taken, 280 German dead were counted in the captured area. The objectives, including Gavrelle Mill, which had been so hotly contested in the Scarpe battles eight weeks previously, were occupied with little difficulty; but the heavy rain interfered with the work of consolidation. The new line gave good observation to the north-east and east, towards Neuvireuil and Fresnes, and to the south-east beyond Greenland Hill.

In the Lens sector, at the junction of the Canadian and I Corps, the attack astride the Souchez river also reached its objectives with little loss. The preliminary occupation of the western slope of Reservoir Hill, north of the river, had been achieved on the evening of the 24th, and patrols following up this success had by next morning advanced nearly to Avion Trench, which was occupied in the early hours of the 28th. Preparations were then made to continue the advance after the general barrage at 7.10 p.m. The 4th Canadian Division (Major-General D. Watson) and the 46th Division (Major-General W. Thwaites), south and north of the river respectively, captured most of Avion village, Eleu dit Leauvette and the German trenches on the eastern slope of Reservoir Hill (Hill 65); while the 3rd Canadian Division (Major-General L. J. Lipsett) succeeded in forming a defensive right flank along the Arleux-Avion road, gaining touch with the 4th in Avion. Inundations from the Souchez river, swollen by the downpour of rain, prevented patrols from reaching the main German defences in the north-eastern part of Avion, and along the railway embankment six hundred yards beyond the objective.[1]

General Horne intended to continue these attacks for the encirclement of Lens during July, including the operation

---

[1] One German division, the *56th*, had been withdrawn from this sector on 22nd June to replace in reserve another sent to the Flanders front, where a British offensive was believed to be imminent. The division in the line had orders to withdraw from the Avion salient to the Avion-Lens railway embankment if attacked.

for the capture of Hill 70, north of the town; but, owing to lack of adequate artillery to complete the destruction of the wire and the defences, the operations were postponed till August.

The threat to Lille from the north by the Second Army did not develop. At the Lillers conference on the 14th June, General Plumer had stated that the extent of such an operation was dependent upon the force the Commander-in-Chief wished him to expend upon it; and as all the reserves of the Second Army would ultimately be required for its share in the Flanders offensive, Sir Douglas Haig decided that its operations towards Lille would have to be limited to the establishment of a good line of defence for the right flank, making use of the obstacles of the river Lys and the adjoining Warneton-Armentières railway.[1] Local attacks, made on the 21st and 26th June by the 3rd Australian Division to drive in strong outposts north of the Douve, met stubborn German resistance, and Major-General Monash suggested to General Plumer that an operation on a bigger scale would be necessary. The intention was to combine it with an attack south of the Douve by the New Zealand Division, to take La Basse Ville and to secure a line of defence covering the crossings of the river Lys; the town of Warneton was to be smothered by a smoke screen during the attack.[2] Such an operation would, it was hoped, create the impression that the passages of the Lys were about to be forced preparatory to an advance north of Lille. Attempts to clear the German advanced posts on the 16th and 21st July, and to dig the jumping-off trenches for these attacks proved, however, very costly, and General Plumer decided to defer the operation until the general offensive at the end of the month.

These feint attacks towards Lens and Lille did not as a matter of fact affect the German defence preparations in

---

[1] See Sketch 5.
[2] North of Warneton the Germans held the *Warneton Line* (their Third Line before the Messines battle) as the main line of defence; but south of that place, where the old line lay east of the river, another line had been constructed on the western bank.

Flanders,[1] but they did assist in diverting German attention from the French front whilst the concentration in Flanders was in progress.

The German Attack at Nieuport, 10th/11th July

The preparations in the coastal sector by the XV Corps (Lieut.-General Sir J. P. Du Cane) were completely upset by a German attack on the bridgehead north of the Yser early in July.[2] The holding of this bridgehead, about eight hundred yards deep between St. Georges and the coast, was an essential part of the coastal scheme. It was the jumping-off ground for the land attack. From it, on the afternoon before the landing operation, the German forward zone was to be captured by the assault of two divisions, and early the next morning (about 3 a.m.), simultaneous with the landing, the advance was to be continued from it across the German Second Line.

The landing was to be made at three places on the open beach : by a right column at Westende Bains, a mile in rear of the German Second Line ; by a centre column three-quarters of a mile farther up the coast on the flank of the German Third Line ; and by a left column a mile and three-quarters beyond, just north of Middelkirke Bains.[3] The three columns were to be specially equipped and organized to be able to advance rapidly " with the greatest boldness

---

[1] Ten German divisions were transferred from the German *Sixth Army* (Lens–Lille sector) to the German *Fourth Army* in Flanders during June alone. *Sixth Army* headquarters did report during June and early July that it expected " with certainty " a major offensive towards Lens, and could therefore spare no more divisions for the Flanders front ; but Crown Prince Rupprecht overruled this opinion, replying that the British had not sufficient strength for two major offensives, and that the attack threatening Lens must be a feint to hold the German artillery from the Flanders front.

[2] See Sketch 9.

[3] The 1st Division was to be specially trained for the landing operations, and, to ensure secrecy, placed in a camp, surrounded with barbed wire, near Dunkirk, where it would be reported to be in quarantine for an infectious disease. All its correspondence was censored, and its rations and other requirements were dumped at the entrance to the camp.

An account of the training and preparations of the division will be found in " The Operations of the 1st Division on the Belgian Coast in 1917 ", by Colonel (Lieut.-General Sir William) Dobbie (then its G.S.O.I.) in the *Royal Engineers Journal* of June 1924.

"and resolution" to seize pre-arranged tactical points.[1] They were to be reinforced by two reserve divisions from Nieuport which were to pass through the two divisions in the German Second Line and carry the attack farther along the coast towards Ostend, fanning out across the polder meadows to gain touch with the Belgian troops on the right advancing from Dixmude.

The land attack depended upon the Yser bridgehead, as the river, deep and tidal, was a hundred to two hundred yards wide. A difficulty arose in taking over from the French. The British guns should have gone into position first; but our Allies would not leave their infantry in the trenches unless covered by French guns; so the 32nd and 1st Division had to relieve the French infantry and go into the line covered by the French guns, then the French guns were removed, and the British infantry was left for some days without much artillery support until its own gunners had settled in. Thus the Germans, gaining earlier notice of the change-over than in a normal relief, of course conjectured that something was on hand, and took measures accordingly. When the bridgehead was taken over from the French on the 20th June, Lieut.-General Du Cane insisted that it "was to be held at all costs". The defences taken over from the French were, however, inadequate, as our Allies had intended, if seriously attacked, to withdraw across the Yser to a defence line along the southern bank. The three lines of built-up breastworks beyond the river gave insufficient protection against shell-fire, and nowhere in this forward area was there any underground shell-proof accommodation for reserves. Tunnellers were at once set to work

---

[1] The 1st Division had had its artillery reduced to three 18-pdr. batteries; but it was reinforced by 9 tanks, 2 cyclist battalions, a motor machine-gun battery and an extra machine-gun company. The three brigade columns were to embark at Dunkirk each in two monitors which would carry 2,500 men apiece. To carry the guns, tanks and vehicles and to land the troops from the monitors, Vice-Admiral Sir Reginald Bacon, commanding the Dover Patrol, had designed floating piers or pontoons, 550 feet in length by 30 feet in beam, with bullet-proof walls extensible for another 125 feet, and they were so shaped that their draft corresponded to the slope of the beach. Each column had one such pontoon made fast by its stern to the two monitors which, lashed together, would push the forward end of the pontoon on to the beach. The troops were to disembark along a gangway kept clear for the purpose, and special tracks were to be carried to enable the tanks to mount the sea-wall. Experiments carried out in the Thames estuary gave results which exceeded all hopes. The pontoons rode out some very bad weather, and were found less difficult to manoeuvre than had been expected.

to construct mined dug-outs in the sand-dunes and made rapid progress[1] and, had time been available, the defence dispositions would have been based on the active intervention of reserves maintained in these dug-outs; but, as matters stood early in July, the greater part of the garrison was still exposed to the full effect of a bombardment.

In the meantime, it was recognized that the safety of the position would depend largely on artillery action, and instructions to that end were issued on the 28th June. Unfortunately, of the 583 guns and howitzers allotted to the Fourth Army for the coastal operation, only 176 had arrived by the 8th July; the remainder, still with the Second and First Armies to support feint attacks and give the impression that the main pressure was to be continued towards Lens and Lille, were not expected until about the 15th.

The German artillery began a bombardment on the 6th July, the day after General Rawlinson and Fourth Army headquarters arrived at Malo les Bains to take over command. The shelling continued on the 7th and 8th, but not to such an extent as to foreshadow an attack. Visibility on these days was poor, with a ground mist and clouds at about nine hundred feet, so few aircraft went up; and no information obtained from other sources gave any indication of the German intentions.[2]

The 10th dawned overcast, with a strong wind from the north-east. From 5.30 a.m. onwards throughout the morning the shelling increased on the entire position. The three floating bridges across the Yser mouth, which were the

---

[1] The 2nd Australian Tunnelling Company, including men accustomed to working through sandy drift, was assisted by working parties of 500 British infantry and later by the 257th Tunnelling Company. A full account of the work of the 2nd Australian Tunnelling Company in this affair is given in A.O.A. iv., pp. 960-5.

[2] Early on the 8th a reconnaissance observer reported movement behind the German lines as normal, and on the 9th no flying took place owing to bad visibility. Air operations were also affected by the destruction caused by a German air raid during the night of the 6th/7th, which bombed the main aerodrome at Bray Dunes (1¼ miles north of Dunkirk) and damaged 12 aircraft.

A prisoner of the *3rd Marine Regiment* captured on the 5th, stated that a British attack was expected shortly and that reinforcements of German artillery were being brought up. Two raids carried out on the night of the 9th/10th succeeded in capturing a prisoner, but he was killed by a shell soon afterwards, so this possible source of information of the German attack also failed.

only communication behind the left, or Dunes, sector, were demolished; and all but one bridge and a footbridge in the right, or Nieuport, sector. By 10.15 a.m. all telephone communication to the forward defences north of the river had failed—the high water-level had prevented the cables from being buried to any depth, and the large number of enemy long-range guns had enabled him to disorganize communications very far back. Wireless also failed to get any reply after about that hour.

At 11 a.m. there was a pause in the shelling. It had been particularly severe against the 1,400-yard sector in the sand-dunes between the Geleide brook and the coast, held by the 2nd Brigade (Br.-General G. C. Kemp) of the 1st Division (Major-General E. P. Strickland) and pretty equally divided between the 1/Northamptonshire and the 2/K.R.R.C., the two battalions in the line.[1] With the bridges behind them demolished, and with no rafts or boats along the banks of the Yser, these two battalions were already isolated. Before noon the destructive phase of the bombardment by the entire array of German artillery and mortars began and continued, except for three pauses of twenty minutes—at 2 p.m., 4 p.m., and 7 p.m.—for observation, until the hour of assault. The narrow breastworks, 7 feet high and only 3 feet thick, soon crumpled up; clouds of sand, thrown up by the shell-bursts and driven by the wind, clogged rifles and machine guns; and a new type of gas shell was used, containing mustard gas (Yellow Cross), which was being saved by the Germans as a surprise against the main Flanders offensive. Several German aircraft, flying as low as 60 feet above the British breastworks, sprayed the forward defence zone and the river bank with machine-gun fire. At 5.15 p.m. messages arrived at divisional headquarters by pigeon from the 2/K.R.R.C. to say that very heavy casualties had been suffered, two companies having lost all their officers, and that movement within the defence zone was no longer possible.

The intensity of the bombardment during the morning had pointed to the imminence of an infantry attack, and the pre-arranged artillery defence involving the bombardment of the German assault assembly trenches was ordered at 9.30 a.m., 11.25 a.m. and 2.10 p.m., and lasted for about an

---

[1] The intention had been to withdraw the 1st Division on 18th July for special training near Dunkirk. See p. 116, footnote 2.

GERMAN SPOILING ATTACKS

hour on each occasion. This retaliation proved insufficient, as the Germans had concrete shelters. The British guns, too, were outnumbered by nearly three to one, and many of them, to avoid disclosing their presence, had not previously registered.[1]

At 8 p.m. the Germans attacked on a frontage of two thousand yards between Lombartzyde and the coast, after sending a strong outflanking party along the shore.[2] The main assault was carried out by five waves of infantry including moppers-up with flame-throwers to fire the dug-outs.[3]

By 8.20 p.m., within twenty minutes, German troops were along the river bank. Isolated parties of British troops offered a stubborn resistance; but survivors estimated that 70 to 80 per cent. of their effectives were killed or wounded before the assault, so that an organized defence was no longer possible. About 8.30 p.m. observers from the south bank saw parties still holding out near the Northamptonshire battle headquarters, and also a counter-attack by the reserve company of the K.R.R.C. in progress, all of which

---

[1] Only 153 guns and howitzers came into action: 18-pdrs., 55; 4.5-inch howitzers, 18; 6-inch howitzers, 10; 8-inch howitzers, 8; 9.2-inch howitzers, 10; 12-inch howitzers, 2; 15-inch howitzers, 2; 60-pdrs, 9; 6-inch guns, 6; 9.2-inch guns, 7; 12-inch guns, 9; 13-pdr. A.A. guns, 9; 3-inch 20 cwt. A.A. guns, 8. Of the remaining guns and howitzers, 28 were put out of action by enemy fire.

[2] When, on 21st June, German patrols reported that British troops had taken over the bridgehead from the French, German O.H.L. decided to forestall the expected British advance up the coast by an attack on the bridgehead. More than 300,000 shells (including gas-shell) were allotted for the operation, and the artillery of the *1st* and *2nd Marine Divisions* were reinforced by three 24-cm. naval guns, 7 siege batteries, 10 mortar batteries, 16 heavy howitzer batteries, 12 light howitzer batteries and 30 field batteries. The attack, to be carried out by two regiments (*1st* and *2nd*) of the *1st Marine Division* supported by the *199th Division*, was to have taken place on the evening of the 9th but the weather was unfavourable for the co-operation of 11 torpedo-boats in the bombardment from off-shore. Although on the 10th the weather was again unsuitable for naval co-operation, it was decided to delay no longer.

[3] The first wave, consisting of groups of a specially trained assault detachment (*Sturmabteilung* of the *Marine Corps*), advanced straight through to the back, or third, British breastwork, cleared it and, after a pause of ten minutes, pressed on to the bank of the Yser; the second wave cleared the dug-outs of the second breastwork and then occupied the third breastwork; the third wave reinforced the first wave and established an outpost system along the river bank, placing machine guns to command the river; the fourth, carrying material for consolidating the position, cleared the dug-outs of the first breastwork and followed on to the third; the fifth occupied and held the second breastwork ("Marine Infanterie Regt. No. 2"; "Trutzig und treu!").

accounted for a number of the enemy before being themselves overwhelmed. Without bridges no assistance could be given, and the loss of the Dunes sector of the bridgehead had to be accepted. During the night 4 officers and 64 other ranks,[1] most of whom had sheltered in the newly-dug tunnels, escaped and swam back across the river, these being the sole survivors from the sector held by two battalions of the 1st Division.

On the front of the 32nd Division (Major-General C. D. Shute), holding from the Geleide brook eastwards to St. Georges, covering Nieuport, only the left brigade, the 97th (Br.-General C. A. Blackader) south of Lombartzyde was attacked. The area behind the second breastwork here lent itself to artificial flooding, and the German infantry was ordered not to go beyond it; but counter-action during the night by the 11/Border Regiment, responsible for this sector, supported by two companies of the 17/Highland L.I. from the north bank of the river at Nieuport, succeeded in regaining all but five hundred yards of their position near the Geleide brook.

At a conference at 10 a.m. on the following morning (11th), General Rawlinson gave instructions to recover the ground lost at the earliest possible moment, including Lombartzyde, in order to turn the flank of the enemy's new front in the Dunes sector along the canal. Lieut.-General Du Cane issued the necessary orders; but in a letter the same afternoon he protested to General Rawlinson, and reminded him of the history of previous British counter-attacks. Those, he wrote, that are made instantly on the initiative of local commanders usually succeed, whereas those ordered by higher authority and made in a hurry usually fail; on the other hand deliberate counter-attacks, with time for adequate preparation, often succeed.[2] He pointed out the difficulties of deployment in the remaining restricted space of the bridgehead and the numerical superiority of the German artillery, adding that even if the lost ground should

---

[1] Three officers and 52 other ranks of the 2/K.R.R.C.; one sergeant and 8 men of the 1/Northamptonshire, and 1 officer and 3 other ranks (out of a party of 50) of the 2nd Australian Tunnelling Company.

[2] It is interesting to note that the same principles were given as fundamental in the German text-book on the defensive battle issued by General Ludendorff on 1st December 1916.

be recaptured the garrison would be exposed to a repetition of the previous day's disaster in the immediate future. He would prefer, he concluded, to remain on the defensive in the existing position until more artillery had arrived, and the main offensive of the Fifth Army and the French had made progress. These objections were allowed; and the counter-attack, planned by the 32nd Division to take place on the following night, was cancelled.

The total casualties of the two divisions (1st and 32nd) in the two days' fighting were approximately 126 officers and 3,000 other ranks. Of the missing included in this total, 50 officers and 1,253 other ranks belonged to the two battalions of the 1st Division, which were practically annihilated.[1]

The War Cabinet were perturbed at this reverse, and, to reassure them, Sir Douglas Haig wrote on the 13th July to the Chief of the Imperial General Staff that the incident would in no way interfere with his main plan, nor did he think it would affect even tactically the intended coastal operation — which was postponed and then abandoned for other reasons. He attributed the loss of the bridgehead to the condition of the defences north of the river and to lack of adequate artillery at the time of the assault, owing to the change from French to British command of the sector being in progress. He was confident, however, that with the superior artillery about to be concentrated, combined with superiority in the air, " we shall be able to overcome " his [the enemy's] guns and then to blow him out of his " position as effectively as he blew us out of ours, and over " a wider area".

The revised plan of General Rawlinson was to attack Lombartzyde from the narrow front still held north of the Yser, and thence to roll up the German defences from the Geleide brook to the coast by a flanking attack shortly afterwards. The coastal attack and the landing operation would then proceed as previously arranged He pointed

---

[1] After the success at Nieuport, Crown Prince Rupprecht wished to make two more " spoiling " attacks; but " in view of the imminent " British offensive it was found that the necessary ammunition could not " be spared ". (G.O.A. xiii., pp. 38-9). The German Crown Prince also wished to make an offensive, but for the same reason was told that he might do no more than slightly improve his *Dauerstellung* (that is a position to be held " for the duration ").

STATE OF GERMANY. JULY

out to Sir Douglas Haig that an essential prelude to the task was complete mastery over the German artillery. On the 18th July, Sir Douglas Haig agreed to the scheme, and told General Rawlinson to work for the 8th August as the date, since he considered that the main offensive would probably have advanced sufficiently by that time to enable the coastal operation to be launched.

The uneasy state of Germany offered some encouragement: the reduction of the bread ration in April was causing riots and disturbances; in July, mutinies took place on several of the battleships; Hindenburg and Ludendorff were already beginning to put the blame for the absence of victory on the civil government, on account of its failure to support the High Command; they threatened resignation unless the Chancellor, Bethmann-Hollweg, retired, and he resigned on the 13th July, being succeeded by Dr. Michaelis, a civil servant.[1]

On the 19th July, the *Reichstag*, by 214 votes to 133, passed a resolution demanding a peace of understanding.

The German general reserve amounted to no more than four to six divisions. It is now known that Major Wetzell, the O.H.L. strategist, was in favour of attacking Italy, as was done later in the year and brought about Caporetto. Ludendorff, relying on the effect of U-boat warfare, did not agree with him; but decided to use the general reserve on the Eastern Front, to smash the Kerenski offensive, begun on the 29th, which it successfully did (8th–28th July).[2]

---

[1] He resigned on 1st November over the question of the Social-Democratic Party instigating a further mutiny in the High Seas Fleet, and was succeeded by the 74-year old Count Hertling, the Bavarian Prime Minister.

[2] It was then used at Riga, 1st September; and in Italy, 24th October.

CHAPTER VIII

THE BATTLES OF YPRES 1917

BATTLE OF PILCKEM RIDGE, 31ST JULY–2ND AUGUST
(Sketches 1, 2, 3, 10, 11, 12, 13, 14)

THE PRELIMINARIES

THE GENERAL PLAN

The Commander-in-Chief outlined at several meetings and conferences the course he hoped that the campaign would follow.[1] It was to open by an offensive on a 15-mile front from Frelinghien on the Lys (3 miles south of Warneton) to the Yser inundations north of Steenstraat. The Second Army (General Sir H. Plumer)[2] was to capture the outpost strongpoints in front of the Warneton Line[3] and to create the impression of an assault on the Warneton Line itself, thereby threatening Lille and holding the German reserves there. The Fifth Army (General Sir H. Gough), together with the French First Army (General Anthoine), was to overrun the German defences on Gheluvelt plateau and Pilckem Ridge. In the subsequent operations,[4] the Fifth Army was to advance north-eastwards, with its right along the high ground of the main Ypres Ridge through Gheluvelt—Becelaere—Broodseinde and Moorslede, to gain the line Thourout—Couckelaere on its way to Bruges.

Sir Douglas Haig did not contemplate a prolonged campaign in the Ypres district and hoped that the Fifth Army would be approaching the Roulers–Thourout railway, fifteen miles from the start in time for the coastal operation by the Fourth Army to catch the high tides on the 7th or 8th August. Then the original offensive, joining hands with the coastal attack and landing, would be continued from the line Thourout–Ostend towards Bruges and the Dutch frontier, south of the Schelde. The Second Army, after

---
[1] See Sketch 1.
[2] See Sketch 3.
[3] That is the German defence line running north from Warneton, west of Zandvoorde and Gheluvelt (see Map 1).
[4] See Frontispiece.

THE YPRES AREA

taking over the defence of Gheluvelt plateau and the main Ypres Ridge as far as Passchendaele, would be ready to develop an advance towards the line Warneton-Menin and, later, to a line Courtrai-Roulers, throwing out a flank guard along the line of the Lys.

THE GROUND[1]

No special difficulties were expected as regards the ground, except in the matter of repairs to roads, and for this, dumps of road metal had been accumulated by the Second Army. It was hoped soon to be well beyond the bombarded area. The Ypres Ridge, extending from Wytschaete to Passchendaele and Staden, is the only feature of the area. But the relief is very slight, Ypres and its canal banks being at the 20-metre contour, and Gheluvelt plateau 55 to 60 metres, with a greatest difference of 131 feet. The minor ridges, so-called, are really no more than "rises"; and the valleys, shallow depressions. In peace-time the land possessed a good drainage system; this had been for the most part damaged or destroyed during the fighting in 1914-15, but had to some extent been restored by the work of the Land Drainage Companies sent out for the purpose. The surface soil was patchy, sometimes clay, sometimes sand, sometimes a mixture of both. The water table is generally near the surface and the trenches often contained water, so that pumps and duck-boards were required. In general, however, the Ypres sector was regarded as not so wet as the Hohenzollern sector near Loos, or the Ploegsteert Wood and Givenchy sectors, where sandbag parapets had to be built up. On the 31st July, No Man's Land was green with grass and weeds; few woods remained, but the land-

---

[1] See Map 1. If the 1 : 100,000 map (Sheets Ghent, Dunkirk, Hazebrouck, Tournai) is examined, it will be seen that from Zeebrugge almost to Dunkirk a narrow belt of dunes extends along the coast. South of this the map shows the "Polder" country, a close labyrinth of thin blue lines, representing drainage ditches known as "Wateringues"; les Moeres, between Furnes and Dunkirk, a reclaimed marsh, with a rectangular system of drainage ditches; and a few canals. This fen country stretches only as far south as Bruges–Ghistelles (7 miles south of Ostend)–Dixmude (Sketch 1 shows the edge of the wet area), thence the Yser borders it as far south as Noordschoote, where the boundary turns west. Thus the area in which the "Third Battle of Ypres" was fought was entirely outside the "low country".

scape was by no means the uniform brown it later assumed.[1]

It will be noticed that numerous streams, starting in small valleys on the Ypres Ridge, the Steenbeek, Stroombeek, Kortebeek, etc., run at right-angles across the line of advance; as their lower courses became obstructed by shell-fire, these tended to become sloughs; this was particularly the case near St. Julien, and, a mile farther north, around the Stroombeek. But it must be borne in mind that the ground was divided into wet zones and dry zones. For instance, even late in the battle, on one half-battalion front a trench could be dug, whilst on the other half only a shell-hole position was possible. As time passed, the bad zones, where there had been fighting or where the line had been stabilized for, say, over a week and had been cut up, were very clearly defined. These bad patches were marked on maps, so that they could be avoided.[2] The movement of large bodies of troops will cut up most surfaces, and for a short time after rain every part was sticky. Finally, it must never be forgotten that the British army in this battle, by its bombardments and barrages, created in front of itself its own obstacle—shell craters and mud, and the Ypres mud was of the consistency of cream cheese. One sank in it.

The Fifth Army Scheme

The "Northern Operations" files which contained the G.H.Q. 1917 plan and the correspondence leading up to it, already summarized, were handed to General Gough by Colonel Macmullen on the 14th May, as a basis for his scheme for the main offensive. The first day's objective, it will be

---

[1] Captain Delvert, the historian of the French First Army in Flanders ("Les opérations de la 1re Armée dans les Flandres, Juillet–Novembre 1917", p. 13), thus describes the ground in the French area :

"The terrain in which the offensive was to develop was that part of "France which lies south of the marshy 'amphibious' region of the "Moeres.

"It is a vast plain of verdure, dotted in this month of July, when the "operations commenced, with the golden rectangles of the harvest. It "was traversed by lines of hedges and rows of trees and speckled with "red roofs, slow turning windmills and high spires. . . . In this terrain "the water-table is a metre below the surface, sometimes less. It was "therefore out of the question to dig a network of trenches and communica-"tions well provided with dug-outs, as on the rest of the front".

[2] See Sketch 28, prepared by the Canadian Historical Section.

GOUGH'S PLAN

remembered, was to be limited to the capture of the German Second Line, an advance of about a mile, so as to enable observation posts to be established on Gheluvelt plateau and beyond the crest of the Pilckem Ridge. There was to be a pause for two days to give time for the forward movement of the field artillery to ensure that observed artillery support would be available for the next advance. Another reason given for the pause was to allow time for the capture and consolidation of the greater part of Gheluvelt plateau before a major advance was attempted farther north across the Steenbeek.[1]

This plan did not appear to provide for the speedy progress which General Gough had understood was required, according to the verbal instructions he had received from Sir Douglas Haig.[2] At conferences with his corps commanders on the 6th and 16th June, a Fifth Army scheme was evolved according to which the first day's objective (the second) was extended another mile, to a third objective, which included the German Third Line.[3] Moreover, without any settled pause along this farther objective, the advance was to be continued if possible, either immediately or within the next few hours, another mile to a fourth objective on the main Ypres Ridge at Broodseinde, with the left flank along Gravenstafel spur to Gravenstafel and Langemarck.[4] The strength of the advance to the fourth objective was left to the discretion of divisional commanders; but as soon as the third objective was reported taken, it was to be reinforced by the battalions which had occupied and remained along

---

[1] See Sketches 10 and 11.

[2] General Sir H. Gough, commenting on this chapter, writes (18th March, 1944): " I have a very clear and distinct recollection of Haig's " personal explanations to me, and his instructions, when I was appointed " to undertake this operation. He quite clearly told me that the plan " was to capture Passchendaele Ridge, and to advance as rapidly as " possible on Roulers. I was then to advance on Ostend. This was very " definitely viewing the battle as an attempt to break through, and more- " over Haig never altered this opinion till the attack was launched, so far " as I know." " The G.H.Q. plan ", General Gough adds, " failed to mass " anything like sufficient forces to carry out so ambitious a task—20 to 30 " divisions were necessary—and the front of attack was too narrow and " directed at the wrong place. It should have been directed farther " south—with its left, say, on Zonnebeke and its right on Messines. It " was also a mistake not to entrust the operation to the General (Sir H. " Plumer) who had been on that front for more than two years, instead " of bringing me over on to a bit of ground with which I had practically " no acquaintance ".

[3] See Note at end of Chapter.

[4] Appendix XIII.

the first objective in the opening assault. As the fourth objective would be beyond effective support of the majority of the field batteries, all available heavy artillery was to be ready to lay a protective barrage in front of the advanced posts along it in the event of an S.O.S. call.[1] If the enemy seriously contested the advance to the fourth objective, it was not to be pressed ; but if little opposition was met, the advance was to be continued the same afternoon, the II Corps on Passchendaele, the XIX Corps on Goudberg, and the XVIII Corps on Poelcappelle. General Gough, however, expected that resistance by German reserves would be met along the fourth objective, and he reckoned on a two or three days' halt to bring up artillery support. The next attack, on the fourth day after the start of the offensive, would, he hoped, gain the Passchendaele–Staden end of the main Ypres Ridge. Thus General Gough, instead of confining his first day's operation to a short fixed advance, was in favour of going as far as he could. It would, as he said, "be wasteful not to reap all the advantages possible resulting from the first attack". Remembering the chance that had been lost at Messines by a limited operation, Sir Douglas Haig was disposed to let the Fifth Army go on, if it could. He therefore approved of the new scheme— it is a sound rule to allow a general to carry out an operation in his own way. He did not in the altered conditions of his offensive consider recalling General Rawlinson and confiding the coastal operations to General Gough.

Although Sir Douglas Haig officially approved the scheme, he yet had some doubts as to the distant objectives given for the first day. The proceedings of the War Cabinet conference in London on the 19th–22nd June had had a moderating influence on his outlook,[2] and a memorandum written by Br.-General J. H. Davidson, head of the Operations Branch G.H.Q., which was handed to him on his return, on the 25th June, criticized General Gough's scheme and recommended strictly limited objectives on the lines of the original G.H.Q. plan. The gist of this memorandum was that no attempt should be made to push the infantry to the maximum depth hoped for in the Fifth Army scheme (i.e., the

---

[1] Appendix XIV gives the 8th Division Operation Order, a typical one, for the battle.
[2] See p. 99.

fourth objective, 5,000 yards). Instead, it advised a succession of deliberate attacks with objectives limited to a depth of about a mile (i.e., the German Second Line), to which distance it had been proved beyond doubt that fresh troops with adequate artillery support could advance without undue loss or disorganization; the artillery destructive fire on this lesser area, too, could be more concentrated. The memorandum pointed out that the eventual line reached, if the Fifth Army scheme were adopted, would probably be a "ragged" one, from which it would be difficult for a fresh attack to start. Immediate counter-attacks by the German reserves were sure to be delivered, and it would be far preferable "to accept battle with those reserves when "we are in an organized state, our guns in position, our "troops not tired and our communications in good state, "than to engage them in some more forward position where "we have none of these advantages". Br.-General Davidson believed that after a succession of effective blows a moment would come when the taking of risks would be justifiable; but, in his opinion, exploitation would not be practicable until at least the first series of reinforcing, or counter-attack, divisions which the enemy would send into the battle had been defeated, and until the enemy was thoroughly demoralized. This result could not be achieved on the first day, the note concluded, and it should not be attempted.[1] In fact, the strength of the British Armies available was not sufficient, as that of the Germans was to be on the 21st March 1918, to attack with unlimited objectives.

General Gough, in a written reply,[1] gave his opinion that preparations on the scale intended should be more fully exploited; and Sir Douglas Haig, after discussing the Davidson memorandum with him and General Plumer at Cassel on the 28th June, had, with General Plumer's support allowed the Fifth Army scheme to stand: it seemed, perhaps, worth trying an all-out attack on the first day. He did, however, remind General Gough that the main battle would be fought on and for the high ground west of Gheluvelt, and that plans should be made accordingly. He stressed the vital importance of the plateau, and impressed on General Gough that the advance farther north should be limited

[1] Appendix XV gives the memorandum in full, and General Gough's written reply.

until the right flank was firmly established upon it ; only then should he push along the ridge to Broodseinde.

This conception of the opening battle of the campaign, which was in fact that of the G.H.Q. plan, was very different to that envisaged in the Fifth Army scheme. Since the front and reserve divisions of the four attacking corps were to be spread out equally along the front of the Fifth Army, General Gough would have been justified in the circumstances in adding strength and depth to the drive by the right (II) corps across Gheluvelt plateau at the expense of his other corps. No alteration was, however, made either to the scheme or to the order of battle ; and Sir Douglas Haig did not press the points he had raised.[1]

A plan can never be regarded as more than a general guide for a campaign. Sir Douglas Haig had frequently pointed out at conferences and in writing, as already mentioned, that the enemy must first be " worn down " by battle ; the only question was whether the Empire forces could afford this wearing-down process ; it was to be reduced if possible. The information given to him by the Intelligence Section on the 20th June was misleading in its conclusion that the offensive would have " a superiority of " two to one in infantry, and in guns and ammunition " greater still, and support in the air even more assured".[2]

---

[1] The Fifth Army Intelligence Summaries during July showed the depth of the German defence both in the artillery and in the infantry dispositions. The weekly summary of 7th July pointed out the strength of the German defences on Gheluvelt plateau, where work was being carried on more intensely than in any other sector, and of the artillery concentration behind them. It added that the Germans would probably endeavour to pivot upon this strongly defended area in the event of their line being driven back farther north, across the Steenbeek. On the 14th, 17th and 21st July the summaries revealed that the field batteries west of the Steenbeek had been withdrawn to east of the stream, to 3,000 yards and more from the front line ; and that the assembly areas for the counter-attack divisions were behind the Gheluvelt plateau and the main (Broodseinde–Passchendaele) ridge.

[2] The statement calculated that of the 25 German divisions in Northern Belgium north of the Lys, 13 were holding the 32-mile front (13 of which were flooded) between the Lys and the coast, with 10 to 12 in reserve. The forecast of Allied strength available for the opening phase of the campaign was 49 divisions (Second Army, 10 ; Fifth Army, 16 ; French First Army, 6 ; Belgian Army, 12 divisions ; Fourth Army, 5). The dispositions showed, however, that the 16 divisions of the Fifth Army which were to make the main offensive would probably be opposed by 5 German front-line divisions, supported by the 10 to 12 divisions in reserve within easy reach. In other words, they might expect to meet equal numbers of infantry; and the Germans still had five weeks to strengthen their defence organization.

In the circumstances, the Commander-in-Chief considered it possible that any one of the strong blows about to be delivered in Flanders might break the German resistance, and he wished to be ready to exploit to the full such an opportunity. It was a case of the Napoleonic maxim, "on s'engage partout et on voit," and he wished to prevent any such missing of opportunity as had occurred on the 1st July at the Somme, when Montauban was taken.[1] With this in mind, Sir Douglas Haig, at a conference on the 5th July, used the words: "in the operations subsequent "to the capture of the Passchendaele – Staden Ridge, "opportunities for the employment of cavalry in masses "are likely to offer"; and in preparation for such a development, the Cavalry Corps was moved from behind the Arras battle front northwards to Merville and St. Pol (25 and 40 miles from Ypres) in July. To his two Army commanders, on the 30th June, separately, he gave advice appropriate to their temperaments. To the thruster, General Gough, he remarked, "the object of the Fifth Army offensive is to "wear down the enemy, but, at the same time, to have an "objective: I have given two: the Passchendaele–Staden "Ridge and the coast". To the sure and steady General Plumer,[2] he said, "be ready to act offensively on the right, "north of the Lys. I shall then have three fronts: one "facing north-east; the centre facing east; and the right "facing south-east. In view of the great possibilities "accruing from the operations, I wish to be able to operate "offensively at will from any of these fronts according to "the manner in which the enemy disposes his forces to "meet me". In this way, he said, he hoped to take the enemy unawares.

On the 27th June, Sir Douglas Haig, on a visit to the II Corps, the right of the Fifth Army, had been asked by the corps commander, Lieut.-General Sir C. W. Jacob,[3] that the southern flank of the attack might be extended to include Tower Hamlets spur, which "lent itself as a jumping-off "place from which the enemy could counter-attack his "right flank in the advance towards Zonnebeke". Sir Douglas Haig, who again emphasized the importance of

---

[1] See "1916" Vol. I, pp. 341–2.
[2] In the South African War, 16 years earlier, Colonel Plumer had the reputation of being the most rapid mover of the column commanders.
[3] See Sketch 16.

securing Gheluvelt plateau to cover the right flank of the offensive, agreed; and arrangements were at once made, through Fifth Army headquarters, to hand over to the II Corps the left division, the 24th, of the Second Army, and a quantity of heavy and field artillery.[1] The southern flank of the Fifth Army was thereby extended on the 4th July to the Klein Zillebeke–Zandvoorde road.

Zero Day Postponed

At the Lillers conference on the 14th June, Sir Douglas Haig gave the approximate date for the main offensive to " secure the Passchendaele–Staden–Clercken Ridge " as the 25th July. On the 1st July, however, General Anthoine, commanding the French First Army, doubted whether he would be ready by that date, owing to lack of labour to make the necessary gun-emplacements and ammunition dumps. Sir Douglas Haig was averse to any postponement, and lent General Anthoine a working party of 7,200 men to assist in building gun emplacements.[2] He further suggested to General Gough that, although the right wing should aim at capturing Gheluvelt plateau, the French and the left wing might be given a less distant objective; but General Gough replied that he would prefer to postpone the offensive rather than modify it.

On the 7th July, at a G.H.Q. conference at Watou, General Gough himself asked for a delay of five days, till the 30th, on account of losses in guns and the late arrival of much of the heavy artillery. With these extra days, he hoped that the German artillery could be thoroughly mastered; batteries could be moved forward to closer range before Zero Day to give better support to the advance from the second to the third objective; and the longer artillery preparation would enable the next advance to be carried out by the same divisions, thereby economizing man-power, and, in the end, saving time. Sir Douglas Haig agreed to postpone the infantry assault for three days, to the 28th.

On the 21st July, General Anthoine wrote to G.H.Q. to the effect that during the past week " only $2\frac{1}{2}$ days of fire "

---

[1] The artillery of the 23rd and 24th Divisions and 13 medium (60-pdr.) and 25 heavy (15 6-inch gun; 5 8-inch and 5 9.2-inch howitzer) batteries.
[2] F.O.A. v. (ii.), p. 653.

had been possible, owing to bad observation due to the dull cloudy weather, and he demanded three more days, till the 31st, for counter-battery work. Sir Douglas Haig was strongly opposed to any further delay. He doubted whether sufficient progress could be made to enable the coastal attack and landing to catch the high tides on the 7th and 8th August. He was anxious, too, about the weather; investigations by the Intelligence Section of the records over eighty years showed that in Flanders, although October was the wettest month, a period of wet weather usually began early in August, and he feared that the initial operations might be hampered. General Gough, although his own preparations would be complete by the 28th, preferred to wait three days for the French rather than alter the plan at the last moment; and General Anthoine persisted in his demand. Sir Douglas Haig yielded to the wishes of the Army commanders; he considered that the French should be given every chance of success, as, in the existing state of tension, France might not stand up to another failure. He decided to postpone the assault for another three days, till the 31st. He expressed doubt as to the wisdom of this decision, and on the 26th informed General Rawlinson, commanding the Fourth Army, that the coastal attack and landing would have to be postponed from the 7th or 8th August till the next high tides.

Thus the delay of six weeks between the Messines battle and the main operation was due in the first place to " Messines ", the arrangements for which were ready, being fought at short notice as a separate engagement in order to draw German attention from the French, before the preparation of the operations as a whole were ready; to time being required to shift guns and material, in particular the guns used in the Lens and Lille diversion attacks; and to the Fifth Army making changes in the mounting of the battle prepared by the Second Army, particularly as regards Gheluvelt; but finally to the postponements asked for by General Anthoine, the French commander.

The Preliminary Bombardment

Facing the entire front of the Fifth Army the German defences, except for a forward observation line, lay on a reverse slope and completely out of sight of ground observers.

The success of the preliminary bombardment consequently depended upon direction from aircraft and shooting by the map based on air photographs; great emphasis, therefore, was laid on gaining mastery of the air in order that assistance by the Royal Flying Corps might be unmolested.

The air offensive, which was to have begun on the 8th July according to a programme issued by Major-General H. M. Trenchard on the previous day, was delayed by bad weather till the 11th. The general idea was to gain air supremacy over an area from the German front line back to the German observation-balloon line, a depth of about five miles on the entire front from the Lys to the coast. The Germans accepted this challenge for air mastery over the battlefield. Early in the month they had had air superiority, and their observed counter-battery fire had seriously delayed and obstructed the emplacement of the artillery. As the fighter strength of the R.F.C. increased during the middle of the month and gradually surpassed that of the Germans in the battle area the artillery situation became easier. The air battles which took place during the last fortnight of July were the most bitter the War had yet produced. Clashes occurred between groups of about thirty aircraft on either side, and on the evening of the 26th July an air battle took place above Polygon Wood involving about ninety-four single-seater fighters at heights from 5,000 to 17,000 feet. Throughout this struggle for air supremacy, and so far as the weather allowed, the British aircraft kept to their programme of artillery co-operation, air photography, reconnaissance and bombing. Towards the end of the month the enemy's opposition declined, nearly all encounters taking place on the enemy side of the line.[1]

The number of aircraft available[2] would have been greater but for the German air raids on London in June and

---

[1] Details of the preparatory air offensive may be read in the official history, "War in the Air" Vol. IV, pp. 139–60.

[2] The allotted strength amounted to 508 British machines, including 230 single-seater fighters; in addition, 200 French (including 100 single-seater fighters), and 40 Belgian machines were available, making a total of 748 aircraft, of which 330 were fighters.

The German *Fourth Army*, holding from Armentières to the coast, had doubled its air strength between 1st and 31st July, by which time it had 600 aircraft (G.O.A. xiii., p. 63), of which one-third were single-seater fighters; so that the Allies had a numerical superiority. These figures do not include either the 104 machines of the Royal Naval Air Service operating along the Belgian coast, or the German naval air arm there of about 63 machines.

THE BOMBARDMENT. 16TH JULY

July. The June raid had resulted in 162 killed and 432 wounded, and on the day following the raid on the 7th July the War Cabinet asked for two good fighter squadrons to be sent to England the next day. A protest by Sir Douglas Haig reduced the demand to one squadron, which was sent, and, in addition, twenty-eight new aeroplanes promised to France for re-equipment were diverted to Home Defence Squadrons.[1]

While the fight for air supremacy was in progress, the bombing squadrons carried out day and night raids on the German aerodromes, on the principal railway junctions and sidings such as those at Ghent, Thourout and Courtrai, on the villages known to be housing German reserves, and on the electricity works at Bruges and Zeebrugge.

The artillery preparation, directed by Major-General H. C. C. Uniacke, M.G.R.A., Fifth Army, began on the 16th July. The total allotment of heavy and medium artillery was 226 guns and 526 howitzers. They were organized into counter-battery and bombardment groups, and were sited in the area Dickebusch (II Corps); western side of Ypres (XIX Corps); Brielen (XVIII Corps); Elverdinghe–Woesten (XIV Corps).[2] The field artillery amounted to 1,098 18-pdr. guns and 324 4.5-inch howitzers, and for the barrage one 18-pdr. gun was available to every 12½ yards of front. The field batteries gradually packed the area about Zillebeke and Verbrandenmolen (II Corps), with forward batteries behind the woods near the front line. Others were in the Potijze–St. Jean area and east of Ypres (XIX Corps) with some batteries immediately behind the canal north of the town. Farther north, most of the battery positions of the XVIII Corps were behind the canal, with forward positions north and north-west of La Brique about twenty-five hundred yards behind the front line. Those of the left corps (XIV) were all west of the canal and mostly

---

[1] See " War in the Air ", Vol. IV, pp. 152–5.
[2] See Sketch 10. The II Corps, with its extra division (24th) and frontage, had three counter-battery and three bombardment double groups of heavy artillery, each single group consisting of four to six siege, heavy or medium batteries. The detail for the corps was 1 15-inch, 6 12-inch, 30 9.2-inch, 54 8-inch, 116 6-inch, 12 4.5-inch howitzers and 1 9.2-inch, 8 6-inch, 66 60-pdr. guns. The XIX, XVIII and XIV Corps each had two counter-battery double groups and three bombardment single groups, one of which was a reinforcing group.

within twelve hundred yards of it.[1] The artillery plan, issued on the 30th June, was modelled upon the precedent of the Messines programme; but most of the advantages of that occasion were lacking. The Fifth Army batteries lay within a salient instead of, as then, firing into one; and they were now overlooked. In the words of Sir Douglas Haig's Despatch: " On no previous occasion had the whole " ground from which we had to attack been so completely " exposed to the enemy's observation ".

The total of the German artillery was not under-estimated. The figures given to Sir Douglas Haig by G.H.Q. Intelligence on the 20th July showed a total of 1,500 guns and howitzers opposed to the 2,299 pieces on the Fifth Army front, a very near calculation of the enemy's strength.[2] His batteries frequently changed position, each having three or more alternative emplacements, with occasionally a single gun firing from them as deception. For this reason, however, the method of calculating batteries destroyed by counting the successful shoots on gun-pits was misleading.[3]

The actual results of the preparatory bombardment and counter-battery work could not be expected to compare with those obtained in the more favourable circumstances of the Messines battle; nor did they justify the optimistic report given to Sir Douglas Haig on the 25th July by Lieut.-General Sir Noel Birch, Artillery Adviser at G.H.Q., that he was " confident the upper hand over the German " artillery had been gained ". His report was particularly at fault in respect of the German artillery concentration in the Gheluvelt area, where, according to a warning by

---

[1] Each infantry division of the II Corps had eight or nine field artillery brigades (including Army field artillery units) to support it, while the divisions of the other three Corps each had six.

[2] On 31st July the German artillery consisted of 345 heavy (252 howitzers and 93 guns) and 392 field (120 howitzers and 272 guns) on the front of Steenstraat–Hollebeke, i.e., approximately opposite the Fifth Army front. Opposite the Hollebeke–Warneton front, i.e., that of the Second Army, they had 127 heavy (55 howitzers and 72 guns) and 176 field (128 howitzers and 48 guns).

G.O.A. xiii., p. 54, puts the German artillery strength at 389 batteries (say 1,556 guns) opposed to 717 Allied batteries (say 2,868 guns).

[3] For example, the Fifth Army reports on the counter-battery results were: for the week ended 20th July, " 42 gun-pits and battery positions " destroyed and 124 damaged, 68 fires and explosions caused "; for the week ended 27th July, " out of 154 shoots carried out with aeroplane " observation, 64 gun-pits and gun positions have been destroyed and 129 " damaged, 113 fires and explosions have been caused. The results, " judged by aeroplane photographs, are very satisfactory ".

Lieut.-General Morland (X Corps), the reported successes of the counter-battery shoots were probably exaggerated owing to the frequent changes of position of the German batteries.[1] Though faced by about double its strength, this important enemy concentration was able to maintain its striking power and caused considerable losses to the II Corps artillery, particularly to the Australian batteries, during the bombardment period.[2]

Failure to neutralize the German batteries added to the great difficulties of the preparatory work under Major-General P. G. Grant, Chief Engineer of the Fifth Army. As German observers overlooked the entire Salient back for over seven miles, and their batteries were firing concentrically into it at observed targets day and night, the preparations were more harassed than those of any previous British offensive. The additional gun platforms, crowded into the area, had to be specially constructed to meet the conditions of the Flanders clay ;[3] and as natural cover was scarce the work had to be done by night, and camouflaged before daylight. Roads and tracks had to be made for the convoys of motor-lorries and wagons which brought the artillery ammunition from the railhead-road refilling points. Both the Royal Engineers and the pioneer battalions earned a special tribute for the successful accomplishment of these preparations, despite the most harassing conditions. Heavy casualties were suffered throughout from the enemy's constant artillery fire and frequent gas shelling, as well as by bombing from the air by night.[4]

---

[1] B.O.A., p. 390, states that this " extremely active and effective mass " of artillery, organized by *Group Wytschaete* about Becelaere, Gheluvelt " and Zandvoorde, was so co-ordinated under a single commander that it " could bring an overwhelming fire-concentration at short notice to crash " (*schlagartig*) on any target within range ". It was at the disposal of *Group Ypres*, for the Steenbeek sector north of Westhoek, if required. The account adds that the organization was employed on several occasions during the preliminary artillery duels to destroy and drive back British batteries which had crossed the Yser canal to the Zillebeke area.

[2] A.O.A. iv., p. 706, gives an eye-witness account of the artillery action against the Australian batteries near Zillebeke Lake.

[3] The platforms were built of stout timbers, anchored to layers of timber bolted and notched together, and in the case of the heavier guns were very elaborate. Concrete was tried ; but the foundations were liable to crack owing to the lack of time for the material to set : quick-setting cement was in its infancy.

[4] During the three weeks, 6th–13th, 13th–20th, 20th–27th, the Fifth Army casualties were 2,275, 5,930 and 7,354, respectively.

The gas shelling, chiefly with the new mustard gas (Yellow Cross), was
Continued at foot of next page.

From the 28th July the full weight of the counter-attack batteries developed, and for three days and nights heavy and field howitzers concentrated on the known German battery positions, while field guns covered the forward battery positions with shrapnel and gas-shell. This concentrated counter-battery action enabled the assaulting divisions to reach their assembly trenches without serious hindrance. On the last night, from midnight until the hour of assault, at 3.50 a.m., gas shelling was extended over all the known battery positions, a procedure which had proved so successful before the Messines assault. By these means, the German initial defence barrage was mostly neutralized; but subsequent events during the day were to reveal that the German artillery still had a great and unmastered reserve of fire-power, particularly in its concentration of guns about Gheluvelt plateau.[1]

The artillery preparation for the opening battle of the Flanders campaign marks the zenith, and for the British, the end of protracted set-piece bombardments following a day-to-day time-table. Both the number of guns employed and the ammunition expended established a record. The growth of the artillery strength of the British Armies can be seen by the comparative figures of 1916 and 1917.[2] The

---

Continued from previous page.
severe in the Fifth Army area. During the night of the 12th/13th, following its use for the first time on the previous day on the Nieuport bridgehead, the town of Ypres was deluged with the new gas, causing 2,014 casualties, mostly in the 15th Division, the majority of whom, however, recovered within seven days. The symptoms were severe pains in the head, throat, and eyes, vomiting and bronchial irritation. The affection was in many cases extremely painful, but caused no permanent damage to the eyes.

[1] By 25th July, the artillery losses of *Group Wytschaete*, which held southwards from Westhoek and astride the Menin Road, are stated to have amounted to 50 per cent. of the heavy guns, 30 per cent. of the heavy howitzers, 17 per cent. of the mortars and 10 per cent. of the 10-cm. guns. (Rupprecht ii., p. 230). A large proportion of these losses were, however, replaced by new or repaired guns before the day of the offensive.

[2] The totals were as follows:

	Frontage Miles	Heavy	Artillery Medium	Field	Ammunition Expended
Battles of the Somme 1916	14	143	284	1,010	1,732,873
Battles of Arras 1917	13	301	662	1,854	2,687,653
Battle of Messines 1917	9	236	504	1,510	3,258,000
Battles of Ypres 1917	15	281	718	2,092	4,283,550

Details of the ammunition expenditure for the bombardment and opening battle (15th July–2nd August) of "Third Ypres" were: 18-pdr., 2,239,608; 4.5-inch howitzer, 728,345; 60-pdr., 255,462; 6-inch gun, 21,354; 6-inch howitzer, 750,119; 8-inch howitzer, 165,975; 9.2-inch howitzer, 113,073; 12-inch howitzer, 8,008; 15-inch howitzer, 1,606. Total, 4,283,550.

ARTILLERY BOMBARDMENT

method, which had been initiated in the spring of 1915 by General Joffre, the French Commander-in-Chief, with the slogan " L'artillerie conquiert, l'infanterie occupe ", and was first adopted by the British for the Battle of Festubert in May 1915,[1] had proved effective up to a point. After two years of experiment, the offensives with the strictly limited objectives of Vimy Ridge and of Messines in 1917 were the most perfect examples of its efficient use; and even then the German centres of resistance had to be overcome by a carefully rehearsed form of battle-drill by the infantry rather than by the simple process of mopping-up, as the slogan implied.

Often the method had been stretched beyond its proper limitations. In the opening offensives at Loos, on the Somme, and at Arras the British artillery had been asked to neutralize the defence on a wider front and to a greater depth than was reasonably practicable with the available resources. Heavy casualties to the assaulting infantry, which the method had been designed expressly to prevent, had been the consequence. Once again, in the battle about to begin, the limitations of bombardment had been left out of account; particularly as the German defence now relied chiefly on immediate counter-attacks by divisions which were held back beyond artillery range. The destruction of the German strongpoints was not practicable and, as the later battles of the campaign were to show, a short concentrated bombardment by heavy and medium artillery, sufficient to stun the garrisons of the strongpoints at the moment of assault, would have been equally effective at a fraction of the cost.

The Yser Canal Crossed North of Boesinghe

Numerous infantry raids, covered by box barrages, were carried out by each corps during the preparatory period. To add to the effect of the bombardment on the German garrison, gas operations were carried out on an extensive scale. On most nights selected areas in the front defences were shelled with both lethal and lacrymatory gas by trench mortars. On the night of the 13th/14th, and again on the 20th/21st, discharges of gas were fired along the whole

---

[1] See " 1915 " Vol. II, p. 47.

front by the Special Companies R.E. from 4,000 projectors on to selected targets in the forward zone back to fifteen hundred yards. For six nights before the assault, too, gas-shell bombardments were carried out by 4.5-inch howitzers on certain known enemy strongpoints, on woods and along the banks of the Steenbeek. The evidence of prisoners tended to show that the day and night bombardment, the harassing machine-gun fire, the gas discharges and shell, and the constant surprise raids had lowered the power of resistance of the German forward garrison almost to breaking point. A further purpose of these raiding parties was to gain warning of a possible German withdrawal from the forward zone before the assault.[1] On the 25th July, patrols, and also artillery observers, on the northern flank reported that they could walk into the German lines, unhindered, in many places.[2] The full meaning of this information was not realized until midday on the 27th, when British air observers reported no trace of the enemy in his front defences opposite the northern sector of the Fifth Army front. During the afternoon patrols sent out by the Guards Division crossed the Yser canal near Boesinghe and occupied the German front trench system on a frontage of about three thousand yards to a depth of five hundred yards, from the Ypres–Staden railway (inclusive) northwards.[3] The French, on the left, also established a new front line on the eastern bank of the canal; but on the right, where Pilckem Ridge becomes more pronounced and offered a reverse slope for shelters out of sight of British artillery observers, patrols sent out by the XVIII Corps met strong opposition, and it

---

[1] On 25th June, General Ludendorff had proposed a withdrawal from Pilckem Ridge to the Third (*Wilhelm*) Line, east of the Steenbeek, before the British offensive, leaving only outposts in the Second (*Albrecht*) Line. The matter was discussed at a *Fourth Army* conference at Courtrai on 30th June, and a counter-proposal by *Fourth Army* headquarters, to hold the existing position was agreed to. See Note at end of Chapter.

[2] The German defences in the low-lying ground along the canal, astride and north of the Ypres–Staden railway, were only lightly constructed for outposts, the first main line of defence being about eight hundred yards east of the canal. On 24th July, front-line regiments of the *49th Reserve Division* reported this outpost zone to be untenable, owing to day and night shelling, and evacuated it. Although its re-occupation was ordered, only a few patrols held it till the 27th. " Res. Regt. No. 226 " ii., pp. 52–7.

[3] At the end of June the French First Army had asked to decrease its frontage by a thousand yards, and the Fifth Army, accordingly, had to extend that distance northwards along the Yser canal, north of Boesinghe and the Ypres–Roulers railway.

was evident that the withdrawal was only local. Nevertheless, the ground gained was valuable, as it eliminated the necessity for the passage of the canal at the outset of the assault, for which intricate preparations had already been made.[1]

On the next day, at 9.45 p.m., after a heavy barrage, the Germans counter-attacked the new line of the Guards Division north of the railway. They were repulsed by artillery and machine-gun fire; the French, too, who had withdrawn during the night to their original breastworks, returned at the request of the Guards Division to protect its left flank. No alteration had to be made to the original objectives for the 31st in consequence of the gain of ground; the battalions concerned were merely ordered to delay their assault till Zero + 34 minutes, in order to allow time for the barrage on their right to come up into line.

NOTE

The German Flanders Position in 1917
(Sketch 12)

The opening offensive of the Flanders campaign was more clearly heralded than any other British or French offensive during the War. In one respect the obviousness of the intention was an advantage; for it caused German O.H.L. to hurry every available man and gun to Flanders instead of taking advantage of the failure of the Nivelle offensive to crush the French army by a counter-stroke.

For nearly two months the Germans, from their dominating observation areas, had carefully watched the deliberate preparations: the rapidly increasing construction of hutments, gun emplacements, tramways and roads and the gradual arrival of new infantry divisions and vast artillery reinforcements and supplies. These activities, confirmed by air reconnaissance, left them in no doubt as to British intentions. Already on the

---

[1] The Guards Division had built a life-size section of the canal to practise bridging and crossing it. A quantity of extemporised canvas-mat bridges, 62 feet long and 5 feet wide, backed by wire-netting and wooden slats, and others made of trench boards on petrol-tin piers, were prepared. They were stored ready for the day of assault in 19 tunnels, dug into the canal bank by the 173rd Tunnelling Company R.E. Arrangements were also made to build a pontoon bridge over the canal at Boesinghe for the passage of field artillery.

12th June Crown Prince Rupprecht of Bavaria, commanding the Northern Group of German Armies, described a British offensive in Flanders as " certain " ; its object, he wrote, would be to free the Belgian coast, and it would be assisted by a landing from the sea. (Rupprecht ii, pp. 195, 199.) The defence against such an operation was made more difficult owing to the narrow back area in this north-east corner of Belgium between the battlefront and the Dutch frontier, and communications were difficult. German O.H.L. appreciated that ground was consequently an important factor, and for any gain by the enemy the maximum cost of men and material was to be exacted. Every effort was to be made to hold the Belgian coast-line, as the collapse of Russia seemed imminent, and the mass of the German Armies could then be transferred to the Western Front for a major offensive.

The defence dispositions deserve special notice, as they incorporate two and a half years of German experience in defensive warfare, and it was the last occasion during the War on which such a defence, with adequate time and resources, was to be organized. The Flanders front, from the Lille–Armentières road to the Belgian coast, was held by the *Fourth Army* (General Sixt von Arnim) ; and on the 13th June, six days after the Messines battle, Colonel von Lossberg was sent to take over as its Chief of the Staff. This notable tactician had become recognized as the " defensive battle expert ". As an Army chief of staff in the Champagne battles in the autumn of 1915, during the Somme campaign in 1916, and in the Scarpe battles in April 1917, his experiences had formed the practical basis of the new German defensive battle textbook. He was now given a free hand to build up the defence organization in Flanders, and he has written in his autobiography[1] that it was the first time he had been able to plan a defence from the outset. In Champagne, on the Somme, and on the Scarpe, he had been brought in after an initial failure. The model which he took was the Hindenburg Position, and the later Wotan Position which he had himself created in front of the Wotan Line during the Scarpe battles (see " 1917 ", Vol. I).

The basic principles of his system were : a deeper defence, no deep dug-outs, and counter-attack by special reserve divisions (*Eingreif-Divisionen*),[2] which were to be close up, " that is in " the zone of enemy long-range fire, so that they, in case of need, " can at once be engaged ".

The system proved a failure in face of General Plumer's

---

[1] See Book List.
[2] See p. 44, footnote 2.

NOTE. GERMAN DEFENCE SYSTEM 143

attacks, as will be seen. In any case, it was exceedingly expensive in man-power, requiring almost as many divisions as the British used in an offensive.

A Flanders Line, begun in February, was one of the five rear (so-called "*eventuel*") positions planned for the Western Front in September 1916. It ran northwards from the Lille defences to Wervicq on the Lys and thence in front of Becelaere, Broodseinde, Passchendaele and Staden to the Belgian coast, half-way between Ostend and Middlekerke. The new Flanders Positions were now built up in front of it. The *Fourth Army* order for the defensive battle which was to be fought within this position was issued on the 27th June; and it crystallized the radical change which had taken place in German defence tactics.

The position consisted of three zones, each 2,000–3,000 yards deep: a forward zone, a battle zone and a rearward zone, the backs of which were marked by the Second (*Albrecht*), the Third (*Wilhelm*) and the Flanders Line, respectively. To avoid heavy casualties in the preliminary bombardment, the forward zone was thinly held. An assault was to be broken up by local counter-attacks with the supports and reserves of the front battalions which garrisoned it; and, more particularly, by the belt of strongpoints and fortified localities (*Stutzpunktlinie*) at the back of it. The Second Line, which was also the artillery protective line, covering the mass of the field batteries, contained the shelters for the reserves of the front regiment. Behind it again were the reserves of the front divisions, ready to advance in time to counter-attack at a moment when the assault was disorganized and exhausted after struggling through the belt of strongpoints in the forward zone. If these reserves failed to recapture the lost ground, there were larger counter-attack formations, the *Eingreif-Divisionen*, ready echeloned in depth farther back, in the rearward zone.[1]

One of these *Eingreif-Divisionen* was normally behind every pair of front divisions. Each of them had one regiment, with its own attached artillery support, in a forward assembly area in the rearward zone at the disposal of the front divisional commander; and its two remaining regiments were in assembly areas two to four thousand yards farther back again.

Behind these super counter-attack divisions, forming a first line of reserves, were other divisions in Army Group reserve ready to take the place of any of the first line ordered forward; but the main clash of the encounter-battle was expected to take place

---

[1] How the system was judged to have failed in September will be found in the Note at the end of Chapter XV.

in the battle zone, as its name implied, between the Second and Third Lines.

In short, the German conception of a defence in depth was a chequered system of strongpoints, to break up and delay an assault, backed by a succession of counter-attack formations ready to recapture any lost ground immediately. *Group Ypres*, for example, had three divisions to hold its 4-mile frontage between the Ypres–Roulers and Ypres–Staden railways. Of the 27 infantry battalions, six garrisoned the forward zone, six were in support near the second line, including the permanent garrisons of the belt of strongpoints, and fifteen were behind the Second and Third Lines ready for an immediate counter-attack. Behind the Passchendaele Ridge as a first line of reserve, were two super counter-attack divisions with advanced regiments (six battalions) near Broodseinde and Westroosebeke ready to advance into the battle zone if the front divisions failed in their task. Such a distribution of the defence force, with the bulk of it behind the forward zone, ensured that a major offensive would meet increasingly strong resistance up to the limit of the range of artillery support. In the Flanders Positions, a counter-attack organization in depth, which the Germans had been striving to achieve since the autumn of 1916, materialized.

The intention was to have belts of strongpoints and defended localities in each of the three zones so that if the forward zone had to be abandoned, the battle zone could be at once transformed into a forward zone and so on ; but the mass of labour and material required to construct the Hindenburg and Wotan Positions during the spring and summer up to early June had limited work on the Flanders Positions, so that by the end of July only the forward zone was complete with concrete battery emplacements farther back ; but a number of farm ruins in the battle zone had been converted into centres of resistance. By that time, too, a Flanders II Line (Terhand–Passchendaele), forming the back of a Flanders II Position had been marked out by wire entanglements behind the main Ypres Ridge from east of Wervicq and through Terhand to join the Flanders I Line west of Passchendaele, and a Flanders III Line (Menin–Dadizeele) was in prospect.

At a conference at *Fourth Army* headquarters on the 30th June the proposal of General Ludendorff to withdraw to the Third (*Wilhelm*) Line before the British assault was discussed. It was considered that to compel the British to make a new artillery deployment would require a withdrawal to the Flanders I Line, which implied giving up the entire system of defended localities in front of it, and no alternative fortified area in depth had yet been constructed behind. *Fourth Army* headquarters considered that the position as it stood was suitable for defence,

NOTE. GERMAN DEFENCE SYSTEM 145

both from an infantry and an artillery standpoint. The defence was to pivot on two specially strengthened features of the main Ypres Ridge—Gheluvelt plateau and Houthulst Forest; and so long as these two bastions held, no considerable British advance eastwards from the Ypres Salient was believed to be practicable. In particular, the artillery concentration behind the Gheluvelt bastion would be able to support the immediate counter-attacks by the counter-attack divisions, either to north or south, with observed fire; and in order to ensure the defence of that important plateau three counter-attack divisions were within easy reach of it. An assurance was given to O.H.L. by Colonel Lossberg that the co-operation of infantry and artillery, and the immediate participation of the counter-attack divisions, had been thoroughly prepared.

On the 6th July Crown Prince Rupprecht recorded that he had ample forces and ammunition to meet the coming offensive, and his confidence was increased by an indiscreet speech by M. Painlevé, the French War Minister, on the 7th July, which made it clear that French assistance would be of a limited character. Not content, however, he asked for more divisions and artillery in order to disorganize the British preparations by local attacks, of which one was delivered on the 10th July to capture the Nieuport bridgehead (Rupprecht ii, p. 214). His proposal, on the 11th July, to attack south of the Menin Road in order to disorganize the British artillery preparations, was, however, rejected by General Ludendorff owing to lack of sufficient troops. British threats on other parts of the front, such as the feint attacks by the First Army and the activities of the Second Army threatening Lille, had played a useful part in that respect. So, too, had the German belief that, as a part of the offensive, the British intended to violate Dutch neutrality by a landing on the coast of Holland, or at least on Walcheren Island; to meet such a move they kept two infantry divisions and one cavalry division in constant readiness in Northern Belgium throughout this period.

On the day of assault the British offensive front was faced by the five corps, called groups, of the *Fourth Army*:

Group Lille held from the southern Army boundary (the Lille–Armentières road) to Warneton on the Lys (inclusive), and was not seriously engaged;

Group Wytschaete carried on the front northwards to the Bellewaarde Lake (exclusive), north of the Ypres–Menin road, with five front divisions (*16th, 18th Reserve, 10th Bavarian, 22nd Reserve* and *6th Bavarian Reserve*);

Group Ypres, with three front divisions (*38th, 235th* and *3rd Guard*), held the adjoining sector to the Ypres–Staden railway;

Group Dixmude, with one front division (*111th*), covered the sector north of the railway to Noordschoote, a large part of which was inundated;

Group Nord, consisting of the *Marine Corps*, held the coastal sector.

As the German *Fourth Army* headquarters did not expect the British offensive to extend south of the Lys nór north of Steenstraat, *Groups Lille* and *Nord* were to find their own reserves; but behind the other three groups a first line of six reserve (*Eingreif*) divisions was assembled close to the Flanders Line. Of these, three (*207th, 12th* and *119th*) were behind *Group Wytschaete*, which had the important Gheluvelt plateau in its sector; two (*221st* and *50th Reserve*) were behind *Group Ypres*, and one (*2nd Guard Reserve*) behind the *Group Dixmude*. Behind this first line of reserve divisions, which were in *Fourth Army* reserve, was a second line of two divisions, one east of Roulers (*3rd Reserve*) and one at Thourout (*79th Reserve*), in the *Group of Northern Armies* reserve, but ready to take the place of any of the first line that might be used. Behind again was *Group Ghent* of two divisions (*23rd* and *9th Reserve*) about Ghent and Bruges which, with the *5th Bavarian Division* in Antwerp, were for defence against a possible landing on the Dutch coast.

Of these twenty divisions, four (*3rd Reserve, 12th, 119th* and *10th Bavarian*) had come from the Eastern Front during May, one (*10th*) from Verdun (*Fifth Army*) in June, and the remaining fifteen, the best available, from the Lille, Arras and Cambrai sectors (*Sixth* and *Second Armies*) during the period May to July.

CHAPTER IX

THE BATTLES OF YPRES 1917
(*continued*)

BATTLE OF PILCKEM RIDGE (*continued*)
31ST JULY
(Sketches 10, 11, 12, 13, 14)

THE CONCENTRATION[1]

Between the 19th and 23rd July Sir Douglas Haig visited all corps headquarters of the Fifth Army, and most of those of the divisions, to examine the details of their preparations; and he expressed his satisfaction. A model, about two acres in size (scale 1 : 50), had been constructed in corps training areas to show the exact lie of the ground to be crossed, and lectures, with practical demonstrations, had been given to company commanders on how to meet various situations which might arise. Each infantry brigade, too, had rehearsed its part thoroughly over taped courses on which were marked the outlines of the trenches and strongpoints to be attacked; special attention was given to the method of overcoming the " pillbox " strongpoints by parties of bombers, supported by Lewis gun fire and rifle grenades, which had proved so effective at Messines.

During the night of the 28th/29th the assaulting brigades began their forward move to the advanced assembly areas. The holding brigade on each divisional front was relieved during the next night, and on the following night the battalions detailed for the assault moved into the line.[2] Owing to the Germans having ground observation over the Ypres Salient, the assembly was hazardous, but it was accomplished uneventfully and apparently unnoticed by the enemy.

---
[1] See Sketch 10.
[2] Battalions detailed for the offensive had been brought up to establishment, averaging 35 officers and 925 other ranks. According to the now usual custom, in order to replace casualties, only an average of 16 officers and 660 other ranks went into action.

The number of men detailed for the capture of the initial objective had been calculated on a basis of 1 man for every 3 yards of front and in addition, a half or one platoon for the capture of each group of farm buildings in the intermediate area.

Under cover of darkness, during the same three nights, the tank brigades which were to participate had moved by stages from their concentration areas at Ouderdom and Oosthoek, eight miles back, to their forward assembly positions about Zillebeke (II Brigade, Colonel A. Courage), Potijze and St. Jean (III Brigade, Colonel J. Hardress-Lloyd) and Frascati, 600 yards north-west of La Brique (I Brigade, Colonel D. D'A. Baker-Carr). They were to be employed in the same manner as at Arras and Messines; but, in view of the shell-cratered state of the ground, full value could not be expected from them in this, the first, engagement of "The Tank Corps".[1] In mid-July Br.-General Elles, commanding the Corps, reported to G.H.Q. that the tanks "could function if there was not intensive shelling". When the attack was postponed until the 31st July, he pointed out to Fifth Army headquarters that the chances for tanks fell with every shell fired. He forecast on the 31st July that 50 per cent. of the tanks would reach their objective, and 48 per cent. did so. Roughly, one-third of the tanks with each corps was to assist in mopping up the German zone of strongpoints in front of the Second Line; one-third was to co-operate in the subsequent advance to the German Third Line; and the remaining third was to be in corps reserve, ready to go through to the final objective. The approach march was difficult, as most of it had to be done without lights, and heavy showers had not improved the roads and tracks;[2] but the dull, cloudy weather was an advantage, and the movement of the tanks, as of the infantry, was unmolested. All but two (134 out of 136) of the tanks reached their positions of deployment in time.[3]

Two cavalry divisions were brought up behind the flanks of the main offensive, one to about Dickebusch (2½ miles south-west of Ypres), and the other to Elverdinghe (4 miles north-west of Ypres), ready to move forward to the Passchendaele–Staden ridge; and, as the operations progressed,

---

[1] The Heavy Branch Machine Gun Corps became The Tank Corps by Royal Warrant on 27th July, 1917. It had been inspected by H.M. the King on 3rd July.

[2] North of Ypres, owing to the absence of bridges over the Yser canal, four causeways had been banked up for crossing it.

[3] The Germans made no special arrangements to deal with tanks. Scared by "Messines", they expected mines: "The opening of the enemy "attack by the explosion of mines had to be taken into account, and at "the most threatened places only sentry posts were left in the front "line" (G.O.A. xiii., p. 54.)

additional cavalry divisions were to be sent as required to these advanced areas from Merville, where, in turn, they were to be replaced from the cavalry concentration about St. Pol.

By 3 a.m. on the 31st the Second, Fifth and French First Armies were in position for the assault. Sir Douglas Haig had already, on the 29th, moved to his Advanced G.H.Q., which was in railway coaches under a row of trees in a siding of the Bergues–Proven railway line near Westcappel (19 miles W.N.W. of Ypres).

The Assault

The Second Army

In view of the dominating observation possessed by the enemy, zero hour had been fixed for sunrise, 3.50 a.m. The morning broke misty, with a moderate westerly breeze driving dense low clouds, 500 to 800 feet up, over the battle area. Under these conditions, the extensive programme for air co-operation had to be cancelled, except as regards progress reports by corps contact squadrons and the bombing of back areas by the Army squadrons.[1] It was still very dark when, on the second of zero hour, the barrage of 18-pdr. shrapnel, one round in four to burst on graze, fell upon the German front line. There it rested for six to ten minutes, whilst the leading infantry crossed the 200-300 yards of No Man's Land, after which the barrage began the forward creep of 100 yards every four minutes.

As at the Battles of the Somme 1916, the assault was made by the infantry of both Armies in waves protected by a moving shrapnel barrage, with "moppers-up" following to prevent any interference from enemy troops passed over and left behind by the first waves.

The Second Army succeeded in advancing its line in many places, in order to gain better observation and to improve the position which had been consolidated after the Messines battle.[2]

---

[1] The intended programme is given in "War in the Air", Vol. IV, Appendix VII.
[2] See Sketch 11.

The II Anzac Corps (Lieut.-General Sir A. Godley) captured the German outpost line west of the Lys, and the New Zealand Division (Major-General Sir A. H. Russell) occupied La Basse Ville. Its main street and houses were cleared with bomb and bayonet within half an hour, dug-outs being left full of dead, and beyond the town small parties of the enemy were killed as they fled along the river bank towards Warneton.[1] The 3rd Australian Division (Major-General J. Monash) occupied a number of outpost strongpoints in front of the Warneton Line about Gapaard. Farther north, the IX Corps (Lieut.-General Sir A. Gordon) advanced its line 500 yards astride the Wambeek and the Roozebeek, and down the spur between those streams. The X Corps (Lieut.-General Sir T. L. N. Morland), astride the Comines canal, took Hollebeke village and advanced 500 to 1,000 yards east of Battle Wood. The further progress of this corps was dependent on that of the Fifth Army, on its left, along the high ground of the main Ypres Ridge towards Gheluvelt, and its bombardment programme was therefore devoted principally to counter-battery work to prevent interference in that area by the German artillery group behind Zandvoorde.

The Fifth Army

The four assaulting corps of the Fifth Army, the II, XIX, XVIII and XIV, made a good start.[2] The German outpost groups were overrun as the barrage went forward, flares of thermit and oil bombs, fired by trench mortars at zero hour, helping the troops to keep direction in the dark.[3]

---

[1] Lance-Corporal L. W. Andrew (2nd Wellington Regiment) was awarded the V.C. for his gallantry in rushing a machine-gun post near Der Rooster Cabaret, on the Warneton road.

[2] See Sketch 13; for the ground, see Map 1; for the German positions, see Sketch 12. The first, second, third and fourth objectives of Sketch 10 coincide, as far as they go, with the German first, second and third lines, and Flanders I Position. The order of battle at end of the volume gives the staffs and formations engaged.

[3] The creeping barrage was formed by approximately two-thirds of the field guns in each corps sector, each gun firing at a rate of 4 rounds a minute, and at half that rate whilst forming the protective barrage, covering the consolidation of the successive objectives. The remainder of the field guns, and all the 4.5-inch howitzers, were employed in laying standing barrages, particularly on the belt of strongpoints in front of the German Second Line, lifting to more distant areas when the creeping
Continued at foot of next page.

FIFTH ARMY. 31st JULY

Ten minutes elapsed before the German defensive barrage came down; and then it was weak and erratic, except on the II Corps front, on the right, where it fell heavily on the woods in No Man's Land on the western edge of Gheluvelt plateau. By 4.40 a.m., when day had broken, the first objectives had been taken, an advance of eight hundred yards across shell-hole pitted Pilckem Ridge; only on the right, in the II Corps sector on Gheluvelt plateau, was there delay.

The leading infantry were now beyond the crest line, and had already captured the principal German observation areas overlooking the Ypres Salient. At 5.5 a.m., fresh companies deployed behind a smoke-screen in the protective barrage, and leap-frogged the leaders on their way to the next objective, a thousand yards beyond. At this stage, as in the Messines battle, strong opposition was expected from the belt of strongpoints covering the German Second Line. This included numerous farm ruins which had been converted into small forts with double walls of concrete and wide loop-holes for machine guns. With a few exceptions, however, the thorough preliminary training in the method of approach by outflanking parties, covered by volleys of rifle-grenades and Lewis gun fire into the loop-holes, and by trench mortar fire, soon forced the garrisons to surrender.[1] The first echelon of 52 tanks had at the last to be held back till daylight, owing to the difficulties of the ground. Although many tanks were ditched or slithered into deep shell-craters as they rumbled to the battlefront, nineteen of this echelon overtook the infantry and gave valuable assistance in gaining the second objective.[2]

Continued from previous page.
barrage arrived within two hundred yards. In addition, back barrages, strengthened by a proportion of 6-inch howitzers and 60-pdr. guns, were placed behind the Second Line to break up local counter-attacks and silence long-range machine-gun nests. These artillery barrages were supplemented by a machine-gun barrage, ahead of the creeping barrage, approximately 64 guns in each corps sector, from positions about five hundred yards behind the British front line.

[1] Here, as at Messines, the Mills No. 23 rifle grenade, with sure and powerful action at a range of 80 yards, proved particularly valuable. A rifle grenadier carried 12 grenades.

[2] In the II Corps sector, owing to difficult conditions, the 16 tanks of the II Tank Brigade arrived late at the front line; but 11 of the 24 tanks of the III Tank Brigade came up in the XIX Corps sector, and 8 out of 12 of the I Tank Brigade, in the XVIII Corps sector. See below for their action in the corps areas.

The II Corps (Lieut.-General Sir C. W. Jacob) had, it was generally recognized, the hardest task of the day.[1] With three divisions, the 24th, 30th and 8th, on a 3-mile frontage from Klein Zillebeke to the Ypres–Roulers railway it was to capture the entire Gheluvelt plateau.[2] The great strength of the German defence in this area, over two miles square, had been repeatedly mentioned in the Fifth Army Intelligence summaries, with full and accurate details. The three main defence zones, backed by the Second, Third and Flanders I[3] Lines, crossed it, and were each only about fifteen hundred yards deep so that the strongpoints were closer together and, the information said, had been completed to a greater depth than on the remainder of the Flanders front. A strong concentration of artillery was known to be massed in support in and around the valleys on the eastern and southern slopes, near Zandvoorde, Gheluvelt, Becelaere and Zonnebeke.

In addition to the constructional strength of the position, it had natural advantages for defence. The outpost system lay through the three woods, Shrewsbury Forest, Sanctuary Wood, and Château Wood, which covered the western extremity of the plateau. Reduced to a wilderness of fallen tree trunks, shell holes and débris, these woods formed an impassable obstacle to tanks, which would have to pass through the narrow defiles between them.[4] At the back of the forward zone, about two thousand yards behind the front line, two re-entrants, formed by the valleys of the Bassevillebeek and the Hanebeek, cut into the plateau from south and north respectively, leaving a narrow waist about

---

[1] See Sketch 14.

[2] The three divisions were faced approximately by four German regiments. The *6th Bavarian Reserve Division* with its three regiments, the *16th*, *17th* and *20th Bavarian*, in the line, had held from Lower Star Post in Shrewsbury Forest to Westhoek since 15th July, and was in course of relief by the *52nd Reserve Division* when the assault was launched. Owing to fear of deep tunnelled mines the outpost system was garrisoned by half the normal strength, and it was to be evacuated back to the Second Line strongpoints in the event of an assault, instead of being held as elsewhere. The remainder of the sector facing the II Corps was held by the flanks of two regiments, that of the *82nd Reserve* (*22nd Reserve Division*) between Lower Star Post and Klein Zillebeke, and that of the *95th* (*38th Division*) between Westhoek and the Ypres–Roulers railway.

[3] See Sketch 12 for these.

[4] It was the obstacle of these woods, it will be remembered, which had compelled the tank authorities to turn down the proposal made by Sir Douglas Haig in February to overrun Gheluvelt plateau with massed tanks. (See p. 25.)

half a mile across. The German Second Line lay across this waist and down the valleys on either side; and machine guns and pillboxes concealed in the undergrowth of the shattered woods about it could, at 400 to 700 yards' range, sweep with fire any advance down the western slopes of both valleys.

The 24th Division (Major-General L. J. Bols), on the right, using all three brigades, was to form a defensive flank across the south-western corner of the plateau, astride the Bassevillebeek re-entrant; its right was to keep touch with the X Corps (Second Army) south of the Klein Zillebeke–Zandvoorde road, while its left gained Tower Hamlets spur and the Menin road west of Gheluvelt. The right brigade, the 17th (Br.-General P. V. P. Stone) reached its objective, 1,000 yards east of Klein Zillebeke; but the 73rd Brigade (Br.-General W. J. Dugan), in the centre, which had to pass through Shrewsbury Forest, was held up by a collection of pillboxes at Lower Star Post, on a rise of ground with a wide clearing round it. The garrison of this fastness, which together with some machine-gun nests in rear resisted throughout the day, not only checked any further advance by the 73rd Brigade, but also prevented consolidation by the 17th Brigade, which had to withdraw to a more sheltered line three hundred yards short of the second objective. The 72nd Brigade (Br.-General W. F. Sweny) succeeded in reaching the Bassevillebeek, at the foot of Tower Hamlets spur; but enfilade fire from Dumbarton Wood, on its left, forced it to return up the western slope of the re-entrant to a line southwards from Bodmin Copse, also a few hundred yards short of its first objective.

The 30th Division (Major-General W. de L. Williams) had the most difficult task in the II Corps. The best available division was needed for the advance across the plateau. The 30th, mostly of Liverpool and Manchester battalions raised by Lord Derby, excellent though it was, had not yet recovered from the severe losses suffered in the Somme and Arras battles. A suggestion, made by G.H.Q., that a fresher division from the centre should replace the 30th Division was not, as time was short, carried into effect; but in compensation, a brigade of the 18th Division was allotted to it, to assist in gaining the more distant objectives. The 21st Brigade (Br.-General G. D. Goodman) was delayed at the exits of its assembly dug-outs by German shell-fire; it reached the starting line soon after the barrage had moved on, but the two leading battalions were unable to catch it up, owing to the wilderness of tree-stumps, shell-holes and barbed wire in Sanctuary Wood. Too heavily laden with equipment to negotiate such an obstacle at the pace of the barrage, the men entirely lost its protection.[1] On reaching the eastern edge of the wood they met fire from intact machine-gun nests on the Stirling Castle ridge, five hundred yards ahead. After an exhausting and costly advance over very heavy and broken ground, in which the support battalions detailed for the next objective became engaged, it was nearly 6 a.m. before the 21st Brigade won this ridge, including the castle ruins, where 44 Germans were captured. The barrage had meanwhile moved on to the second objective on the far side of the Bassevillebeek valley. Time after time attempts were made to press on without artillery support down the slope from Stirling Castle; but machine-gun fire from the belt of strongpoints and concealed emplacements a few hundred yards away across the valley checked all of them with severe losses. A line was then consolidated approximately along the first objective from Bodmin Copse northwards to Stirling Castle. In the 90th Brigade (Br.-General J. H. Lloyd) the advance was slowed by its left battalion losing direction: instead of attacking Glencorse Wood it strayed northwards into Château Wood, and made matters worse by reporting that it had captured Glencorse Wood. Finally this brigade, also, was checked, along its first objective, by machine-gun fire from the strongpoints covering the German Second Line across the waist of the plateau between Inverness Copse and Glencorse Wood.

From 5 a.m. onwards a persistent and intense German barrage fell on Sanctuary and Château Woods on a scale which showed the importance placed by the enemy on holding this high ground.[2] It caused a complete breakdown in the communication arrangements, so that no definite

---

[1] On 29th July Major-General Williams had told the Fifth Army commander that he considered the rate of the creeping barrage, 25 yards a minute, too fast for the infantry in his sector and advised 20 yards a minute. The following morning he repeated the request for the alteration to the corps commander, who replied that it was too late.

[2] On the three final days of the intense phase of the counter-battery programme against the German artillery concentration on and behind Gheluvelt plateau visibility had been poor; and now, on the battle day itself, the counter-batteries had to fire blind with little aircraft assistance owing to the low clouds, and with no ground observation.

information about the progress of the battle was known at divisional or corps headquarters till after 10 a.m.[1] At 10.40 a.m., thirty minutes after the barrage had begun its forward creep from the second to the third objective, Major-General Williams sent a message to II Corps headquarters at Hoogeraaf, south of Poperinghe, that the situation was vague—" apparently we are not on the Black [Second] " Line anywhere, but hold the Blue [First] Line intact ".[2]

Fortunately Major-General Williams had suspected from various reports received up to 9 a.m. that the second objective had not been reached ; and he had mentioned this to Major-General R. P. Lee (18th Division), whose 54th Brigade was to carry on the advance in his sector from the third to the fourth objective. That brigade was recalled ; but the other units of the 18th Division, two battalions of the 89th Brigade (Br.-General W. W. Norman), attached, and two of the 53rd Brigade (Br.-General H. W. Higginson), detailed to take the third objective, had already gone forward. Delayed and losing a number of men by the constant German shelling of Sanctuary Wood, they missed the barrage which had already moved on to the third objective by the time they reached the first at about 8 a.m. Renewed efforts to advance both down the slope to the Bassevillebeek and across the waist of the plateau without artillery support were in vain. Units were by this time so mixed up on the western edge of the plateau that eight different battalions were represented in the dug-outs near Clapham Junction on the Menin road. On the left, a slight but expensive advance carried the line forward three hundred yards to the cross-

---

[1] Telephone cables back from forward artillery observers and from the advanced signal stations were cut almost without exception ; wireless failed owing to the persistent shelling and damage to instruments ; power buzzers were found unworkable owing to the damp ground ; and visual signalling was very difficult owing to the bad light. Pigeons and messengers alone remained as a means of communication back from the front line ; many of the pigeons sent failed to reach their destination and, although runners did excellent work, some hours necessarily elapsed before they could cover the bad ground back to a telephone headquarters.

[2] Previous to this, at 9.50 a.m., a message had been received from a contact aeroplane that it had been fired at by machine guns and rifles in Inverness Copse (which was short of the Second Line) and that no British troops were seen nor answers given to signals thereabouts. Messages sent by pigeon from the front line near Stirling Castle—at 8.30 a.m. to 30th Division headquarters stating the position, and at 9 a.m. to 30th Division and divisional artillery headquarters asking that the barrage be re-opened from the Blue to the Black Line—did not reach their destination.

tracks south of Westhoek, where it was again halted by machine-gun fire from Glencorse Wood.[1]

The 8th Division (Major-General W. C. G. Heneker), the left division of the II Corps, also had trouble. In the initial assault Bellewaarde Lake had been captured by a simultaneous move up the spurs on either side of it, whilst keeping its banks under a bombardment of thermit shells from trench mortars. Beyond, however, the barrage was very nearly lost by the infantry as it struggled towards the higher ground through the tangle of fallen trees and barbed wire in Château Wood. The resource and initiative of a company commander were largely responsible for the advance being kept going.[2] The first objective, on the open ground of the Bellewaarde ridge beyond the wood, was occupied in time to enable the support battalions of the two assaulting brigades to follow the barrage through to the second objective. This objective, reached about 6 a.m., was on a forward slope, and both brigades soon came under heavy machine-gun fire from concealed emplacements on the opposite side of the Hanebeek valley, at 500–800 yards' range, and also from Glencorse Wood, on the right flank, which the 30th Division had failed to take.[3] In such circumstances the new line, southwards beyond Westhoek village, was found to be untenable, so that the 24th Brigade (Br.-General H. W. Cobham), and the right of the 23rd Brigade (Br.-General G. W. St. G. Grogan), but not the left, had to be brought back about five hundred yards to the shelter of the Westhoek ridge.

---

[1] The reserve battalion of the *239th Reserve Regiment* from Becelaere arrived in Inverness Copse about 9 a.m. with orders to recapture the Stirling Castle high ground, but, owing to the protective British barrage and machine-gun fire, they were unable to do more than reinforce the garrison of the Second Line. Half the support battalion of this regiment had sheltered in a long tunnel dug under the Menin road, west of Inverness Copse, but when the assault began the tunnel was blown in by the Germans.

[2] 2nd Lieut. (acting Captain) T. R. Colyer-Ferguson (2/Northamptonshire), with six men was able to keep close to the barrage, and reached the Bellewaarde ridge (first objective) ahead of the rest. The garrison withdrew on a wide front, and with a captured machine gun he killed 35 of a party of Germans who counter-attacked, and dispersed the remainder. He was awarded the V.C. for " an amazing record of dash, gallantry and " skill for which no reward can be too great having regard to the importance " of the position won ". This officer was killed shortly afterwards.

[3] Major-General Heneker, in his proposals for the assault, wrote on 10th July : " I would point out that the whole success of my attack depends " on the 30th Division on my right ; should they be held up at any point, " the remainder of my advance, i.e., beyond the second objective, will be " seriously exposed to commanding enfilade fire from the Stirling Castle– " Polygon Wood ridge ".

The II Tank Brigade had been unable to improve the situation on the plateau. Its difficulties were due primarily to the failure to gain an area of deployment east of Sanctuary Wood and other near-lying woods by a preliminary operation, as intended by Tank Corps headquarters, before attempting a deeper advance. The failure of the 30th Division to capture the strongpoint immediately northeast of Clapham Junction was most unfortunate. Many efforts by heavy batteries to destroy this gigantic pillbox, which commanded the length of the main approach route along the Menin road from Hooge, had been in vain, and approaching tanks had been knocked out one after another by an anti-tank gun within it. Seventeen derelict tanks soon dotted the ground in this area, later to be known as " the " tank graveyard ". Of the total 48 fighting tanks detailed to assist the II Corps, only 19 reached the front line and came into action ; and, after fighting with great gallantry and inflicting considerable losses on the enemy, all but one became casualties.[1]

The XIX Corps (Lieut.-General H. E. Watts) had no wooded obstacles to delay its assault, but the gentle slopes of Pilckem Ridge had become a barren expanse of shell-holes.[2] The 15th (Scottish) Division (Major-General H. F. Thuillier) reached the second objective, for the most part up to the barrage. Its right brigade, the 44th (Br.-General F. J. Marshall), was in touch with the 8th Division

---

[1] Of the 16 tanks of the first echelon, only 4 had succeeded in running the gauntlet of the gaps in the woods and reaching the foremost infantry, 4 being knocked out in the Hooge gap alone by anti-tank guns. Of the 24 in the second echelon detailed to assist in the capture of the third objective, 14 had come into action ; a proportion of these had travelled along the edges of Dumbarton Wood, Inverness Copse and Glencorse Wood, where they had silenced several machine guns and broken up assemblies for local counter-attacks ; but they were unable to deal with a number of machine guns concealed in low concrete emplacements with loop holes at ground level, and owing to the fire from these guns, attempts by the infantry to follow them had failed. Of the 8 tanks of the third echelon detailed for the fourth objective, only 1 came into action, and that, too, became involved in the fighting between the first and second objectives. Of the 52 fighting and supply tanks of the brigade which had started from the assembly areas, 19 were hit by shells or anti-tank guns, and 22 were ditched or broke down mechanically.

[2] See Sketch 15. The XIX Corps was opposed approximately by the inner flank regiments of the *38th* and *235th Divisions* (*94th and 456th*, respectively). The *38th* completed the relief of the *17th Division* on 28th July, and the *235th* had taken over from the *233rd Division* by the 27th.

(II Corps) on the Ypres–Roulers railway; and the 46th Brigade (Lieut.-Colonel K. J. Buchanan, acting) had its left on the Steenbeek, though a stiff fight for the redoubt in Frezenberg village—where two tanks, working past either flank, saved the infantry heavy losses—had caused delay till after 9 a.m. The 55th (1st West Lancashire) Division (Major-General H. S. Jeudwine) had, as planned, gained a foothold east of the Steenbeek from Pommern Redoubt to within six hundred yards of St. Julien; but only after stiff fighting. Square Farm, an extensive ruin with vaulted cellars, in the belt of strongpoints, had held up the advance of the 165th Brigade (Br.-General L. B. Boyd-Moss) till after 9 a.m., when, after several assaults, it was captured with 130 prisoners. Pommern Redoubt, too, in the second objective, though entered at 6.5 a.m., held out in places for another three hours; and Bank Farm, also in the German Second Line, held out until the arrival of a tank. The 166th Brigade (Br.-General F. G. Lewis), in spite of a number of costly fights against machine-gun nests on the way, had reached its objective up to the barrage; but Spree Farm, another strongpoint in the German Second Line, gave trouble until two tanks succeeded in silencing its machine guns.[1]

After pausing an hour on reaching the first objective, the two northern corps, the XVIII and XIV, together with the French First Army, which had advanced successfully on the left, were, in order to form the northern defensive flank, to move forward to the Steenbeek, whose valley, with marshes bordering the stream, and with its drainage upset by shelling, offered one of the bad patches of the battlefield.[2] Covered by a smoke-screen, support battalions of the leading brigade had come forward over the crest of Pilckem Ridge,

---

[1] One tank reached Border House, beyond the objective and 400 yards south-east of St. Julien, at 7.50 a.m.

[2] See Sketch 16. The 4 assault divisions of the 2 northern corps of the Fifth Army were faced by approximately 4 German regiments in the line: *455th (235th Division)*, *392nd* and *100th (23rd Reserve Division)* and *73rd (111th Division)*. These divisions had two regiments in the line and one in reserve behind the Flanders I Line. Each regiment in the line had one battalion in the forward zone, one in support about the Second (*Albrecht*) Line and the third in reserve behind the Third (*Wilhelm*) Line. The two regiments of the *23rd Reserve Division* were in course of relief by the *3rd Guard Division* when the assault was launched.

and so accurate was the shrapnel barrage, flicking up the earth along a uniform and unmistakeable line, that they were able to follow safely at fifty yards' distance ; but the heavy showers of the preceding days had made the ground very slippery, and it was hard work to keep up the pace. The gentle slope down to the Steenbeek, beyond which outposts were to be established, has no marked irregularities ; and the stream itself, about fifteen feet wide between low banks, was at the moment shallow and, in spite of mud, fordable.

The two divisions of the XVIII Corps (Lieut.-General Sir I. Maxse) established a forward line along the stream on a frontage of 3,000 yards, from St. Julien (inclusive) to within three hundred yards of the Pilckem–Langemarck road. The 39th Division (Major-General G. J. Cuthbert) occupied St. Julien with its 116th Brigade (Br.-General M. L. Hornby), the 13/R. Sussex taking prisoner 17 officers and 205 other ranks from cellars and dug-outs.[1] Parties of the 117th Brigade (Br.-General G. A. Armytage), covered by a barrage from Stokes mortars and by rifle grenades, outflanked and rushed the entrances of the three pillboxes at Regina Cross, bayoneted the machine-gunners and killed or captured thirty Germans. The Alberta strongpoint threatened to hold up the advance ; but two tanks which arrived opportunely, crushed the uncut wire and by their fire drove the garrison to cover until dealt with by the infantry. By 8 a.m. both brigades had reached their objective, and their front companies were consolidating a defence along the eastern bank of the Steenbeek.

The 51st (Highland) Division (Major-General G. M. Harper) met with stiffer resistance, but mopped up large numbers of Germans crouching in shell-holes throughout the forward zone.[2] The capture of McDonald's Farm by the 152nd Brigade (Br.-General H. P. Burn) was a good example of infantry and tank co-operation ; a shower of

---

[1] Two tanks assisted in the capture of the village and knocked out a battery near by. During the advance, 2nd Lieut. D. G. W. Hewitt (14/Hampshire) was awarded the V.C. for his courage and leadership, despite a severe wound. He was subsequently killed by a sniper while the position was being consolidated.

[2] A battalion of the *Lehr Regiment* (*3rd Guard Division*) was taking over the forward zone from the front battalion of the *392nd Regiment* at the time of the assault.

rifle grenades from two platoons into the building, and six shells from a tank on the right, brought out the German survivors, 70 being taken prisoner and a 4.2-inch howitzer and two machine guns captured. The arrival of a tank also assisted in silencing machine guns in Ferdinand Farm, and in dispersing parties of Germans in shell-hole positions nearby.[1] On approaching the Steenbeek, machine-gun fire from the opposite bank swept the advance, and the intention to establish an outpost bridgehead on the eastern bank at Maison du Rasta had to await a better opportunity.[2] Great courage and initiative were shown by individual officers and men in dealing with the increased opposition met by the 153rd Brigade (Lieut.-Colonel H. G. Hyslop, acting)[3] throughout its advance. Machine guns in Cane Wood and Rudolphe Farm caused heavy casualties before they were cleared out and 70 prisoners taken. Resistance from François Farm and from a blockhouse in a cemetery beyond it added to the delay; but by 10.30 a.m. outpost groups had been established by the 1/6th Black Watch on the rising ground east of the stream.

The two divisions of the XIV Corps (Lieut.-General Lord Cavan) on either side of the Ypres–Staden railway had another eighteen hundred yards to reach the Steenbeek, and were each to use their reserve brigade for the final eight hundred yards. The 38th (Welsh) Division (Major-General C. G. Blackader) was also faced by a fresh garrison.[4] In the

---

[1] Of the second echelon of 12 tanks of the I Tank Brigade which were to assist the XVIII Corps beyond the second objective, five came into action successfully.

[2] German machine guns sixty yards beyond the river were playing on the right battalion, the 1/6th Gordon Highlanders, and Private G. McIntosh of the battalion crossed the river alone, without orders, armed with a revolver and a Mills grenade and worked round behind a machine-gun emplacement. He threw the bomb into it, killed two Germans, wounded a third and brought back the two light machine guns. He was awarded the V.C.

Sergeant A. Edwards (1/6th Seaforth Highlanders) was awarded the V.C. for locating and leading his men against a machine-gun emplacement, killing all the team and capturing the gun. Although twice wounded, he continued to show a high example of coolness and determination in the subsequent advance and consolidation of the ground gained.

[3] Br.-General A. I. Gordon had been killed by a shell on the 29th while inspecting his assembly trenches. Br.-General A. T. Beckwith assumed command of the brigade on 2nd August.

[4] The *Guard Fusilier Regiment (3rd Guard Division)*, popularly known in Berlin, its hometown, as " The Cockchafers ", had completed the relief of the *100th Reserve Regiment* on the previous day.

initial stage the 114th Brigade (Br.-General T. O. Marden) had heavy losses before it took the pillbox and defended shell-craters near the Iron Cross road junction, where 20 of the garrison were killed, and 40 prisoners and three machine guns taken. The 113th Brigade (Br.-General L. A. E. Price-Davies), after capturing the several concrete machine-gun nests in Pilckem village,[1] suffered severely, particularly in officers, from machine-gun fire from the railway embankment on its left flank. Although the barrage was lost, the objective was gained by short rushes. Of the two battalions of the reserve brigade, the 115th (Br.-General G. Gwyn-Thomas), the 11/South Wales Borderers reached the stream in good time, by 9.53 a.m. A pillbox on the east bank with a garrison of 2 officers and 30 other ranks in the ruins of a roadside inn, Au Bon Gite, was captured as well as two adjacent strongpoints.[2] The 17/R. Welch Fusiliers was delayed at the start by machine-gun fire from the left flank. Fighting its way most gallantly without artillery support, it reached the stream at 12.30 p.m. with its strength reduced to 4 officers and two hundred other ranks.

North of the railway the Guards Division (Major-General G. P. T. Feilding) had taken full advantage of its occupation, on the 27th, of the eastern bank of the canal. Shortly after zero hour the German artillery had concentrated upon and destroyed most of the extemporized bridges over the canal; but others, re-made from the broken material and wire-matting, were placed by 5.20 a.m., in time for the support battalions to cross and deploy behind the smoke barrage for their advance to the third objective. The shrapnel and the machine-gun barrage, the combined effect of which was described as " magnificent", was closely followed. The 2nd Guards Brigade (Br.-General J.

---

[1] During this action Corporal J. L. Davies (13/R. Welch Fusiliers) gained the V.C. He advanced through the barrage and, single-handed, attacked a machine-gun emplacement which was causing serious losses, bayoneted one of the crew and brought in another with the captured gun. Although wounded, he then led a bombing party to assault a defended house. He died of wounds received during the engagement.

[2] Sergeant I. Rees (11/South Wales Borderers) gained the V.C. on this occasion. He worked round the flank of and rushed from twenty yards a machine gun which was inflicting many casualties, shot one of the team and bayoneted another. He then bombed a large concrete shelter, killing 5 and capturing 30 prisoners, including 2 officers, in addition to an undamaged machine gun.

Ponsonby), on the right, which had already suffered considerable casualties from machine guns in pillboxes both in Artillery Wood and Wood 15[1] before they were mastered, was temporarily checked by fire from emplacements on the north side of the railway embankment. This opposition was overcome with the help of the support companies, three officers and 50 other ranks being captured thereabouts.[2] The 3rd Guards Brigade (Br.-General Lord Henry Seymour) had to hold back its left, as the French 601st Regiment was checked in front of Colonel's Wood; but elsewhere the Guards Division occupied its entire sector of the third objective in the allotted time, soon after 8 a.m. Two battalions of the 1st Guards Brigade (Br.-General G. D. Jeffreys) had meanwhile moved up and, at 8.50 a.m., they passed through towards the Steenbeek, eight hundred yards distant. The right of the 2/Grenadier Guards, affected by the check to the 38th Division, south of the railway, was held up within eighty yards of the stream by machine-gun fire which caused considerable losses. The remainder of that battalion and the 2/Coldstream Guards, on the left, reached the stream by 9.30 a.m., and established outposts on the eastern bank. The barrage had become thin and ragged at this stage, and as the Langemarck–Weidendreft road was evidently strongly held, the intention to push out patrols towards it was abandoned.[3]

The French First Army, attacking with two divisions of its I Corps, had carried out the advance in touch with the left of the Guards Division. The machine-gun nests in Colonel's Wood, near their point of junction, were not cleared till about 2.30 p.m., but on the remainder of the 3,000-yard frontage, northward to Steenstraat and the

---

[1] Sergeant R. Bye (1/Welsh Guards) gained the V.C. here. On his own initiative, he reached one of the blockhouses and put the garrison out of action, and later, after the attack had passed on, he volunteered to take charge of a party to clear up a line of blockhouses, which he did, showing remarkable initiative, and took many prisoners.

[2] Private T. Whitham (1/Coldstream Guards) was awarded the V.C. for conspicuous bravery here. On his own initiative, he worked round an enemy machine gun which was enfilading the battalion on the right. Moving from shell-hole to shell-hole under heavy fire, he captured it, including an officer and two other ranks. His action saved many lives and enabled the advance to be continued.

[3] The rallying line of the *73rd Regiment* along this road had in fact been reinforced by two sections of the divisional (*111th*) machine-gun brigade.

inundations, the objective was gained, and in places passed, the outskirts of Bixschoote being reached.[1]

The capture of the second objective had been the signal for a forward movement by a number of field batteries. On the XVIII Corps front, six field batteries had advanced and were in action by 9 a.m. alongside the eleven forward "silent" batteries; similarly on the XIV Corps front, three brigades of field artillery were ready about the same hour to give closer support for the consolidation of the defensive flank along the Steenbeek and, if necessary, to support a further advance. In the sectors of each division, too, a squadron of cavalry was to advance, as soon as the second objective had been captured, to reconnoitre ahead of the foremost infantry and exploit any local success. Some of these units did attempt to reach the Steenbeek; but most of their horses were killed in a gallant effort to carry out their orders. The squadron, 1/King Edward's Horse, in the sector of the 51st Division advanced as far as a hundred and fifty yards short of the Steenbeek before the survivors dismounted and took up a position near Ferdinand Farm, where they remained till the following morning.

Otherwise in the XIX, XVIII and XIV Corps all had gone as well as the most optimistic could have expected; but at the vital place, Gheluvelt plateau, progress had been small.

---

[1] For a detailed account of the French assault see F.O.A. v. (ii.), pp. 670-5.

CHAPTER X

THE BATTLES OF YPRES 1917 (*continued*)

BATTLE OF PILCKEM RIDGE (*concluded*)
(Sketches 11, 12, 14, 15, 16)

THE MAIN OFFENSIVE CONTINUED

Up to about 9.30 a.m. (31st July), the assault had proceeded according to plan, except in a small sector south of the Menin road. The capture of the observation areas on the western edge of Gheluvelt plateau and along the entire crest line of Pilckem Ridge was a valuable achievement. The Germans were now deprived almost entirely of observation over the Ypres district.[1] The menace which every British soldier in the Salient had felt for over two years was at an end, and the situation reversed. While men and traffic could now move about the Ypres Salient in daylight with comparative impunity, British ground observers could see deep into the German position.

As at Messines, the thinly held German forward zone, over a mile in depth, had been captured with little loss. During the further advance, the casualties, however, had increased; but local counter-attacks by support and reserve units of the German front divisions had been dispersed by the protective barrage and by machine-gun fire, particularly from the many pillboxes about the original German Second Line, which had been converted at once for fire in the opposite direction.[2] But the defence showed no sign of cracking; on the contrary, the reports bore out the German text-book statement, emphasized in Fifth Army Intelligence summaries during the two previous months, that the resistance would probably stiffen the deeper the attack penetrated.

It must be noted that if the operational decisions of the Paris Conference of the 4th May had been followed, the

---

[1] They still held a small area of high ground near Clapham Junction, on the Menin road, from which part of the Ypres area could be seen.
[2] After one of these local counter-attacks two hundred German dead were counted in front of the second objective north of Frezenberg in the sector of the 165th Brigade alone.

day's fighting would have ended at this stage.[1] Leaving outpost groups, machine-gun nests and artillery observers in the forward area, the mass of the assaulting brigades should have been withdrawn behind the original front line. Before the next step of another mile into the German position was taken, the great advantage already gained would have been consolidated, artillery moved forward and communications laid. The G.H.Q. plan had allowed two days for this preparatory work after the capture of the observation areas; and the same recommendation had been made by the Operations Branch G.H.Q. on the 25th June.[2] According to the Fifth Army scheme, however, the main offensive by the two southern corps, the II and XIX, was to be resumed within a few hours, as soon as the northern defensive flank had been formed, and events seemed to justify such an aggressive course : the advantage gained was to be exploited at once. At the time-table hour, 10.10 a.m. (Zero+6 hours 20 minutes), the barrage again began its forward creep.

Meanwhile, in the II Corps, the reserve brigade of the 8th Division, the 25th (Br.-General C. Coffin), had moved up to the Westhoek ridge, and was ready at 10.10 a.m. to carry on the attack to the third objective.[3] After advancing a few hundred yards, the leading battalions were checked by machine-gun fire from across the re-entrant and from Glencorse Wood, like the 24th and 23rd Brigades had been, and had to fall back approximately to their starting line, the right in touch with the 30th Division about five hundred yards south of Westhoek. Even then, it was due to the presence in the front line and "very gallant conduct "under the heaviest fire" of Br.-General Clifford Coffin, which earned him the Victoria Cross, that this line of shell-holes was held in the face of continuous machine-gun and rifle fire.[4] The 24th and 30th Divisions were also unable to

---
[1] See p. 24.
[2] See pp. 128-9.
[3] See Sketch 14.
[4] Major-General Heneker, in his subsequent report on the battle, wrote that he considered "the position chosen for the Black Line [second "objective] as a halting place was wrong. Being on a forward slope to "the enemy, it involved too many casualties to consolidate, and the "troops attacking the Green Line [third objective] suffered heavy casual-"ties as they crossed the Westhoek ridge and went down the slope".
Continued at foot of next page.

make any progress. The deadlock on the entire II Corps front was apparent, and Lieut.-General Jacob, at 1.30 p.m., informed Fifth Army headquarters accordingly.

The divisions of the XIX Corps[1] made very good progress. The reserve brigade of each division had now to advance about another mile into the German position in order to reach the third objective, which included the German Third Line. This lay on the reverse slope of the Zonnebeke–St. Julien spur, which branched out north-westwards from the main Ypres Ridge diagonally across the corps front beyond the Steenbeek. At 10.10 a.m., when the barrage resumed its forward creep, the two infantry brigades, covering the corps frontage of 3,000 yards, followed close behind, each with two battalions leading.[2] About this time the clouds cleared and the sun broke through for a short time, it became oppressively hot and sultry, and a mist from the damp ground soon made visibility difficult again.

The 45th Brigade (Br.-General W. H. L. Allgood), covering the front of the 15th Division, had its right exposed at the outset owing to the check to the 8th Division. As a result of heavy machine-gun fire from that flank, its right, the 6/7 R. Scots Fusiliers, after heavy losses, had to halt for cover about Potsdam House, west of the Hanebeek; but the left companies of the battalion succeeded in reaching Bremen Redoubt, near Zevenkote in the German Third Line, about 11.30 a.m. The 6/Cameron Highlanders, on the left, out of effective range of this fire, pressed on relentlessly, and at 11.45 a.m., after a sharp fight for the defences on Hill 37, a dominant feature of the spur, where 150 prisoners were taken, gained the objective; patrols then occupied Dochy and Otto Farms beyond the Zonnebeke–Langemarck road.

Continued from previous page.
This comment applies equally to the first objective on the whole II Corps front. The same report asked that " all lines to be consolidated for defence " should, as far as possible, be on reverse slopes to the enemy ". The usual British and German practice was to have an observation line near the crest or on the forward slope to the enemy, and the main line of defence on the reverse slope.

[1] See Sketch 15.

[2] By 9.25 a.m. thirteen field batteries had advanced to near the original British front line to give closer support; but the barrage itself was noticeably thinner.

The 164th Brigade (Br.-General C. I. Stockwell), advancing on the front of the 55th Division, met stubborn resistance as it moved up the slope. Its sector was a bad patch in the artillery preparation, for most of the strongpoints were still intact; and, although the majority of the German field batteries had been withdrawn during the long halt along the second objective, several still remained in concrete emplacements near these defended localities and continued to fire into the advancing lines. On the right, the 1/4 Loyal North Lancashire was delayed at Somme Farm and again at Gallipoli Farm, at both of which places a German battery had to be captured by platoon outflanking attacks before the garrison capitulated. Hill 35, another feature of the spur, was crossed and farther on, at Kansas Cross in the German Third Line, a battery which continued to fire point-blank at a hundred yards was rushed, and a number of prisoners taken.[1] The 2/5 Lancashire Fusiliers, on the left, was also held up by a battery and machine guns at Pond Farm early in the attack and lost the barrage; but Pond Farm, and Hindu Cottage beyond it, were both occupied after bitter fighting. As the attack reached the back slope of the spur beyond Hindu Cottage, it met strong machine-gun fire from Schuler Farm, another intact strong point with a supporting field battery near the Zonnebeke–Langemarck road. This fire at close range disorganized the advance, until the battalion commander personally rallied the foremost companies, which took the place by envelopment.[2] A line of wire and trenches, covering some empty battery positions west of the road between Schuler Farm and Kansas Cross, was mistaken for the German Third Line, really six hundred yards farther on, and the surviving Fusiliers stayed there; but the platoon detailed to occupy advanced posts on the Gravenstafel spur crossed the valley and reached Aviatik Farm, where a German officer and 50 other ranks were taken prisoner. Both battalions of the brigade had already lost more than half their strength, and the two support battalions had merged into them.

---

[1] Corporal T. F. Mayson (1/4 King's Own) was awarded the V.C. for his remarkable valour and initiative in destroying a machine gun and its crew single-handed on two occasions in this advance.

[2] Lieut.-Colonel B. Best Dunkley, 2/5 Lancashire Fusiliers, was awarded the V.C. for conspicuous bravery. The *London Gazette* added that it was doubtful if the left of the brigade would have reached its objective but for his determined leadership. He died of wounds received in the action.

Simultaneously with the advance of the two brigades of the XIX Corps from the second objective at 10.10 a.m., the 39th Division, the right division of the XVIII Corps, had sent forward three battalions of its reserve brigade, the 118th (Br.-General E. H. C. P. Bellingham), to connect the left of the main attack with the defensive front along the Steenbeek. The 1/6 Cheshire, after crossing the Zonnebeke–Langemarck road, came under heavy machine-gun fire from the right rear, owing to the delay of the 164th Brigade. Despite heavy losses, it pressed on to the German Third Line west of Aviatik Farm, at the extremity of Gravenstafel spur, where a large number of Germans behind a mass of uncut wire were holding up their hands in surrender. The 1/1 Hertfordshire, advancing through St. Julien, suffered considerable casualties from enfilade fire from its left flank, before reaching the objective east of the St. Julien–Poelcappelle road. The 4/5 Black Watch continued the line west of the road from Triangle Farm to the right of the 51st Division on the Steenbeek.

The battered condition of the banks of the Steenbeek had hindered the progress of the second echelon of 24 tanks of the III Tank Brigade, detailed to assist the advance of the XIX Corps to the third objective. Only nine came into action, and they were too late to take part in the actual assault.[1]

The German Counter-Attacks[2]

By noon the deadlock in the II Corps sector had narrowed down the main offensive from the intended 7,000-yard frontage to one of 3,500 yards, held by the XIX Corps, between the Ypres–Roulers railway and St. Julien, whence the XVIII and XIV Corps formed a defensive flank. The responsibility for the decision as to whether the opposition was sufficiently weak to justify a continuation of the offensive to the main ridge (fourth objective) on either side of Broodseinde had been left to divisional commanders; but a long delay occurred before definite information that the third objective had been reached was received at the respective

---

[1] Two tanks with the XIX Corps reached the third objective, one at Kansas Cross and another at Winnipeg; and one with the XVIII Corps reached it at Springfield.

[2] See Sketches 16 (on which the counter-attacks are shown), 14, 15.

divisional headquarters, west of Vlamertinghe, six miles back.[1] In the XIX Corps, as in the II Corps, signal communications had been seriously affected by the bad visibility, and information from the leading brigades was limited to messages by runner, which took one to two hours to reach cable-heads in the original British front line.[2] Advanced signal stations had been opened at both the first and second objectives by 10 a.m.; but the cables were so constantly broken either by traffic or by shells that they were unreliable. The results obtained by contact aircraft, too, had been disappointing, for, apart from difficulties of visibility during most of the day, the foremost infantry were disinclined to show their positions, as ordered, by flares, as these, too often, either brought down enemy artillery fire upon them, or gave their positions away to the German contact patrols in the neighbourhood.

In the XIX Corps, the check to the 45th Brigade near Potsdam House before 11 a.m. was not known to 15th Division headquarters till 1.13 p.m., when the arrangements for the advance to the fourth objective in its sector were at once postponed. Information of the arrival of the 164th Brigade at the third objective was not received at 55th Division headquarters till 2.30 p.m., when orders were at once given to the two battalions on the first objective to close up to the second objective preparatory to pushing through to the fourth objective, as previously arranged.[3] At 3.10 p.m. these instructions by the divisional commanders were overruled by General Gough, who, on hearing that the third objective had been reached on the XIX Corps front, ordered it to be

---

[1] Preparations had been made to move the two divisional headquarters to Ypres (15th Division) and to dug-outs in the canal bank north of the town (55th Division) as soon as the third objective was consolidated.

[2] Messages by pigeon from the tanks which reached the third objective gave little information beyond that of their own position.

[3] The orders for the next advance, to the fourth objective, on the XIX Corps front were that the protective barrage in front of the third objective was to cease at 12.10 p.m. (Zero+8 hours 20 minutes), when infantry patrols, accompanied by troops of the North Irish Horse, were to advance and occupy positions on the high ground of the Passchendaele ridge, north-west of Keerselaarhoek (15th Division), and about Wolf Farm on the Wallemolen spur beyond the Stroombeek (55th Division). To support these patrols, the two battalions of each division which had captured the first objective in the first stage of the assault were to advance to the second objective as soon as the third objective was reported captured, from which they would reinforce, and later relieve, the patrols on the fourth objective.

reinforced by all available troops of the corps. The execution of this order was anticipated by the course of events.

As a consequence of the delay in communication, the three advanced brigades of the XIX and XVIII Corps had received neither reinforcement nor support for some hours after their arrival at or near their third objective, about 11 a.m. They were widely strung out, owing to heavy casualties, and ammunition was running short. The protective artillery barrage ceased soon after mid-day, and the few tanks which had reached the third objective had returned to their base as ordered.

Air reports gave no warning to Army or corps headquarters of the approach of the larger German counter-attack formations from behind the Broodseinde–Passchendaele ridge.[1] The earliest news came from a forward artillery observer with the 45th Brigade, who, on approaching the Bremen Redoubt, near Zevenkote in the German Third Line, at 11.30 a.m., saw, two thousand yards ahead, " a vast amount of " German infantry going along the Passchendaele Ridge " ; but his message did not reach 15th Division headquarters till 12.53 p.m. From 1 p.m. onwards messages began to arrive from ground observers all along the battle front that the enemy was massing for a counter-attack. Soon afterwards drizzling rain set in, and messages ceased. The supporting artillery did not yet know the exact line which had been gained, forward artillery observers lost touch with the batteries, and observers along the second objective could no longer see what was happening ahead.

About 2 p.m. an intense German artillery barrage fell upon all that part of the German Third Line between the Ypres–Roulers railway and east of St. Julien—that is mainly the

---

[1] As no adequate air programme had replaced the original one abandoned in the early hours owing to bad visibility, corps squadrons had confined their action to reporting the progress of the infantry, whilst the Army squadrons roved over the German back areas machine-gunning and bombing ground targets, such as troops on the move, transport and airfields, at the pilots' discretion. Although this work was done in a most courageous and effective manner, as the German regimental histories admit, the messages sent back gave no clue to the probable relation to the battle of the enemy formations encountered, and no advantage was taken of the clear period of visibility before midday to search the back area for the expected advance of the counter-attack divisions. The need for a closer co-operation between the squadrons of the Royal Flying Corps and the ground operations was emphasized by Major-General Trenchard in a circular letter after the battle.

THE GERMAN COUNTER-ATTACKS. 31ST JULY

XIX Corps front. Battalion diaries state that it was mainly enfilade fire from the right flank, from behind Zonnebeke and from Gheluvelt plateau. Shortly afterwards waves of German infantry approached from front and flanks.[1]

The first clash came against the left flank of the break-in. The left and centre of the 118th Brigade (4/5 Black Watch and 1/1 Hertfordshire) of the 39th Division, astride the St. Julien–Poelcappelle road, unable to withstand the onslaught, fell back gradually to their second starting-line east of the Steenbeek, and in front of St. Julien.[2] The right of the brigade, the 1/6 Cheshire on the extremity of Gravenstafel spur, was thereby exposed, and swung back its left flank. A number of prisoners who had previously held up their hands in surrender took advantage of this movement to pick up their rifles again and open fire. Any aggressive action on their part, however, was promptly averted owing to the intensity of the German barrage, falling at this moment on friend and foe alike along the German Third Line; the Germans took shelter from it, while the Cheshire, losing heavily, withdrew gradually towards St. Julien and Border House.

The withdrawal of the 118th Brigade exposed the left flank of the 164th Brigade (55th Division) and at 2.15 p.m. Br.-General Stockwell ordered a defensive flank to be formed from Schuler Farm back to Border House; but just as this movement was beginning six waves of German infantry appeared over the crest of Zonnebeke spur. They were preceded by a barrage directed by Very-pistol rockets fired by the leading infantry, whilst, in addition, three aircraft cruised low along the line of the defenders, machine-gunning

---

[1] The information received at German *Fourth Army* headquarters by 11 a.m. was that British troops were advancing towards the Third Line on a wide front between Zonnebeke and Langemarck. The two *Eingreif* divisions in *Group Ypres* sector were thereupon ordered to counter-attack against the flanks of the break-in, astride the Zonnebeke–Winnipeg and the Poelcappelle–St. Julien roads.

[2] The counter-attack here was delivered by two regiments of the *50th Reserve Division*, the northern counter-attack division of *Group Ypres*; the *231st Reserve* north of the Poelcappelle–St. Julien road, and the *230th Reserve* south of it. From their assembly area near Westroosebeke (2¼ miles N.E. of Poelcappelle) they had marched to their position of deployment south-west of Poelcappelle. Their first objective was the original German Second Line on either side of St. Julien, the left of the counter-attack passing Schuler Farm.

and dropping bombs on them.[1] No more was heard of the advanced posts beyond the Zonnebeke–Langemarck road and on Gravenstafel spur; and the hard won defended localities at Kansas Cross and Schuler Farm had to be abandoned.[2]

Gallant efforts were made by the four battalions of the 164th Brigade to form a new front as they fell back through the German battle zone; but they were hampered both by a shortage of ammunition and by lack of any artillery support. At 4.53 p.m. Major-General Jeudwine, commanding the 55th Division, ordered the 164th Brigade to hold a line Hill 35–Somme Farm–Border House, and a protective barrage was to be placed three hundred yards in front of it; at the same time, the 165th and 166th Brigades were to prepare to hold the second objective at all costs, and to push out to support the 164th Brigade where possible. Before even this message was despatched, the Hill 35–Border House line was in German hands, and the captured enemy battery positions in and behind it had been lost. Only a party of about thirty men of the two left battalions of the brigade returned to the second objective, other survivors, who attempted to hold the Border House–Somme Farm line, being surrounded. The remnants of the two right battalions, narrowly escaping envelopment about Hill 35, also withdrew to the second objective, and the ruins of St. Julien were abandoned.

As the 164th Brigade withdrew parties of Germans began to move behind the left of the 45th Brigade on and south of Hill 37.[3] About 2.30 p.m. after a short stand on Hill 37,

---

[1] This incident is one of the earliest examples of the close support of an infantry attack from the air. The German order stated: "The *45th Flight* will support our counter-attack with two or three aircraft. These "will fly in front of the assaulting troops, will stimulate the offensive "spirit of the men by flying low, and will weaken the enemy's power of "resistance by dropping bombs and opening machine-gun fire."

[2] The counter-attack across Zonnebeke spur was delivered by 2 battalions of the *60th Reserve Regiment* (*221st Division*), the southern *Eingreif* division of *Group Ypres*. From its assembly area behind Broodseinde it had deployed north-east of Zonnebeke station at 1 p.m., and moved down the depression between Gravenstafel and Zonnebeke spurs. It overran the British advanced posts, and when the left reached Dochy Farm, the two battalions swung half-left across the Zonnebeke–Langemarck road into the Third Line on Zonnebeke spur. After a pause, the advance was then continued with its left on the Kansas Cross–Wieltje road, and with the original Second Line, about the Steenbeek, as the next objective.

[3] The intention of *Group Ypres* was to counter-attack with two regiments astride the Zonnebeke–Langemarck road; but the *1st Ersatz Reserve*,

Continued at foot of next page.

the latter troops had to fall back to avoid envelopment. No more was heard of the patrols at Dochy and Otto Farms, and by 4.15 p.m. the survivors of the 45th Brigade also were back about the second objective, with an advanced post at Iberian Farm. Its right, held up in the morning about Potsdam, withdrew to a position dug during the afternoon by the support battalion four hundred yards in front of the second objective, and in touch with the 8th Division south of the railway.

The later part of this withdrawal from the third objective was carried out in drenching rain; for, soon after 4 p.m., the drizzle which had persisted through the afternoon had turned into a steady downpour. Visibility was consequently very poor; but time had been given to make thorough defence preparations, the backbone of which lay in the artillery and the machine-gun organization.[1] The German advance as it approached the Steenbeek was slowed down by the strengthening opposition as well as by the heavy rain and the consequent state of the ground near the stream, the worst patch on the whole battlefield, as already mentioned. In many places the men were seen to be up to their knees in mud and water, and it was not until 6 p.m. that the foremost Germans reached within three hundred yards of the second objective.[2] At that hour the artillery and machine-gun barrage opened on S.O.S. signals as arranged, and under its withering fire the Germans turned and withdrew up the slope, leaving many casualties in their track; but they held on to the ruins of St. Julien. The barrage was maintained for four hours in front of the second objective on the XIX Corps front, south of St. Julien, and harassing fire (200 rounds per battery) was kept up throughout the night along the barrage line and three hundred yards east of it.

Continued from previous page.
which was to have been on the left of the *60th Reserve*, and would have come up against the 45th Brigade, lost direction and arrived too late to take part in the counter-attack.

[1] In the event of an attack on the second objective an artillery protective barrage was to be laid down three hundred yards in front, reinforced by a machine-gun barrage by eight machine guns in each brigade sector firing indirect from about the first objective. Any of the attacking enemy who penetrated this wall of metal were to be dealt with by direct fire of twelve machine guns in each brigade sector near and behind the second objective.

[2] The histories of the German regiments concerned state that the majority of the rifles and light machine guns were by this time choked with mud, and unserviceable.

The three brigades which had withdrawn from the third objective had lost an average of 70 per cent of their strengths,[1] and at 10 p.m. they were ordered back to the original British front line to reorganize, leaving the defence of the second objective to the brigades which had earlier captured it.

The success achieved in the centre had been an encouragement to the enemy to press his counter-attacks on both flanks.[2] Between 2.30 p.m. and 3 p.m. waves of German infantry advanced down the slopes on either side of Langemarck towards the position of the northern defensive flank along the Steenbeek. In the sector of the 51st Division (XVIII Corps) the defence had been consolidated for several hours and an intense artillery barrage, combined with a fusillade from machine guns, Lewis guns and rifles changed the German advance into a disorderly flight.[3] Taking advantage of this retirement, parties of the 152nd Brigade, which had waited for some hours for a favourable moment to establish a bridgehead across the stream, waded over and rushed the strongpoint in the ruins of Maison du Rasta; another party occupied Maison Bulgare, two hundred yards to the south. Later in the evening the Steenbeek became almost a torrent owing to the heavy rain, and these advanced posts were withdrawn.

Opposite the 38th Division, the Germans, after suffering heavy casualties near the ruins of Langemarck from the artillery barrage, made only slow progress across the open ground west of the village in face of continuous machine-gun fire. About 5 p.m., however, the bridgehead at Au Bon Gîte had to be abandoned, the garrison withdrawing to the line already consolidated west of the stream.[4] The Guards

---

[1] The casualties of the three brigades were:

	Officers	Other Ranks
45th Brigade ...	43	1,122
164th Brigade ...	70	1,300
118th Brigade ...	70	1,450

For full list of casualties, see pp. 177-8.

[2] See Sketch 16.

[3] These Germans were the left companies of the *231st Reserve Regiment* advancing north of the Poelcappelle–St. Julien road.

[4] This counter-attack was delivered by the *229th Reserve Regiment*, the *Stossregiment* of the *50th Reserve Division*, which had been handed over to the *3rd Guard Division* at 7 a.m. Its history states that enfilade fire from machine guns in the pillbox of Au Bon Gite (garrisoned by the
Continued at foot of next page.

THE GERMAN COUNTER-ATTACKS. 31st JULY

Division, north of the Ypres–Staden railway, succeeded in holding the line it had gained during the morning; while, farther north, the French not only resisted a counter-attack from about St. Janshoek but advanced beyond their original objective, obtaining a firm footing in Bixschoote.[1]

In the southern part of the battle area, too,[2] during the afternoon, local counter-attacks were delivered by the enemy against the new front of the II Corps, south of the Ypres–Roulers railway. Determined efforts, made by him about 2 p.m. and again at 7 p.m., against the sector of the 8th Division in order to recapture the second objective on the Westhoek ridge, had a temporary success[3]; but units of the 25th Brigade re-occupied the lost ground, after which the brigade was relieved and withdrawn behind Bellewaarde ridge into reserve. The divisional front was now left to the care of the 23rd and 24th Brigades, which had carried out the morning assault. Farther south again, astride the Menin road and in the Bassevillebeek re-entrant, after the repulse of local counter-attacks delivered by the German front divisions,[4] Major-General Williams, commanding the 30th Division, had ordered a renewal of the attack against the second objective to take place at 6.30 p.m. At 5.30 p.m., however, II Corps headquarters ordered the consolidation of the ground already gained; the attack was cancelled and units of the 18th Division engaged in the sector of the 30th Division were withdrawn.

On the front of the Second Army[5] a strong counter-attack

Continued from previous page.
11/South Wales Borderers) was mainly responsible for holding up both its leading battalions, which lost 19 officers and 614 other ranks in this counter-attack. The help of heavy artillery had to be asked for before the pillbox could be assaulted.

[1] The *77th Reserve Regiment, Stossregiment* of the *2nd Guard Reserve Division*, which was handed over to the front division, the *111th*, during the morning, counter-attacked early in the afternoon with its right on St. Janshoek and its left on Weidendreft. About 4.30 p.m. the two remaining regiments came up on either flank, the *91st Reserve* opposite the Guards Division between Weidendreft and the Ypres–Staden railway and the *15th Reserve* opposite Bixschoote. This division relieved the front division (*111th*) during the night.

[2] See Sketch 14.

[3] A battalion of the *41st Regiment* (*221st Division*), which had advanced to the Polygon Wood area in the morning, participated with the *95th Regiment* in this counter-attack.

[4] As the assault had not reached the Second Line in this sector, the three German *Eingreif* divisions of *Group Wytschaete* remained unused and intact.

[5] See Sketch 11.

to re-capture La Basse Ville took place at 3.30 p.m., after an intense bombardment; but it was checked by artillery fire and a machine-gun barrage, and the ground gained in the morning by the New Zealand Division was held. The X Corps, too, successfully repulsed a local counter-attack at 7 p.m. north of the Comines canal, where a bitter fight had continued throughout the day to retain a hold on the main ridge about Klein Zillebeke.

Heavy rain set in on the evening of the 31st. This added to everyone's discomfort and limited further operations to local efforts to improve the newly established front. When, however, in the early hours of the 1st August, the German garrison withdrew from the strongpoint near Lower Star Post in Shrewsbury Forest, which had dislocated the attack of the 24th Division, the movement was detected and the place occupied by the 73rd Brigade.

The roads west of the canal had not been much damaged; east of it they were patched quickly either by filling the holes or laying sleepers, slabs or half-round timbers.[1] But one of the effects of the rain was to drive all traffic off the fields on to the roads and tracks as far as they extended; this slowed all movement and, by concentrating it on certain arteries, offered easy targets for the harassing fire of the German artillery and aircraft. Near the front the carrying parties were forced to go across country and thus greatly added to their labours and, as half the total strength of the divisions in reserve was employed on this service, it tended to reduce their battle value.

Notwithstanding ground hindrances, during the afternoon of the 1st August in the XIX Corps area, the Germans made a determined effort to regain their original Second Line along the Steenbeek, south of St. Julien, in order to strengthen the northern flank of their position on Gheluvelt plateau. At 3.30 p.m., groups of infantry, covered by a smoke screen and by an intensive artillery barrage, gained a footing in the sector of the 15th Division on a frontage of three hundred yards about Beck House, north of Frezenberg, until two

---

[1] A Note on road and track communications will be found at the end of Chapter XI.

battalions of the 45th Brigade advanced from the first objective and re-occupied the lost ground about 9 p.m. A similar attack, delivered at 1.30 p.m. the following afternoon (2nd August) against the front of the 55th Division about the Pommern Redoubt, was broken up by an artillery barrage and machine-gun fire, the enemy retiring behind Hill 35. During the 2nd, too, Germans were reported to be massing opposite the 39th Division; the area was at once heavily shelled, after which the 116th Brigade occupied the ruins of St. Julien without serious opposition, and later in the day a chain of posts was established east of the Steenbeek northwards from the village. In places here, owing to the state of the river banks, the men were up to their waists in mud and water.

The remainder of the new battle front was maintained intact during this period, although consistent German artillery fire, particularly against the II Corps front on Gheluvelt plateau, interfered considerably with the work of consolidation. The sodden ground, due to continued heavy rain, added to the hardships and exhaustion of the troops in the forward areas, and exceptional patience and endurance were needed, and devoted, to clear the battlefield of wounded.[1]

Results of the Battle

In a note written on the 4th August for transmission to the War Cabinet, which he kept regularly informed, Sir Douglas Haig described the fighting on the 31st July as "highly satisfactory and the losses slight for so great a "battle". Compared with the first day of the Battles of the Somme 1916, when eleven divisions of the Fourth and Third Armies had been engaged in the front line, as against fourteen of the Fifth and Second Armies in the present case, when the casualties reported were 61,816 (reduced later by the return of absentees to 57,540), the losses, 31,850 (for the

---

[1] For exceptional bravery and devotion to duty, Captain N. G. Chavasse, V.C., M.C., R.A.M.C., (attached 1/10th King's), was awarded a bar to the Victoria Cross he had gained at Guillemont on 9th August 1916. Despite serious wounds from which he subsequently died, he continued to go out repeatedly under heavy fire to search for and attend the wounded, and assisted in carrying in many of them across most difficult ground. He was the only recipient of both the V.C. and a bar to the V.C. in the War.

three days 31st July–2nd/3rd August), were moderate, although in themselves severe.[1]

A general advance of about three thousand yards had been made, whereas at the Somme only three divisions on the right had made fair, but less, progress, and two others only achieved small isolated advances.

Although expectations had not been entirely realized and considerable casualties had been suffered, valuable results had been gained. The enemy's observation areas on the highest part of Gheluvelt plateau (near Clapham Junction) and along the long rise via Bellewaarde to Pilckem had been captured, and nine of his divisions had been badly mauled. Apart from an unusually large number of German dead on the battlefield, over six thousand prisoners (including 133 officers) and 25 guns had been captured.[2] It is now known, as might have been expected, that the front divisions had been so badly shattered that they had to be replaced within a few days by fresh divisions. This relief implied the provision of a new complement of counter-attack divisions in close support. Thus began that steady stream of German divisions to the Flanders front which was to drain the

---

[1] See " 1916 " Vol. I, p. 483.

The total casualties of the Fifth Army for the period 31st July to 3rd August were 27,001 all ranks (including 1,223 officers), of which total 297 officers and 3,400 other ranks were killed. The casualties of the divisions engaged from right to left (including field artillery and machine-gun companies) were :

	Officers			Other Ranks			Total
	Killed	Wounded	Missing	Killed	Wounded	Missing	
24th Division	41	68	3	345	1,434	351	2,242
30th ,,	31	114	7	434	2,348	431	3,365
8th ,,	43	117	—	372	2,176	368	3,076
18th ,,	11	30	—	117	728	59	945
15th ,,	45	110	19	343	2,258	668	3,443
55th ,,	32	109	19	417	2,193	677	3,447
39th ,,	38	107	13	401	2,537	775	3,871
51st ,,	10	51	—	268	1,268	129	1,726
38th ,,	21	90	—	373	2,036	402	2,922
Guards	25	69	—	330	1,363	177	1,964
	297	865	61	3,400	18,341	4,037	27,001

The casualties of the Second Army for the period 31st July to 2nd August were :

	Officers			Other Ranks			Total
	Killed	Wounded	Missing	Killed	Wounded	Missing	
IX Corps	26	60	15	335	1,186	381	2,003
X Corps	18	60	—	128	1,277	11	1,494
II Anzac Corps	9	31	1	253	1,036	22	1,352
	53	151	16	716	3,499	414	4,849

[2] The losses of the German *Fourth Army* for the third of a month period, 21st–31st July, are given as " 30,000 in round numbers " ; as " wounded " whose recovery was to be expected in a reasonable time" are not included, by our reckoning the total should be about 40,000.

THE RESULTS

resources of the enemy during the next four months, and keep him from attacking the French.

The situation was, however, only relatively satisfactory. The nine leading divisions of the four corps of the Fifth Army had been intended to reach the third and fourth objectives on the first day, and then to carry out the subsequent advance to the Passchendaele–Staden ridge before relief. Actually, they were less than half-way to the first day's objectives, and had already lost 30 per cent. to 60 per cent. of their fighting strength. Of the available fighting tanks, too, which it was hoped would play a vital part in the later stages of the battle, about half (48 per cent.) had been knocked out or had fallen out.[1]

The strength of the German defence, particularly the striking power of the counter-attack divisions and of the supporting artillery, had been underestimated, as had been the case in the French offensive under General Nivelle in April. One result was that the assaulting divisions, which had easily captured the German forward zone to a depth of a mile in the first three hours, had had to remain throughout the day in a forward area exposed to observed artillery and machine-gun fire ; as two months earlier at Messines, most of the casualties were suffered not in the assault, but in the new positions won.

Apart from actual losses the conditions under which the battle was fought were most exhausting for all the troops concerned. The postponement of the assault till the 31st July had lengthened the bombardment by six days, and the effect of artillery fire on this unprecedented scale on the rain-softened ground was to convert a good part of the area which the assaulting troops had to cross—and this included the valleys of the Bassevillebeek, the Hanebeek

---

[1] Appendix XVI gives the Tank Corps instructions for the salvage of immobilized tanks in the battle area.

Of 117 fighting tanks which had gone into action, 77 had been ditched, bellied or had broken down mechanically, and 42 of these, including those receiving direct hits by shell, had become a total loss.

The gun-carrier tank, for which the design had been started in July 1916, made its first appearance in this offensive. Intended to transport across country a 60-pdr. or a 6-inch howitzer, the tank had its engine (105 h.p. Daimler) in rear, and in front was a platform ; this could be drawn out and lowered to form a ramp up which the gun was hauled, by a winding gear attached to the engine, into its position for transit. The length of the G.C. tank was 30 feet (43 feet with tail) ; width over all 11 feet 6 inches ; weight 27 tons unloaded or 34 tons (maximum) loaded with gun and its ammunition.

and the Steenbeek—into a sea of shell-holes, soon to be full of semi-liquid, clayey mud, and through which a way had to be picked.

The labours of the artillery, too, particularly that of the II Corps (Br.-General A. D. Kirby) and XIX Corps (Br.-General W. B. R. Sandys), which had to face the retaliation from the German artillery concentration behind Gheluvelt plateau, had been as gruelling as that of the infantry, and, judged by the proportion of casualties, nearly as hazardous. The gun detachments had practically no relief throughout the preparatory bombardment period, and were exposed to frequent and intense German barrages of high explosive and gas shell. The magnificent efforts of the artillery arm were also handicapped by the excessive demands on its limited resources: the batteries were called on to spread their fire over the entire German position back to the Flanders I Line, with its multiplicity of alternative and dummy battery emplacements, involving a record expenditure of shell and long hours in continuous action.

The Fifth Army Scheme Not Altered

During the afternoon of the 31st July, Sir Douglas Haig had visited Fifth Army headquarters. He instructed General Gough to continue carrying out the original scheme. The next advance, he said, was to be made as soon as possible, but only after adequate bombardment, and after domination of the enemy artillery had been obtained. In the meantime, the ground gained was to be consolidated, and the positions improved where necessary to facilitate the next operation.

When, therefore, later, at 5.43 p.m., definite information was received at Fifth Army headquarters that both the II and XIX Corps were back about the German Second Line,[1] General Gough ordered the two corps to be ready to renew the offensive to the third objective by the morning of the 2nd August. At 8.45 p.m. this order was slightly modified, to ensure that the German Second Line on Gheluvelt plateau should be taken by the II Corps before the advance farther north, beyond the Steenbeek, was continued.[2] The II Corps was to carry out this attack on the 2nd August, and two

---

[1] See Sketch 12.
[2] See Sketch 12 and Appendix XVII.

PLAN FOR CONTINUATION. 1st AUGUST 181

days later the II, XIX and right of the XVIII Corps were to resume the offensive to the third objective. At the same time,[1] the left of the XVIII, with the XIV and the French First Army, were to carry forward the northern defensive flank to the Winnipeg (1,000 yards east of St. Julien)–Langemarck–Weidendreft road, as a preliminary to a major offensive at a later date.

This decision was confirmed by a G.H.Q. order issued the following morning;[2] but that same day the Operations Branch G.H.Q. wrote for Sir Douglas Haig a memorandum commenting upon the situation.[3] It advised that the attack by the II Corps should not be hurried—the Fifth Army had ordered it to be delivered next day—and should be carried out by fresh divisions: the present front divisions of the II Corps were already exhausted and greatly depleted, and it was pointed out that the use of tired troops had generally been a cause of failure. The memorandum also recommended that the artillery preparation should be allowed two or three days of clear visibility in order to make full use of the observation areas occupied on the 31st July.[4] The Fifth Army could not hope, it added, to advance from the Steenbeek until its right, the II Corps, had both gained and consolidated the greater part of Gheluvelt plateau; and the capture of the Inverness Copse–Westhoek area (second objective) by the II Corps was not considered sufficient for the purpose. In conclusion it was suggested that since the Germans clearly regarded the bastion formed by Gheluvelt plateau as the most important tactical feature on the battle front, a large-scale counter-attack to regain any lost ground there was to be expected.[5]

---

[1] See Sketch 16.
[2] Appendix XVIII.
[3] Appendix XIX.
[4] Two captured German maps had disclosed concealed machine-gun emplacements in the areas to be attacked, and accurate shooting by the heavy howitzers would be necessary for their destruction.
[5] The Germans did indeed regard the fortified area on Gheluvelt plateau as the key to their Flanders position. In his diary on the evening of the Pilckem battle, 31st July, Crown Prince Rupprecht wrote that " the " results of the day's fighting were all the more satisfactory because the " counter-attack divisions of *Group Wytschaete* behind Gheluvelt plateau " had scarcely been used ".
On 5th August, too, an order of *Group Wytschaete* stated that " the " enemy cannot continue his intended break through north-eastwards " towards Roulers until he has gained freedom for his right flank by " pressing back the *52nd Reserve Division* on Gheluvelt plateau. The next

Continued at foot of next page.

In short, the memorandum repeated the opinion given by Sir Douglas Haig himself to General Gough on the 28th June, to the effect that the main battle would have to be fought on and for Gheluvelt plateau. This, too, was the opinion of the corps commanders of the Fifth Army.[1] The question of reinforcing the II Corps was considered, and resulted, as will be seen, in two divisions being sent to it.

Continued from previous page.
" blow may therefore be expected to be delivered with the utmost strength " against the *52nd Reserve* and *12th Divisions* " (holding between Shrewsbury Forest and Westhoek).

[1] It will be remembered that the same recommendation was an essential feature of both the 1916 and 1917 plans.

CHAPTER XI

THE BATTLES OF YPRES 1917
(continued)

THE FAILURE AT GHELUVELT PLATEAU (10TH AUGUST)
AND THE
BATTLE OF LANGEMARCK (16TH–18TH AUGUST)
(Sketches 12, 17, 18, 19, 20, 21)

RAIN HOLDS UP OPERATIONS

The rain which had set in on the evening of the 31st July continued three days and nights almost without cessation.[1] For the time being it converted the shelled areas near the front into a barrier of swamp, four thousand yards wide, and this had to be crossed in order to reach the new front line. The margins of the overflowing streams were transformed into long stretches of bog, passable only by a few well-defined tracks which became targets for the enemy's artillery; and to leave the tracks was to risk death by drowning. The mud-covered roads, practically unrecognizable, though constantly repaired, were pitted with shell-holes three or four feet deep. For the moment tank support was impracticable.

Br.-General Elles, commanding the Tank Corps, suggested to Fifth Army headquarters on the 2nd August that the remaining tanks should be kept for employment in bulk for distant objectives at a later stage of the campaign, and it was agreed that they would not be called upon to assist in the attacks ordered for the next few days, nor until after a spell of dry weather.[2]

On the 2nd August, the operations ordered had been postponed. On the 4th the rain ceased, and on the following

---

[1] See Note I, at end of Chapter.
[2] They got into action again on 17th August, as will be seen . During 3rd/4th August Br.-General Elles and his chief staff officer, Lieut.-Colonel J. F. C. Fuller, together with Colonel J. Hardress-Lloyd (III Tank Brigade), very properly drafted alternative schemes for initiating a tank attack on some other part of the battle front. These will be dealt with in the volume on the Battle of Cambrai 1917.

day, although the weather remained stormy and unsettled, with no sun or drying wind, and more rain forecast, Fifth Army headquarters fixed the 9th for the II Corps operation against Gheluvelt plateau, and the 13th for the resumption of the main offensive. The intervening period was dull and misty, and on the evening of the 8th a violent thunderstorm, accompanied by heavy rain, again turned the sodden battle area into a temporary quagmire. Both operations were consequently postponed for 24 hours, zero hour for the 10th being fixed for 4.35 a.m. In spite of weather and ground difficulties, the battle had to go on; for progressively during July and through August and September the first consideration with Sir Douglas Haig was the dangerous condition of the French army: that army must be preserved, and the Germans must be kept from it by attack.

Failure at Gheluvelt: 10th August[1]

The preparations for the proposed operations were hampered, and their prospect of success spoilt, by the undiminished strength of the German artillery concentration on and behind Gheluvelt plateau. This mass of guns continued to harass, by day and by night, the 6,000-yard frontage and the back areas of the II and XIX Corps between Stirling Castle and St. Julien, whilst those of the XVIII and XIV Corps northwards from St. Julien were left in comparative quiet. The counter-batteries of the Fifth Army, on the other hand, continued to spread their fire over the whole Army frontage of 12,000 yards in preparation for the renewed general offensive. In addition to the disadvantage of this dispersal of artillery power, the counter-batteries had the further handicap of having to work on old and often incorrect registrations, for the periods of good visibility were too few to check by air reconnaissance the shifting of German batteries to any of their three or four alternative emplacements. As a result, the German artillery concentration opposite the II Corps remained unmastered. From the evening of the 31st July onwards it pounded the new battery emplacements, so that their construction and occupation became a long and costly task, which was not completed until the 8th August. Artillery casualties were

---
[1] See Sketch 17.

severe both in men and in guns, and as early as the 4th August many batteries were reduced to half-strength; and some brigades had to be reorganized from four into two batteries. The recurring wastage of artillery fire-power, due to the German counter-battery work, was a severe handicap to the artillery programme. The ground in this period was so rain-sodden that digging was not practicable, and battery detachments lived in shell holes, covered by sheets of corrugated iron; periods of rest were arranged with detachments at the wagon lines, or during the replacement of destroyed and worn-out guns. The state of the ground, as well as the shelling, made the laying of plank roads and duckboard tracks for the supply of ammunition to the new battery positions, which was now taken in hand, exceptionally troublesome, and when laid they were exposed to fire. The wagon drivers and emergency carrying parties, even though they moved only by night, had continually to run the gauntlet of German artillery fire, because in the darkness the enemy shelled in particular, frequently with mustard gas, the mass of wheeled transport and pack animals which had to pass through the road bottle-neck at the Menin Gate of Ypres.

Conditions for the infantry, too, in the forward areas were most trying. Apart from weather and ground conditions, persistent German barrages, generally on the three zones simultaneously, on the front line and its approaches, and on the support and reserve trenches about the original British front line, made reliefs of the front garrison and the transport of supplies across the shell-swept zone an exceedingly hazardous task. For these reasons, whereas on the quieter sector north of St. Julien the divisions of the XVIII and XIV Corps were not relieved until between the 5th and 8th August, those of the II and XIX, between Stirling Castle and St. Julien, had to be taken out of the line on the 1st or, at latest, the 4th August.[1] The relieving divisions of the II Corps detailed to carry out the preliminary operation on the 10th August, were consequently in or near the

---

[1] The 8th Division was relieved by the 25th on 1st August; and the 30th, 15th and 55th Divisions by the 18th, 16th and 36th on 4th August. The 24th Division, which was to remain on the defensive behind the Bassevillebeek, was not relieved.

In the XVIII and XIV Corps, the 38th Division was relieved by the 20th on 5th August, the 39th Division by the 48th on 6th August, and the Guards and 51st Divisions by the 29th and 11th Divisions on 8th August.

front line for over a week before the assault took place, and were already exhausted.

The main task of the II Corps,[1] the storming of Gheluvelt plateau, was allotted to its centre division, the 18th (Major-General R. P. Lee). By an advance of eight hundred yards two of its brigades were to capture the belt of strongpoints across the waist of the plateau and secure the German Second Line, including Inverness Copse and Glencorse Wood. In order to allow the 18th Division to close up on its assault frontage of twelve hundred yards, the 24th Division, on the right, on the 7th August extended its front northwards from Bodmin Copse to south of Stirling Castle. The 25th Division (Major-General E. G. T. Bainbridge) was to co-operate on the left of the 18th by a simultaneous advance of a few hundred yards, with one brigade, to re-occupy the German Second Line on the reverse slope of the Westhoek ridge, including Westhoek village, which had been given up during the battle on the 31st July.

The assault was to be carried through without a pause : the barrage time-table allowed 46 minutes for the 18th Division and 25 minutes for the 25th Division to complete the operation. A general bombardment on the whole front of the Fifth Army was to be maintained for the duration of the assault. On the 8th both Inverness Copse and Glencorse Wood were shelled with 3,000 rounds from heavy and medium howitzers, and the bombardment was continued during the 9th, the first fine day of the month.

The attack of the II Corps met with fair success, reaching the objective line on the left, including Westhoek village, but failing to hold it on the right. Although it was seen that many of the strongpoints, particularly those at the south-west and north-west corners of Inverness Copse, were still intact,[2] the thinly held German forward zone, eight hundred yards in depth, was overrun by the assault groups which, at 4.35 a.m., followed the barrage. The ground was difficult to cross. Water-filled shell-craters abounded and in Glencorse Wood the broken tree trunks lay on black, slimy mud ; but the Germans offered little resistance, and

---

[1] See Sketch 17.
[2] These pillboxes, designed for two or three machine guns, were built of reinforced concrete, 4 feet thick, and to smash them required a direct hit by a heavy howitzer shell.

many came forward to surrender.[1] However, the objective was easier to reach than to hold. Soon after 6 a.m. a German barrage, formed by field guns and heavy machine guns, was laid along the British starting line between Stirling Castle and Westhoek, which boxed in the assaulting battalions and cut them off from reinforcements and supplies; and shortly afterwards the immediate local counter-attacks by the German support battalions were launched.

The 7/Queen's, covering the 400-yard frontage of the 55th Brigade (Br.-General G. D. Price) along the eastern edge of Inverness Copse, had its southern flank exposed owing to the failure of its right company, which should have formed a defensive flank along the southern edge of the wood. Held up at the start by machine-gun fire from an intact strongpoint at the south-western corner of the copse, it could make no progress. Both this company and its support company had been seen by German sentries crossing the crest of the Stirling Castle ridge in bright moonlight, about 1.30 a.m., to their starting line; and they had suffered heavy losses, including most of their officers, from artillery and machine-gun fire before zero hour. Threatened with envelopment, the companies of the Queen's fell back through the northern sector of the copse, followed closely by the Germans, who re-occupied the western edge, including the machine-gun nest at the north-west corner. Renewed efforts of the Queen's to advance were in vain.[2]

The 11/Royal Fusiliers and 7/Bedfordshire, covering the front of the 54th Brigade (Br.-General C. Cunliffe Owen), had reached their objective in greater strength and with more cohesion. They occupied the pillbox shelters of the German Second Line on either side of Fitzclarence Farm and along the sunken track near the eastern end of Glencorse Wood, and from this line, although all the officers of the Fusiliers had fallen, they were able to check the immediate counter-attacks. But the German box barrage interrupted the supply of food, water and ammunition, and as the day passed the need for fresh troops to hold the objective became urgent. The other two battalions of the

---

[1] The front battalion commander of the *239th Reserve Regiment*, who was taken prisoner, said his men were demoralized after heavy losses in the Pilckem battle and subsequent days, and that he had reported shortly before the attack that he could not guarantee to hold the sector.

[2] The casualties suffered by the 7/Queen's in this attack were 10 officers and 272 other ranks.

brigade, exhausted after holding the line for ten days in very trying circumstances and weakened by casualties, were not considered fit to go into action. At 7.40 a.m., when the brigadier asked that the 53rd Brigade, in divisional reserve about Dickebusch, south of Ypres, might be moved up in closer support, his request was not granted. Only one division, the 56th, was in corps reserve, ten miles distant at Poperinghe, and Major-General Lee wished to keep his reserve brigade, the 53rd, fresh to take over the divisional front at nightfall; he feared, too, that overcrowding in the forward area might lead to unnecessary casualties from the German barrage. For these reasons, the 53rd Brigade was not ordered to move till 3.20 p.m., and its two leading battalions, the 8/Norfolk and 6/R. Berkshire, did not reach the assembly area, west of Sanctuary Wood, till 7 p.m.

Soon after 5 p.m. the Germans were seen assembling in Polygon Wood and Nonne Bosschen, and also in Inverness Copse, on the right flank. About 7 p.m. intense artillery fire deluged Glencorse Wood and its vicinity, and shortly afterwards, under cover of a smoke cloud, German infantry advanced against the front, and from Inverness Copse against the right flank.[1] The survivors of the two battalions, having little ammunition left, withdrew on the right to their starting line, south-west of Glencorse Wood; but the north-west corner of the wood was held. The brigadiers, in their battle reports, complained of the weakness of the protective barrage arrangements against the counter-attacks, and were of opinion that the allotment of only one aeroplane, equipped with wireless, to each corps to watch for counter-attacks was not enough.[2]

On the left, the short advance on the Westhoek ridge had been carried out successfully. The four battalions in line of the 74th Brigade (Br.-General H. K. Bethell) overran the German outpost groups; and Westhoek village, with two intact strongpoints within it, was rushed by the 2/R.

---

[1] For this counter-attack the German front-line regiment, *238th Reserve*, was reinforced by a battalion of the leading (*Stoss*) regiment, *6th Reserve*, of the *Eingreif* (*9th Reserve*) division from Reutel.

[2] The casualties of the two battalions during the action were:

	Officers	Other Ranks
11/Royal Fusiliers	17	335
7/Bedfordshire	6	255

Irish Rifles.[1] A stretch of deep mud, in places thirty yards wide and covered by water a foot deep, in the Hanebeek valley, formed an obstacle to counter-attack; but the German artillery continued to shell the Westhoek ridge throughout the day, and the casualties of the brigade were considerable.[2]

At 11.55 p.m. Lieut.-General Jacob ordered the existing front line to be consolidated, adding that the capture by the 18th Division of the day's objective was to be carried out as soon as practicable. Br.-General Higginson (53rd Brigade), who had just taken over the divisional front, whilst complying, at once pointed out the difficulties of a renewal of the attack: the night had been dark, and *inter alia*, one of the three battalions sent up lost direction by crossing to the north of the Menin Road by mistake. The attack was accordingly postponed for 24 hours, and eventually cancelled; and although the barrage was laid, the assault of the other two battalions was stopped in time.

Battle of Langemarck: 16th August

The logical consequence of the failure of the preliminary operation of the II Corps on the 10th should have been another postponement of the offensive proposed for the 14th; and on the 12th, Lieut.-General Jacob did ask that the main attack be delayed, as the situation on Gheluvelt plateau was still unsatisfactory: he wished that, at the least, the objective aimed at on the 10th should be reached before another offensive was launched.[3] There were the unpleasant facts

---

[1] Facing the 74th Brigade was the left regiment, *90th Reserve*, of the *54th Division*, which had taken over from the *38th Division* on 3rd/4th August.

[2] The casualties of the 4 battalions concerned during the period 5th–11th August amounted to about 50 per cent. of their battle strength: 47 officers and 1,271 other ranks (of whom 12 officers and 146 other ranks were killed) out of a battle strength of 96 officers and 2,397 other ranks.

The Germans suffered still more severely whilst concentrating in the Hanebeek valley preparatory to a counter-attack. The result of a succession of British artillery barrages upon them was seen by Br.-General Coffin, who walked over the ground on the 16th. He saw German dead lying on both sides of the streams more thickly than the dead on any battlefield in his experience; and he considered that they had been lying out about six days.

[3] He had received a letter that morning from Major-General Heneker (8th Division), asking that Glencorse Wood and Nonne Bosschen might be occupied as a preliminary operation, as the failure and heavy losses suffered by his division on 31st July had been due to enfilade fire from those woods on the higher ground on the right flank.

that the counter-batteries had not yet mastered the German artillery concentration at the back of Gheluvelt plateau, and that the replenishment of the forward infantry dumps with ammunition and supplies was behind-hand owing to the constant shelling and to the tracks through Sanctuary and Chateau Woods being obliterated. The local man-power situation, too, had become acute. All the eight divisions in reserve to the four attacking corps had been moved up into the line, and the two divisions in Fifth Army reserve had been sent up as a partial replacement.[1] To provide more divisions for corps reserve, the Second Army was asked to transfer three of its best divisions to the Fifth Army[2]; but as these divisions were to be held back for subsequent operations, the renewed offensive was to be carried out by the divisions in hand. As will be seen, the fresh divisions were soon involved in the fighting.

Fifth Army headquarters still had in mind the original scheme, and further delay would affect the coastal operations, which had either to catch the high tides at the end of the month or wait another four weeks. General Gough therefore agreed to postpone the action for 24 hours only, in order that essential reliefs might be completed.

During the afternoon of the 14th, however, a thunderstorm, with heavy rain, again soaked the battle area, so that zero hour was delayed a further 24 hours, until daybreak on the 16th. On that day, after a very dark night, a ground mist limited visibility to three hundred yards; but the assaulting brigades, which had to cross muddy and very broken ground to reach the forming-up line, were all in position along the tapes at 4.45 a.m. when the barrage opened. Gradually the mist cleared and the morning became bright and sunny.

The Main Attack[3]

The II Corps was to reach the German Third Line from Polygon Wood (inclusive) along Anzac Farm spur to the Ypres–Roulers railway, an average advance of fifteen

---

[1] The 56th Division had been handed over to II Corps on 6th August; and the 61st Division to XIX Corps on 14th August.

[2] The 47th and 14th Divisions (the latter less artillery) went to the II Corps on 14th and 15th August, respectively; and the 23rd Division to XVIII Corps on the 15th.

[3] See Sketch 18.

hundred yards; a southern defensive flank was to be formed by capturing and consolidating eight selected strongpoints at intervals between Stirling Castle and Black Watch Corner (the south-western corner of Polygon Wood). The distance to be covered was about double that aimed at on the 10th, but the assaulting battalions were on a narrower frontage, 250 instead of 400 yards, and a halt of twenty minutes was to be made along an intermediate line, where the support battalions of each brigade would leap-frog them. Eight tanks had been allotted to assist the II Corps; but on the 15th the approaches, owing to the rain and the heavy shelling, were found to be impassable, and tank co-operation was cancelled. The II Corps artillery was approximately the same strength as that which had supported the assault on the 10th: the creeping barrage, lifting 100 yards every 5 minutes, was provided by 180 18-pdr. guns on the corps front; standing barrages, by 72 4.5-inch howitzers and 36 18-pdr. guns, were laid on targets in and beyond the area to be occupied; and the 8 machine-gun companies of the two divisions were grouped to fire overhead on two barrage lines, one on the objective and another east of it, through the north-eastern corner of Polygon Wood to south-west of Zonnebeke village.

The 56th (1st London) Division (Major-General F. A. Dudgeon) used all three brigades. The 53rd Brigade (Br.-General H. W. Higginson)—handed over by the 18th Division to the 56th on relief—was to form the southern defensive flank;[1] but at the outset a barrage of high-explosive shell from German batteries to the south-east, from the direction of Zandvoorde, fell among the leading companies of its two assaulting battalions, causing delay and heavy casualties. The survivors were then brought to a halt by intense machine-gun fire from Inverness Copse, particularly from the intact pillbox at the north-western corner, known to contain three machine guns with a wide

---

[1] Br.-General Higginson had pointed out on the 12th, and again on the 14th, that, owing to severe losses in holding the front of the 18th Division from 10th–12th August, the brigade was not in a fit state for its task. On the 15th, two extra battalions were given to him, the 7/Bedfordshire of the 54th Brigade, which had only 3 days' rest after its action in Glencorse Wood, and the 1/4th London, from the 168th Brigade, in 56th Division reserve. These two battalions were given the task of forming the flank.

field of fire to front and flanks, and from Fitzclarence Farm across the open plateau. A special bombardment of the pill-box by heavy artillery, ordered for two hours from 5 p.m. to 7 p.m. on the previous evening, had not taken place owing to a misunderstanding, and the preparatory shelling by 4.5-inch howitzers had been ineffective. In consequence a later effort by the support companies also failed. Farther north, the two London brigades had a better start and gained the first objective, the 169th Brigade (Br.-General E. S. de D. Coke) occupying the line of pillbox shelters in the sunken track in Glencorse Wood, and the 167th Brigade (Br.-General G. H. B. Freeth), the edge of Nonne Bosschen. After the halt on the intermediate objective, however, the support battalions of both brigades, which passed through, at once met increasing opposition, especially from machine guns in a number of old gunpits; and as the ground became exceptionally soft, the barrage was lost. Only isolated parties reached the objective—the shelters, in the German Third Line, in Polygon Wood and along Anzac Farm spur south of Iron Cross Redoubt.

The 8th Division (Major-General W. C. G. Heneker), which had relieved the 25th Division on the 14th, was back in its old sector after less than fourteen days' rest for reorganization.[1] Its assaulting brigades, the 25th and the 23rd, after crossing the muddy bed of the Hanebeek by portable bridges, stormed up the eastern slope of the valley and reached the objective. Iron Cross and Zonnebeke redoubts in the German Third Line, and also Anzac Farm, were occupied; only the left was checked, machine-gun fire from Potsdam preventing any considerable movement immediately south of the Ypres–Roulers railway.

The battle reports of the two London brigades of the 56th Division in Polygon Wood and east of Nonne Bosschen emphasize that the lack of preparation and the need for fresh troops close at hand to consolidate the ground gained became evident soon after the objective was reached. The protective barrage, too, was weak; much of the shrapnel had the burst-on-graze fuze, effective enough on hard ground,

---

[1] It had suffered over three thousand casualties in the Pilckem battle on 31st July. Divisional commanders, later in the month, protested to Fifth Army headquarters that at least four, preferably six, weeks should be allowed for a division to replace casualties and to train the new drafts.

II CORPS. 16TH AUGUST

but useless on the muddy patches and water-filled craters ahead of the troops. Groups of Germans managed to infiltrate behind the isolated detachments of the four front battalions,[1] and by 6 a.m. most of the latter found themselves surrounded. About that hour also an intense German artillery barrage crept forward with German infantry following it. After a short struggle, the few survivors of the London battalions were rallied about 7 a.m. behind shelters along the sunken track in Glencorse Wood, where machine guns of the 9/London halted the counter-attack, and along the western edge of Nonne Bosschen. On receipt of news of the progress of the enemy counter-attack, an order by Br.-General Higginson for a support battalion of the 53rd Brigade to form a southern defensive flank by an attack southwards from the southern edge of Glencorse Wood was at once cancelled.

The recapture intact by the Germans of their machine-gun emplacements in the northern end of Nonne Bosschen enabled them to enfilade the foremost companies of the 25th Brigade to the north, which were consolidating their objective on the open slope of Anzac Farm spur. The very situation feared by Major-General Heneker had arisen.[2]

About 9.30 a.m. German reinforcements, which had been seen earlier in the distance dismounting from motor-lorries, began to advance in strength across the crest of Anzac Farm spur.[3] Smoke used in the German barrage which covered this counter-attack hid the Very light S.O.S. signals from the British ground artillery observers and, although the day was fine and visibility good, only one air-call, and that indefinite, denoting enemy infantry, was received. Consequently artillery support was not given until 10.15 a.m., when it was too late.[4] The 25th Brigade, attacked in front and enfiladed from its right, withdrew to the Hanebeek after

---

[1] Opposite the 56th Division, the *34th Division* had relieved the *52nd Reserve Division* on 11th/12th August, with the *67th Regiment* in Inverness Copse and astride the Menin Road, and the *145th Regiment* in Glencorse Wood and Nonne Bosschen. These fresh regiments each had one battalion in the forward zone.

[2] See p. 189, footnote 3.

[3] The *34th Regiment (3rd Reserve Division, Eingreif)*, from Droogenbroodhoek (2 miles east of Zonnebeke), reinforced the *27th Reserve Regiment (54th Division)* opposite the 8th Division at this hour.

[4] In their reports on this battle, divisional artillery commanders suggested that at least two aircraft should be detailed to each divisional front for the sole purpose of watching for, and giving warning of, the enemy's counter-attacks.

suffering heavy losses; and the Germans, following up, began to envelop the right flank of the 23rd Brigade, which then joined in the general retirement. Both brigades, which had become considerably intermixed, were rallied a few hundred yards in front of their starting-line, west of the Hanebeek, with the left battalion, the 2/Middlesex, slightly forward at the point where the stream passed under the Ypres–Roulers railway.

The German artillery repeated the standing barrage used on the 10th along the Stirling Castle–Westhoek line to box in the brigades which had made the assault. The shelling continued throughout the day, and was intense from noon onwards, barring the way for carrying parties with ammunition and food. About 4 p.m. a German counter-attack developed through and on both sides of Polygon Wood against the two brigades of the 56th Division.[1] The survivors of the 169th Brigade, holding the sunken track through Glencorse Wood, having expended all their ammunition, fell back to their starting-line near the western edge of the wood; the 167th Brigade, enfiladed by machine-gun fire from this exposed flank, was forced to conform. A body of German infantry, estimated at over a thousand, began to follow up; but artillery fire on S.O.S. signals checked it with severe losses. Later in the evening, in order to avoid further losses from enfilade machine-gun fire, the advanced units of the 8th Division along the Hanebeek also withdrew nearly to their starting line.[2]

To reach its objective, the original German Third Line on Anzac and Zonnebeke spurs, the XIX Corps (Lieut.-General H. E. Watts) had to cross a mile of open ground, chequered with pillboxes and strongpoints. The two divisions selected to lead, the 16th (South Irish) and the 36th (Ulster), were

---

[1] All three battalions of the *90th Reserve Regiment* (*54th Division*), which had been withdrawn to reserve at and north of Becelaere after relief on the 12th, were sent up during the morning to reinforce the counter-attacks in the Glencorse Wood and Nonne Bosschen sectors.

[2] The total casualties incurred by the 56th and 8th Divisions in this action were:

	Officers			Other Ranks			
	Killed	Wounded	Missing	Killed	Wounded	Missing	Total
56th Division ...	20	62	13	250	1,153	677	2,175
8th Division ...	8	7	12	244	1,274	566	2,111

The 56th Division was relieved on the night of the 17th/18th by the 14th Division. The 8th Division (previously short of officers) was relieved by the 47th Division on the night of the 18th/19th.

hardly in a fit state for such a task. They had taken over the line only on the 4th August; but, whilst in corps reserve, at least half their infantry had been continuously employed in the forward area as carrying parties and on other duties since the last week in July; they had lived and worked throughout a most trying fortnight in the quagmire of the Hanebeek and Steenbeek valleys, overlooked by German machine-gunners and artillery observers on the opposite spurs, and subjected to a shelling almost as intense as that on the II Corps sector. Casualties and sickness had consequently reduced the battle-strength of the two divisions by one-third, some of the battalions, indeed, being down to half their establishment. The loss of efficiency had been cumulative, and, owing to the need for frequent inter-battalion reliefs, all units had been equally affected.[1]

The waves of the assaulting troops were so thin that, in the words of a participant, the operation looked more like a raid than a major operation. Although resistance was met at once from the German strongpoints, two to eight hundred yards ahead,[2] the leading companies, torn and raked by bullets from front and flanks, continued on up the bare shell-pitted slope.

The 16th Division (Major-General W. B. Hickie) engaged two brigades; the 48th (Br.-General F. W. Ramsay) was badly cut up by machine guns in Potsdam, Vampir and Borry Farms.[3] Mopping-up parties were so scarce and strung out that the Germans were able to bring out machine guns from these shelters, and fire into the backs of the leading men. Even so, observers saw isolated parties arrive within a hundred yards of the German Third Line, their objective. The 49th Brigade (Lieut.-Colonel K. C. Weldon,

---

[1] The casualties incurred in the 16th Division during the period 1st–15th August amounted to 107 officers and 1,957 other ranks; whilst those of the 36th Division during the same period approximated to 70 officers and fifteen hundred other ranks.

[2] For each of the two assaulting divisions the creeping barrage was laid by 14 18-pdr. batteries; and standing barrages by 24 4.5-inch howitzer batteries. Forty machine guns of each division fired overhead barrages on three successive lines from positions immediately west of the Frezenburg–St. Julien road.

[3] The series of short concentrated bombardments by heavy artillery at a range of 6,000 to 8,000 yards had failed for the most part to hit these pin-point targets. The use of gas shell to neutralize their garrisons immediately before the assault, as suggested by a brigade commander, was not tried.

acting)[1] also encountered stiff opposition. The right was soon held up at Borry Farm (estimated to be garrisoned by a hundred men and 5 machine guns), although costly but unsuccessful efforts were made to take the place. The left of the brigade, after overrunning Iberian and Delva Farms, was checked four hundred yards from the summit of Hill 37.[2]

The 36th Division (Major-General O. S. W. Nugent) experienced similar difficulties. The leading waves of the 108th Brigade (Br.-General C. R. J. Griffith) were swept from the outset by machine-gun fire from Gallipoli and Somme Farms, and finally checked by a new and strong wire entanglement set diagonally across the front, covering those two places, gaps cut in it during the preparatory bombardment being commanded by German machine guns either in the strongpoints or in neighbouring emplacements. This wire prevented bombing parties from working round the flanks of the strongpoints.

The first part of the advance of the 109th Brigade (Br.-General A. St. Q. Ricardo) entailed wading through a swamp caused by the flooded Steenbeek, during which the assaulting units came under machine-gun fire from Pond Farm and Border House. The barrage was lost, and the advance checked ; but the left managed to occupy Fortuin, a slight eminence four hundred yards from the starting tapes.

About 9 a.m. waves of German infantry streamed over the crest of the Zonnebeke–St. Julien spur against the 16th and 36th Divisions, preceded by an intense artillery barrage, described in the diaries as " crushing ". No warning had been given by air-observers to the artillery of the assembly of a strong German force of infantry in the dip behind the spur, and smoke shells in the German barrage hid the counter-attack from the ground artillery observers.[3] The XIX Corps diary states that the " weather conditions were

---

[1] Br.-General P. Leveson-Gower and most of his staff were gassed on the evening of the 15th. He did not return to command the brigade till 23rd August.

[2] Private F. E. Roon (2/Royal Irish) was awarded the V.C. for his courage and fearlessness as a stretcher-bearer in saving the lives of many of his comrades.

[3] The *5th Bavarian Division* held the line opposite the XIX Corps with two regiments and one in reserve (*21st Bavarian*). The counter-attack previously planned in detail as " Scheme F ", was delivered by the three battalions of the reserve regiment, with elements of the *Eingreifdivision* (*12th Reserve*) from Passchendaele.

"ideal, good visibility with a westerly wind"; but co-operation between air observers and the artillery was as inadequate as in some other sectors. Many of the advanced elements of the 16th Division, men of the 7/R. Irish Rifles and 9/R. Dublin Fusiliers (48th Brigade), with parties of the 8/R. Inniskilling Fusiliers (49th Brigade), who, by great gallantry and determination, had nearly reached the objective, fought till killed or overrun. Other survivors of the two divisions, their rifles and Lewis guns jammed with mud, fell back to the starting line. During the following hour the tragic events which had taken place on the same ground during the afternoon of the Pilckem Ridge battle were repeated. At 10.15 a.m. the corps commander, after discussion with the two divisional commanders, decided reluctantly to bring back the barrage to the starting line, even though scattered detachments were known to be still holding out in the German position.

At 2.8 p.m. Fifth Army headquarters ordered a line Borry Farm–Hill 35–Hindu Cottage, at least, to be captured; the left of the XIX Corps to gain touch with the right of the XVIII Corps at Winnipeg. The remainder of this order was for "the II Corps to clear up the situation " on its right flank," while, on the left of the XIX Corps, the XVIII and XIV Corps were to reconnoitre a line 500 to 1,500 yards beyond the objective, "with a view to a " further advance at the earliest possible moment ". At 4 p.m. Lieut.-General Watts, in passing this order to his divisional commanders, asked when they proposed to carry it out. Major-General Nugent suggested the following morning at the earliest; but both he and Major-General Hickie were averse to the scheme. Reports from the brigadiers and battalion commanders showed that all four brigades which had carried out the assault were exhausted, and that no brigade was able to muster as many as five hundred men. Already, too, the reserve brigade of each division had been sent forward to assist in holding the starting line. In view of these reports, Lieut.-General Watts informed Fifth Army headquarters at 8 p.m. that he was unable to carry out the attack ordered.[1]

---

[1] The casualties of the 16th Division during the period 1st–20th August were 221 officers and 4,064 other ranks, of which total 115 officers and 2,042 other ranks occurred during the battle period 16th–18th August (26 officers killed, 61 wounded, 28 missing; 254 other ranks killed, 1,098 wounded, 690 missing). *Continued at foot of next page.*

The Northern Flank

The assault by the XVIII and XIV Corps to form the northern defensive flank, along the western sector of the Gheluvelt–Langemarck line,[1] was launched in more favourable circumstances, as work on the systematic organization of the back areas had been little molested. A record of what had been accomplished is available. It states that in each area an 18-foot timber road[2] led from a spur of the broad gauge Ypres–Staden railway which had been extended across the Yser canal on a causeway. From the roadheads and railheads, light railways, with branches or trench tramways, connected the artillery group rail stations with the gun positions and enabled the artillery preparation to be carried out methodically. Plank roads, duck-board walks and mule tracks for pack transport had been laid forward to the front line from the Yser canal; and supplies had reached the holding battalions regularly. For infantry the plank roads were abandoned as time passed in favour of duck-boards, as being less conspicuous and more easily laid and repairable, trestles to carry them being put into the shell craters when necessary. For the artillery, branch cross-country tracks were eventually made from the main roads to the gun positions, as timber roads and tramlines to them were frequently damaged by shell-fire. Pack animals (not generally used for gun ammunition till early October) blocked and damaged the duck-walks; so they were driven across country, the leader finding a way between craters.[3] As the front trenches along the Steenbeek were waterlogged, sleeping accommodation was provided either in small steel shelters, each with room for 4 or 5 men, or in old German concrete pillboxes and dug-outs. Water was brought up in watercarts and petrol tins until pipe lines could be laid; for at this date the Ypres water supply had not yet been repaired.

Continued from previous page.
The 36th Division lost 144 officers and 3,441 other ranks during the period 2nd–18th August, of which total 81 officers and 1,955 other ranks occurred during the battle period 16th–18th August (19 officers killed, 55 wounded, 7 missing; 299 other ranks killed, 1,203 wounded, 453 missing).

[1] See Sketch 19.

[2] Constructed with $2\frac{1}{2}$-inch beech slabs or railway sleepers, or else with fascines and 6 inches of broken brick or large stones, on which road metal was laid.

[3] See Note II at end of Chapter. There is further information about communications in Chapter XIII.

XVIII CORPS. 16TH AUGUST

By local actions on the 11th, 12th and 14th August, outposts had been established on the eastern bank of the Steenbeek, except at Au Bon Gîte, where a pillbox still held out; so that most of the leading companies were able to form up for attack on the eastern side of the stream. The whole area, a mile wide, between the stream and the objective, the worst patch on the battlefield, as already noticed, was a muddy waste, pitted with water-filled shell holes, and the assaulting groups quickly broke up into small parties, picking their way in single file, many men sinking into the slime up to their knees.

The 48th and 11th Divisions of the XVIII Corps (Lieut.-General Sir I. Maxse) each assaulted with one brigade, the remaining brigades being in reserve behind either flank. Eight tanks, allotted to assist, had been warned not to use the roads owing to the congestion of traffic; but an approach march across country was impracticable owing to the soft condition of the ground, and the order for their co-operation was cancelled. The 145th Brigade (Br.-General D. M. Watt) of the 48th (1st South Midland) Division (Major-General R. Fanshawe), had a hard fight to overcome a strongpoint in the most northerly house of St. Julien, where forty Germans and a machine gun were captured; the advance then met a heavy cross fire as the leading wave topped the rise of ground about two hundred yards east of the Steenbeek. This opposition came from machine guns in intact strongpoints at Hillock Farm and Maison du Hibou, a couple of hundred yards ahead, and further attempts to advance only resulted in additional casualties. Small parties were seen to reach Springfield Farm, near the objective; but none of the men returned. The check here affected the right of the 34th Brigade (Br.-General S. H. Pedley), covering the front of the 11th Division (Major-General H. R. Davies), which was held up in front of the Cockcroft and Bülow Farm; but its left gained the final objective near the White House.[1]

---

[1] The casualties incurred in the two brigades concerned in the action amounted to:

	Officers	Other Ranks
145th Brigade	38	873
34th Brigade	32	749

The ground to be crossed by the XIV Corps (Lieut.-General Earl of Cavan), lower down the Steenbeek valley, was much the same as that which confronted the XVIII Corps, but arrangements were made for cleaned rifles to be passed to the front during the advance to replace those choked with mud, armourers' shops being established well forward for the purpose. The barrage was very thorough,[1] and as it approached the Germans scuttled away in large batches or readily surrendered.[2] The troublesome strongpoint at Au Bon Gîte, in the sector of the 20th Division (Major-General W. Douglas Smith), was captured at zero hour,[3] and the two assaulting brigades followed the barrage through to the objective. A slight delay occurred to the 61st Brigade (Br.-General W. E. Banbury) near Langemarck, where the ground between the Steenbeek and the débris of Langemarck village was a water-covered swamp, and isolated centres of resistance caused some casualties; but the advance of the 60th Brigade (Br.-General Hon. L. J. P. Butler), on the right, outflanked this opposition, and the farther side of Langemarck was reached.[4]

---

[1] In addition to the heavy artillery groups, each division of the XVIII and XIV Corps was supported by approximately 6 field artillery brigades, in 2 groups, comprising in all 108 18-pdr. guns and 36 4.5-inch howitzers. The two groups supporting the 11th Division alone fired during the 24 hours from midnight to midnight on 16th August, 47,000 18-pdr. shells and 13,409 4.5-inch howitzer shells. An overhead machine-gun barrage was fired by 4 machine-gun companies on each divisional front from positions immediately west of the Steenbeek, and 32,000 rounds of small arms ammunition were dumped near the gun positions.

[2] Opposite the XIV Corps was the *79th Reserve Division*, which had been in the line since it had relieved the *3rd Guard Division* on 4th August. Its heavy losses in the operations against Vimy Ridge in April (see " 1917 " Vol. I, p. 341 footnote) had been made up mainly with drafts of the 1918 class (19-year olds), who, according to the regimental histories, could not stand up to heavy continuous shelling. The division was due for relief when the assault was launched.

[3] It had been arranged for an aeroplane to fly low over and machine-gun the strongpoint one minute before zero hour, to draw the attention of the garrison, while two specially trained companies of the 11/Rifle Brigade, left behind for the purpose by the 59th Brigade, advanced close up and threw smoke bombs at it. The assault which followed captured the strongpoint and its garrison of one officer and fifty men.
    Sergeant E. Cooper (12/K.R.R.C.) rushed forward alone to a German blockhouse, and, by firing his revolver into the opening, silenced the garrison, 45 Germans and 7 machine guns being captured in it. A serious check to the advance was thereby avoided. He was awarded the V.C.

[4] Private E. Edwards (7/K.O.Y.L.I.) was awarded the V.C. for conspicuous bravery. By his splendid example in throwing bombs through loopholes in a German blockhouse, he saved a critical situation, and captured 36 prisoners.

In the sector of the 29th Division (Major-General Sir B. de Lisle), north of the railway, the strongpoints along the Langemarck–Weidendreft road fell to the 88th Brigade (Br.-General D. E. Cayley); and blockhouses offering resistance near Montmirail Farm were outflanked by units of the 87th Brigade (Br.-General C. H. T. Lucas).[1] The objective was reached by 8.30 a.m. The XIV Corps had captured in its advance, 26 officers and 774 other ranks, in addition to 10 field guns and howitzers and 56 machine guns.

Farther north, too, the French First Army, with its I Corps, had reached its objective along the line of the Kortebeek and St. Jansbeek, north-westwards to the inundated area about Langewaade, although several of the strongpoints were only taken after prolonged fighting. On the extreme left, the ruins of Poesele and Drie Grachten, on the eastern side of the Yser canal, were also occupied.[2]

The Germans made no serious effort to regain the lost ground opposite the northern defensive flank;[3] but, with the good observation they still possessed from the higher ground, their artillery and machine guns were able to inflict heavy losses on the garrison of the new line, particularly in the sector of the 20th Division.[4]

---

[1] Sergt. W. H. Grimbaldston (1/K.O.S.B.) was awarded the V.C. for extraordinary courage and boldness. In the face of heavy fire from a blockhouse, although wounded, he reached the entrance and, by threats with a hand-grenade, he forced the garrison of 36 Germans with 6 machine guns to surrender.

C.S.M. J. Skinner (also of the 1/K.O.S.B.) was awarded the V.C. for his dash and gallantry in clearing two blockhouses with the help of 6 men, and capturing sixty Germans and 3 machine guns within them.

[2] F.O.A. v. (ii.), pp. 675–86.

[3] German *Fourth Army* headquarters still based its defence on holding the bastions of Gheluvelt plateau and Houthulst Forest. They considered that so long as these were held a British advance in between was of small consequence. (Rupprecht ii., p. 267.)

[4] The casualties suffered by the two attacking divisions of the XIV Corps amounted to:

	Officers			Other Ranks			
	Killed	Wounded	Missing	Killed	Wounded	Missing	Total
20th Division (6th–19th August)	27	103	10	446	2,296	322	3,204
29th Division (15th–18th August)	16	43	1	238	1,088	66	1,452

LANGEMARCK

THE BATTLE DIES DOWN

At a conference at Fifth Army headquarters on the following day, the 17th, the corps commanders were told by General Gough that the whole of the objective given for the 16th was to be reached by a resumed offensive on the 25th. He mentioned that another major offensive to take the section of Passchendaele ridge between Broodseinde and Westroosebeke would be launched as soon as possible afterwards. In the meantime, local attacks were to be made on the 22nd to establish a starting-line for the 25th: the II Corps was to take Inverness Copse,[1] and the XIX and XVIII Corps were to advance to within a few hundred yards of the Gheluvelt–Langemarck Line, their next objective, which the XIV Corps had already reached.[2]

Both the 17th and 18th August were fine, with a drying breeze, and at 4.45 a.m. on the 20th, seven tanks, moving along the St. Julien–Poelcappelle road, covered by a smoke and shrapnel barrage, with a high-explosive barrage ahead, succeeded in capturing four of the strongpoints near it which had held up the 48th Division on the 16th. These places—Hillock Farm, Maison du Hibou, Triangle Farm (¼ mile east of the last) and the Cockcroft—were at once occupied by platoons of infantry, who were signalled forward as soon as the Germans showed signs of surrender.[3]

On the 22nd, with zero hour at 4.45 a.m., the 48th and 11th Divisions of the XVIII Corps, though assisted by tanks, were able to advance only a few hundred yards, but captured one strongpoint east of the Kerselaere cross-roads, and another east of Bülow Farm.[4] The simultaneous attack

---
[1] See Sketch 18.
[2] See Sketch 20.
[3] Twelve tanks of the I Brigade started, but 5 were ditched near St. Julien. Hillock Farm was reached at 6 a.m. and the garrison ran away. Maison du Hibou could not be approached nearer than 80 yards, owing to boggy ground; but a male tank fired 50 shells at it with its two 6-pdr. guns, and twenty Germans who ran out were machine-gunned by the female tank, half of them being killed. At Triangle Farm the garrison was kept under cover by a tank while the infantry entered and killed most of the occupants. A female tank was ditched within 50 yards of the Cockcroft at 6.45 a.m., as a hundred Germans ran out of the buildings and adjacent dug-outs; many were killed and the strongpoint was occupied. Five of the 7 tanks returned safely and the infantry casualties were slight, with 1 officer and 2 other ranks killed.
[4] Tanks were to have formed the spearhead, a thin wave of infantry following behind to mop up; but of the 10 tanks detailed to assist the
Continued at foot of next page.

by the XIX Corps was a more costly experience with little better results. Two fresh divisions were employed: the 15th (Major-General H. F. Thuillier) and the 61st (2nd South Midland, Major-General C. J. Mackenzie) which had relieved the 16th and 36th Divisions on the 17th. Two brigades, the 45th and the 44th, covered the front of the 15th Division, and one brigade, the 184th (Br.-General Hon. R. White), that of the 61st Division. The concrete pillboxes in the farm ruins were as intact as on the 16th August, and, being re-covered with mud each night by the German garrisons, both they and the intervening machine-gun nests were invisible to the infantry till it was close up. The 15th Division was checked soon after the start in front of Potsdam, Vampir, Borry and Iberian Farms; parties seen to infiltrate beyond, near to the objective, were never heard of again. ·The left of the division, assisted by two tanks, made some progress up the slope of Hill 35 till halted by the Gallipoli Farm strongpoint.[1] The 61st Division advanced its line about six hundred yards to include Somme Farm and Hindu Cottage. Thus, on the whole, little was gained by the XIX Corps.[2]

More important for the campaign as a whole was the renewed effort by the II Corps to occupy Inverness Copse on Gheluvelt plateau.[3] It was made a few hours later than the attacks of the XVIII and XIX Corps, at 7 a.m. by a brigade of the 14th Division (Major-General V. A. Couper), which, on arrival from the Second Army,

---

Continued from previous page.
48th Division, 6 were ditched or hit whilst circumventing water-filled shell-holes on the St. Julien–Winnipeg road before reaching the front line. The remaining 4 tanks on the Poelcappelle road helped in the capture of Springfield, which was retaken shortly after by the enemy; and 2 with the 11th Division were mainly responsible for the capture of Bülow Farm.

[1] Four tanks which were to have supported the right brigade, the 45th, were all ditched on the way up on the badly-holed Frezenberg–Zonnebeke road; and of the remaining 6, which left their starting-point west of Pommern Redoubt five minutes before zero, 4 were ditched about the redoubt, in the front line.

[2] The casualties incurred during the fighting and in holding the gains the next day were:

	Officers			Other Ranks			
	Killed	Wounded	Missing	Killed	Wounded	Missing	Total
44th Brigade ...	10	22	3	111	697	209	1,052
45th Brigade ...	6	23	8	103	609	270	1,019
184th Brigade ...	9	26	6	126	488	259	914

[3] See Sketch 18.

had relieved the 51st Division on the 17th/18th. The objective was limited to the copse and the open plateau north of it, including Fitzclarence Farm. The 43rd Brigade (Br.-General P. R. Wood) used two battalions for the assault on a frontage of eight hundred yards. The 6/Somerset L.I. followed the barrage through the copse in a masterly manner, taking 130 prisoners; but the 6/Cornwall L.I., on the open plateau to the north, was soon held up by heavy machine-gun fire from the strongpoint in Fitzclarence Farm and from an L-shaped farm, two hundred yards north of it. The Somerset, with thinned ranks and their left flank exposed, were counter-attacked almost at once from three sides, and had to fall back to a line half-way through the copse, where two tanks coming along the Menin Road gave support.[1] This line, gradually strengthened by the remainder of the brigade, was held against three counter-attacks in the afternoon; at 7 p.m., indeed, a message from the Somerset claimed that with two fresh battalions the eastern edge of the copse could be reached and held. This message, however, crossed a 9 p.m. order from II Corps headquarters, that the line reached in the copse was to be consolidated, whilst the left flank, the Cornwall L.I., with the help of four tanks, was to capture both Fitzclarence Farm and the L-shaped farm the next morning at 4 a.m. Heavy rain fell during the night, and three of the tanks were ditched on the way up; so the infantry attack did not take place; but the fourth tank, which arrived late, gave valuable help in repelling a renewed German attack at 6.50 a.m. along the northern side of the copse.

Major-General Couper's intention had been to relieve the 43rd Brigade by the 41st that night (23rd/24th), and the necessary orders had been given at 9 p.m. on the evening of the 22nd. Next morning, however, the corps commander told him to hold back the 41st Brigade for the proposed offensive on the 25th, and the relief had to be cancelled. The II Corps, although on the decisive flank, had at this time no division in reserve, as the 15th and 47th Divisions[2] had been absorbed; on hearing of the XIX Corps' decision,

---
[1] The two tanks were ditched near the Menin road about this time, and the other two, farther north, finding themselves unsupported by the Cornwall L.I., returned to base.

[2] See p. 190.

Lieut.-General Jacob protested to Fifth Army headquarters that he had not enough infantry to carry out the proposed offensive on the 25th to gain Fitzclarence Farm and Nonne Bosschen, as the 23rd and 25th Divisions, promised to him, were earmarked for the subsequent operation to gain the Polygon Wood line.

Early on the 24th the fight for Inverness Copse flared up afresh. About 4 a.m. an intense German barrage fell on the copse and north of it as far as Glencorse Wood ; but it did little damage. Half an hour later German infantry attacked.[1] South of Glencorse Wood parties of bombers and others, with portable flame-throwers, broke into the Cornwall's defence, and the battalion fell back to the starting-line of the 22nd. In Inverness Copse the assault had less cohesion, and although groups of the defenders fell back in places to the western edge, the lost ground was quickly retaken. The line half-way through the copse could probably have been held throughout the day ; but the exact situation of the front line, owing to the withdrawal of the Cornwall on the left, was not clear to the supporting artillery, and a steady shelling of the western part of the copse was maintained throughout the morning. Several urgent messages were sent back to lengthen the range ; but all telephone communication had been cut, and it was nearly 2 p.m. before the artillery fire died down. By that hour the holding infantry, exhausted after three days and nights of great strain, had withdrawn from the copse, and on the cessation of the shelling the Germans re-occupied the western edge, except for the north-western corner.[2] On hearing the news

---

[1] The *67th Regiment* (*34th Division*) stood approximately opposite the 43rd Brigade ; the *32nd Division*, an *Eingreifdivision*, with its leading (*177th*) regiment, east of Becelaere. By the night of the 23rd all 3 battalions of the *67th Regiment* had moved up to reinforce the forward zone. To lead the deliberate counter-attack planned for daybreak on the 24th, a battalion of the *177th Regiment* was sent up, in addition to a company of the *4th Assault Battalion*, a specially trained formation of *Sturmtrupps* under the direct orders of the Army commander. " Regt. No. 67 " ii., p. 71, states that the barrage formed by the combined artillery of three divisions fell short, causing heavy casualties, and broke up the assault. It adds that eleven counter-attacks were delivered to re-occupy the copse during these three days, but does not give the casualties.

[2] The casualties of the 43rd Brigade during the action were 59 officers and 1,464 other ranks, of which 24 officers and 194 other ranks were killed, 33 officers and 1,088 other ranks wounded, and 2 officers and 182 other ranks missing.

of the withdrawal, Major-General Couper placed two battalions of his reserve brigade (41st) at the disposal of Br.-General Wood, who intended to use them for a counterattack to regain the copse, believing that the Germans would be disorganized; but an alarmist report, that the Stirling Castle ridge had been lost, delayed the issue of the order until it was too late in the day for action.

Principal Rôle Transferred to General Plumer

The loss of Inverness Copse ended the third fruitless and costly effort to gain ground on Gheluvelt plateau since the Pilckem Ridge battle on the 31st July. The Germans still held the waist of the plateau between the sources of the Bassevillebeek and the Hanebeek, and the greater part of it was still available for their artillery observers, and for batteries which could sweep the lower ground on either flank with observed artillery fire.[1]

The news of failure, which had reached G.H.Q. in the course of the afternoon, was a great disappointment to Sir Douglas Haig, and he came to the conclusion that the principal rôle must be transferred from the Fifth to the Second Army. On the following morning, he visited Second Army headquarters at Cassel. After relating General Gough's lack of success, he recalled to General Plumer the importance of Gheluvelt plateau, and announced his intention to concentrate his maximum resources for its capture. In order to compel the dispersal of the fire of the German artillery massed behind it he wished to extend the attack frontage southwards to include Zandvoorde;[2] and as it was very desirable to carry out the operation under one command, he proposed that the Second Army should take back from the Fifth Army the frontage of the II Corps. He asked General Plumer to prepare at once to attack from this frontage of 6,800 yards, between the Ypres-Comines canal and the Ypres–Roulers railway; and, changing his tactics, he agreed that the operation should take the form of a succession of

---

[1] On 19th August the Fifth Army Intelligence Summary gave the following estimate of the German artillery array on the Army front: in the Zandvoorde–Gheluvelt–Zonnebeke area, 88 batteries (238 guns); Zonnebeke and Poelcappelle, 50 batteries (132 guns); between Poelcappelle and Houthulst Forest (inclusive), 62 batteries (188 guns).

[2] See Sketch 22.

MINOR ACTIONS. 25TH–27TH AUGUST

attacks with strictly limited objectives until the Zandvoorde–Polygon Wood–Broodseinde position had been gained.

At a conference later in the day at G.H.Q., Sir Douglas Haig elaborated his new scheme to General Plumer, in the presence of General Gough, and it was decided that the Second Army should take back the front of the II Corps early in September. General Plumer asked for three weeks in which to make his preparations, and this request was granted. In the meantime the Fifth Army was to continue to be active and press the enemy: its right, the II Corps, before being handed over to the Second Army, was to occupy Inverness Copse, Glencorse Wood and Nonne Bosschen, and its left was to continue to advance towards Poelcappelle.

The Fifth Army order for a general offensive on the 25th was therefore cancelled; and the actions which took place on the 27th in accordance with the decision that activity should be continued were minor affairs; but they resulted in considerable further casualties and very little gain of ground.

Zero hour for the II Corps was at 4.45 a.m. and heavy rain had fallen throughout the night. Four tanks were to co-operate with the 41st Brigade (Br.-General P. C. B. Skinner), of the 14th Division attached temporarily to the 23rd Division (Major-General J. M. Babington), in order to gain a footing in Inverness Copse and Glencorse Wood, half a company of infantry being allotted to each tank. All four were ditched near the front line, about Clapham Junction, and the few parties of infantry which did succeed in reaching the objective were either killed or forced to fall back.

For the three northern corps, zero hour was later in the day, at 1.55 p.m. The assaulting battalions were marched up by night from their assembly areas, in spite of the rain, and in the last stages the men, standing up to their knees in mud and water in the shelled area, had to wait for ten hours until the hour of assault. Twenty minutes before this the rain, which had ceased for a while during the morning, came on again in torrents with a driving wind, and most of the smoke candles, of which each man carried three, to form a smoke screen, could not be lit. The ground, too, was so slippery from the rain, and so broken by the water-filled shell holes, that the pace was slow and the protection of the creeping barrage was soon lost.

In the XIX Corps sector,[1] the 15th and 61st Divisions were brought to a halt within a hundred yards of the enemy's outpost groups between Gallipoli and Schuler Farms; and after attempts to advance farther had cost a third of the men and half of the officers engaged, the survivors withdrew to about their starting-line.

In the XVIII Corps sector the Germans at first showed every inclination to surrender; but, on seeing the slow progress of the infantry struggling over the slippery ground, they opened rapid fire at close range. Only a small advance was made, but it included the capture of Springfield and Vancouver Farms by the 48th Division, made with the help of three tanks, which had come up by the St. Julien–Poelcappelle road; and the 11th Division, on the left, was able to advance its line slightly near Pheasant Farm.

The XIV Corps, attacking with one brigade of the 38th Division, was to occupy the six hundred yards of the Gheluvelt–Langemarck line still uncaptured on either side of the road-junction at Schreiboom.[2] Here, too, the attacking troops of the 115th Brigade were unable to keep pace with the barrage owing to the mud, and were exposed to frontal fire, and enfilade fire from the strongpoint at White House. By evening the survivors were back in their original line.

As the following day was also one of rain and gale, in the evening Sir Douglas Haig ordered the limitation of further operations by the Fifth Army until the Second Army was ready.[3] An exception was made of the attack, under Fifth Army orders, by the II Corps on Gheluvelt plateau; but as the weather continued wet, that operation was cancelled on the 31st. The capture of the woods on this front was to be included either as preliminary to or as part of the main offensive by the Second Army, after the corps and its frontage had been transferred from the Fifth Army.

CASUALTIES AND RESULTS OF THE MONTH'S FIGHTING

The casualties during the four weeks of August (31st July–28th August) since the opening day of the main offensive

---

[1] See Sketch 20.
[2] See Sketch 19.
[3] Appendix XX.

CASUALTIES. 31ST JULY—28TH AUGUST

had amounted to 3,424 officers and 64,586 other ranks;[1] and the expenditure of artillery and munitions had eaten deeply into the available reserves.[2] In all, 22 British divisions (including one twice) had been engaged on the Fifth Army front, of which 14 had been relieved and withdrawn to refit:[3] and, in spite of the large nucleus of officers and men withheld from battle to reconstitute the units, these 14 divisions could not be considered fit to be engaged for some weeks. The casualties alone do not give the full picture of the situation; for, apart from actual losses, the discomfort of the living conditions in the forward areas and the strain of fighting with indifferent success had overwrought and discouraged all ranks more than any other operation fought by British troops in the War, so that, although the health of the troops did not suffer,[4] discontent was general: the soldier hates discomfort more than he fears danger. The memory of this August fighting, with its heavy showers, rain-filled craters and slippery mud, was so deeply impressed on the combatants, who could not be told the reason for the Commander-in-Chief's persistency, and such stories of it were spread at home by the wounded, that it has remained the image and symbol of the whole battle, overshadowing the subsequent successful actions

---

[1]
Officers			Other Ranks			
Killed	Wounded	Missing	Killed	Wounded	Missing	Total
684	2,563	177	9,582	47,598	7,406	68,010

[2] In the II Corps sector alone the artillery ammunition expenditure between 25th June and 31st August amounted to 2,766,824 rounds, 85,396 tons.

[3] The total of 22 divisions is made up as follows:
    II Corps: 24th, 30th, 8th, 18th, 25th, 14th, 47th, 56th.
    XIX Corps: 15th, 55th, 16th, 36th, 61st.
    XVIII Corps: 39th, 51st, 48th, 11th, 23rd.
    XIV Corps: 38th, Guards, 20th, 29th.

On the coast, under the Fourth Army, were the 1st, 32nd, 33rd and 66th; at Salonika, 4; in Palestine, 6; in India, 3; in Mesopotamia, 1; in Egypt (for France, 75th), 1; leaving in France 24 British divisions, the Canadian and the two Anzac Corps for the First, Second and Third Armies and reserve.

[4] "The sickness during the period of the battles was comparatively "slight, . . . and the wastage from sickness considerably less than the "wastage from wounds". Medical Services, General, iii., p. 171.

Conditions, according to German authorities (e.g. Kuhl ii., pp. 112–3) were much worse on their side, and the toll of sickness very heavy: "The "Hell of Verdun was surpassed. The Flanders battle was called the "greatest martyrdom of the World War". There were no trenches and no shelters except the few concrete blockhouses: "in the water-filled "craters cowered the defenders without shelter from weather, hungry and "cold, abandoned without pause to overwhelming artillery fire".

of the campaign and preventing the true estimation of them, even in some cases stopping any knowledge of them from reaching the public ear.

The credit side of the balance sheet, even at this stage, was not inconsiderable. During the period 25th July to 28th August, 23 German divisions (17 in the first three weeks)[1] had been exhausted and withdrawn out of the 30 which had been engaged (two of them twice) opposite the Fifth Army alone on the front Hollebeke–Weidenreft (near Langemarck) ;[2] and, northwards to Merckem, 7 more with heavy losses, opposite to the French First Army.[3] Of this total of 37 divisions—as against 26 Allied (4 French, 22 British) divisions—9 had come from Champagne and Alsace–Lorraine, thereby relieving anxiety in that direction; information, too, had been received by G.H.Q. of a diminution of 70 per cent. in the German heavy gun ammunition in the French sector, indicating that the Germans had had to concentrate their available heavy artillery ammunition in Flanders. More important than this, Sir Douglas Haig's purpose to draw all available German reserves to the British sector was proving effective. The French battle-front had been left unmolested, and German plans for an attack on the Russian front had had to be postponed.[4]

---

[1] Kuhl ii., p. 114. French and German divisions had only 9 battalions to the British 12.

[2] See Sketch 19.

[3] In this period only the French 1st, 2nd, 51st and 162nd Divisions were engaged, the 29th and 133rd, which earlier had been on the coast, having been sent there to rest.

[4] Ludendorff writes: " From 31st July 1917 till well into September " was a period of tremendous anxiety. . . . The fighting on the Western " Front became more serious than any the German army had yet experi-" enced, while in the East we had to keep on hammering at Russia in " order to bring about the fall of the Colossus. . . . On 31st July the " fighting caused us very heavy losses in prisoners and stores, and a large " expenditure of reserves ; and the costly August battles imposed a great " strain on the Western troops. I was myself being placed in a serious " predicament. The state of affairs in the West appeared to prevent the " execution of our plans elsewhere. Our wastage had been so high as to " cause grave misgivings, and exceeded all our expectations. The attack " on the Duna [Hutier's Riga offensive] in Russia had to be postponed " repeatedly. Indeed, it became a question whether we could continue " to bear the responsibility of retaining those divisions [4 divisions sent " in June from the French sector of the Western Front to deal with the " Kerenski offensive] in the East "

NOTE I

RAINFALL

In criticism of Sir Douglas Haig it has been asserted that " Flanders was the wettest area on the front ", that " in Flanders the weather broke early each August with the regularity of the Indian monsoon ", and that the offensive of the 31st July was " a reckless gamble . . . on the chance of a rainless autumn on the Flemish coast ".[1]

Neither experience nor meteorological statistics go to confirm these assertions, for which no authority is given. Bigourdan's " Le Climat de la France ", the authoritative work at the time, founded on fifty years' records, gives the average annual rainfall of the four frontier Departments in which the British operated as : Nord (which includes French Flanders), 28.5 inches (722 mm.) ; Pas de Calais, 30.1 (766), Aisne, 28.6 (728) ; Ardennes, 33.8 (859). Flanders had therefore the lowest average. August is described as having " normal " fall ; September " increasing " ; of October it is said, " this month is very "generally that which gives everywhere most rain. This is " particularly true for the Nord region and for the coastal " region "—but " the ground is generally dry enough to absorb " most of the rain quickly ". The average rainfall at Dunkirk was 28.2 inches ; Arras, 26.7 ; Paris, 22.0. Plate 14 of the " Atlas de France " shows Flanders as having the second lowest rainfall, between 23 and 31 inches (600 to 800 mm.). In England the average of the years 1881–1915, according to *Whitaker's Almanack*, was 32.67 inches. In fact, there seems to be very little difference between Flanders and south-eastern England, with its normal showery August, fine September and wet October ; and this is confirmed by the isohyets (equal rainfall lines) in all meteorological atlases.

The autumn of 1914, when Sir Douglas Haig was fighting at Ypres, was, as already mentioned, exceptionally fine ; no statistics are available, the local stations having been abandoned in the face of the enemy and no others established ; but in 1915 the Meteorological Officer of the B.E.F.[2] had a station at St. Omer,

---

[1] It seems almost unnecessary, particularly after the " summer " of 1946, to point out that there is no regularity about the weather of England and Northern France. So irregular is it that the Secretary of the Royal Meteorological Society stated on 4th August 1946 (in the *Sunday Times*) that " there is some doubt whether consistently accurate *24-hour forecasts* " will be feasible ".

A letter in *The Times* newspaper of the 10th September 1946 states that, until 1946, the highest August rainfall in Kent for the 73 years during which records had been kept, was in the year 1917.

[2] Colonel E. Gold, C.B., D.S.O., O.B.E., F.R.S., M.A., now Deputy Director, Meteorological Office, Air Ministry, who has provided me with the statistics here given.

NOTE I. RAINFALL

which registered in July 2.12 inches; in August, 1.5 inches; in September, 5.11 inches. In 1916 he had five stations:

	Hesdin	First Army	Second Army	Third Army	Fourth Army
July	1.48	.94	1.02	(not available)	1.93
August ...	3.51	3.31	2.91	4.14	3.03
September ...	3.24	2.09	2.20	2.83	2.95
October ...	5.43	3.18	2.72	3.47	3.81
Total ...	13.66	9.52	8.85	10.44	11.72

Thus the Second Army area (Flanders) had the lowest for the four months.

For 1917 the records of three representative stations in the northern area gave:

	Vlamertinghe	Hazebrouck	Béthune
July	3.14	3.22	3.77
August	5.00	5.07	3.85
September	1.58	.55	.70
October	4.21	3.97	4.37
	13.93	12.81	12.69

These figures are above the average.[1]

In any case, the rain, perhaps caused by the heavy firing, was not, and could hardly have been, foreseen on the available records, and it did not interfere with Sir Douglas Haig's main purpose of keeping the German reserves in Flanders; for as long as the British continued to attack the enemy could not move any troops away to attack the French; but it did prevent the full use of aircraft and of tanks, and was a drag on all movement.

---

[1] In Earl Lloyd George's "War Memoirs" iv., p. 2207 (for the source of his information see Book List under "Lloyd George"), from which the quotation at the beginning of this Note is taken, the average rainfall " in the lowlands of Flanders" [the station or stations are not stated, nor is the source of the statistics] for the four years 1914–17 is given for the months of July, August and September, but not for October. The figures in inches are:

	July	August	September	Total
1914 ...	4.88	1.57	2.95	... 9.40
1915 ...	2.91	4.21	2.56	... 9.68
1916 ...	3.86	2.79	3.07	... 9.72
1917 ...	4.095	4.17	.629	... 8.89
	15.745	12.74	9.209	

Colonel Gold, to whom these figures were submitted, states "There are " undoubtedly some mistakes in the table, e.g., August was very definitely " wetter than July, whereas the table suggests the reverse". For 1916 the British figures for the three months at the five stations in and near Flanders are 6.34, 6.13, 6.97 for the northern stations, and 8.23 and 7.91 for Hesdin and the Somme—nothing like 9.72.

The British figures as a whole show that 1917 was wetter, not drier, than the preceding three years—and those who fought in Flanders will probably agree. The omission of October in the table, the month when operations were definitely influenced by weather, seems to deprive the "War Memoirs" table of any point or military value.

NOTE II

THE ROAD AND TRACK COMMUNICATIONS
(Extracted from a report of Colonel E. F. W. Lees,
D.S.O., R.E., C.R.E. Guards Division.)

On any day on which a definite advance was attempted, track-tracing parties, four in number, each under an officer, followed close on the heels of the attack; the probable lines of the traces were taken from the map and aeroplane photographs, and broadcast to the troops beforehand. The track-tracing parties marked the routes from duck-walk heads, with white tapes raised on white posts when not under direct observation by the enemy, and on low unpainted pickets when under direct observation; the traces were freely notice-boarded with place-names, map references and objectives, the notice boards being prepared beforehand. The greatest determination was shown by these track-tracing parties, and they never failed to arrive on the final objective, usually within 20 minutes to half an hour of its capture, unless the casualties were too great. On one occasion (Railway Street trace, 31st July) only one sapper of the party survived; but with all his own carrying to do in the final stage, and with the aid of a sketch partially obliterated by the blood of his officer, who was killed, he got his trace through.

The value of these traces was proved by the constant stream of traffic up and down them, as the tapes moved forward; the moves of supports and reliefs, the evacuation of the wounded, and the supply of ammunition were much facilitated. The notice-boards were especially valuable in enabling troops to locate themselves; the troops always seemed rather hazy as to their whereabouts on the battlefield, especially when it came to a question of identifying Green, Blue, etc., lines [the objectives] on the ground, such lines being usually in a devastated zone. On the 31st July, 48 notice-boards were erected and distributed among the four traces forward.

The duck-walks followed these traces as quickly as possible, deviation from the original line selected being avoided unless absolutely necessary, as the troops " knew where they were " if the original traces were adhered to; alteration of trace meant alteration of notice-boards, and runners especially regarded the notice-boards as friends.

Construction of the duck-walk depended, of course, on supply and labour; supply was good, and labour was sufficient because the brigades realised the necessity of these duck-walks: no appeal for extra assistance, over and above the " ordered " working ·parties, was ever refused: brigade commanders, on their own initiative, kept individual men (little notice was taken of individuals by day in the forward area) carrying trench-boards from forward dumps up the trace throughout the hours of daylight. The average amount of duck-walk construction was between 800 and 900 yards per 24 hours; 5,000 yards were completed in the 5 nights 10th to 15th October, excluding the night 12th/13th, when no work was done. Forward dumps were kept filled by infantry carrying parties, often under most unpleasant conditions of shelling and weather; but a steady flow of material forward was maintained, and we usually left a good supply in our forward dumps on handing over to a relieving division: for example, on coming out of the line on October 16th there were 2,100 yards of duck-walk stores in one forward dump, and 2,200 yards in the other.

One pair of duck-walks was selected as the " priority route ", and the full allotment of labour and stores was always made to this route; the second pair might or might not get their full allotment of both, and it was from the second pair that labour was diverted in emergencies.

Maintenance of the duck-walks was not too difficult; daylight patrols were maintained, and small dumps of spares were kept filled; the duck-walks were never out of action, except for very short periods. The enemy took a dislike to certain sections and this dislike became known and could be catered for; one section, for instance, the section near Vee Bend, was blotted out by shell-fire on 3 occasions in 6 days.

This obvious dislike of certain sections by the enemy was useful in that, if an attack were contemplated involving the moving forward of a large number of troops to their assembly positions, it was possible to lift and relay a section likely to be badly shelled; on one such occasion, as a " set-piece ", 1,300 yards of duck-walk (Bridge Street) were moved 300 yards north between dusk and the time when the troops moving up to their assembly positions were due to pass over the section. I went down this track soon after the attack and before the battlefield was cleared: there were only two dead men on the whole of the reconstructed length.

A very useful adjunct to the " traces " in front of duck-walk heads were the " Mats ": these, consisting of strips of canvas and rabbit wire netting, held together by wooden slats, were a lighter version of the mats which had been used to enable raiding parties, in the period prior to the 27th July, to wade across the muddy bottom of the Canal; they were used on noticeably muddy parts of the " traced tracks ", and, though their life was short, they were of real value; 355 of these mats were used, for instance, in front of the duck-walk head during the period 9th to 15th October, and the Field Company commanders were always demanding far more than could be manufactured and sent forward.

NOTE II. COMMUNICATIONS

Infantry bridges were an accessory to the duck-walk tracks which were much used to carry the track over trench lines and individual craters : in the period 9th to 15th October, 180 of these bridges were used.

On the whole it may be said that the construction and maintenance of the duck-walks were not outside the capacity of the division ; we kept them going forward at a reasonable pace, breaks were quickly dealt with, and I do not think that it can be said that the division was ever held up by the impossibility of moving men and man-loads across country.

Roads. Reference has already been made to the fact that, west of the Canal, the roads were not so badly knocked about as might have been expected, and the main traffic route within the divisional area was quickly through to the Canal Bank, and capable of carrying heavy traffic.

East of the Canal, the damage to roads outside the " devastated zones " (except at certain obvious traffic junctions) was serious, but the roads could be patched up quickly ; no attempt was made to do more than make them passable, since no road metal was available ; re-making the road was naturally left to the corps. The main object of the Field Company commanders was to get some form of drainage going again, as soon as the holes in the road were filled.

The badly shelled " traffic junctions ", being limited in length, were dealt with by making good the surface and laying beech-slabs, sleepers (if any could be spared from the tramways) and half-round logs : the trace of the road was adhered to, as the " turn-offs " to deviations appeared to have such a serious effect on slowing up traffic.

In the devastated zones, deviation was sometimes inevitable, but every endeavour was made to avoid such deviations for the reason given in the last paragraph ; on one occasion traffic movement practically ceased for six hours, and the trouble was traced to two " turn-offs ". Generally, however, traffic kept moving without unreasonable delays, and the occasion referred to was the only one on which, so far as I can remember, no engineer stores got to the rendezvous where the carrying parties to the forward dumps were waiting.

The amount of labour and transport necessary to get the roads going was very great, and the supply of road-surfacing materials appeared to be limited ; this may, however, have been due to lack of transport behind the division, not to actual lack of material. The French on our left made great use of fascines ; I used them when I could get hold of the material to make them, but the local resources were very limited. On several occasions I endeavoured to find out, from my opposite number with the French division, the sources of their supply, but with no success.

Both beech-slab and sleeper surfaces proved very slippery in wet weather, and it was difficult to keep them clear of mud; we endeavoured to avoid the use of either on any marked slope, using half-round logs in such places.

For the use of the division there was only one " through " road, and this had not been designed to carry two lines of traffic on a dark night; delays were inevitable; every endeavour was made to control the traffic at the Canal Bank, so that the vehicles which had to go the greatest distance forward crossed first. The first part of the night usually proceeded smoothly, but side traffic coming in from the batteries frequently upset the most carefully designed programmes. The ideal aimed at was practically the creation of one-way traffic; everything UP until a certain hour of the very early morning, and after that everything DOWN; but there was a natural reluctance to remain longer than absolutely necessary in the forward area.

The road problem (repair, maintenance, and traffic control) was not an easy one, but, as I have said in regard to duck-walks, the difficulties could be, and were, dealt with.

Tramways. These were the most efficient form of transport under the circumstances, and an agent which was used to the utmost capacity; our efforts were limited only by the amount of tramway material available. Tramway construction, like one of the two pairs of duck-walks, was a " priority " job and sufficient men were provided each 24 hours to ensure that all the material available was used.

The iron sleepers, provided with the track, proved quite inadequate to carry the line in many parts of the battlefield, and it was necessary to use wooden sleepers every yard, and a wider formation, for long lengths; this added largely to the quantity of tramway material which had to be got up, and to the amount of labour required.

In very bad places the track was carried on trestles: in the Broembeek valley the line was carried for 80 yards in this manner.

The rate of progress was roughly 300 yards of track laid per 24 hours: formation and bridge construction were kept well in front of tramway-head.

Maintenance of tramways was always a heavy item; the enemy evidently put a high value on this form of transport, and the bursts of artillery fire were frequent, heavy, and well distributed during the earlier part of each night. On the night of 30th/31st July, there were 22 breaks and 2 smashed bridges in the section between X line and Boesinghe village.

In addition to enemy efforts, we had to contend with the damage caused by the movement of the artillery; the gunner treated the duck-walks with consideration, but appeared to

NOTE II. COMMUNICATIONS

think that he could bump over the tramways: probably they were difficult to see in the dark.

Maintenance of the tracks was, however, carried on by the sappers and their attached troops with the greatest determination, and the tramways were seldom out of action for long. More anxiety was attached to the maintenance in working order of a sufficient number of trucks. Damage by shell fire was frequent; but a break in the line any time after 4 a.m. in the morning was most dreaded by the tramway officers since this meant the probable marooning of some trucks in the forward area with, apart from the danger of damage by shell fire, a consequent shortage of trucks at the commencement of the next night's traffic.

A very strict control was necessary to ensure that a full and proper use was made of the tramways, especially in regard to quick turn-round: a control station was established at the Canal Bank early in August, and a sapper officer was detailed in charge of this station; he lived at the control station and had a very unpleasant time until the enemy was pushed farther back, as it was impossible entirely to conceal the existence of this station from the enemy. This officer dealt with the allotment, loading, and despatch of the trucks, and had to be prepared to alter his programme at a moment's notice, if a serious break were reported. One of his most important duties was to see that units sent back their trucks the same night. At first, certain units had the bright idea of hanging on to their trucks until the following evening, when they sent them down " against " the traffic, in the hope that, on arrival at the Canal, they would be allowed to load up these trucks again and " repeat the process ". This officer was responsible for the repair of damaged trucks, and for making " one out of two " when returning empties brought in badly damaged trucks, or bits of them; he maintained also the main depôt of spares for the repair of the lines, and sent forward material to keep full the small repair dumps, and he met emergency demands. As this officer controlled the truckage available, the proper provision of maintenance stores could be ensured. He was not responsible that the maintenance gangs should keep him informed of any serious break in the line—i.e., one that would take more than an hour to repair: up to this limit, we found that unloading, carrying the truck round the break, and reloading did not cause too great a lag.

Artillery and Pack Transport Tracks.[1] The weather was all against the maintenance of such tracks: they became so quickly churned up into a mass of mud as to be useless.

---

[1] A track was a cross-country road without any artificial surface, such as stone or timber.

We speedily abandoned all idea of artillery tracks: outside the badly shelled zones, if the weather forecast were at all favourable, we endeavoured to help the gunners by making short lengths from the main traffic artery; provided that an elaborate system of notice-boarding was adopted, these tracks were used as being the quickest way to definite positions; they went out of action directly the rain came down.

Pack transport on the main artery was such a nuisance that for a time we made every effort to make and maintain tracks for its use—with little result, and it appeared far better to let such transport make its own way across country, keeping in sight of the duck-walks: the animals became clever at getting about, provided they were allowed to "spread", though they did not compare with the "packs" of donkeys which I saw being used on various occasions in the French area on our left; these animals showed a wonderful aptitude for getting about the country (however much cut up) and kept the general direction laid down by their leader extraordinarily well.

CHAPTER XII

THE OPERATIONS NEAR LENS

BATTLE OF HILL 70
15TH–20TH AUGUST
(Sketch 21)

ALTERNATIVE OFFENSIVE FRONTS

During the last fortnight of August bitter fighting had also been in progress thirty miles to the south, in front of Lens. It will be remembered that before the Battle of Messines, Sir Douglas Haig, foreseeing that the Flanders campaign might be forbidden or stopped by the War Cabinet, had turned over in his mind alternative fronts for operations on a less ambitious scale. One of these was the Lens front, in the sector of the First Army, and he had therefore encouraged General Sir Henry Horne to continue the series of attacks begun at the end of June for the envelopment of the town.[1]

At that time, owing to the transfer of a number of heavy batteries to Flanders and Italy,[2] an important part of the programme, the capture of Hill 70, north of the town, had been postponed. On the 10th July, however, orders were issued by the First Army for the Canadian Corps (Lieut.-General Sir A. W. Currie) to take over the front opposite Hill 70 from the I Corps, and to formulate a scheme for the capture of Lens from the north-west on or before the 30th, in order to draw pressure both off the Ypres sector and off the French Aisne front. Next day (11th), orders were issued by the Canadian Corps for the 1st and 2nd Canadian Divisions to complete all preparations to carry out the operations for the capture of Hill 70. This objective was selected because it gave observation far into the German lines and its possession would be so intolerable to the enemy that he could not submit to it and must react. By the 16th the Canadian Corps had taken over from the I Corps, the 2nd Canadian Division in the sector from Lens to the Loos

---

[1] See Sketch 21.
[2] Ten 6-inch howitzer batteries (there were only 152 in France) were sent to Italy in April and 3 more in July.

Crassier and the 1st Canadian Division, thence to Bois Hugo. On the 27th, the 4th Canadian Division came into the line, relieving the 2nd of the part of its front opposite Lens; but as zero day (30th) approached, it was seen that the destruction of the wire was incomplete. The Commander-in-Chief at a conference at corps headquarters, having given the assurance that the operations in the north fixed for the 31st July were quite independent, and that there was no necessity to assault before both infantry and artillery were satisfied that preparations were complete, the operation, after being set for the 1st August, was postponed for 48 hours, and then for a further 24 hours, on account of the wet weather. Then notice was given by the First Army that zero day would not be before the 6th August, and later that it could not be before the 15th.

Capture of Hill 70 by the Canadian Corps: 15th August

This hill, described in a previous volume,[1] is an eminence east of Loos at the end of one of the many spurs reaching out north-eastwards from the Artois plateau. On the lower part of its southern slope are the town and suburbs of Lens; but the summit is a barren expanse of chalk down with commanding views over the open fields of the Douai plain to the east. The capture of the summit had been the constant pre-occupation of those responsible for the sector ever since the Battle of Loos on the 25th September 1915, when it had been overrun, but not held.

The objective was an old German trench, dug arc-shape around the reverse, or eastern, slope of the summit from Cité St. Elisabeth to Bois Hugo, an assault frontage of two miles. The battered trenches on the hill, with their deep dug-outs, were now used by the Germans only as shelters against bombardment and the weather; the defensive battle would evidently be fought from machine-gun nests and open shell-hole positions in the intermediate areas of the old lines. But this particular trench formed a useful objective, as it was sufficiently forward to protect the proposed artillery observation posts about the summit, and would, in the hard chalk subsoil of the hill, be easy to consolidate for immediate defence.

---

[1] "1915" Vol. II, p. 145. See Sketch 21.

Every detail of the operation had been frequently rehearsed by the units selected for the assault over a taped-out course on similar ground near Aix Noulette. As it was expected that the Germans would rely on a succession of immediate counter-attacks by fresh troops from behind their thinly held forward zone to retake any lost ground, countermeasures had been carefully worked out. It was hoped by the full use of artillery power in all stages of the battle to reduce infantry casualties to a minimum. Concentrations of fire both by heavy and divisional artillery were to be laid on the probable lines of advance on the enemy's counter-attack formations and on their assembly areas about Cité du Grand Condé, Cité St. Auguste and Bois des Dames; and forward artillery observers with the leading infantry, and air observers in 2-seater Sopwiths,[1] had the special task of watching the back areas for enemy concentrations as targets for artillery. The importance of mopping up at once isolated machine-gun nests and infantry groups in shell-holes in the captured area was also stressed at the rehearsals; and the 48 Vickers machine guns attached to the assaulting brigades were to reach pre-arranged positions, in close support of the foremost line, as rapidly as possible. These positions, selected to give mutual support, were to be converted into platoon strongpoints for at least 25 men, and consolidated immediately. A party of engineers was detailed to each for the construction of blocks and the erection of wire.

The postponement had enabled the artillery preparations, under Br.-General E. W. B. Morrison, commanding the Canadian Corps artillery, to be very thorough;[2] and in a region of well-built mining villages, collieries and factories this was most necessary. Counter-battery work by three

---

[1] No. 43 Squadron R.F.C., from an advanced airfield, patrolled, with groups of 3 machines at a time, throughout the day over an area 7,000 yards wide and 1,500 to 2,500 yards from the front line, through which German counter-attack formations would have to pass. No. 16 Squadron furnished contact patrols for the attack.

During the three days, 15th, 16th and 17th, a total of 240 reports of German batteries firing resulted in as many shoots by counter-batteries supporting the Canadian attack.

[2] His Staff officer was Major A. F. Brooke (later Field-Marshal Lord Alanbrooke); Commander H.A., Br.-General R. H. Massie; Counter-battery Staff Officer, Lieut.-Colonel (later General) A. G. L. McNaughton. Commanders Divisional R.A., Br.-Generals H. C. Thacker (1st); H. A. Panet (2nd); J. H. Mitchell (3rd); C. H. Maclaren (4th); and H. M. Campbell (46th).

heavy artillery groups,[1] assisted by the heavy artillery of the I Corps on the northern flank, begun in mid-July, and destructive shoots by three bombardment groups[2] and 13 field artillery brigades, begun during the latter half of July, were not interrupted by the postponements or by the enemy's destructive retaliation, but continued up to the eve of the assault, by which time it was estimated that of the 102 enemy batteries, only 63 were still active.

Since it was obvious that the enemy was expecting an attack, the preparatory programmes were so drawn up as to make it appear that the front of assault would be directly west of Lens. As a further measure of deception, during the 14th, the I Corps, on the left of the Canadians, bad weather favouring, carried out assault demonstrations with dummy tanks.

Heavy thunder showers which fell during the afternoon of the 14th cleared in the evening, and the night was fine, but dark. At zero hour, 4.25 a.m., dawn was just breaking when the barrage crashed on the German defences.[3] At the same time, drums of burning oil were fired from projectors on the right flank on to Cité St. Elisabeth, and the dense smoke from them was carried by a south-westerly breeze up over Hill 70; whilst on the left flank, smoke bombs, fired from 4-inch Stokes mortars, neutralized German observers on the rise of ground about Hulluch.[4]

---

[1] The II Canadian, XV and L. H.A.G.'s.
[2] I Canadian, LXIII and LXIV, H.A.G.'s.
[3] The creeping barrage was formed by 9 field artillery brigades, 4 to support the 2nd Canadian Division, and 5 the 1st Canadian Division; each field gun to cover a front of twenty yards. Four hundred yards ahead of the creeping barrage was a jumping barrage of 4.5-inch and 6-inch howitzers, and beyond that a moving barrage of heavy howitzers which dealt in succession with enemy strongpoints.

The machine-gun creeping barrage, inaugurated so successfully by the Canadian Corps in the Vimy Ridge assault, was to be repeated: on the front of assault 160 Vickers guns, in 4 groups, were to lay barrages along the objectives and to be ready to answer subsequent S.O.S. calls.

The ammunition expenditure shows the scale of the artillery support. From zero hour to midnight on 15th August, 67,000 rounds of 18-pdr. and 12,000 rounds of 4.5-inch howitzer shell were fired by the artillery of the 1st Canadian Division alone; the 18-pdr. total averaged 713 rounds per gun.

[4] Eighteen of these mortars were installed for the purpose in the sector of the 46th Division (I Corps) and fired by No. 4 Special Company R.E.

The Assault

Protected by the barrage and the clouds of smoke which shrouded the battle area, the Canadian infantry broke down all resistance. Although the Germans were expectant and ready,[1] such was the swiftness and strength of the onslaught that the trench garrisons were overwhelmed, and within twenty minutes the first objective beyond the Lens–La Bassée highway, an average advance of six hundred yards, had been reached by the two divisions.[2]

On the right, the 4th and 5th Brigades of the 2nd Canadian Division (Major-General H. E. Burstall), with a combined frontage of seventeen hundred yards, had forced their way, without check, through the débris of the mining villages of Cité St. Edouard and Cité St. Laurent. After a half-hour pause for consolidation, the 4th Canadian Brigade (Br.-General R. Rennie), using the same battalions (18th, 21st and 20th), followed the barrage through the ruins of Cité St. Elisabeth, and formed a defensive flank facing the northern edge of Lens town.[3] The 5th Canadian Brigade (Br.-General J. M. Ross) had farther to go, and, replacing the 25th and 22nd Battalions with the 24th and 26th, pressed on through Cité de St. Emile to the final objective, which was reached by 6 a.m., or soon afterwards.

The assault by the 1st Canadian Division (Major-General A. C. Macdonell) had been marked by the same dash and

---

[1] There is plenty of evidence of this: "All signs pointed that the British attack would take place on the 15th" ("Res. Regt. No. 10", p. 139); "on the evening of 14th August, the brigade warned us that a great attack would take place on the 15th". ("Regt. No. 165", p. 150); "at 3 a.m. the *II Battalion* reported from the front trenches that the enemy lay ready for the assault in wave after wave" (*idem*); "the resting battalion *1/65*, as divisional reserve of the *185th Division*, was from 14th August in permanent alarm and ready to march at a moment's notice". ("Regt. No. 65", p. 248.)

In consequence of the 3 a.m. warning, 3 minutes after zero the German artillery put down a scattered barrage, but it soon dwindled away under the well-directed fire of the counter-batteries covering the attack.

[2] The two Canadian divisions were faced by approximately 2 German regiments of the *7th Division*, the *165th*, which had only been in the line for some twelve days, and the *26th*, which held a 1,600-yard frontage across the summit of Hill 70, its right north of Bois Hugo. In expectation of the attack, the reserve battalions of both regiments had been moved forward overnight to the brickworks in the southern corner of Cité St. Auguste and to Mortar Wood, respectively.

[3] Sergeant F. Hobson (20th Battalion) was awarded the V.C. for valour during a strong enemy counter-attack, saving a serious situation with a Lewis gun, although not a gunner; he was killed shortly afterwards.

thoroughness of execution. The 2nd Canadian Brigade (Br.-General F. O. W. Loomis), with the 5th and 10th Battalions assaulting, gained the summit of the hill, and the 3rd Canadian Brigade (Br.-General G. S. Tuxford), attacking with the 16th, 13th and 15th Battalions, occupied the western edges of Bois Rasé and Bois Hugo. The 3rd Brigade then carried through for another four hundred yards to its next and final objective. On the 2nd Brigade front, the fresh 8th and 7th Battalions pressed on to their intermediate objective along the German Second Position, and successfully accomplished that part of their task; numbers of Germans who ran back were killed by the barrage, and enemy machine guns in Bois Hugo, after causing some casualties, were quickly silenced by bombing parties working round the flanks.[1]

By about 6 a.m. the operation had been completed according to plan, with the exception of a further advance of five hundred yards to be made by the 2nd Brigade down the eastern slope of the hill. The smoke was now clearing, and this final stage would probably have been easier if carried out without a pause, taking advantage of the bad visibility and temporary demoralization of the defence. During the halt of twenty minutes allowed by the artillery time-table, the Germans had steadied along the front of Cité St. Auguste, and in the clear daylight they were ready to meet the resumed advance. Almost at once both battalions, the 8th (Manitoba) and the 7th (British Columbia), met an intense machine-gun and rifle fire which swept the glacis slope, and the movement was slowed down to individual rushes from shell hole to shell hole. The barrage lost its protective value and casualties rapidly mounted. The 8th Battalion, on the right, on a frontage of four hundred yards, made little progress, except with its right company, and only the left company of the 7th Battalion, whose objective was a strongly defended shallow chalk quarry in the side of the hill,[2] reached it. In these circumstances, the 7th Battalion withdrew to the previous objective, leaving about fifty men to hold the northern end of the quarry; the 8th Battalion conformed. Casualties had

---

[1] A German trench-mortar battery was captured with 500 shells, and, after one of the prisoners had been compelled to explain the mechanism, all the shells were fired at the enemy in the course of the day.

[2] This quarry was the principal German supply dump in the Hill 70 sector.

been heavy, the 7th Battalion being able to muster only 4 officers and 120 other ranks, or less than a quarter of its original battle strength.

THE GERMAN COUNTER-ATTACKS

The morning was cloudy, but visibility was good as soon as the smoke had cleared. The forward artillery observers could now overlook the panorama of Douai plain to the east and north-east of Lens, and messages which came in from ground and air observers from 6.30 a.m. onwards gave a detailed picture of the enemy's movements and of his active batteries in the back areas.

Between 7 a.m. and 9 a.m., whilst the captured ground was being consolidated,[1] local counter-attacks, as foreseen, were delivered by German reserves against the new front from Bois Hugo, from the wood near the Chalk Quarry, from the Brick Works and from Lens, but were broken up by observed artillery fire according to plan, and finally checked by machine-gun and rifle fire.[2] Later in the morning masses of enemy infantry were seen advancing in extended order on a wide front behind Cité St. Auguste, and the Canadian infantry, from their commanding position on the hill, were able to witness the very heavy casualties and disorganization caused by the observed barrages of both heavy and field batteries on these targets.[3]

---

[1] The defended line of observation was to be along the final objective, with the main line of resistance along the intermediate objective immediately east of the Lens–La Bassée road. About and behind the main line of resistance strongpoints were constructed under the supervision of parties of engineers. The Vickers machine guns with each brigade took up pre-arranged positions in close support in the intervening zone.

[2] The reserve battalions of the two German regiments on either flank of the assault frontage were also brought up to counter-attack: that of *156th Regiment* (the right of *11th Reserve Division*) counter-attacked from Lens towards Cité St. Elisabeth, and that of *393rd Regiment* (the right of *7th Division*) counter-attacked towards Bois Hugo. Both failed with heavy losses.

[3] By about midday 7 German battalions had reinforced the 8 battalions along the assault frontage: *Group Loos* had ordered forward at once the *4th Guard Division*, the *Eingreif* division behind Hill 70 sector, to assist in the recapture of the hill. The advanced (*Stoss*) regiment, *93rd Reserve*, reached the Bois de Dix-huit at 9.15 a.m., and reinforced the line at and north of the Chalk Quarry; the other two regiments, together with a resting battalion of the *65th Regiment*, belonging to the *185th Division*, holding north of Hulluch, marched at once from the Bauvin–Carvin area. The counter-attack was ordered to begin at 11 a.m., *I Battalion* of the

Continued at foot of next page.

Subsidiary Operations

Subsidiary operations were carried out by the 4th Canadian Division (Major-General D. Watson) on the front opposite Lens, in order to divert attention from the 1st and 2nd Divisions. At zero hour gas projectors fired bombs into the enemy defences opposite Avion (2 miles south of the centre of Lens). At 8.25 a.m., as pre-arranged, the 11th Canadian Brigade (Br.-General V. W. Odlum) made an advance, and when the 2nd Canadian Division reported the capture of its objectives, strong patrols of the 11th Brigade, under an 18-pdr. barrage, pushed forward on the front between the Souchez river (½-mile south of Eleu) and the Lens railway. Heavy fighting ensued, and the patrols were driven back by counter-attacks. The casualties of the 11th Brigade were 9 officers and four hundred other ranks; but the enemy was undoubtedly deceived, as he employed a considerable force of artillery and infantry against the 11th Brigade, which might have been engaged against the right flank of the 2nd Canadian Division.

Further Counter-attacks

From 12.45 p.m. counter-attacks by these larger formations developed against the whole length of the new Canadian line. Four waves of infantry which moved against the 3rd Brigade in Bois Rasé and Bois Hugo were checked, and practically annihilated by artillery and machine-gun fire. Another attack in strength from Cité St. Auguste against the 2nd Brigade made no headway, and, farther south about Cité St. Elisabeth, a slight loss of ground was regained later in the afternoon. In all, eighteen counter-attacks were repulsed

---

Continued from previous page.
65*th Regiment* and the *Fusilier Battalion* of the *5th Guard Grenadier Regiment* against the Cité St. Emile sector; the 3 battalions of the *93rd Reserve* against the hill from Cité St. Auguste, and the 3 battalions of the *5th Guard Fusilier Regiment* against Bois Hugo, with two battalions of the *5th Guard Grenadier Regiment* in reserve.

The histories of these regiments confirm their heavy losses during the advance, and state that they marched across the open " through fountains " of earth sent up by the heavy shells ", and later, " through a hail of " shrapnel and machine-gun bullets ". Owing to disorganization and delay, the counter-attacks were not delivered till the afternoon, and then piecemeal. The *4th Guard Division* headquarters complained that the order to counter-attack was not given till too late by *Group Loos*, whose excuse was that the division had been kept in hand as the last reserve.

with what must have been terrible slaughter, and not a German soldier reached the Canadian line alive.

The final objective of the 2nd Brigade, in front of Cité St. Auguste, had not yet been gained ; and Br.-General Loomis, at 1.35 p.m., ordered zero hour to be 4 p.m., later postponed to 6 p.m. At that hour, the barrage crept forward to and beyond the objective ; but no infantry attack followed. The two battalions concerned had suffered heavy losses and were exhausted, and as the responsible front line commanders had seen strong German reinforcements reach the objective trench, they had cancelled the order on their own initiative.[1] That night, the 5th (Western Cavalry) and 10th (Alberta) Battalions took over, with orders to capture the objective at 4 p.m. next day. The morning of the 17th August was quiet, and the attack, following an intense bombardment, was made under a rolling barrage by short rushes down the four hundred yards of open slope. The objective was gained, but at a considerable cost of life, as the Germans were found in force and in the act of massing for a counter-attack. Fierce close fighting took place, especially at the Chalk Quarry, where the Germans left behind a hundred dead, in addition to a hundred wounded and 30 prisoners. At 7.15 p.m. a series of unsuccessful counter-attacks—originally planned for 6 p.m. —took shape, lasting an hour and a half. With the assistance of well-directed artillery and machine-gun fire, the line of the quarry was held ; but, farther south, the 5th Battalion, greatly reduced in strength and short of ammunition, had to fall back to a shell-hole position about two hundred yards short of the final objective where the 2nd Canadian Division had been established.[2]

---

[1] The 7th and 8th Battalions had, together, only 8 officers and less than two hundred men fit to go forward, and if that small force, on a front of eight hundred yards, had been further weakened, the summit of the hill might have lain open to the German counter-attack, seen to be imminent. Headquarters of the *4th Guard Division*, on hearing of the failure of the counter-attack, had, in fact, ordered another attempt to recapture the hill to be made at 6.25 p.m. It was repulsed all along the line ; and " Garde Gren. Regt. No. 5 ", which attacked south of Cité St. Auguste, states that its companies were " deluged (*überschüttet*) with artillery fire ".

[2] The losses of the 2nd Brigade during the action totalled 249 killed (including 13 officers), 1,177 wounded and 225 missing.

Private M. J. O'Rourke (7th Battalion) was awarded the V.C. for unceasing devotion to duty as a stretcher bearer under heavy fire throughout the operation.

Private H. Brown (10th Battalion) was awarded the V.C. for conspicuous bravery, passing through an intense barrage to deliver a message from the front line. He died of wounds a few hours later.

The Germans continued their efforts to regain the hill on the following days. In the early hours of the 18th, after a concentrated bombardment of the batteries of the 1st Canadian Division with Yellow Cross (mustard) gas shell,[1] counter-attacks were delivered against the divisional front, in particular on the quarry. But the gaps in the line of the 1st Canadian Division south of the quarry had been closed and consolidated by the 1st Brigade, which had relieved the 2nd on the night of the 17th, and neither this attack nor another made on the afternoon of the 19th was able to loosen the Canadian hold on this stubbornly contested area with its many underground shelters.[2]

SUBSEQUENT FIGHTING

On the 18th, Lieut.-General Currie had decided to clear up the situation in front of Lens town, on the lower half of the long southern slope of the hill. The town itself was a mass of ruins with scarcely a house standing, and few of its streets were recognizable. The 4th Canadian Division, which faced the western outskirts, had, as we have seen, sent forward strong patrols on the 15th without their being able to enter the town.[3] The intention now was to close in on the town from west and north by occupying the German front line on a frontage of three thousand yards from Eleu, on the Arras–Lens road, to east of Cité St. Émile. The operation was to be carried out at 4.35 a.m. on the 21st by the inner brigades (10th and 6th) of the 4th and 2nd Canadian Divisions.

It was still dark when the assault took place, and again the Canadian attack coincided with an enemy counter-attack.

---

[1] Heavy casualties to the 1st Division artillery, amounting to 4 officers and 179 other ranks, were caused by this gas, and the guns of 3 batteries received direct hits.

[2] Major O. M. Learmonth, M.C. (2nd Battalion) was awarded the V.C. for most conspicuous bravery during these counter-attacks. Though mortally wounded, he continued to direct the defence, standing on the parapet of the trench, catching bombs thrown at him by the enemy and throwing them back.

[3] The *11th Reserve Division*, holding Lens, had suffered such losses during the bombardment in these attacks that two regiments of the *220th Division* (*55th Reserve* and *99th Reserve*) were given to it to reinforce the lines along the western side of Lens, south of Cité St. Elisabeth. Both regiments had had heavy casualties when, on the night of the 20th/21st, the *1st Guard Reserve Division* began to take over the sector. Part of this latter division took part in the fighting on the 21st.

The 2nd Division found the Germans either advancing or fully ready to advance.

The 10th Brigade (Br.-General E. Hilliam), after hand-to-hand fighting in the houses, gained and retained all its objectives in the western environs of Lens, except on the left, immediately south of the Lens–Béthune road, where the 50th Battalion had been caught in a barrage thirty minutes before zero.[1] North of that road the two assaulting battalions of the 6th Brigade (Br.-General H. D. B. Ketchen), also caught in the German barrage, became involved in difficult fighting. The 27th (Winnipeg) Battalion was confronted by the strong defence area in the triangle between the Lens–Béthune and the Lens–La Bassée roads ; the 29th (Vancouver) Battalion, south of Cité St. Emile, at once met a strong force of German infantry, many loaded with bombs and without rifles, waiting ready to assault. After a desperate struggle in the dim light and ground mist, lasting fifteen minutes, two companies of the 29th, using their bayonets, forced back double the number of the *1st Foot Guard Regiment* beyond the trench which was the Canadian objective.[2] Hard fighting continued throughout the morning. The Canadians of the 2nd Division had behind them five hundred yards of open ground constantly shelled and swept by bullets, whereas the Germans had at their backs deep cellars for shelter and concealed communication trenches by which reinforcements of men and supplies could arrive ; but this disparity was to some extent reduced by the heavy and superheavy artillery shelling the city all day.[3] At 3.30 p.m. a strong counter-attack in greatly superior strength led to both Canadian battalions of the 2nd Division being deliberately withdrawn, and by 7.30 p.m. they were back on their starting line. All other objectives were held, and German efforts to gain more ground towards Cité St. Emile failed.[4]

---

[1] Corporal F. Konowal (47th Battalion) was awarded the V.C. for conspicuous bravery and leadership in mopping up the cellars, craters and machine-gun nests in his sector.

The untaken 200-yard sector of the German front trench was captured four days later, after a more thorough bombardment.

[2] C.-Sergt.-Major R. Hanna (29th Battalion) was awarded the V.C. for leading a successful assault upon a strongpoint, personally bayoneting three of the garrison and capturing a machine gun, after three assaults upon it had failed and all the officers of his company had become casualties.

[3] The *5th Guard Grenadier Regiment* was reinforced at 12.30 p.m. by a battalion of the *190th*, the remaining regiment of the *220th Division*.

[4] The casualties of the 6th Brigade on this day were 106 killed (including 10 officers), 638 wounded and 72 missing.

THE CASUALTIES

The fighting on the slopes and summit of Hill 70 had been as bitter as any experienced by the Canadian Corps—though it had Mount Sorrel and the Somme in 1916 to remember—and the casualties had been heavy: a total of 304 officers and 8,114 other ranks.[1] The Germans had spared no efforts to recapture this vital observation area, which opened the way to the encirclement of Lens; but in spite of the employment of three additional divisions, including two *Guard* divisions, and a personal visit by General Ludendorff to the battle area on the 18th, they had failed with heavy losses, including 24 officers and 1,345 other ranks taken prisoner. At a time when the Western Front was being combed by the Germans to meet the great demands for Flanders, five of their divisions had been engaged and broken up by three Canadian divisions in a few days. The respective strengths in the assault had been 14 Canadian battalions, with 2 in support and reserve, against 6 German battalions, with 15 more employed in the counter-attacks, that is 16 against 21.

Unsettled conditions continued till the end of the month in this area without any change in the situation. Early in September a scheme was put forward by General Horne to complete the capture of Lens town and cut off the retreat of its garrison by a concentric advance north-east from Eleu towards the Sallaumines high ground, and south-east from Hill 70. Sir Douglas Haig, desiring, above all, to divert the enemy's attention and reserves from the French front, approved the scheme, and preparations were ordered for its execution about the 15th October; but from lack of troops this could not take place.

---

[1] This total was for the period 15th–23rd August for the Hill 70 operation. The casualties of the divisions engaged during that period (less gas casualties, 27 officers and 1,095 other ranks) were:

	Officers			Other Ranks			
	Killed	Wounded	Prisoners	Killed	Wounded	Prisoners	Total
1st Canadian Division	33	65	1	848	2,081	7	3,035
2nd Canadian Division	34	75	—	729	1,875	11	2,724
4th Canadian Division	19	39	3	362	871	138	1,432
	86	179	4	1,939	4,827	156	7,191

Corps troops and units attached to the 1st Canadian Division lost 8 officers and 97 other ranks.

CHAPTER XIII

THE BATTLES OF YPRES 1917 (continued)

BATTLE OF THE MENIN ROAD RIDGE[1] 20TH–25TH
SEPTEMBER 1917
(Sketches 11, 22, 23)

GENERAL SITUATION AT THE END OF AUGUST

The general situation during August, partly favourable to the Allies, partly adverse, made it evident that there could be no relaxation of the British effort, and that the British Armies in Flanders, with some assistance from the French, might be called upon to withstand the onslaught of the mass of the German Armies. Little could be expected of the American Armies before 1918, only two divisions (Regular troops and Marines) having actually arrived. "The "acts of collective indiscipline" in the French Second, Fourth, Fifth, Sixth and Tenth Armies on the Aisne front of the early summer were dying away ;[2] but General Pétain was still pessimistic, and told Sir Douglas Haig that not very much could be expected of his troops, and that the British offensive must be maintained. In redemption, however, of his promise to give what assistance he could, he had, on the 26th August, staged an offensive of the French Second Army (General Guillaumat) at Verdun.[3]

The Russian Armies, despite their short-lived "Kerenski "Offensive" in July, which, at any rate, showed good will, were fast disintegrating, and revolutionary outbreaks were spreading.

---

[1] This battle for Gheluvelt plateau was known to the troops as the Battle of the Menin Road. In the narrative the word "Ridge" of the official title has been dropped.

[2] See pp. 28-30.

[3] See F.O.A. v. (ii.), pp. 828–910. Planned on the lines recommended by General Pétain at the Inter-Allied Conference held on 4th May (see pp. 23-24). It was launched after an 8-day bombardment by the French Second Army on a front of eleven miles astride the Meuse. The strictly limited objectives, 2,000–4,000 yards distant, were gained, including the important heights of Mort'Homme and Hill 304, which the Germans had captured at so great a cost in their February 1916 offensive. Heavy casualties, including 10,000 prisoners, were inflicted on the Germans during the fighting, which continued into September. There was no counter-attack or counter-offensive, as the German *Eingreif* divisions had been sent to Flanders, and there were barely enough troops to hold the line in passive defence.

The Italians, certainly, on the 17th August had begun the Eleventh Battle of the Isonzo, and had made such progress that the Austrians were being driven from their last hold on the Bainsizza plateau, and were appealing to Germany for help. It was clear, however, that the Germans and Austrians would soon be able to reduce their forces on the Eastern Front and from their central position were able to send reinforcements to aid any ally and to any front which might be menaced. Except for Allied holdings at Salonika and in Albania, the Central Powers were in occupation of the Balkans (Bukarest had capitulated on the 6th December 1916), and General Sarrail's offensives from Salonika had failed—he was soon to be recalled. In Palestine, General Allenby's victories were yet to come (Third Gaza was begun on 27th October). In Mesopotamia, however, Bagdad had been occupied in March, and other successes had followed.

To exhaust Germany, whose troops provided the *Korsettenstangen* (corset bones) of her feeble allies, seemed the best hope. If her aid were withdrawn from Austria, Turkey and Bulgaria, they would soon collapse.

In his report of the 21st August to the War Cabinet, after reviewing the latest operations, Sir Douglas Haig wrote, "I am well satisfied with them, although the gain of "ground would certainly have been much more considerable "but for the adverse weather conditions." He emphasized the heavy wastage of the German troops, and expressed the opinion that there was good reason to hope that very considerable results would soon follow with more rapidity than might appear likely, and the new position then gained would greatly facilitate clearing the coast.

In the circumstances, he felt that "the right course to "pursue is undoubtedly to press the enemy in Flanders "without intermission and to the full extent of our power." Two weeks later, in his report on the 2nd September, he explained, and regretted, the necessary delay of three weeks in the operations, till the third week in September, and mentioned the shortage of artillery ammunition, especially of 6-inch howitzer shell.[1] At the same time, he repeated

---

[1] At a G.H.Q. conference on 22nd August, Vice-Admiral Sir R. H. Bacon said that the Admiralty was particularly anxious that at least the coastal strip between Westende and Middelkirke should be occupied. Heavy 15-inch naval guns mounted on shore could then range Bruges at 31,000 yards, and Zeebrugge at 34,000 yards ; the whole length of the Zeebrugge–
Continued at foot of next page.

his conviction that the best, if not the only, way to surmount the crisis and the temporary inaction of the French army was to continue the campaign with all available resources.

Review of the Flanders Situation

On the other hand, the Prime Minister considered that the time had arrived to review the situation. The Cabinet Committee, when sanctioning the Flanders campaign on the 8th June, had, it will be remembered, made the reservation that if at any time the results appeared unsatisfactory, the situation would be re-examined with a view to the cessation of the campaign and the adoption of an alternative plan. At a conference in London on the 4th September, which Sir Douglas Haig attended, Mr. Lloyd George expressed the opinion that, as Russia would probably be of no further help and as the French could take no active part in the War until the following year, it would be better to husband resources during the remainder of 1917, and to embark only on minor operations, such as the support of the Italian offensive against Austria. On the 26th August, General Cadorna, the Italian Chief of the General Staff, had warned the French and British Governments that, although the Austrians were in a precarious state, the Italian offensive could not be continued, owing to lack of heavy artillery and munitions. Mr. Lloyd George now proposed that the British and French should support this offensive which promised so well; and, as a beginning, he asked for the despatch of a hundred more heavy guns from the Flanders front to Italy.[1]

Sir Douglas Haig, in reply, repeated his conviction that to withdraw a single man or gun from Flanders—or from

---

Continued from previous page.
Bruges canal could be brought under fire, and the locks destroyed, and great additional security could then be given to the Dover and Dunkirk cross-Channel traffic during the long winter nights. Sir Douglas Haig replied that he was not prepared to undertake the coastal operation until the Passchendaele–Staden ridge had been occupied and the enemy's hold on the coast seriously threatened; the first week of September was now too soon, and he proposed to postpone the operation till the first week of October, when the tides would again be suitable. He added that he could not countenance a landing to capture the coastal strip north of the Yser as a separate operation unless the naval situation was so serious as to justify great risks.

The operation never took place; but the 1st Division, which was to have carried it out, did not leave the coast until 20th October.

[1] See p. 219. In August a 9.2-inch howitzer was sent. The French had sent a dozen heavy batteries.

the Western Front—would be a most unsound policy. In his opinion, the Prime Minister's proposal to sit still for the remainder of 1917 would give the enemy the initiative and allow him to strike a blow at one or other of the Allies which might prove disastrous.[1] From a military point of view, it was preferable to fight the Germans on ground where the British Armies were already established, with their supply services intact and close to the coast, than to be forced to send divisions hurriedly to support a tottering French or Italian battle front at any one or more points the enemy might choose. After a discussion, the majority of the Cabinet Committee proved to be in favour of allowing the operations in Flanders to continue; but, on further pressure from Mr. Lloyd George, Sir Douglas Haig agreed to discuss with General Pétain the despatch of some more heavy artillery to Italy.

Although Sir Douglas Haig did not doubt that the right course was to continue the offensive in Flanders, he saw the possibility that rain and mud might bring operations to a standstill. Another disquieting factor was the lack of reinforcements. On the 17th August, General Sir William Robertson had written to G.H.Q. that probably less than eight thousand men would arrive in France as drafts during September. This figure would do little more than replace normal wastage, and at a G.H.Q. conference on the 21st August, Sir Douglas Haig told his Army commanders that the British divisions in France would probably be a hundred thousand men below establishment by the end of October.[2]

The problem which faced the Commander-in-Chief early in September was to decide on his course of action should these factors of man-power and weather limit large-scale operations in Flanders. A memorandum on the subject written by the Operations Branch G.H.Q. on the 16th Sept-

---

[1] With a general reserve of no more than six divisions thrown in, the Germans crushed the "Kerenski offensive" in July, were to break the Russian front at Riga (1st–5th September), and the Italian front at Caporetto (24th October).

[2] Although departmental corps had been "combed", and 2nd line Yeomanry units and cyclists battalions drafted, the heavy losses incurred during the earlier battles of 1917 (Arras, the Scarpe, Bullecourt and Messines) had not yet been made good; and on 11th August a General Staff memorandum showed that the deficiency in infantry alone was 85,000 men, an average of 1,650 in each division. The total infantry establishment of the 52 divisions, each of 12 battalions, in France was 605,280 of all ranks, and, in addition, 44,325 for the 44 pioneer battalions.

cmber assumed that the advance in Flanders might have to be halted along a line Polygon Wood (a little east of Westhoek)–Broodseinde–Gravenstafel–Poelcappelle,[1] and it advised that preparations should be made to switch troops and guns rapidly from Flanders to other sectors where offensive schemes were ready. Two such sectors were mentioned: the Lens area, where the capture of the town had been planned by the First Army, and Lombartzyde, the occupation of which would strengthen the hold of the Fourth Army on Nieuport.[2] On that day, too, the 16th, the commander of the Third Army (General Hon. Sir Julian Byng) gave Sir Douglas Haig fuller details concerning the scheme for the capture of the Flesquières salient with the help of tanks, and an advance on Cambrai, and had asked that five of his divisions, which averaged 3,000 men under strength, might be brought up to establishment for the operation. Sir Douglas Haig thought well of this scheme, and promised all the support he could afford; but he added that no date could be fixed as long as the Ypres operations were in progress.

Throughout these deliberations, Sir Douglas Haig's chief concern was to divert German attention, particularly from the French front. The limited French attack at Verdun, promised by General Pétain on the 2nd June for the end of July, had indeed been carried out, as we have seen, at the end of August; but within four weeks, on the 19th September, the French Commander-in-Chief was again imploring that the offensive in Flanders should be continued without further delay. During this special visit to British headquarters he assured Sir Douglas Haig that between the British right and Switzerland he had not a man upon whom he could rely. Not only, he said, had the French army ceased to be able to make any considerable offensive, but its discipline was still so bad that it would be unable to resist a determined German offensive: France was nearing the limit of her man-power, and the danger existed that the French Government would—as indeed G.H.Q. had feared in the two preceding winters—demand a separate peace rather than withstand another German offensive and its

---

[1] For these places, see Sketch 2.
[2] See Sketch 9.
  Belgian Army headquarters asserted that if control was lost of the canal locks at Nieuport, the Yser inundations would become tidal, and great damage might be caused to the Belgian defences.

resulting casualties.[1] Even after making allowance for General Pétain's pessimistic outlook[2]. Sir Douglas Haig appreciated the urgency of his repeated requests for a breathing-space for the recovery of the French army. The imperative need to retain France as an active partner in the War was evident, and her decision on this vital matter had become the dominant factor in the situation.

The Revised Scheme

As a result of the firmer control of operations adopted by Sir Douglas Haig after the 24th August,[3] effect was given to his own advice to General Gough two months earlier that the main battle of the campaign should be fought on and for Gheluvelt plateau. Although the general plan remained unaltered the tactical scheme was radically revised. The fullest possible weight of the Second Army was to be massed against the plateau, the occupation of which was to be carried out by a succession of assaults, or " steps " as they were called, with strictly limited objectives. Each step would ease the simultaneous and corresponding advance of the Fifth Army over the lower ground to the north, and across the muddy Steenbeek valley. The Second Army was to maintain the chief pressure of the offensive against Gheluvelt plateau until its eastern edge was occupied. This entailed an advance of four thousand yards, including the capture of Polderhoek, Gheluvelt and Tower Hamlets spurs, which dominate the south-eastern and southern slopes. The Fifth Army, on the left, was to capture the Zonnebeke–Gravenstafel sector of the Ypres Ridge ;[4] and, with its right flank covered by the Second Army, it would then proceed to complete the occupation of the Passchendaele–Staden sector, as originally planned, and be ready to exploit strategically any opportunities which

---

[1] A memorandum written by G.Q.G. for the Minister of War on the state of the French army at the end of September 1917, stated that any reverse would provoke anew, and this time probably beyond remedy, the dangerous crisis through which the army had passed in May and June. (Painlevé, " Comment j'ai nominé Foch et Pétain ", p. 215.)

[2] Maréchal Joffre, in his Memoirs, writes : " Pétain est trop négatif, " trop timide . . . des idées quelquefois un peu fausses, quelquefois de " facheuses paroles de pessimisme et de découragement ". See also his attitude in March 1918 (" 1918 " Vol. I, p. 539).

[3] See Sketch 22 and Map 1, and p. 206.

[4] See Sketch 23.

might occur. Although the objectives with which the campaign had started were still far distant, Sir Douglas Haig hoped that any one of the heavy blows he proposed to deliver might yet demoralize and crack the German defence, with far-reaching consequences.

The Second Army scheme was submitted by General Plumer to G.H.Q. on the 29th August, after a conference with his corps commanders on the 27th. The operation to capture Gheluvelt plateau was to be carried out by two corps, the X (Lieut.-General Sir T. L. N. Morland) and the I Anzac (Lieut.-General Sir W. R. Birdwood), with the II Anzac (Lieut.-General Sir A. J. Godley) in reserve for use in the later fighting.[1] The southern flank, between the right of the X Corps and the Comines canal, was to be guarded by the IX Corps (Lieut.-General Sir A. Gordon) with one division (19th); southwards from the canal, the remaining $7\frac{1}{2}$ miles of the Second Army frontage[2] were to be occupied defensively with the least possible force consistent with safety, another division of the IX Corps to hold as far as a line just north of Messines, and the VIII Corps (Lieut.-General Sir A. Hunter-Weston), with two divisions, thence to the Lys, south of Frelinghien (3 miles south of Warneton).

General Plumer's intention was to capture the plateau by four separate steps, with an interval of six days between each to allow time to bring forward artillery and supplies; the distance of each step, governed by the need to meet the strong German counter-attacks with fresh infantry supported by an effective artillery barrage, was to be limited to about fifteen hundred yards.[3] For the first step he considered a thousand yards to be the maximum frontage for each division:[4] the X Corps and the I Anzac Corps had five and four divisions, respectively; allowing two divisions as reserve to each corps and one division of the right corps (X) to assist in forming a southern defensive flank, four divisions remained to make the first step.

General Plumer also pointed out that, as the Fifth Army would be attacking simultaneously on the left, the wide front of attack required by Sir Douglas Haig in order to make the Germans disperse their artillery fire would be

[1] See Sketch 22.
[2] See Sketch 11.
[3] That is, a little less than the 2,000-yard limit he had suggested in May. See p. 16.
[4] See Sketch 22.

obtained without the inclusion of an attack against Zandvoorde: the state of the ground in the Bassevillebeek valley would make an attack from the west against that village very difficult; he therefore urged its postponement till a later stage of the operations: by omitting it, the Second Army attack frontage of 6,800 yards, proposed by Sir Douglas Haig, would be shortened by two thousand yards. After further discussion, the Commander-in-Chief, on the 30th August, agreed that the Fifth Army should take over eight hundred yards of front south of the Ypres–Roulers railway. In this way the Second Army was able to array four divisions, two of the X and two of the I Anzac Corps, on a frontage of four thousand yards, to make the first step of fifteen hundred yards, the right division (39th) of the X Corps joining the 19th Division of the IX Corps in the formation of a southern flank to the penetration. Compared with the assault on the 31st July, double the force was to be employed to cover half the frontage.[1]

The new plan laid special emphasis on the need for heavy and medium artillery both to smash the concrete shelters and machine-gun nests during the preparatory bombardment and to engage in effective counter-battery work before and during the assault. General Plumer asked for a total of 1,339 guns and howitzers, and received actually for his offensive front, 1,295 (575 heavy and medium and 720 field guns and howitzers).[2] This quantity of heavy and medium artillery was more than double the allotment to the same frontage for the offensive on the 31st July (282 heavy and medium, and 576 field guns and howitzers).[3]

The estimate of artillery ammunition needed for a seven days' bombardment and the first day's assault was $3\frac{1}{2}$ million

---

[1] On 31st July, the II Corps had 3 divisions on a frontage of 6,200 yards to make an advance of over three thousand yards.

[2] The total artillery allotment to the Second Army, including the defensive fronts of the IX and VIII Corps, amounted to 33 heavy artillery groups and 46 brigades of field artillery. The detail of heavy and medium guns and howitzers was 1 12-inch gun, 3 9.2-inch guns, 20 6-inch guns, 2 15-inch howitzers, 18 12-inch howitzers, 82 9.2-inch howitzers, 126 8-inch howitzers, 296 6-inch howitzers, 180 60-pdr. guns; the field artillery consisted of 826 18-pdrs. and 276 4.5-inch howitzers.

[3] The growth of the proportion of heavy and medium to field artillery had been one of the striking features of artillery progress during the War. At Neuve Chapelle in March 1915 the proportion was 1 to $4\frac{1}{2}$ (80 heavy and medium to 378 field guns and howitzers), for Arras–Vimy (April 1917) about 1 to 2 (989 heavy and medium to 1,809 field), and for Menin Road as above) it was 1 to less than $1\frac{1}{2}$.

rounds. Taking into account that the distance to the objective was shorter by half, the allotment would give a density of shells on this important sector of the German position nearly four times as great as on the 31st July.

These material demands show General Plumer's determination to ensure by all reasonable means that the conquest of Gheluvelt plateau should be as thorough as had been that of Messines Ridge.

THE NEW ATTACK ORGANIZATION

The Second Army operation orders for the first step were issued in two parts, on the 1st and 10th September;[1] the probable date for the assault was given to corps commanders as the 20th.

The artillery instructions, issued on the 29th August and 13th September,[2] made it clear that success would depend primarily on the action of the artillery. In the first two years of the War not only German tactics and engineering skill but also the provision of material, particularly artillery material, had managed to keep ahead of the British; but the respite afforded by the continued resistance on the Russian front had at last enabled sufficient guns and shells to be accumulated to give the British gunner a better chance—and he took it.[3] The gathering artillery potential had been

---

[1] Appendices XXI, XXII.
[2] Appendix XXIII.
[3] Mr. Winston Churchill became Minister of Munitions on 22nd July 1917. Taking over from Dr. C. (later Lord) Addison, he reorganized the Ministry. During the previous seven months of the year the great national projectile factories had come into full operation, and the output of shells had already outrun the supply of guns, which were manufactured—for both army and navy—solely by the armament firms. Some of the shell factories were diverted to the repair of worn guns, as the delivery of new weapons, particularly those of the heavier types, had fallen short of demands, especially the 6-inch howitzer, which was in great favour. The deliveries in France during 1917, compared with those during 1916 (given in brackets) were: 18-pdrs. 2,091 (1,492), 4.5-inch howitzers 562 (553), 60-pdrs. 449 (640), 6-inch guns 65 (9), 6-inch howitzers 1,267 (691), 8-inch howitzers 441 (142), 9.2-inch guns 11 (4), 9.2-inch howitzers 203 (199), 12-inch howitzers 48 (24).

The official records state that the weekly expenditure of artillery ammunition during the Third Battle of Ypres averaged above 3,200,000 rounds; and the weekly expenditure of the heavier natures of shell (43,300 tons) was nearly double that during the Somme battles (25,394 tons) twelve months before. The deliveries of guns were held up partly by some being sent to Russia and Italy; but the ammunition supply from British
Continued at foot of next page.

shown in the battles for the Vimy and Messines Ridges, where the frontage and depth of the area attacked had been within the power of the artillery to overwhelm with shell; now the German position on Gheluvelt plateau presented a similar opportunity.[1]

The keynote of the Second Army plan was the systematic concentration of fire on definite targets such as strongpoints, battery positions and counter-attack formations, both before and during the assault, the fire-power being directed by every means of observation from the ground and the air. In addition, a barrage of artillery and machine-gun fire a thousand yards deep was to move ahead of the infantry, in order to keep down any enemy troops lying in shell holes in the open.

Even with the weight of concentrated artillery fire now possible on this narrow assault frontage, General Plumer fully appreciated the limitations of artillery protection. The infantry would still have to fight skilfully across the shell-cratered ground in order to overcome the strongpoints, and fresh troops would have to be close at hand to consolidate any objective that was reached and hold it against immediate counter-attacks. From the lessons learnt in the Messines battle, General Plumer had worked out a more flexible attack organization for the infantry to deal with the new German method of defence. His proposals, summarized in a memorandum sent to G.H.Q. on the 12th August,[2] were approved, and they were incorporated in the training of both the Second and Fifth Armies for the coming offensive.

Radical changes were made in the scheme of attack. The assault was to be led by one or two lines of skirmishers, at 5-paces' interval, to act as an advanced guard in order to afford freedom of manoeuvre to groups in rear. The loose distribution of the infantry in groups for the purpose of outflanking enemy strongpoints and fortified shell holes

---

Continued from previous page.
factories alone enabled the expenditure to be maintained and a reserve established as well. The issue to the War Office of 18-pdr. shell (H.E. and shrapnel) in 1917, for example, was 47,992,000 rounds and the expenditure 38,086,000 rounds; the issue for the 4.5-inch howitzers was 13,028,000 rounds and the expenditure 10,664,000 rounds.

[1] For the Vimy Ridge operation one gun or howitzer stood to every 9 yards of the offensive front; for the Messines battle there had been one to 7 yards of front; but now, for the Menin Road battle, one gun or howitzer stood to every 5.2 yards of the offensive front.

[2] Appendix XXIV.

became a recognized battle drill; each group had its task and was trained as an organized fighting unit, success depending largely on the resolution with which junior commanders handled these small columns. Mopping-up parties, also in groups, following close behind the assault units, were trained to garrison definite areas and strongpoints as soon as these were cleared. The chief drawback of this training was that it did not prepare the infantry sufficiently for a battlefield so utterly barren and bare of cover—except shell-holes—as that on which they were about to fight.

In each step the operation was to be carried out in three bounds. The assault to the first objective was to be the longest, about eight hundred yards, and made by a comparatively weak force, normally one battalion on each brigade frontage, sufficient to overrun the German companies in the outpost zone. After a halt for 45 minutes, to give time for the mopping-up parties to clear the areas, the advance to the second objective would take place; it would encounter stronger opposition from the concrete pillboxes in the belt of strongpoints, so it was to be shorter than the first, about five hundred yards, and made by a fresh battalion, which would leap-frog the troops on the first objective. A longer halt, about two hours, was to be made on reaching the second objective, in order to allow time for consolidation against counter-attack by the local reserves of the German front divisions. The advance to the final objective was to be still shorter, about three hundred yards, and was to be made by the two remaining battalions of each assaulting brigade (double the strength of the original attack), which had been kept back in order that the ground gained could be consolidated as rapidly as possible for defence against the expected organized counter-attack by the enemy's *Eingreif* divisions, now probably reaching the battlefield.

Another change affected the use of infantry reserves. A marked defect in the Messines battle had been the crowding on the ridge, owing to the engagement of the reserves by time-table regardless of the situation.[1] The employment of reserves was now to be left to the commanders on the spot, the guiding principle being that fresh troops should always be at hand, ready to meet the succession of German counter-attacks wherever they might fall. One quarter of each

---

[1] See p. 71.

assaulting unit (company and battalion) was to move in close reserve, ready to give support at once, at the discretion and on the initiative of its own commander, either to assist in overcoming local opposition or to occupy a fire position if the troops in front were being forced back. Larger counter-attack reserves, as they were called, up to the strength of a brigade in each assaulting division, were to be held ready to ensure the hold on the final objective in the event of the assaulting units being too disorganized or weakened by losses to resist a determined counter-attack. The employment of these reserves was also to be left to the discretion of local commanders, acting on the information at their disposal. The echelons of the assaulting divisions extended back for eight miles opposite Gheluvelt plateau, and in rear of each assaulting division was a division in reserve, near enough to reinforce or to relieve it the same night or the following morning if required.[1] As a consequence of this re-organization of reserves, the echelons of the assaulting divisions corresponded approximately to the echelons in depth of the German counter-attack formations.[2]

During the three weeks' interval in September, every unit in the Second and Fifth Armies detailed for the operation was given intensive training in this new attack organization; and every attack exercise was designed to produce at some stage a counter-attack situation, so that the local reserves could be practised in dealing with them.[3]

PREPARATIONS

Details of the plan were explained at a Second Army conference on the 31st August, and the necessary changes

---

[1] The reserve divisions were about eight miles from the front line: the 21st and 33rd, in X Corps reserve, were at Caestre and Westoutre, respectively; and the 5th and 4th Australian, in Anzac Corps reserve, at Reninghelst and Steenvoorde. (The places are not on any sketch map in this volume.)

[2] See Note at end of Chapter VIII.

Each British company had a platoon in reserve, corresponding to the German *Stoss-trupp*, and each battalion a company (like the German *Stoss-kompagnie*). The reserve brigade of each division was also organized in echelons (as were the German regiments in divisional reserve): for example, behind the two assaulting brigades of the 41st Division, the reserve brigade had two battalions about Armagh Wood (1,200 yards behind the front line), one battalion near Larch Wood, east of Verbrandenmolen (1,200 yards behind again), and its fourth battalion west of Voormezeele (3,000 yards farther back).

[3] Appendix XXV.

in the dispositions of the divisions were carried out during the next few days.[1] The VIII Corps (Second Army reserve) took over the sector astride the Douve from the II Anzac Corps, which withdrew with its divisions for special training to the Lumbres area, west of St. Omer. The IX Corps, with its right on a line just north of Messines, extended its left northwards from the Comines canal for a thousand yards, so that the X Corps would have to use only one division to protect its southern flank during the advance. The II Corps and its frontage were taken over by the Second Army from the Fifth Army at noon on the 3rd September. The staff of the II Corps headquarters was relieved on the 5th, leaving its divisions (24th, 30th and 8th) at the disposal of the X, and I Anzac Corps. These divisions, however, remained in their sectors, and continued to hold the line until a few days before the assault.

The dispositions of the Fifth Army remained unaltered, with the exception that the staff of the XIX Corps headquarters was relieved on the 7th September by V Corps headquarters, from the Fifth Army reserve.[2] The three tank brigades which had been in the battle area throughout August were withdrawn on the 11th September, leaving four battalions (3 of the I and one of the II Brigades) to be maintained at full strength to meet any demands for co-operation in the coming battle.[3]

The minor attacks made by the Fifth Army early in September, in accordance with G.H.Q. instructions of the 28th August to limit the operations to gaining the Glencorse line, continued to be unsuccessful. An attack made by the 42nd and 61st Divisions of the XIX Corps on the 6th September, at 7.30 a.m., to occupy the strongpoints at Borry Farm, Beck House (300 yards north of Borry Farm), Iberian

---

[1] See Sketch 11.
[2] See Sketch 23. The 9th Division, from the Third Army, took over the right sector of the V Corps, astride the Ypres–Roulers railway, on 18th September; and the 55th Division about the same date returned to its old sector, after replacement of its casualties of 31st July.
[3] On 7th September, Br.-General Elles (Tank Corps) wrote to G.H.Q. that, on account of the state of the ground, there was " no prospect of " using tanks until the end of this month ", and then all would depend on the amount of shelling and the amount of rain. He asked for, and obtained, permission to withdraw 5 of the 8 battalions from the forward area for training and preparation for winter accommodation. He mentioned that there were possibilities for the employment of tanks on the First and Third Army fronts, and suggested raids.

Farm, and the gun-pits on Hill 35, failed, as also did another attempt by the XIX Corps to capture the Hill 35 position; Beck House and Iberian Farm were both captured, and a German counter-attack during the morning was repulsed; but another more determined effort in the afternoon, with strong artillery support, retook both places, and by nightfall the infantry were back along their starting line, except for a small gain south of Borry Farm, and on the slope of Hill 35, near Gallipoli Farm. The casualties of the attacking units during the day were 16 officers and 395 other ranks. A renewed attack against Hill 35 on the morning of the 10th was carried out by the 61st Division, also without success. Sir Douglas Haig then ordered the Fifth Army commander to stop minor attacks; and those planned by the V, XVII and XIV Corps for the 13th, 11th and 15th September, respectively, were cancelled.

The interval of three weeks, not due to the weather, but asked for by General Plumer and sanctioned by G.H.Q.,[1] was calculated on the time necessary for the construction of roadways to bring forward the immense quantity of artillery ammunition and supplies required, and for the burying of the main telephone lines. Emplacements, too, had to be made for this great array of guns, including the majority of the II Corps' barrage batteries, which had to be moved to more advanced positions to support the offensive.[2] Light railways—under the Director of Light Railways, Br.-General G. H. Harrison—were to be connected up for the supply of ammunition from the two railheads, Pacific and Fuzeville

---

[1] This pause deceived the enemy. On 13th September Crown Prince Rupprecht's Chief of the Staff recorded : " My inmost conviction that the " battle in Flanders is at an end is more and more strengthened ". His view was confirmed by a captured British airman and other prisoners, who " stated definitely that the offensive in Flanders was over, and that " an attack would be made farther south ". It was therefore deduced that " the enemy was regrouping in order to attack at another place ". G.O.A. xiii., p. 71.

[2] Apart from the artillery taken over with the II Corps on 3rd September, the surplus was made up by further weakening the artillery strength of the Third and Fourth Armies, and of the right (VIII) corps of the Second Army.

The total number of guns and howitzers transferred to the Second Army between 28th August and 12th September to make up the required allotments for the offensive front was 54 18-pdr.; 186 4.5-inch howitzers; 60 60-pdr.; 180 6-inch howitzers; 12 6-inch guns; 64 8-inch howitzers; 56 9.2-inch howitzers; 13 12-inch howitzers, and 1 15-inch howitzer.

(5 miles west and south-west of Ypres, respectively) ;[1] they had a combined capacity of 9 or, at the most, 11 trains a day, and since the quantity required was 54,572 tons, or 156 train-loads, in addition to normal expenditure, the actual dumping was expected to occupy at least seventeen days. Considerable stocks were, however, already available at railheads, and the dumping was completed in 13 days. The light railways were easily and quickly laid from the standard gauge lines west of Ypres, and were intended to be the principal means of transport for the ammunition ; quick repairs to them after shell damage were, however, difficult, and a large proportion of weight of shell had eventually to be taken by road.

Major-General F. M. Glubb, Chief Engineer of the Second Army, was responsible for preparatory work on roads and tracks ; and on its satisfactory completion the success both of the first and subsequent steps of the operation would necessarily depend. The wet weather and the intense shelling during the August battles had left the roads and tracks in a bad state, in spite of the energy of the repair squads. On the plateau itself, east of Hooge, the original tracks, including the Menin road, were scarcely recognizable ; in parts, water-filled shell holes lay almost crater to crater, and a few upright poles were all that remained of the woods on the slopes. In both the X Corps and I Anzac Corps areas, where the bulk of the traffic was expected, one-way circuits were planned with transverse connecting links, one behind and one in front of the original British line, under the supervision of corps and divisional engineers, respectively[2]. The new roads were constructed chiefly of planks, as they were quicker to lay than road-metal and were less conspicuous ; they were also easier to repair, and constituted a less weight of material.[3]

---

[1] See Sketch 4.
[2] See Sketch 22 and Map 1.
For example, in the I Anzac Corps area the roads out of Ypres and Menin and Verbrandmolen (2 miles S.S.W. of Hooge) were used behind the original front line, with a transverse connecting link through Zillebeke (a mile south-west of Hooge) to Hooge and Hell Fire Corner (1¼ miles west of Hooge) ; forward from Hooge 3,200 yards of plank road was built across the crater field through Château Wood, and thence around Bellewaarde Lake back to the Menin road at Birr Cross Roads (800 yards west of Hooge).
[3] Road-metal dumps were formed along the road sides out of Ypres, a large one being near the Menin Gate ; but, owing to an acute shortage of

Continued at foot of next page.

In addition to the engineers and pioneers of the corps and divisions concerned, and the technical railway construction units, 12,500 men of the Labour Corps and a thousand men of the British West Indies Regiment were employed on the work. Fortunately the first three weeks of September were mostly fine sunny days, with a drying wind, so that the sea of mud in the forward area gradually turned into a brown dusty desert; the plank-roads, which at first almost floated, began to settle down on a firm foundation. Even so, owing to shortage of transport and time, they were only single-track, with passing places, and breakdowns and direct shell hits caused numerous traffic jams; but not until October, when the fine weather broke, did transport which left the roads get into serious trouble. The patience and endurance of the drivers, under shell fire through Ypres and beyond, in such circumstances, and particularly of the horse transport used in the forward areas by night, is to their lasting credit.

Road repairs and extensions were always in hand. In the I Anzac Corps area, for instance, eighty motor lorries each took three tons of planks daily at dusk from Ouderdom railway siding through Ypres and along the Menin road to Hell Fire Corner and Birr Cross. As soon as these lorries were clear of Ypres on their return journey, a hundred and twenty 2-horse wagons drove out through the town to these roadside dumps, and took the planks forward to the working parties. By the exertions of all concerned, mostly in darkness and frequently under fire, the road circuits were completed by the 19th September, the day before the assault.

The working parties also had to construct numerous additional duck-board tracks for the increased number of infantry units in the area, from the ramparts of Ypres and from the Yser canal right up to the front line. These tracks

---

Continued from previous page.
tip-up dump carts, G.S. wagons had to be used to take metalling to the working parties. The stone had to be shovelled into and out of these wagons, which was very wasteful both in time and labour.

The planks, chiefly of elm and beech, were about 9 feet long, 1 foot across and 2½ inches thick. Four or five planks, laid lengthwise (runners) formed the base of the track, and others, laid crosswise and spiked to the runners, formed the surface; half-round pine logs along each edge formed a kerb and kept the wheels on the track. Underlying shell-holes were first filled in with earth from a draining trench dug along either side of the road. Daily at 2 p.m. a special train arrived at Ouderdom station (4½ miles out of Ypres), with 240 tons of planks for the I Anzac Corps alone.

led either alongside the already beaten paths, or apart through the long grass of the derelict fields.

A desultory bombardment to "soften", as it is now called, the German defences began on the 31st August, immediately after the approval of the artillery plans drawn up by Major-General C. R. Buckle, Major-General R.A., Second Army. Emphasis was laid on the importance of being able to concentrate at will a large volume of fire on either selected or fleeting targets, a policy made practicable by improved organization and better liaison. The heavy and medium artillery were formed into bombardment, counter-battery, barrage and "fleeting opportunities" groups, allocated to corps and divisions. Close liaison was ensured by officers, not below the rank of major, who lived at the headquarters of the corps and divisions which their group was covering, with direct telephonic communication to the groups. The field artillery was grouped in a similar way, with liaison officers attached to the headquarters of the brigade and battalion which their batteries were to support. Battery positions, pillboxes, machine-gun nests, observation posts, telephone exchanges, were systematically bombarded by the aid of information obtained from air photographs, prisoners' statements, ground observation and other means—counter-battery fire was particularly assisted by the work of the four sound-ranging sections of the 2nd Field Survey Company R.E., using bases east of Ypres, at Zillebeke, on the Wytschaete ridge and on Hill 63 (Ploegsteert), covering the whole Second Army area. Both by day and night slow barrages on the approaches to the forward area and the battery positions partially isolated the German gunners from supplies and reliefs. These barrages were formed by two tiers of fire, those up to six thousand yards' range being dealt with by field artillery and machine guns, and the more distant, up to the German battery positions, by 60-pdr. and 6-inch guns, supplemented by 6-inch howitzers. The ammunition allotted for isolating fire was expended, two-thirds by night and one-third by day. During the last seven days from the 13th September onwards, the bombardment was intensified ; and on each of these days, in order to wear down and exhaust the enemy, two practices of the barrage scheme, lasting from 30 to 100 minutes on either the whole Army or a few of the corps fronts, crept across the German defence system. Infantry raids were made during these practice barrages for the capture of prisoners, in order to confirm the enemy's order of battle. As at Messines, the last two days were devoted chiefly to counter-battery work; air observation greatly assisted these concentrated shoots on located enemy batteries, wireless communication being established either direct to batteries or to the Army Report Centre.

The signal communication arrangements back to the Army Observation and the Report Centres, which had proved so successful in the Messines battle, were repeated, including an organized chain of observers both on the ground and in balloons, five Balloon Companies R.F.C. being available in the Second Army. The Report Centre was again at Locre (7½ miles south-west of Ypres); it had a wireless installation and a dropping-ground for aeroplane messages. Trunk telephone cables were laid from it through the Army and corps areas with central exchanges to serve groups of headquarters. These buried trunk lines were continued into the forward area in readiness for the expected advance of the Army.

The Fifth Army artillery preparation, under Major-General H. C. C. Uniacke, Major-General R.A. Fifth Army, followed former lines, with the exception that the preliminary bombardment was to consist of a " really intense " and hurricane bombardment for the last twenty-four " hours ", instead of a systematic shelling for a period of seven days. General Gough, at a conference on the 10th September, explained that he thought surprise was more likely to be obtained in this way.

The Royal Flying Corps, of which twenty-six squadrons were now available in the battle area of the Second and Fifth Armies,[1] played a vital part in the preparation, particularly as the location of targets relied mainly on air reconnaissance and photographic reports. Night flying was also carried out on an extensive scale for the bombing of villages known to house German reserves, and for the dislocation of railway stations and junctions on the only two lines leading behind the front into Western Belgium.

---

[1] Seven corps squadrons, two fighter reconnaissance squadrons, twelve single-seater fighter squadrons, three day-bomber squadrons and two night-bomber squadrons. See " War in the Air " iv., p. 181.

PREPARATIONS. SEPTEMBER

Enemy interference with the preparations was limited, owing to the loss of ground observation over the Ypres district during the August battles. The German artillery, with a four to six inferiority in numbers,[1] had to rely for targets on information from their balloon observers and from the occasional reconnaissance aircraft which broke through by day. Consequently most of their fire which was directed against artillery positions consisted of widely spread area shoots; and although battery positions, dumps and hutments lay thick on the low ground about Ypres in the Second Army area the casualties suffered were comparatively slight. The majority of the Second Army casualties during this period occurred among the infantry and the labour gangs in the forward area on the plateau[2] where they were in view of the enemy's ground observers, so that much of the work had to be done by night. These conditions were accentuated on the front of the Fifth Army, where the whole of the front area for some two to three thousand yards, except on the extreme right which was sheltered by the Zonnebeke ridge, lay on a forward slope under direct enemy observation crossed only by a few duck-board tracks and beaten paths. All relief parties and supplies to the front had to run the gauntlet of the enemy's artillery and machine-gun fire. Thus it happened that the casualties of the Fifth Army during the preparatory period were nearly double those of the Second Army.[3]

On most nights during September German aircraft crossed the line to bomb the camps in the Ypres neighbourhood, and the communications as far back as St. Omer. A succession of aircraft, one at a time, bombed the crowded shelters, Nissen huts and horse lines in the back areas throughout the night, preventing sleep even if they did little damage; but carried out on clear nights, the bombing occasionally caused severe losses: in one attack a battalion at Locre camp lost

---

[1] To avoid gun casualties during the bombardment period the Germans withdrew a number of batteries into reserve, using men and material to maintain those which remained in position up to strength.

The *3rd Bavarian Ersatz* and *121st Divisions*, which held the greater part of Gheluvelt plateau and Tower Hamlets spur, had between them 106 heavy and 160 field guns and howitzers; added to these was the corps artillery group for the special defence of this key position.

[2] During the 3-week period 30th August–20th September (exclusive), the Second Army casualties were 299 officers and 5,198 other ranks.

[3] During the three weeks, up to 20th September (exclusive), the Fifth Army casualties were 521 officers and 10,135 other ranks.

nearly a hundred men. Seldom, if ever before, had bombing from the air produced such a definite moral and material effect. To check these raiders, and also the series of night raids on England which were being made at the same period by German squadrons operating from Belgian airfields,[1] a defensive-offensive system was worked out—and described in a handbook on anti-aircraft gunnery (September 1917)—to co-ordinate the action of the night pilots, searchlights and anti-aircraft guns.[2] Although no night raiders were brought down behind the line, these counter-measures foiled them; they soon turned their attention to the French and Belgian fronts, and their few visits soon came to be regarded as an annoyance rather than a danger, with the certainty and satisfaction that conditions on the enemy's side of the line in the matter of night bombing were very much worse.

Zero Hour

By the 18th September all the brigades of the Second and Fifth Armies detailed for the assault had moved up from their training areas to within easy reach of the front line. At dusk on the 19th the approach march began. Well-signposted tracks had been made for each brigade, mostly across country, so as to leave the roads clear for the nightly stream of wheeled traffic. On nearing the line, white tapes, laid after dusk, guided battalions and companies to their destinations.

After a fine sunny day a drizzle set in at nightfall, increasing to steady rain by 11 p.m. The troops were soon wet through; and the tracks, where not duck-boarded, became slippery and difficult. Soon after midnight, however, the rain ceased leaving a clear starlit sky.

About 11 p.m. General Gough had telephoned to General Plumer's headquarters, under which he had been placed for

---

[1] See "War in the Air" iv., p. 196.
The principal Belgian airfields concerned at Gentrode (east of Ghent) and St. Denis Westrom (south-west of Ghent) were hit with bombs up to 230-lbs. weight, and night fighters attempted to intercept the German raiders.

[2] Five Searchlight Sections R.E. were employed in the Second Army area, and 34 anti-aircraft guns (3-inch and adapted 13-pdr. guns) and 56 specially detailed machine guns were in action.
The anti-aircraft defences in the Fifth Army area consisted of 5 Searchlight Sections R.E., and twenty-two 13-pdr. and two 3-inch guns.

any matter requiring settlement at the last moment, proposing that, on account of the rain, the attack should be postponed. General Plumer said that before deciding he would like to consult "Meteor" (Lieut.-Colonel E. Gold) as to the weather, and his corps commanders and, at their suggestion, some divisional commanders, as to the state of the ground. On learning that apart from a risk of thunderstorms the weather would probably be mainly fair in the immediate future, and that the ground was "go-able," he informed the Fifth Army that the attack should proceed.

The order and silence of the approach march impressively confirmed the excellence of the arrangements. The jumping-off tapes were close to, in places within 150 yards of the opening barrage line which was the line of the German sentry-groups, and it was hoped to have the area about the British front line clear of troops in a few minutes, before the expected German counter-barrage came down upon it. The battalions for the first objective moved out into the crater-field of No Man's Land and those for the second objective deployed about the front line. The successive lines of groups were close-packed at first; but they were to shake out to their proper distances as the German position was entered. The battalions for the third and final objective assembled about a thousand yards or more in rear; here they were to remain for about two hours, so timing their advance as to be able to go straight through to their objective.[1]

At 4.30 a.m., before the assembly was complete, a German barrage came down for twenty minutes and caused some confusion in the I Anzac Corps sector, but heavy casualties were avoided by a process of squeezing-up. At 5 a.m. the barrage was repeated on the same area without effect.[2]

---

[1] For various local reasons there were exceptions. The 1st Australian Division, for example, had the battalions for all three objectives well forward, those for the third objective being close behind the front line. In this way, the divisional commander hoped to get all his assault units clear of the German barrage from the start, and to have them near at hand in close support.

[2] The enemy had been puzzled by the long lull during the first weeks of September; but by 17th September German *Fourth Army* headquarters was convinced that an offensive in the Ypres sector was imminent. A.O.A. iv., p. 758, states that about 3 a.m. on the 20th an officer of the 2nd Australian Division who went beyond his assembly position in the front line by mistake in the dark, was captured by a German patrol, and on him was found an operation order for the attack by the two Australian divisions on either side of the Ypres–Ménin road. The German division

Continued at foot of next page.

Four minutes before zero hour brilliant flares from German rockets lit up the centre of the I Anzac Corps sector, followed by the fire of German field batteries on the assembled assault troops of the 2nd Australian Division. Before serious harm could result, the British barrage crashed down on the German position, and as the counter-batteries deluged the German batteries with gas-shell the waiting infantry rose and moved forward close behind the barrage.

Zero hour had been fixed for 5.40 a.m. as being the moment when it would probably be light enough to see two hundred yards ahead. The eastern horizon was already tinged with red, but a thick ground mist after the rain made visibility poor and, in the words of a German diarist, the British infantry suddenly came upon the defenders " like spectres out of the mist ".

The battle will be described under three headings: the main attack of the Second Army, the Southern Flank, and the co-operation of the Fifth Army.

Continued from previous page.
concerned (*121st*) ordered an artillery barrage on and behind the front line of the 2nd Australian Division which faced it. A general warning was sent out by wireless, and both *Group Ypres* and *Group Wytschaete* headquarters warned their *Eingreif* divisions to be ready. The German regimental histories admit, however, that the information was circulated too late for effective artillery counter-measures.

CHAPTER XIV

THE BATTLES OF YPRES 1917 (*continued*)

BATTLE OF THE MENIN ROAD RIDGE (*concluded*)
THE SECOND ARMY MAKES THE FIRST STEP (20TH SEPTEMBER)
(Sketches 22, 23)

THE MAIN ATTACK

Four divisions, the 41st (Major-General S. T. B. Lawford), the 23rd (Major-General J. M. Babington), the 1st Australian (Major-General H. B. Walker) and the 2nd Australian (Major-General N. M. Smyth), each with two brigades leading, assaulted on the 4,000-yard frontage of Gheluvelt plateau.[1] During August many thousands of British troops had moved forward over this same ground when zero hour arrived with high hopes of success, but on this occasion they were inspired with more than the usual confidence. Behind them was the new deep organization of supports and reserves already described; in front, they were screened to a depth of a thousand yards by an artillery barrage of an extent and weight beyond all precedent. General Plumer's insistence on a great increase in the proportion of heavy and medium howitzers enabled the bombardment groups to form two belts of heavy high-explosive shell to creep ahead of the two field artillery belts of the barrage. Thus, together with the machine-gun barrage, which lay between the heavy and the field artillery barrages, five belts of fire, each accountable for two hundred yards, preceded the infantry.[2] Beyond the barrage belts lay the

---

[1] See Sketch 22.

[2] The first (A) belt was a shrapnel barrage laid by about one half of the available 336 18-pdr. guns; the second (B) belt consisted of high-explosive shell, fired by the remainder of the 18-pdr. guns and by 114 4.5-inch howitzers. (The two divisions of the X Corps had 174 18-pdr. guns—41st, 90; 23rd, 84—and the two Australian divisions, 162—1st Australian, 90; 2nd Australian, 72.) The 41st, 23rd and 1st Australian Divisions had 30 4.5-inch howitzers each, and the 2nd Australian Division, 24. Half the ammunition issued to the 18-pdr. guns was H.E., the fuzes being in the proportion of 70 per cent. instantaneous and 30 per cent. delay action. *Continued at foot of next page.*

fire of the four heavy artillery counter-battery double groups, consisting of 222 guns and howitzers covering a 7,000-yard frontage; they were ready to neutralize with gas and H.E. shell any German batteries which might open fire.[1]

Massively supported in this manner, it is no wonder that the four assaulting divisions advanced with the utmost resolution. The three sunny weeks of September had hardened the ground between the shell-craters, and, although it was slippery after the night's rain, the infantry were able to pick their way and generally keep pace with the artillery time-table. The barrage, described by eye-witnesses as magnificent both in accuracy and volume, covered the first two hundred yards rapidly, in lifts of 50 yards every two minutes, and in an initial rush the infantry, following within two hundred yards of or closer to the barrage, took the German outpost and local counter-attack groups by surprise. Overrun in the mist, many parties were caught in their shelters, or on the point of emerging from them, and both hand-grenades and inflammatory phosphorus bombs proved most useful for clearing dug-outs and shelters and forcing a quick surrender. The pace of the barrage then slowed to lifts of 100 yards every 6 minutes, and the rate of fire of the field batteries was halved to two rounds a gun a minute.[2]

Continued from previous page.

The third (C) belt was fired by 240 machine guns under corps control (128 behind the divisions of the X Corps, and 112 behind those of the I Anzac Corps), to keep the German local counter-attack reserves in their shelters.

The fourth (D) belt was made by 120 6-inch howitzers, and the fifth (E) belt by ¹26 60-pdr. guns, and 28 8-inch and 14 9.2-inch howitzers. For the 6-inch, 8-inch and 9.2-inch howitzers the proportion of fuzes was 50 per cent. of the No. 106 burst-on-graze fuze and 50 per cent. delay action, as many as possible of the No. 106 fuze being kept for the barrage.

The XIV Corps had experimented with this form of barrage in its attack on 28th August (see p. 200, footnote 1).

[1] In the original artillery plan, the German batteries were to be neutralized with gas shell (70 per cent. lacrymatory and 30 per cent. lethal) for four hours before zero hour; but at a Second Army conference on 15th September it was considered that such action might arouse the enemy's suspicions and the order was cancelled. The heavy and medium guns and howitzers of the four counter-battery groups of the X and I Anzac Corps consisted of 114 6-inch howitzers, 32 8-inch howitzers, 30 9.2-inch howitzers, 10 12-inch howitzers and 36 60-pdr. guns.

[2] The pace on 31st July had been 100-yard lifts every 4 minutes.

The forward movement of the barrage itself gave the general direction for the advancing infantry; but, owing to the prevalence of mist, keeping direction by compass bearing had been specially practised in the preliminary training. Smoke shells, one by every field gun, were fired in the barrage, as the signal as each objective was reached.

THE MAIN ASSAULT. 20TH SEPTEMBER 255

The western half of the plateau was soon covered with small assault groups, worming their way in single file between the shell craters deep into the German defence system. In general, unnerved and stunned by the concentrated blast of the heavy high-explosive shell in the two forward belts of the barrage, many of the Germans in the front line, and even in more distant lines, were completely demoralized. Although only a few of the concrete shelters and pillboxes had been smashed by direct hits and many of the machine-gun emplacements had escaped destruction, their occupants were found dazed and inactive, gunners sitting beside their unfired guns. Those who were still capable of action had but the one idea, to surrender as soon as possible, and ran forward, waving handkerchiefs and pieces of white bandage to meet the approaching infantry. On the few occasions when opposition was encountered the mist helped the attacking troops to pass round the flanks, whilst the new attack organization, especially the immediate use of the local reserves, maintained the forward impetus, although frequently at a high cost in casualties, in the few places where a strong resistance was offered.[1]

Of the four divisions making the main assault, the right (41st) division had to cross the difficult valley of the Bassevillebeek before gaining Tower Hamlets spur, and only three of them, the 23rd of the X Corps and the two Australian divisions of the I Anzac Corps, had a straightforward advance across the high ground of the plateau, and these three will be dealt with first.

In the sector of the 23rd Division, the left division of the X Corps, a single strongpoint in Dumbarton Wood (just west

---

[1] The German defences across Gheluvelt plateau were held by 3 German divisions, *9th Reserve, 3rd Bavarian Ersatz* and *121st*, from Lower Star Post–Zandvoorde road to Zonnebeke, a frontage of nearly four miles. They had, all three, been in the line for over 3 weeks, since the 20th, 28th and 19th August, respectively, and were to be relieved in the next few days.

The 41st and 23rd Divisions (X Corps) were faced by the right (*395th Regiment*) of the *9th Reserve Division*, and the left and centre (*28th Ersatz* and *4th Bavarian Reserve Regiments*) of the *3rd Bavarian Ersatz Division*. Opposite the 1st and 2nd Australian Divisions were the right (*15th Bavarian Reserve Regiment*) of the *3rd Bavarian Ersatz Division*, and the left and centre (*56th Reserve* and *7th Reserve Regiments*) of the *121st Division*. Each of these divisions had all its three regiments in the line, with one battalion in the outpost zone, one in support in and behind the original Third (*Wilhelm*) Line, and one in reserve behind the Flanders I Line.

of the lakes) caused heavy casualties to the 68th Brigade (Br.-General G. N. Colvile) ;[1] but despite this temporary check and the difficulty of keeping direction in the dense clouds of smoke and dust raised by the artillery barrage, the first objective beyond the marshy ground north of Dumbarton Lakes was reached a few minutes after the barrage and a defence consolidated along the upper reach of the Bassevillebeek. The 69th Brigade (Br.-General T. S. Lambert), faced at once by the remains of Inverness Copse, was able to penetrate the litter of wire and débris without great difficulty; small parties of Germans, however, who remained hidden in covered shell holes till the leading infantry had passed, opened fire on the battalions moving up behind, in artillery formation, ready to leap-frog to the subsequent objectives, and inflicted severe losses on them. Sixty Germans who resisted in this manner were killed by the moppers-up. Beyond the first objective a line of dug-outs north of Kantinje Cabaret on the Menin road gave trouble and groups of Germans in them, about forty in all, only surrendered after a tough struggle, in which the brigade trench mortars took a prominent part. These dug-outs were taken by the 9/Green Howards, whose success is the more praiseworthy as they had lost heavily in passing through Inverness Copse, eight of the sixteen company officers, including two company commanders, having been killed or wounded.

Four tanks of A Battalion, II Tank Brigade, were to have assisted in the advance along the Menin road; but one failed to reach the starting point and the pace of the infantry was too fast for the other three across such broken ground. One received a direct hit whilst on the Menin road, and the other two assisted in bringing up ammunition and engineer material.

The two Australian divisions, dividing the 2,000-yard sector north of the Menin road, were to occupy ground which had already, in August, been twice overrun and lost by British troops. Of the 1st Australian Division, the 2nd Brigade (Br.-General J. Heane), with its right directed on Fitzclarence Farm, crossed Glencorse Wood, which " was

---

[1] All the company commanders of the 11/Northumberland Fusiliers became casualties. The opening barrage had fallen beyond this stronghold.

" found to offer no impediment ",[1] and quickly stifled any resistance. Some machine guns which opened fire at close range through the mist from the southern edge of the wood were promptly rushed or attacked from the rear;[2] the garrison of Fitzclarence Farm was forced to keep under cover by firing rifle grenades into the loopholes of this strongpoint, whilst other groups, working round to the back, rushed in and captured an officer and forty other ranks. The 3rd Brigade (Br.-General H. G. Bennett) met trouble about the concrete shelters in the sunken track at the northern side of the wood, the scene of previous fighting in August. Machine-gun fire from the roof of one of these shelters swept and temporarily checked the advance, with many casualties, until support groups, moving in close reserve, quickly surrounded the area and, after a savage encounter, numbers of Germans who emerged from the shelters were killed or taken prisoner.[3] Mopping up was completed whilst the leading assault companies hurried on to regain the barrage. The waste of Nonne Bosschen was crossed by keeping to the lips of the water-filled shell craters,[4] and the second objective along the western edge of Polygon Wood, recognizable only by a thin growth of saplings among the shell craters, was gained up to time, about 7.45 a.m.;[5] the pillboxes and con-

---

[1] A.O.A. iv., p. 763.

[2] 2/Lieut. F. Birks (6th Battalion) was on this occasion awarded the V.C. for his wonderful coolness and personal bravery. Accompanied only by a corporal, he rushed a strongpoint in Glencorse Wood which was holding up the advance. The corporal was wounded, but 2/Lieut. Birks went in alone, killed the machine-gun crew with a bomb and captured the gun. Shortly afterwards, with a small party, he attacked another strongpoint occupied by about twenty-five Germans, of whom 15 were captured and the remainder killed.

[3] This action was fought by the 11th and 10th Australian Battalions.

Private R. R. Inwood (10th Battalion) was awarded the V.C. for conspicuous bravery and devotion to duty on this occasion. He went forward alone through the barrage and captured an enemy strongpoint, killing several Germans and capturing 9 others. Early the next morning, the 21st, he again went forward alone and bombed a machine-gun crew, which had been causing casualties, killing all but one, whom he brought back with the gun.

[4] Thus A.O.A. iv., p. 765. A photograph, taken on 1st October 1917, opposite p. 771, shows a bare broken surface, like that of a slightly rough sea, with a number of hard sharp-cut water-filled craters; the wrecks of a few pillboxes are shown, but only two skeleton trees—even the stumps of the others have disappeared.

[5] The distance to be covered by each division varied; but the barrage time-table allowed a maximum of 43 minutes to reach the first objective, and averaged 35 minutes for the second advance, with a halt of 45 minutes in between.

crete shelters in the Third (*Wilhelm*) Line being rushed or surrounded. Here, as in the belt of strongpoints about the Second (*Albrecht*) Line, the garrisons were found dazed and at least nine machine guns were captured unfired, together with the crews, listless alongside them.[1]

The 2nd Australian Division with its two brigades, the 7th (Br.-General E. A. Wisdom) and 5th (Br.-General R. Smith), on either side of the Westhoek–Zonnebeke road moved down into the Hanebeek valley with the near bank of the stream as a first objective. The German outpost companies, which had bayonets fixed, seemed too surprised to use them; and five machine guns which opened fire at close range were silenced almost at once. Beyond the first objective, up the farther slope of the valley, the vigour and determination of the Australian advance carried all before it, the Germans surrendering wholesale without firing a shot. Visibility through the mist was now 200–300 yards; and on reaching the top of the slope, on the Anzac House spur, machine-gun fire from two formidable strongpoints in the *Wilhelm* Line, Albert and Iron Cross redoubts, was quickly smothered by smoke grenades, the garrisons being chased with Lewis gun fire as they ran away. On the extreme left 15 Germans in the two-story Anzac House pillbox, which was a principal German artillery observation post, were overpowered as two machine guns were being dragged into position in the open.[2]

On the arrival of the 23rd Division and 1st and 2nd Australian Divisions along the second objective about 7.45 a.m., a fresh breeze from the south-west rolled away the mist, and the value of the morning's achievement was apparent. The sight which met the eye brought that thrill of victory always hoped for but so seldom experienced in previous offensives. The strongly defended neck of the plateau between the Bassevillebeek and the Hanebeek re-entrants which had defied all the August assaults had been forced, and the 23rd Division by its capture of the Kantinje Cabaret

---

[1] The concrete shelters (*Mebus*) were enclosed except for the back entrances; but the pillboxes were loopholed for machine guns.

[2] Anzac House blockhouse, of special interest to the Australians owing to its name, had two large lower rooms, and a small upper room reached by a ladder. Loopholes in the upper room gave extensive views over the target areas of the artillery groups concerned. A field wireless set was found there.

area was firmly established at the root of the Tower Hamlets spur. Inverness Copse, with its bitter memories, was left behind. Ahead in the clear morning sunlight the two Australian divisions could see across the brown wilderness of shell-holes and shattered tree-stumps to the farthest limits of the plateau about Broodseinde; and by the capture of Anzac House they had removed the chief German artillery observation post overlooking the Steenbeek valley to the north.

Strong counter-attacks had been expected to develop during the two-hour halt on the second objective; but the belts of fire of the protective barrage which swept up to 2,000 yards into the enemy's back areas delayed or checked such as were attempted before they reached the foremost line of the infantry.[1] While carrying out their tasks of consolidation many of the men threw away their cigarettes in favour of German cigars, found in abundance in the captured dug-outs, but were not allowed to smoke them long in peace; for accurate sniping from machine-gun nests and pillboxes became increasingly harassing, both at long and close range, from the far end of Polygon Wood and from inside the protective barrage. This firing also retarded the action of the fresh troops moving up to carry on the advance to the third and final objective. These battalions had passed through gaps in the thin and disjointed German barrage on the back areas with little loss, but as they approached the front their casualties began to mount up. Local action was taken at once to silence the sniping fire, and a number of deeds of exceptional valour were done as parties worked round the nearer centres of resistance and forced their garrisons to surrender. Strongpoints occupied in this manner included Black Watch Corner at the south-western corner of Polygon Wood, and Garter Point, two hundred yards east of Anzac House, both of which fell to Australian troops, the former being taken by the 5th Battalion, and Garter Point by the 18th Battalion.

---

[1] The five belts of fire, after remaining stationary for 14 minutes, advanced a further 400 yards, and here those of the shrapnel and machine-gun barrages stayed, the 18-pdr. guns slowing down to one round a minute per gun; the other three belts of fire then swept the ground ahead up to 2,000 yards, keeping their distances. All the fire belts eventually came back to the second objective line in time to begin the new creeping barrage to the next objective.

At 9.53 a.m. the barrage started its forward creep to the final objective three to four hundred yards distant. As the machine guns were now outranged, they dropped out of the barrage until they had advanced to nearer and pre-arranged positions, when they again took their place in the final protective barrage as before. The 23rd Division found the crossing of these last few hundred yards difficult and costly. A succession of pillboxes in ruined cottages along the Menin road were only taken after hard fights, and the resistance offered by a few concrete dug-outs in Veldhoek and a strongly held hedgerow in front of it had to be outflanked before the stubborn defenders surrendered or made their escape. A dozen pillboxes in the *Wilhelm* Line caused heavy casualties to the left brigade, the 69th, before they were cleared about noon, and the final objective was gained. There the ground was found favourable for digging.

The two Australian divisions reached their final line within half an hour. Resistance had been expected from the machine-gun nests and strongpoints which had been firing during the halt; but the garrisons, stunned by the renewed impact of the barrage, appeared, like those of the front lines, glad to surrender. The few casualties suffered by the 1st Australian Division were caused chiefly by the keenness and closeness with which the barrage was followed. The two right battalions (7th and 8th) of the 1st Australian Division which captured a number of pillboxes and shelters in the Third Line south of Black Watch Corner (Polygon Wood) lost 4 officers killed and a number of men from this cause. There was complaint that a number of the barrage guns, both heavy and field, were firing short in this final phase of the barrage; but the two battalions covering the front of the 2nd Australian Division were certainly fired on by enemy artillery and machine-gunned from the air[1] during their short advance to complete the capture of Anzac House spur; they reached their objective with little loss, and, making use of the shell craters and any existing trenches, began to consolidate.

---

[1] According to " F.A. Regt. No. 241 ", two batteries fired at the advance over direct sights at 1,500 yards from near Molenaarelsthoek.
Eight German aircraft, which had managed to break through the Royal Flying Corps' screen, flew over the line at this time; and they also machine-gunned the field batteries in rear. One of them was shot down by Lewis gun fire.

Meanwhile, the right division of the main assault, the 41st, had failed to gain the third objective, beyond the Bassevillebeek–Tower Hamlets spur, which stands out prominently for nearly a mile southwards from the main body of the plateau. The right brigade, the 124th (Br.-General W. F. Clemson), had met stiff opposition at the outset from hidden machine-gun nests in the Bassevillebeek valley, and amid the considerable confusion thus caused the barrage was lost. The beek was nevertheless crossed, but, finally, as the men moved up the eastern slope of the valley, machine-gun fire became so intense that no further headway could be made. This fire came mainly from a strongly defended locality in the shape of a quadrilateral, four hundred yards long and a hundred deep, enclosing three ruined cottages, at the southern extremity of the spur, apparently little affected by the barrage. It commanded not only the slope to the front, but also the whole length of the spur to the north as far as the mass of concrete dug-outs and pillboxes known as " Tower Hamlets " on the highest part. After several costly attempts to advance, the 124th Brigade abandoned further effort.

The 122nd Brigade (Br.-General F. W. Towsey), on the left, after overcoming determined resistance in the Bassevillebeek valley, was also checked near the top of the eastern slope, opposite Tower Hamlets defences, by enfilade machine-gun fire from the quadrilateral; its right battalion then swung back to link up with the 124th Brigade, and, on the left, the 23rd Division threw back a flank to connect on that side.[1]

The Southern Flank

The action of the 39th Division (Major-General E. Feetham), whose task was to form the left sector of the southern defensive flank of the X Corps southwards from the Bassevillebeek up the western slope of the valley to near Groenenburg Farm—the 19th Division (IX Corps) continuing the flank to the Comines canal—suffered from the misfortunes of its neighbour on the left, the 41st Division.

---

[1] According to German regimental histories, the front battalions of the *395th* and *28th Bavarian Ersatz Regiments*, holding Tower Hamlets spur, were practically annihilated, and of the support battalions only remnants survived (70 of the *395th Regiment*, holding the spur south of Tower Hamlets) when relieved on the night of the 21st/22nd.

Assaulting with one brigade, the 117th (Br.-General G. A. Armytage), on a frontage of 750 yards, the left battalion, the 16/Rifle Brigade and its support, the 17/K.R.R.C., were both raked with machine-gun fire from the left flank throughout the eight hundred yards of their advance, particularly from the hidden dug-outs in the Bassevillebeek valley, which had checked the 124th Brigade. They incurred severe casualties, the left company of the 16/Rifle Brigade losing all its officers and 95 other ranks, and the 17/K.R.R.C. eventually having two of its companies commanded by corporals;[1] but despite this, the objective was gained by the two battalions, which then swung back their flank to get into touch with the right of the 124th Brigade still just short of the stream. The two right battalions, the 17th and 16/Sherwood Foresters, after a steady advance over very soft ground, also gained their objective along the eastern side of Bulgar Wood, a number of dug-outs on the western side being outflanked.[2]

The 19th Division (Major-General G. T. M. Bridges), on the right of the 39th, successfully formed the southern flank between Groenenburg Farm and the Comines canal by an average advance of six hundred yards on a 1,600-yard frontage.[3] The right of its 58th Brigade (Br.-General A. E. Glasgow) came under enfilade fire from the railway embankment alongside the canal, and the centre was checked

---

[1] Sergeant W. F. Burman (16/Rifle Brigade) was awarded the V.C. for most conspicuous bravery in this action. Seeing his company held up by an enemy machine gun, he went forward alone to what seemed certain death, killed the German gunner and carried forward the gun to the objective, where he subsequently used it with great effect. Later, seeing the battalion on his right held up by enfilade fire, he went forward with two others and outflanked the enemy party, killing 6 and capturing 2 officers and 29 other ranks out of about 40.

Corporal E. A. Egerton (16/Sherwood Foresters) was awarded the V.C. for his gallantry and initiative. Owing to the mist, some German dug-outs were not cleared by the leading groups, and fire from them was causing heavy losses. When volunteers were called for, Corporal Egerton at once dashed to the dug-outs under heavy fire at short range, and shot 3 of the Germans, after which 29 surrendered. His bravery relieved in less than thirty seconds an extremely difficult situation.

[3] The artillery barrage supporting the 19th Division, of less strength than for the main assault, consisted of a creeping barrage, with a searching barrage 300 yards ahead of it, by the field artillery (132 18-pdrs. and 32 4.5-inch howitzers) and a standing barrage distributed in depth beyond the searching barrage by heavy and medium batteries (32 6-inch howitzers, 6 8-inch howitzers, 4 9.2-inch howitzers and 18 60-pdrs.). A machine-gun barrage 300 yards ahead of the searching barrage was laid by 82 machine guns. A smoke screen was maintained on the German observation posts on Zandvoorde Hill for four hours.

FIFTH ARMY. 20TH SEPTEMBER 263

by frontal machine-gun fire from Hessian Wood; but both these sources of resistance were soon silenced, and the objective along the eastern edge of Hessian Wood reached.[1] The 57th Brigade (Br.-General T. A. Cubitt) met with deep mud in front of Belgian Wood and so lost the barrage; but by 8.10 a.m., when the mist lifted, the entire objective of the 19th Division had been gained, although at a heavy cost. Patrols were at once pushed out to clear the immediate foreground. About midday the division suffered further serious loss, as Major-General Bridges, who had gone forward to congratulate his brigadiers, was severely wounded, losing a leg. The C.R.A., Br.-General W. P. Monkhouse, assumed temporary command in his place.[2]

THE FIFTH ARMY CONFORMS[3]

General Gough's Fifth Army, moving abreast of the Second Army, was to capture the *Wilhelm* (Gheluvelt–Langemarck) Line in the sector of its right corps, the V; its centre corps (XVIII) was to complete the occupation of that line, from east of Schuler Farm to east of Langemarck, and then advance 500-800 yards towards Poelcappelle; and the left corps (XIV) was to form a northern flank with its right division. Additional artillery brought from the First, Third and Fourth Armies had been concentrated to support the advance of the Second Army across Gheluvelt plateau, but the artillery allotment to the Fifth Army remained unchanged.

Of the three corps, the V (Lieut.-General E. A. Fanshawe)

---

[1] A platoon of the 9/Cheshire, the left battalion of the brigade, outflanked the Hessian Wood machine-gun nest from the north. 2nd Lieut. H. Colvin (9/Cheshire) was awarded the V.C. in this gallant action. Seeing the battalion on his right held up by machine-gun fire he led a platoon to its assistance, cleared a number of dug-outs one after the other, entering them alone, and forced the occupants to surrender. He took about fifty prisoners in all. The citation in the London Gazette adds that "the "complete success of the attack in this sector was mainly due to 2nd Lieut. "Colvin's leadership and courage".

[2] For casualties see the summary for each division given on p. 279.

The opposition in front of the 39th and 19th Divisions consisted of regiments of 2 German divisions: the *6th Reserve* and *19th Reserve* (*9th Reserve Division*), and the *213th Reserve* and part of the *209th Reserve* (*207th Division*). The *9th Reserve Division* had been in the line since mid-August, and the *207th* since 2nd August.

[3] See Sketch 23.

had the toughest task.[1] Its objective, entailing an average advance of twelve hundred yards, was the same as the IX Corps had twice essayed in vain during August. Most of the fortified farms and pillboxes on the open slopes east of the Hanebeek and Steenbeek, sited in depth and each supporting its neighbours by cross-fire, which had successfully held the British attacks, were still intact, despite the persistent efforts of the heavy artillery to smash them. In order to seize them and all the known pillboxes, farms and dug-outs, the usual lines of moppers-up were replaced during the training rehearsals by special detailed parties, up to half a platoon, in the leading assault waves, the gaps thus caused in the waves being filled by groups from behind.[2] But amongst the legacy of experience gained during the fruitless August attacks was the axiom that it is not only necessary to capture strongpoints at once, but also to occupy them, and this the parties were instructed to do.

The artillery allotment of the V Corps was less in heavy guns and howitzers (159 against 208) than that of the I Anzac Corps, on its right; but in field pieces it was larger (360 against 216). Thus, as its two assaulting divisions had nearly double the frontage of the Australians (1,800 compared with 1,000), the barrage support was considerably weaker, the belts of fire being reduced to three.[3]

---

[1] See Sketch 23. Opposite the V Corps were parts of 4 German regiments: the *66th (121st Division)*, and the *77th Reserve, 15th Reserve* and *91st Reserve (2nd Guard Reserve Division)*. As already mentioned, the *121st Division* had been in the line since 19th August and was expecting relief, but the *2nd Guard Reserve Division* was comparatively fresh, having only been in the line since 13th September.

[2] This procedure was also followed in the divisions of the XVIII Corps, and was soon to become the general practice throughout the Fifth Army.

[3] A creeping barrage of 18-pdrs. at the same general rate of advance as in the Second Army barrage, a combing barrage by 18-pdrs. and 4.5-inch howitzers, to search the area from 100 to 400 yards ahead of the creeping barrage, and a neutralizing barrage, formed by 6-inch howitzers and 60-pdrs., to sweep the area from 450–1,200 yards in advance of the creeping barrage, the 60-pdrs. firing shrapnel. The remainder of the heavy and medium artillery not engaged in counter-battery work was to form standing barrages on special danger areas, such as Windmill Cabaret (Hill 40) and Hill 37; also on the known assembly areas for the larger German counter-attack formations in the hollows behind Zonnebeke and Gravenstafel.

The heavy and medium artillery of the V Corps, organized into two double bombardment and four counter-battery groups, comprised 66 6-inch howitzers; 16 8-inch howitzers; 14 9.2-inch howitzers; 4 12-inch howitzers; 1 15-inch howitzer; 48 60-pdrs.; 8 6-inch guns and 2 9.2-inch guns. The field artillery totalled 270 18-pdrs. and 90 4.5-inch howitzers. A number of these guns and howitzers were put out of action by noon of the 21st, including 19 60-pdrs. and 47 18-pdrs.

Immediately in front of the 9th (Scottish) Division (Major-General H. T. Lukin) was the muddy valley of the Hanebeek; the course of the brook itself, choked by the constant bombardment, had become a belt of swamp and water-filled shell-holes. Each of the two leading brigades, the 27th (Br.-General F. A. Maxwell) and South African (Br.-General F. S. Dawson), sent forward two battalions, and, half-way to the final objective, the support battalions were, after a pause, to leap-frog through and continue the advance. The first belt of the creeping barrage, on the insistence of Major-General Lukin, consisted of high explosive and smoke shell instead of shrapnel, refinements being introduced to assist the capture of the more strongly held centres of resistance.[1] In front of the 27th Brigade, for example, Hanebeek Wood, which contained a number of pillboxes, was kept under a high-explosive and smoke barrage, leaving a wide lane clear for an infantry company to move round behind it. When the barrage lifted to beyond the wood, the place was at once stormed from front and rear by the 6/K.O.S.B. (27th Brigade), fifty prisoners and four machine guns being taken.

Borry Farm, the locality which had given so much trouble to the XIX Corps and now lay in the direct path of the South African Brigade, was successfully treated in a similar manner by the 4th South African Regiment. The mist favoured the mopping-up parties, and the majority of the strongpoints were easily overrun; an exception was the group of four pillboxes about Potsdam House, which caused many casualties before it was eventually rushed from three sides. Seventy prisoners and a number of machine guns were taken by the 12/Royal Scots, the left battalion of the 27th Brigade, assisted by a detachment of South Africans from the left rear. The commanding officer of the 1st South African Regiment, which was moving in support of the 3rd, seeing that heavy casualties were being inflicted on both battalions from Potsdam House, gathered some thirty men and with two Lewis guns and a machine gun attacked the

---

[1] Major-General Lukin, who had commanded the South African Brigade when it joined the 9th Division in April 1916 and became the divisional commander in the following December, had already tried this form of creeping barrage satisfactorily in the Battles of Arras 1917 (see "1917" Vol. I, p. 227); renewed success on this occasion led to its employment later by the 3rd and 59th Divisions when they took over the front of the V Corps.

pillboxes in rear. This small party alone captured 25 prisoners and 7 machine guns.

Although further delay was caused to the centre of the division by numerous machine-gun nests along the Ypres-Roulers railway, south of Potsdam House,[1] the whole of its first objective had been gained by the time the barrage resumed its forward creep at 7.8 a.m.

The 55th (1st West Lancashire) Division (Major-General H. S. Jeudwine), temporarily deficient in man-power and training, was to have the most costly struggle of the day.[2] The 165th and 164th Brigades (Br.-Generals L. B. Boyd-Moss and C. I. Stockwell) led. At the outset considerable confusion was caused by, and many casualties were suffered from, an intense German barrage which crashed on the assembled units about zero hour, and by a hail of bullets from machine guns and rifles at close range which swept their ranks when they rose to follow their own barrage.[3] After this unlucky start, the leading lines, handicapped by the mist, omitted to search a number of dug-outs and strongpoints; and soon afterwards Germans emerged from them armed with machine guns and rifles. The supporting waves were checked, and the advanced elements, hearing the firing behind them, either halted or turned back. Thus the barrage was lost and the first objective was not reached.

At 7.8 a.m., when the advance of the V Corps to the final objective was due to start, its situation was critical; and, to make matters worse, the lifting mist gave the defence a good field of fire. Strange to say, however, the Scottish regiments of the 27th Brigade, having the 2nd Australian

---

[1] Captain H. Reynolds, M.C. (12/Royal Scots) was awarded the V.C. for most conspicuous bravery in overcoming this resistance. He proceeded alone from shell hole to shell hole under machine-gun fire and forced a phosphorus grenade inside a pillbox entrance, setting the place on fire and causing the death of or surrender of the 11 occupants; 8 were taken prisoner with 2 machine guns. He then led his company on to the final objective, despite continuous machine-gun fire from the left flank, taking seventy more prisoners and another 2 machine guns.

[2] The division had lost 135 officers and 3,720 other ranks on 31st July in this same sector, and the replacement of its casualties at St. Omer had been slow and piecemeal. About a thousand men arrived too late to be trained for the attack and had to be left behind.

[3] Prisoners stated that the attack was expected, and that the jumping-off tapes had been seen. " Res. Regt. No. 91 ", which faced the 55th Division, states that as a precautionary measure, its front battalion was relieved during the night of the 18th/19th, and that the machine-gun companies were relieved without loss during a lull of the bombardment on the night of the 19th/20th, a few hours before the assault.

Division (Second Army) moving forward on the higher ground on their right, met with little opposition. The South African Brigade, on the other hand, its left flank in the air, covered the distance only at great cost; the two fresh battalions, carrying on beyond the first objective, were swept by machine-gun fire from Hill 37, north of the Zonnebeek, where the 55th Division should have been, and the 2nd S. African Regiment, on the left, lost half its strength.[1] In the end, the brigade captured Bremen Redoubt and Waterend House, in the Zonnebeek valley, where seventy prisoners were taken, and formed a defensive flank back to the first objective, with machine-gun posts covering the low marshy ground of the Zonnebeek.[2]

The 55th Division meanwhile had continued to struggle towards its first objective without much artillery support. The headquarters of the three brigades and of the two artillery groups were all in close touch in the tunnelled dug-outs in Wieltje, and connected by cable with divisional headquarters at the (Ypres) Canal Bank. Information from the front line, however, was scanty and slow; the German artillery barrage had cut all wires between the forward stations and cable-heads, casualties among the runners were heavy, and visual communication was obscured for some hours by the mist and then by smoke. The situation had to be guessed, and by 10 a.m. both the 165th Brigade about Gallipoli Farm and the 164th Brigade in front of Schuler Galleries (a line of dug-outs three hundred yards long connected by a concrete gallery and strongly wired) had been reinforced by a battalion of the 166th Brigade (Br.-General F. G. Lewis) from divisional reserve. With this assistance, the first objective, including the galleries but excluding Schuler Farm, was gained by mid-day. By this time the units were disorganized; local fighting was still in progress on Hill 35, and advanced elements which had reached Hill 37 had been driven off by a counter-attack at 11.30 a.m. A nest of machine guns had at once been

---

[1] Lce.-Corporal W. H. Hewitt (2nd S. African Regiment) was awarded the V.C. on this occasion. Though twice wounded, he eventually managed to get a bomb through the loophole of a pillbox which dislodged the occupants and so enabled the advance to proceed.

[2] In this action, from midnight 19th/20th till its relief on the night of the 21st/22nd, the S. African Brigade lost 51 officers and 1,204 other ranks (of which 16 officers and 237 other ranks were killed) out of a strength of 91 officers and 2,488 other ranks assembled for the attack.

established in the Schuler Galleries and another of nine guns near Keir Farm and these played a leading part in checking further counter-attacks. By 5 p.m., after the remainder of the divisional reserve had been sent up, Hill 35 and Hill 37, the dominating features of Zonnebeke spur, were cleared and held. Touch was established with the S. African Brigade at Waterend House; but the centre and left of the division still hung back some 500 yards behind the final objective.

The two divisions of the XVIII Corps (Lieut.-General Sir I. Maxse) were to gain a footing on Gravenstafel and Poelcappelle spurs, which reach out westwards from the main Ypres Ridge. They assembled with difficulty east of the Steenbeek, between St. Julien and Langemarck, the low ground being not only muddy but also pitted with shell holes filled with water from the obstructed channels of the Steenbeek and its tributaries.[1]

The 58th (2/1st London) Division (Major-General H. D. Fanshawe) had to advance a thousand yards to gain the strongpoints on the western extremity of Gravenstafel spur. As a previous frontal attack had failed chiefly owing to the state of the ground, the main attack was now to be made with the left brigade (174th, Br.-General C. G. Higgins), from that flank, moving south-eastwards up the rising ground of the spur, while the right brigade (173rd, Br.-General B. C. Freyberg) on the lower ground limited its action to attracting the enemy's attention.

The holding attack of the 173rd Brigade, made with the 2/4 London, achieved its purpose and, further, led to the occupation of the Winnipeg cross-roads.[2] The 174th Brigade delivered the main thrust with three London battalions following one another on a battalion frontage. The strongpoints immediately ahead, in front of Vancouver Farm and

---

[1] Thirty tanks of the I Tank Brigade were allotted to the XVIII Corps to assist in the capture of the strongpoints within reach of the St. Julien–Winnipeg and St. Julien–Poelcappelle roads. Two companies of E Battalion were to support the 58th Division and one company of D Battalion the 51st Division; but the ground was impassable and only one tank succeeded in reaching its objective, Delta House, and helped in its capture by the 51st Division.

[2] An additional task, to assist in the capture of Schuler Farm, on the right boundary of the division, with the help of two tanks failed. The tanks stuck in the mud before their arrival on the scene, and the platoon of infantry was held up by machine-gun fire from the farm.

Keerselaere, were overrun, the only resistance coming from Hubner Farm at the edge of the spur where the garrison, including over seventy unwounded men, surrendered to an enveloping attack. The two rear battalions then passed through, swinging half-right up the rise of the spur. Keeping to the high ground, they took in reverse the several strong-points along the spur and reached the dominating area about Wurst Farm, their objective, close behind the barrage.[1] A definite objective, pillbox or emplacement, had been allotted to each platoon or section to clear and occupy; and once outflanked a strongpoint was as good as captured. Six officers and 285 unwounded prisoners were taken, as well as 50 machine guns. Outpost groups then fanned out to the left to the divisional boundary across the Stroombeek valley. The success of this difficult operation, carried out by the 2/8 (P.O. Rifles), 2/5 (London Rifle Brigade) and 2/6 (Rifles) London battalions in that order, was mainly due to the thoroughness of the preliminary training. The creeping barrage was described as excellent; and smoke-shell, which formed a large proportion of the protective barrage in front of each objective, had, together with the mist, concealed the progress of the operation from the German artillery observers until it was completed. Standing barrages of gas shell, too, on approaches, valleys, and tracks had served to isolate and dishearten the German forward garrison.

The advance by the 51st (Highland) Division (Major-General G. M. Harper) to gain a footing on the Poelcappelle spur was also made by one brigade, the 154th (Br.-General J. G. H. Hamilton). The going was at first very heavy; but most of the bad patches were known and avoided. Advancing on a 1,400-yard front, the two leading battalions, the 1/9 R. Scots and the 1/4 Seaforth Highlanders, met strong resistance almost at once from the remains of the long trench-breastwork of the *Wilhelm* Line, known in this sector as "Pheasant Trench", along the westernmost edge of Poelcappelle spur. A number of newly constructed machine-gun emplacements were sited about forty yards in

---

[1] Sergeant A. S. Knight, 2/8th London (Post Office Rifles), was awarded the V.C. for his extraordinarily good work, exceptional bravery and initiative during this advance. Single-handed, he rushed twelve of the enemy in a shell-hole, bayoneted two, and shot a third; the remainder scattered, leaving behind a machine gun. Shortly afterwards he alone rushed an enemy machine-gun crew in action, bayoneted the gunner and captured the gun.

front of it, and although the position had been battered by the barrage and by the preliminary 24-hour bombardment,[1] the enemy fought stubbornly: in a two hundred yards' stretch of the trench, 150 German dead were counted. After this final hand-to-hand encounter, no further noteworthy opposition was met, and by 8.25 a.m. the final objective was occupied across the Poelcappelle spur within a thousand yards and within sight of the village.

By this double success the XVIII Corps had gained a favourable jumping-off line for its next offensive, with good observation towards Poelcappelle and up the valleys of the Lekkerboterbeek and Lauterbeek on either side; the capture of the German observation areas on Gravenstafel and Poelcappelle spurs also enabled the valley of the Steenbeek to be used for gun positions for forward batteries.[2]

The short advance to be made by the 20th Division (Major-General W. Douglas Smith) of the XIV Corps (Lieut.-General Earl of Cavan) to establish a northern flank between Poelcappelle spur and the Ypres–Staden railway was to be made by two brigades, each with two battalions leading, on a frontage of fourteen hundred yards. Only the left battalion of the left brigade, the 59th (Br.-General H. H. G. Hyslop), reached the objective. The right of the 61st Brigade (Br.-General W. E. Banbury) made some progress until it was checked by the failure of the inner flanks of both brigades at the outset to overrun Eagle Trench, the northward con-

---

[1] The extent of the artillery support may be gathered from the ammunition expenditure. The 22 18-pdr. batteries supporting this brigade attack in the 51st Division's sector fired 67,000 rounds between noon on the 19th and noon on the 20th; the six 4.5-inch howitzer batteries fired 14,000 rounds during the same period; the 12 6-inch howitzer batteries fired 5,561 rounds between 5.30 a.m. and 9.35 a.m. on the 20th, and 3 batteries of 9.2-inch howitzers fired 685 rounds. In addition to 60-pdrs. and other medium and heavy artillery, 16 trench mortars fired 2,700 rounds.

[2] The German regiments facing the XVIII Corps were the *175th, 128th* and the *5th Grenadiers* of the *36th Division*. They had been in the line since 8th September, each regiment occupying a frontage of 800–900 yards with one battalion in the outpost zone, one in support and one in reserve in and behind the Flanders Line. "Gren. Regt. No. 5." (opposite the left of the 154th Brigade) states that its average company battle strength at this time was 2 officers, 10 n.c.o's. and 65 men; and that the regiment had 35 heavy and 32 light machine guns, and 12 trench mortars (*Minenwerfer*), much of which material was broken or made unserviceable during the bombardment. Of the 280 all ranks of the front battalion only about twenty, mostly wounded, survived the day.

tinuation of Pheasant Trench.[1] The barrage was lost, and the situation remained at a deadlock throughout the morning. At 1.30 p.m. Major-General Douglas Smith ordered another attack to be made at 6.30 p.m. with a repetition of the artillery programme, including a smoke-shell barrage on Eagle Trench.

The German Counter-attacks[2]

By midday the Second Army had completed its first step across Gheluvelt plateau, and the Fifth Army was up alongside on the left. General Plumer had every reason to believe that the Germans were committed to their system of defence by counter-attack. He had expected that the enemy's thinly held forward zone, to a depth of two thousand yards, would be captured, and that the test of the infantry and artillery organization would be the holding of it against the onslaught of the German counter-attack divisions.

The defence of the captured ground had been consolidated as soon as the successive objectives were gained. Large stocks of German shovels and wire found in the area were of service. The selected strongpoints were generally a German pillbox or machine-gun emplacement, and machine guns placed in them formed the framework of the infantry defence. The final objective became the line of observation for the foremost sentry groups, and the second objective became the main line of resistance, advantage being taken of reverse slopes and folds in the ground for concealment. As a rule, both these lines were merely an irregular chain of small groups of men taking cover in shell holes; but some of the Australian brigades dug continuous trench lines for both observation and resistance. Although the trenches simplified control and lateral communication, they received most of the German shelling—which the groups in shell holes escaped.

A pre-arranged system of visual signal communication was

---

[1] Blazing oil from 290 projectors was discharged on Eagle Trench, known to be strongly held, at zero hour; but the projectors had a probable range-error of about 200 yards, and eye-witnesses state that the drums fell immediately beyond the breastwork, leaving the garrison unaffected and lighting up the advancing British infantry.
The 20th Division was faced by the *185th Regiment* (*208th Division*), which had been in the line since 5th September.

[2] See Sketch 22.

at once established back from the forward area, with the alternatives of runners, messenger dogs and pigeons.[1] Wireless and power-buzzer sets were erected at each brigade headquarters, working back to the corps directing station, and also at the forward artillery observation posts, one to each heavy and field artillery group, to group headquarters and batteries; but great difficulty was experienced in reading ground wireless signals during heavy firing. Telephone cables, even for short lengths, had proved unreliable in the wake of an attack, and it was not until the following afternoon that buried cables were completed in the captured area, visual signalling, chiefly by Lucas lamp, being used forward from the cable heads.[2]

General Plumer's main concern after the objective had been gained was for his artillery, and he made many enquiries during the afternoon as to how the gun detachments were standing the strain. In continuous action, they had been laying the barrage for over eight hours, and would probably have to continue till nightfall; their casualties from German counter-battery action, particularly in the Zillebeke–Verbrandenmolen area, had been heavy;[3] but they stuck to their task, and the local counter-attacks by the reserve battalions of the German front-line regiments which had attempted to regain the lost ground between 10 a.m. and 1.30 p.m. had all been checked by the protective barrage and machine-gun fire.

More such attacks, however, were likely to come. It was known that there were three German divisions in reserve opposite the two British Armies waiting the moment to be put into the battle. By 1.48 p.m., when the protective barrage was timed to end, they had not appeared, and the barrage ceased; but information had reached the Second Army report centre that strong enemy formations were

---

[1] Sixteen pigeons were allotted to each infantry brigade and 12 to the forward observers of each divisional artillery; they proved very valuable as a means of communication.

[2] Two tanks fitted with wireless had also been lent to the Second Army for subsidiary inter-communication with the forward area. One, attached to the X Corps, was sent up to Clonmel Copse, and the other, with the I Anzac Corps, to the south-western corner of Glencorse Wood, where it received a direct hit by a shell almost at once. Actually, owing to the clear weather, visual signalling proved adequate without wireless assistance.

[3] The artillery casualties are given on p. 279. The artillery ammunition expenditure of the Second and Fifth Armies during the battle period is given on p. 292.

GERMAN COUNTER-ATTACKS. 20TH SEPT.

moving forward from the Flanders III Line, from about Menin, Moorslede, and Westroosebeke.[1]

The day was now clear and sunny, and co-operation between air observers and artillery, due to better weather conditions and to an improved technique, showed a marked improvement.[2] A stream of wireless messages began to flow in from the air observers in the seven R.F.C. squadrons allotted, one to each corps, to watch for counter-attacks and other important targets. Soon after 3 p.m. a force estimated at three battalions was reported to be advancing north of the Menin road up the Reutelbeek valley towards Polderhoek against the sector of the X Corps; another force of about the same strength, accompanied by field batteries, was seen moving up on to the plateau from the east towards Polygon Wood and Anzac House spur against the I Anzac Corps; and another, estimated also as a regiment, was coming down Poelcappelle spur from Westroosebeke against the centre of the Fifth Army.[3] The searching barrages laid down at once

---

[1] For these places see Frontispiece and Sketch 12.

The Second Army Intelligence Summary of 16th September stated that the main effort of the German counter-attack divisions was to be expected against the Gheluvelt plateau; the probable lines of approach were given as towards Tower Hamlets spur, up the Reutelbeek valley, and against Polygon Wood.

This forecast was correct. Two of the three divisions mentioned in the text were directed to Gheluvelt plateau, to recapture the *Wilhelm* Line. Crown Prince Rupprecht wrote in his diary the following day (21st) that it was evidently the British intention to gain Gheluvelt plateau as the preliminary to a break-through northwards, combined with a landing on the Belgian coast.

[2] A total of 394 wireless messages was received during the day from these air observers, and about a third led to immediate artillery fire.

Continuously from zero onwards a patrol consisting of a contact aeroplane and another to watch for counter-attacks, both fitted with wireless, was maintained over the battle area in each corps sector. Great strides had been made at this period in improving the haphazard methods hitherto adopted both by battery commanders and pilots, which were unsuited to the rapid growth of the artillery and air strengths. The transmission of signal codes by wireless from aeroplane to battery wireless-masts had been standardized, and more attention to the training both of pilots and battery officers in this vital part of their work was ordered in the instructional schools both in the United Kingdom and in France.

[3] See Sketch 23.

These formations were the leading regiments of the three divisions in reserve; the *21st Bavarian Reserve* (*16th Bavarian Division*), from Gheluwe; the *458th* (*236th Division*), from Moorslede; and the *452nd* (*234th Division*), from Oostnieuwkerke. A typical account of their advance is given in " Das Buch der 236 Inf. Division ", p. 98.

German accounts state that the counter-attack divisions were held back in anticipation of a further British advance, when they would have a better chance of success.

by all available heavy and medium batteries on these areas were so effective that the columns were soon forced to deploy. Harried and delayed by this artillery fire, the Germans arrived about 5 p.m. within machine-gun range, the strong but scattered artillery barrage which supported them falling mostly behind the foremost British units.[1]

Visibility during the late afternoon became exceptionally good. Looking back from the battle area every detail of the gaunt ruin of the Old Cloth Hall within the ramparts of Ypres could be seen lit up by the setting sun. Clearer still to ground observers, with the sun at their backs, was the detail in front; no movement on Gheluvelt plateau and on the long western slopes of the Broodseinde–Passchendaele ridge could escape the eye. Under such conditions, with every disadvantage, were the enemy counter-attacks launched.

The German advance up the Reutelbeek valley against the 23rd and 1st Australian Divisions had been watched by the foremost infantry for an hour or more, and every preparation had been made to smash the counter-attack with machine-gun and rifle fire. At 7.2 p.m. just when the moment for action seemed to have arrived, an intense barrage by field artillery and machine guns, in answer to an S.O.S. call, descended on the Germans gathering a few hundred yards away, the artillery barrage within half a minute of the signal, and the machine-gun barrage within a few seconds.[2] For forty to sixty minutes, the area in front of both divisions was combed and recombed by fire, and the result was devastating. For the infantry awaiting the onslaught the reaction to this fire success was one of disappointment. An Australian officer, however, said afterwards that his men, south of Polygon Wood, simply sat back and laughed when they saw the opportunity they had been praying for snatched away at the last minute by the guns: they knew that the Germans would be unable to pass through such a barrage, and in fact no further sign of movement was seen that evening.

---

[1] According to the German artillery diaries they were still very uncertain as to the actual line the British had gained.

[2] S.O.S. rockets were sent up by infantry headquarters, from brigade downwards, in the line, and confirmed by the forward artillery observers by signal or telephone. The new S.O.S. signal, a firework rocket which burst into three single lights red, green and yellow floating one above the other in the air for several minutes, was unmistakeable.

North of Polygon Wood the S.O.S. signals for artillery support were sent up on Anzac House spur soon after 6 p.m. From here, too, Germans in considerable strength had been seen moving out of Molenaarelsthoek on the plateau towards the northern end of Polygon Wood against the 2nd Australian Division, and were also observed farther north coming down the slope from Broodseinde and across the Zonnebeek valley towards the position of the 9th Division. The barrage which fell instantly in compliance with the S.O.S. signal continued for forty minutes, and no further sign of either counter-attack was reported.[1] On the southern flank of the plateau, too, Bavarians, filtering forward in twos and threes from shell-hole to shell-hole, reinforced the garrison on Tower Hamlets spur and made efforts to reach the Bassevillebeek across the southern end of the spur. Two attempts made between 6.30 and 7 p.m. against the sector of the 39th Division were, like the others, smashed by an effective artillery barrage, laid on S.O.S. signals, and by machine-gun fire.[2]

The counter-attack against the Fifth Army had no more success.[3] About 5.30 p.m. large numbers of Germans were seen moving down the western slope of the main ridge about a mile in front of the new line of the 55th, 58th and 51st Divisions. Collective fire by machine guns and rifles had been organized on the probable lines of approach and ranges given out. In the centre, in the sector of the 58th Division, machine-gun and Lewis gun fire was opened shortly before 6 p.m. at fifteen hundred yards whereupon the numerous small German columns deployed into extended formation. Rifle fire was opened when the Germans, estimated at two thousand opposite this division alone, arrived at 650 yards' range, by which time they were already thinned out by casualties. On their coming within a hundred and fifty yards of the foremost strongpoint the barrage came down. An eye-witness with the 58th Division states that the effect was "beyond description and the enemy stampeded"; and

---

[1] The *457th Regiment* (*236th Division*), from about Beythem (six miles east of Broodseinde), joined in this counter-attack north of Polygon Wood, with orders to retake the *Wilhelm* Line on Anzac spur. (See " Das Buch der 236 Inf. Div.", p. 100.)

[2] The *14th Bavarian Reserve Regiment* attacked in the Tower Hamlets spur sector; all its three battalions were engaged.

[3] See Sketch 23.

it was after sunset before German patrols returned and occupied an outpost position.

In front of the 55th Division too, on the right, a strong counter-attack from about Gravenstafel directed against Hill 37 was crushed by the artillery barrage and by enfilade machine-gun fire from Keir Farm and Schuler Galleries.[1]

Opposite the 51st Division, on the left, the counter-attack down Poelcappelle spur, about 5.30 p.m., was supported by a barrage of unusual intensity. South of the Lekkerboterbeek, though pressed until 7 p.m., it was checked in front of the new line with very heavy casualties; but in the left sector, the thousand yards between the stream and the Langemarck–Poelcappelle road, the 1/4 Gordon Highlanders reinforced by the 1/8 Argyll & Sutherland Highlanders ran out of ammunition and at 6.30 p.m. withdrew to Pheasant Trench. There they were rallied and, after collecting ammunition from the wounded, went forward again, and the enemy counter-attack was brought to a stop about the first objective of the morning assault, six hundred yards from the original line gained. Defensive flanks were established by the units on either side of this minor break-in.[2]

By nightfall it was evident to the British staffs that the three *Eingreif* divisions had spent their force and incurred heavy losses, and that their onset was not likely to be repeated without a lengthy preparation.[3] Some of the corps commanders wished to take advantage of the situation. They proposed to send forward lightly equipped infantry to pursue and destroy the counter-attacking units which had been

---

[1] This counter-attack was made by the *459th Reserve Regiment*, the right of the *236th Division*, with orders to reach the Steenbeek. "Res. Regt. "No. 91" (which the *459th Reserve* reinforced in the front line), states that "every effort made to press the attack failed owing to the terrible "artillery barrage and machine-gun fire, which tore great gaps in the "advancing companies and caused complete disorganization".

[2] The counter-attack against the 58th and 51st Divisions was carried out by the *234th Division*. Its leading regiment, the *452nd*, had halted near Poelcappelle, and continued its advance soon after 5 p.m., when the wo remaining regiments came up on its left; all three regiments of the division then carried out the counter-attack in line on a front of 2,500 yards, their objective being the recapture of the *Wilhelm* Line.

The history of the *234th Division* (" Hohe Hausnummern an der West-"front", pp. 94–111) gives a full account of this counter-attack from the German side. It admits the very heavy losses suffered, some of the battalions losing 60 per cent. of their officers and up to 50 per cent. of their strength.

[3] The *3rd Reserve* and *50th Reserve Divisions*, about Menin and behind Roulers, were known to be a second echelon of divisions in reserve behind the battlefront.   *Continued at foot of next page.*

beaten ; but others and some of the divisional commanders advised more caution. Major-General H. S. Jeudwine (55th Division) pointed out that the enemy still had numerous strongpoints mutually supporting each other and probably garrisoned, and that to pursue into this zone would be to court heavy losses, that as soon as the depth of the prepared position had been penetrated, but not before, open fighting would be possible, and that then the maxim to pursue a defeated counter-attack could be developed to the full.

During the next five days a number of local attempts were made by the Germans to improve their position at various parts of the line, but they were frustrated by artillery and machine-gun fire. Chief of these was an attack, begun at 6 p.m. on the 21st against the 55th Division's sector, in order to regain Hill 37. Behind a heavy barrage, the enemy advanced in several waves, followed by small columns, and penetrated the position in a few places, despite an intense counter-barrage ; enfilade machine-gun fire, however, checked any deep entry, and by 9.15 p.m. the line had been completely restored by the local supports.

Final Operations

Two more attempts, one by the 41st Division and the other by the 20th Division, were made to gain the two small portions of the final objective not reached on the 20th September. On the 21st, at 9.30 a.m., the 41st Division (X Corps) attacked Tower Hamlets spur with its reserve, 123rd Brigade ; but the quadrilateral, south of the Hamlets, which

---

Continued from previous page.
Crown Prince Rupprecht wrote in his diary (23rd September) that the problem of launching the counter-attack divisions against such a dense artillery barrage, which cut all communications with the forward areas, was difficult to solve. During the previous battles a number of weak spots in the barrage had been easy to locate and the counter-attack formations had been able to get through, whereas now the British barrage, concentrated on a narrower attack frontage, was so dense that no infantry could penetrate it. He quotes a Bavarian officer who was on the plateau on the 20th, and also in the Verdun battles, that the weight of the barrage on the 20th had surpassed all precedent.

G.O.A. xiii., p. 75, sums up : " The German *Eingreif* divisions were at " 8 a.m. assembled at their stations in readiness to move at any moment. " In spite of this, the counter-attacks did not take effect until the late " afternoon ; for the tremendous British barrage fire caused most serious " loss of time and crippled the thrust power of the reserves ".

had checked the advance on the previous day still resisted, despite a previous heavy shelling.[1] The 20th Division (XIV Corps, Fifth Army), on the extreme left, made a first attempt to capture Eagle Trench, its original first objective; but the tanks co-operating with it came to grief in Langemarck village, and the operation was cancelled. At 7 a.m. on the 23rd, in a second attempt, an assault was made by detachments of the 12/K.R.R.C. and 10/Rifle Brigade, after a 3-minute hurricane bombardment by 3-inch Stokes mortars. The infantry then bombed along the breastwork trench, covered by a barrage of rifle grenades, and cleared it, taking 86 unwounded prisoners and 10 machine guns.

Thus ended, with complete success except at Tower Hamlets, the first step in Sir Douglas Haig's first trial of step-by-step advance; the much vaunted new German defence tactics had failed to stop the new method. The change was not appreciated in England or in France, and the success was underrated by the public, but not by the troops themselves, or by their adversaries.

The Commander-in-Chief was encouraged to go on, in spite of the lateness of the season. As a first measure, within seventy-two hours of the substantial capture of the final objective on the 20th September, all the six divisions which had made the main assault, those of the X and I Anzac Corps of the Second Army and the V Corps of the Fifth Army, had been relieved by the divisions in close reserve. The general opinion of the troops was that if every attack could be carried out so cleanly and be followed by relief so quickly, the men would be well content.[2]

During the period of the assault and counter-attacks, 3,243 prisoners had been taken and very heavy losses inflicted in killed[3] and wounded, in addition to the capture of a quantity of booty; but the outstanding gain was that the Germans had been driven from the major part of their key position on Gheluvelt plateau.

---

[1] On the 21st, Br.-General F. A. Maxwell, V.C., commanding the 27th Brigade (9th Division), whilst superintending consolidation, was killed by a sniper at 40 yards' range. A born leader, he had always been regardless of personal safety and was at the time sitting on the front of the parapet watching wiring.

[2] A.O.A. iv., p. 790.

[3] In the sector of the 23rd Division alone, astride the Menin road, over a thousand German dead were buried within the British lines.

NOTE

CASUALTIES 20TH–25TH SEPTEMBER

The total casualties, all arms, of the Second Army for the period 20th–25th September were 672 officers and 11,460 other ranks, of which total 132 officers and 1,642 other ranks were killed. The total casualties, all arms, of the Fifth Army for the period 20th–21st September (48 hours) were 386 officers and 7,923 other ranks, of whom 96 officers and 1,221 other ranks were killed.

The casualties of the Second Army artillery for the period 20th–25th September were:

	Officers	Other Ranks
Heavy Artillery	29	555

(20 per cent. of the officers and 15 per cent. other ranks, killed.)

	Officers	Other Ranks
Field Artillery	51	691

(31 per cent. of the officers and 14 per cent. other ranks, killed.)

The casualties of the divisions engaged (Fifth Army figures include Army field artillery) were as follows:

	Officers Killed	Officers Wounded	Officers Missing	Other Ranks Killed	Other Ranks Wounded	Other Ranks Missing	Total
Second Army:							
19th Division	15	58	1	325	1,265	269	1,933
39th ,,		(Total—47)			(Total—929)		976
41st ,,	40	98	12	394	2,069	510	3,123
23rd ,,	20	52	—	392	1,313	357	2,134
1st Australian Division	31	72	5	348	1,584	312	2,352
2nd ,, ,,	23	50	1	302	1,167	230	1,773
Fifth Army:							
9th Division	21	56	24	374	1,594	122	2,191
55th ,,	27	78	7	143	1,507	182	1,944
58th ,,	19	36	—	237	773	171	1,236
51st ,,	12	27	4	173	827	141	1,184
20th ,,	17	46	4	235	938	169	1,409
							20,255

The Second Army total of infantry casualties (excluding machine-gun companies) was 494 officers and 8,671 other ranks out of a total strength of 9,278 officers and 218,652 other ranks (239 battalions). The percentage of killed to the total casualties was 17 per cent. for officers and 13.5 per cent. for other ranks; and the percentage of casualties to total strength was 5.3 per cent. for officers and 3.9 per cent. for other ranks. The machine-gun companies had a large percentage of losses and of killed. Out of a total strength of 806 officers and 13,584 other ranks (73 machine-gun companies), the casualties were 58 officers (7.2 per cent.) and 537 other ranks (3.9 per cent.) and the percentage of killed to the total casualties was 24 per cent. for officers and 23 per cent. for other ranks.

CHAPTER XV

THE BATTLES OF YPRES 1917
(continued)

BATTLE OF POLYGON WOOD[1]
26TH SEPTEMBER
(Sketches 24, 25)

OUTLINE FOR THE FINAL PHASE OF THE CAMPAIGN

On the 21st September, Sir Douglas Haig gave instructions for the execution of the second step across Gheluvelt plateau in accordance with the plan of action already arranged on the 15th with General Plumer.[2] The main attack, to be made by the I Anzac Corps, was intended to carry the line forward another twelve hundred yards in order to include the whole of Polygon Wood and the southern part of Zonnebeke village. The right was to be covered by the X Corps, which was to attack with two divisions on either side of the Menin road; and the left was to be secured by the Fifth Army, which was to reach the line Zónnebeke–Kansas Cross roads, including the dominating Hill 40 north of Zonnebeke station.

The complete success of the attack on the 20th encouraged Sir Douglas Haig to forecast the subsequent stages of the campaign, and on the 22nd he sent an explanatory map to the commanders of the Second and Fifth Armies.[3] Assuming the second step to have been completed on the 26th, he intended that the Second Army, using the II Anzac Corps from its reserve, should take over the V Corps frontage from the Fifth Army.[4] This second extension of the Second

---

[1] The official date of this battle is 26th September–3rd October. As the minor actions early in October belong to the events developing into the Battle of Broodseinde (4th October), they have been relegated to the next chapter.

[2] See Appendix XXVI and Sketch 24.

[3] See Sketch 25.

[4] General Plumer had intended this arrangement from the first; but Lieut.-General Birdwood had doubted whether the divisions of his I Anzac Corps would last out to make the third step, in which case the II Anzac Corps was to have taken over from them. The 1st and 2nd Australian Divisions were, however, still so fresh that it was agreed at a conference of corps commanders on the 21st to keep the I Anzac Corps in the line.

Army front would bring the main Ypres Ridge as far north as Passchendaele (inclusive)[1] within its sector of attack. The third step, at a date to be decided upon by the two Army commanders, was to include the capture by the two Anzac corps of the Broodseinde sector of the main ridge and Gravenstafel spur, whilst the X Corps consolidated the defence of the eastern edge of Gheluvelt plateau to cover the right flank of the Australians. In a subsequent operation, the fourth step, the Second Army was to occupy the main ridge northwards from Broodseinde as far as Passchendaele (inclusive). It would thereby complete its task of gaining a secure defensive position to cover the right flank and rear of the Fifth Army for a resumed advance north-eastwards. The Fifth Army, conforming to these steps, would then be facing north-east along a front Goudberg–Spriet–St. Janshoek.

Sir Douglas Haig still hoped that any one of the blows he intended to deliver might cause disintegration of the German opposition, and all available British strength in France, including the five cavalry divisions, was to be assembled ready to exploit any opportunity thus created by pushing through the new Fifth Army front north-eastwards towards Roulers and Staden. In accordance with the original plan of February 1917, too, the Fourth Army, in the coastal sector, was to be ready to attack across the Yser, and landings at Ostend and Middelkirke were still to be regarded as a possibility.

THE PREPARATION FOR THE SECOND STEP AND ENEMY INTERFERENCE

General Plumer had issued the warning order for the second step on the evening of the 20th, a few hours only after the first step had been completed.[2] To enable the I Anzac Corps to limit the attack frontage of each of its two leading divisions to a thousand yards, as before, the X Corps was to take over the six hundred yards south of Polygon Wood, making the Black Watch Corner–Reutel track the boundary. A corresponding northward shift was to be made by the IX Corps, and the VIII Corps was to extend to cover the frontage vacated by the IX.

---
[1] See Sketch 25.
[2] See Sketch 24.

The most important of the preparations for the forward move of most of the supporting artillery—about two thousand yards—was the maintenance and strengthening of the new plank roads on and behind the western edge of the plateau. The transverse roads and light railways north and south of Zillebeke connected with the highways out of Ypres formed the basic framework for the lay-out of the new battery positions of the bombardment and counter-battery heavy artillery groups. Other roads,[1] two thousand yards nearer the front, served the same purpose for the field batteries: that from Observatory Ridge through Sanctuary Wood, behind the Stirling Castle high ground, for the X Corps, and that in front of Hooge and Bellewaarde Lake, behind the Bellewaarde ridge, for the I Anzac Corps. On the plateau itself a transverse road was laid northwards from Clapham Junction along the Westhoek track, past the western side of Glencorse Wood.

The general advance of the artillery actually began on the afternoon of the 20th. The following days being fine with a drying breeze, the preparations were completed as planned during the next four days. The artillery bombardment and counter-battery work followed the routine adopted for the first step, and similar practice barrages swept the German defences at least once each day. The artillery of the VIII and IX Corps, on the southern flank, simulated the preparation for an attack on Zandvoorde, and also demonstrated against Warneton (4 miles S.S.W. of Zandvoorde).

The infantry divisions for the assault took over the line during this period under cover of darkness.[2] In the X Corps sector the 39th Division side-stepped northwards on the night of the 22nd/23rd to take over from the 41st Division in order to make another effort, simultaneous with the main attack, to gain the eastern edge of Tower Hamlets spur. The 33rd Division, moving up from corps reserve, relieved the 23rd Division on and north of the Menin road during the night of the 24th/25th. The 5th and 4th Australian Divisions, from I Anzac Corps reserve, took over from the 1st and 2nd Australian Divisions on the nights of the 22nd and 23rd.

A well-organized German counter-attack delivered in the

---

[1] See Sketch 22.
[2] See Sketch 24.

GERMAN SPOILING ATTACK. 25TH SEPTEMBER

early morning of the 25th against the 1,800-yard sector between the Menin road and Polygon Wood threatened seriously to delay the further progress of the preparations.[1] The 33rd Division (Major-General P. R. Wood) was about to take over this sector from the 23rd Division, and the relief of the front battalions had just been finished when, at 5.15 a.m., German heavy and field batteries opened an intense bombardment on the forward area, using high-explosive, shrapnel and some gas shell. The morning was fine but hazy, and soon after 5.30 a.m. large numbers of Germans were seen three to five hundred yards away approaching in group formation.[2] Although the position and ground were quite strange to the defending troops, the attack was held in the centre, south of the Reutelbeek, and had only slight successes on the flanks: on the right, north of the Menin road, the 1/Queen's of the 100th Brigade (Br.-General A. W. F. Baird) yielded about two hundred yards; on the left, the 1/Middlesex, covering the front of the 98th Brigade (Br.-General J. D. Heriot-Maitland) north of the Reutelbeek, fell back six hundred yards; reinforced there by the 1/Argyll and Sutherland Highlanders it established a new front during the afternoon southwards from Black Watch Corner.[3] The right of the I Anzac Corps held

---

[1] Crown Prince Rupprecht states in his diary on the 23rd that he feared the British would complete the capture of Gheluvelt plateau in their next advance, and that it was essential to gain time in order to bring up sufficient reserves to ensure that the counter-attack system of defence should not fail again, as it had done on the 20th. He adds that as an effort to delay the preparations for the next British offensive for a few days, he ordered a counter-attack to be delivered against the southern flank of the plateau position on the 24th (later postponed till the 25th). The object was the recapture of the pillboxes and shelters of the *Wilhelm* Line now occupied by the foremost British troops.

[2] The attack was delivered by two regiments of the *50th Reserve Division*, which had relieved the *3rd Bavarian Ersatz Division* four days earlier. The *230th Reserve* and *229th Reserve Regiments* advanced south and north of the Reutelbeek, respectively, each with one battalion leading. The supporting artillery had been increased, particularly in the Terhand area (See Sketch 12), to 20 heavy and 44 field batteries, nearly four times the normal allotment to a division, the greatest concentration of artillery, it is believed, in any one German divisional sector.

The assault was to have started simultaneously with the barrage, at 5.15 a.m., from 500 yards east of the *Wilhelm* Line; but the barrage fell short on the assembled infantry, according to the history of the *230th Reserve Regiment*, and they had to fall back and wait till it lifted at 5.30 a.m.

[3] The greatest difficulty was to keep the front line supplied with small arms ammunition, owing to the intense and continuous German artillery barrage which boxed in the area. At times, the supply was seriously low, and was maintained only by individual actions of great gallantry.

Continued at foot of next page.

stubbornly the southern edge of Polygon Wood as a defensive flank, and with machine guns and Stokes mortars forced the Germans to take cover.[1] That the enemy losses during the day were severe was evident from his repeated efforts to reinforce the leading battalions, which were seen by the forward artillery observers, and effectually defeated by protective artillery barrages.

Owing to the dislocation in the 33rd Division caused by the fighting, General Plumer agreed to a modification of its operations for the following day: the 98th Brigade alone was to cover the right flank of the I Anzac Corps, whilst the 100th Brigade was to regain the lost ground; but, as will be seen, the 98th proved too weak to carry out the duty required of it.

The Assault

The enemy's desperate attempt to delay the next step forward across Gheluvelt plateau did not make it necessary even to change the zero hour, fixed for 5.50 a.m. the next morning (26th). The 5th and 4th Australian Divisions of the I Anzac Corps which were to carry out the main attack were ready on the starting line when the five belts of the barrage, a thousand yards in depth, fell on the German position. The ground was now so powdery and dry that the bursts of the high explosive shell raised a dense wall of dust and smoke, and a morning mist adding to the obscurity, direction had to be kept by compass-bearing; but so closely did the Australians follow the dust cloud that most of the German machine-gun detachments were rushed or out-flanked before they could fire a shot. Bursts of fire from a few isolated places along the 2,000-yard assault frontage, however, caused considerable casualties before these centres of resistance could be quelled.[2]

Continued from previous page.
Lce.-Corporal J. B. Hamilton, whose battalion (1/9 Highland L.I.) was north of the breaks-in, was awarded the V.C. for his fearlessness in carrying bandoliers of ammunition several times through the enemy's barrage to his front line, and distributing it in full view of the enemy's snipers and machine guns at close range.

[1] The 58th Australian Battalion, reinforced by a company of the 60th, held this southern flank of the 5th Australian Division.

[2] The I Anzac Corps was faced mainly by the *49th* and *2nd Reserve Regiments* (*3rd Reserve Division*). This division had arrived from the Russian front in June and had completed the relief of the *121st Division* on 24th September. The southern part of Polygon Wood was defended by the right company of the *229th Reserve Regiment* (*50th Reserve Division*).

Each Australian division employed two brigades, and each brigade one battalion for the first objective and two for the following short advance of about four hundred yards to gain the final objective and consolidate it against counter-attacks. In the 5th Australian Division (Major-General J. Talbot Hobbs) the plan of action was slightly deranged by the unexpected need for the 15th Brigade (Br.-General H. E. Elliott) to protect a long southern flank, for, as is explained later, the 98th Brigade (33rd Division) had not been able to push forward to do this as arranged. After a pause till 7.30 a.m. along the first objective, eight hundred yards from the start, the advance was resumed. Some confusion arose when the so-called " racecourse " in Polygon Wood (actually the driving-track of a former Belgian artillery school) was mistaken for the final objective; by 9.45 a.m., however, the 15th Brigade had reached its allotted position,[1] and the 14th Brigade (Br.-General C. J. Hobkirk) was up alongside with its left on a hamlet four hundred yards south of Molenaarelsthoek. This brigade had captured in its stride the important German observation station on the Butte in Polygon Wood, some of the garrison running away, and about sixty surrendering from the dug-outs in its back slope. The backbone of the new line consolidated by the division was formed by the captured German shelters of the Flanders I Line, east of Polygon Wood.

The 4th Australian Division (Major-General E. G. Sinclair-Maclagan) carried on the line to the north, having gained its objective, involving an advance of twelve hundred yards, without any serious check.[2] It had crossed the depression at the source of the Steenbeek with comparatively few casualties, and its new front lay along Tokio spur, a feature

---

[1] Private P. Bugden (31st Australian Battalion) was awarded the V.C. for most conspicuous bravery in this action. On two occasions during the advance of the battalion to the final objective he led small parties of men through heavy machine-gun fire to attack strongly held pillboxes which were holding up the advance. He successfully silenced the machine-gunners with bombs and captured the garrison at the point of the bayonet. Later in the action he was killed whilst rescuing wounded men under machine-gun fire, after having brought back five.

[2] At the end of August Lieut.-General Birdwood, commanding the I Anzac Corps, had asked General Plumer to allow the 4th Australian Division to be transferred from the II to the I Anzac Corps, so that the Australian divisions could be sent into battle in pairs. This arrangement was approved, two British divisions being allotted to the II Anzac Corps to make up its complement of four divisions.

parallel to its old line on Anzac House spur. The 4th Brigade (Br.-General C. H. Brand) faced Molenaarelsthoek, and the 13th Brigade (Br.-General T. W. Glasgow) had reached with its left the ruins on the southern outskirts of Zonnebeke village.[1]

The failure of the 98th Brigade (33rd Division) to keep abreast and cover the right flank of the 15th Australian Brigade caused some very natural ill-feeling, as the extent to which the fighting on the previous day had dislocated the arrangements of the 98th Brigade was not appreciated at the time.[2] The two battalions which were detailed, the 1/4 Suffolk and the 5/6 Scottish Rifles (on loan from the 19th Brigade in divisional reserve), were to assemble along a north-south line through Verbeek Farm and advance some five hundred yards at 5.15 a.m. in order to reach, and take forward with them, at 5.50 a.m. (zero hour), the remnants of the troops of the division still holding on to the Black Watch Corner line. Unfortunately one battalion lost direction on the way up to the assembly position, and about 5 a.m., before it was established there, the Germans started to shell the area. As the moon had set and mist had begun to blanket the ground, which neither battalion had seen in daylight, the forward movement was postponed until 5.30 a.m. By that hour the German shelling had become an intense barrage, and the waiting groups were ordered to take cover.[3] Owing to this further delay the barrage, which started at 5.30 a.m., was lost, and the advance was unable to proceed beyond the line of Black Watch Corner, nearly a thousand yards short of its assigned location.

On hearing of this check Major-General Wood, the divisional commander, sent up yet another battalion from the 19th Brigade, the 2/R. Welch Fusiliers, to assist the

---

[1] Sergeant J. J. Dwyer (4th Company, Australian Machine Gun Corps), was awarded the V.C. for his courage. On reaching the final objective, he rushed his gun forward to within thirty yards of a German machine gun which was enfilading troops to the flank, and he fired point-blank at it. Killing the detachment, he brought back the German gun to the front line. He also commanded his guns with great coolness and effect on both that and the following day in repelling German counter-attacks.

[2] A.O.A. iv., p. 832.

[3] The Germans had gathered from prisoners captured the previous day that another offensive would be launched early the following morning; and an artillery concentration was ready to cover the gain they had made on the 25th south of Polygon Wood.

98th Brigade. It was to move into the Australian area in Polygon Wood and thence attack south-eastwards, at noon, in co-operation with a frontal attack from the Black Watch Corner line. No artillery assistance was given to this attack, as some men were known to be still holding out in the forward area. Although heavy machine-gun fire was encountered, most of the ground lost on the previous morning was reoccupied, but not before 2 p.m.[1] Meanwhile, the 100th Brigade after a struggle which continued into the afternoon, regained the ground lost north of the Menin road the previous day, fifty Germans being taken prisoner and as many killed.

South of the Menin road the 39th Division (Major-General E. Feetham) was unable to complete the capture of Tower Hamlets spur. The chief obstacle, as foretold in divisional orders, turned out to be The Quadrilateral,[2] at the southern extremity of the spur, which had given so much trouble to the 41st Division on the 20th. It had been subjected to a systematic bombardment from the 23rd onwards to zero hour, and two tanks, moving south down the Tower Hamlets track, were to co-operate in its capture. On the left, the groups of shelters and machine-gun nests on the crest of the spur, known as Tower Hamlets, were overrun by the 116th Brigade (Br.-General M. L. Hornby), whose objective was gained by 6.30 a.m.; but the 118th Brigade (Br.-General E. H. C. P. Bellingham), on the right, lost the barrage, being delayed by the morass in the Bassevillebeek valley, where the men had often to pull each other out of the deep mud. In spite of this bad beginning, little enemy opposition being met, The Quadrilateral was entered, parties of the 4/5 Black Watch and 1/1 Cambridgeshire then pressing on through the objective to its eastern edge. The two tanks, unable to negotiate the shell-torn ground off the Menin road near the Dumbarton Lakes, failed to arrive; and before the infantry could consolidate their gains they were swept by machine-gun fire at close range from the southern face and south-eastern corner of The

---

[1] " Res. Regt. No. 230 " states that the mist had lifted by this time, and that all available heavy machine guns fired " at this incredibly " favourable target, at 1,000–1,800 yards' range, with annihilating effect ". The account adds that seven machine guns alone fired over 20,000 rounds in a short period.

[2] For this, see Sketch 22.

Quadrilateral, followed immediately by a determined counter-attack from shelters close by. The leading companies had to withdraw to a new line established in the ravine a couple of hundred yards short of the western face.[1] The Quadrilateral thus remained in the possession of the enemy, and its prolonged resistance gave support to the theory that a system of defended localities, with their own counter-attack troops to secure the perimeter, might well be more effective for breaking up an assault than a number of isolated strongpoints, or pillboxes, which fell easily when surrounded.

The northern flank of the main attack was established by the V Corps of the Fifth Army as planned, with the exception that the important observation area on Hill 40, north of Zonnebeke station, remained in enemy hands. The 3rd Division (Major-General C. J. Deverell) assaulted with two brigades on its 1,500-yard frontage. The 76th Brigade (Br.-General C. L. Porter), keeping in touch with the Australians throughout, consolidated a position south of the railway, including the western outskirts of Zonnebeke. The advance of the 8th Brigade (Br.-General H. G. Holmes), north of the railway, was dislocated by the marshy Zonnebeek stream, which crossed its front half-way to the objective and was in places impassable. In the mist some confusion was inevitable, and the barrage was lost. Eventually the brigade was brought to a standstill by machine-gun fire near the foot of Hill 40, six hundred yards from the objective.[2]

The 59th (2nd North Midland) Division (Major-General C. F. Romer) advanced steadily under an effective barrage. The two assaulting brigades, the 176th (Br.-General T. G. Cope) and the 178th (Br.-General T. W. Stansfeld),

---

[1] Most of Tower Hamlets spur was in the sector of the *50th Reserve Division*, and was held by its left regiment (*231st Reserve*). The Quadrilateral itself, however, at the southern end of the spur, was in the sector of the *25th Division*, with a first-class reputation. " Reg. No. 115 " (holding The Quadrilateral) states that " the attack was enfiladed with " machine-gun fire from the south, and the two counter-attack companies " cleared the enemy out of the position ".

[2] Unfortunately, the commanding officer of the 2/Royal Scots, Lieut.-Colonel N. McD. Teacher, D.S.O., was killed whilst reorganizing his battalion preparatory to its advance on Hill 40. The divisional commander's battle report states that the loss of this promising officer was to a large extent the cause of the failure to capture the hill.

divided the 2,000-yard sector, Waterend House–Schuler Farm. The care and time spent in their preliminary training was well repaid ; for the enemy strongpoints were overcome at once, and the final objective was reached behind the barrage with but few casualties.[1]

It was intended to take the opportunity of the general attack to make an advance of about eight hundred yards up Gravenstafel spur to the vicinity of Aviatik Farm, employing the right brigade of the 58th Division. This brigade, the 175th (Br.-General H. C. Jackson), moved with its right up the north Hanebeek valley, in touch with the 59th Division ; but, owing to loss of direction in the mist and a lack of cohesion, progress on the higher ground of the spur ended a quarter of a mile short of the objective.

FAILURE OF THE GERMAN COUNTER-ATTACKS

The capture of the thinly held German forward zone had not been difficult and, as on the 20th September, the main task of the day, especially for the artillery, was to anticipate and crush the onset of German counter-attacks. The arrangements to meet this, such as the inclusion of the more important observation areas in the objective, had been as carefully elaborated as they had been on the 20th. Tower Hamlets spur commands the southern slope of Gheluvelt plateau towards Zandvoorde ; the heads of the valleys of the Reutelbeek and Polygonebeek overlooked the enemy's assembly areas in the low ground north of the Menin road ; and from the top of the Butte de Polygone the remainder of the plateau east and north-east to Becelaere and Broodseinde could be observed. By the immediate consolidation of the position with local reserves against counter-attack echeloned in great depth, it was hoped to ensure the security of these observation areas.[2]

---

[1] The left regiment (*34th Fusilier*) of the *3rd Reserve Division*, and the right and centre regiments (*102nd Reserve* and *392nd*) of the *23rd Reserve Division*, faced the two divisions of the V Corps. The left regiment (*100th Reserve*) of the latter division faced the 58th Division (XVIII Corps), astride Gravenstafel spur. The *23rd Reserve* had relieved the *2nd Guard Reserve Division* on 23rd September.

[2] For example, to act as reserves against counter-attack, each of the two attacking Australian divisions kept back one brigade in divisional reserve in the Hooge area (on the western slope of the plateau), and, in turn, each of the four attacking brigades kept back one battalion as

Continued at foot of next page.

By noon the sun had broken through, and the day became hot and visibility ideal. From that hour onwards wireless messages from air observers began to reach the Army and corps report centres, all to the effect that German troops were moving up against the whole front of attack: the roads and tracks leading westwards through Gheluwe (on the Menin road, 10 miles from Ypres), Becelaere and Moorslede (4 miles E.N.E. of Zonnebeke) were reported to be crowded with enemy infantry. Between 1 p.m. and 2 p.m. the infantry and forward artillery observers confirmed these reports: large numbers of the enemy were crossing the shoulder of the spur north of Becelaere and were appearing on the eastern edge of the plateau south of Broodseinde, whilst, farther north, they were massing on the Broodseinde–Passchendaele ridge. The assembly places and ways of approach to them were roughly as foreseen in the counter-attack maps issued with Second Army Intelligence Summaries shortly before the battle, and this early information enabled the areas in question to be heavily shelled and the enemy formations disorganized before they could fully deploy. The series of counter-attacks which followed, supported by a number of low-flying aircraft firing machine guns, were in consequence disjointed.

At 3.25 p.m. S.O.S. signals were sent up in the sector of the 4th Australian Division, north of Polygon Wood, and the protective barrage came down so promptly and effectively that the counter-attack which threatened on either side of Molenaarelsthoek did not materialize.[1] Half an hour later, about 4 p.m., a succession of waves of German infantry were seen coming over Reutel spur (a mile west of Becelaere), a thousand yards to the fronts of the 98th Brigade (33rd

---

Continued from previous page.
brigade reserve in and behind the day's starting line. To the attacking battalions, one to each brigade, fell the task of consolidating the first objective. In addition, each of the two battalions in each brigade following up the initial attack to carry on the short advance of four hundred yards to the final objective kept back one company, and each company, one platoon.

Defence in depth, organized in this manner during the attack, now became the normal training procedure throughout the Second and Fifth Armies. About a quarter of the 70–80 machine guns with each division was available for the defence of the final objective on its 1,000-yard frontage, the rest being allotted to the creeping and protective barrages, and for the occupation of strongpoints in depth throughout the position.

[1] The protective barrage on S.O.S. signal had been tested shortly before on each brigade front (between 1.30 and 2.30 p.m.).

Division) and the 5th Australian Division; at the same time, air observers reported a mass of enemy troops on the roads north of Reutel. By the orders of the I Anzac Corps, protective artillery and machine-gun barrages, including gas shell, were put down on these ways of approach and also on the German battery positions in the Holle Bosch (wood) north of Becelaere. Some of the forward companies, which had run out of ammunition, fell back about a quarter of a mile from abreast of Cameron House, south of Polygon Wood, to their support position on the Black Watch Corner line; but the barrage alone sufficed to disperse the counter-attack, many Germans being seen running back towards Reutel.

South of the Reutelbeek three German battalions were seen moving up the valley against the 100th Brigade (33rd Division) soon after 4 p.m.; one battalion was leading in extended order, with two supporting in closer formation. This force was so severely handled by observed artillery fire that only a fraction of it approached the front line west of Polderhoek. The survivors met with machine-gun and rifle fire, and some, who persisted, were quickly dispersed with the bayonet. At 5 p.m., and again at 6 and 6.40 p.m., enemy troops were reported to be assembling farther south, opposite Tower Hamlets, where the new line had suffered a heavy German bombardment throughout the day; but here, too, the artillery and machine-gun barrages prevented any serious attack from developing.

At 6.50 p.m. S.O.S. signals gave warning of a final combined effort by the enemy on a wide front from Tower Hamlets to Polygon Wood, and also north of the wood. In places his infantry did penetrate the barrage, only to be annihilated by machine-gun and rifle fire, and the losses were exceptionally heavy. Br.-General Elliott's 15th Australian Brigade (5th Division) held stubbornly to the south-eastern edge of Polygon Wood, despite its long weak southern flank; and on the remainder of the Australian front northwards to Zonnebeke the German counter-attackers could do no more than reach their own front line on either side of Molenaarelsthoek. North of the Zonnebeek the enemy counter-attack, moving down the slope from the Broodseinde–Passchendaele ridge, reached Hill 40 about 6.30 p.m., just at the moment when the renewed attack upon it by the 3rd Division was beginning; no progress was made by either side, so the hill remained for the time being in German hands.[1]

After 8.30 p.m. the Germans ceased all effort to regain the lost ground, and a quiet night followed. Early next morning (27th) an Australian patrol occupied Cameron House, south of Polygon Wood; and during the afternoon the 98th Brigade (33rd Division) gained the whole of its modified objective north of the Reutelbeek near Cameron Covert.

Results of the Second Step

Although the frontage attacked was considerably less than on the 20th (8,500 yards compared with 14,500 yards) the demands made on the artillery during the Polygon Wood battle were said to be proportionately as great, and the forward move of the majority of the heavy and field batteries added a longer carry to the difficulties of the ammunition supply.[2] It had been necessary for the protective artillery barrages, especially those laid by the I Anzac Corps, to be maintained almost without break from dawn to dusk; in addition, the X Corps artillery had been heavily engaged during most of the 25th. The Second Army artillery casualties, too, were nearly double those incurred on the

---

[1] The German remarks on the counter-attacks (G.O.A. xiii., p. 77) are: "The *Eingreif* divisions for the most part again struck against an already well dug in (*eingenistete*) enemy, in some places against new enemy attacks. "... In the face of the British barrages they took 1½ to 2 hours to advance one kilometre, their formation broken and their attack-power lamed".

Three German divisions were engaged: the *17th* thrust with its *75th Regiment* through the sector of the *50th Reserve Division* between the Menin road and the Reutelbeek, with its *90th Fusilier Regiment* north of the Reutelbeek, and with its *89th Grenadier Regiment* against the southern part of Polygon Wood. The *236th* attacked in the sector of the *3rd Reserve Division* with all its regiments (*457th, 459th, 458th*) towards the line Polygon Wood–Zonnebeke. The *4th Bavarian* advanced through the *23rd Reserve Division* in and north of Zonnebeke and against Hill 40 with two regiments (*5th* and *9th Bavarian Reserve*), which together lost forty officers and thirteen hundred other ranks during the day's fighting.

[2] The expenditure of ammunition by the bulk of the Second and Fifth Army artillery during the week 23rd–30th September was as follows, the expenditure for the preceding week (16th–23rd) being given in brackets:

	Second Army		Fifth Army	
18-pdr. ...	508,347	(982,916)	539,038	(905,292)
4.5-inch how. ...	127,182	(262,631)	127,996	(235,158)
60-pdr. ...	51,819	(77,637)	48,773	(69,240)
6-inch how. ...	134,696	(209,953)	93,600	(130,324)
8-inch how. ...	28,846	(50,599)	18,610	(23,435)
9.2-inch how. ...	28,859	(45,574)	14,293	(17,660)

20th;[1] many of the batteries were now established on the western end of the plateau, visible to German ground and balloon observers, and to support the organized counter-attack on the 25th[2] the German artillery strength had been reinforced by the employment of reserves of guns in the Terhand area.

Three German divisions had been sent in on the battle day to support three front divisions, compared with three sent up to support six front divisions on the 20th September, and despite this added density of infantry, the German system of defence by organized counter-attack had again completely failed. Not a yard of ground lost by the enemy had been recaptured, and the counter-attack divisions had to be utilized to reinforce the new line to which the front divisions had been withdrawn.[3]

Not only had the objective of the second step been gained and held, but the destruction also of German divisions and artillery was being carried out faster than they could arrive through the bottle-neck of communication into Western Belgium. The great advantage in the choice of

---

[1] The casualties suffered by the artillerymen in the Second Army during the week ended 26th September–3rd October were as follows, those incurred during the previous week (20th–26th September) being given in brackets:

	Officers		Other Ranks	
Royal Field Artillery ...	79	(51)	1,145	(691)
Royal Garrison Artillery ...	40	(29)	1,147	(555)

[2] The German artillery concentration to support the defence of Gheluvelt plateau on 25th and 26th September was estimated by Second Army Intelligence to amount to the equivalent of ten divisional artilleries.

[3] The casualties incurred on 26th September by the British divisions engaged were as follows:

	Officers			Other Ranks			
	Killed	Wounded	Missing	Killed	Wounded	Missing	Total
39th Division ...		(Total—57)			(Total—1,520)		1,577
33rd ,, ...	24	75	8	420	1,592	786	2,905
5th Aust. Div. ...		(Total—135)			(Total—3,588)		3,723
4th ,, ,, ...		(Total—77)			(Total—1,452)		1,529
3rd Division ...	34	100	3	463	2,573	859	4,032
59th ,, ...	33	105	7	143	694	128	1,110*
58th ,, ...	10	11	2	88	309	79	499

15,375

For once G.O.A. (xiii, p. 77) admits that the German losses 11th–30th September, that is including the battles of the 20th and 26th, were greater than the British, putting them at 38,500 (to which 30 per cent. should be added for lightly wounded) and the British at 36,000.

* From the " Q " diary, it is evident that the figures of the officer casualties given above are for the period 20th/21st—30th/1st, during which other ranks' casualties were 470 killed, 2,194 wounded, and 438 missing.

Flanders as the battlefield area which accrued from this limitation of enemy entry was now manifest.[1]

Major-General C. H. Harington, Chief General Staff officer of the Second Army, in a summary of the situation compiled after the battle, wrote that " the desperate efforts made by " the enemy to retain his position between Tower Hamlets " and Polygon Wood indicate the importance he attaches to " denying us ground observation facilities from the heads of " the valleys between Gheluvelt and Becelaere, and how " much he was willing to pay to hold that area ". The summary added that the dispositions of the enemy's counter-attack divisions and the promptness with which they were set in motion showed that he fully realized the threat to that part of the plateau still remaining to him north of Becelaere, " where our line is now within a short distance of looking " over the eastern edge " ; and it gave a warning that stronger efforts than ever might be made in order to hold this area, behind which the enemy could still bring up and assemble troops under cover.

NOTE

German Change in Defensive Tactics

Ludendorff (ii, p. 480) bitterly complained that " the enemy " managed to adapt himself to our method of employing counter- " attack divisions ".

" The failures (*Misserfolge*) of the 20th and 26th September " caused the German High Command to review their defensive " tactics. The main reason for this was the experience that the " *Eingreif* divisions arrived too late to strike the enemy in the " midst of his assault and take advantage of the confusion in " his ranks ". Systematic artillery support for the counter-attack could not be organized, as the exact situation of the enemy and German front lines was usually not known until next morning at the earliest. It was therefore decided to hold back the *Eingreif* divisions on the day of assault and engage them only on the following day in a systematic counter-attack. The first condition for such procedure was naturally that the position divisions had sufficient fighting power to stop the first onrush of the enemy at the line of main resistance, " a condition that did

---

[1] On 24th September, Crown Prince Rupprecht wrote in his diary : " It " is to be hoped that another attack will not follow too quickly, as we have " not sufficient reserves behind the front ". Owing to lack of fresh divisions at hand, the *236th Division*, already used to counter-attack on the 20th, had been put in a second time.

"not always obtain to its full extent". The position divisions were therefore to be strengthened by giving them more machine guns. These were to be taken from the back areas of the position; the machine guns of the standing-by and reserve battalions were also to be moved to the front. These two categories of battalions were also pushed to the front as soon as, or before, the battle began, so as to catch the enemy whilst consolidating. Finally, " each *Eingreif* division was to send up one battalion behind " each regiment of a position division, as far as the artillery " protection position ". (Flandern 1917, pp. 120–1.)

The Germans were in fact returning to their pre-war axiom in field fortification : " one line and a strong one ".

As a first step it was laid down on the 22nd September that there must be :

(1) " increased artillery counter-preparation before the battle, " not only against the enemy's artillery but also, about half, " against his infantry ", massed behind a screen of outposts.

(2) More offensive raids to make him strengthen his front lines and incur loss.

(3) Strengthening of artillery observation in the German battle area, so that fire would be effective when he entered it.

(4) Speeding up of the counter-attacks. (G.O.A., xiii, p. 75.)

CHAPTER XVI

THE BATTLES OF YPRES 1917 (*continued*)

BATTLE OF BROODSEINDE
4th October
(Sketch 26)

PREPARATIONS

The outstanding success of the first two steps across Gheluvelt plateau, together with the rapid wastage of the enemy's divisions, led Sir Douglas Haig to make special preparations for the long awaited opportunity of a break-through. G.H.Q. at this time was of opinion that the Passchendaele–Staden ridge, as a minimum, could be gained by the end of October, and that much more might be achieved if the fine weather held: the German defence in Flanders was thought to be near breaking point and, with Russia still holding out, no appreciable reinforcements from the Eastern Front to bolster it up could be expected.[1]

At a conference on the 28th September, Sir Douglas Haig informed Generals Plumer and Gough that the next step, the capture of the eastern end of Gheluvelt plateau and Broodseinde, would complete a definite stage of the offensive: he intended that the objective for the following step, about the 10th October, should, in order to permit of exploitation, be less strictly limited. An opportunity might, he explained, occur after the defeat of the enemy's counter-attacks, provided that a general withdrawal on his part seemed indicated: fresh reserve formations would have to be held ready to push through with all speed on the heels of the retreating Germans; and, supported by artillery, cavalry and tanks, they would move in pursuit either eastwards towards Moorslede, or northwards to turn the enemy's

---

[1] More than one-third of the German divisions were still on the Russian front (145 on the Western Front, 82 in Russia, 9 on the Danube and 2 in Macedonia), and G.H.Q. Intelligence estimated that even if Russia made a separate peace, only 36 divisions could be spared immediately, and they would require 16 weeks for transfer at the maximum rate of 2 divisions a week, given the existing conditions of the German railways.
Between 1st November 1917 and 21st March 1918 the Western Front was actually strengthened by 34 divisions from the East. Kuhl ii., p. 6.

HAIG'S INSTRUCTIONS. 28TH SEPTEMBER 297

flank on the main ridge, the cavalry operating towards Roulers.[1] He asked the Army commanders for their requirements.

General Plumer sent in the statement of his requirements in men and material for the next stage on the 30th September, and General Gough did so on the 1st October, each writing a covering letter, independently, to the effect that he believed any idea of extensive exploitation to be premature. Both commanders considered that the main ridge from Passchendaele to Westroosebeke would first have to be gained, and that the capture of this high ground would probably take at least two more steps at three days' interval after the 10th October, followed by three or four days' pause in order to repair the roads from the rear, before any considerable exploitation could be contemplated. General Gough pointed out that the step-by-step method of attack with advances up to only fifteen hundred yards would leave the enemy's artillery fairly intact, so he could not think that the general situation on the 10th would offer an opportunity to push forward under approximately open warfare conditions with advanced guards supported by field artillery.

Sir Douglas Haig's comment on these covering letters was that he did not mean that exploitation must necessarily follow the attack on the 10th October; but he did wish the reserve formations to be ready to go through should the situation develop satisfactorily; and, if it did not, the same arrangements would hold good for a later date. At a further conference on the subject, on the 2nd October, he explained that he was anxious not to repeat the mistake made by the Germans on the 31st October, 1914, when they failed to take advantage of the exhaustion of the British forces after their repeated attacks on this same battle-ground at "First Ypres": he had decided to abandon projects for operations elsewhere (e.g., Cambrai) and to employ all available strength for the Ypres operations so long as weather conditions permitted. Six divisions, he said, were to be taken from other sectors of the front in order to reinforce the Fifth Army, and the Canadian Corps (four divisions) was to be brought up from Lens to the Second Army about the 20th October.

The arrangements for the immediate exploitation of any

---

[1] See Frontispiece.

outstanding success of the attack proposed for the 10th October were agreed upon at this conference. Each division was to have a reserve brigade, lightly equipped, in readiness to move up to the front line, accompanied along selected routes by its own mobile artillery, consisting of two 60-pdr. batteries, two 6-inch howitzer batteries and four R.F.A. brigades. If within, say, four hours after zero the leading brigades of the morning assault reported the situation to be favourable, these reserve brigades were to carry on the advance early in the afternoon to more distant objectives, to be reached before nightfall, those of the Second Army to well beyond Passchendaele,[1] beyond the slopes of the main ridge both to the north and to the east. The reserve brigades of the I Anzac Corps were to reach Droogenbroodhoek, on the Moorslede road, three thousand yards beyond Broodseinde; those of the II Anzac Corps were to have their right at Passchendaele station, on the Moorslede road, and their left, in touch with the Fifth Army, north of Passchendaele, on the Westroosebeke road.

A reserve division of each corps was to be ready to entrain at Godewaersvelde (Second Army) and Abeele (Fifth Army), each brigade in two trains (1,800 men to a train); those of the Second Army were to use the Poperinghe–Ypres line to Zillebeke and stations along the Roulers branch towards Zonnebeke, those of the Fifth Army the Proven–Boesinghe line and its extensions. Major-General P. A. M. Nash, the Director-General of Transportation, stated that, with three hours' notice, he could have the reserve divisions on the battlefield within $3\frac{1}{2}$ to 4 hours. These divisions would be in a position to continue the advance on the following morning from the line gained by the reserve brigades if the resistance was found to be crumbling. Two cavalry divisions, the 1st with the Second Army and the 5th with the Fifth Army, would be allotted to co-operate with the reserve divisions, the remainder of the Cavalry Corps remaining west of the Yser canal until the Passchendaele ridge was clear of the enemy. Two tank battalions were allotted to the Second Army, and a tank brigade (3 battalions) to the Fifth Army, Sir Douglas Haig explaining: " The firmer ground and better going beyond the shell-torn " area, which we hope shortly to reach, will give the tanks a

---

[1] See Sketch 26.

"better chance, and will permit their employment in large "numbers."

These arrangements for exploitation did not affect the third step, which, as previously ordered, had a strictly limited objective. The main assault was to be made by four divisions of the two Anzac corps. The I (Lieut.-General Sir W. R. Birdwood) was to capture the Broodseinde ridge, on a frontage of two thousand yards astride the Moorslede road, from its junction with Gheluvelt plateau about Noordemdhoek, northwards to Nieuwemolen (exclusive); whilst the II (Lieut.-General Sir A. J. Godley), on a frontage of three thousand yards, overran Gravenstafel spur. The Fifth Army was to attack on the left, towards Poelcappelle, with four divisions, their left resting on the Ypres–Staden railway.

The right flank of the operation was to be buttressed and protected by a simultaneous advance of the X Corps (Lieut.-General Sir T. Morland) to the eastern edge of Gheluvelt plateau, an average distance of twelve hundred yards, thus including the dominating observation areas near Reutel and In de Ster. General Plumer stated that he intended to use both reserve divisions of the X Corps (7th and 21st) on the 1,400-yard frontage of the attack. Sir Douglas Haig, stressing the need to secure also the south-eastern corner of the plateau, both for observation and for a more effective defence, suggested that the objective north of the Menin road which had not been gained on the 26th should be included. General Plumer insisted that for this another fresh division would be required, and it was agreed to transfer the 5th Division from the Fifth Army to the X Corps for this purpose. The southern flank, south of the Menin road, was to be established by one division, the 37th, of the IX Corps. In all, twelve divisions were to be employed on a frontage of fourteen thousand yards.

The date proposed for the operation was the 6th October, in order to allow ample time for the preparations of the II Anzac Corps, which had taken over the V Corps sector on the 28th September. Sir Douglas Haig, however, feared a break in the long spell of dry weather, and, on enquiry, both General Plumer and General Gough said they hoped to be ready, given reasonable conditions, by the 4th October.[1]

---

[1] This anticipated a German counter-attack with two divisions against the Gheluvelt sector planned for the 8th, but coincided with the date of an operation against Zonnebeke by a regiment. (G.O.A. xiii., p. 78.)

The Second Army orders for the battle and the artillery plan were issued on the 28th September, and the necessary adjustments of the corps sectors were made during the three following days: the X Corps took over from the I Anzac Corps to the north-eastern corner of Polygon Wood, in order to limit to a thousand yards the assault frontages towards Broodseinde ridge of the two Australian divisions. The IX Corps, as compensation to the X Corps, extended its left on Tower Hamlets spur northwards to the Menin road. After the transfer of artillery units from the V Corps, the Second Army artillery support amounted to 796 heavy and medium and 1,548 field guns and howitzers.[1] The bulk of the battery positions had to be advanced another thousand to fifteen hundred yards, and, as before, most of the preparatory work consisted in the construction of plank roadways and tracks for ammunition supply, and the laying of buried cable for communications.[2] A number of duck-board tracks, too, had to be laid forward in the II Anzac Corps area across the swampy ground of the blocked watercourses of the Haanebeek, Steenbeek and Zonnebeek, the latter two being bridged with duck-boards at seven points on the front of the 3rd Australian Division alone.

The Second Army artillery plan was designed to mystify the enemy as to the day and hour of the infantry assault. The Menin Road battle (20th September) had been preceded by a 7-day bombardment, the Polygon Wood battle by a 24-hour bombardment, but it was intended to launch the assault on the 4th October without any artillery preparation apart from the normal intensive counter-battery work and the deliberate destruction of strongpoints. The barrage was to be laid with massed strength at the actual zero hour: the

---

[1] For the main assault the I Anzac Corps had 152 heavy and medium and 192 field guns and howitzers (96 of the latter to each division), and the II Anzac Corps, 227 heavy and medium, with 384 field. These figures gave a theoretical concentration of 985 guns and howitzers of all calibres on the 5,000-yard attack frontage; owing to wear and casualties, however, the proportion was considerably lower than the figures imply. The Second Army gun casualties for August for the 18-pdrs. alone were 234; for September, 350; and for October, 249. Replacement was only gradual.

[2] In the I Anzac and X Corps sectors, the transverse circuit road behind Glencorse Wood to Clapham Junction was nearly ready, the cable head being at Iron Cross Redoubt (1,000 yards north-west of the centre of Polygon Wood). In the II Anzac Corps, however, the plank road ended at Frezenberg, some 5,000 yards from the objective. The buried cable head, by a fine effort of the labour parties, working at night and at a cost of numerous casualties, was continued another 3,000 yards, five to seven feet deep, from Verlorenhoek to Zevencote, before the battle.

form, a thousand yards deep, was not changed, but, as a deceptive measure, full-scale practice barrages, including gas shell, were laid at various hours on several days from the 27th September onward.[1]

As General Plumer had foreseen, the Germans made desperate final efforts to maintain their hold on the eastern end of Gheluvelt plateau, and also to delay the onset of the next British step, which was designed to capture it. The fine weather held over the turn of the month ; warm sunny days were followed by bright moonlit nights, but as a thick ground mist shrouded the district in the early morning hours, the Germans took advantage of it for their counter measures. At 4.30 a.m. on the 30th September a heavy bombardment by enemy artillery and trench mortars suddenly fell on the right brigade, the 70th (Br.-General H. Gordon), of the 23rd Division, between the Menin road and the Reutelbeek.[2] Half an hour later infantry emerged from the mist along the 800-yard frontage of the brigade, held by the 8/K.O.Y.L.I. and 11/Sherwood Foresters. Preceded by assault groups using liquid flame throwers, smoke bombs and hand-grenades the Germans came on boldly, only to be met at once by rapid fire from every rifle, Lewis gun and machine gun in the front line. Owing to the mist, S.O.S. signals for artillery support could not be seen, and messages sent back by runner took two hours to reach brigade headquarters in Sanctuary Wood. Nevertheless, the two battalions stood firm, and the Germans, breaking under the withering fire of the defence, fled in confusion. A feebler repetition of the attack, at 6 a.m., suffered the same fate.

---

[1] The first belt was laid 150 yards in front of the jumping-off tapes. After 3 minutes the barrage was to creep forward by 100-yard lifts every 4 minutes for the first 200 yards, and then every 6 minutes to the first objective protective line, 200 yards in front of the infantry halt. During the pause the barrage was to wander a thousand yards deeper into the German position to break up counter-attacks, and then suddenly return. At Zero+130 minutes it was to creep forward again in front of the infantry by 100-yard lifts every 8 minutes to the final objective line, whence, after a pause, it was to creep forward at intervals of about an hour fifteen hundred yards deeper into the position. The protective barrage by the first two belts (field artillery) was to cease at 11.20 a.m. apart from S.O.S. signals, and the two back belts (heavy and medium artillery) at 1.44 p.m. The rates of fire were to be two rounds a gun a minute for the 18-pdrs., 1¼ for the 4.5-inch howitzers and one to two for the heavier guns and howitzers.

[2] The division had taken over from the 33rd Division on 27th September, after only two days' rest.

On the following morning, the 1st October, a hurricane bombardment was opened at 5 a.m. by the enemy on the 1,500-yard frontage from the Reutelbeek northwards to Polygon Wood (half of it inclusive), smothering with shell the whole area back to a thousand yards. Three brigades were in position in this sector: the 69th (Br.-General T. S. Lambert) of the 23rd Division, about Cameron Covert; the 110th (Br.-General Lord Loch) of the 21st Division, and the 22nd Brigade (Br.-General J. McC. Steele) of the 7th Division, in front of Polygon Wood. At 5.30 a.m. German infantry in strength appeared, particularly in the Polygon Wood sector. The 1/R. Welch Fusiliers, holding the line of the 22nd Brigade, earned special commendation for its quick and stubborn response. The 9/Leicestershire, covering the 110th Brigade, gave ground slightly at first, causing the 9/Green Howards to swing back its left in Cameron Covert. Immediate and most courageous counter-attacks by these two battalions, however, regained the lost ground, with the exception of a couple of pillboxes in Cameron Covert.[1] After making two more efforts during the course of the next three hours the Germans fell back to their original shell-hole position. Their artillery continued to shell very heavily throughout the day the area they had attacked, and infantry formations continued to move up as if assembling for another effort. Intense rifle and machine-gun fire, together with prompt and accurate artillery barrages on S.O.S. calls, however, broke up these concentrations with severe losses, so no further attack developed.

Thanks to the stout defence, against specially trained German shock-troops, these costly enemy attacks neither delayed nor interfered with the preparations for the third step to gain Gheluvelt plateau northwards to Broodseinde.[2]

---

[1] Lieut.-Colonel P. E. Bent (9/Leicestershire) earned the V.C. on this occasion for bravery and inspiring leadership. He saw the right of his battalion, with the battalion on its right, being forced back east of Polygon Wood, and personally led forward all available reserves at hand, made a successful counter-attack and regained the position, which was of essential importance for subsequent operations. He was killed at the objective, after giving his orders for re-consolidation.

[2] The German attacks on 30th September and 1st October were made by regiments of two fresh divisions, the *8th* and *45th Reserve*, supported by 12 sections of specially trained assault groups of the *Sturmbataillon* of the *Fourth Army*. They had orders to retake the shelters and observation points lost on 26th September.

The failure and heavy losses suffered in these attacks made it necessary
Continued at foot of next page.

The Third Step

The Second Army

At dusk on the 3rd the assaulting brigades began the march up to the line; most of the Australians, of whom three divisions were going into battle side by side for the first time, passed out of Ypres by the Menin Gate.

The chief concern was a probable break in the weather. The sunset had been stormy, and in the late evening a strong gale rose from the south-west, bringing showers of rain, as the forecast had predicted, and heralding the arrival of the second turning point in the campaign, really bad weather, the assignment of the major rôle to General Plumer having been the first. The approach march during the midnight hours was made across ground rendered greasy by the rain, and for the most part the duckboard tracks had to be used to enable units to reach their destinations up to time. In the opinion of an infantry brigadier opposite Poelcappelle " the going was not too bad on the 4th, infantry had no " difficulty and we had no tanks ditched, in fact they [the " tanks] were elated. Shells ricochetted too, showing the " ground was hard in places."

A full moon was hidden by clouds when, by 4 a.m. on this 4th October, the first of the admittedly " black days " of the German army,[1] the men lay crowded on the wet ground behind the jumping-off tapes. Brigades had assembled well forward to escape the expected German defensive barrage about zero hour; but at 5.20 a.m., forty minutes earlier, intense German artillery fire suddenly fell on most of the front of the two Anzac corps. It seemed that the waiting mass of men had been detected, and, in order to minimize losses, they were squeezed still closer to the German outpost groups, taking any available cover in shell holes. The 11th Australian Brigade on Windmill Hill (Hill 40) was crowded into a belt of ground only a hundred yards deep. Even so, heavy casualties were suffered during forty minutes' shelling, particularly by the brigades of the I Anzac Corps, which

---

Continued from previous page.
to reorganize the major counter-offensive which the Germans had planned for 3rd October north of Polygon Wood. It was postponed 24 hours, till daybreak on the 4th.

[1] *Flandern 1917*, p. 122.

lost, it was estimated, one man in seven killed or wounded before the assault started.[1]

At 6 a.m. the British barrage suddenly crashed down on the whole depth of the German position. The infantry stood up, unperturbed by their ordeal, and, lighting cigarettes, the men surged across No Man's Land to escape a renewal of the German shelling. The companies then shook out into groups and small columns, with their proper distances and intervals, as rehearsed. It was twilight, and a drizzling rain, driven by a south-west wind, limited visibility to about thirty yards.[2]

The two assaulting divisions, the 1st and 2nd Australian, of the I Anzac Corps, from their starting-line on Tokio spur, had to cross the depression of the upper Zonnebeek before climbing the sharp slope on to Broodseinde ridge. Their first objective, the pillboxes of the Flanders I Line, which lay on a natural terrace below the crest, was about eight hundred yards away, the final objective being on the far slope, four hundred yards beyond. Before the leading companies had crossed No Man's Land they saw in the dim light, close ahead, lines of men rising up from shell-holes. Some were already on the move forward with bayonets fixed, and the Australians opened fire. The assault was only momentarily delayed. As the Australians advanced they found Germans in every shell-hole waiting for the signal to advance.

Although the first two belts of the barrage were noticeably thinner and more ragged than on the 20th September, owing

---

[1] The German bombardment was preparatory to an organized counter-attack to be made by three battalions (*212th Reserve Regiment*) on a 2,000-yard frontage, Polygon Wood–Zonnebeke (inclusive), backed by the three regiments of the *4th Guard Division* (holding the sector). The object was to retake the observation areas lost on 26th September, particularly those on Tokio spur. The assault was timed to start at 6.10 a.m. As mentioned earlier, it had been postponed for 24 hours, owing to dislocation caused by the failure of the counter-attack on the 1st. The operation had been rehearsed on the 2nd, and again on the 3rd, in the presence of the corps and divisional commanders.

[2] As on 20th September, each division employed two brigades for the assault, each brigade using one battalion to gain the first objective, and two for the short advance to the final objective to ensure that a strong force of fresh infantry should be available to meet the expected German counter-attack. The fourth battalion of each brigade was held close at hand as a reserve against counter-attack.

Battalions attacked on a 3-company frontage, with one company held as reserve against counter-attack, and each company had one platoon extended to follow the barrage, two platoons as moppers-up, with one platoon in reserve, all moving in small groups of section columns.

to the weakened artillery support,[1] the same confident resolution and determined driving power which had characterized the assault by these two Australian divisions on the 20th September quickly gave them mastery of this unexpected situation. Many of the enemy would not face the onslaught and fled back, risking the barrage, whilst numerous sharp and merciless encounters took place with any survivors who offered resistance. The area was soon littered with German dead, and the large number who bore bayonet wounds was evidence of the bitterness of the encounter.[2]

After the leading waves of German infantry had been overpowered, opposition to the advance of the 1st Australian Division (Major-General H. B. Walker) came chiefly from the numerous strongpoints. Some of these, indeed, were taken easily. An Australian officer captured 31 prisoners single-handed from one blockhouse, and the garrison of another surrendered with three machine guns as soon as the attack began. But such incidents were exceptional. Battalions of the 1st Australian Brigade (Br.-General W. R. Lesslie) found a number of pillboxes in the marshy ground near Molenaarelsthoek, and lost many men before they could outflank and capture them; and machine-gun fire from Retaliation Farm caused loss to the 2nd Australian Brigade (Br.-General J. Heane) before the garrison was bombed out. The 1st Brigade tended to advance obliquely to the slope, through the tree stumps of Romulus and Remus Woods (two copses north of Molenaarelsthoek), and overlapped into the sector of the 2nd Brigade. The two brigades arrived together on the first divisional objective at 7.15 a.m. The order was to halt there for an hour; but many of the leading companies, flushed with victory, continued to chase the routed Germans over the crest, the barrage being so thin

---

[1] Instead of the support of eight field brigades, made up of the divisional artillery of the 1st and 5th Australian Divisions and three Army brigades R.F.A., as on 20th September, the attack had to rely on the help of the five brigades of field artillery belonging to the 3rd Australian Division. The eight brigades had been transferred, on relief, to the II Anzac Corps, and, in addition, a double bombardment group had been sent to help the X Corps to deal with the valleys on the southern flank.

[2] Crown Prince Rupprecht's First General Staff Officer recorded in his diary: " Quite the heaviest battle to date ". (G.O.A. xiii., p. 79.)

The *212th Reserve Regiment*, about to launch the attack on Tokio spur, lost 36 officers and 1,009 other ranks during the battle, some companies losing 95 per cent. of their effective strength; and the casualties of the three regiments of the *4th Guard Division*, holding the line, were in the same proportion.

that the smoke shell marking the objective was not noticed.[1] The divisional commanders, in their battle reports, questioned the value of the hour's halt along this first objective. They considered that it was tactically unnecessary, and enabled numbers of the enemy to get away, with trench mortars and machine guns, who might otherwise have been overtaken.

The bare open ridge south of Broodseinde is hog-backed, and the many craters and lengths of old trench near the paved highway along the narrow summit had been used by the Germans as sites for various command and observation posts. Machine-gun fire from a few nests of resistance covering these posts was soon located. Parties of bombers, covered by rifle grenades, Lewis guns and trench mortars firing at the loopholes of the emplacements, worked along the old trenches and shell craters and enveloped them. In this manner, two battalion headquarters staffs were captured after twenty minutes' resistance, and a number of machine guns silenced. Thereby the way was cleared for the advance by the supporting battalions to the final objective at 8.10 a.m., which was gained with little further trouble.

In the sector of the 2nd Australian Division (Major-General N. M. Smyth), Germans were met at the outset advancing with fixed bayonets, and as summarily dealt with as the troops opposing the advance of the 1st Division. Zonnebeke "Lake", a brackish water-hole a couple of hundred yards wide, was by-passed, and with great skill and courage numbers of machine-gun detachments who resisted stubbornly in the ruins of the village were overcome. The 6th Brigade (Br.-General J. Paton), following close on the heels of the retreating Germans without pausing on the first objective, overran four anti-tank field guns in position near the highway, beyond the crest, which were firing at point-blank range along the ridge. Some of these advanced companies were brought back by their officers to the first objective. Here, too, the thrust on to the ridge itself had paved the way for the advance to the final objective, including the heap of rubble marking the site of Broodseinde hamlet, which was easily gained. The troops of the 7th Brigade (Br.-General E. A. Wisdom), after clearing the ruins of Zonnebeke in a most skilful and rapid manner, met a

---

[1] A suggestion that coloured smoke should be used for the purpose, as easier to distinguish, had not been adopted.

withering machine-gun fire as they topped the crest of the ridge, and were finally checked immediately east of the highway.

The ridge broadens out north of Broodseinde, and, partly because of fire which came from Daisy Wood three hundred yards ahead, and partly because the lie of the ground seemed exactly suitable for defence, the local Australian commander decided to consolidate along the old trench line which had been reached, about two hundred yards short of the final objective. This old trench was part of the British front line of the winter of 1914-15, and as the Australians dug in they found scraps of khaki uniforms belonging to British soldiers who had given their lives to hold this gateway to Calais and London three years earlier. The gathered strength of the Empire had now arrived to make good the gallant defence by that small British force.[1]

The task of the II Anzac Corps, to capture the Zonnebeke and Gravenstafel spurs, was as formidable as that of its sister corps, the open slopes in front of it being chequered with strongpoints. The final objective, General Godley was instructed, was to be held in such strength as to ensure its security as a jumping-off line for the next step on to the Broodseinde-Passchendaele sector of the main ridge. To make early provision for this northward shift of the axis of the campaign, and in view of his corps holding a greater frontage by a thousand yards than the I Anzac Corps and having a more distant objective, General Plumer had given him additional artillery support.[2]

A number of duck-board bridges across the streams and their marshy margins, particularly the Zonnebeek, already practically impassable otherwise, had eased the assembly of the two assaulting brigades of the 3rd Australian Division (Major-General Sir John Monash), and, although little time had been allowed for the corps artillery commander (Br.-General E. W. M. Powell) to make his preparations, the barrage was acclaimed as excellent. Strong opposition, met at the outset on Windmill Hill (Hill 40), was at once crushed

---

[1] See "1914" Vol. II and "1915" Vol. I.
[2] The II Anzac Corps had 1½ times as much heavy artillery as that of the I Anzac Corps (227 as against 152 guns and howitzers) and double the number of field guns and howitzers (384 as against 192). The XIX Corps, to support its attacks during August in the same sector, had 147 heavy and medium guns and howitzers.

by the weight of the barrage and by the ruthless determination behind the infantry assault.[1] Bayonets were freely used against the large number of Germans found assembled, 350 dead being counted later in the first five hundred yards of one brigade sector alone.[2] As the Australians swept on down the back of Windmill Hill and **over** the Haanebeek, Germans were seen ahead of them, running into the high-explosive barrage, which, in the dawn light, looked, to quote an observer, like " a wall of flame ". After a halt till 8.10 a.m. on the far side of the stream, fresh battalions began the advance up Gravenstafel spur.[3]

The Flanders I Line here lay diagonally across the front of the 3rd Australian Division, and the battalions of its right brigade, the 11th (Br.-General J. H. Cannan), met resistance at once from several of its pillboxes. Delay was caused whilst parties, covered by volleys of rifle-grenades, outflanked these centres of resistance, in which they captured a battalion headquarters and over fifty prisoners. The 10th Brigade (Br.-General W. R. McNicol) was also checked about the same time by intense machine-gun fire from Abraham Heights, until a company, working round by some sheltered ground, finally outflanked the position. A series of most gallant individual acts contributed largely to the capture of these strongpoints, and, although the barrage had been lost by both brigades, the defence was broken.[4] Large numbers of Germans were mopped up in a maze of dug-outs which had been tunnelled into the banks of the railway cutting in the sector of the 11th Brigade, and Nieuwemolen cross-roads, on the main Broodseinde ridge, was reached soon after 9 a.m. About that hour, too, the two brigades attained their final

---

[1] Lce.-Corporal W. Peeler (3rd Australian Pioneer Battalion) went ahead of the first wave of the assault and accounted for over thirty Germans in various shell-hole positions, including snipers and a machine-gun detachment, which were opening fire on the advance. His valour and fine example, for which he was awarded the V.C., greatly assisted the assault.

[2] That of the 10th Brigade, on the left. The assembled Germans formed the northern wing of the proposed counter-attack which was to force the British back across the Zonnebeek in this area.

[3] The II Anzac Corps was faced mainly by the *20th Division*, recently arrived from the Russian front. It had taken over the sector on 28th September. Behind it was the *4th Bavarian Division* (*Eingreif*).

[4] One of these gallant acts was that of Sergeant L. McGee (40th Australian Battalion), who was awarded the V.C. for most conspicuous bravery. Armed only with a revolver, he rushed a machine-gun emplacement which was causing severe casualties to his platoon, shot some of the detachment and captured the rest. He was foremost in the subsequent advance.

objective, after occupying all the pillbox defences of the Flanders I Line in their sector across the western breast of the main ridge and down to the Ravebeek.

The aggressive spirit of the troops of the New Zealand Division (Major-General Sir A. H. Russell), next on the left, carried all before it. The chief opposition was encountered along the crest of Gravenstafel spur. Abraham Heights were overrun by battalions of the 4th Brigade (Br.-General H. E. Hart). Gravenstafel itself was then mopped up, a hundred prisoners being taken by one company alone. On the left, the 1st New Zealand Brigade (Br.-General C. W. Melvill) took Boetleer Farm, on Hill 32, a prominent feature near the western extremity of the spur. The advance was continued across the spur into the upper Stroombeek valley, leaving its trail of German dead; and 1,159 prisoners with 59 machine guns were captured by the division.[1] The final objective, near the Ravebeek, was reached close behind the barrage.[2] On the high ground across the valley could be seen the pillboxes of the Flanders I Line on Bellevue spur, the objective for the next attack.[3]

THE FIFTH ARMY

The Fifth Army had kept abreast of the main attack. The German position was now astride Wallemolen and Poelcappelle spurs, with the supporting field artillery about the Flanders I Line, some three thousand yards back. The objective included the outpost zone to a depth of twelve hundred yards.[4]

---

[1] Large numbers lying out in shell-holes were killed by the barrage, as few were wearing their steel helmets. In the sector of the 1st Brigade alone the German dead were estimated at eight hundred.

[2] A vivid description of the firing of the barrage from the point of view of a gunner is given in N.Z.O.A. ii., p. 260.

[3] The casualties suffered by the divisions of the I and II Anzac Corps during the period of the battle to date were:

	Officers	Other Ranks	Total
1st Australian Division ...	124	2,324	2,448
2nd Australian Division ...	92	2,082	2,174
3rd Australian Division ...	66	1,744	1,810
New Zealand Division ...	110	1,533	1,643
			8,075

[4] The two corps of the Fifth Army were opposed, approximately, by two German divisions, the *10th Ersatz* and *6th Bavarian*, with the *187th* in close reserve as *Eingreif* division.

The XVIII Corps used three brigades of two different divisions. Warwickshire battalions of the 143rd Brigade (Br.-General G. C. Sladen), covering the front of the 48th (1st South Midland) Division (Major-General R. Fanshawe), gained up to time most of the objective assigned to their brigade, situated on the muddy southern side of the Lekkerboterbeek, with their right resting on Wallemolen spur, though the centre was held up about three hundred yards short by resistance encountered at a farm situated in the objective. Four hundred prisoners were taken.[1] The two brigades advancing on the front of the 11th Division (Major-General H. R. Davies) were well supported by ten tanks of D Battalion (I Tank Brigade, under Colonel C. D'A. Baker-Carr) in their advance up the gradual slope of Poelcappelle spur. Fire from a number of strongpoints swept the area with machine-gun bullets, causing heavy casualties, and the corps diary states that the "success of the operation was "due to a very large extent to the part played by the tanks."[2] Poelcappelle was entered by units of the 34th Brigade (Br.-General B. G. Clay),[3] and of the 33rd Brigade (Br.-General F. G. Spring)[4] and, although the objective included only the western half of the village, tanks continued to hunt the enemy down the main street and drove the garrisons from a number of pillboxes beyond the eastern exit, killing numbers of them with 6-pdr. guns and Lewis guns as they

---

[1] Private A. Hutt (1/7 R. Warwickshire) was awarded the V.C. for his courage and initiative on this occasion. When all the officers and n.c.o.'s of his platoon had become casualties, he took command and continued the advance. Held up by a strongpoint, he ran forward in front of the platoon, shot an officer and 3 men in the pillbox, and the remaining forty or fifty occupants of the strongpoint surrendered to him. Later in the day he went forward four times, under heavy fire, to bring in wounded men lying in front of the line, no stretcher bearers being at hand.

[2] The diary adds that "the moral support their presence gives to the "infantry and the apparent awe with which they are regarded by the "enemy, show that if they can arrive at the appointed place, resistance "there is speedily overcome".

[3] Sergeant H. Coverdale (11/Manchester) was awarded the V.C. for gallantry in attacking a number of strongpoints and killing two machine-gun detachments. He showed an utter disregard of danger throughout the operation, setting a splendid example of fearlessness to his men.

[4] Corporal F. Greaves (9/Sherwood Foresters) won the V.C. for his initiative and gallant leadership. His platoon was checked by machine-gun fire from a strongpoint, and, seeing his commander and the sergeant were casualties, he at once rushed forward to the rear of the building and bombed the occupants, killing and wounding the garrison and capturing 4 machine guns. It was solely due to his personal courage that heavy losses were not incurred here and the assault checked.

ran away. Orders issued at noon to exploit the success by a further local advance were cancelled, owing to a German counter-attack on the right about 1 p.m.[1]

The XIV Corps formed the northern flank. On the left, the marshy-edged Lauterbeek was successfully crossed, and the 29th Division (Major-General Sir B. de Lisle), using one battalion, the 1/R. Dublin Fusiliers, gained its objective, overlooking the Broembeek valley.[2] The 4th Division (Major-General T. G. Matheson), with its 11th Brigade (Br.-General R. A. Berners) and 10th Brigade (Br.-General A. G. Pritchard), on a 1,400-yard front, crossed 19 Metre Hill, only a few hundred yards short of their objective, although the protective barrage was very ragged. About noon, both brigades, lying on the forward slope, were raked by machine-gun fire, especially from the left flank. Despite gallant efforts by the 1/Rifle Brigade and the 2/Seaforth Highlanders (which lost a high proportion of its officers), the advanced companies had to withdraw to the western slope of the hill, and all later efforts to reach the final objective were made in vain.[3]

---

[1] The tanks were able to use the macadamized, though cratered, St. Julien–Poelcappelle road, and elaborate preparations were made to carry forward timber and fascines, to the limit of each tank's capacity, for filling the holes in it. Many large trees felled across it by the Germans were negotiated by swinging the tank at them at an angle. Only one tank and two of the personnel became casualties during the action. See Note at end of Chapter.

[2] Sergeant J. Ockenden (1/R. Dublin Fusiliers), seeing the platoon on his right held up by machine-gun fire, rushed the gun and killed the detachment. Later, he led his section against a strongpoint, under heavy fire, and after killing four of the garrison, the remaining 16 surrendered. He was awarded the V.C.

[3] The casualties in the four assaulting divisions of the Fifth Army for the period 4th–6th October were:

	Officers			Other Ranks			
	Killed	Wounded	Missing	Killed	Wounded	Missing	Total
48th Division:							
Artillery	—	4	—	6	31	—	} 1,205
Infantry	12	27	3	242	741	139	
11th Division:							
Artillery	2	6	—	16	66	—	} 1,430
Infantry	5	20	—	201	1,015	99	
4th Division:							
Artillery	2	6	—	7	44	—	} 1,338
Infantry	9	43	16	219	929	63	
29th Division:							
Artillery	—	1	—	5	19	—	} 310
Infantry	—	11	2	41	192	39	
							4,283

The Right Flank Guard

The advance to the eastern edge of Gheluvelt plateau was successfully accomplished by the X Corps. Side by side with the Australians, the 7th Division (Major-General T. H. Shoubridge) assaulted with two brigades, each on a frontage of five hundred yards. The first objective, the Reutel–Broodseinde track, was approximately the line the division had held in mid-October 1914:[1] the battle of " First Ypres " was now being fought in reverse. The 20th Brigade (Br.-General H. C. R. Green) reached the plateau edge between Noordemdhoek and In de Ster Cabaret, a total advance of fifteen hundred yards, with the 8/Devonshire, 2/Border Regiment and 2/Gordons, while south of the Cabaret, the 1/South Staffordshire and 21/Manchester of the 91st Brigade (Br.-General R. T. Pelly) arrived about the same time, Germans streaming down the slope ahead of them. Large numbers of Germans were found dead in their camouflaged shell-holes, killed by the barrage, and most of the six hundred prisoners taken were thoroughly demoralized.[2] The two brigades of the 7th Division, though short of the final objective, now overlooked the broad Heulebeek depression between the plateau and Keiberg spur to the north-east, and saw deep into the German back areas in the Flemish lowlands towards Dadizeele. Under this observation it seemed impracticable that any considerable German counter-attack against the southern flank of the newly-captured Broodseinde ridge could develop.[3]

---

[1] At a parade held four weeks later, only 115 officers and 948 other ranks who had landed with the division in Belgium were still with it.

[2] The division was opposed by the left regiment (*93rd Reserve*) of the *4th Guard Division*, which had been in the line since 27th September; it had already suffered heavy losses and was due for relief. Two more regiments, the *93rd* (*8th Division*) and the *94th Reserve* (*22nd Reserve Division*) were sent up from close reserve to assist in holding the artillery protective line below the ridge.

[3] The admirable arrangements by the commander of the X Corps artillery (Br.-General H. L. Reed) contributed in great measure to the success.

The artillery support and the barrage were on the same scale and intensity as that for the previous steps across the plateau. The heavy artillery consisted of 226 guns and howitzers, organized into 3 double bombardment groups (119) and 2 counter-battery groups (107); and the 258 18-pdrs. and 84 4.5-inch howitzers were in 3 field artillery groups, one to each division. The pace and depth of the barrage were unchanged. A pause of 1 hour 40 minutes was to be made at the first objective. To ensure liaison with the infantry, an artillery lieutenant-colonel, with a staff officer, was at each infantry brigade headquarters (near Hooge) and two artillery officers went forward with each attacking battalion headquarters.

X CORPS. 4TH OCTOBER

The southern flank of the X Corps operation was to be established by its centre and right divisions between Polygon Wood and the Menin road. This sector was broken by the Polygonbeek (between Reutel and Cameron Covert) and the Reutelbeek, which drain this south-eastern corner of the plateau. Normally a few feet wide and a few inches deep, the beds of these brooks, broken by shell-craters, had become belts of oozing mud of uncertain depth; joining near the objective, they formed a muddy valley of well over half a mile wide between Reutel village and Polderhoek spur to the south.

The centre division, the 21st (Major-General D. G. M. Campbell), to which four tanks were allotted, used two of its brigades, each of which deployed one battalion for the first objective and two for the follow-through. The 3rd/4th Queen's, of the 62nd Brigade (Br.-General C. G. Rawling), in action for the first time, and the 9/K.O.Y.L.I. of the 64th (Br.-General H. R. Headlam) crossed the slough of the Polygonbeek in the face of fire from a number of unsuspected pillboxes on the opposite bank. Despite heavy casualties, with the support of one tank which moved by the Hooge–Reutel road, these two battalions most gallantly worked round and captured these strongpoints—an outstanding feat in the circumstances. The support battalions then passed through to the edge of the plateau, the Germans fleeing ahead.[1]

This success gave possession of a dominant position overlooking the Reutel valley to the south-east, and so completed the security of the southern flank of the main Broodseinde battlefront. The value of the position was not altered by the fact that later in the day, owing to constant machine-gun and artillery fire from Polderhoek spur, at a thousand yards' range across the valley, the right brigade,

---

[1] Lieut.-Colonel L. P. Evans (Black Watch), commanding the 1/Lincolnshire (62nd Brigade), was awarded the V.C. for gallant leadership through the enemy barrage and in the subsequent assault. Seeing casualties being caused by an enemy machine gun, he went forward himself, and firing his revolver through the loophole of the emplacement, forced the detachment to surrender. Though severely wounded, he continued to lead his battalion to the objective until, after its consolidation, he collapsed through loss of blood.

Captain Clement Robertson (Queen's, attached Tank Corps) was awarded the V.C. for outstanding valour in leading his tanks in attack under heavy fire. He guided them on foot across most difficult ground to their objective, and thereby ensured their successful action. He was killed shortly after the objective had been reached.

after suffering severe losses, had to withdraw slightly to more sheltered ground. The final objective was not gained, but the casualties show with what stubborn courage this important sector of the battlefield, at the eastern edge of Gheluvelt plateau, was captured and held.[1]

The right division of the X Corps, the 5th (Major-General R. B. Stephens),[2] was able to occupy Cameron Covert (at the head of the Reutelbeek re-entrant) with its left brigade, the 95th (Br.-General Lord E. C. Gordon-Lennox), an advance of eight hundred yards, a tank helping the 1/Cornwall L.I. to capture the pillboxes within it.[3] The 13th Brigade (Br.-General L. O. W. Jones), with its right on the Menin road, had the difficult task of occupying Polderhoek spur. The château and its park, then a waste of churned-up mud at the eastern end of the spur, give command over the valley to the north and lay within the brigade's final objective. These two localities had been converted into a strong defended area; in the château ruins was a concrete fortress, and numerous pillboxes had been built in the park covering all the approaches. Despite all difficulties, several of the pillboxes were occupied, and several parties of the 1/K.O.S.B. entered the château; but by nightfall some of the gains, including the château, had to be given up. Farther south, the right battalion of the brigade, the 1/R. West Kent, advancing north of the Menin road, gained a little ground towards Gheluvelt.[4]

The IX Corps, south of the Menin road, kept in touch with the 5th Division with the left brigade, the 111th (Br.-General C. W. Compton), of its 37th Division (Major-General

---

[1] Of the 86 officers of the 62nd Brigade who went into action, 74 became casualties during the period 3rd–8th October. The three leading battalions each lost over 40 per cent. of their effective strength, and no battalion had more than six officers left in action by 8th October. Before midday on the 4th, the 12/13 Northumberland Fusiliers had lost its commanding officer and all four company commanders.

The casualties suffered by the 64th Brigade were equally heavy, totalling 61 officers and 1,293 other ranks in the few days of the battle period.

[2] The 5th Division had relieved the 23rd in this sector on 2nd/3rd October.

[3] This tank was one of the four allotted to the 21st Division. It eventually stuck in the marshy ground at the junction of the two brooks near the objective. The 5th Division was not provided with tanks, owing to the state of the ground.

[4] The sector between Polygon Wood and the Menin road was defended by the *19th Reserve Division*, with the *17th Division* in close reserve.

THE RESULT

H. Bruce Williams), but failed to capture Gheluvelt Wood. The right brigade of this division, the 63rd (Br.-General E. L. Challenor), renewed the attempt to capture the defended locality on Tower Hamlets spur ;[1] but the 8/Somerset L.I. and 8/Lincolnshire, which entered it, were swept by machine-gun fire from front and flanks, as in previous attempts, and had to fall back to their starting-line.[2] Heavy losses were incurred, and intense German shelling, together with the muddy condition of the Bassevillebeek valley, prevented the arrival of sufficient reinforcements in time to resume the attack.[3]

EXPLOITATION POSTPONED

Early reports which had come in gave clear evidence of the morning's achievement, but by noon it was obvious that " an overwhelming blow had been struck and both sides " knew it ".[4] The main objectives had been gained, and the number of prisoners was exceptionally large, the Second Army alone having taken over four thousand.[5] In the opinion of officers of long experience on the Western Front, the number of dead Germans seen on the battlefield exceeded

---

[1] The line here was held by the *25th Division*, backed by the *16th Bavarian Division*.

[2] Private T. H. Sage (8/Somerset L.I.) was awarded the V.C. for saving the lives of a number of men by throwing himself on a bomb dropped by a neighbouring soldier who was shot down when about to throw it.

[3] For the Bassevillebeek see Sketch 22. The casualties suffered by the assaulting divisions of the X and IX Corps were :

		Officers			Other Ranks		
	Killed	Wounded	Missing	Killed	Wounded	Missing	Total
7th Division ...	22	66	2	351	1,517	165	2,123
21st ,, ...	10	51	10	364	1,699	482	2,616
5th ,, ...	17	51	3	(Total—2,486)			2,557
37th ,, ...	11	16	2	167	529	93	818
							8,114

The casualties incurred by the Second Army during the period 4th–8th October, by arms, were :

	Officers			Other Ranks			
	Killed	Wounded	Missing	Killed	Wounded	Missing	Total
Artillery, R.F.A. ...	12	47	1	128	573	30	791
Artillery, R.G.A. ...	1	8	—	75	305	1	390
Infantry	135	347	36	2,197	6,106	2,041	10,862
Machine-gun Coys.	4	22	—	89	325	15	455
							12,498

[4] A.O.A. iv., p. 875.

[5] The Second Army captured during the day's fighting 114 officers and 4,044 other ranks ; the Fifth Army, 12 officers and 589 other ranks.

that observed in any previous British assault of the war, and messages stressed the demoralized state of the survivors.[1]

Br.-General Charteris, head of G.H.Q. Intelligence Branch, after an interview with Sir Douglas Haig, went from Advanced G.H.Q. to the Second Army headquarters, nearby in Cassel, to discuss the possibilities of exploitation. General Plumer preferred to stand by the original plan. The latest information at Second Army headquarters, confirmed by G.H.Q. Intelligence, he said, was that eight German divisions stood in close reserve behind the battle sector, and that another six were in reserve, not far off, in Belgium:[2] the Commander-in-Chief had stressed that exploitation should not be attempted until the German counter-attacks had been defeated; and it was evident that all the available divisions had not yet been engaged. Demoralization, he thought, had probably affected only the six front divisions which had been subjected to the barrage; the German artillery, at any rate, was showing an undiminished strength:[3] the Terhand (Flanders II) and Dadizeele (Flanders III) lines, long stretches of which were known to be wired and to contain strongpoints, could be effectively held by the resting divisions unless the troops of exploitation

---

[1] Ludendorff (p. 490) writes: "The battle on the 4th October was "extraordinarily severe, and again we only came through it with enormous "losses. It was evident that the idea of holding the front line more "densely, adopted at my last visit to the front in September, was not the "remedy".

"Flandern 1917" calls it, "the black day of October 4th". Opposite the I Anzac Corps alone, where the German attack was forestalled, the *45th Reserve Division* lost 83 officers and 2,800 other ranks (not including lightly wounded), and the *4th Guard Division*, 86 officers and 2,700 other ranks. "Foot Guard Regt. No. 5" described it as the worst day yet "experienced in the War".

G.O.A. (xiii., p. 80) sums up: "The new [Lossberg] battle scheme had "not stood the test (*nicht bewährt*) on the 4th October". On 7th October the commander of the *Fourth Army* ordered "the foremost line of shell "craters, if no natural obstacle was available, to be occupied by a quite "thin screen of posts with light machine guns. A main line of resistance "was to be constructed 500 to 600 yards behind this screen".

[2] This information was approximately correct; but an additional division (*22nd Reserve*) was not taken into account.

[3] The German artillery had been reinforced about the end of September in anticipation of the major counter-attacks which were to be delivered in the first days of October. A prominent tactical feature was the intensive use of enfilade fire, the batteries north-east of Passchendaele firing south-west and those about Tenbrielen and Comines (respectively 3 and 5 miles south of Gheluvelt) firing, almost entirely, north and north-west. The guns were widely dispersed, well hidden in houses and huts, and smoke screens were used to conceal them further when in action.

were closely supported by guns ; the dominating factor, he concluded, was that no artillery advance was practicable until the two miles of mud of the shelled area had been negotiated. About 11 a.m., however, General Plumer did consider the possibility of exploitation. He then ordered the I Anzac Corps to push eastwards to Keiberg spur, and the II Anzac Corps to co-operate. Lieut.-General Godley, commanding the latter corps, favoured an advance northwards along the main ridge towards Passchendaele.[1] Lieut.-General Birdwood, the commander of the I Anzac Corps, on the other hand, was strongly opposed to any further advance until the artillery was in a position to give close support, and the supply communications had been improved ;[2] he also told General Plumer that the fighting had been stiffer than appeared from the early messages, and that casualties had been heavy. A scheme was put forward at midday by Lieut.-General Morland, commanding the X Corps, for the exploitation of the situation by an advance northwards from the In de Ster promontory against the southern flank of the Germans opposite the I Anzac Corps, but this was opposed by Major-General Shoubridge (7th Division), on the grounds of the uncertainty of the situation and the heavy losses of the 21st Division in the Reutelbeek valley on his right flank. At 2 p.m. General Plumer abandoned any idea of exploitation.

On the Fifth Army front, General Gough, at 10.30 a.m., told his corps commanders to push on, if possible : the XVIII Corps another five hundred yards astride Wallen-molen spur to the eastern edge of Poelcappelle, the XIV Corps conforming ; and at noon a definite order was given for the attack to be continued at 5 p.m. Meanwhile, however, the withdrawal of the 4th Division at 19 Metre Hill had caused some confusion at the inner flanks of the two corps, and the order was cancelled.

---

[1] Information subsequently received would seem to indicate that an immediate advance during the morning hours to Keiberg spur would have met with little resistance, and an Intelligence summary issued later by II Anzac Corps states that Passchendaele village itself might have been captured with slight opposition. Early in the afternoon, however, the arrival of enemy reinforcements would have stiffened the prospects of resistance, and the artillery support and supplies available for these advanced troops would have been very meagre.

[2] The closest field guns were 5,000 yards from Broodseinde. In the Messines battle, the 18-pdrs. were given a range of 6,200 yards as the safe maximum, and the 4.5-inch howitzers, 7,000 yards.

The German *Fourth Army*, following its decision of the 29th September,[1] held back its counter-attack divisions as a whole, but sent forward a number of single battalions or regiments to fill the gaps caused by the heavy losses of the front divisions.[2] From the observation areas gained by the morning assault the approach towards the In de Ster promontory of these single units could be clearly seen, also across Keiberg spur towards Broodseinde and, two miles farther north, towards the ruins of Passchendaele. In contrast to the brown, devastated wilderness over which the British troops had just struggled, the enclosed countryside which they now overlooked on this eastern slope of the ridge was green and undamaged by shell-fire. The many small woods and hedges afforded the advancing German infantry excellent cover, of which full use was made. All progress, however, was made at the expense of heavy casualties, owing to the prompt British artillery response to the S.O.S. signals, and to accurate machine-gun and rifle fire.[3]

The only substantial counter-attack was launched against the southern flank, from behind the shelter of Polderhoek spur, about 3 p.m. Moving up the Reutelbeek valley the Germans re-occupied Reutel and Cameron Covert, and replenished with machine guns and ammunition the garrison of Polderhoek Château.[4] The chief German reaction, however, lay in persistent shelling of the captured ground, particularly of Gheluvelt plateau and Broodseinde ridge, which considerably aggravated the difficulties of consolidation and supply.

---

[1] See p. 295.

[2] This change in the German defence tactics was forecast by Second Army Intelligence (Lieut.-Colonel C. H. Mitchell) in its Summary issued on 1st October. It was suggested that after the recent failures of his major counter-attacks, the enemy would probably hold back his forces and would " deliver organized counter-attacks twelve or more hours after " the assault, and make the utmost use of his artillery, especially in " enfilade ".

[3] Battalions from five counter-attack divisions had reinforced the line: from the *8th* and *22nd Reserve Division*, opposite In de Ster promontory; from the *45th Reserve* and *4th Bavarian*, opposite Broodseinde ridge; and from the *16th* through and north of Passchendaele, opposite the XVIII Corps at and south of Poelcappelle.

[4] The objective of the British main attack was believed by the Germans to be Becelaere, and this counter-attack, delivered by a composite force of battalions drawn from all three regiments of the *Eingreif* (*17th*) division, together with reserve battalions of the front division (*19th Reserve*), was intended to strike into the southern flank of the advance. It was finally broken up with heavy losses by the artillery barrage, and by the machine-gun fire of the 21st and 5th Divisions.

A strong south-westerly wind, with occasional showers and low clouds down to 400 feet, had restricted air co-operation throughout the day.[1]

NOTE

Tank Operations (General)

The following extracts are taken from Notes which were issued by the headquarters of the Tank Corps (4th October, 1917), based on experience during the fighting from April to October 1917.

(1) *Limitation of the Tank and the Crew.* The main limitations of the tank are :

(a) Its weight, which militates against its going over heavily shelled wet ground.

(b) Its speed, which over heavily shelled ground is 10 yards a minute, over unshelled ground from 1 mile to 5 miles an hour.

(c) The difficulty of maintaining direction on account of limited visibility.

(d) The exhaustion of the crew, due to heat and the difficulties of driving.

From these limitations experience has led to the following conclusions :

(a) If the ground over which the tanks are to proceed has been heavily shelled, they will cross it slowly ; but if it is also soaked with rain the majority of them will not cross it. Therefore, to employ tanks on such ground is to throw them away (e.g., the tanks of the First Army, operating on Vimy Ridge, 9th April, 1917).

---

[1] For details of the work of the Royal Flying Corps, see " War in the " Air " iv., pp. 202–4. On pp. 201–2 of the same volume is a summary of Sir Douglas Haig's memorandum on the work of the Royal Flying Corps in the Ypres battles during the month of September. During thirty days 226 day and night bombing attacks had been made on enemy targets, in which 7,886 bombs of a total weight of 135 tons had been dropped, compared with 969 bombs dropped by German airmen on targets within British lines. In co-operation with the artillery, air observers and pilots had helped to range on 9,559 targets, chiefly German batteries ; and 14,678 photographs had been taken from the air. The Germans had concentrated a great force of aircraft on the Flanders front early in September, and were very active over the British lines ; but towards the end of the month they had withdrawn behind their own lines, thanks to the continuous offensive action of our fighter patrols, so our artillery observation machines were able to carry out their work of ranging almost unmolested during the battles in the latter part of the month.

(*b*) Tanks cannot keep up with infantry until the zone of heavy bombardment has been crossed. This zone is approximately 3,000 yards deep. To expect tanks to co-operate in initial attacks in this zone is to expect the impossible (e.g., tanks with the Second Army operating against the Dam Strasse, 7th June, 1917).

(*c*) Tanks cannot proceed with any certainty during the dark or in twilight over ground intersected with trenches or broken by shell fire unless such ground has been reconnoitred.

(*d*) Mist and smoke will bring tanks almost to a standstill. So will dust; not only the dust thrown up by shells but that picked up by the tracks and blown into the face of the driver.

(*e*) On a hot day the temperature in the tanks will rise to 120 deg. F. in the shade, causing vomiting and exhaustion in the crews. Eight hours' continuous work is about the limit of the crew's endurance, after which the men require 48 hours' rest.

(*f*) A tank can only work for 8 continuous hours. Its circuit of action is 8 miles.

(*g*) Tanks cannot operate through thickly wooded country or over ground covered with tree stumps.

(*h*) Tanks can crush down wire entanglements sufficiently to allow infantry to cross at a walk and in single file (e.g., action at Bullecourt, 11th April, 1917).

(*i*) Tanks cannot pass through barrages with safety. High-explosive barrages are the most dangerous for them (so far as the tank is concerned, H.E. should not be mixed with shrapnel in the creeping barrage. The progress of tanks would also be facilitated if heavy artillery and trench mortars were not used on the enemy's trench system).

(2) *Tank objectives*

The selection of tank objectives is the foundation of the whole tank operation. Although it is necessary that infantry and tank objectives should be the same, it does not follow that tanks can advance over the same kind of ground as infantry. Consequently if the greatest value is to be obtained from tanks, the infantry objectives should be selected as much from the point of view of tank limitations as for those of artillery limitations.

Generally speaking, the following types of objectives have been found bad :

(*a*) Objectives within 2,000 or 3,000 yards of our front line.

(*b*) Heavily shelled ground.

(*c*) Interior of villages.

(*d*) Woods.

TANK ACTION

(e) Marshy ground, valleys, heads of streams.
(f) Deep sunken roads.
(g) Objectives which can only be approached through narrow defiles.

An objective should be clearly seen from the starting point. The line of approach to it should be direct, any attempt to follow winding trench lines leads to loss of direction. By having well-defined fixed objectives co-operation between tanks and infantry is considerably increased.

(3) *Tank Formations*

Tank units should be formed in echelons in depth, the number of echelons being equal to or more than the number of objectives. Sections should not be split up, and companies and battalions should, as far as possible, be given well-defined and restricted areas to operate in, so that concentration after the fight is facilitated.

(4) *Decentralization in Command*

The duty of the tank is similar to that of the gun ; consequently the command of tank units can be made to approximate very closely to that of artillery units. The senior tank commander and the senior subordinate commanders under him should act in the dual capacity of an adviser to the commander of the formation with which they are operating and as commander of their own units, their action being based on what the infantry commander considers his men can do. The one object of the tank or the guns is to reduce resistance to the infantry advance.

(5) *Tactical Action and Distribution*

The main tactical principles to remember are : Tanks must be used in echelons according to the objectives. They must be used in mass so as to obtain concentration of power and effort, mutual protection and certainty of action. The employment of tanks in small " packets " leads to their destruction in detail ; their desultory use, and dribbling them forward on indefinite objectives, to decimation of power and loss of organization. In close country, unless order is maintained, the result may be that tanks will on occasion fire into our own infantry.

A strong reserve should be held in hand to turn the accidents of battle to our favour. If continuity of action is aimed at, tank units should be formed in sufficient depth to enable the leading echelon to be withdrawn and refitted, so that it may be ready to return into action a little before the last echelon is exhausted.

Minor points to remember are that if tanks work up and down trenches they should remain on the parapet side so as to obviate firing into our own infantry. Dug-outs should be fired into by 6-pdr. guns. Destruction of guns should be left to the sappers. The tank commanders shall be acquainted with the infantry S.O.S. signal. Prisoners should be left for others to take.

(6) Co-operation with Other Arms

Time co-operation between infantry and tanks is based on the infantry understanding what the tank can do, and the tank commander understanding what the infantry can do.

The best possible liaison must exist between the tank units and the infantry. This co-operation must be established right down to the tank commanders and the infantry battalions, so that a tank commander can re-organize the troops with whom he is working. The infantry should know the approximate routes and objectives of the tanks. The crew number should be painted on the rear of the tank, and this should be known to the infantry with which the tank is operating.

Infantry should be warned not to bunch behind the tank nor be led off their objectives if tanks are moving diagonally across their front; neither should the infantry wait for the tanks if the tanks are late.

The greatest assistance in the location of tanks during operations can be rendered by the R.F.C. When a tank is ditched, a white square 18 inches by 18 inches, if spread on the top of the tank, can be used to notify the aeroplanes that the tank is broken down.

Counter-battery work is as essential to tanks as to infantry as long as the enemy's guns are in position, but once they move or are captured, this form of protection becomes needless. In such circumstances, the only likelihood of a continuance of the infantry advance will come from the tank which will afford local protection against hostile machine guns.

CHAPTER XVII

BATTLES OF YPRES 1917 (*continued*)

BATTLE OF POELCAPPELLE
9TH OCTOBER
(Sketches 26, 27)[1]

THE PLAN

The events of the 4th October added urgency to the arrangements approved on the 2nd[2] for the continuation of the campaign. It was intended to make the next step in two stages: first, a morning assault by the leading brigades, to reach more than half-way to the day's objective; and then, if the situation indicated a general withdrawal on the part of the enemy, the reserve brigades were to follow through in the afternoon.

In the Second Army, the I Anzac Corps was to attack on the right with the 1st and 2nd Australian Divisions, with the 4th and 5th in reserve; and, on the left, the II Anzac Corps was to employ the attached 66th and 49th Divisions,[3] with the New Zealand and 3rd Australian Divisions in reserve. The infantry of the four divisions in reserve, which were some fifteen miles behind Ypres, were to be ready to entrain for the front on the day of attack. The Fifth Army proposed to employ the XVIII and XIV Corps. The 1st and 5th Cavalry Divisions were to be assembled on the eve of the attack within a day's march of the battlefield, allotted respectively to the Second and Fifth Armies should these require them. The remainder of the Cavalry Corps was to be assembled in readiness to follow.

In reply to a question asked by G.H.Q., General Plumer gave his opinion that not more than two tank battalions

---

[1] In the Battle of Poelcappelle only small gains of ground were made; so no special sketch map is provided. The places mentioned will be found on Sketch 26 for the Second Army and Sketch 27 for the Fifth Army.
[2] See p. 297.
[3] Both these divisions came from the Fourth Army on the coast.

could be usefully employed on the Second Army front. They were concentrated at Voormezeele (2 miles south of Ypres). General Gough considered that the brigade of tanks allotted to him would be sufficient for the needs of the Fifth Army : " the firmer ground and better going beyond the shell-torn " area we hope shortly to reach will ", he added, " give the " tanks a better chance . . . and will permit of their being " employed in larger numbers ". One company each was allotted to the XVIII and XIV Corps for the initial attack.

When the time came, General Plumer decided not to send any tanks up, and owing to the state of the ground the Fifth Army tanks never arrived on the scene at all.

In the general plan, the leading brigades of the Second Army were to pursue the retiring enemy northwards well beyond Passchendaele, and drive him off the slopes of the main ridge to the north-east and east, whilst those of the Fifth Army were to gain the Flanders I Line about Spriet.

The G.H.Q. Intelligence Summaries issued on the 5th and 6th, showed that the nine German front divisions, all battered and demoralized by the assault on the 4th, had been relieved, and that the new practice of holding back the counter-attack divisions had alone enabled any reliefs to be found. Provided one or two more similar blows could be struck at a few days' interval it was considered, with good reason, that the Germans would be unable, with their available reserves and the limited railway resources into the Belgian corridor, to maintain sufficient troops to provide for the reliefs for their front divisions.[1] In order to give them no time to recover, Sir Douglas Haig advanced the

---

[1] German O.H.L. had intended to launch an offensive against Italy in September, in order to bolster up its Austrian ally and at the same time to ease the pressure in Flanders. Owing to the difficulty of mustering the required 9 divisions (6 only were eventually sent, and a seventh was improvised from *Jäger* battalions), mostly from the Eastern Front, to support the Austrian troops, the offensive had to be postponed till the end of October. How few were available from the Western Front is shown by the fact that one of the divisions selected, the *195th*, which had been withdrawn into reserve from the Cambrai sector and specially equipped and trained during September for a campaign in Italy, was on 1st October ordered to hand back its special equipment and proceed at once to Flanders. It did not reach Italy till the middle of December.

Ludendorff, writing of this period, about mid-October, states : " The " wastage in the big actions in Flanders was extraordinarily high. Two " divisions which had been held in readiness in the East and were already " on their way to Italy were diverted to Flanders. The Italian operation " [Caporetto] could not be started before 22nd October, and the weather " held it up till the 24th. These days were the culminating point of the " crisis ".

next step by twenty-four hours, to the morning of the 9th, and it was hoped to gain Westroosbeke by another blow on the 12th.

The Change of Weather

The prospects of the fulfilment of the plan visualized in this programme depended upon the weather. The rain which had set in during the afternoon of the 4th continued in a steady drizzle, with occasional heavy showers, throughout the next two days, and on the 7th came squalls of cold drenching rain. That evening, at a conference at G.H.Q. the two Army commanders told Sir Douglas Haig that, though willing to continue, they would welcome a closing down of the campaign. Sir Douglas Haig, however, hoped at least to drive the Germans from their dominating position along the Passchendaele–Westroosbeke sector of the main ridge, whence they still overlooked the Steenbeek valley, and wished to gain the good lateral highway and more easily drained ground on the summit before the winter. He considered that the longer the operation was delayed, the better prepared would be the enemy's defences and reserves, and the more difficult and costly would be the task. Let the reader, looking at the prospect as it appeared at noon on the 4th October, ask himself, " in view of the results of " three step-by-step blows, what will be the result of three " more in the next fortnight ? ".[1]

A weightier reason for this momentous decision of the Commander-in-Chief was the need to continue to divert German attention from the other Allied fronts. The recovery of the French Army had been in large measure due to the granting of extra leave, amounting to ten days every four months, a concession which had resulted in the permanent reduction of its effective strength by some 340,000 men, about a quarter of its establishment. Consequently the French front was so thinly held that on the 25th September the British Government had been asked to take over an additional frontage of six divisions, to the line of the Oise.[2]

---

[1] These are the words of the Australian Official Historian (A.O.A. iv., p. 881).

[2] Sir Douglas Haig was not present at the meeting when this matter was discussed, and his subsequent protests were in vain. At a meeting with General Pétain on 18th October, however, it was agreed to transfer the 4 British divisions of the Fourth Army (on the coast) to relieve 4 divisions of the French Sixth Army on the British right flank. The relief took place in January 1918. (See " 1918 " Vol. I, p. 47.)

Fresh onslaughts were also expected against the Russian and Italian fronts, and, both to protect these Allies and to ease the task in 1918, Sir Douglas Haig was convinced that the pressure in Flanders should not be relaxed, quite apart from any progress which might be made in terms of ground gained. His opinion was strengthened by the persistent and urgent pleas of General Pétain to continue the Flanders operations in order to ensure that the flow of German reserves should be diverted from the French front. A French limited attack, delivered in Champagne on the 23rd October at Malmaison, was, in consequence, entirely successful.[1]

At the end of September the Prime Minister had visited G.H.Q. and asked for the Commander-in-Chief's views on paper as to the rôle of the British forces in the event of Russia being unable to maintain an active part in the War— even making a separate peace—and having regard to the weakened condition of France and Italy. In a statement, dated 8th October, Sir Douglas Haig gave his opinion that if the power of resistance of the German Armies were broken, or was " even manifestly on the point of breaking " down, Germany and her Allies would gladly accept such " terms of peace as the Allies might offer " ; that Germany could only be beaten on the Western Front, and that none of the alternative courses offered any prospect of defeating her. He continued that the collapse of Russia would release a considerable proportion of the forces of the Central Powers for use elsewhere ; but this would be balanced by the arrival of American troops. The Austrians would be able to transfer sufficient reinforcements to throw Italy on

---

[1] The battle was delivered on a 7½-mile frontage, after a bombardment for 6 days and 6 nights, by 6 divisions. In 4 days a maximum advance of 3½ miles was made, 11,157 prisoners were taken and 180 guns were captured.

The German line was very thin and weak. Kuhl (ii., p. 114) states, " about the middle of October the greater part of the divisions which " stood on the rest [other than Flanders] of the frontage of the " Crown Prince Rupprecht's Group of Armies had already been engaged " in Flanders several times. On the whole front except Flanders only " the most indispensable defence garrisons against partial attacks could " be provided, even at the most threatened places like Lens and St. " Quentin ". Crown Prince Rupprecht even considered withdrawing in Flanders to a shorter line, and made preparation to do so, in spite of the loss of ground and moral disadvantages involved. Then rain came to his assistance. He seems, like the British public and army, to have been still ignorant of the state of the French army.

the defensive : " we cannot assist her without compromising " the success of our own plans ". As regards France : " neither the French Government nor the military authori- " ties will venture to call on their troops for any further " great and sustained effort, at any rate before it becomes " evident that the enemy's strength has been definitely and " finally broken ". The Commander-in-Chief pointed out the wastage of the German Armies, but under-estimated the number of enemy divisions (179 ; it was 210) which might be placed on the Western Front in 1918. Finally, he begged that no more frontage should be taken over from the French, that drafts to replace wastage should be trained and sent to France, and that the Cabinet should have " firm faith in " the possibility of final success "—three conditions which were not vouchsafed to him[1].

In the circumstances Sir Douglas Haig was most anxious that the morning assault on the 9th should not be postponed unless absolutely necessary, but it was agreed to cancel the afternoon attack by the reserve brigades. During the night (7th/8th) the rain ceased, and a drying wind held through the 8th till about 4 p.m., when the rain came down again in torrents. The weather reports showed more stormy weather approaching, and no improvement in sight. Three hours later, at dusk and in pouring rain, the assaulting brigades began their approach march to the line.

The roads and tracks across the battle area had gravely deteriorated. Three months of persistent shelling had blocked the watercourses, and the mass of shell-holes frustrated every effort to drain the water away. It must be emphasized, however, that the chief engineers of the corps and the divisional C.R.Es. are unanimous in stating that up to the 4th October there had been no serious difficulty in maintaining the communications to the front, weather and ground conditions being tolerable and damage done by the enemy being readily repairable. Some even say this was the case until the 12th ; but in certain areas conditions did become impossible. The entire valley of the upper Steenbeek and its tributaries (behind the II Anzac Corps) was, in the words of one divisional C.R.E., " a porridge of mud ".

---

[1] There were in the United Kingdom on the 1st January, 1918, 966,673 trained ' A ' men, excluding Dominion troops, of whom 607,403 were available. See " 1918 " Vol. I, pp. 50–2 and Appendices 3, 4 and 7.

On such a foundation, despite the concentrated and untiring efforts of the engineers of the two Anzac corps, no progress could be made with the plank roads for the forward move of the guns: the planks either sank in the mire or floated away.[1] The field batteries of the II Anzac Corps which were to have been near the Zonnebeke–Winnipeg road to support the main attack had to remain west of the Steenbeek on hurriedly constructed and unstable gun-platforms. Until these were made many of the guns were up to the axles in mud, and some even to the muzzles.[2] The morning objective of the 9th would be at their extreme range (6,000 yards); Passchendaele village, whose church spire was visible from many of the battery positions, was seven thousand yards distant, so the mass of German field batteries which were about and behind that locality would be beyond reach.[3] The field batteries of the I Anzac Corps, too, were to have advanced another mile, to behind Anzac House and Tokio spurs. Only a few batteries had reached Anzac spur, when the single plank road available, overlaying the Westhoek–Zonnebeke track, gave way beneath the traffic, and the remainder of the guns had to remain alongside the road a short distance from their former positions.[4]

The ammunition supply to the advanced field batteries

---

[1] General Plumer ordered the X Corps to provide 6 infantry battalions to assist in the construction of light railways and roads in the two Anzac corps areas; but even this help was of little avail.

[2] Each gun-platform had to have a foundation of fascines and road metal, on which was placed a double-decked platform of beech-slabs nailed together. It required two days' hard work to make, and a temporary plank road had to be built from the platform to the main roadway for the ammunition supply by pack transport. Even after this labour, many of the platforms began to sink into the mud after a few rounds had been fired.

[3] The field batteries in support of the right (66th) division had to be placed mostly alongside the Frezenberg–Zonnebeke road within a few hundred yards east of Frezenberg: one brigade (331st) was unable to come into action till after the assault had started; but in combination with the other (330th) only 25 guns took part, and they were over a mile in rear of their intended position. The batteries to support the left (49th) division were alongside the Wieltje–Gravenstafel road between Wieltje and the Steenbeek, with a few batteries forward beyond the stream and behind Hill 35 alongside the same road. See Sketch 26.

[4] On 5th October Lieut.-General Birdwood (I Anzac Corps) informed General Plumer that, so far as his corps was concerned, the far-reaching proposals for exploitation, including the capture of Keiberg spur, were not practicable, as neither the light railway nor the Westhoek–Zonnebeke road could be completed in time to carry the quantity of heavy and field artillery necessary.

was a formidable task, made possible only by selecting battery sites within 100–150 yards of the main roadways. Shells and supplies had to be carried by pack animals from the wagon lines to the guns, and this journey, which normally took about an hour, now required any time from six to sixteen hours. The mules and pack horses frequently slipped off the planks into the quagmire on either side, where they sometimes sank out of sight, and the shells generally arrived coated with slime, and unusable till cleaned. The dug-outs at the wagon lines and the shelterless gun platforms were soon flooded, and the men had to sleep on wet blankets or sodden straw,[1] resulting in a rapid dwindling of the effective artillery strength through sickness and exhaustion. The system of reliefs for the gun detachments from the wagon lines failed from lack of personnel at a time when work was being doubled and men were most needed. The heavy artillery suffered from disabilities almost as great as the field. Yet, as a whole, as already mentioned, " the sickness during the battles [of Ypres] was compara- " tively slight ".[2]

These conditions affected equally the infantry in the forward area. " Baby elephant shelters "[3] of corrugated iron were issued to shelter the forward troops. The only passable supply routes were the signposted duck-board tracks, of which one was available for each brigade sector to within about a mile of the front line. This last stretch was marked by a taped row of stakes, on which lamps were hung at night ; but the constant tread of pack animals had trampled long stretches of the tracks out of sight.[4] The difficulty was to get the assaulting troops up to the jumping-off tapes at all, and in some sort of condition to make an attack. The chief cause of the great discontent during this period of the Flanders fighting was, in fact, the continuous demands on regimental officers and men to carry out tasks which appeared physically impossible to perform, and which no other army would have faced. It must be em-

---

[1] Tin hip-baths, sent up from Ypres, were a luxury for a few to sleep in.
[2] Medical History, General, iii., p. 171.
[3] So called from their appearance : grey, half-cylindrical with larger corrugations than ordinary corrugated iron.
[4] The C.R.E. of the 49th Division states that the construction of the plank road from Wieltje was greatly hampered by the " masses of pack " animals absolutely fighting to get on to any part of the track before it " was completed ".

phasized again, too, that in all that vast wilderness of slime hardly tree, hedge, wall or building could be seen. As at the Somme no landmarks existed, nor any scrap of natural cover other than the mud-filled shell-holes. That the attacks ordered were so gallantly made in such conditions stands to the immortal credit of the battalions concerned.

The Attack

The Second Army[1]

The two brigades of each of the two assaulting divisions (66th and 49th) of the II Anzac Corps which were to carry out the main attack had already assembled east of Ypres, behind Frezenberg and Potijze, and it was estimated that they could cover the 2½ miles to the jumping-off tapes in five hours, so as to arrive by midnight; but the difficulties were greatly under-estimated. The night was inky dark, and the rain poured down. During the last mile of the duck-board tracks the men had to struggle through mud above their ankles and often up to their knees, with occasional bursts of German shell-fire over them. At 2.30 a.m.[2] both divisions reported to corps headquarters that some of their battalions would be late for zero hour, 5.20 a.m.; and, despite every effort to hurry on the less exhausted, large gaps existed along the jumping-off tapes when the barrage began its forward creep. As a result of circumstances already mentioned, a large number of guns and howitzers failed to participate, and others fired inaccurately from their unstable platforms. Indeed, so weak and erratic was the barrage that no edge was apparent or visible to guide the infantry; and the high-explosive shells, which formed a high proportion of the total, buried themselves in the mud and soft ground, losing most of their effect. Regardless of this scant artillery protection, battalion commanders, spreading out their companies to cover the wide gaps in the line, ordered the advance.

No previous attack organized by the Second Army in the War had such an unfavourable start. The left division, the 49th (1st West Riding) (Major-General E. M. Perceval), after its exhausting night march, detailed to move up

---
[1] See Sketch 26.
[2] "Summer Time" had come to an end on the 8th.

Wallemolen spur (on which Bellevue stands) on to the main ridge north of Passchendaele, was confronted at the outset by the Ravebeek, the bed of which had become a morass 30 to 50 yards wide, waist-deep in water in the centre.[1] Only a few parties of the two leading Yorkshire battalions of the right brigade, the 148th (Br.-General R. L. Adlercron), were able to cross this obstacle. The West Yorkshire battalions of the left brigade, the 146th (Br.-General M. D. Goring-Jones), had less difficulty, the inner flanks of the two brigades using the bridge and causeway of the Gravenstafel road. A few hundred yards beyond the morass the advance came under heavy machine-gun fire from a number of pillboxes on the higher ground ahead, about Bellevue, and it was finally checked after severe losses by belts of low wire entanglement, 25 to 40 yards wide, which stretched intact in front of the pillboxes and across the whole front of the division. The pillboxes themselves, too, were seen to be protected by newly made apron fences of barbed wire.[2] The main resistance, however, came from the fire of rifles and machine guns hidden in shell holes, hard to locate and even harder to suppress by artillery fire. The cause of the deadlock which now occurred, about 9.30 a.m., was not appreciated at divisional headquarters, and battalions sent up from brigade and divisional reserves to press on the attack either shared the same fate as the leaders, or were held back by local commanders on their own initiative, west of the Ravebeek, on Gravenstafel spur. By the afternoon both brigades were back, very near their starting-line, leaving parties of the 146th Brigade well forward close to the wire. The division had lost over two thousand, five hundred of all ranks in casualties.[3]

The 66th (2nd East Lancashire) Division (Major-General Hon. H. A. Lawrence), the right wing of the II Anzac Corps,

---

[1] Sketch 28 gives some idea of the conditions.

[2] The wire entanglement, recently repaired, and the pillboxes were part of the Flanders I Line still uncaptured, from the Ravebeek northwards to Spriet and beyond. Although both wire and strongpoints were clearly marked on the maps issued to all concerned and could be seen from Gravenstafel spur, the artillery preparation had made little impression on them.

[3] An aeroplane observer reported at 1.20 p.m. that flares were being shown by advanced parties of the 49th Division near the final objective. An order from divisional headquarters to push forward in strength to the line indicated failed to reach the units concerned, as the messengers became casualties on the way. The observer was probably mistaken in his locations.

in serious action for the first time,[1] was to advance along the main ridge with its left on the Ravebeek, the objective being seven hundred yards short of Passchendaele village. No wire barred its progress, as the Flanders I Line in its sector had been occupied on the 4th by the 3rd Australian Division. The left brigade, the 198th (Br.-General A. J. Hunter), was, however, hampered by the mud and by a number of wide and deep water-filled derelict trenches on the lower slopes above the Ravebeek ; it was also enfiladed by machine-gun fire from the uncaptured pillboxes across the valley, near Bellevue, at a range of 500–800 yards. For these reasons, the leading East Lancashire battalions were finally halted about three hundred yards short of the first objective, and the supporting battalions, in their turn, could make no more headway. The 197th Brigade (Br.-General O. C. Borrett), on the higher and drier ground on the right, though delayed for over an hour at the start, made rapid progress along the main ridge, with its right on the Roulers railway, to which the corps boundary (previously the chord of the curve of the railway between Zonnebeke and Passchendaele) had been shifted to simplify the keeping of direction. The sandy ground on the ridge top made easier going, and although the weak barrage had long since passed on, the 2/8, with elements of the 3/5, Lancashire Fusiliers reached the final objective about 10 a.m. An officer's patrol which, passing through Flanders II Line, entered Passchendaele village, found the ruins deserted. Scattered groups of Germans sheltering in shell holes had surrendered readily during the advance ; but the rain now ceased, and, with clear visibility, German machine guns began to rake the leading units with enfilade fire from the right flank. Some enemy field batteries, seen to be firing over open sights south of Passchendaele, also took a steadily rising toll of the brigades.[2]

---

[1] This second-line division had arrived in France in March 1917 ; the 49th Division had been in France since April 1915.
[2] German *Fourth Army* headquarters, after the disastrous policy of attempting to hold the front line in great strength on 4th October, reverted temporarily, on the recommendation of General Ludendorff the following day, to the former method of weakly held outpost zones. The foremost line of outpost groups was still to be liberally supplied with light machine guns. Opposite the II Anzac Corps was the *195th Division*, and its left regiment, the *233rd Reserve*, had relieved its front battalion only a few hours before the attack was launched.

The 2nd Australian Division (Major-General N. M. Smyth), which was to have covered the right flank of the 66th Division (now the right wing of the II Anzac Corps) south of the railway, with its 5th Brigade (Br.-General R. Smith) and groups of the 17th and 20th Battalions, reached the final objective along the north-western part of Keiberg spur, 1,200 yards distant. But before the 66th Division arrived on the objective this flank protection had to withdraw; for although the opposition had been slight, the battalions, averaging only about one-half establishment at the start, had been unable to mop up numbers of Germans hiding in shell holes during the advance, and as enemy reinforcements were filtering through to these pockets of resistance, the 5th Australian Brigade withdrew eight hundred yards in order to avoid encirclement. As the battalions fell back, suffering further heavy casualties, they saw the men of the 197th Brigade (66th Division) advancing towards Passchendaele, north of the railway; by the time that they were reinforced, the men of the 197th Brigade nearest to them had withdrawn, so the Australians remained where they were on the first objective.

The 6th Australian Brigade which was to have occupied Daisy and Dairy Woods on the right of the 5th Brigade, was checked soon after the start by machine-gun fire from these places.[1] On the right again, a raid on Celtic Wood by men of the 1st Australian Division found the enemy well prepared, and only 14 of the 85 officers and men engaged returned unwounded.

About mid-day the leading units of the 197th Brigade in front of Passchendaele, finding no support on either side, as a precaution, swung back both flanks. The centre, mistaking this manœuvre for a general withdrawal, also fell back, and the whole line, moving in good order, halted along the first objective, where it gained touch with the 2nd Australian Division south of the railway, and with the 198th Brigade north of the Ravebeek. At 5.10 p.m. a German counter-attack was checked in front of this line by machine-gun fire and by an S.O.S. artillery barrage. Before nightfall the G.O.C. of the 66th Division ordered another

---

[1] On the right, Br.-General Smith sent two companies of the 19th Battalion southwards from the 5th Brigade sector, behind the two woods, and these were mostly cleared before dark.

slight withdrawal to a line about five hundred yards in front of the starting line, in order to conform to the front of the 49th Division (the left wing of the II Anzac Corps), and to avoid enfilade fire from the Bellevue strongpoints north of the Ravebeek.[1]

South of the two Anzac corps a barrage had been laid on the remainder of the Second Army front to simulate a general offensive. On Gheluvelt plateau, the X Corps had, in addition, attacked with two divisions in order to hold the German reserves about Becelaere and Gheluvelt. The 5th Division made another effort to capture Polderhoek Château. Owing to heavy enfilade fire from the right flank, from about Gheluvelt, and the consequent confusion which caused loss of direction, little progress was made by the 15th Brigade (Br.-General N. M. Turner); and the 95th Brigade astride the Reutelbeek was unable to advance beyond the eastern edge of Cameron Covert.[2] On the left, the 7th Division, which had extended its front southwards to Black Watch Corner (south-west corner of Polygon Wood) in order to relieve the 21st Division, occupied the final objective given to that division for the 4th October, including Reutel village and the commanding observation area thereabouts. This successful advance was made by the 2/1 H.A.C. and 2/R. Warwickshire of the 22nd Brigade.

The Fifth Army[3]

North of the main attack, the Fifth Army was to co-operate by putting in the XVIII Corps to advance another

---

[1] The casualties suffered by the front-line attacking divisions in the day's fighting were:

	Officers			Other Ranks			
	Killed	Wounded	Missing	Killed	Wounded	Missing	Total
II Anzac Corps:							
49th Division ...	37	62	14	386	1,614	472	2,585
66th Division ...	24	76	9	477	2,059	474	3,119
	61	138	23	863	3,673	946	5,704
I Anzac Corps:							
2nd Australian Division ...		(Total—75)			(Total—1,178)		1,253
							6,957

[2] Br.-General Turner attributed the failure of his brigade to capture Polderhoek spur to the omission of Gheluvelt in the attack frontage. The place was neither bombarded nor attacked.

[3] See Sketch 27.

twelve hundred yards up to Poelcappelle spur and towards the main ridge about Westroosebeke. The assaulting battalions of both the 48th and 11th Divisions, found by the 144th and 32nd Brigades, respectively, were, however, raked by machine-gun fire at the outset.[1] Already exhausted by the march up on the previous night (7th/8th), lasting 14½ hours through mud and rain, they were not in a fit state to meet the unexpected severity and suddenness of this opposition. The barrage was lost, and little progress was made.[2]

The northern flank of the operation was to be formed by an advance by the XIV Corps to the southern edge of Houthulst Forest, the French First Army co-operating on its left. The low-lying ground, though swampy, had been less damaged by shell fire than that farther south, and the jumping-off tapes were reached in good time and without difficulty. The final objective, a distance of four thousand yards from the field batteries, was within their effective range, and the ammunition supply was ample and well organized.[3] The main anxiety had been in regard to the passage of the Broembeek, about three feet deep, which crossed the front of the centre and left divisions. The assaulting companies, however, were able to wade across it, and the planks and light bridges which were carried forward

---

[1] A fresh German division, the *16th* (known by repute as " The Iron " Division "), had been put into this sector to cover the Passchendaele–Westroosebeke high ground, which was now the principal German observation area. Its orders were to hold the foremost line, and outpost groups, with numerous machine guns, had occupied during darkness shell-hole positions so close to the jumping-off tapes that the opening barrage fell behind them.

A German division at this time had 120 heavy and 72 light machine guns for its 2,500-yards' frontage; included in this number were those of the S.S. (Marksmen) machine-gun detachment, attached to each division in the line, which were sited about the Second (artillery protective) Line, and laid an overhead barrage on the assault.

[2] Corporal W. Champ (6/Green Howards) was awarded the V.C. for most conspicuous bravery in capturing alone a pillbox by throwing bombs into it, and bringing back a machine gun and 20 prisoners under heavy fire from snipers. He was killed later in the day by a sniper's bullet.

[3] For the artillery barrage, with 100-yard lifts every 6 minutes, forty-nine 18-pdr. batteries (312 guns), organized into 3 groups, were engaged, the left group, covering the Guards Division, containing 23 batteries; and the available heavy and medium artillery, as for previous attacks, was dispersed in 3 bombardment and counter-battery groups. The machine-gun barrage was described as " superlative ".

were not required.[1] On the right, the 4th Division, which attacked with one brigade, the 12th (Br.-General A. Carton de Wiart), on its 800-yards' frontage, was held back by the failure of the XVIII Corps, on its right, to advance beyond Poelcappelle. A front line was, however, eventually consolidated immediately east of the Poelcappelle–Houthulst road. The 29th Division reached its final objective astride the Staden railway up to time, about 8 a.m., with the 2/Royal Fusiliers covering the front of the 86th Brigade (Br.-General G. R. H. Cheape) and the Royal Newfoundland Regiment, that of the 88th Brigade (Br.-General H. Nelson) north of the railway.[2] In the sector of the Guards Division (Major-General G. P. T. Feilding), too, the deep artillery and machine-gun barrage was intense and accurate; and this protective fire kept the defenders, who were mostly in open shell holes, under cover till the assault was upon them. Although each of the two attacking brigades carried forward with them over two hundred light bridges and bridge mats for crossing the Broembeek, which at this lower part of its course was ten to fifteen feet across and two to six feet deep, with sloping banks, few had to be used. After a successful advance of 2,500 yards, the objective on the western extremity of the long Veldhoek-Vijwegen spur, facing the southern edge of the forest, was gained and consolidated. The right of the 1st Guards Brigade (Br.-General C. R.

---

[1] The *227th* and the *18th Divisions* faced most of the XIV Corps. The *227th Division* had taken over the 2,500-yards' sector of the *6th Bavarian Division*, south of Houthulst Forest, by 4 a.m. on the morning of the assault, a fact which is given in the German accounts as an excuse for the slight resistance offered.

[2] Three Victoria Crosses were awarded to men of the 29th Division in this action.

Private F. G. Hancock (4/Worcestershire) worked his way alone to behind a pillbox holding up the advance, entered it and threatened its occupants with a Mills bomb. Shortly afterwards he reappeared with an enemy machine gun under his arm, followed by forty Germans, who had surrendered to him.

Sergeant J. Lister (1/Lancashire Fusiliers) also went ahead of his men to silence an enemy machine gun in a shell hole in front of a pillbox. He shot the gunners, and then shouted to the garrison of the pillbox to surrender, whereupon a hundred Germans emerged from it, and from neighbouring shell holes, with arms raised. One man who declined he shot dead. This act of bravery and initiative enabled the advance to be continued behind the barrage in the battalion's sector.

Sergeant J. Molyneux (2/Royal Fusiliers) prevented a check to the assault by at once organizing a bombing party to clear a trench of the enemy, and then captured the house behind it in a hand-to-hand fight during which twenty to thirty prisoners were taken and a number of the enemy killed and wounded.

Champion de Crespigny) was near to the cross roads, les 5 Chemins, on the summit of the spur, and the left of the 2nd Guards Brigade (Br.-General B. N. Sergison-Brooke) at the (Faidherbe) crossroads, five hundred yards east of Veldhoek.[1]

The French First Army also gained its objective, carrying on the line from the British left westward to the old position.

Apart from a local counter-attack during the afternoon from the south-western corner of Houthulst Forest against the Faidherbe crossroads, which was repulsed by the 1/Coldstream Guards, the Germans made no great effort to recover the lost ground south of the forest. The forest itself was a German defended locality of great artificial strength, with numerous pillboxes and machine-gun emplacements concealed within it, and its defences were kept garrisoned by all available man-power.[2]

Thus the gains of ground on the 9th October, except on the left flank, had been small and were confined to those near Reutel, opposite Passchendaele and near Houthulst Forest.[3]

---

[1] Lance-Sergeant J. H. Rhodes (3/Grenadier Guards) was awarded the V.C. for his initiative in entering a pillbox single-handed in the face of machine-gun fire, and forcing the occupants to surrender, including a forward observation officer connected by telephone with his battery, and nine men.

[2] The casualties suffered by the Fifth Army during the period 9th–14th October are given on p. 345, footnote 2.

[3] The Germans attribute their comparative success on 9th October to the presence of " a comparatively fresh division ", but add " the German " losses were, however, very (*recht*) considerable ", and " the sufferings " of the troops bore no relation to the advantage obtained ". (G.O.A. xiii., p. 83.)

It was in this period that the first mention is made (7th October) that the commander of the German Armies in Flanders advanced suggestions and made preparations for a retirement, as mentioned in the preface. This was not approved by Ludendorff, as such a movement meant the abandonment of the U-boat bases.

CHAPTER XVIII

THE BATTLES OF YPRES 1917 (concluded)

The Battles of Passchendaele
12th October–10th November
(Sketches 27, 28)

First Battle of Passchendaele[1]
12th October

Prospects and Weather

On the evening of the 9th October General Plumer, aware of the anxiety of Sir Douglas Haig that the operations should continue and the higher ground about Passchendaele should be reached, informed G.H.Q. that, in his opinion, the II Anzac Corps had gained in the day's fighting " a sufficiently good jumping-off line for the next " attack on the 12th", on which date, he added, there was every reason to hope that Passchendaele would be captured. His letter was in reply to a request, made by G.H.Q. on the 6th October, for his suggestions as to the best use that could be made of the Canadian Corps, which was to be transferred from the First to the Second Army in the middle of the month. General Plumer proposed that the Canadians should relieve the II Anzac Corps after the capture of the Passchendaele–Westroosebeke ridge on the 14th October: they could, after improving the position there by an advance towards Moorslede, then relieve the X Corps north of the Ypres–Menin road, and carry out the capture of Becelaere and Gheluvelt, whilst the IX Corps, on its right, attacked Zandvoorde from the north.[2]

General Plumer's sanguine expectation that Passchendaele would be captured in the next attack was based on misleading information. The failure of the main attack on the 9th against Poelcappelle was assumed to have been due to the mud, and it was not until the morning of the 11th that reports from patrols of the brigades of the 3rd Australian

---
[1] See Sketch 27.
[2] See Sketches 25 and 26 for these places, and then Sketch 27.

and New Zealand Divisions (which, in order to make the next advance, had relieved the 66th and 49th Divisions overnight) disclosed the strength of two formidable and continuous belts of new wire entanglements. This obstacle, thirty yards in breadth, protected the pillboxes of the Flanders I Line on Wallemolen spur, and in fact had been the real stumbling-block to the advance. It was also disclosed that, although the 49th Division had held the lower slope of the spur east of the Ravebeek, the 66th's line was about the pillbox 'shelters from which its assault had started. The conditions, too, were lamentable. The sodden battleground was littered with wounded who had lain out in the mud among the dead for two days and nights; and the pillbox shelters were overflowing with unattended wounded, whilst the dead lay piled outside.[1] The survivors, in a state of utter exhaustion, with neither food nor ammunition, had been sniped at by Germans on the higher ground throughout the 10th, with increasing casualties.[2]

On receipt of the reports from the relieving brigades, the opening barrage line for the 3rd Australian Division, on the right, had, in consequence of the withdrawal of the 66th Division, to be brought back 350 yards. At the same time, the C.R.A. of the New Zealand Division, on the left, reported that, owing to the difficulties of getting batteries across the Steenbeek and the instability of the gun platforms, effective artillery support for his division could not be depended upon. These adverse facts were not at once known at Second Army headquarters. Nor had G.H.Q. any knowledge of the changed situation which they revealed: that same afternoon (11th) Sir Douglas Haig told a meeting of war correspondents that mud alone had caused the failure on the 9th: " we are practically through the enemy's defences," adding, " the enemy has only flesh and blood against us, not " blockhouses; they take a month to make."

Showery weather continuing during the 10th and 11th, little progress could be made on the plank roads. The field batteries were unable to advance farther, and the heavy

---

[1] A stretcher case required up to sixteen men for the carry back across the mile of mud to the duck-board tracks and advanced dressing stations.
[2] The normal ammunition expenditure in one attack was estimated to be 70 rounds per rifle and 25 magazines for each Lewis gun. It had not been possible, however, to send up the considerable extra supplies for the period of consolidation, so that the rounds carried by each man were soon expended.

FIRST PASSCHENDAELE

batteries, in vain efforts to move to forward positions, found little time for counter-battery work or for destroying the wire and pillboxes on Wallemolen spur. Both wire entanglement and pillboxes could be seen from Gravenstafel spur, and the forward artillery liaison officers with infantry brigades pressed throughout the day for their destruction by heavy artillery before the assault was launched. No action, however, could be taken until the late afternoon, when a few heavy batteries opened up on the Bellevue sector for a short time, but with negligible results.[1]

At 6 p.m. on the 11th the infantry brigades of the 3rd Australian and New Zealand Divisions (II Anzac Corps) which were to make the main assault moved up from their assembly areas behind Pilckem Ridge, five miles from the front. The evening was cold and bleak, and a leaden sky added to the desolation of the muddy and cratered belt which the battalions had to cross. At nightfall they broke up into a series of Indian files, each man holding on to the equipment of the man ahead in order to keep to the duckboard in the dark. About midnight, wind arose, bringing a drizzling rain, and, for the second time, General Gough rang up Second Army headquarters to ask for a postponement of the attack. General Plumer, after consulting his corps commanders, decided to carry on. As the leading battalions crossed Gravenstafel spur in pitch darkness they were deluged with gas, which caused considerable inconvenience but very few casualties, the wind helping to disperse it.[2] The duckboards, as no gain of ground had been made on the 9th, now reached nearly to the front line, and in the left sector the morass of the Ravebeek had been bridged by five coconut-mat crossings, laid by night by the 1st Field Company, New Zealand Engineers, and at 3 a.m. the battalions were along their jumping-off tapes. About zero hour, 5.25 a.m., the wind increased in strength

---

[1] German regimental histories note that effective counter-battery fire almost ceased between the 9th and 12th.

[2] The gas shelling was part of a planned German gas-shoot, named *Mondnacht*, arranged for the night of the 2nd, and delayed owing to the late arrival of the ammunition. G.O.A. (xiii., pp. 84–5) states that from midnight to 2 a.m. a belt of ground 800 to 1,100 yards deep behind the Allied front from Messines to Dixmude was shelled with gas, principally mustard gas, in order to catch the troops moving through it to attack. British accounts, it adds, do not mention this gassing, so " on account of " the muddy ground and unfavourable weather the effects must have " been small ".

and the drizzle turned to heavy rain, which, with a brief respite during the morning, was to fall steadily throughout the day.[1]

The Attack

The Second Army

The final objective for the main assault was the same as that given for the afternoon advance by the II Anzac Corps on the 9th October, just beyond Passchendaele.[2] The village stands on one of the highest parts of the main ridge, and the eventual corps frontage of three thousand yards was to run through its eastern outskirts, with the left astride the summit at the head of the re-entrant north of Goudberg. The 3rd Australian Division (Major-General Sir J. Monash) was to take the village, whilst the New Zealand Division (Major-General Sir A. H. Russell), on its left, overran the Bellevue and Goudberg defences on the high ground of Wallemolen spur. Long halts of two and one hours, respectively, were to be made at the first and second objectives, which also were the same as those given for the morning assault on the 9th.

Owing to the difficulties mentioned above, the artillery barrage intended to support the advance of the New Zealand Division, weak and erratic at the start, became even thinner and more ragged as the troops advanced up the slope, howitzer shells burying themselves in the sodden ground and merely splashing the pillboxes with fountains of mud. In consequence, the New Zealanders found themselves confronted with broad belts of unbroken wire entanglements, and with small means or hope of passages being cut through them, or of silencing the machine guns sited in the numerous pillboxes and emplacements beyond the wire. It was evident that any progress made would be only at the cost of heavy losses in men. Making most courageous efforts to cut their way through the wire, the Otago and Canterbury battalions of the 2nd Brigade (Br.-General W. G. Braithwaite) were raked by murderous machine-gun fire, and the four battalions of the 3rd (Rifle) Brigade (Br.-General A. E. Stewart), attacking north of the Gravenstafel–Meetcheele road,

---

[1] Crown Prince Rupprecht notes in his diary on this day (12th) : "sudden change of the weather. Most gratifying—rain : our most effective ally ".
[2] See Sketch 27.

suffered in the same way.[1] As had happened so many times before, the first belt of wire became a death-trap for hundreds of gallant men, and those who did struggle on to the second belt suffered a like fate. This splendid division lost a hundred officers and 2,635 other ranks within a few hours in brave but vain attempts—its only failure—to carry out a task beyond the power of any infantry with so little support, and had gained no ground except on the left.

Although the 3rd Australian Division, on the right, met stiffer resistance at the outset than did the 66th Division three days previously on the same ground, the course of its progress was similar. The 10th Brigade (Br.-General W. R. McNicol), south of the Ravebeek, was checked about the first objective by enfilade machine-gun fire across the valley from the Bellevue pillboxes. The 9th Brigade (Br.-General C. Rosenthal), on the main ridge, overran the machine-gun nests near the first objective and pressed on astride the highway to the second objective in front of Passchendaele, finding wounded men of the 66th Division still hiding in shell-holes thereabouts.[2] One patrol reached the village, which it found still deserted, and numbers of Germans were seen retreating from Wallemolen spur across the highway to the north; but the Australian attack was not strong enough to weaken appreciably the opposition facing the New Zealanders. At 10.50 a.m., as soon as the facts of the situation became known at the headquarters of the 3rd Australian Division, Major-General Monash decided to make an enveloping attack with the reserve battalion (38th) of his 9th Brigade past the western side of Passchendaele, and asked that the New Zealand Division should meanwhile bombard the Bellevue position with every available gun. He then learnt that, by order of Lieut.-General Godley, the corps commander, the New Zealand Division would once

---

[1] Each brigade assaulted with one battalion leading, two behind to leap-frog through to the second and third objectives, with the fourth battalion held back as reserve against counter-attack.

[2] Captain C. S. Jeffries (34th Australian Battalion) was awarded the V.C. for conspicuous bravery. With a small party of his company, he captured a pillbox from which machine-gun fire was holding up the advance, taking 4 machine guns and 35 prisoners. Later, he organized another successful attack on an emplacement, capturing 2 machine guns and thirty more prisoners, subsequently leading his company forward under heavy artillery and machine-gun fire to the objective. This gallant officer was killed later in the day, after his inspiring influence and his initiative had prevented the centre of the Australian advance from being held up.

more assault, in conjunction, at 3 p.m. Before this hour, however, the situation had gravely deteriorated. By noon the enfilade fire raking the 10th Australian Brigade south of the Ravebeek morass had caused such heavy casualties that the senior surviving officer, seeing no hope of silencing it, had ordered withdrawal to the starting-line. By groups of fours and fives, the movement was completed by 3.30 p.m. The leading units of the 9th Brigade, on the summit, pounded by German field guns firing over open sights and swept by fire from machine guns and snipers, saw themselves faced with annihilation in their advanced position. They, too, on the order of the senior officer in the line, withdrew soon after 3 p.m. almost to the starting line, a new front being established there before nightfall. On hearing of the withdrawal and the heavy losses sustained, the corps commander's order for a renewed effort at 3 p.m. was cancelled.[1] It had in fact little prospect of success, owing to the strength of the German artillery and reserves behind Passchendaele.

The 4th Australian Division (Major-General E. G. Sinclair-Maclagan) was to have protected the southern flank with advanced outpost groups, to be established across Keiberg spur by two battalions of its 12th Brigade. The objective was gained with considerable difficulty and loss, but had to be abandoned on the withdrawal of the 9th Brigade north of the railway.

THE FIFTH ARMY

The task of the Fifth Army on this day, the 12th October, was to establish the northern flank of the main assault. In the XVIII Corps sector, the 9th (Scottish) Division (Major-General H. T. Lukin), which had returned to the line after two weeks' rest, was to advance on to the main ridge north of the Goudberg re-entrant, a distance of two thousand yards, whilst the 18th (Eastern) Division (Major-General R. P. Lee) conformed on the left, north of the Lekkerboterbeek. The 9th Division assaulted with its 26th Brigade (Br.-General J. Kennedy), and the 18th Division with the 55th Brigade (Br.-General G. D. Price). Here, too, the barrage was thin and erratic; thirteen field batteries were

---

[1] The news of the withdrawal of the 10th Brigade and its serious losses was flashed back by lamp signal soon after noon from a captured pillbox near the Ravebeek, where a report centre had been established by the 40th Australian Battalion.

to have advanced to positions on either side of the Winnipeg–Langemarck road, within two thousand five hundred yards of the front line, but a high proportion of the guns had been unable to reach their allotted positions, and the machine-gun barrage was more or less ineffectual, owing to the mud which clogged the mechanism both of guns and rifles and prevented the re-filling of belts. The German machine-gun detachments, in dry emplacements, on the higher ground in advance of the Flanders I Line, had no such trouble, and opened an intense fire on the leading battalions struggling through deep mud towards them. The barrage was lost; attempts to push on by short rushes from shell-hole to shell-hole gradually ceased. Very heavy losses soon resulted, and much progress in such circumstances was hardly to be expected. Though touch was maintained by the 9th Division with the New Zealanders about Wallemolen, the XVIII Corps' front remained but slightly in advance of its starting-line, and isolated parties of both brigades reported by air observers at 5 p.m. to be near the final objective, were withdrawn during the night.

The XIV Corps succeeded in extending its perimeter northwards towards Houthulst Forest, as the supporting artillery and machine guns had fewer difficulties to contend with and the barrage was much more effective. The 4th Division (Major-General T. G. Matheson), using one brigade, the 12th (Br.-General A. Carton de Wiart), met with little resistance, except on its right wing, which was held back owing to the check of the 18th Division on the eastern outskirts of Poelcappelle; the left of the brigade, however, gained its final objective, an advance of seven hundred yards across the flats north-west of the Poelcappelle-Staden road.[1] Opposite the 17th (Northern) Division (Major-General P. R. Robertson), also, the Germans were in no mood to face the barrage, and most of the final objective on both sides of the Staden railway was gained by its leading brigade, the 51st (Br.-General C. E. Bond), despite mud and considerable casualties from snipers. The Guards Division (Major-General G. P. T. Feilding), on the left, gained the whole of its final

---

[1] Private A. Halton (1/King's Own) was awarded the V.C. for his courage in going forward alone under heavy fire about three hundred yards and capturing a machine gun and its detachment which was causing heavy casualties.

objective.[1] Using the 3rd Guards Brigade (Br.-General Lord H. C. Seymour), the line was advanced across the western extremity of Vijwegen spur to the edge of the forest.[2]

SECOND BATTLE OF PASSCHENDAELE
26TH OCTOBER–10TH NOVEMBER

PROSPECTS

At a G.H.Q. conference at Second Army headquarters in Cassel on the following morning, the 13th, it was agreed to postpone all further attacks until an improvement in the weather made the construction of roads practicable for the forward movement of the artillery and, consequently, a more prolonged and effective bombardment feasible. Sir Douglas Haig again stressed the importance of gaining Passchendaele and the main ridge northwards to Westroosebeke as a winter position. He wished, too, to help the French attack in Champagne (23rd October) by keeping German attention fixed on the operations in Flanders. He mentioned also that he was engaged in the consideration of an alternative operation against Cambrai before winter put a stop to active operations; five hundred tanks were being collected, and infantry divisions were being specially trained to co-operate with them. General Hon. Sir Julian Byng, commanding the Third Army, said he hoped that his preparations would be

---

[1] The Guards Division thereby made the record of gaining the final objective allotted to it in every assault in this campaign. From the Yser canal to Houthulst Forest its successive advances had, to quote the divisional diary, "been made so quickly and so quietly that its achievement is in danger of being forgotten".

[2] The casualties suffered by the divisions of the Fifth Army engaged in the fighting during the period 9th–14th October were:

	Officers			Other Ranks			
	Killed	Wounded	Missing	Killed	Wounded	Missing	Total
48th Division	12	14	3	170	527	154	880
11th ,,	11	13	5	260	935	250	1,474
9th ,,	21	53	5	130	884	28	1,121
18th ,,	18	54	4	260	1,051	282	1,669
4th ,,	5	49	—	98	841	8	1,001
29th ,,	11	38	—	139	778	146	1,112
17th ,,	11	40	1	147	844	164	1,207
Guards ,,	24	64	1	420	1,678	188	2,375
XVIII Corps Artillery	—	6	—	6	41	—	53
XIV Corps Artillery	—	6	—	11	61	3	81
	113	337	19	1,641	7,640	1,223	10,973

complete by mid-November, and asked that, if the Cambrai scheme was approved, the Flanders operations should be continued as long as possible, in order to give him every chance of success.

For these reasons Sir Douglas Haig had no intention of closing down the Flanders campaign, despite the appalling condition of the battle area.[1] He was kept regularly informed of the condition of the ground by his liaison officers and by the staff officers of the G.O.C. Royal Artillery and of the Engineer-in-Chief; and occasionally members of his own Operations Section flew over the battlefield and their reports did not minimize the bad conditions. Nearly one-half of the area in front of Passchendaele was water or deep mud, the most serious difficulty being that the valley of the Ravebeek was impassable—except by bridging of some sort —even for infantry, and for the first mile split the front where the Canadian Corps was to operate in the next attack (26th October) into two halves, each a defile. Arrangements were made to continue the struggle. The Canadian Corps (Lieut.-General Sir A. W. Currie), from the Lens–Vimy front, was to take over from the II Anzac Corps about the 18th October, and then gain possession of the Passchendaele area by three short advances at three or more days' interval. The Fifth Army would then capture Westroosebeke to make the position secure for the winter.

At a conference on the 16th, Lieut.-General Currie pointed out that the date of the next attack depended upon the artillery protection and the state of the roads: the cutting of the wire and the bombardment of the pillbox strongpoints had already begun: if the required artillery and ammunition could be moved up to about the Zonnebeke–Winnipeg road, as originally intended, within two thousand five hundred yards of the enemy's most advanced positions, by the night of the 21st/22nd, he agreed to carry out the first attack on the 26th, given reasonable weather.[2] He proposed to make the second attack, with the same infantry brigades, after a three days' interval, and asked for a minimum of four days

---

[1] Sketch 28, copied from a map prepared by the Historian of the Overseas Forces of Canada, Department of National Defence, shows the area.

[2] Lieut.-General Currie wished to have six 6-inch howitzer batteries, two 60-pdr. batteries and three brigades R.F.A. of his southern artillery groups brought forward to near Hill 40 (Windmill Hill), and four brigades R.F.A. of his northern groups behind Gravenstafel spur by the night of the 21st/22nd, with 8,000 tons of ammunition near at hand. See Sketch 25.

between the second and the third attacks, to permit of the necessary inter-divisional relief. Sir Douglas Haig impressed on General Plumer that Lieut.-General Currie should not be forced to start until he was confident that the conditions were such as to ensure success. In the interval, in order to maintain the pressure, the Fifth Army was to co-operate with the French First Army in an attack on the 22nd, to gain further ground towards Spriet and Houthulst Forest.

On the 17th/18th October the Canadian Corps artillery headquarters (Br.-General E. W. B. Morrison) relieved those of the II Anzac Corps, the guns being handed over in their positions, crowded alongside the tracks behind Hill 40 and about Kansas Cross and Winnipeg.

After the middle of October the weather improved. The German artillery, however, became more aggressive in its efforts to hinder progress in the laying of plank roads, and to delay other offensive preparations, which could be seen from Passchendaele Ridge. Almost nightly from the 14th October onwards to mid-November enemy aircraft bombarded the back areas with high-explosive, and drenched the low ground of the Steenbeek valley with gas shell. Sneezing gas (blue cross=diphenyl chlorarsine), which made it difficult to keep on the respirators, was followed by mustard gas (yellow cross=dichlorethyl sulphide), which blistered the body and damaged the throat and eyes. Although only a few deaths were caused, some thousands of men of the infantry in support and reserve positions, of the artillery and of the working parties were disabled during this period. Large areas, too, including battery positions and bivouacs, became saturated with mustard oil and could not be reoccupied for some time.

Despite this nightly ordeal, in addition to frequent shelling by day, the plank roads and battery positions were ready by the appointed date.[1] The apparently hopeless task of extending the long stretch of plank road to Hill 40 was solved by the discovery that the pavement of the Frezenberg-Zonnebeke road still existed under a deep covering of mud; this was removed and the road surface repaired, the circuit

---

[1] The average daily labour employed on the forward roads in the Second Army area at this time was 2 infantry battalions, 7 pioneer battalions, 10 field companies R.E., 7 tunnelling companies, 4 Army Troops companies R.E. and 2 labour companies. The proportion of casualties in these working parties approximated to that of infantry in battle.

being completed by pushing forward the Westhoek–Zonnebeke plank road to join it. From the 21st onwards systematic wire-cutting and the bombardment of the strongpoints were intensified, as well as counter-battery work, and on each day preparatory barrages in depth combed the enemy's position.[1]

On the 22nd, at 5.35 a.m. (Fifth Army zero hour), the artillery action was opened along the whole front of the Fifth and Second Armies, in order to give the impression of a large-scale offensive. In the attack of the Fifth Army which followed, in combination with the French,[2] some progress was made on both the XVIII and XIV Corps fronts, though some of the gains were lost later in the day.[3]

On the 23rd, the 50th Battalion, the extreme right of the

---

[1] The artillery placed at the disposal of the Canadian Corps amounted, nominally, to a total of 227 heavy and medium guns and howitzers, and was about the same as that at the disposal of the II Anzac Corps at the Battle of Broodseinde on 4th October, but actually there were never more than 139 in action. This total included : 48 (in action, 16–23) 60-pdrs. ; 106 (in action, 83 or less) 6-inch howitzers ; 32 (in action, 23–25) 8-inch howitzers ; 26 (in action, 11–16) 9.2-inch howitzers ; with 17 brigades R.F.A., totalling, nominally, 306 18-pdrs. and 102 4.5-inch howitzers, but with never more than 230 and 75, respectively, in action.

[2] The French 1st Division covered the left of the attack, using one regiment and some patrols, which gained all objectives (F.O.A. v. (ii.), pp. 713, 4).

[3] The total casualties incurred by the Fifth Army during the day amounted to : officers, 2 killed, 21 wounded ; other ranks, 58 killed, 377 wounded, 21 missing. About 125 Germans were taken prisoner.

The German *Fourth Army* had, by an order dated 11th October, introduced yet another variation in its defence dispositions, which was now tried for the first time. The main line of resistance was put back as far as eight hundred yards or more from the British front, the intervening area (*Vorfeld*) being manned only by a few outpost groups, or patrols at night, who were to withdraw to this line in the event of an attack. The idea was to afford opportunity for the artillery and the heavy machine guns to lay a barrage in front of the main line of resistance, to become the first line of defence, and hold up the impetus of the attack at this stage. The line was to be held at all costs, or, if lost, to be retaken by immediate counter-attack. On the present occasion, it was sited generally behind the British objective, and the counter-battery gas shelling more or less neutralized the German artillery barrage.

The new procedure, if noticed, was not reported : the garrisons (about thirty men, with machine guns, rifles and grenades) of the pillboxes—many built for shelter only—hurried out as soon as the barrage lifted to man adjoining emplacements and slit fire-trenches ; but our men followed the barrage so closely that the Germans were often caught in the pillboxes, and one of their captured officers complained, in English, that " your men " attacked so closely upon the barrage that they seemed mixed up with their own shell fire ".

Canadian Corps, pushed out posts three or four hundred yards along the top of the ridge towards Passchendaele.[1]

THE ATTACK OF THE 26TH OCTOBER
THE SECOND ARMY

On the 26th the Canadian Corps attacked at 5.40 a.m. with two divisions in the sectors which had previously been occupied by the II Anzac Corps. The operation was given the appearance of a general offensive on the whole battle front by simultaneous attacks on the flanks, in order to pin down the enemy's reserves and force him to disperse his artillery fire. The previous day had been fine and cool, with good visibility, and the belts of wire across Wallemolen spur were seen to have been well broken, although the pillboxes on the Bellevue spur and on the front of the right division were still intact. From midnight onwards, as the assaulting brigades were forming up along the jumping-off tapes, and throughout the morning, it rained steadily and continually. Despite the appalling ground conditions, the 4th Canadian Division (Major-General D. Watson), on the right, using one battalion, the 46th (South Saskatchewan) of the 10th Brigade (Br.-General E. Hilliam), to cover the 1,300-yard frontage south of the Ravebeek, keeping close behind the barrage,[2] gained the whole of its objective, an advance of four hundred yards. Consolidation was carried out under heavy artillery fire from German batteries south-east of Passchendaele, and two counter-attacks were beaten off. But the line being enfiladed from Laamkeek, a heavy barrage fell on the area in the afternoon, and casualties mounted to 70 per cent. of the 420 men on the position. In the face of a third counter-attack, the survivors of the 46th Battalion fell back to within a hundred yards of the original line. Then the 44th and 47th Battalions came up to reinforce, and by 10 a.m. on the 27th the line of the original first objective had been regained.

On the left, the 3rd Canadian Division (Major-General L. J. Lipsett) used two brigades for its difficult task. The 9th (Br.-General F. W. Hill) followed the barrage across the

---
[1] About 26th October " intelligence came to hand that England was " preparing an immediate attack from the sea in grand style against " Flanders. In consequence, a corps headquarters and two-thirds of two " divisions were held ready to deal with it ". (G.O.A. xiii., p. 89.) Nothing of the kind was on hand.

[2] The barrage moved by 50-yard lifts every 4 minutes.

broken wire, and at 6.30 a.m. men of its left battalion, the 43rd (Cameron Highlanders of Canada), were seen on the sky-line about the pillboxes north of Bellevue. The 58th Battalion (Central Ontario), on the right, was, however, checked about the Laamkeek defences, and by 8 a.m. an intense German artillery and machine-gun barrage on the area, covering a counter-attack, caused heavy casualties and brought the advance to a standstill four hundred yards short of the final objective, which had earlier been reported as captured. Heavy rain was falling, and for some hours a repetition was feared of the two previous failures in this sector. The 52nd Battalion (Manitoba), in support, was sent up to reinforce the crest north of Bellevue, which it reached about noon, and found there fifty men of the 43rd Battalion. The going was easier on the sandy soil on top of the spur, and, fighting southwards with great perseverance and skill under the most arduous conditions, these battalions outflanked in turn the remaining pillboxes near Bellevue and Laamkeek, enabling the assaulting battalions to consolidate the positions won.[1] By 3.30 p.m. the Germans had been driven from the Flanders I Line defences from the Ravebeek northwards to Wolf Copse, where touch was gained with the 8th Brigade (Br.-General J. H. Elmsley), whose leading battalion, the 4th Canadian Mounted Rifles, after penetrating the position, had halted for the troops on both flanks to come abreast.[2]

The line gained by the 3rd Canadian Division, though only an average advance of five hundred yards, and still five hundred yards short of the day's objective, included a

---

[1] The award of two V.C.'s commemorates this incident. One was to Captain C. P. J. O'Kelly (52nd Battalion), who, after the first attack had failed, led two companies of his battalion across a thousand yards of open ground under heavy fire and, without an artillery barrage, reached the enemy position on the crest of the hill, and then personally organized and led a series of attacks against pillboxes, his company alone capturing 6 of them with a hundred German occupants and 10 machine guns.

The other V.C. was awarded to Lieut. R. Shankland (43rd Battalion), for rallying his command and holding the position gained on the crest against German counter-attacks, thereby enabling the supporting troops to come up unmolested. His courage and splendid example inspired all ranks, and undoubtedly saved a very critical situation.

[2] Private T. W. Holmes (4th Canadian Mounted Rifles) was awarded the V.C. for conspicuous bravery and resource. On his own initiative and single-handed, he ran forward and threw two bombs, killing the crews of two machine guns which were holding up the advance. Later, he went forward alone under heavy fire and threw a bomb into the entrance of a pillbox, causing the 19 occupants to surrender.

portion of the Flanders I Line across Wallemolen spur, and, in spite of counter-attacks, the Canadian Corps was now established on the drier high ground of the main ridge to the south-west and west of Passchendaele village. Over five hundred prisoners had been taken.[1]

In the diversion attacks on the flanks,[2] the X Corps on Gheluvelt plateau had made a third attempt with its 7th and 5th Divisions to capture Gheluvelt and Polderhoek spurs, as well as Tower Hamlets Quadrilateral, on the extreme right. Although Polderhoek Château was captured by the 15/R. Warwickshire (13th Brigade), from the very outset only very slow and laborious headway could be made in mud so soggy that in places the men, knee-deep, became stuck fast and easy targets for German snipers. After superhuman efforts, this most gallant attempt to achieve the impossible was abandoned, and all ground won was given up later in the day. The casualties had been heavy, amounting in the two divisions to 119 officers and 3,202 other ranks.

The Fifth Army

On the northern flank, the troops of the Fifth Army met with no success. The XVIII Corps used the 63rd (Royal Naval) Division (Major-General C. E. Lawrie) and the 58th (2/1st London) Division (Major-General A. B. E. Cator) in a renewed effort to advance up the valley of the Lekkerboterbeek. Here, too, the mud, knee-deep, checked progress to a crawl of rather less than a yard a minute. The barrage was lost, rifles became quickly clogged, and the men fell back, if they could, to the starting line, or were cut off. The XIV Corps,[3] which attacked with the 57th (2nd West Lancashire) Division (Major-General R. W. R. Barnes) and 50th (Northumbrian) Division (Major-General P. S. Wilkinson), was also unable to advance ;[4] but on the extreme left

---

[1] The *11th Bavarian Division* held the front opposite the Canadian Corps, with the *238th Division* in close reserve.

[2] See Sketch 26.

[3] On 29th October, the XIV Corps headquarters was relieved by the XIX.

[4] The casualties incurred by the four divisions in the XVIII and XIV Corps which attacked on this day were:

		Officers			Other Ranks		
	Killed	Wounded	Missing	Killed	Wounded	Missing	Total
63rd Division	8	14	–	223	427	277	949
58th „	5	28	4	94	561	669	1,361
57th „	11	35	–	215	992	381	1,634
50th „	13	30	7	228	815	365	1,458
	37	107	11	760	2,795	1,692	5,402

the 1st and 133rd Divisions of the French First Army, after three days' bombardment, made a little headway under great difficulties towards the south-western corner of Houthulst Forest.

Divisions Sent to Italy

In the evening (26th), in consequence of the collapse of the Italians at Caporetto and their headlong retreat, G.H.Q. received an order from London, given by the Prime Minister, which directed Sir Douglas Haig, as a preliminary measure, to send two divisions to Italy as quickly as possible. This was an unpleasant shock in the midst of battle, but the order had to be obeyed. The 23rd and 41st Divisions of the X Corps, about to be relieved, were selected, with Lieut.-General Lord Cavan (XIV Corps) as commander; corps artillery, other corps troops and air units were also detailed. The advance parties left Flanders on the 28th.

It may be added that on the 8th November, in accordance with a further order, the 7th and 48th Divisions were selected to go to Italy, under Lieut.-General Sir R. Haking (XI Corps), and left soon afterwards, and that on the 14th November two more divisions, the 5th and 21st, were warned, but the order to the 21st was cancelled. The 2nd and 47th Divisions were also warned to be ready to go to Italy, but it was not found necessary to send them. The British Armies in France, however, lost five divisions they could ill spare.

The Communications

It was intended to make another bound on the 30th, but it was evident that further progress was dependent on whether the leading Canadian troops could be supplied with rations, trench munitions and engineer stores. In order to ensure this, the Canadian Corps organized a train of 250 pack animals per brigade, and in each brigade sector a track was made of fascines, planks and corduroy, which led from rear brigade headquarters to the forward area. By day its use was impracticable, being overlooked by the enemy, and by night many of the animals missed their footing and were lost or drowned in the mud alongside. Gun ammunition, too, had to be brought forward by pack transport from the wagon lines west of Ypres to the main dumps near Frezenberg and

CANADIAN CORPS. 27TH–30TH OCTOBER

Wieltje and thence to the battery positions. These exhausting tasks, carried out under frequent artillery fire, entailed a heavy toll of casualties; but there was no shortage of supplies and stores, and no lack of ammunition at the guns, even at times of heaviest expenditure.[1]

The weather improved on the 27th, and that night the 10th Canadian Brigade made a slight advance and consolidated new forward posts. Elsewhere on the ground, comparative infantry quiet reigned; but, as a consequence of fine weather, air activity was intense, aircraft observing for the artillery shoots on 116 enemy batteries, besides bombing front areas and taking photographs.

The 28th was also fine; but the lines were fog-enshrouded most of the day, and at night, in retaliation for the previous day's bombardment, the enemy heavily shelled the battery positions with mustard gas. The 29th, the eve of the next attack, was, except for intermittent shelling, quiet; but at night there was considerable bombing of the British back areas.

THE ATTACK ON THE 30TH OCTOBER

On the 30th, at daybreak, 5.50 a.m., the Canadian Corps advanced to complete the capture of the objective of the 26th on the left brigade front, and to establish a position on the southern edge of Passchendaele for the final assault.[2] In spite of the bright moonlight and the proximity of the Germans, the forming up was carried out successfully, the enemy sending over only twenty shells. Advanced posts having been withdrawn, the barrage came down exactly to time.

Until about 11 a.m. the weather was fine, but it was very cold, with a high wind blowing; rain in the afternoon seriously interfered with consolidation and supply. The 4th

---

[1] During the 24 hours from noon 5th November, including the attack on the 6th, the average expenditure per gun was 267 18-pdr. shells and 197 4.5-inch howitzer shells. The 1st Canadian Division records that its field batteries were issued with 116,125 18-pdr. shells and 17,868 4.5-inch howitzer shells during the period 3rd–12th November, and that the transport of this quantity of ammunition from the main dump to the batteries alone represented a total of 18,990 animal trips.

[2] The *238th Division* had relieved the *11th Bavarian*, opposite the Canadian Corps sector on the night of 26th/27th October. The *39th Division* was now in close reserve.

Canadian Division, using its 12th Brigade (Br.-General J. H. MacBrien), reached the outskirts of Passchendaele on both sides of the ridge highway with the 85th (Nova Scotia Highlanders), 78th (Winnipeg Grenadiers) and 72nd (Seaforth Highlanders of Canada) Battalions. All obstacles were overcome, and the objective was gained according to time-table, including Crest Farm, won and lost by the 9th Australian Brigade on the 12th October, which the 72nd Battalion, following in the wake of an excellent barrage, now rushed before the defenders could man their guns. The 3rd Canadian Division, which had relieved its 9th Brigade by the 7th (Br.-General H. M. Dyer), reached Meetcheele, but the Princess Patricia's Canadian L.I. and the 49th (Edmonton) Battalions had had hard and costly fighting along the narrow summit of Bellevue spur. The 8th Brigade, with the 5th Canadian Mounted Rifles leading, advanced about eight hundred yards and gained a footing at Vapour Farm, on the western tip of Goudberg spur. The fighting on this day was marked by many individual actions of great gallantry.[1]

During the afternoon the 3rd Canadian Division received no less than five counter-attacks from the north of Passchendaele; but all were successfully repelled.

On the left flank, the XVIII Corps, using the 63rd and 58th Divisions, again made only slight progress up the boggy slope on either side of the Lekkerboterbeek, despite heavy losses in the 190th Brigade (Br.-General A. R. H. Hutchinson) of the 63rd Division. Up to their knees in mud, the men were unable to follow the barrage, and were caught in

---

[1] Five of the six assaulting battalions lost over 50 per cent. of battle strength. Three V.C.'s were awarded to soldiers serving in the 7th Canadian Brigade for outstanding courage during the day:

Lieut. H. Mackenzie (7th Company, Canadian Machine Gun Corps) rallied and took command of an infantry company in which all the officers and n.c.o.'s had become casualties, and then led it in attacks against two pillboxes, both of which were captured.

Sergeant G. H. Mullin (P.P.C.L.I.) climbed on top of a pillbox, shot two machine-gunners with his revolver and caused the garrison of ten to surrender.

Private C. J. Kinross (49th Battalion, Edmonton) rushed a machine-gun detachment single-handed, killed the six men and captured the gun.

Major G. R. Pearkes (5th Canadian Mounted Rifles, 8th Canadian Brigade) also received the V.C. for bravery and skilful leadership. Though wounded early in the day, he personally led an attack on a strongpoint, which was captured and held against repeated counter-attacks, thereby enabling the battalion on his left to gain its objective.

that of the enemy's artillery. The Artists Rifles (28/London) suffered particularly severely, and the casualties in the brigade amounted to nine hundred all ranks.

Isolated and unsuccessful counter-attacks by the enemy on the Canadians continued from early morning throughout the 31st. On this day, General Plumer received instructions to take over from the Fifth Army the XVIII Corps front and troops, so that the forthcoming further operations should be under one command. This left General Gough with only the XIV Corps. On the 2nd November Lieut.-General Sir Claud Jacob, with the II Corps Staff, relieved Lieut.-General Sir Ivor Maxse (XVIII Corps).

General Plumer ordered vigorous counter-battery work to be carried on by all corps of the Second Army from the 31st October, and the Canadian and II Corps to take some preparatory measures and make every endeavour to get guns forward whenever possible. It was intended to carry out the next two stages of the operations (eighth and ninth) on the 6th November and, probably, on the 10th, in order to allow time for the Canadian Corps to carry out inter-divisional reliefs, and on the 3rd November, the 2nd Canadian Division relieved the 4th Canadian Division, and next day the 1st Canadian Division relieved the 3rd Canadian Division.

The Attack on the 6th November

The objective of the Canadian Corps on the 6th November was a wide arc east and north-east of Passchendaele.[1] The II Corps was not to participate in the operation except by artillery fire; whilst the I Anzac, IX and VIII Corps were to do their utmost to simulate attacks on Droogenbroodhoek spur (2,000 yards east of Broodseinde), Becelaere, Gheluvelt and Zandvoorde.[2] The artillery plan for the attack on the 6th was the same as on previous occasions, with the exception that, as the enemy had ceased to crowd troops into the front system, no reason existed for making the rear portion of the barrage closer and thicker than the rest. Preliminary barrages and bursts of fire in depth were to be fired on the evenings of the 1st, 2nd and 3rd, and on the evening of

---

[1] See Sketch 28.
[2] See Sketch 26 for these places.

the 5th bursts were to be fired by all guns and howitzers on the Canadian Corps front.

Minor operations were undertaken by the Canadian Corps on the nights of the 1st/2nd November and the 3rd/4th November, with the object of improving its position by the capture of certain enemy strongpoints. These attacks, though they met with strong opposition, were successful. In retaliation, on the night of the 2nd/3rd the Germans made a determined attack near the Australian–Canadian junction, and succeeded in regaining a small wood in the Ravebeek valley; elsewhere they were repelled. At 5 a.m. on the 3rd November, half an hour after the 2nd Canadian Division had completed the relief of the 4th, another German effort to dislodge the Canadians from the main ridge north of the Roulers railway succeeded in entering the position in a few places; but by 11 a.m. the line had been restored.

The Canadian assault against Passchendaele and the high ground north of it was launched at 6 a.m. on the 6th November on a two-divisional frontage, the I Anzac Corps providing flank protection on the right and the II (late XVIII) Corps on the left. The weather was at first fine and cold, then overcast, with occasional showers. By forming up in No Man's Land, the Canadians escaped the German barrages which fell at 4.30 a.m. and one minute after zero.

On the right, the 2nd Canadian Division (Major-General H. E. Burstall) used its 6th Brigade (Br.-General H. D. B. Ketchen), which put in three battalions on a 750-yard frontage, the 27th (City of Winnipeg), 31st (Alberta) and the 28th (North West). By 7.10 a.m. the Canadians were streaming through, and past either side of, Passchendaele in large numbers, bayoneting Germans in the ruins and along the main street. Resistance from pillboxes and shell-holes, particularly at the northern exit, was at once engaged by covering fire of Lewis guns and rifle grenades, and then outflanked. By 8.45 a.m. the entire objective along the eastern crest beyond the village had been gained behind the barrage, which was described in messages as "splendid".[1] The right flank was formed by the 5th

---

[1] Private J. P. Robertson (27th Battalion) was awarded the V.C. for his gallantry in rushing an enemy machine gun, killing the detachment of 4 Germans single-handed, and then, turning the gun on the retreating enemy, inflicting many casualties. Carrying the gun, he led his platoon, which had lost all its leaders, to the objective.

Brigade (Br.-General J. M. Ross), which used one battalion, the 26th (New Brunswick), for the purpose. The 2nd Canadian Division, alone, took prisoner 21 officers and 430 other ranks in an advance of eight hundred yards.[1]

On the left, the 1st Canadian Division (Major-General A. C. Macdonell) kept abreast of the 2nd, north of the village. As large areas of mud and water in the Goudberg re-entrant were impassable, the attack frontage of the division was limited to the 380-yard width of the Bellevue–Meetcheele spur to its junction with the main ridge. The task was given to two battalions, 1st (Western Ontario) and 2nd (Eastern Ontario) of the 1st Canadian Brigade (Br.-General W. A. Griesbach), with a flanking attack eastwards astride Goudberg spur entrusted to its 3rd (Toronto) Battalion. The battalions got well away and, though meeting at once with machine-gun fire, overran all opposition.[2] The garrison of Mosselmarkt was surrounded, and a shell-hole position behind, which covered that strongpoint and offered stubborn resistance, was outflanked and silenced by trench-mortar fire. Two field guns and four machine guns, with four officers and fifty other ranks, were captured there. The objective was reached by 7.45 a.m., the inner flanks of the two divisions resting on the ridge highway, a couple of hundred yards north of the northern exit of Passchendaele, with the left at the western tip of Goudberg spur. At 9.30 a.m. enemy reinforcements were seen advancing, but were successfully dealt with by artillery fire alone.

Although the German artillery and machine guns, assisted by bombing, concentrated on the captured area and its approaches throughout the morning and early afternoon, making supply hazardous and communications difficult, every effort by the enemy to retake the lost ground was frustrated. The Canadians, disposed in depth and taking cover in shell-holes, suffered very few casualties. From 5.30 p.m. the shelling became intense, and at 6.45 p.m. the S.O.S. signals went up along the whole Canadian Corps

---

[1] The *11th Division* held the front opposite the two Canadian divisions, with the *44th Reserve Division* in close reserve. The *11th* had arrived from Champagne on the 3rd, and taken over the sector during the night of the 5th/6th from the *39th Division*.

[2] Corporal C. Barron (3rd Battalion) was awarded the V.C. for his bravery and determination in rushing 4 enemy machine guns single-handed which were holding up the advance. His action enabled the advance of the battalion to be continued.

front. German patrols were seen, but no attack developed, and by 7.30 p.m. the front was comparatively quiet.

During the next three days preparations for a further advance, by the 1st Canadian Division only, were in hand, and no incidents of importance occurred except that on the 8th November General Plumer handed over the command of the Second Army to General Sir Henry Rawlinson, and left next day to take over command of the British forces in Italy.

The Attack on the 10th November

On the 10th, the 1st Canadian Division extended its hold northwards for another five hundred yards along the main ridge east of the highway; the 2nd Canadian Division and the 1st (British) Division (II Corps) on the left were made responsible for flank protection. The attack was made at 6.45 a.m. in a rainstorm by the 2nd Canadian Brigade, with its 7th (British Columbia) and 8th (90th Rifles) Battalions, supported by the 20th (Central Ontario) Battalion (4th Brigade, 2nd Canadian Division) on the right, and the objective was gained by 7.45 a.m. Despite the fact that the Germans were again able to concentrate their artillery on the narrow attack frontage, the gains were held against a series of counter-attacks, and the Canadian main line of resistance was consolidated, in a precarious salient astride the main ridge, but with advanced outpost groups in shell-holes and short lengths of trench on the eastern slope of the ridge, so disposed as to give the enemy's artillery no good target. This was the line handed over to the VIII Corps when the Canadian Corps returned to the Lens–Avion–Mericourt front. Rain continued to fall heavily during the day, and a note in the records of the Australian Corps pays a fine tribute to the Canadian battalions: " The " night had been vile, and the day too. If the Canadians " can hold on they are wonderful troops ".[1] They did hold on; although, on the northern flank, the II Corps was unable to maintain its gain on the main ridge north of the Goudberg re-entrant.

In the II Corps sector the 1st Division reached the crest of the main ridge north of Goudberg, on the left of the Canadians, with both its leading battalions. The right

---
[1] A.O.A. iv., p. 935.

battalion, the 1/South Wales Borderers, had, however, veered off to the right, leaving a considerable gap; and when, soon after 7 a.m., the Germans counter-attacked, they penetrated at this gap before the situation could be rectified. The majority of the left battalion, the 2/R. Munster Fusiliers, were cut off: of the 17 officers who took part only 4 returned; and four hundred other ranks were killed, wounded or missing. By 1 p.m. the Borderers, after heavy casualties amounting to 10 officers and 374 other ranks, had been forced to withdraw their exposed flank from Goudberg Copse to the starting line.

The capture and retention of the Passchendaele high ground reflects the high standard of the staff work and training of the Canadian Corps and its four divisions. Once again, as at Vimy Ridge and on Hill 70 earlier in the year, the tenacity and endurance of Canada's splendid contribution to the British Imperial Forces were manifest.[1]

The impression made on Ludendorff by the attacks of the Second Army is shown in his *Memoirs*. Writing of this period, he says that " on the 26th and 30th October and " again on the 6th November the fighting was of the severest " nature. The British charged like a wild bull against the " iron wall which kept them from the submarine bases. They " threw their weight against positions along the entire front " —obviously, he had been deceived by the diversion attacks.

END OF THE BATTLES OF YPRES 1917

The intention to complete the capture of the main ridge northwards to Westroosebeke as a winter position could

---

[1] The total casualties suffered by the Canadian Corps during these actions in the period 26th October–11th November were:

	Killed		Wounded		Taken Prisoner		Gas Fatal		Gas Non-Fatal		Totals	
	Off.	O.R.	Off.	O.R.	Off.	O.R.	Off.	O.R.	Off.	O.R.	Off.	O.R.
1st Canadian Division	42	871	63	1,746	–	5	1	6	10	242	116	2,870
2nd ,, ,,	34	924	71	1,715	2	3	–	6	6	201	113	2,849
3rd ,, ,,	58	1,171	88	1,964	–	3	–	2	16	229	162	3,369
4th ,, ,,	36	792	70	1,679	–	9	–	3	8	353	114	2,836
Canadian C'ps Troops	6	94	9	298	–	–	–	1	1	86	16	479
TOTALS	176	3,852	301	7,402	2	20	1	18	41	1,111	521	12,403

not be put into effect. On the 9th, the II Corps artillery headquarters asked for a pause of ten days, till the 19th, so that it could advance its field batteries another thousand yards, east of the Winnipeg–Langemarck road, before the next attack; and then other factors intervened. The despatch of five British divisions, under General Plumer, to the Italian front, with the prospect of at least three more following them, had greatly crippled the British Armies in France, which never, at any time, had adequate reserves. Sir Douglas Haig's proposal to use these divisions to strengthen the blow he intended to deliver at Cambrai, on the ground that a notable success on the Western Front would at once ease the Italian situation, was not accepted by the War Cabinet. In addition to the departure of these five divisions, the four divisions of the Fourth Army in the coastal sector, relieved by the French, were, by arrangement between the two Governments, to take over forty miles of the French front on the British right, south of the Somme, and, therefore, were also lost to the British offensive effort.[1]

As the operations near Cambrai were due to start in a few days, Sir Douglas Haig decided on the 20th, in the circumstances, to close down the Flanders campaign. It had served its purpose. On the 14th, the Fifth Army front was handed over to the Fourth (formerly the Second) Army, Fifth Army headquarters being withdrawn into G.H.Q. reserve.

Casualties of Both Belligerents

The total battle and trench wastage casualties in the Second and Fifth Armies for the period of the "Third "Battle of Ypres", 31st July–10th November, 1917, were, as rendered week by week at the time, 238,313.[2] Except in the case of the report of one Army for one week, this total includes "Missing" (of whom there were 29,036), some of whom subsequently returned. The figures submitted to the

---

[1] See "1918" Vol. I, p. 47. This was the front attacked by the Germans on 21st March 1918.

[2] Details are given in a Note at end of Chapter. The infantry casualties in the various battles only amount to 170,534 all ranks (A.G.'s Returns). The balance, 67,779, is made up by the other arms and the trench wastage in the periods between the battles.

CASUALTIES 361

Supreme War Council on the 25th February, 1918, by the British Section of the Military Representatives were:

31st July–3rd October	138,787
4th October–12th November	106,110
Total	244,897[1]

This total includes normal wastage. For the Battles of the Somme 1st July–18th November, 1916, the unadjusted casualties were 419,654.[2]

The British losses in the period were increased by the deliberate shelling and bombing of casualty clearing stations and other medical establishments behind the front, though duly marked by the Red Cross.[3] It must also be borne in mind, in considering the human casualties, that according to the Medical History thousands of lightly wounded men were included in the totals, and that 64 per cent. of the total wounded returned to duty at the front and 18 per cent. to the Lines of Communication, garrison or sedentary occupations, total 82 per cent.[4] In the German Army in 1914–15, 75 per cent. of the wounded rejoined; in later years, the percentage (not given) was not so large.[5]

In spite of the very adverse weather and ground conditions, there was very little sickness in Flanders. The Medical History states:[6]

"The sickness during the battles [of Ypres 1917] was "comparatively slight. Most of the patients were treated "in divisional or corps rest stations, although an average "of 0.3 to 1.0 per cent. of strength had to be evacuated to "the base". The sick rate in France and Flanders in 1917 was less than in any year of the War except 1916, when ground conditions were worse: the daily percentage sick

---

[1] The clerk-power to investigate the exact losses was not available. It will be recalled that on the first day of the Battles of the Somme, the total casualties originally reported were 61,816, with 17,758 missing. Later investigation—requiring 6 months for a single day—reduced these figures to 57,470, with 2,152 missing and 585 prisoners of war. (See "1916" Vol. I, p. 483.)
[2] See "1916" Vol. I, p. 497.
[3] A list of those bombed is given in "Medical History", General, Vol. III, pp. 163–4.
[4] "Medical History", Casualties & Medical Statistics, p. 20.
[5] Sanitätsbericht ii., pp. 178–9.
[6] "Medical History", General, Vol. III, p. 171.

off the strength was, in 1914, 0.26; in 1915, 0.24; in 1916, 0.13; in 1917, 0.15; and in 1918, 0.16.[1]

Let us now turn to the enemy's side.

The German losses have never been divulged. They must be conjectured. The official Bavarian History of the War, published in 1921,[2] puts the British losses on the Flanders battlefield at 400,000; and these figures have subsequently appeared in all German books.[3] In 1916 the German wireless announced the British casualties on the Somme (419,654) as 600,000, which were nearly the figures (582,919) of the losses of the Germans. Suspicion is therefore raised that their losses in Flanders were the 400,000 at which they assess the British, the more so that this very figure has been arrived at by statistical enquiry, the elements of which are indicated below.

The nearest approach to a confession of heavy losses is in the history written by General von Kuhl,[4] who was Chief of the General Staff on the Flanders Front. He speaks of the campaign as " the greatest martyrdom of the World War. " No division could stick it out in this hell for more than " fourteen days. It must then be relieved. . . . Foot and " bowel complaints ravaged the troops ". It is common knowledge that no German division was relieved until it had lost half or more of its initial strength.

The German monograph divulges that on the 3rd August the *2nd Guard Reserve Division* " had a strength of 2,208, " of whom six hundred were sick. Significant signs of stress " were manifest in other divisions: the *38th Division* " requested relief, as it had lost two-thirds of its strength ".[5]

---

[1] " Medical History," Casualties & Medical Statistics, p. 59.
[2] B.O.A., p. 410.
[3] Also in some English books, including the late Earl Lloyd George's Memoirs (iv. p. 2233), with such erroneous statements as " the losses " finally exceeded even the terrible losses on the Somme ".
[4] Kuhl ii., pp. 113–5.
[5] On the subject of wastage Kuhl (ii., pp. 113–15) says :
" During the period 15th June–15th December 1917, 77 divisions were " transported to the *Fourth Army* front [from the Lille–Armentières road " to the Belgian coast], and 63 transferred from it. . . . From the begin- " ning of the battle on the 31st July to the 20th August, that is in the " first three weeks, 17 divisions were used up (*verbraucht*) ", and he adds that, by the end of November, " the average strength of battalions on the " Western Front was about 640 men, and all reinforcements have been " used up except the 1899 Class of 18-year olds, and recovered wounded " sent to the front ". *Continued at foot of next page*

CASUALTIES

The German Official Account puts the losses of the *Fourth Army* from 21st July to 31st December at " 217,000 " in round numbers, of whom 35,000 were killed and 48,000 " missing "[1]—the British took 26,631 prisoners. For comparison with British statistics the total would be about 289,000 ; but this is by no means all, for several divisions rendered their returns after they had left the *Fourth Army*, and others belonging to the Rupprecht Group of Armies, but not to the *Fourth Army*, were engaged.

The establishment of a German division in 1917 was about 12,000 ;[2] taking an average loss of 4,000 before relief, that is only one-third of the divisional establishment, or one-half the infantry and machine-gunners, and assuming that reinforcements balanced the wastage by sickness, one has 88 divisions multiplied by 4,000 = 352,000, from which the losses in the period 15th June–30th July, say 15,000, should be deducted, which leaves 337,000, without any addition for the 11th–15th November.

Approaching the subject on the datum that the average strength of the infantry battalions was down at the end of November to 640, the reduction in infantry alone comes to 285,120. Allowing 100 men reinforcements per battalion, the loss of the infantry alone comes to 364,320. There seems every probability that the Germans lost about 400,000.

The general result of the battles is discussed in the next chapter.

Continued from previous page.
Crown Prince Rupprecht in his Order of the Day at the end of the battle, says that " 88 divisions [? 77 fresh and the original garrison] were " engaged, 22 of them twice ".

[1] G.O.A. xiii, p. 96. A footnote gives the losses by 10-day periods, the largest total is for 1st–10th October, and is 35,000. These tri-monthly returns sent to O.H.L. do not include " wounded whose recovery was to " be expected within a reasonable time " ; for these, as already pointed out, at least 30 per cent. must be added.

[2] The establishment of a British division in 1918, after the infantry battalions had been reduced from 12 to 9, was 16,035.

NOTE

THE BATTLES OF YPRES 1917

Total Battle and Trench Wastage by Weeks in the Fifth and Second Armies
31st July–10th November

(Extracted from the Summaries of Operations Furnished Weekly to G.H.Q. by these Armies)

FIFTH ARMY.

Week Ended.	Officers. Killed.	Officers. Wounded.	Officers. Missing.	Officers. Total.	Other Ranks. Killed.	Other Ranks. Wounded.	Other Ranks. Missing.	Other Ranks. Total.	Grand Total.
3rd Aug.	298	1,154	64	1,516	2,633	12,637	2,893	18,163	19,679
10th ,,	154	544	27	725	3,087	14,606	3,405	21,098	21,823
(1) 17th ,,	74	441	35	550	1,177	7,980	854	10,011	10,561
24th ,,	125	568	41	734	1,971	11,835	2,397	16,203	16,937
(2) 31st ,,	68	255	33	356	1,178	6,558	1,456	9,192	9,548
(3) 7th Sept.	12	89	—	101	287	1,861	49	2,197	2,298
14th ,,	17	144	5	166	507	3,742	212	4,461	4,627
21st ,,	18	120	1	139	438	2,373	260	3,071	3,210
(4) 28th ,,	105	364	15	484	1,319	7,980	862	10,161	10,645
(5) 5th Oct.	20	162	4	186	538	2,490	91	3,119	3,305
12th ,,	65	220	6	291	839	4,348	480	5,667	5,958
20th ,,	105	311	20	436	1,395	6,595	1,472	9,462	9,898
26th ,,	23	178	3	204	557	3,649	314	4,520	4,724
2nd Nov.	59	283	7	349	1,044	5,111	1,431	7,586	7,935
9th ,,	10	65	—	75	133	1,336	16	1,485	1,560
Total	1,153	4,898	261	6,312	17,103	93,101	16,192	126,396	132,708

SECOND ARMY.

2nd Aug.	53	151	16	220	716	3,499	414	4,629	4,849
9th ,,	26	80	6	112	487	2,076	570	3,133	3,245
16th ,,	7	53	1	61	240	1,124	14	1,378	1,439
23rd ,,	12	49	1	62	235	985	17	1,237	1,299
30th ,,	2	29	2	33	61	380	8	449	482
6th Sept.	7	54	—	61	117	573	26	716	777
13th ,,	13	77	—	90	200	1,211	37	1,448	1,538
20th ,,	30	117	1	148	451	2,369	66	2,886	3,034
27th ,,	148	605	7	760	2,090	9,083	2,173	13,346	14,106
4th Oct.	122	493	32	647	1,930	8,464	1,215	11,609	12,256
(⁵) 12th ,,	81	262	11	354	1,621	6,128	1,368	9,117	9,471
19th ,,	207	536	51	794	3,855	14,833	3,295	21,983	22,777
26th ,,	68	301	10	379	1,308	6,119	663	8,090	8,469
2nd Nov.	114	344	31	489	1,606	7,736	1,615	10,957	11,446
10th ,,	75	349	22	446	1,693	6,915	1,363	9,971	10,417
Total	965	3,500	191	4,656	16,610	71,495	12,844	100,949	105,605

FIFTH AND SECOND ARMIES TOTAL.

| Total | 2,118 | 8,398 | 452 | 10,968 | 33,713 | 164,596 | 29,036 | 227,345 | 238,313 |

(1) Add additional casualties for 16-8-1917—Officers, 253 ; O.Rs., 5,242, not detailed.
(2) Estimated casualties during operations—Officers, 94 ; O.Rs., 2,840, some of which may be included in W./E. 31-8-17.
(3) In addition estimated casualties for 6-9-1917—Officers, 16 ; O.Rs., 395.
(4) Does not include casualties for 20-9-1917.
(5) Includes casualties for 20-9-1917.
(6) Eighty-six accounted for as rejoined, killed or wounded, not missing.

CHAPTER XIX

RETROSPECT

THE GENERAL RESULT

No great victory had been won; it was—to use a German distinction—an ordinary, not an annihilating victory; but it resulted in the Allies being in possession of the crest of the Ypres Ridge[1] from Messines via Wytschaete and Gheluvelt plateau to beyond Passchendaele, and had ensured the security of the French Armies whose front, in spite of their very serious internal troubles, was intact and whose morale had been raised by the successes at Verdun and Malmaison. The Flemish coast, however, was still in possession of the enemy.

To achieve this gain of ground and to keep the German hosts on the Western Front fully employed, the British losses incurred had been heavy and the misery endured by the troops very great. Was what had been achieved worth the cost? Our Allies and our foe have no doubt whatever about it.

A theory has obtained circulation that had it not been for the exhaustion of the British Armies in the " Passchen-" daele " operations, the German onslaught of the 21st March 1918 would never have succeeded to the extent that it did. The Germans, however, as indicated in the Preface, take the opposite view; they believe that complete success would have been theirs in the spring of 1918 had it not been for the exhaustion, practically the destruction, of their best divisions in Flanders. In the words of one of them the fighting had resulted in " the gradual disappearance of infantry equal in " quality to that of their opponents, and the tragic feeling " of inferiority to the artillery and air forces of their " opponents ".[2] Perhaps what was of more importance the trained German reserves had almost totally disappeared; so that sick men and half-trained lads of 18 and under had to be thrust into both the war-hardened divisions already in

---

[1] See Map 1.
[2] Bath, p. 177.

FLANDERS 1917 367

France and into the less experienced and less sternly disciplined divisions brought to France from the Russian front. For the British retirement in March 1918 cogent reasons other than the alleged moral and physical exhaustion in 1917 have been adduced;[1] for instance the lack of reinforcements, of which there were plenty in England ; the forced reduction of infantry brigades from 4 to 3 battalions by order from London ; the absence, from paucity of divisions, of a G.H.Q. or central reserve ; and, in spite of insufficient troops, the compulsory taking over of 30 miles of the French front by order of the War Cabinet, so that a weak British Fifth Army had to meet, at short notice and in a singularly poorly developed French system of trenches, a desperate German assault, a gambler's attempt to finish the war by one colossal stroke.

After every campaign it can be argued that if something else had been done, or something not done, the result might have been different. In the present case it might be argued that had General Plumer's successful advances—called by the names of Menin Road, Polygon Wood and Broodseinde, on the 20th and 26th September and 4th October respectively —been begun on the 31st July, nearly two months earlier, Sir Douglas Haig's plan might have brought complete success, and the Flanders coast would have been cleared. In that July, however, the Germans were fresh, which they were not at the end of September, and had ample reserves, which they had not at the end of September, and we do not know what their reaction would have been ; they might have allowed General Gough to thrust well into their position and, as was actually suggested, might have " enticed the enemy " [British] into a trap and then struck a mighty and deadly " blow from both flanks ", or driven him up against the coast and into the sea.[2] Here therefore what might have been will not further be considered, but the main elements of the problem will be set forth and certain criticisms discussed.

THE DECISION TO UNDERTAKE AN OFFENSIVE
AFTER THE NIVELLE FAILURE

Although the Nivelle offensive on the Aisne failed to achieve the decisive results promised and expected of it,

---
[1] See " 1918 ", Vol. I and the Sketch opposite its page 1.
[2] Bath, p. 180.

and came to an end on the 20th April, and although the British Arras battle, undertaken as a diversion to assist the French, was obviously approaching stalemate about that date, the French and British Governments were in full accord that the initiative must not be allowed to pass into the hands of the enemy. At the Conference in Paris, 4th/5th May, on the conduct of operations, it was decided by the two Governments, with the full agreement of the military commanders, to continue the Aisne and Arras offensives as far as possible, and to carry out the northern offensive (that is the Flanders operation). The British actually had this last—the Messines operation, the preliminary step—in preparation since early 1916 as an alternative to the Battle of the Somme ;[1] but from lack of labour the preparations on the Ypres front were far from complete.

The British Prime Minister was foremost in demanding that "the enemy must not be left in peace for one "moment. . . . We must go on hitting and hitting with all "our strength until the Germans end, as they always do, "by cracking ". Among the conclusions of the Conference were : "it is indispensable to continue offensive operations "on the Western Front. . . . A purely defensive attitude "would be the gravest imprudence ".[2]

It was specifically added, "the methods to be adopted "and put into practice, the choice of time and place of the "different attacks are the business [*ressort* in the French "text] of the responsible generals, and these latter must "from this moment examine and find solutions for these "questions ".

THE CHOICE OF FLANDERS

Sir Douglas Haig from the moment of assuming the chief command of the British Armies in France and Flanders in December 1915 had been in favour of attacking in Flanders, causing General Joffre to say of the British, "operations "dans le région d'Ypres qui semble toujours leur tenir en "cœur ". Haig fought on the Somme only in deference to the wishes of General Joffre, who desired that the British

---

[1] See " 1916 " Vol. I, pp. 21, 31–3.
[2] Procès verbal of the Allied Conference in Paris, 4th and 5th May 1917. Great Britain was represented by Mr. Lloyd George, Lord Robert Cecil, Admiral Jellicoe, Sir Douglas Haig, Sir William Robertson, Major-General F. Maurice (Operations).

should make their effort alongside his army. Indeed, Joffre's sole reason for attacking where he did was that the two Allied contingents should attack side by side. As if to reinforce the British Commander-in-Chief's views, on the 23rd November, 1916, Mr. Asquith, then Prime Minister, handed to him a typewritten letter, in which it was said: " There is no operation of war to which the War Committee " would attach greater importance than the successful " occupation, or at least the deprivation to the enemy, of " Ostend, and especially Zeebrugge ".

Joffre's two attempts in 1915 to cut off the German salient in France by attacking on both sides of it, in Champagne and near Arras, had achieved nothing; in 1916 the Germans had been unable to break in at Verdun; the Allies on the Somme had gained little ground, but had done so much to wear down and exhaust their enemy, that rather than face another such battle the German High Command had given up a large extent of territory, and had decided to stand on the defensive and trust to unrestricted U-boat warfare to finish the war. For the moment, defence seemed harder to overcome than offence.

Strategically the northern sector was the best place for the Allies to attack. It was there that the enemy's most dangerous U-boat bases were situated, and he would not drop back without a struggle. The outer flank would be protected by the neutral territory of Holland, and if penetration of the enemy's front were accomplished, the rest of his line might be rolled up southwards. Anywhere else—except on the French right wing near Switzerland, where both sides regarded the ground as impossible under existing conditions of armament—a success must at first produce a salient, vulnerable on both sides, the perils of which were obvious and were to be clearly exhibited in 1918.[1]

The Germans were fully aware of the danger in the north and, besides the normal front garrison and reserve, kept a cavalry division and 2 divisions (sometimes as many as 5) near the Dutch frontier under General von Moser[2] to deal with a possible landing in that quarter, and, as has been

---

[1] Much of the original Cambrai salient was lost to counter-attacks in 1917, and what remained had to be abandoned by the British, after most of its garrison had been gassed (see " 1918 " Vol. I, pp. 249, 303, 304); the enemy in succession had to evacuate the Soissons salient, the Amiens salient, the Lys salient, and the St. Mihiel salient.

[2] See his " Aufzeichnungen ".

narrated, rushed large reinforcements to Flanders as soon as the Nivelle danger was over.

In 1917 Sir Douglas Haig would have preferred to make the Flanders offensive his first and principal task, and to begin operations early in the year;[1] but General Nivelle had other views and the British Commander-in-Chief was ordered to conform to them, after an attempt had been engineered at the Calais Conference of 26th February, 1917,[2] to make him completely the military subordinate of the Frenchman. General Nivelle recognized the importance of an advance in Flanders; but confident of the success of his Aisne plan wrote, as already mentioned, to Sir Douglas Haig[3] " it is " certain that the Belgian coast will fall into our hands as a " result of the retreat of the German Armies, [after their ex- ".pected defeat on the Aisne] and without attack. If, on the " contrary, our attacks fail, it will still be possible to carry " out *in fine weather* the operation projected in Flanders ". [The compiler's italics. Evidently General Nivelle did not expect heavy rains.]

After the failure of the Nivelle offensive the French proposed to organize " a Franco-Belgian Army of 12 divi- " sions, 6 of them French, with the mission to cover the left " of the offensive of the British in Flanders ", which was then sanctioned.[4]

The French Mutinies

The outbreak of " acts of collective indiscipline " in the French Armies put a totally different complexion on the situation. The French Government stated officially that their forces would not be able to co-operate in an offensive. General Pétain, who had succeeded Nivelle, sent first his Chief of Staff, General Debeney, on the 2nd June, and then went himself to tell Sir Douglas Haig, behind closed doors and without witnesses, as a military secret, of the deplorable state of the French Armies and of their inability to play any part in the year's operations, either offensive or defensive. Except for a matter of a few divisions, they would stand on the defensive " until the Americans and

---

[1] See " 1917 " Vol. I, pp. 20–22.
[2] See " 1917 " Vol. I, pp. 55–57.
[3] The whole letter translated is in " 1917 " Vol. I, Appendix 2.
[4] F.O.A. v. (ii.), p. 617.

"tanks arrived", and he begged that the British should continue to attack. He even threatened to "run out" if the French were attacked.[1] To secure that the enemy should not exploit this temporarily enfeebled condition of the French became the first and immediate purpose of the British Commander-in-Chief, and continued to be so until the end of the year.

Alternatives to Flanders

On the 8th June, that is after the report of the victory at Messines had come to hand, the newly formed Cabinet Committee on War Policy met to consider the future conduct of the war. They were not told of the desperate state of the French army, but were aware that our Ally could not co-operate in any great offensive, and that little American help would be forthcoming in 1917. They examined Sir Douglas Haig's plans, and heard the statement of the First Sea Lord who "insisted on the clearing of the Belgian "coast as a vital necessity",[2] and who said, as before mentioned, that "if the army cannot get the Belgian ports, "the Navy cannot hold the Channel and the war is as good "as lost". The Committee came to no decision at the time, being inclined to leave the responsibility for decision to the military authorities; but six weeks later on the 21st July, only 10 days before the British offensive was due to start, they gave formal approval to the Commander-in-Chief's plan and promised full support.

Alternatives to Flanders were of course considered. Proposals to leave the Western Front on the defensive until the American army should be ready, and take action to

---

[1] A few months later, in March 1918, he had to be prevented from "running out" by the appointment of General Foch. See "1918" Vol. I, pp. 450 and 539.

Marshal of the Royal Air Force Viscount Trenchard, at the time Commander of the Royal Flying Corps in France, was one of the few foreign witnesses of what he calls "the awful demoralization of the French army "and people". He was quartered behind the French Aisne front at various times in the summer of 1917 for reconnaissances in connection with the establishment of a base for an independent air force in an eastern area, and saw soldiers and civilians alike, continually streaming back southwards along all the roads in fear of a German attack. His car was held up six hours in a village, the road being completely blocked by a rabble of soldiers and refugees with their belongings.

[2] These words occur in a report of the Secretary of the War Cabinet.

knock out Turkey or Austria were made. Not many divisions nor much material could be spared from France, even if a strict defensive were imposed; sufficient shipping was not available; the theatres in which Turkey could be effectively attacked, the Balkans, Asia Minor and Palestine, entailed long sea communications, and it was not by the capture of Jerusalem, or even the occupation of Constantinople, that the Germans were to be defeated. Austria, except for a narrow coastal strip leading to Trieste, could be got at only by crossing the Alps and their south-eastern outlyers. All these theatres, too, were rugged in their features and poor in railways and roads. Besides, the past operations at Gallipoli and Salonika, and the Italian 2-years' struggle on the rocks of the Carso and Bainsizza, did not offer an encouraging prospect. And to weaken the Western Front in the then state of the French Armies would be to invite what would now be called a gigantic " Dunkirk ".

The proposal to reinforce the Italians looked the most hopeful; but the Chief of the Imperial General Staff pointed out that a British contingent if sent to Italy, must be interpolated among Italian troops and would come under the command of General Cadorna, of whom few held a high opinion, and who, in four months' time, to justify Robertson's objection, was to suffer at Caporetto one of the greatest defeats in history. Nothing more, therefore, was then said about a campaign against Austria, but it was settled that Salonika, Palestine and Mesopotamia were to be kept alive.

On the Western Front, where the British frontage extended from the French left near St. Quentin to the Belgian right at Boesinghe, a little north of Ypres, the choice of a front of attack was small. Various sectors: the Somme (with a devastated area), Arras, and Loos (Lens) all south of the La Bassée canal, had been tried. North of the canal lay the flat, waterlogged district between the Deule and the Lys, the site of a large ancient lake, the scene of the disappointing engagements of Festubert, Neuve Chapelle and Aubers. Beyond were Messines and the Flanders sector, the strategic advantages of which have been mentioned, and which, being on the extreme northern wing, was the most difficult for the enemy to reinforce. The selection of this sector seems obvious.

THE NATURE OF THE GROUND AND NORMAL WEATHER CONDITIONS IN FLANDERS[1]

The ground—the Ypres Ridge at any rate, and even beyond—was not unknown to Sir Douglas Haig and to many British officers. In October 1914 the 7th Division and 3rd Cavalry Division, falling back on Ypres from the east after landing at Ostend and Zeebrugge, had passed all over it and had stood on the ridge at Passchendaele; the 2nd Division, coming from the Aisne, had been on the ridge at Broodseïnde. The First Battle of Ypres which followed left no impression of special muddy conditions. In that year, 1914, the autumn weather had been propitious, and in 1915 and 1916 there was no unusual weather in the Ypres Salient; in 1915 bad weather is not mentioned until the 5th October, when, at the battle of Loos, operations had temporarily to cease: for " owing to the state of the ground " any forward movement would be impossible for several " days ";[2] but by the 13th the weather was bright and sunny again. Similarly at the Somme in 1916, already referred to, it was not until 11 a.m. on the 2nd October that autumn rain set in, and not until the 4th that " heavy " rain now compelled a postponement of the operation ".[3]

Were the nature of the ground and the weather to be expected in August and the following month such as to make successful operations in Flanders out of the question? The answer is in the negative, supported by the fact that really serious difficulty did not supervene until the early part of October, although, before that date, rain, as in most of the 1915–18 battles, did cause temporary postponements, and led General Gough to suggest that operations should be stopped; but there was a difference between the August rains and the October rains: the former dried up fairly quickly, but the latter soaked the ground, and it remained soaked.

---

[1] Besides what has been said in this volume, particularly about the patchy condition of the ground surface, a description of Flanders will be found in " 1914 " Vol. II, p. 74, *et seq.*, and of the country around Ypres on p. 128 *et seq.* One sentence only need be quoted:

" One of the remarkable features of all parts of Flanders is the sub-
" surface water, which, always fairly high, rises considerably as autumn
" progresses: any excavation or depression, whether natural feature,
" ditch, trench or crater, soon fills with water, and its sides then fall in ;
" whilst the surface of the ground is rapidly churned by traffic into the
consistency of cream cheese ".

[2] " 1915 " Vol. II, p. 371.

[3] " 1916 " Vol. II, pp. 432–3.

In March 1935 the opinions—of which the compiler had been contemporaneously aware—were obtained in writing from 51 of the Chief Engineers of Armies and corps and of the C.R.Es. of divisions engaged. They may be summed up in the words of the Chief Engineer of the Second Army: " there was no trouble at all [with communications] until " about the 5th October ". Some of the others put the date as " after the 4th October "; others—varying with the sector in which they were employed—make it after the 7th, the 9th and even the 12th. That last day happens to be the date fixed by Crown Prince Rupprecht of Bavaria, commanding on the other side, who records in his diary, " Rain. Our best ally ". Perhaps the most interesting statement is from the C.R.E. of the XIV Corps,[1] on the left, notoriously the worst sector. He wrote: " I never saw " anything to make me consider communications really bad " and any of our attacks inadvisable ". The final success of the Canadians at the end of October substantiates this opinion.

The artillery records are equally conclusive. According to them it was not until October that conditions became really difficult and resort had to be had to pack animals to carry up ammunition—as it had at the Somme in the same month, October, of the previous year. The following extract is made from a typescript " History of the Develop- " ment of the British Artillery in France 1914–1918, " Compiled from Records in the Office of the Major-General " Royal Artillery, G.H.Q. ", by the late Lieut.-Colonel S. W. H. Rawlins, who was chief of the staff to the Major-General R.A., Sir Noel Birch:

> " Meanwhile, since early in October, Napoleon's
> " ' fifth element '—mud—had become a factor of the
> " gravest importance. Even August had been un-
> " usually wet, and since then the ground, always water-
> " logged and now thoroughly cut up, had steadily got
> " worse and worse. The mere movement of artillery
> " and supply of ammunition under peace conditions
> " would have been a herculean task; it was scarcely
> " possible to walk off the duckboards. All ammunition
> " supply to the more advanced batteries was perforce

---

[1] A most dependable officer. He was in January 1918 promoted and brought to G.H.Q. as one of the two Deputy Engineers-in-Chief.

"carried out by packing, mules were constantly
"engulfed, and even guns in considerable numbers
"were swallowed up in the sea of mud ".[1]

The French Official History, likewise, mentions no difficulties on account of mud or rain until the 12th October, and then in connection with the passage of the lower Steenbeek; but it adds that this was effected " convenable-
"ment ". On the 26th October, it has " the last operation
"of the autumn suffered from touches (atteintes) of bad
"weather; the sector is a sea of mud, and supplies come up
"irregularly by the cut-up roads, and have to be carried on
"men's backs ".[2]

It was late in October, not in August, that General Foch said " la boue is bad, and le Boche is bad—but the two
"together . . ."[3]

The Mud

Several eminent civilian critics with the ear of the public have spread the mud legend, and maintained that on account of the mud Sir Douglas Haig should never have initiated a campaign in Flanders at all, and should certainly have stopped operations in August.

Mud there certainly was most of the time, but not of the degree to justify calling Third Ypres " The Campaign of
" the Mud ".[4] Even to call it "A Campaign in the Mud " would be little more than to call it an autumn campaign. Whenever great armies carry on operations in European autumns and winters, or in tropical rainy seasons, be it in Flanders, Holland, Poland (Napoleon fought the Pultusk campaign in spite of the " fifth element "), Spain (" les
" infâmes boues de l'Espagne ", said Napoleon), Italy (in 1944), Burma, or Virginia (" have you been ' through '

---

[1] The brigade records confirm this. Only one brigade used packing before October, and then in August; on the other hand, one brigade did not use it until November.

It was not until 15th October that the ingenious Lieut.-Colonel Nissen (of the hut), then C.R.E., G.H.Q. Troops, was sent up to Ypres, to see how communications to the very front could be improved. He devised a mud punt, but it was not found necessary to employ any such device.

[2] F.O.A. v. (ii.), pp. 704 and 714.

[3] Charteris, p. 274; but according to Hanotaux, Tome 15, p. 239, the alliteration was " la pluie " and " les pillboxes ".

[4] The chapter heading in Earl Lloyd George's " War Memoirs " and the sub-title of his pamphlet.

376 FLANDERS 1917

" Virginia ? " was an army jest in 1861–65)—there is mud. Yet no one has blamed Marlborough, Napoleon, Grant, or the generals of 1939–45 for carrying on over soft ground and under adverse weather conditions. Flanders was not even the worst " pitch " on the Western Front, as legend would lead us to suppose : old hands would give the palm to Hulluch or Givenchy. The C.R.E. of the 56th Division has recorded : " Some accounts of the Passchendaele campaign " leave the impression that it rained continuously for weeks " and months, and that the terrain was a morass. This was " not my experience. I have been wetter and muddier on " the Somme in 1916, October especially. What is true, " I think, is that around Ypres the shell holes were more " numerous to the acre than on the Somme ". Another C.R.E., speaking of October, has pointed out that the whole battlefield was not devastated : " where ground had been " lost and won, or where the line had been static for, say, a " week, it was badly cut up, but between these zones, the " damage was not excessive ". The Australians, as their historian has shown,[1] considered the mud at the Somme worse than that at Passchendaele, as it truly was. He wrote :

> " In the interval [that is between the 12th and " 26th October] the conditions approximated to those " of the previous winter on the Somme, but with the " difference that the excellent position on Broodseinde " Ridge, the immense work on roads, railways and " duckboard tracks, and the employment of pack " transport almost up to the front line, rendered the " plight of the forward infantry, at least in the Anzac " sector, *far less trying* ".

He recalls the talk of the troops :[2]

> " on our way up the duckboards [on 9th October] " we met an officer . . . who said that the mud was " nearly as bad as Flers [where tanks were first used in " the Somme battle]. Murdoch asked if it were quite " as bad. He shook his head—' Oh, no—we've never " had anything as bad as that ' ".[3]

---

[1] A.O.A. iv., p. 930.
[2] A.O.A. iv., pp. 890–1.
[3] The following will be found in Lord Newton's " Retrospection ", p. 229. He was on an official visit to the Western Front as Controller of the Prisoners of War Department : " Nothing could exceed the depression
Continued at foot of next page.

The main difficulty in the last stage was getting ammunition to the guns, so that the heavy artillery, at least, had to keep close to the roads, and the guns were strung out one behind the other, in file, an easy target.

Reports and photographs clearly indicate that the mud in Holland in the winter of 1944–45 was far and away worse than any experienced in 1917 in Flanders—or at any time on the Western Front. As one officer has put it, in Holland there was "hard mud, soft mud, gravel mud, mud with "ice in it, and also the sort you can't say if it's mud or "dirty water". Clogs were found better than boots, but even they were sucked in.

As regards the conditions in Burma, the following appeared in *The Times* newspaper on the 1st December, 1945, in an appreciation of the Fourteenth Army:

> "None of them [other Armies] have had to face such "a combination of toils and hazards, such an alliance of "the pitilessness of nature with the ferocity of man as "the Army which followed General Slim. . . . It "encountered all the scourges that can make campaigning in the tropics a long agony: sweltering heat, "the almost unending length of the steaming monsoon "*rains*; jungles where the enemy might lurk at arm's "length away; that exhausting 'fifth element' of warfare, the *mud* of Arakan and Lower Burma".

And the campaign lasted as many years as Third Ypres lasted months.

The Continuation of the Battle in October After the Break in the Weather

By October order had been re-established in the French Armies, and in any case it was too late in the year for the Germans to carry out large scale and rapid operations against them. But Pétain continued his appeals, and

---

Continued from previous page.
" of the scene: a flat country, enveloped in fog and soaked in rain; prac-
" tically every house destroyed; trees without branches, and the ground
" so pitted with shell holes that there was sometimes barely standing room
" between them. Mud everywhere." The date is 3rd October, 1916, not 1917, and the locality is the Somme battlefield with an attack impending, not Flanders.

Reference should be made to "1916" Vol. II, pp. 444, 457, 536–8, where the appalling conditions on the Somme in October and November 1916 are described.

Plumer's successes had given Sir Douglas Haig hopes of a substantial victory which would clear the Belgian coast.

By his nature, he possessed exceptional persistence and tenacity; it had been dinned into him, too, at the Staff College that "the man who gives the last kick wins. . . . " Conditions on the enemy's side are often worse than your " own ". And he had studied Marlborough's campaigns in the Netherlands. He had not forgotten that the Duke had captured the fortress of Dendermonde in 1706, when the weather turned out to be much worse than expected and the watery conditions were terrible—Louis XIV had said " the English must have an army of ducks to take it ". Haig was well aware that in most of Marlborough's Low Country sieges the trenches were knee-deep in mud. In October 1706, when the Duke proposed to besiege Mons, the Dutch refused co-operation, as they said it was too late in the season and their troops would be ruined.[1] In 1707, that "most unprosperous" year, the Allied troops were kept in the field well into October. In 1708 (Oudenarde) the Duke carried on until December and January (Lille city surrendered 22nd October, the citadel on 9th December, Ghent capitulated 2nd January), a most extraordinary thing in those days (as improper as Wellington attacking Ciudad Rodrigo in January 1812, whereby he caught the French quite unprepared). In 1709 (Malplaquet, 11th September) operations were stopped early owing to bad weather, rain beginning at the end of August. But in 1710, after a struggle in the marshes of the Lys and the capture of St. Venant, which fell on the 29th September, the campaign went on despite heavy rains until the 8th November, when Aire surrendered. " Our poor men are up to their knees in " mud and water, a most grievous sight ", wrote the Duke.

To come to a recent date, just a year before, on the 13th November, 1916, the Fifth Army had fought at the Somme, in the mud, the very successful battle of Beaumont Hamel, after days of pouring rain.[2]

Well informed of the miserable conditions at the front, still, as the medical reports showed that sickness among the troops was "comparatively slight ", Sir Douglas Haig

---

[1] Atkinson's " Marlborough " (p. 303), from which the other information is also taken.
[2] See " 1916 " Vol. II, p. 480, second paragraph, *et seq.*

decided to carry on. He rightly gauged that the conditions on the enemy's side were much worse.[1]

Tanks

Was the Passchendaele sector " hopeless for tanks " and did the Staff of the Tank Corps protest and declare it to be " utterly unsuitable for tanks " ?   It will have been seen in the narrative that tanks co-operated successfully in the attacks made as late as the end of September. The late General Sir Hugh Elles, in 1917 commanding the Tank Corps, has recorded :

> " There was never any question of ' protest ', merely the expression of increasing misgiving. . . . After reconnaissances we reported that we could function if there was not intensive shelling. When the attack was postponed from the original date to the 31st July, I pointed out to the Fifth Army G.S. as strongly as I could that our chances fell with every shell fired. My official forecast on the 31st July was that we would get 50 per cent. of tanks to their objectives. In the event, we got 48 per cent. G.H.Q. and Fifth Army were perfectly frank upon the point that they regarded any success by tanks as a windfall [remember, they were the tanks of 1917]. Guns were the big thing [this, of course, was the German view, as proved on the 21st March, 1918], and tanks must take their chance. Every resource was to be put in, whether it pulled its weight or not ".

It was the shell craters rather than the mud which interfered with the tank, both in its travel to the front and its use in action.

On the 7th September Major-General Elles wrote to G.H.Q. :

> " The state of the ground is such that it will not be possible to use tanks until the line is advanced

---

[1] G.O.A. (xiii., p. 86) says that on 21st October the German *Fourth Army* reported that the troops could not carry on much longer in defence, owing to " the psychological impressions to which even the bravest troops are liable, and particularly the case with the infantry, which is exposed to continued enemy fire and the rigour of the weather in mud-filled shell craters, without its being possible to secure for it in any useful degree sufficient rest, as enemy attacks followed so quickly one after the other ".

"1,000–1,500 yards [that is clear of the shell-beaten zone].

"When this is done there will be considerable difficulties, unless the weather is exceptionally good, which will prevent the use of tanks in large masses.

"There is, therefore, no prospect of using tanks until the end of the month. They must then be used east and north of the line Broodseinde–Poelcappelle. This is dependent on amount of rain and shelling.

"At present there are 8 tank battalions in the Ypres forward area. Allowing a safe margin, 3 battalions only appear to be necessary for operations.

"I request I may be allowed to withdraw remaining 5 battalions from the forward area as soon as possible, in order that training may be continued.

"Reinforcements both in tanks and personnel are available to keep the 3 battalions up to strength, and additional battalions could be railed to the forward area in ample time should necessity arise.

"If this is approved [it was], I should be able to carry on training (most necessary), make arrangements and reconnaissances for the possible employment of tanks on other fronts, and prepare winter accommodation.

"As regards employment of tanks on fronts other than those of the Second and Fifth Armies, there are possibilities on both the First and Third Army fronts ".[1]

In the then pattern of the tanks, their slowness of movement even on good ground, their vulnerability, their poor gun-power (the " male " tank carried a 6-pdr. and the " female " tank only machine guns), and the general feeling that they attracted fire, and were in the way—the Australians said they would rather be without them[2]—there was no good reason to abandon the strategic advantages of the Flanders sector and relinquish a chance of freeing the Flanders coast in order to provide harder ground for the mass employment of tanks. In all their later employment

---

[1] Major-General Elles particularly favoured the Lens area ; but General Horne (First Army) declined to co-operate there unless his divisions—reduced to a minimum—could be reinforced ; and the tanks went to Cambrai.

[2] A.O.A. iv., p. 385. See also p. 274.

in 1917 and 1918 after Third Ypres their casualties were equally heavy with equally small, though very valuable, local successes sometimes in exchange.[1]

Liaison

The Commander-in-Chief spent most of his time visiting various headquarters, and he was throughout kept fully informed of the conditions at the front. As already pointed out, he had his own G.H.Q. liaison officers, and he utilized the staffs of the G.O.C. Royal Artillery and of the Engineer-in-Chief. These envoys did not minimize the state of the battlefield in October, and there was much plain speaking. Major-General J. H. Davidson (Operations, General Staff), in mid-October, after flying over the area, reported more water than ground. The senior staff officer of the G.O.C. Royal Artillery, Lieut-Colonel S. W. H. Rawlins, at the same date told Sir Douglas Haig plainly : " If this offensive goes on, there will be no artillery for the spring offensive." The R.E. representative told him that the duckboard tracks could be kept going, as they were difficult targets and easily repairable, but that the roads near the front could not be maintained, and that the cost in casualties was very heavy. Despite these conditions, the Canadians in October, as we have seen, fought their way to Passchendaele—with sufficient communications over the mud—so persistence was justified.

Tactics : Limited or Unlimited Objectives

In the autumn of 1917 the machine gun still ruled the battlefield, and ground observation for the artillery was all-important—the French would never attack unless the light and weather were favourable for ground and captive balloon observation. Such aircraft observation as could be provided was used for distant targets, not for spotting machine-gun nests and pillboxes, with which, if the barrage had not knocked them out, tanks were to deal. To capture ground which gave the enemy good observation, not only to the front, but also to the flank, was of the first importance.

---

[1] At Cambrai the sudden opening of the barrage for the infantry advance, without previous registration or preliminary bombardment, may have been quite as much a factor in the initial success as the tanks.

The outstanding value to the Germans of Gheluvelt plateau —which performed the function of a bastion and flanked the lateral valleys on either side—was well known, and frequently mentioned at the conferences preceding the battle ;[1] but it was not made the foremost objective by the Fifth Army in the opening phase of the battle. The assault on the first day was a general advance of equal strength on the whole front, in waves covered by a narrow belt of barrage in the Somme style, without reference to the features of the ground. Modern defences cannot, any more than those of old style fortresses with deep ditches and high parapets, be taken by the chests of the infantry.

Whether the advance should be by short bounds or unlimited was very fully discussed, and, as has been seen, the General Staff (Operations) made protest against any advance beyond the support of the artillery.[2] The method adopted must, of course, depend on the strength of the enemy's defences. In March 1918, against the thin line of Gough's Fifth Army without a single pillbox and without reserves, with the certainty that the French would not hurry to help the British,[3] Crown Prince Rupprecht ordered " a relentless advance as far as possible without a pause :[4] each unit and formation was to push on regardless of what was happening on its right and left : success, it was said, " would depend on the speed of the operations ". Against semi-permanent fortifications, perfected during a period of two and a half years, bristling with pillboxes, instead of high parapets, and guarded by belts of wire instead of deep ditches, practically siege operations were required. Given the wave formation employed and the German deep defence, near objectives covered by the ordinary barrage could generally be secured ; whether anything more was possible depended upon the enemy's attitude. It would naturally be a mistake to be content with a near objective if the enemy and the ground offered opportunities. The success at Messines had been wasted, Sir Douglas Haig considered, to the extent that advantage had not been taken of the

---

[1] See Chapter VIII.
[2] See pp. 128-9.
[3] See " 1918 " Vol. I, p. 145. The Chief of the Staff of the *Eighteenth Army* wrote in his appreciation : " It need not be anticipated that the " French will run themselves off their legs and hurry at once to the help " of their Entente comrades."
" 1918 " Vol. I, p. 150.

immense initial success of siege methods. But the one thing that the infantry generals were agreed upon was that any further advance must be made by fresh troops, leaving the original attackers to hold the trenches won and become the new reserve. This meant that there must be substantial reserves, and that they must be close up, conditions rarely possible.

Profiting by his knowledge of the ground and the insight obtained into the enemy's new methods, General Plumer improved on the procedure adopted at Messines; he adhered to short bounds, even shorter than at first discussed, and developed his offensive into a succession of them—as, indeed, the General Staff (Operations) had advised on the 25th June; and he attacked on a selected and tactically important part of his front only, and with a very deep barrage. Unfortunately the October rains interfered with the bringing forward of his artillery and after three successful bounds, the fourth, Poelcappelle, was a failure; but, narrowing his objective, in the subsequent two bounds, Passchendaele, on the top of the Ypres Ridge, was secured.

Relations of Haig and His Generals

Having settled on the general plan at conferences, and discussed and decided on general principles, Sir Douglas Haig seldom interfered with his Army commanders as regards methods or details of execution; indeed, he often gave way to them and their wishes in spite of his better judgment—notably, he yielded to General Gough as regards distant objectives and the neglect of Gheluvelt plateau; in the following March, General Byng was to resist G.H.Q. orders to evacuate the Cambrai salient before the German attack, and thus to incur unnecessary losses.[1] The Commander-in-Chief exercised his authority by personal visits rather than by written orders, the formal G.H.Q. operation orders merely recording what had been already settled. The one exception in the policy of non-interference was when he transferred from General Gough to General Plumer the principal rôle in the battle. On the other side, Ludendorff constantly and habitually interfered with Army and corps commanders, not always through their hierarchal

---

[1] See "1918" Vol. I, p. 249.

seniors, the commanders of the Groups of Armies—usually with disastrous results; for he had not the intimate knowledge of the ground and the situation possessed by men on the spot. Maréchal Foch, though he constantly visited the higher headquarters, did not interfere except to incite his subordinates to action: his words to General Maud'huy at Arras in September 1914 have passed into history: "There are three courses: retreat, stay where you are, "attack. I forbid the first, take your choice of the other "two". Knowledge of the character and talents of a subordinate is the only guide to the way he can be successfully handled.

Selection of General Gough for the Principal Command

General Hubert Gough, commander of the Fifth Army, was selected by Sir Douglas Haig to play the principal part:[1] he had been selected by him at the Somme to command the Reserve Army and lead the exploitation of the hoped-for success.[2] He was only 47 years old and much the youngest of the Army commanders. In August 1914 he was commanding the 3rd Cavalry Brigade, and had received rapid promotion, commanding a cavalry division, a division and a corps in swift succession, on the 22nd May, 1916, being advanced to an Army, which he commanded with judgment and discretion throughout the Battles of the Somme. He was a personal friend of the Commander-in-Chief and had all the qualities which might be expected to ensure that he would seize any chance to exploit a success if an opportunity occurred—many have said since what a pity it was that he was not in command of the cavalry at Cambrai. The Commander-in-Chief did not want a repetition of the loss of opportunity at Messines, a battle which General Gough himself called only "another big raid". His natural temperament, his cavalry training, his quickness of judgment and his impatience of delays and his drive—qualities which made the late General George Patton, U.S. Army, also a cavalryman, remarkable in 1944–45—caused Gough to be less suitable for the "siege operations in the field", which required long preparation

---
[1] See p. 19.
[2] See "1916" Vol. I, p. 267.

and usually made slow progress. It will be recalled that when he came to siege work in the Peninsula, the Duke of Wellington handed operations over to his artillery and engineer officers until they could inform him of a practicable breach. It must be held, in any case, that it was an error of judgment on the part of the Commander-in-Chief in the first instance to supersede General Plumer and his staff, who knew the ground—" every puddle " in the Ypres Salient, it was popularly said—by a general and a staff unacquainted with it. This change over was also the cause of the loss of precious time, as the Second Army's long thought-out plans and careful preparations did not suit General Gough's ideas, and thus considerable new work was involved. The Commander-in-Chief, however, realized his initial mistake, and at the end of August, set about handing the principal rôle in the Salient back to General Plumer, and eventually the Fifth Army was reduced to a single corps. This change of command, however, again led to loss of precious time, and, still worse, to the waste of the fine weather in September; for General Plumer required three weeks to make his preparations: that the pause led the Germans to think that the battle was over the British could not know. From the 16th August onwards, on account of the conditions of the ground, General Gough had urged that " tactical success " was not possible, or would be too costly under such " conditions, and advised that the attack should now be " abandoned ",[1] but he admits that Sir Douglas Haig's reasons for continuing on account of the general situation were " valid ".

Loss of Time Between Messines and "Third Ypres"

The unfortunate interval between the 14th June and the 31st July was not solely due to the change of Army commanders at Ypres. Time was required to shift artillery from the Messines and Lens areas northward—Sir Douglas Haig had never received the heavy artillery he had asked

---

[1] Gough, p. 205. In March 1918, when on the 28th it was obvious that a decisive victory could not be gained, some of Ludendorff's generals advised that the offensive should be stopped and a decision sought elsewhere. See Major-General Freiherr von Schoneich's " Die Front in den " Krisen des letzten Kriegsjahres ".

for, and had not enough for two offensives simultaneously, or even for an offensive and a colourable feint by guns elsewhere.[1]

The final postponements from the 25th July to the 28th and then to the 31st were due partly to the late arrival of much of the heavy artillery, and partly to the French, General Anthoine after various postponements asking for three days more in order to complete counter-battery work. The late consent of the War Cabinet did not affect the date.

The delays at the last moment resulted in the bombardment begun on the 16th lasting fifteen days, so that the ground was more cratered—that fatal obstruction to the tanks—than it need have been.

COMPARATIVE STRENGTH OF THE TWO OPPONENTS

It used to be reckoned in Germany that to turn out of a position an "*ebenbürtigen*" foe—that is a foe equal in all respects, courage, training, morale and equipment—required threefold numbers. Certainly in the battles of 1870, at Spicheren, at Colombey, at Mars la Tour, and Gravelotte, with about equal numbers, no tactical decision was obtained; in all the early battles against the French army the proportion of German infantry to French varied from 5 to 1 down to 2 to 1, and in artillery the Germans were immensely superior.

It has already been stated that in the July–August 1917 fighting, 26 French and British divisions were opposed by 37 German; in the whole period of the fighting in Flanders, 51 British and Dominion divisions and 6 French, total 57, drove back 88 German divisions (Crown Prince Rupprecht of Bavaria's figures). Nearly every British division was engaged; for in November 1917 there were on the Western Front under Sir Douglas Haig, in all only 50 British divisions,

---

[1] " In June 1916, as soon as the Ministry of Munitions was prepared to receive a new order, Sir Douglas Haig wrote home stating the " organiza-" tion that he was going to adopt and the amount of guns that he required " —and neither this proposed organization nor his demands were after-" wards altered. His demands were never fully met and it therefore took " him much longer than was expected to defeat the German artillery. " Until 1918 he was unable to demonstrate with his artillery at several " places along the line in order to deceive the enemy as to his real point " of attack, nor punish the German artillery to the extent he desired ". From a report prepared in 1919 by General Sir Noel Birch, as G.O.C. Royal Artillery.

4 Canadian, 5 Australian and 1 New Zealand, total 60, with 5 cavalry divisions and 2 Portuguese divisions not engaged at the front ; and he could not count on the support of more than 6 divisions of the French Armies.

The wonder is not that complete success was not achieved, but that so much was done by so few to break the spirit and reduce the numbers of the enemy. That any progress was made under such conditions and with such numerical inferiority was due to the unfailing staunchness and the infinite courage of the infantry, engineers and pioneers, and to the outstanding technical superiority of the French and British artillery. A nation cannot expect great and immediate victories unless it supplies the means, the men and the material.

SKELETON ORDER OF BATTLE[1]

SECOND ARMY

G.O.C.	General Sir Herbert Plumer
Major-General G.S.	Major-General C. H. Harington
D.A. & Q.M.G. ...	Major-General A. A. Chichester
M.G.R.A.	Major-General G. McK. Franks to 7th July, then Major-General C. R. Buckle
C.E.	Major-General F. M. Glubb

FIFTH ARMY

G.O.C.	General Sir Hubert Gough
Major-General G.S.	Major-General N. Malcolm
D.A. & Q.M.G. ...	Major-General H. N. Sargent
Major-General R.A.	Major-General H. C. C. Uniacke
C.E.	Major-General P. G. Grant

I Corps

G.O.C.	Lieut.-General Sir Arthur Holland
Br.-General G.S. ...	Br.-General G. V. Hordern
D.A. & Q.M.G. ...	Br.-General N. G. Anderson
Br.-General R.A. ...	Br.-General M. Peake (k. 27.8.17)
Br.-General H.A. ...	Br.-General A. Ellershaw
C.E.	Br.-General E. H. de V. Atkinson

II Corps

G.O.C.	Lieut.-General Sir Claud Jacob
Br.-General G.S. ...	Br.-General S. H. Wilson
D.A. & Q.M.G. ...	Br.-General R. S. May
Br.-General R.A. ...	Br.-General A. D. Kirby
Br.-General H.A. ...	Br.-General D. F. H. Logan
C.E.	Br.-General C. Godby

V Corps

G.O.C.	Lieut.-General Sir Edward Fanshawe
Br.-General G.S. ...	Br.-General G. F. Boyd
D.A. & Q.M.G. ...	Br.-General H. M. de F. Montgomery
Br.-General R.A. ...	Br.-General R. P. Benson
Br.-General H.A. ...	Br.-General A. M. Tyler
C.E.	Br.-General A. J. Craven

---

[1] The sketch maps show the corps in either Army and the divisions in any corps at the different periods of the campaigns.

IX Corps

G.O.C.	Lieut.-General Sir Alexander Gordon
Br.-General G.S. ...	Br.-General J. S. J. Percy
D.A. & Q.M.G. ...	Br.-General B. H. H. Cooke
Br.-General R.A. ...	Br.-General G. Humphreys
Br.-General H.A. ...	Br.-General G. B. Mackenzie
C.E.	Br.-General G. P. Scholfield

X Corps

G.O.C.	Lieut.-General Sir Thomas Morland
Br.-General G.S. ...	Br.-General A. R. Cameron
D.A. & Q.M.G. ...	Br.-General W. K. Legge
Br.-General R.A. ...	Br.-General H. L. Reed, V.C. to 11th October, then Br.-General G. Gillson
Br.-General H.A. ...	Br.-General H. O. Vincent
C.E.	Br.-General J. A. S. Tulloch

XIII Corps

G.O.C.	Lieut.-General Sir William McCracken
Br.-General G.S. ...	Br.-General I. Stewart
D.A. & Q.M.G. ...	Br.-General S. W. Robinson
Br.-General R.A. ...	Br.-General R. A. C. Wellesley
Br.-General H.A. ...	Br.-General L. W. P. East (k. 6.9.17)
C.E.	Br.-General E. P. Brooker

XIV Corps

G.O.C.	Lieut.-General Earl of Cavan
Br.-General G.S. ...	Br.-General Hon. J. F. Gathorne-Hardy
D.A. & Q.M.G. ...	Br.-General H. L. Alexander
Br.-General R.A. ...	Br.-General A. E. Wardrop
Br.-General H.A. ...	Br.-General F. G. Maunsell
C.E.	Br.-General C. S. Wilson

XV Corps

G.O.C.	Lieut.-General Sir John Du Cane
Br.-General G.S. ...	Br.-General H. H. S. Knox
D.A. & Q.M.G. ...	Br.-General G. R. Frith
Br.-General R.A. ...	Br.-General B. R. Kirwan
Br.-General H.A. ...	Br.-General C. W. Collingwood
C.E.	Br.-General C. W. Singer

XVIII Corps

G.O.C.	Lieut.-General Sir Ivor Maxse
Br.-General G.S.	Br.-General S. E. Hollond
D.A. & Q.M.G.	Br.-General P. M. Davies to 14th Aug., then
	Br.-General B. Atkinson (acting) to 8th Nov.
Br.-General R.A.	Br.-General D. J. M. Fasson
Br.-General H.A.	Br.-General H. E. J. Brake
C.E.	Br.-General H. G. Joly de Lotbinière

XIX Corps

G.O.C.	Lieut.-General H. E. Watts
Br.-General G.S.	Br.-General F. Lyon to 25th Sept., then
	Br.-General C. N. Macmullen
D.A. & Q.M.G.	Br.-General A. J. G. Moir
Br.-General R.A.	Br.-General W. B. R. Sandys
Br.-General H.A.	Br.-General C. G. Pritchard
C.E.	Br.-General A. G. Bremner

Canadian Corps

G.O.C.	Lieut.-General Sir Arthur Currie
Br.-General G.S.	Br.-General P. P. de B. Radcliffe
D.A. & Q.M.G.	Br.-General G. J. Farmar
Br.-General R.A.	Br.-General E. W. B. Morrison
Br.-General H.A.	Br.-General R. H. Massie
C.E.	Br.-General W. B. Lindsay

I Anzac Corps

G.O.C.	Lieut.-General Sir William Birdwood
Br.-General G.S.	Br.-General C. B. B. White
D.A. & Q.M.G.	Br.-General R. A. Carruthers
Br.-General R.A.	Br.-General W. J. Napier to 14th Oct., then
	Br.-General W. A. Coxen
Br.-General H.A.	Br.-General L. D. Fraser
C.E.	Br.-General A. C. Joly de Lotbinière

ORDER OF BATTLE

II Anzac Corps

G.O.C.	Lieut.-General Sir Alexander Godley
Br.-General G.S. ...	Br.-General C. W. Gwynn
D.A. & Q.M.G. ...	Br.-General A. E. Delavoye
Br.-General R.A. ...	Br.-General E. W. M. Powell
Br.-General H.A. ...	Br.-General A. S. Jenour
C.E.	Br.-General A. E. Panet

Guards Division (Major-General G. P. T. Feilding):
1 Gds., 2 Gds., 3 Gds. Brigades

1st Division (Major-General E. P. Strickland):
1, 2, 3 Brigades

3rd Division (Major-General C. J. Deverell):
8, 9, 76 Brigades

4th Division (Major-General T. G. Matheson):
10, 11, 12 Brigades

5th Division (Major-General R. B. Stephens):
13, 15, 95 Brigades

7th Division (Major-General T. H. Shoubridge):
20, 22, 91 Brigades

8th Division (Major-General W. C. G. Heneker):
23, 24, 25 Brigades

9th (Scottish) Division (Major-General H. T. Lukin):
26, 27, South African Brigades

11th (Northern) Division (Major-General H. R. Davies):
32, 33, 34 Brigades

14th (Light) Division (Major-General V. A. Couper):
41, 42, 43 Brigades

15th (Scottish) Division (Major-General H. F. Thuillier):
44, 45, 46 Brigades

16th (Irish) Division (Major-General W. B. Hickie):
47, 48, 49 Brigades

17th (Northern) Division (Major-General P. R. Robertson):
50, 51, 52 Brigades

18th (Eastern) Division (Major-General R. P. Lee):
53, 54, 55 Brigades

19th (Western) Division (Major-General C. D. Shute acting to 19th June, then Major-General G. T. M. Bridges, wounded 20th September; Br.-General W. P. Monkhouse acting to 22nd September, then Major-General G. D. Jeffreys):
56, 57, 58 Brigades

20th (Light) Division (Major-General W. Douglas Smith):
59, 60, 61 Brigades

21st Division (Major-General D. G. M. Campbell):
62, 64, 110 Brigades

23rd Division (Major-General J. M. Babington):
68, 69, 70 Brigades

24th Division (Major-General L. J. Bols):
17, 72, 73 Brigades

25th Division (Major-General E. G. T. Bainbridge):
7, 74, 75 Brigades

29th Division (Major-General Sir B. de Lisle):
86, 87, 88 Brigades

30th Division (Major-General W. de L. Williams):
21, 89, 90 Brigades

33rd Division (Major-General P. R. Wood):
19, 98, 100 Brigades

36th (Ulster) Division (Major-General O. S. W. Nugent):
107, 108, 109 Brigades

37th Division (Major-General H. Bruce Williams):
63, 111, 112 Brigades

38th (Welsh) Division (Major-General C. G. Blackader):
113, 114, 115 Brigades

39th Division (Major-General G. J. Cuthbert to 20th August, then Major-General E. Feetham):
116, 117, 118 Brigades

41st Division (Major-General S. T. B. Lawford):
122, 123, 124 Brigades

47th (2nd London) Division (Major-General Sir George Gorringe):
140, 141, 142 Brigades

48th (1st South Midland) Division (Major-General R. Fanshawe):
143, 144, 145 Brigades

ORDER OF BATTLE

49th (1st West Riding) Division (Major-General
E. M. Perceval) :
146, 147, 148 Brigades

50th (Northumbrian) Division (Major-General
P. S. Wilkinson) :
149, 150, 151 Brigades

51st (Highland) Division (Major-General G. M. Harper) :
152, 153, 154 Brigades

55th (1st West Lancashire) Division (Major-General
H. S. Jeudwine) :
164, 165, 166 Brigades

56th (1st London) Division (Major-General F. A. Dudgeon) :
167, 168, 169 Brigades

57th (2nd West Lancashire) Division (Major-General
R. W. R. Barnes) :
170, 171, 172 Brigades

58th (2/1st London) Division (Major-General H. D. Fanshawe
to 6th October, then Major-General A. B. E. Cator) :
173, 174, 175 Brigades

59th (2nd North Midland) Division (Major-General
C. F. Romer) :
176, 177, 178 Brigades

61st (2nd South Midland) Division (Major-General
C. J. Mackenzie) :
182, 183, 184 Brigades

63rd (Royal Naval) Division (Major-General C. E. Lawrie) :
188, 189, 190 Brigades

66th (2nd East Lancashire) Division (Major-General
Hon. H. A. Lawrence) :
197, 198, 199 Brigades

1st Canadian Division (Major-General A. C. Macdonell) :
1 Cdn., 2 Cdn., 3 Cdn. Brigades

2nd Canadian Division (Major-General H. E. Burstall) :
4 Cdn., 5 Cdn., 6 Cdn. Brigades

3rd Canadian Division (Major-General L. J. Lipsett) :
7 Cdn., 8 Cdn., 9 Cdn. Brigades

4th Canadian Division (Major-General D. Watson) :
10 Cdn., 11 Cdn., 12 Cdn. Brigades

FLANDERS 1917

1st Australian Division (Major-General H. B. Walker) :
1 Aust., 2 Aust., 3 Aust. Brigades

2nd Australian Division (Major-General N. M. Smyth) :
5 Aust., 6 Aust., 7 Aust. Brigades

3rd Australian Division (Major-General Sir John Monash) :
9 Aust., 10 Aust., 11 Aust. Brigades

4th Australian Division (Major-General W. Holmes, killed 2nd July ; Br.-General C. Rosenthal acting to 16th July, then Major-General E. G. Sinclair-Maclagan) :
4 Aust., 12 Aust., 13 Aust. Brigades

5th Australian Division (Major-General J. Talbot Hobbs) :
8 Aust., 14 Aust., 15 Aust. Brigades

New Zealand Division (Major-General Sir Arthur Russell) :
1 N.Z., 2 N.Z., 3 N.Z. (Rifle), 4 N.Z. Brigades

NOTES

8TH DIVISION :
25th Brigade. Br.-General C. Coffin was awarded the V.C. on the 31st July, 1917.

9TH DIVISION :
27th Brigade. Br.-General F. A. Maxwell, V.C., was killed in action on the 21st September, 1917. Lieut.-Colonel H. D. N. Maclean acting till Br.-General W. D. Croft took over on the 23rd.

21ST DIVISION :
62nd Brigade. Br.-General C. G. Rawlings was killed in action on the 28th October, 1917 ; Colonel G. M. Sharpe acting till 1st November, when Br.-General G. H. Gater assumed command.

29TH DIVISION :
86th Brigade. Br.-General R. G. Jelf was invalided on the 16th August, 1917. Lieut.-Colonel H. Nelson acting till the 24th August, when Br.-General G. R. H. Cheape assumed command.

41ST DIVISION :
123rd Brigade. Br.-General C. W. E. Gordon was killed in action on the 23rd July, 1917. Br.-General W. F. Clemson (124th Brigade) acting until the arrival of Br.-General E. Pearce Serocold on 3rd August.

49TH DIVISION :
    146th Brigade. Br.-General M. D. Goring-Jones left on the 18th October. Br.-General G. A. P. Rennie assumed command.
    148th Brigade. Br.-General R. L. Adlercron left on the 24th October ; Br.-General L. F. Green-Wilkinson assumed command.

58TH DIVISION :
    173rd Brigade. Br.-General B. C. Freyberg, V.C., was wounded on the 19th September, 1917. Lieut.-Colonel W. R. H. Dann acting till 3rd October, when Br.-General R. B. Worgan assumed command.

NEW ZEALAND DIVISION :
    1st Brigade. Br.-General E. H. J. Brown was killed in action on the 8th June, 1917, Br.-General C. W. Melvill taking over on the same day.

PROJECT FOR COMBINED NAVAL AND MILITARY OPERATIONS ON THE BELGIAN COAST WITH A VIEW TO PREVENTING THE ENEMY USING OSTEND AS A SUBMARINE BASE

GENERAL STAFF MEMORANDUM
12TH NOVEMBER 1915
(Sketch 1)

1. *Main object of the proposed operations.* On the 28th October the Admiralty expressed a wish that the question of joint naval and military operations on the Belgian coast should be considered. In accordance with this desire the question was discussed at a meeting of the General Staff and Admiralty War Staff on the 8th November. The Admiralty War Staff were of opinion that it was of the utmost importance in the interests of the Expeditionary Force to deprive the enemy of his submarine bases at Ostend and Zeebrugge, because the use of these ports by the Germans constituted a growing danger to the transport of troops and supplies across the Channel, owing to the ease with which enemy submarines could now sow mines within the Straits of Dover, a danger likely to be accentuated during the long winter nights. Combined naval and military operations undertaken for the object of destroying the enemy's base at Ostend, or of preventing its use by him, would therefore serve a definite military purpose.

2. *Possible plan of operations.*

(1) In order to secure effective naval support for the proposed operations, it would appear essential that our ships should be able to approach within effective range of the enemy's positions along the dunes. This at present they are unable to do owing to the fire of a German battery of heavy guns which is situated a little to the south of Mariakerke. It is hoped, however, that this battery will shortly be silenced by the fire of the Fleet, supported by Allied guns and howitzers in position east and south of Nieuport.

(2) When this has been effected it is suggested that the enemy's lines between the Nieuport–Bruges road and the coast should be attacked, and that this attack, so far as is possible, should be a surprise. In order to obtain this result it would be necessary to draw off the enemy's attention by an offensive in some other quarter, such as the Ypres area. Good concealed positions for guns can be found in the dunes east of Nieuport, and artillery could be increased in that district without the enemy's knowledge.

Even if the presence of the guns were discovered, it is doubtful whether the Germans would suppose that anything more than a feint attack was in contemplation, for it has been a constant practice to make demonstrations in this direction when an offensive was being undertaken elsewhere. The primary objective of this attack would be the enemy's second position, that is the line Westende Plage–Westende–Ketsbrug,[1] and thence along the branch canal between the Plaaschendaele Canal and the Bruges highroad. This would mean an advance of a little more than 2,000 yards at the widest point. It is thought that this extent of ground might be gained in the course of one attack, if supported by the enfilade fire of the guns of the Fleet.

(3) The advantage of securing this line would be twofold :—

(a) By increasing the depth of the position east of the Yser it permits of greater freedom of movement and facilitates the concentration of troops and guns east of Nieuport for a further offensive.

(b) The capture of the locks at Ketsbrug would allow of the flooding of a certain extent of ground on both sides of the Plaaschendaele Canal.

(4) This line having been secured the question then arises, " What further steps could be taken to exploit this success ? "*

It is suggested that a further advance along the coast might not prove a very difficult operation in view of the support which could be rendered by the enfilade fire of the Fleet.

Such an advance, however, in order to achieve success would not only have to be made along the whole front between the sea and the Bruges road, but would have to be combined with a Belgian advance west of the Yser. If a forward position such as Westende Plage could be secured it would render it very difficult for the enemy to maintain himself in the low ground on both sides of the Plaaschendaele Canal. His positions in that area consist at the present time of fortified houses and farms which could be destroyed with comparative ease by fire both from front and flank once the French had obtained the commanding ground referred to above. It has already been mentioned also that some of this country could be flooded once the locks at Ketsbrug were in the hands of the French.

It is therefore probable, in view of the ease with which all the low ground can be enfiladed from the dunes, that the enemy would have to relinquish a broad stretch of country south of the dunes.

If he did so, he would no doubt flood it in order to prevent the French using it. The French and German front would then

---

[1] Ketsbrug is at the junction of the Plaaschendaele Canal and its branch near Nieuport.

*Note.—The attack on the enemy's position from Westende Plage to the Bruges road could be most conveniently undertaken by the French, who are already in position. The question whether British troops should be employed for a further advance is one wihch must be left to the decision of the Commander-in-Chief in France.

be restricted to the narrow belt of dunes. At first sight an advance along this belt would seem a very difficult operation, but on the other hand, the enemy's position in this quarter would be extremely precarious. He would be bombarded from the front by a great concentration of guns which could be concealed among the dunes east of Nieuport, and would also be bombarded in flank from the sea. It is true that the French advance would also be enfiladed from the south by long range fire, but a certain amount of shelter could be obtained from this fire on the north side of the dunes where the beach would provide a covered means of approach and the German guns would in turn be bombarded from the Belgian front. It is thought possible that, if the advance were pushed forward as far as Westende Plage, a landing might then be effected at Middelkerke Bains. That would mean the clearing of the enemy off the dunes as far as Middelkerke Bains, the possession of which is of great importance, as it commands a very wide extent of ground. East of Middelkerke the dunes become so narrow that it is difficult to see how the Germans could maintain themselves there and they would probably have to retire altogether, in which case they would no doubt flood the country round Ostend to prevent our occupying it. Our object would then be gained, for the enemy would be unable to use the port.

(5) In the event of the above operations proving unsuccessful in clearing the whole coast as far as Ostend, they would none the less seem to be justified providing the primary objective, Westende Plage–Westende–Ketsbrug to the Bruges road, could be attained. This line would, as already explained, render the French position at Nieuport far more secure, and would give them advanced gun positions from which the harbour at Ostend could be bombarded and thus increase the enemy's difficulties in using it.

3. *Ulterior objects of the operations* : The effect of the operations, if successful, would not be confined merely to preventing the enemy using Ostend. If Ostend could be occupied, long range guns could be mounted for the bombardment of Zeebrugge. The operations would furthermore exercise a very marked moral effect in Holland, a factor which may prove of great importance at a later stage of the war when there may be a chance of inducing that country to intervene on our side. In view of the probable decisive effect which such intervention would exercise, no chance should be lost of impressing Holland with our ability to secure the Belgian coast line as a preliminary to driving the enemy out of Belgium.

A. J. MURRAY,
Lieut.-General,
Chief of the Imperial General Staff.

APPENDIX II

COMMANDER-IN-CHIEF'S INSTRUCTIONS FOR PREPARATION OF PLAN FOR NORTHERN OPERATIONS

7TH JANUARY, 1916

1. Plan for landing and capture of Ostend to be worked out in detail.

2. The success of the operation will depend on *surprise* of enemy.

With this in view, plans for engaging enemy in order to cause him to withdraw his reserves from the Ostend area will also be worked out—e.g., attack on Fôret d'Houthulst : advance on Middelkerke.

3. The date on which these operations will take place must depend on the plans of the G.O.C.-in-C. French Army.

D. HAIG.

APPENDIX III

GENERAL SIR HENRY RAWLINSON'S PROPOSALS FOR THE ATTACK BY THE FOURTH ARMY AGAINST THE YPRES FRONT

27TH FEBRUARY, 1916
(Sketch 2)

General Remarks

1. This means an advance by the Fourth Army on a front of about six and a half miles widening out to a front of 9½ miles.

2. Any such advance will have to be made by definite stages, with intervals of time allowed for the preparations necessary for undertaking each subsequent advance. The first three stages only will be dealt with in these proposals, as beyond that it is impossible to make a definite forecast.

3. The advance of the Fourth Army should be supported on its right by an advance of the Second Army to cover the right flank.

4. The original front being a narrow one, and the positions for artillery being limited in the initial stage, a large force will not be required in the front line for the first advance. But, as these troops become exhausted, and as the front widens, the number of troops required will increase considerably.

5. To commence with, the object of the advance of the Fourth Army must be to widen the base to give room to manoeuvre, so that more troops and artillery can be employed for the later stages of the operations.

6. Till this base has been widened the Second Army on the right, south of the Roulers–Ypres railway, will only require to keep the enemy employed, but as soon as the above object has been attained the Second Army should push its attack simultaneously with the Fourth Army.

7. An advance along the seashore from Nieuport can either be made at the same time as the initial advance south of Steenstraate or can be made simultaneously with the second stage of the attack.

8. There are three questions that require to be gone into in more detail before it can be said for certain that these proposals are practicable :

(*a*) The feasibility of attacking the enemy's position east of the canal between Boesinghe and Steenstraat. That is to say whether it is possible to force a passage across the canal which is some 25 to 40 metres wide, and at present is reported to hold 1 to 2 metres of water and 1 metre of mud.

(*b*) Whether the French are prepared to hand over to us the front up to Steenstraat six weeks or two months prior to the attack, and also the sector now held by the French 38th Division at Nieuport.

(*c*) Whether there are enough roads, railways and rolling stock available in this area for supplying a large number of troops with food and ammunition.

An answer in the affirmative to these three questions is essential if these proposals are to be practicable.

9. Assuming that the answer to these three questions is satisfactory, I would suggest the plan given in the following paragraphs.

Preliminary Preparations

10. The first step is to bring up into position sufficient heavy guns and howitzers to dominate the enemy's artillery which covers the front south of Steenstraat. Till this is done any preliminary arrangements and preparations will be difficult, if not impossible, owing to the present predominance of the German artillery in this area. These guns should be in position at least two months before the actual attack takes place.

11. At the same time or shortly after the above heavy artillery comes into position the areas now occupied by the French between Boesinghe and Steenstraat and at Nieuport should be taken over by us.

APPENDIX III

(*a*) One corps (" B ") between Boesinghe and Steenstraat.

(*b*) Another corps (XIV, called "A" corps in this scheme) on a 3-division front, continuing to hold the line from the Roulers–Ypres railway to Boesinghe.

(*c*) Two divisions at Nieuport.

12. As soon as these troops have taken over, the necessary preparations for the attack should be begun with every available man. The preparations of the XIV Corps should be put in hand at once and reconnaissances for gun positions carried out as soon as possible for the whole front.

13. At a somewhat later period a third corps (" C ") should move up into the area west and south-west of Poperinghe.

First Stage of the Advance

14. Leaving out, for the moment, the Nieuport attack, the first stage of the advance should be made by two corps, the right ("A") with two divisions, the left corps (" B ") with either two or three divisions in the front line.

(*a*) Right corps ("A") between Hill 29 and Boesinghe (front 3,200 yards), the remaining division holding a defensive line from the Roulers–Ypres railway to the Ypres–Langemarck road (front 4,000 yards approximately).

(*b*) The left corps (" B ") between Boesinghe and Steenstraat (front 3,500 yards). The first objective in each case being . . . [about 800 yards into the German position].

15. At the end of the first stage a readjustment of corps and divisions will be necessary, and an interval of at least seven days for this, and for moving part of the artillery closer up, before the attack in the second stage will be required.

Second Stage of the Advance

16. The second stage of the advance should be made by 3 corps :

(*a*) Right corps (" C ") to attack the German front line system between the Ypres–Roulers railway and Hampshire Farm [1,500 yards north of Wieltje].

(*b*) Centre corps ("A") to attack from Hampshire Farm (exclusive) to the Ypres–Langemarck railway, including Hill 29 and Pilckem.

(*c*) Left corps (" B ") to attack from the Ypres–Langemarck railway (inclusive) to the Ferme Cheurot [near Bixschoote] (inclusive).

The objectives being in each case . . . [about 800 yards distant to include the capture of the crest of Pilckem ridge from Verlorenhoek to near Bixschoote].

17. For the protection of the right flank of the Fourth Army during the second stage there should be a simultaneous attack on Bellewaarde Farm by the Second Army.

18. A further and longer interval will now be required for the re-arrangement of troops and the moving forward of artillery before the third stage of the advance is undertaken. The majority of the heavy artillery will have to be moved forward during this interval.

19. A fourth corps (" D ") should now be brought up and will probably be required to take over part of the line held by the left and centre corps (" B " and "A"), prior to the third stage being undertaken.

Third Stage of the Advance

20. The third stage will comprise an attack on the enemy positions through Frezenburg–St. Julien–Langemarck–Bixschoote.

This is a front of approximately 13,000 yards, and will require four corps for the attack.

21. The fronts to be attacked by the 4 corps would be approximately :

(*a*) Right corps (" C ") : Roulers railway to Fortuin [600 yards south of St. Julien] (inclusive).

(*b*) Right centre corps ("A") : St. Julien–the Haanebeek [1,200 yards south of Langemarck] (inclusive).

(*c*) Left centre corps (" D ") : Langemarck (inclusive)– point where Bixschoote–Langemarck railway crosses the Steenbeek.

(*d*) Left corps (" B ") : Point where Bixschoote–Langemarck railway crosses the Steenbeek–Bixschoote.

22. Beyond this third stage it is impossible at present to forecast. If the attack in the third stage is successful a further advance will be made on Passchendaele–Poelcappelle and Houthulst Forest, the right of the Fourth Army keeping touch with the left of the Second Army.

23. Probably the best time for the attack by the two divisions at Nieuport will be simultaneous with the second stage of the Fourth Army attack.

Whether to be made on a two division or one division front I am not yet prepared to state definitely, but probably the latter.

The front of attack here will narrow as it progresses, and the advance might be greatly assisted by the fire of guns from the sea. Further reinforcements beyond the two divisions should, therefore, not be required.

24. As already pointed out, the number of hostile guns and howitzers in the area south of Steenstraate is very considerable, and in order to gain predominance over them we shall require

a very strong force of heavy howitzers. The exact number, however, that will be required I am not yet prepared to state, but there is no question but that every heavy gun and howitzer that can be made available for this operation can be made use of and will add to the probabilities of a successful result.

H. RAWLINSON,
General, Commanding Fourth Army.

APPENDIX IV

G.H.Q. MEMORANDUM
PROJECT FOR OPERATIONS IN FLANDERS AND BELGIUM

5TH MARCH, 1916
(Sketches 1 and 2)

1. The object in view is to defeat or drive back the hostile forces in North-West Belgium, occupy the country north and west of the general line Ypres–Roulers–Bruges and free the Belgian coast line.

2. Apart from tactical or topographical considerations, two factors have to be considered:

(a) The normal distribution of the German forces in the area between the Lys and the sea is:

Holding the line ...	105	battalions
In local reserve ...	66	,,
Resting in rear ...	45	,, (includes XXVII Corps)
Total ...	216	,,

(b) The approximate line to be held, if eventually required to be held as a "line", is approximately 60,000 yards and will require (say) 8 corps. All of this will be new line and the net increase over the length of line now held will be about 45,000 yards.

3. From the above it is obvious that, in order to achieve the object laid down in paragraph 1:

(a) The French must take over again a certain portion of the line now held by us.

(b) That not only the French but all our Allies should attack simultaneously in order to hold and use up the hostile strategic reserves.

(c) That our operations themselves must be designed with a view to holding the hostile troops all along our front and, if possible, drawing the German reserves away from our main line of advance.

APPENDIX IV

Outline of Proposed Operations

First Stage:

(a) *Operation:* Secure the ridge east of the Ypres Canal on the approximate line Hill 29–Ferme des Ponts–Steenstraat.

Object: To deny observation to the Germans and enable dispositions for a fresh advance to be made.

Troops: Engaged—4 to 5 divisions.
          Reserve—2 divisions.
Time: *Preparation*—3 weeks.
          Operation—2 days.

(b) *Operation:* Capture the Messines–Wytschaete Ridge.

Object: Secure the flank of the Ypres Salient to protect and cover the period required for the concentration for the main attack, deny observation and gun positions to the enemy and obtain gun positions and observation over the Lys valley, hold Germans and attract and use up reserves.

    N.B.—It may well happen that the Germans will now think that this is really the main attack, and in any case the possession of the Ridge is of such importance that strong counter-attacks are practically certain, thus achieving one of the objects of the operation.

Troops: Engaged—9 divisions.
          Reserve—3 divisions.

    N.B.—It will not be possible for the Germans to tell that the troops concentrating for the main attack north of Ypres are not concentrating to press the Messines attack.

Time: *Preparation*—Ample time is available if commenced at the same time as for (a).
          Operation—Will probably automatically continue until merged into part of the main operation by the operations in fourth stage.

Second Stage:

Operation: Secure the German front trenches on a wide front between Neuve Chapelle and Bois Grenier [19 and 12 miles south of Ypres, respectively].

Object: To hold Germans, use up hostile local reserves, and if possible induce the idea that the attack north of Ypres is only a feint. Also to cover the period necessary to prepare for a fresh advance from the line reached in first stage (a).

Troops: Engaged—4 to 6 divisions.
          Reserves—local.
Time: *Preparation*—as for first stage (a) or less.
          Operation—to follow about 48 hours after first stage (a) and last about three days.

Third Stage:

Operation: Continuation of the attack north of Ypres.

Object: To secure the general line ... [Bellewaarde to Bixschoote], i.e., generally speaking, to penetrate German second line and advance our line as far as it can go without moving forward our heavy artillery.

Troops: Engaged—9 divisions.
Reserve—6 divisions.

Time: Preparation—4 or 5 days only can be allowed, i.e., that covered by the period occupied by the attack on front trenches in second stage.

Operation—About 2 days, after which heavy guns must be advanced and troops brought up for main attack.

Fourth Stage:

Operation:
   (a) Whilst holding the Messines-Wytschaete Ridge against counter-attack, endeavour to advance the left north-east along the ridge running roughly from Wytschaete towards Broodseinde.
   (b) *Main Attack*—To the approximate line Frezenberg-St. Julien-Langemarck to inundated area north-east of Bixschoote.

Object:
   (a) Secure the right flank of the main advance.
   (b) Complete capture of second line and strongpoints and place right on Passchendaele Ridge and left on inundations.

Troops: Engaged—(a) 1 corps; (b) 4 corps.
Reserve—(a) 1 corps; (b) 4 corps.

Time: Dependent on time taken to advance heavy artillery and bring forward troops, and on progress of attack under (a) above.

Fifth Stage:

Operation: Continuation of main attack:
   (a) Secure the Passchendaele position.
   (b) With the right on Passchendaele, advance in the general direction of Staden.
   (c) Simultaneous with the above an advance from Dixmude should be made.

Object: To secure the redoubts and positions at Passchendaele and throw forward the line to Staden and Zarren.

Troops : (say), 7 corps.

N.B.—A mobile force to be held ready, this force to move on, say, Thourout, after fifth or during sixth stage, according to the situation.

Sixth Stage :

From the above line an advance to be made on Roulers–Thourout. An attack from Nieuport to be made simultaneously with this advance and followed, if Germans are falling back, by the special operation.

APPENDIX V

G.H.Q. LETTER TO SECOND ARMY

6TH JANUARY, 1917
(Sketch 1)

With reference to your G.352 dated the 12th December, 1916, giving your plan for offensive operations north of the river Lys, the Commander-in-Chief desires me to draw your attention to the following points with a view to recasting the plan.

1. The operations north of the river Lys will not take place until after the subsidiary British attacks elsewhere and main French offensive operations have been carried out. It is therefore to be anticipated that the enemy will have been severely handled and his reserves drawn away from your front before the attacks north of the Lys are launched.

Under these circumstances, it is essential that the plan should be based on rapid action and entail the breaking through of the enemy's defences on a wide front without any delay.

2. The plan, as submitted by you, indicates a sustained and deliberate offensive such as has been carried out recently on the Somme front. In these circumstances the enemy will have time to bring up fresh reinforcements and construct new lines of defence.

3. The object of these operations is to inflict a decisive defeat on the enemy and to free the Belgian coast.

The immediate intention is to break through the enemy defensive systems on the approximate front Hooge–Steenstraat with the object of securing the line Roulers–Thourout and, by advancing in a north-easterly direction, to threaten the coast defences in rear.

The Belgians and French will co-operate by attacking from Dixmude and Nieuport respectively.

4. The operations naturally divide themselves into two sectors and will be organized under two separate Army commands :

(*a*) The attack on the Messines–Wytschaete Ridge and Zandvoorde, with the object of forming the defensive flank for the decisive attack, will be carried out by the Southern Army.

(*b*) The decisive attack, from the approximate front Hooge–Steenstraat with objectives Roulers and Thourout, will be executed by the Northern Army. It is essential that this attack should be carried out with the least possible delay. The Belgians will co-operate by attacking from Dixmude in the direction of Clercken and Zarren.

5. Will you please submit your plans by the 31st January, giving your recommendations as to how these operations should be carried out.

The scheme should include :

(*a*) Your recommendations as to the point of junction between, and the areas allotted to, the two attacking Armies.

(*b*) Your estimated requirements in divisions, guns and tanks, assuming that a total of ten corps headquarters will be allotted for the operations.

(*c*) Any further railway construction you may consider necessary.

L. E. KIGGELL,
Lieut.-General,
Chief of the General Staff.

APPENDIX VI

G.H.Q. INSTRUCTIONS FOR THE FORMATION OF A SPECIAL SUB-SECTION OF THE OPERATIONS SECTION OF THE GENERAL STAFF

8TH JANUARY, 1917
(Sketch 1)

Lieut.-Colonel C. N. MACMULLEN.

1. You will form a special sub-section, with [Major Viscount] Gort, in the Operations (A) Section of the General Staff, with the object of working out a plan of operations to take place north of the river Lys.

2. I attach a paper showing the organization and duties of O.A. [not printed].

3. You will find all the papers necessary to show the general scope of the operations. Gort will assist you in collecting these papers, which you should keep under lock and key in a separate box in my room.

Shortly, the idea is for the British to operate on the Vimy, Arras and ancre fronts, in conjunction with attacks by the French armies. If the French are successful in driving the Germans back, we shall put all our efforts in to help them and there will be no necessity for the operations north of the river Lys taking place.

If, on the other hand, the French do not succeed in their efforts to force the Germans back and thus fail to clear the Belgian coast, the French will take over from us probably up to the Ancre river, and we shall switch as rapidly as possible to carry out our operations on a large scale north of the river Lys.

4. The object of our operations north of the river Lys is to clear the Belgian coast this summer. The War Cabinet attaches the greatest importance to the liberation of this coast.

5. The idea is to attack from south of Messines to about Steenstraat (British), from Dixmude (Belgian), from the Nieuport sector (either British or French), and the landing near Ostend (British).

The attack on the present Second Army front to be divided into two sectors:

Southern Sector (Second Army: Sir Herbert Plumer).
Objectives: Messines–Wytschaete, Zandvoorde, and protect the northern sector attack.

Northern Sector (Fourth Army: Sir Henry Rawlinson).
Objectives, in the first instance: Roulers, Thourout, astride the two railways, thence north-east to clear the coast and get in rear of the German coast defences. (Consider the advisability of taking over from the Belgians up to Steenstraat.)

Belgian Attack. From Dixmude. *Objectives:* Clercken, Zarren.

6. Sir Herbert Plumer made out a scheme for the northern and southern sector attacks in the shape of a steady, deliberate advance similar to the Somme battle. The Commander-in-Chief rejected this. The whole essence is to attack with rapidity and push right through quickly. It must not be forgotten that this attack will be delivered subsequent to attacks by the whole of the French armies and a portion of the British army. The Germans are likely to be disorganized and weak.

Sir Herbert Plumer is recasting the scheme, to be submitted by the 31st January.

Neither Sir Herbert Plumer nor Sir Henry Rawlinson have been told officially what their own tasks are to be.

APPENDIX VI

7. The Southern Sector attack is comparatively simple, but the Northern Sector attack requires careful thought owing to the difficulty of massing troops and guns in the Ypres Salient, also in the crossing of the canal north of the Salient. (Charteris [Head of Intelligence Section] has information on this latter point.)

8. You should get to work at once to make out the whole plan, in collaboration with the Second Army headquarters. When your scheme is completed and approved by the Commander-in-Chief, then Sir Henry Rawlinson will be made acquainted with it and allotted a headquarters (probably Lovie Château), and he can work out the details.

9 and 10. [These paragraphs deal with the subjects to be studied and the individuals to be consulted.]

11. The idea is to shift the Fourth Army bodily round to the north. Propose on Z Day of the Arras attack pulling out the XIV and III Corps headquarters, each with one division, ready to send off. Also extend the First Army up to the river Lys and shift the II Anzac Corps north of the river Lys. It is of the greatest importance to make the switch as rapidly as possible and to get everything cut and dried, so that the moment the Commander-in-Chief knows that the operation south of Vimy will not produce the results required he can carry out the switch with the greatest rapidity.

There would be in the north :
    <u>VIII, XIV, III</u>, X, IX, II Anzac
and we could send, probably at short notice,
    XIX, XVIII, <u>IV, XV, I Anzac</u>
those underlined being allotted to the Northern sector.

12. Consider the possibilities of surprise attack with tanks in the Northern Sector. The O.C. Tanks is carrying out a reconnaissance of this area.

13. Remember that the Field-Marshal Commanding-in-Chief will command and control all the attacking forces—British (naval and military), Belgian and French, and conduct the operations as one whole.

Consider the system of command. The date of attack will probably not be before the 15th June. [Note advance of date.]

14. When you have studied all the papers, etc., and understand the whole project thoroughly, please speak.

                        J. H. DAVIDSON,
                        Br.-General, General Staff.

APPENDIX VII

MEMORANDUM BY OPERATIONS SECTION, GENERAL STAFF G.H.Q.
(Submitted 14th February, 1917)
(Map 1 ; Sketches 1 and 2)

Summary of the Proposed Northern Operation in Chronological Order

1. To take over from the Belgians up to Noordschoote [2½ miles north-west of Bixschoote] immediately the switch from the south is decided on.

2. To take over from the French at Nieuport as soon as possible after the switch from the south is decided on.

3. The capture of the enemy's front line from Ontario Farm [a mile west of Messines] to Peckham (Spanbroekmolen) by Second Army as soon as possible after the switch from the south is decided on.

4. On Zero Day a simultaneous attack by the Second and Fourth Armies on a front from St. Yves to Lizerne [½ mile south of Steenstraat] with the object of penetrating to a depth of approximately 1,500 to 2,000 yards.

5. On Zero + 2 Day, or earlier, if found possible, an attack by the Fourth Army on the enemy's third line north of the Ypres–Roulers railway, combined with an attack supported by a strong force of tanks on to the Becelaere–Broodseinde line. Second Army to push forward simultaneously to a line running from the Ypres–Comines railway by Gheluvelt to Becelaere.

6. The attack on Zero + 2 Day to be followed immediately by a rapid continuation of the advance by the Fourth Army towards the line Roulers–Thourout, Second Army taking over the defensive flank up to Broodseinde.

7. An attack at Nieuport as soon as the main advance has reached the neighbourhood of Cortemarck [7 miles north of Westroosebeke], or earlier if the enemy shows signs of great demoralization.

8. The continuance of the attack at Nieuport on the following day, combined with a landing on the coast at and south-west of Middelkerke Bains.

N.B.—Administrative arrangements have not been discussed in this note, though they have been considered. The most important in them is the time estimated as necessary for completion of railway construction required for the operations at Ypres. This amounts to three months after the plan is approved and labour actually provided on the ground. Completion should be timed for at least fifteen days before Zero Day, making a total of three and a half months.

APPENDIX VII

DISCUSSION OF PROPOSALS FOR THE NORTHERN
OPERATIONS WHICH HAVE FOR THEIR OBJECT
THE CLEARANCE OF THE BELGIAN COAST

General Idea

1. The operations proposed take the form of breaking through the enemy's defences on the front from St. Yves to Steenstraat (approximately 30,000 yards), the formation of a defensive flank along the Messines–Wytschaete Ridge and on via Gheluvelt, Becelaere and Broodseinde to Moorslede, and an advance north-east via Roulers and Thourout. After a definite stage has been reached in the main advance an attack is proposed at Nieuport and a landing on the Belgian coast.

Roles of the Second and Fourth Armies

2. Generally speaking, the rôle of the Second Army is the formation of the defensive flank and that of the Fourth Army the main advance. Some modification of this on the northern part of the defensive flank is necessary in the initial stages and will be discussed later.

Boundaries

3. The Steenvoorde–Poperinghe–Ypres–Hooge–Menin Road as far as Clapham Junction (common to both Armies as far as Abeele and thence inclusive to the Fourth Army), and thence a line running east along the Reutelbeek is proposed as the most suitable initial boundary between the two Armies.

The Poperinghe–Ypres road will form part of one of the main through roads available to Fourth Army in their advance, and, as such, should be allotted to Fourth Army from the outset. The proposed boundary on, and in advance of, our present front line is that which is considered most suitable in view of the objectives to be reached and most commensurate with the respective facilities of each Army in matters of artillery support and of assembly places for troops and tanks.

The southern boundary of the Second Army should be on the river Lys; it will only be necessary to hold the front south of the front of attack very lightly.

Our present boundary with the Belgians does not give the Fourth Army a sufficiently broad base of attack, nor enough area in rear, and it is recommended that we should take over from the Belgians as far as Noordeschoote. Although it is desirable to do this as soon as possible in order to create less suspicion and afford time for the necessary preparations to be made in the area taken over, it does not appear probable that the necessary troops can be made available before Zero Day of the Arras attack. A division could then be found from Fourth Army, but it would be undesirable to transfer this till the decision to switch had been reached in case of a great success in the south. The recommendation made, therefore, is that we should take over this area immediately the decision is made to switch and that meantime we should open negotiations with the Belgians in order to prepare plans and allow of reconnaissance.

The boundaries between Second and Fourth Armies and areas allotted are shown on Map A. [not reproduced].

Objectives

4. The objectives proposed for both Armies are shown on Map B. [not reproduced].

(a) The capture by the Second Army of the enemy's front line system from Ontario Farm to Peckham (Spanbroekmolen) is proposed as a preliminary operation. This is not essential but would greatly facilitate the subsequent task of Second Army and should render possible the attainment in one bound of the objective proposed on Zero Day. It is very desirable that the operations of the Second Army should be carried through without a check and the G.O.C. Second Army is doubtful whether the objective shown can be reached in one day if a start is made from our present front line.

This preliminary operation should, however, only take place if it is carried out immediately, or very soon after, the decision is made to switch and at least a month before the main operation. There is then some chance of it being considered a demonstration made with a view to hold up enemy reserves destined to oppose the southern operations. Resources would probably admit of it being carried out at the time proposed.

It should be noted that the G.O.C. Second Army considers that " a prolonged occupation of a small sector might be " unduly costly in men and ammunition ". It is thought that, in view of the conditions which will then be existing, there is very little force in the above argument, if the position is held in accordance with the methods which have been found successful in holding exposed positions elsewhere.

(b) The objectives proposed for the main attacks of Second and Fourth Armies entail the capture of the enemy's first line and most of his second line on the whole front of attack on Zero Day and of his third line on the front of Fourth Army on Zero + 2 Day or earlier. The most formidable task is undoubtedly the capture of that part of the position between Observatory Ridge and the Ypres–Roulers railway south of Frezenberg owing to the difficulty of arranging for adequate artillery support and for the assembly of troops.

Second Army accordingly proposed to relegate this portion of the attack to a subsequent phase, but it seems unsound to postpone our gaining a secure hold of the high ground, a matter admittedly of first importance to subsequent operations.

APPENDIX VII

As an alternative it is proposed that the capture of the line shown in dot and dash shall be carried out by a body of tanks with infantry in support. The scope of this attack will be limited to the extent required to deprive the enemy of the whole of his observation over the salient and so afford us freedom of action there on and after Zero Day. The capture of this line will also permit of the assembly in forward positions of the large number of tanks with which it is proposed that Fourth Army shall capture the Becelaere–Broodseinde line on Zero + 2 Day.

A preliminary reconnaissance regarding the employment of tanks on the above lines has been carried out by the Tank Corps and a favourable verbal report made. O.C. Tanks is now going further into the matter and will submit a detailed plan.

The left flank of the Fourth Army attack on Zero + 2 Day has been left undetermined for the present as Sir H. Rawlinson desires to consider further his proposal that it should extend only as far as Langemarck in view of the fact that one of the two railways and two of the four roads available to him for his advance pass through that point.

It is suggested that the Second Army should take over from Fourth Army the front Becelaere–Broodseinde as soon as possible after its capture together with the troops concerned, leaving the Fourth Army free to carry out their subsequent operations relieved of all concern for the safety of their flank as far as Broodseinde.

In the same way Second Army might subsequently extend their left flank as far as Moorslede as soon as Fourth Army has progressed thus far.

Allotment of Troops

5. The enemy's defences on the front of the Second Army are more powerfully organized than on that of the Fourth Army and the initial frontage of attack is greater by some 4,000 yards (17,000 yards as opposed to 13,000 yards), but on the other hand, artillery support to the Second Army attack is easier on most of the front, it will be aided by a powerful mine system and its objective is limited.

It is thought that the attack should be carried out on a frontage of eleven divisions and that three divisions will be sufficient in immediate reserve.

An allotment of four corps comprising fourteen divisions is proposed therefore for Second Army (Second Army proposed eleven divisions attacking, seven in corps reserve and a further corps of three divisions in Army reserve).

In addition, one corps, of three divisions in G.H.Q. Reserve, should be located in Second Army area. This would be available as a reinforcement to the Second Army in case of necessity but should be regarded as primarily intended as a reservoir of reinforcement for the Fourth Army in the later stages of their operations.

Although Fourth Army can draw reinforcements in later stages from the above reserve corps and also from divisions which have taken part in the Second Army attack and are immediately withdrawn and reorganized, it is essential that they should have sufficient troops prior to the attack to undertake the first stage of the advance after the break through. Exclusive of cavalry, the minimum required for this appears to be six corps comprising eighteen divisions of which four corps, each of four divisions, will be attacking and two corps, each of one division, will be in reserve. The detailed allotment of troops is shown below.

Timing of Attacks

6. It has been suggested that the Second Army attack as far north as Observatory Ridge should precede that of the Fourth Army in view of the facts that :

(*a*) The assembly of troops for and launching of this attack are easier than that of the Fourth Army.

(*b*) The subsequent operations of the Fourth Army are dependent on success by the Second Army.

(*c*) A prior attack by the Second Army might draw off local reserves which might oppose the Fourth Army.

It is submitted, however, that these considerations are outweighed by the value of dispersal of hostile artillery fire resulting from attack on the broadest front possible, a factor which becomes of increased importance when attacking from a salient.

Moreover, an attack by the Second Army as a first phase is opposed to the idea underlying the whole scheme, which is a heavy surprise attack followed by a rapid break through, and such local reserves as might be attracted to the Second Army front would probably be replaced by others drawn from a distance immediately the serious nature of the Second Army attack was realized.

It is considered, therefore, that the Zero Day for both Second and Fourth Army attacks should be the same.

Role of the Belgians

7. The British operations should be in no way dependent on co-operation by the Belgians and need not be so. Any operation which the latter can undertake with a view to dispersal of the enemy's forces, or even subsequently to co-operate with the main attack, should be regarded as an additional asset, but no diversion

APPENDIX VII 415

should be made of British resources, which can be profitably employed either on the Ypres front or at Nieuport.

A reduction of floods on the Belgian front should not be carried out unless it can safely be done at least fifteen days before the Zero Day of the Arras attack. Carried out then it would be regarded as a feint but later would merely call attention to the proposed operations.

The Nieuport Attack and Landing

8. This operation appears to offer good prospects of success and might lead rapidly to very striking results. The paramount necessity is that it should be kept secret, especially the landing, and the method of landing now proposed renders this easy. It appears worth considering whether a report of an intended landing north of Ostend should be spread abroad prior to the Arras attack. When this is proved false subsequent rumours of operations on the coast might obtain less credence.

It is proposed that the enemy's front line system at Nieuport should be captured in the afternoon and that his second line should be attacked about 3 a.m. on the following day. Simultaneously with the attack on the second line a landing would be effected at three points at and south-west of Middelkerke Bains by a force embarked after dark the previous evening at Dunkirk.

Zero Day for the Nieuport attack should be when the main advance has progressed so far as to afford a reasonable chance of early tactical co-operation between the two forces. This might be when our troops have reached the neighbourhood of Cortemarck or earlier if the enemy showed signs of great demoralization and disorganization.

The rôle of the landing force would be to push forward rapidly with the greatest boldness and resolution to seize certain tactical points, including those giving control of the power to inundate, and the force would be specially organized with this end in view.

The points of landing, routes of advance and objectives are shown on Map C. [not reproduced].

The landing force would be reinforced at its objectives by two reserve divisions from Nieuport which will push through as soon as the attack there has penetrated the defences, the task of these two divisions being to extend further the line gained.

(It may be possible to put ashore a second echelon of the landing force shortly after the first.)

The minimum strength of the first echelon of the landing party at each of the three points will be 5,000, and it may be possible to increase these numbers. The method of landing is from two monitors at each point by means of special pontoons under cover of a smoke screen. Tanks and other vehicles will be carried on the pontoons and the issue of troops from the pontoons will be preceded by tanks if necessary.

The initial number of divisions required for this operation is five, i.e., two to attack, two in reserve and one as the foundation of the landing force.

The latter should be a specially selected division, earmarked well in advance and not tried too high beforehand.

It will not be necessary to take over from the French at Nieuport till the switch is decided on, but the transfer should be carried out as soon after that as troops can be made available. It will be necessary to discuss the matter with them well in advance so that plans may be prepared.

It is considered that the operations at Nieuport and the landing should be directly under G.H.Q.

Proposed Initial Allotment of Corps Headquarters, Divisions and Heavy Artillery

	Corps H.Q.	Divisions	6-inch, 8-inch and 9.2-inch howitzers	Other Heavy Artillery
Second Army	4	14	385	175
Fourth Army	6	18	270	120
G.H.Q. Reserve in Second Army area	1	3	—	—
Nieuport attack and landing	1	5	70	30
	12	40	725*	325*

* Heavy guns and howitzers available in excess of the above numbers o be allotted to Second and Fourth Armies in proportion of 7 to 5.

N.B.—The above allotment of divisions leaves 25 surplus on a basis of 65. Assuming 7 or 8 to be required to hold the front between the Lys and the Scarpe, this leaves 18 or 17 to carry on the battle in the south. The degree of energy with which it will be possible to do this will be dependent on the amount of front taken over by the French.

APPENDIX VIII

SECOND ARMY OPERATION ORDER NO. 1
OF 10TH MAY, 1917
(Sketch 2)

1. Under instructions from the Commander-in-Chief and with a view to enforcing the enemy to withdraw reserves from the main battle front (Vimy–Arras), the Second Army will capture the Messines–Wytschaete Ridge on a date (Zero) which will be fixed later.

APPENDIX VIII

2. The troops allotted for the operations are :

II Anzac Corps	3rd Australian, New Zealand, 25th, 4th Australian Divisions.
IX Corps	36th, 16th, 19th, 11th Divisions.
X Corps	41st, 47th, 23rd, 24th Divisions.
Reserve Corps (XIV)	Guards, 1st, 8th, 32nd Divisions.

3. The objects of the operations are :

(a) To capture the enemy position from St. Yves to Observatory Ridge.

(b) To capture as many as possible of the enemy guns in the vicinity of Oosttaverne and north-east of Messines.

(c) To consolidate a position to secure our possession of the Messines–Wytschaete Ridge and establish a series of posts in advance.

4. The final objective of each corps is shown generally on attached map by a Black Line,[1] the intermediate stages being shown by Red and Blue Lines, together with timings at each stage. It is imperative, in order to effect surprise and to capture enemy guns, that the attack should be pushed through without delay in one day.

5. The attack will be made at dawn (the exact hour will be notified later).

6. The initial advance will be assisted by the explosion of mines on each corps front. The mines will be fired at zero hour.

7. Two battalions of the Heavy Branch Machine Gun Corps [Tanks] will assist the operations.

8. The preliminary bombardment will be 5 days.

The allotment of artillery to corps, the artillery policy to be pursued from now onwards, the method of carrying out the preliminary bombardment and the general artillery plan have been issued to corps concerned.

9. A subsidiary operation will be carried out by VIII Corps in connection with the above attack.

10. H.Q. Second Army will be at Cassel.

11. Acknowledge.

C. H. HARINGTON,
M.G.G.S. Second Army.

Issued at 9 p.m.

---

[1] Not reproduced. Sketch 2 gives the objectives.

SECOND ARMY OPERATION ORDER NO. 2
OF 19TH MAY, 1917
(Sketch 3)

1. In continuation of Second Army No. 1, the scope of the operations set forth therein will be extended to include the capture of the Oosttaverne Line by a deliberate attack.

2. The Blue Line [second intermediate objective] will be captured by Zero + 1.40 where a pause of two hours will be made.

3. At Zero + 3.40 the advance to the Black Line [first day's objective] will be made which will be captured by Zero + 5. Steps will be taken to ensure that this line is consolidated effectively without delay.

4. The attack on the Oosttaverne Line will be made from the Black Line at Zero + 10 by fresh troops brought forward for the purpose.

5. Immediately the Black Line is captured all heavy available artillery will be employed against the Oosttaverne Line and on counter-battery work, and a protective barrage will be maintained in advance of the troops engaged in consolidating the Black Line.

6. During the interval between Zero + 5 and Zero + 10, as much field artillery as possible will be brought forward to positions previously selected and communications adjusted.

Patrols and reconnaissances will be pushed out as far as the artillery barrage permits.

7. O.C. II Brigade Heavy Branch M.G.C. will arrange direct with corps for the employment of the Tanks allotted in G. 691 dated 18.5.1917 to assist

(a) In the capture of the Black Line,
(b) in the capture of the Oosttaverne Line and enemy guns.

8. An artillery plan in connection with the capture of the Oosttaverne Line will be issued shortly.

9. Acknowledge.

C. H. HARINGTON,
M.G.G.S. Second Army.

Issued at 12 noon.

APPENDIX X

ALLOTMENT AND EMPLOYMENT OF TANKS

SECOND ARMY ORDER OF 18TH MAY, 1917
(Sketch 5)

IX Corps
X Corps
II Anzac Corps
II Brigade Heavy Branch M.G.C.

Tanks will be allotted and employed as under in the forthcoming operations.

1. The main objects of the operations are:
  (a) The capture and consolidation of the Messines–Wytschaete Ridge.
  (b) The capture of the Oosttaverne Line.
  (c) The capture of the enemy guns in the area between (a) and (b).
In all of the above it is hoped that tanks will be able to assist.

2. It is thought that tanks can best be employed in the first instance to assist in the pressure being put on the enemy from the northern and southern flanks, viz., from Dam Strasse and Messines.

Not only tactically will this be of advantage, but the ground is more suitable for the employment of tanks in the above directions.

3. The allotment of tanks will be as under:

To X Corps (Northern Tank Bn.)	3 sections for Dam Strasse attack to operate under the orders of X Corps commander.
To IX Corps (Northern Tank Bn.)	1 section to operate under the orders of G.O.C. IX Corps for 19th Division.
	2 sections in corps reserve.
To II Anzac Corps (Southern Tank Bn.)	1 section to co-operate with 25th Division under orders of G.O.C. II Anzac.
	1 section to assist attack of 36th Division (arrangements to be made between IX and II Anzac Corps).
	1 section in corps reserve.
	3 sections for capture of Messines to work under G.O.C. II Anzac for assisting New Zealand and 3rd Australian Divisions.
In Army Reserve	3 sections Northern Tank Bn.
	3 sections Southern Tank Bn.

420   APPENDIX X

4. It is intended that the above (less Army reserve) should be used for the capture of the Black Line [first objective]. It will therefore be necessary for the tanks in corps reserve to move forward as soon as possible to assist in the above.

The advance from the Blue [second intermediate objective] to Black Line will be made at Zero + 3.40 hours. It is hoped that the Black Line will be captured by Zero + 5 hours.

5. The attack of the Oosttaverne Line will be made by fresh troops at Zero + 10 hours and will be assisted by such tanks as can be rallied from the attack on the Black Line and by the tanks in Army reserve, which will be allotted to corps for the purpose.

IX Corps and II Anzac Corps will each include the passage of 3 sections of the above through their areas.

6. The commander, 2nd Heavy Brigade, will arrange to move forward the tanks in Army reserve (24) at such time and by such routes as will insure their getting to the Black Line in sufficient time to operate in the attack of the Oosttaverne Line which attack will commence from the Black Line at Zero + 10 hours.

He will consult with the corps commanders as to the places of assembly and routes required to give effect to the above.

C. H. HARINGTON,
M.G.G.S. Second Army.

APPENDIX XI

MACHINE GUNS IN THE ATTACK
GENERAL PRINCIPLES
(Issued by G.H.Q. before the battle of Messines)

1. The nature of the ground over which the attack will proceed necessitates the division of the tasks of machine guns allotted for covering fire into three categories:

(*a*) A creeping barrage, either direct, enfilade or oblique in front of the artillery barrage. The object of this barrage is to catch anyone rushing back from the heavies or sheltering in shell holes or ditches between the trenches.

(*b*) Guns detailed for fire on selected targets, such as strong-points, cuttings or ravines.

(*c*) Guns to sweep from the commencement of the attack all the ground in front and rear of the enemy's main line of resistance on the Ridge and other advanced localities commanding his front lines.

All guns will have a protective barrage line in order to cover the pause at the intermediate objectives.

APPENDIX XI

2. Guns for (a) and (b) will be more or less on a line about 1,000 yards behind our front line.

Guns for (c) will be on a line as far forward as possible so as to obviate a change of position before the Ridge is secured.

3. It is proposed that the guns from each brigade should form a group. Definite tasks will be allotted to each group. The Group Commanders will be under the control of the divisional M.G. officer. This officer during operations to be located at the most convenient brigade H.Q. where he will be in communication with each group, his own and flank divisions and with the corps.

The guns in each divisional sector will be under the control of the division, with the proviso that the barrage guns or their tasks once approved, will not be altered without the authority of the corps.

4. The division will see to all the necessary work being carried out, supply materials, and make arrangements for supply of ammunition, maps or charts, etc.

5. Arrangements are being made for the fixing of a "Depression Stop" on each gun. A plan is enclosed of a portable platform for the emplacement.[1]

6. The scheme attached allots from the reserve division a certain number of guns to each divisional sector. The task of these guns will be completed when the Ridge is secured and they will then come under the orders of the corps. The same applies to the motor machine guns.

7. The scheme provides for the searching of all important features between the reserve line and the final objective and for a large number of guns being ultimately available for holding the Ridge.

The searching of the ground between the trenches is a most important factor which is often overlooked; and perhaps much more important than the trenches themselves. Machine guns are very effective weapons for this purpose, and this will be their chief rôle until the objectives are reached and secured. Their next rôle is to put down a protective barrage against attack.

The schemes provide only a general idea. Exact targets and times for lifts will be worked out in detail later on. They cannot be laid down until the artillery programme is settled.

8. *Ammunition* At Zero the following scale of ammunition per gun should be established:

3,500 rounds in belts at the gun;
8,000 rounds in boxes at the Belt-filling Depot;
8,500 rounds in boxes at Reserve Dump;
4,500 rounds in boxes in the ammunition limbers.

---

[1] Not reproduced.

Ammunition not consumed by the guns of the reserve division will be available for the other guns.

9. The construction of the emplacements and preparation of maps can be begun immediately. The maps or charts can be so drawn as to allow of any alteration of targets without altering the gun positions, and they will also allow of an enormous concentration of fire on any particular locality.

10. During the artillery bombardment machine guns should co-operate for the purpose of :

(1) Lowering the efficiency of the enemy working-parties.

(2) Making the transport of material, and especially trench mortar ammunition, difficult.

(3) The deterioration of the enemy's morale. This will be obtained by firing on :

(a) The targets engaged during the day by the artillery and wire.

(b) Communication trenches and avenues leading to the above.

(c) The points of assembly of working-parties, dumps, etc.

(d) Trench railways, roads and tracks ; especially those leading to trench mortar emplacements.

(e) Searching of reverse slopes.

(f) Anti-aircraft defence.

11. The following points are some of the lessons learnt by one corps and deserve very careful consideration :

(a) *Guns going forward*

Most divisions allotted 8 guns (some 12) to go forward for early consolidation.

Each machine gun was given a definite locality to be reached at a definite stage of the operation.

The time for going forward varied from Zero to Zero + 2 hours.

Guns pushed forward with the first wave were destroyed.

The machine guns must avoid becoming mixed up with the assaulting waves.

They should cross No Man's Land as early as possible and then progress behind the assaulting troops. If not across before the hostile barrage begins there is no object in trying to push on ; get on when the shelling permits. Battalions have a large number of Lewis guns to rely on if resistance is met. Machine guns in an advance cannot quickly come into action apart from the impossibility of firing over our own men at very close range.

It is desirable that some guns should reach points of

APPENDIX XI 423

observation as soon after their capture as possible. They may have good targets in the fleeing enemy.

The machine-gun defensive organization *must* be in depth.

Avoid old German trenches. Get 100 yards away in a shell hole or depression.

(b) *Ammunition*

Ammunition marked " J " is unserviceable. That marked " T " gives some trouble. There was no trouble with that marked " E " and " K.N."

When the dumps are established they should be marked by boards or flappers.

Pack trains are essential for getting ammunition forward. Yukon carriers most efficient.[1]

(c) *Miscellaneous*

Use flappers as an arrangement for timing of lifts. Place sandbags on ground to receive empty belts. Rainproof shelters required for belt fillers.

APPENDIX XII

MEMORANDUM ON THE PRESENT SITUATION AND FUTURE PLANS
WRITTEN FOR THE WAR CABINET BY THE COMMANDER-IN-CHIEF
12TH JUNE, 1917

My action since the 1st May has been in accordance with the views and intentions expressed in my Nos. O.A.D. 428 of that date, and O.A.D. 449 of the 16th May.[2]

A modified pressure has been maintained, with good results, on the Arras and Vimy fronts and arrangements to continue this for the present have been made.

The first phase of the operations for the clearance of the Belgian coast (capture of the Messines–Wytschaete Ridge) has been carried out with complete success, and is of considerable importance in facilitating preparation for a further advance and in improving our defensive position round Ypres.

Arrangements have been made to take over from the French, at an early date, the sector now held by them on the Belgian coast.

French troops have already taken over my southern front as far north as the Omignon river; and by arrangement with

---

[1] With a Yukon carrier the weight of the burden on the back was taken by a brow-band. See p. 67.
[2] Not printed; the gist has been given in the text.

General Pétain, instead of relieving my troops between the Omignon river and Havrincourt as proposed by me, French troops will take over a portion of the front now held by the Belgians on my immediate left and will co-operate in my Northern Operations.

General Pétain is also arranging for offensive operations on other portions of his front, on a sufficient scale to prevent withdrawal of German forces to oppose my advance; and, well prepared and supported by artillery, the operations intended by him should prove effective in wearing down the enemy opposed to him.

It will be seen, therefore, that, with one exception, the conditions specified by me in my memorandum of the 1st May have been, or are being, fulfilled.

The one exception I allude to is the completion of my divisions to establishment and the provision of guns required to complete my Armies to the scale agreed upon.

With the drafts and guns already promised, however, I consider, on present indications, that it will be possible to carry through at least a portion of the operations intended, and my plans and preparations are being made to advance by stages so arranged that, while each stage will give a definite and useful result, it will be possible for me to discontinue the advance if and when it appears that the means at my disposal are insufficient to justify a further effort.

Success in the first stage alone will improve our positions round Ypres so greatly that the saving in normal casualties there during the winter will probably far more than counterbalance the casualties to be expected in capturing the objectives aimed at. Moreover, from the experience of previous attacks made by us this year, the German casualties in defence are likely to exceed ours in attack, while the moral gain from another defeat of the Germans will count for much, and at the present stage of the war may open up far-reaching possibilities.

I am accordingly pushing on my preparations for the Northern Operations, but these cannot be complete for some time and the scope of my plans can and will be adjusted as may be necessary to future developments in the situation.

I take this opportunity to submit for the consideration of the War Cabinet the following remarks on the general situation and the deductions I draw as to the conduct of the campaign in France.

According to reports, the endurance of the German nation is being tested so severely that discontent there has already assumed formidable proportions. The German Government, helped by the long disciplinary training of the people, is still able to control this discontent; but every realization of the failure of the submarine campaign increases the difficulty of doing so, and further defeats in the field may have unexpectedly great results, which may come with unexpected suddenness.

The German army, too, shows unmistakeable signs of deterioration in many ways and the cumulative effort of further defeats may at any time yield greater results in the field than we can absolutely rely on gaining.

From a careful study of the conditions, I feel justified in stating that continued pressure with as little delay as possible certainly promises at least very valuable results; whereas relaxation of pressure now would strengthen belief that the Allies are becoming totally exhausted, and that Germany can outlast them. Waning hope in Germany would be revived, and time would be gained to replenish food, ammunition and other requirements. In fact many of the advantages already gained by us would be lost, and this would certainly be realized by, and would have a depressing effect on, our Armies in the field, who have made such great efforts to gain them.

The depressing effect in France would be especially great and especially dangerous. At the present crisis of the war French hope must have something to feed on. The hope of American assistance is not sufficient for the purpose. It is still too far distant and the French at the moment are living a good deal on the hope of further British successes. They can and will assist in these by keeping the enemy on their front fully employed, wearing him down, and preventing him from withdrawing divisions to oppose us. But they feel unable to do more at present than this, and it is useless to expect it of them— although any considerable British successes and signs of a breakdown in the German power of resistance would probably have an electrifying effect.

That the British Armies in France are capable of gaining considerable further successes this year I am confident, as are all ranks under my command—it is only the extent of the success possible that is in doubt, and that depends mainly on three factors, viz. :

First, on whether the War Cabinet decides to concentrate our resources on the effort.

Secondly, on the degree of help given by Russia.

Thirdly, on the extent to which the German resolution and power of endurance stand the great strain they are undergoing.

The first of these factors lies within the power of the War Cabinet. The second to some extent, and the third to a very great extent, depend on their decision.

It is my considered opinion, based not on mere optimism but on a thorough study of the situation, guided by experience which

I may claim to be considerable, that if our resources are concentrated in France to the fullest possible extent the British Armies are capable and can be relied on to effect great results this summer—results which will make final victory more assured and which may even bring it within reach this year.

On the other hand I am equally convinced that to fail in concentrating our resources in the Western theatre, or to divert them from it, would be most dangerous. It might lead to the collapse of France. It would certainly encourage Germany. And it would discourage our own officers and men very considerably. The desired military results, possible in France, are not possible elsewhere.

I am aware that my motives in stating this may be misunderstood, but I trust that in the interests of the Empire at what is undoubtedly a critical period in the war, whatever value the War Cabinet may attach to my opinion may not be discounted by any doubt of such a kind. I have reason to believe that the commanders-in-chief of British forces in other theatres of war are entirely in agreement with the view that the Western Front always has been and will remain the decisive one.

The correct strategy to pursue, in accordance with the teaching of every great exponent of the art of war, is clear under such conditions.

In my opinion the only serious doubt as to possibilities in France lies in the action to be expected of Russia, but even that doubt is an argument in favour of doing our utmost in France with as little delay as possible.

Russia is still holding large German forces and every week gained makes it more impossible for the enemy to transfer divisions to the West in time, if we act promptly.

There is still room for hope of increased Russian assistance, and successes in the West will surely increase the prospects of it.[1]

A passive attitude in the West, or more minor successes, would not encourage the Russians; and delay under such conditions may make matters worse in Russia instead of better.

In conclusion, I desire to make it clear that, whatever may be placed at my disposal, my undertakings will be limited to what it is reasonably possible to succeed in.

Given sufficient force, provided no great transfer of German troops is made, in time, from East to West, it is probable that the Belgian coast could be cleared this summer, and the defeats on the German troops entailed in doing so might quite possibly lead to their collapse.

Without sufficient force I shall not attempt to clear the coast,

---

[1] The Kerenski offensive took place in July.

APPENDIX XII

and my efforts will be restricted to gaining such victories as are within reach, thereby improving my position for the winter and opening up possibilities for further operations hereafter if and when the necessary means are provided.

A definition of the term "sufficient force" must depend on developments in the general situation; but provided that does not grow less satisfactory than at present I estimate that even the full programme may not prove beyond reach with the number of divisions now at my disposal, if brought up to and maintained at establishment of men and guns. An increase in the forces available would, of course, give still greater prospects of complete success.

D. HAIG,
Field-Marshal,
Commanding-in-Chief, British
Armies in France.

NOTE ON THE STRATEGIC SITUATION WITH SPECIAL REFERENCE TO THE PRESENT CONDITION OF GERMAN RESOURCES AND PROBABLE GERMAN OPERATIONS

1. The distribution of the hostile strength in the various European theatres of war is at present [11th June]:

	Western.	Russian.	Italian.	Danube.	Macedonia.	Total.
German	157	66	—	9	2	234
Austrian	—	$37\frac{1}{2}$	$38\frac{1}{2}$	$2\frac{1}{2}$	2	$80\frac{1}{2}$
Bulgarian	—	—	—	$3\frac{1}{2}$	$8\frac{1}{2}$	12
Turkish	—	1	—	2	1	4
	157	$104\frac{1}{2}$	$38\frac{1}{2}$	17	$13\frac{1}{2}$	$330\frac{1}{2}$

It is noteworthy that the total number of hostile divisions on the Eastern Front has, since the beginning of May, only been reduced by 2 German divisions, 2 Austrian divisions, making a total of 4 divisions.

2. From a study of the movements of German divisions from East to West and West to East since February of this year, it seems established that:

1st: The Germans do not intend to reduce the total number of divisions on the Eastern Front at the present time.

2nd: They are sending to the Eastern Front either units of inferior quality, or else units which they desire to save from heavy casualties (e.g., Saxon units) for political purposes.

Even if the position in Russia should change for the worse in the immediate future, there appears no reason to anticipate that Russia will make a separate peace, and, therefore, for the reasons given in Ia/33796,[1] it is improbable that more than 20 divisions could be spared from the Eastern Front for the Western Front. These 20 divisions could not arrive at a greater rate than 2 divisions in every 6 days.

3. *Wearing out of Divisions in the Western Theatre*

The total number of German divisions on the Western Front is at present 157. Of these, 105 divisions have passed through the mill of battle, and although some of them may be used again in defence, none will be of full fighting value for offensive operations. Only 52 divisions on the Western Front remain fresh, and of these 17 are Landwehr divisions unsuitable for offensive operations.

Thus, at the present moment, if Germany were to anticipate offensive operations, she could not rely on more than 35 fresh divisions on the Western Front, and 20 fresh divisions which might be brought from Russia and replaced by tired divisions from the Western Front.

4. *German Available Man-Power*

The situation as regards the various classes in the German army is summarized as follows:

All classes up to 1918 have been exhausted in the sense that they can afford no further recruits.

The 1915 and 1916 classes together form about 15 per cent. of the infantry in the German field units.

The 1917 class is now at its maximum in fighting units and alone represents between 12 and 15 per cent. of the fighting infantry. A few more recruits of this class may be available for drafts, but the proportion will be small.

The 1918 class is now coming to the front in large numbers and provides the bulk of the immediate reserves in the advanced field depots. It represents about 5 per cent. of the fighting infantry.

The 1919 class is now at the home depôts.

The 1920 class is being examined prior to being called up.

It is noteworthy that while the systematic drafting of recruits from the depôts on the Eastern Front to the Western Front, rendered possible by the inactivity of Russia, has retarded the rapid flow of the 1918 class, still the exhaustion of this class is proceeding at approximately the rate which was anticipated in previous studies of man-power. Prisoners taken in the recent fighting show a remarkable absence of further drafts of "combed" men reaching the German infantry.

The only remaining source of man-power, beyond the annual classes specified above, consists in returned wounded from

---

[1] Not printed.

APPENDIX XII

hospital. This may be expected to provide about 50,000 a month as a maximum figure, leaving a balance of between 100,000 and 200,000 a month to be provided by the younger classes during the ensuing months of heavy fighting.

Experience has shown that, even in the first years of the war, when Germany was receiving large drafts of " combed " men and men previously unfit, still the average of $2\frac{1}{2}$ annual classes was required to maintain the units in the field at their fighting strength. In the present year, with an increased number of divisions in the field and with a greatly reduced if not entire cessation of drafts of " combed " men and men previously unfit, it is a fair deduction that not less than 3 annual classes, and probably $3\frac{1}{2}$, will be required to maintain the forces in the field at their establishment. That is to say, by the end of this year Germany will be fighting with her 1920 class in the field depôts and with the home depôts either empty or filled by the 1921 class —boys who will then be less than 17 years of age.

These estimates of man-power are borne out by definite indications which have come to light during the past few months, viz :

(1) Reduction of the establishment of German battalions in the field army.

(2) The breaking up of the regiments of the second series of new divisions formed in Germany, and now forming drafts for field units.

(3) The generally reduced physique of the men in the field units, as exemplified by the prisoners captured by us.

The question of man-power may be summed up in one sentence, viz. :

Germany is now within four to six months of the total exhaustion of her available man-power, if fighting continues at its present intensity.

At the end of this time, it can be definitely asserted, she will be unable to maintain the strength of her field units at even their present reduced establishments.

5. *Economic Conditions*

During the past few months perfectly definite indications of the pressure of economic conditions on the military strength of the German army have come to light, viz. :

(1) Captured order pointing out that worn-out guns cannot now be replaced as rapidly as required.

(2) Captured order substituting iron cartridge cases for brass cartridge cases in rifle ammunition.

(3) Captured order laying down the severest economy in telephone and telegraph equipment and wires.

(4) Captured order reducing field rations by one-third.

In addition to these direct evidences of the stringency produced by the blockade and the general exhaustion of the country, captured correspondence has shown beyond any possibility of doubt that the economic conditions in Germany itself are pressing with great and ever-increasing severity on the people.

A study of the tables of exchange shows that since the commencement of the year the exchange of the mark has fallen according to the following extent:

Place.	December, 1916.	April, 1917.	June, 1917.
Amsterdam	38.88	38.43	34.80
Stockholm	56.75	52.25	49.75
Copenhagen	59.76	54.50	50.70
Berne	79.90	78.60	73.10

6. *Effects of Previous Battles of 1917*

A reliable informant has given the total casualties suffered by the German army in the battles of Arras, Champagne and the Aisne up to the beginning of this month as 400,000. If to this are added the ordinary casualties from sickness and casualties from other theatres, it is probable that the total casualties to the German army since the beginning of April are not less than 500,000, an average of nearly 250,000 a month.

7. *Morale*

The most definite evidence that can be obtained with regard to the state of morale of an army in the field is the opinion entertained of it by the army to which it is opposed.

There is no doubt that at the present moment the British troops are convinced that in every respect they are better fighting men than the German army. This is a very marked difference from the opinions which were openly expressed before the battle of the Somme.

Further evidence of the fall of German morale can be found in captured correspondence, of which samples have been printed and issued from time to time.

But the greatest evidence is probably the small number of casualties with which positions, fortified by every possible means and which the Germans intended to defend to the last, have been captured by our army.

8. *Summary*

These general conditions can be summed up as follows:

(1) The course of events in Russia has not, so far, justified Germany in moving any considerable number of troops from the Eastern to the Western theatre.

(2) Even if events in Russia should take a marked turn for the worse, it is unlikely that Germany could move more than

20 divisions at an average rate of 2 divisions per week from the Eastern to the Western Front.

(3) Of the divisions at present on the Western Front not more than 35 remain fresh for offensive operations. 105 divisions have been worn out by the battle and have probably lost an average of not less than 40 per cent. of their infantry.

(4) Germany is within four to six months of a date at which she will be unable to maintain the strength of her units in the field.

(5) The pressure of economic conditions on the nation at large is increasing and has definitely extended to the ranks of the army.

(6) There is a marked and unmistakable fall in the morale of the German troops.

From all these definite facts, it is a fair deduction that, given a continuance of circumstances as they stand at present and given a continuation of the effort of the Allies, then Germany may well be forced to conclude a peace on our terms before the end of the year.

G.H.Q. France,
   11th June, 1917.

APPENDIX XIII

FIFTH ARMY INSTRUCTIONS FOR THE OFFENSIVE OF THE 31st JULY, 1917, DATED 27th JUNE, 1917

Addressed to II, VIII, XIV, XVIII, and XIX Corps

(Sketch 10)

At a series of Conferences held by the Army commander, on the 26th June, 1917, the following points, connected with the forthcoming operations, were definitely fixed and the decisions arrived at are to be taken as orders:

1. The barrage will open at Zero on the enemy's front line. It will lift off the front line at Zero + 6 minutes and will then creep forward at an average rate of 100 yards in 4 minutes.

2. The barrage will be kept upon each successive objective until the last infantryman is in a position to assault. The whole of the objective will then be carried simultaneously all along our front.

3. The Green Line [third objective] is to be the main objective of the day's operations. The protective barrage will remain in front of this line for one hour after the time at which the infantry is to reach it.

At this stage of the operations all commanders, including the Army commander, will resume control of their troops. It is more important to ensure perfect control than to gain advantages of ground.

4. So soon as this final protective barrage is lifted, all barrage arrangements will be placed under corps control; but great care must be exercised by G.Os.C., R.A., to ensure that arrangements at all points of junction are made in consultation with the corps concerned.

Patrols are then to be sent out to reconnoitre the enemy and to make good any ground and tactical points which he has vacated. The patrols and their objectives should be definitely told off by corps before the beginning of operations. They should be taken from fresh troops if possible. In sending them forward it is to be remembered that it is all-important for us to have a clearly defined line from which to start the next advance whenever it may be ordered.

5. Finally, the Army commander impressed upon all corps commanders, and directed them to press on their subordinates, the fact that if we are to achieve the results expected of us, we must be prepared to fight a series of organized battles on a wide front and on a large scale. If we are to do this successfully the reorganization after each attack must be very carefully thought out beforehand and must be executed with the utmost possible rapidity.

6. A time-table of lifts is attached,[1] also remarks by the Army commander on each corps scheme, for the consideration of corps commanders.

7. Acknowledge.

N. MALCOLM,
Major-General, M.G.G.S. Fifth Army.

---

[1] Not reproduced.

8TH DIVISION OPERATION ORDERS OF THE 22ND JULY, 1917

(Sketches 10, 22)

1. (*a*) On Zero Day the II Corps is to attack the enemy on its front line; it will attack with the following divisions in line from right to left :

    1st and 2nd Stages ... 24th Division, 30th Division, 8th Division.
    3rd Stage ... ... 24th, 18th and 8th Divisions.
    4th Stage ... ... 18th, 8th Divisions.

(*b*) The 25th Division will be in reserve ready to exploit a great success on the 8th Division front.

(*c*) The 15th Division (XIX Corps) will be attacking on the left of and simultaneously with 8th Division.

2. The objective of the II Corps is to secure the following general lines :

    (i) [First objective] Shrewsbury Forest–Stirling Castle–Bellewaarde Ridge (Blue Line).

    (ii) [Second objective] Dumbarton Lakes–Herentage Château–Westhoek Ridge (Black Line).

    (iii) [Third objective] Tower Hamlets–Veldhoek–Polygon Wood–Potsdam (Green Line).

    (iv) [Fourth objective] If opportunity arises, the Molenaarelsthoek–Broodseinde Ridge (Red Line).

3 and 4. [Boundary and objectives in detail.]

5. The attack on the Blue and Black Lines [First and Second objectives] will be made by the 24th Brigade (on the right) and 23rd Brigade (on the left).

6. The attack on the Green Line [Third objective] will be made by the 25th Brigade which will advance from its dug-outs at Halfway House not later than Zero + 4 hours, but in such time as to be formed up behind the Westhoek Ridge by Zero + 6 hours. They will then advance up to the line of the protective barrage so as to follow close up to it when it lifts at Zero + 6 hours 28 minutes.

7. At Zero + 7 hours 10 minutes, the 24th Brigade will take over the whole of the Black Line [Second objective] from 23rd Brigade which will be ready to move forward on receipt of orders about Zero + 7 hours 50 minutes to a position of readiness east of the Haanebeek.

8. The advance to the Red Line [Fourth objective] will be in three stages and will be carried out by the reserve battalion, 25th Brigade, assisted by tanks and B Squadron 1/1st Yorkshire Dragoons.

The advance at each stage will consist of pushing out strong cavalry and infantry patrols with tanks, supported by larger bodies to secure localities.

The patrols, their objectives and those of the tanks will be definitely told off before the commencement of operations.

Should the enemy be found in weak strength to be contesting our advance, he will be driven in by the troops mentioned above: should he be found to be in strength, it is NOT the divisional commander's intention to attack him on Z Day; the leading troops of the 25th Brigade will establish themselves in that case on a line within assaulting distance of whatever line the enemy is holding.

9. G.O.C. 23rd Brigade will keep in close touch with G.O.C. 25th Brigade from Zero + 7 hours 50 minutes onwards, and will, on receipt of information from him that any of the objective lines east of the Green Line [Third objective] has been secured or that the advanced troops 25th Brigade have established themselves within assaulting distance of the enemy, at once move forward troops to consolidate the line gained. The actual line to be consolidated is left to the discretion of the G.O.C. 23rd Brigade, but it will be approximately the line farthest east that the advanced troops 25th Brigade have been able to secure. On relief, the latter, less Squadron 1/1st Yorkshire Dragoons which will then automatically come under orders of G.O.C. 25th Brigade, will at once rejoin 25th Brigade.

10. Two brigades 25th Division will from about Zero + 5 hours occupy all trenches and dug-outs in 8th Division assembly area except those occupied by Signal personnel, dumps, dressing stations, and the Brigade H.Q. at Railway Wood. In the event of the Red Line [Fourth objective] being gained by 8th Division, these two brigades will in all probability be at once ordered forward to take over and consolidate the Red Line.

11. The approximate lines to be consolidated are as follows:

(i) The Blue Line [First objective] by 24th and 23rd Brigades until Zero + 5 hours.

(ii) The Black Line [Second objective] by 24th and 23rd Brigades until 24th Brigade take over the line from 23rd Brigade, when 24th Brigade will be solely responsible for consolidation.

(iii) The Green Line [Third objective], which as the main objective of II Corps, must be held at all costs by 25th Brigade.

APPENDIX XIV 435

(iv) The most advanced line gained east of the Green Line by 23rd Brigade.

12. (a) The artillery barrage will lift normally at the rate of 100 yards in 4 minutes.

(b) It will be put down on enemy's front line at Zero and will remain on it till Zero + 5 minutes. It will then lift 100 yards and remain on that line till Zero + 8 minutes : it will then lift 100 yards and remain on that line till Zero + 10 minutes : it will then lift 100 yards and remain on that line till Zero + 14 minutes, after which lifts and times will be normal.

(c) Protective barrages will be put down as follows :
    (i) 300 yards east of Blue and Black Lines respectively.
    (ii) 500 yards east of Green Line.
    (iii) 500 yards east of Noordemdhoek–Broodseinde road from Red Line.

[12 (d) and (e) deal with artillery support.]

13. [Deals with artillery support and machine-gun barrage.]

14. (a) 1 section of No. 3/A Bn. Tanks will co-operate with each of the 23rd and 24th Brigades, if the attack on the Black Line is held up at any point.

(b) No. 2 Coy. of A Bn. Tanks will co-operate with 25th Brigade in its advance from the Black Line to the Green Line.

(c) 1 section No. 3 Coy. A Bn. Tanks will co-operate with 25th Brigade in its advance from the Green Line to the Red Line.

15. No. 3 Special Company R.E. will fire 1,000 Thermit 4-inch Stokes mortar shells at the bank on the west edge of Zillebeke Lake from Zero to Zero + 10 minutes.

16. [Road repairs.]

17. Contact aeroplanes will be sent over the lines to receive signals as to the positions of the leading troops at the following hours :

(a) At Zero + 1 hour (15 minutes after reaching the Blue Line).

(b) At Zero + 2 hours (30 minutes after last man reaches Black Line).

(c) At Zero + 8 hours (30 minutes after last man reaches Green Line).

(d) At Zero + 9 hours (20 minutes after patrols have gone forward from Green Line).

18. All troops will be in their assembly zones by 1 a.m. Zero Day ; troops detailed for the attack of the Blue and Black Lines

[First and Second objectives] will be in their assembly positions by Zero — 1½ hours.

19. Arrangements as to synchronization of watches, information as to Z Day and zero hour will be issued later.

20. Divisional headquarters will be at Scottish Camp on Z Day.

21. Instructions have been issued in amplification of these orders : in cases of any difference, these orders will be considered as overriding the instructions.

22. Acknowledge.

Issued at 7 p.m.

E. BEDDINGTON,
Lieut.-Colonel, General Staff.

APPENDIX XV

MEMORANDUM DATED 26TH JUNE, 1917, BY BR.-GENERAL J. H. DAVIDSON (OPERATIONS SECTION O.a) ON THE FORTHCOMING OPERATIONS (31ST JULY, 1917) AND REPLY DATED 28TH JUNE BY GENERAL SIR HUBERT GOUGH (COMMANDING THE FIFTH ARMY)

I am of opinion that in the operations of the Second and Fifth Armies which are shortly to take place we should not attempt to push infantry to the maximum distance to which we can hope to get them by means of our artillery fire, our tanks, and the temporary demoralization of the enemy. Experience shows that such action may, and often does, obtain spectacular results for the actual day of operations, but these results are obtained at the expense of such disorganization of the forces employed as to render the resumption of the battle under advantageous circumstances at an early date highly improbable.

An advance which is essentially deliberate and sustained may not achieve such important results during the first day of operations, but will in the long run be much more likely to obtain a decision.

By a deliberate and sustained advance, I refer to a succession of operations each at two or three days' interval, each having as its object the capture of the enemy's defences, strongpoints, or tactical features, to a depth of not less than 1,500 yards and not more than 3,000 yards.

It has been proved beyond doubt that with sufficient and efficient artillery preparation we can push our infantry through to a depth of a mile without undue losses or disorganization, and I recommend strongly that the operations for the capture of the Passchendaele–Staden Ridge should be conducted on the principle of a series of such operations, following one another at short intervals, in such a manner as to avoid at any particular period wholesale reliefs, wholesale displacement of artillery, and the wholesale hurrying forward of guns, troops, ammunition, and supplies over ground which is practically devoid of communications.

The Germans will bring forward their reserves to stop our advance whether the latter is rapid or deliberate. It appears to be much more advantageous to us to accept battle with and engage those reserves when we are in an organized state, our guns in position, our troops not tired, and our communications in a good state, than to engage them in some more forward position where we have none of the advantages referred to. We shall not be in a position to obtain a victory or exploit success until we have thoroughly demoralized the enemy and defeated at all events the first series of divisions which he will bring up as reinforcements to the battle.

In considering the manner of carrying out the operations as recommended above, the following points require close study:

1. *Communications*

In order to carry out offensive operations of any description successfully we require to have good communications, both for purposes of troop movements and for supplies and ammunition. Roads and light railways must be constructed. It is not possible to do this at a very rapid pace.

2. *Displacement of Artillery*

In order to give the enemy no rest and to preserve continuity of artillery action, there must be no great displacement of artillery on any one day. The great majority of the guns must always be in action. The displacement must therefore be gradual. Any abnormal displacement of artillery dislocates the whole mechanism of movement, supply, and the construction of the communications.

3. *Continuity of Artillery Action*

There should be little or no diminution in the action of the artillery. When the preparation of the first operation is completed and the assault is delivered the destructive preparation of the next zone will be commenced at once. For this purpose it will be advisable in each phase of the operations to have a few guns well forward and masked. A certain amount of displacement of artillery will always be proceeding. As soon as the objective on the first day has been reached, such field artillery as it is necessary to move will be moved forward and the practice barrage commenced at once.

The destructive counter-battery work will be continued unceasingly and without any pause. Neutralizing counter-battery work will be more limited.

4. *Intensity of Artillery Fire*

There will not be such long periods of intense barrage fire. This should materially help to save gun lives. It will be necessary only to keep up the intensity of barrage fire during the period of attack, which will be comparatively short.

5. *Concentration in Artillery Preparation*

Since the zone of preparation will not be so deep, the artillery fire for the purposes of destruction will be more concentrated.

6. *Line of Departure*

The line of departure in each successive step of the operations must not be ragged, that is to say, the objectives on any day of attack must be fully reached. It often happens that, if the advance of the infantry is carried to any great depth, the line that is reached is ragged, and it is not only difficult for the infantry to start forward to a fresh attack but it is also impossible for the field artillery to put down a satisfactory barrage. The best means of securing a good line of departure for the next operation is to ensure that the infantry are not pushed too far and that the objectives are well within their reach.

7. *Casualties*

A large proportion of the casualties which are incurred are due to the density of the infantry which is necessitated by the intention of penetrating the enemy's position to a great depth. The less the depth to be penetrated, the less the depth of the troops required. Divisional reserves instead of being close up can be kept at some distance, immune from losses and fresh for the next effort.

8. *Reliefs*

With short and frequent advances, reliefs of large formations will be avoided owing to the fact that attacking troops can cover a wider front. This is an important factor and one which will reduce disorganization and confusion, and ensure continuity of action by avoiding the long delays which are inseparable from wholesale reliefs.

9. *Morale of the troops*

There is nothing the troops themselves dislike so much as great depth in an attack. The less the depth in attack, the greater is the confidence of the troops in their ability to reach their objectives, and the fewer will be the casualties. These facts tend to raise the morale of the troops since they feel confident of succeeding in their task.

10. *Sustained nature of the fight and effect on the enemy's morale*

By the means described above the fight can be sustained under conditions which are entirely to our advantage. The enemy will be allowed no respite. The first day's operations, which will probably aim at the capture of the enemy's second line of defence, will throw him into a state of disorganization, destroy a considerable portion of his forces, and cause him to withdraw his artillery. Our experience shows that the enemy does not recover from this state of partial demoralization for a period of two or three days ; if, therefore, we are in a position to deliver a second and well-organized attack during that period we shall already have secured very great advantages. These advantages are likely to increase as the process continues. The great danger in missing the advantages gained by a local and temporary disorganization of the enemy lies in the serious delays which are inseparable from over-reaching our strength and our organizing capabilities on the first day.

By the process described above and by a succession of successful operations deliberately planned and deliberately executed, there should come a moment when we will be justified in taking a certain amount of risk. Such risk should not, however, be undertaken until we have positive proof of the enemy's demoralization, which must be of more than a local and temporary character. This local and temporary character of the enemy's demoralization will probably change and become more widespread with the congestion of his troops and the disorganization in rear. Rapid and effective blows struck at him one after the other at short periods are likely to destroy his troops at a far greater pace than spasmodic efforts. It is the pace at which we can destroy the enemy's troops that will cause the greatest disorganization in his rear by congesting the areas with defeated troops and necessitating the reinforcements arriving too rapidly on his railways.

11. *Tanks*

The most satisfactory period for using tanks is that in which we are operating over ground which has not been destroyed by shell fire, when the enemy is partly demoralized, and when he has not been able to establish his anti-tank defences. With the exception of a few tanks which may be used at the outset of the operations for the purposes of rounding up pockets, etc., the greater bulk of the tanks should be reserved for use against the enemy during the later stages of the battle, when we are beginning to feel ourselves justified in taking risks.

APPENDIX XV

MEMORANDUM BY GENERAL SIR HUBERT GOUGH

In its broad principles, I am in agreement with this paper, in so far as it advocates a continuous succession of organized attacks.

The point for discussion is the application of this principle, as regards place and time, and particularly as regards the first day's attack. Should we go as far as we can the first day, viz.: certainly up to the Green Line, and possibly the Red Line, or should we confine ourselves to the Black Line on the first day and attack again in three days to gain the Green Line, and again to gain the Red Line at a further interval of three days?

It is important to recognize that the results to be looked for from a well-organized attack which has taken weeks and months to prepare are great, much ground can be gained, and prisoners and guns captured during the first day or two.

After the first attack, long prepared, one cannot hope to gain similar results in one attack as long as the enemy can find fresh reserves, and the depth of ground gained and guns captured usually decline in subsequent attacks.

I think therefore that it would be wasteful not to reap all the advantages possible resulting from the first attack.

If we only go as far as the Black Line on the first day and then make two more attacks with intervals on the Green and Red Lines, we would have to move many guns at least twice instead of only once as would be the case if we can take the Red Line on the first day. The delay in moving artillery is not caused by the length of time taken to traverse the distance covered so much as by the time taken to rearrange everything in the new position.

If we take the whole of the Red Line or only the Green Line, it is calculated that all our field artillery can be in position behind the captured line with 400 rounds per gun, and all our heavy artillery in position approximately on the line of No Man's Land, within three days of the first attack, ready to support an advance of fresh infantry. Owing to the number of divisions allocated by the Chief for this attack, we are enabled to fight a division with another division immediately behind it, ready to take up the same frontages, and the two divisions always acting in the closest liaison with each other. This provides us with great depth along our whole front and will enable reliefs to be carried out with greater facility and rapidity than has usually been possible.

It is necessary to draw the correct conclusions from past operations for future use, and it seems to me that it is an error to suppose that the delays and spasmodic attacks which we have witnessed have been entirely due to the disorganization of the forces engaged.

APPENDIX XV

It seems to me to have been due more to the failure to recognize in this war of masses and great depth of reserves, that immediately the organized battle has been fought, it is necessary to plan and prepare for a second organized battle, and after that, without delay, a third, and even a fourth.

Owing to this not being very clear in all minds, delays have arisen, in some cases because of the tendency to stay on a good position once captured and not advance into this " low ground " or into that " salient ".

In other cases, a tendency to think that one battle settled the fate of the operations and that nothing further was necessary than to advance against an enemy believed (erroneously) to be disorganized, and this has led to disappointments and delays owing to disjointed attacks and insufficient artillery support, no plan having been at once made to fight another and an " organized " battle on a grand scale.

I do not think, however, if the necessity for fighting a succession of organized battles is quite clear in everyone's mind, and if the plans for these battles are made, and are made without delay, that it will in any way militate against a sustained and deliberate advance, because all the ground that can be captured is seized as a result of the first day's attack, or indeed of any succeeding attacks.

The operations for the capture of Passchendaele–Staden Ridge envisaged by me, and put I trust clearly before my corps commanders, do in truth constitute a succession of organized attacks at short intervals.

I think we should certainly aim at the definite capture of the Green Line, and that, should the situation admit of our infantry advancing without much opposition to the Red Line, it would be of the greatest advantage to us to do so.

I do not say that we shall always be able to make organized attacks every 3 days, but I do look forward to making deliberate and organized attacks on a large scale every 10 days as long as our strength lasts, or until the enemy is exhausted. If it is previously and clearly recognized by every commander engaged in these operations that one successful battle is not sufficient to ensure success for the whole operation, and that we must prepare, mentally as well as materially, for a continuous succession of organized attacks, I do not think that there should be much danger of our giving battle with the German reserves until our troops are in an organized state and our guns in position.

In reference to this point, and to the great importance of rapidity, even though our attacks are of an organized nature, I would refer to the suggestion put forward by the D.L.R. for training special troops for laying light railways. I think the provision of these troops may be of incalculable value, and the men employed on this work for a few weeks during these operations may be the equivalent of 3 to 6 times their numbers brought up to fight later.

APPENDIX XVI

INSTRUCTIONS FOR RECOVERY OF TANKS DAMAGED IN ACTION

(ISSUED BY THE HEADQUARTERS OF THE TANK CORPS)
20TH JULY, 1917

1. OBJECT

The object of all Unditching and Salvage operations is to keep the maximum number of tanks in action with the minimum disorganization of the fighting crews.

2. MEANS

The means disposable are:
(a) The fighting crews
(b) Reserve crews (to relieve fighting crews of protective duties)
(c) Salvage companies
(d) Workshops personnel
(e) Tunnellers
(f) Unskilled labour.

3. PRINCIPLES

The principles to work by are:
(a) No tank will be abandoned. The tank commander is responsible for the safety of his tank until he has been relieved of this responsibility by his section or company commander.
(b) A ditched tank will not be considered as a tank out of action.
(c) Reorganization is not to be delayed by employing exhausted fighting crews on unditching operations.
(d) Work will first be concentrated on tanks which can be most speedily unditched or brought into action.
(e) The company commander is responsible for the safety of his tanks as long as they are borne on his charge.
(f) Salvage companies, as long as they are attached to brigades, will be considered as integral parts of them, and in order to carry out their work rapidly and with method they must be informed what the tank operations are and what they may demand.

APPENDIX XVI

(g) Salvage will be carried out by organized squads of men working in definite areas.

(h) Each brigade will be responsible for salvage of all tanks in its area of operations.

(i) Salvage squads will not be sent forward until information has been received as to what tanks are ditched, etc., and their whereabouts.

4. Distribution and Organization of Salvage Companies

Salvage companies will be distributed as follows:
No. 1 Company to the 2nd Brigade.
No. 2 (less one section) to the 3rd Brigade.
One section No. 2 Company to the 1st Brigade.

Tunnellers will be attached to salvage companies as follows:
No. 1 Salvage Company, 60 tunnellers from those allotted to 2nd Brigade.
No. 2 Salvage Company (less 1 section), 60 tunnellers from those allotted to 3rd Brigade.
One section of No. 2 Company, 40 tunnellers from those allotted to 1st Brigade.

Salvage companies will be organized for operations so as to permit of rapid salving of tanks with maintenance of the endurance of the salvage personnel which will require to be reassembled and rested at stated times.

Salvage sections will be organized in two or more salvage squads (preferably 3 so that when occasion arises for a section to be attached to a tank battalion, one squad may work with each tank company) to which will be attached a number of tunnellers.

When possible each squad will be placed under a competent leader who understands Salvage. (A suggested organization is given in Appendix A.)[1] The length of time the tunnellers should remain attached to the salvage companies must be left to the decision of the brigade commanders. On occasion, if much carrying work is likely, it may be necessary to supplement the tunnellers allotted to salvage companies by unskilled labour.

When considered necessary a small workshops detachment should be attached to each company to work in connection with the salvage operations.

5. Duties

Fighting crews

(a) If circumstances render the work possible crews will at once set to work to unditch a ditched tank or bring a

---

[1] Not reproduced.

disabled one into action again, a sentry having first been posted to watch in the direction of the enemy.

(b) If in the opinion of the tank commander this work is impossible and that it is unnecessary for the whole of the crew to wait with the tank, a sentry and his relief will be posted over or in the vicinity of the tank and the remainder of the crew withdrawn, a message being sent forthwith to the section commander giving the number of the tank, map location and extent of damage.

Reserve crews

Normally reserve crews will be employed in relieving the fighting crews of protective duties on the completion of a specific operation. This will enable the fighting crews to assemble, rest and reorganize.

Workshops personnel

(a) The duty of the battalion workshops is to maintain the maximum number of tanks in fighting condition by work in the workshops.

(b) The duty of the company workshop detachments is to see their company's tanks over our own front line and to carry out light mechanical repairs in the field. They should never be employed on unditching operations.

Salvage companies

(a) The duty of the salvage company is to relieve the battalions of work which would prevent them fighting the maximum number of tanks. This duty will be subdivided as follows :

(i) During an action to assist crews to unditch their tanks.

(ii) After the action to bring back to railhead tanks which are so disabled that the battalion workshops are unable to make them ready for action again in useful time.

(iii) To recover material from tanks which are total wrecks.

(b) The O.C. salvage company will render a weekly statement up to and including Saturday, showing the result of salvage operations during the week. This return will reach Advanced H.Q. Heavy Branch each Monday.

6. Special Salvage Measures

(a) Tanks which are handed over to the salvage company will be struck off the strength of the battalion concerned, the O.C. salvage company being advised by wire, and the wire repeated to Advanced H.Q. Heavy Branch. Such wires must state : manufacturer's and battalion's numbers, detail of injury and exact map location of tank.

APPENDIX XVI

(*b*) No receipts will be given by salvage units for derelict tanks lying in the battle area, or for the equipment which they contain; but salvage companies will safeguard them as far as it lies in their power.

(*c*) All salved tanks received by the central workshops will be taken on their strength and will be shown as received from the salvage companies on the " position of tanks at central workshops" statement sent to H.Q. Heavy Branch daily. They will continue to appear on this statement day by day together with remarks as to their repair until transferred to some other category.

(*d*) In all cases where tanks are dealt with by a salvage company, tank log books will be sent by the battalion which has struck the tank off its charge direct to the central workshops, which will issue them to the battalion taking over the tanks after repair.

(*e*) If the tank is ditched but otherwise mechanically sound, the company commander will issue instructions as to what equipment will be removed; generally this will consist of:

Lewis guns, Lewis gun spare parts, clock, compass and periscopes. No tools or tank parts which are essential to the salving of the tank will be taken away.

(*f*) When a tank has been handed over to a salvage company and time does not permit of immediate salvage taking place, the tank will be locked up and camouflaged, and a notice bearing G.R.O. 2294 hung on the lock.

J. F. C. FULLER,
Lieut.-Colonel, General Staff.

APPENDIX XVII

FIFTH ARMY OPERATION ORDER NO. 11 OF THE 31st JULY, 1917

(Sketch 12)

After consulting corps commanders, the Army commander came to the following decisions:

1. On August 2nd the II Corps will complete the capture of the Black Line [Second objective].

2. On August 4th the II, XIX and right of the XVIII Corps will attack and capture the original Green Line [Third objective].

3. At the same time the left of the XVIII and the XIV Corps will attack and capture the line Weidendreft (northern end)-

Langemarck (inclusive)-Langemarck-Winnipeg Road (inclusive) to its junction with the Green Line [Third objective].

4. The Red Line [Fourth objective] to be taken as a separate objective at a later date.

5. The task of the French First Army being as before, to cover our left flank, G.O.C. French First Army will be asked to co-operate in both attacks, and to state what line he proposes to take as his objective in each case.

6. The Red Line [Fourth objective] on the left of the XIV Corps front to be modified as required to meet the French objective line.

7. The date August 4th will be worked to by all concerned. Bad weather or other unforeseen difficulties may render a postponement desirable. Corps will report at once if they will not be in a position to attack on this date.

8. Acknowledge by wire.

N. MALCOLM,
Issued at 8.45 p.m.   Major-General, General Staff.

APPENDIX XVIII

G.H.Q. INSTRUCTIONS OF 1st AUGUST, 1917, TO THE FRENCH FIRST ARMY, FIFTH ARMY AND SECOND ARMY

1. The results of the attack made yesterday by the French First Army and the British Second and Fifth Armies are highly satisfactory.

Important positions of great strength have been captured and very heavy casualties have been inflicted on the enemy, who has already been compelled to throw a large proportion of his available reserves into the fight.

2. Armies will consolidate the positions gained and make ready to continue the infantry advance, in accordance with the general plan of operations already communicated, as soon as the necessary artillery preparation has been carried out.

3. The objectives of the next infantry advance will be arranged by the G.O.C. Fifth Army in direct communication with the G.O.C. French First Army, the arrangements proposed being reported to Advanced G.H.Q. in due course.

4. In addition to its primary task of continuing to assist the Fifth Army by all means in its power, and especially by vigorous

counter-battery action against all hostile guns within range which can be used against the right flank of the main advance, the Second Army will endeavour to maintain the impression of an intended advance to capture Lille.

L. E. KIGGELL,
Lieut.-General,
Chief of the General Staff.

APPENDIX XIX

MEMORANDUM ON THE SITUATION ON THE II CORPS FRONT BY G.H.Q. (OPERATIONS)

1st August, 1917
(Sketch 12)

1. The next objective is their original Black Line [Second objective]. The difficulties of this operation are :

(a) The corps has at present a ragged front line which has to be adjusted.

(b) One division at least (i.e., the 8th) is being relieved. Probably the 30th and 24th Divisions will be ordered to attack again. They will certainly be ordered to do so if the attack has to take place in a very short time.

(c) The ground will be heavy for several days after the rain stops.

(d) A good many scattered concrete machine-gun emplacements in the vicinity of Inverness Copse must be engaged with carefully observed fire.

2. Favourable circumstances in connection with the attack are as follows :

(a) The objective is a very limited one.

(b) We have now got full and detailed information as to the position of machine-gun emplacements, etc., in the objective, and have secured in many places direct observation, whereas hitherto no direct observation on this line has been possible.

(c) The whole artillery of the corps can concentrate on the preparation for this objective. (Hitherto the same guns have had to prepare three objectives simultaneously.)

3. The reasons for attacking as early as possible are :

(a) All further operations on the Fifth Army front are held up until this attack has been successfully carried out.

(b) The enemy will be gaining time to strengthen his rear defences.

(c) Our hold on Westhoek will be precarious until we have advanced to the Black Line, and this is the most important tactical point on the Army front at the present moment. In addition there is always a probability of a German counter-attack on a large scale on the whole of the II Corps front.

We know from experience, however, that in these subsidiary operations, hurried preparations and the use of part-worn troops are generally the cause of failure, and that failure involves waste of valuable time and personnel.

In this particular case we want to make absolutely certain of the artillery preparation, which will require very careful control and accurate shooting and two or more days good flying weather prior to the attack.

To ensure success, which is all-important at this stage, the corps ought really to attack with three fresh divisions and not put the 30th and 24th in again. If the Army presses for an early operation, the 30th and 24th will probably be used and will certainly be of no further use for offensive operations. If pulled out now they should both of them be ready to fight again early in September at the latest.

The use of three fresh divisions in the II Corps for the operation against the Black Line will enhance the probability of success, and lessen the delay between the operations against the Black Line and the Green Line [Third objective].

Situation on the Rest of the Fifth Army Front

The situation on the rest of the Fifth Army front is satisfactory. Three divisions, viz., the 15th, 39th and 55th, have suffered heavily, but if relieved and given a fortnight to three weeks' rest should be fit for offensive operations.

Situation on the Second Army Front

The 14th, 23rd and 47th Divisions are at present in reserve. They should perhaps be placed in G.H.Q. Reserve or the Second Army Commander asked not to place them in the line without first referring to G.H.Q. They may be required to feed the Fifth Army.

J. H. Davidson,
Br.-General, General Staff.

APPENDIX XX

G.H.Q. ORDER OF 28TH AUGUST, 1917, LIMITING THE OPERATIONS OF THE FIFTH ARMY

(Sketch 12)

With reference to O.A.D. 606, dated the 26th instant,[1] it may be expected that the Second Army preparations for attack will be complete in about three weeks.

In view of the unfavourable weather, of the inadvisability of pushing forward too far on your centre and left before the capture of the main ridge, and of the need that you should have in hand a thoroughly efficient force for the capture of the Staden Ridge hereafter in combination with the advance of the Second Army, the Commander-in-Chief considers it inadvisable that you should attempt any operations on a great scale before the Second Army is ready to co-operate.

He therefore desires that in the present circumstances your operations may be limited to gaining a line including Inverness Copse and Glencorse and Nonne Bosschen Woods, and to securing possession, by methodical and well-combined attacks, of such farms and other tactical features in front of your line farther north as will facilitate the delivery of a general attack later in combination with the Second Army. Proceeding on this principle he trusts that you will be able so to arrange for reliefs, and for the rest and training of your divisions, as to ensure having a fresh and thoroughly efficient force available for the severe and sustained fighting to be expected later. He considers these questions of relief, rest and training to be of great importance.

L. E. KIGGELL,
Lieut.-General,
Chief of the General Staff.

APPENDIX XXI

SECOND ARMY OPERATION ORDER NO. 4 OF THE 1ST SEPTEMBER, 1917

(Sketches 22, 25)

1. The task allotted to the Second Army [see Sketch 25] is the capture of the southern portion of the Passchendaele Ridge

---
[1] This order directed the Second Army to take over the Fifth Army front as far north as the Ypres–Roulers railway and gain possession of Gheluvelt plateau.

from Broodseinde southwards to Hollebeke, including the Polderhoek and Tower Hamlets Ridges at an early date in order to facilitate the further advance and at the same time protect the right flank of the Fifth Army.

The Fifth Army will advance simultaneously with the above operations.

2. The operations will be carried out by the following troops:

I Anzac	...	1st, 2nd, 4th and 5th Australian Divisions
X Corps	...	21st, 23rd, 33rd, 39th and 41st Divisions
IX Corps	...	One division north of Ypres–Comines Canal (19th Division)
II Anzac (In Reserve)		New Zealand, 3rd Australian, 7th and 49th Divisions.

3. The boundaries between corps will be:

* * * * *

Back boundaries of corps are shown on Area Map issued to corps.

4. The first stage of the operations should aim at the capture [see Sketch 22, which gives the objectives] of:

(a) The line J.3.a.2.9–Black Watch Corner–Carlisle Farm [¼ mile south-west of Cameron House]–J.15.d.3.9 by I Anzac.

(b) Thence via J.21 central–J.26.b.9.0–Groenenburg Farm by X Corps.

(c) Groenenburg Farm–P.1.a.6.5–Canal by IX Corps.

5. Subsequent stages will entail the capture of Polygon Wood and Molenaarelsthoek by I Anzac Corps, while the X Corps protect the right flank by the capture of Polderhoek and Cameron Covert.

6. I Anzac and X Corps will each retain two divisions in corps reserve in the initial stages of attack.

7. The principles on which the Artillery Plan will be based have been issued to corps.

8. Corps will submit their plans of attack based on the above as soon as possible, showing approximately the various stages they consider can be gained with the troops at their disposal.

9. H.Q. Second Army will be at Cassel.

10. Acknowledge.

C. H. HARINGTON,
M.G.G.S., Second Army.

Issued at 12 noon.

APPENDIX XXII

SECOND ARMY ADDENDUM OF 10TH SEPTEMBER, 1917, TO OPERATION ORDER NO. 4 OF 1ST SEPTEMBER, 1917

1. In continuation of Second Army Operation Order No. 4 of the 1st September, the Second Army operations will be carried out as shown on attached map.[1]

2. The various stages of the first phase of the operations are shown by Red, Blue and Green Lines [First, Second and Third objectives].

3. The date of the operations will be notified later. The hour of attack will be between 5 and 6 a.m.

4. The operations will be carried out as under:
   (i) The barrage will be put down 150 yards in front of our front line.
   (ii) The barrage will advance after three minutes.
   (iii) The barrage will cover the first 200 yards at the rate of 100 yards in 4 minutes.
   (iv) The barrage will then advance to the Red Line at the rate of 100 yards in 6 minutes.
   (v) There will be a halt of 45 minutes on the Red Line.
   (vi) The barrage will advance from the Red to the Blue Line at the rate of 100 yards in 8 minutes.
   (vii) There will be a halt of 2 hours on the Blue Line.
   (viii) The barrage will advance from the Blue to the Green Line at the rate of 100 yards in 8 minutes.

5. The barrages that enable the infantry to enter the Red, Blue and Green Lines, respectively, will contain a proportion of smoke shell to indicate to the infantry that these lines have been gained.
The screen afforded by this smoke will also enable officers and n.c.o.s to see that the lines are reorganized.

6. On arrival at the Green Line which is the final objective of the first day (the Blue Line for IX Corps and southern division of X Corps) a protective barrage will be put down 200 yards in advance of the line gained, and the programme of searching barrages as given in Second Army G. 705 of 8th September[2] will be carried out.
Posts will be pushed out to a distance of about 100 yards in advance of the line that is being consolidated.

---

[1] Not reproduced, see Sketch 22.
[2] Not printed.

7. The Fifth Army are arranging to attack simultaneously with the Second Army, the objective of the right of the V Corps being the capture of Zonnebeke Redoubt, joining with our Blue Line about Anzac House.

8. South of the Ypres–Comines Canal IX and VIII Corps will by demonstration and smoke simulate attacks on Houthem and Warneton.

9. The First Army are arranging to co-operate.

10. Corps and Army barrages will be carried out in accordance with Second Army G. 697 and G. 721 of 8th September.[1]

The Fifth Army are arranging to co-operate in the barrages at the junction between Armies.

11. The Artillery Plan as issued will be carried out commencing on a date to be notified later.

12. Acknowledge.

Issued at 12 noon.

C. H. HARINGTON,
M.G.G.S., Second Army.

APPENDIX XXIII

SECOND ARMY INSTRUCTION OF THE 29TH AUGUST, 1917

GENERAL PRINCIPLES ON WHICH THE ARTILLERY PLAN WILL BE DRAWN

PRELIMINARY BOMBARDMENT

1. To break down obstacles which are impassable for infantry, but in doing so to create as few new obstacles as possible. To bombard strongpoints.

2. To isolate from the rear the enemy's batteries and front systems so that he cannot bring up ammunition or replace guns and cannot bring up food or stores without suffering serious loss. To keep him short of food. To reduce his morale.

3. To teach the enemy to lie at the bottom of his shell holes or dug-outs whenever any barrages are going on. After one barrage has passed over him he must always expect others. In doing this, cause as many casualties as possible to reduce his morale. This will be effected by working a succession of dense creeping barrages of every available nature of gun and howitzer over the whole area to a depth of 2,000 yards beyond the last objective.

---

[1] Not printed.

APPENDIX XXIII

4. To carry out observed destructive shoots on hostile batteries from now on. As soon as batteries are isolated, *vide* 2 above, to begin intense counter-battery work.

ATTACK

5. The attack will be made behind 5 barrages which will cover a depth of about 1,000 yards.

6. Immediately prior to and during the attack all known hostile battery positions will be neutralized.

PROTECTIVE MEASURES AFTER GAINING THE OBJECTIVE

7. Barrages to a depth of about 800 yards will be prepared beforehand which can be put down when the enemy counter-attacks, and arrangements will be made for all or any portions of these barrages to creep forward so as to embrace the whole of the enemy reserves.

ADDITIONS OF THE 14TH SEPTEMBER, 1917

[Nos. 1, 2, 3 and 4 deal with the allotment and distribution of artillery ammunition.]

COUNTER-BATTERY WORK

5. From now on the hostile batteries will be systematically destroyed by observed fire from the air or ground.

6. For 7 days prior to the attack day intense counter-battery work and isolating fire will be carried on. Every means of observation should be used to its utmost capacity and concentration shoots should be carried out when means of observation are not available.

7. The hostile batteries will be neutralized with gas shell (if weather conditions are suitable for their employment) for the four hours immediately preceding zero hour on the day of attack. If weather conditions are not suitable for use of gas shell, H.E. or shrapnel will be substituted.

The hostile batteries will be neutralized with gas shell (if the weather permits) in a similar manner from 2 a.m. to 6 a.m. on C Day, i.e., for the four hours immediately preceding the *second* preparatory barrage on the whole Army front. H.E. or shrapnel will be substituted if weather conditions are unsuitable for gas shell.

During the preparatory barrage which starts at 6 a.m. on C Day the enemy batteries will be neutralized to the same extent as they will be from zero hour on the day of attack.

8. Preparatory barrages and any necessary bombardment will be carried out during the five days preceding the attack.

9. Isolating fire will be carried out by day and night throughout the whole period. The approaches to the front systems and the hostile batteries will be closed by two tiers of fire.

The field artillery and machine guns will deal with the area up to a range of 6,000 yards from their battery positions, the 60-pdrs. and 6-inch guns supplemented if necessary by some 6-inch howitzers will keep all approaches beyond the hostile batteries under fire. As a rule the ammunition allotted for isolating fire will be expended two-thirds by night and one-third by day, but when the weather is such that the air service cannot keep the approaches under observation the amount fired by day must be increased. Arrangements will be made by Second Army for crossing the fire of adjacent corps on such back approaches as can be enfiladed by this means.

10. On the first day of bombardment communication trenches will be blocked by knocking in a length of about 10 yards; places which are under observation from O.P.s should be selected for this purpose when possible.

11. Wire which is known to exist will be cut early in the bombardment.

12. Known machine-gun emplacements and strongpoints will be bombarded by the heavy artillery using delay action fuses.

13. Telephone exchanges will be destroyed.

14. The morale of the enemy will be reduced by frequently passing a succession of barrages over his shell hole system and dug-outs instead of by the bombardment of trenches. For method of using these barrages see Appendix 2 attached.[1]

15. All known hostile O.P.s should be destroyed not later than two days before the day of attack.

16. Gas shell should be used against the hostile battery positions and on shell holes, dug-outs and localities which are believed to be occupied when atmospheric conditions are favourable. They should also sometimes be used in the last portion of a barrage. Gas shell should always be preceded by H.E., the proportion of gas shell being gradually increased.

The Attack

17. The infantry will advance under an 18-pdr. barrage which will be preceded by at least 4 other barrages on the principles indicated in Appendix 1 attached.[1] If considered desirable the 18-pdr. and 4.5-inch howitzer barrage (B) and the machine-gun barrage (C) can be combined and readjusted to form 2 mixed barrages in lieu of the method shown. If greater depth is

---

[1] Not reproduced.

APPENDIX XXIII

required the several barrages may be as much as 300 yards apart instead of 200 yards. From the moment the attack commences every battery position believed to be occupied will be neutralized. As many planes as are available and can be employed without jamming should be used for sending down zone calls throughout the day.

18. The rate of fire of 18-pdr. guns for the first two minutes will be increased to four rounds per gun per minute : during the pauses in the advance it will be one round per gun per minute. The barrages will be thickened by smoke shell if necessary.

19. In cases where high ground within 2,000 yards of the objective has considerable command over the ground that the creeping barrages will traverse such as the Zandvoorde Ridge, it may be necessary to keep this high ground under fire, withdrawing the necessary guns from the barrages.

20. The field artillery should be so allotted to barrages that about one-third can be withdrawn at any moment without making a gap in the barrage, to deal with LL and G.F. calls and fleeting opportunities. The same system should be adopted in the heavy artillery with 60-pdr. guns and 6-inch howitzers.

21. Protective barrages in depth should be prepared beforehand. In addition to a barrage along the whole front, more concentrated barrages should be arranged to be put down on certain areas over which a counter-attack may be expected.

Fuses

22. The proportion in which fuse No. 106 will be supplied is 50 per cent. of No. 106 and 50 per cent. delay for all 6-inch howitzers, 8-inch howitzers and 9.2-inch howitzers. As few No. 106 as possible should be used for C.B. work and in bombardment in order that as many as possible may be available for barrages.

23. With the 18-pdr. 50 per cent. of the ammunition will be H.E., the fuses for which will be 25 per cent. with delay and 75 per cent. without delay.

Liaison

24. *Field artillery and infantry*

A senior officer of the field artillery supporting it should live with the headquarters of each attacking infantry brigade. Field artillery liaison officers should also be attached to headquarters of each assaulting battalion.

Heavy artillery and division commanders

A heavy artillery officer not below the rank of major from the Bombardment Group which is covering the divisional front should live at divisional headquarters with a direct telephone line to the Bombardment Group and through this Group to the Counter-Battery Office.

Heavy artillery with R.F.C.

A senior officer of the heavy artillery should live with the corps R.F.C. squadron.

Resting Personnel

25. Very careful arrangements must be made to give the personnel of batteries sufficient rest throughout the operations.

Protection of Ammunition

26. The protection of ammunition from weather is most important.

27. Acknowledge.

C. H. Harington,
Major-General,
M.G.G.S., Second Army.

APPENDIX XXIV

SECOND ARMY'S REMARKS OF 12th AUGUST, 1917, ON G.H.Q. MEMORANDUM DATED 7th AUGUST, 1917,[1] ON THE BEST METHOD OF MEETING THE LATEST SYSTEM OF DEFENCE ADOPTED BY THE ENEMY

Your O.B./2089 dated 7th August, 1917.[1]

The tactical notes forwarded with the above letter raise the question as to the best method of meeting the latest system of defence adopted by the enemy so as to carry out our offensive, and maintain positions gained, with the greatest loss to them and the least to ourselves, especially in the early stages of the operation.

The tactics of the enemy when meeting an offensive are no longer to rely on lines of trenches or clearly defined localities, but

(*a*) to have as their first system of defence a few troops with machine guns scattered about in shell holes, and other well-concealed places ;

(*b*) to have at hand small bodies of picked troops ready to deliver local counter-attacks whenever opportunities offer, and

---

[1] Not available.

APPENDIX XXIV

(*c*) to have in close reserve formations amounting to a division in different sectors of their defence for counter-attacks of an organized character.

To successfully overcome these we must have :

(*a*) A thoroughly effective system of " mopping-up " by the advanced troops.

(*b*) Small supports and reserves sufficient and near enough to deal with local attacks.

(*c*) Reserves capable not only of beating off an organized counter-attack but of crushing it.

And for all these phases the dispositions should be such as to ensure the effective use of rifle, machine-gun and artillery fire.

Each section of the defence must naturally be dealt with according to the character of the ground, but speaking generally the first advance can certainly be a longer one than has been customary hitherto, supported as it will be by the full density of artillery and machine-gun barrages and with no organized line of resistance to overcome ; but on the other hand the halt after the first advance should be much longer than formerly to admit of the whole area which has been traversed being thoroughly cleared, and of the advance certainly of machine guns and possibly of field artillery.

The second advance, i.e., after the first halt, must be shorter than the first and should be carried out by different troops to those engaged on the first. If any field guns have moved forward (as they certainly should have if possible), the artillery barrage will be somewhat thinner and the machine-gun barrages probably less also. No " front line " opposition is likely to be met with, but there will probably be " strongpoints " and defended localities, and local counter-attacks may be expected, and small supports or reserves must be in readiness and machine guns carefully disposed to deal with these and time allowed for this.

The halt after the second advance must also be a prolonged one, and might advantageously be on an irregular rather than on a regular line, the field artillery barrage being advanced well beyond it and sweeping backwards and forwards to some considerable depth. It will gradually become thinner as more guns move forward.

During the first two advances the heavy artillery would be engaged almost entirely and continuously on counter-battery work as being of primary importance to the progress of the infantry.

The third advance should be even shorter than the second and should be aimed at reaching positions (not necessarily a connected line) where an organized counter-attack can be met by fresh infantry, machine-gun and field and heavy artillery fire, and will be the final objective of the day's operations.

The dispositions to carry out an offensive on these lines successfully must involve considerable depth, and taking the division as the unit, would mean an attack on a brigade front only, each of the three brigades having the task of one advance assigned to it.

In support of each division there should be another division ready to crush organized counter-attacks and to take the place of the leading division before physical exhaustion of their infantry sets in.

The length of each advance and the duration of each halt (apart from the characteristics of the ground to be traversed) must be calculated on :

(i) The distance beyond our starting point to which field and heavy artillery and machine-gun support can be given and the time required to bring forward guns so as to make it really effective in dealing with counter-attacks.

(ii) The time required by the infantry to deal effectively with the opposition between each halt.

(iii) The time required to have sufficient reserves ready to deal with counter-attacks.

(iv) The physical powers of the infantry to carry out the tasks assigned to them.

The physical capability of the infantry depends undoubtedly not so much on the distance traversed as on the intensity of the hostile fire to which they are subjected and the length of time the nervous strain involved lasts, and in operations on a large scale this strain is sure to be greater on some sections than on others. It follows, I think, that unless it be accepted that the general advance must be governed by the progress made where the opposition is heaviest, an irregular wave rather than a regular line must be expected at the close of a day's operations and there seems very little, if any, disadvantage in this.

If an attack is to be carried out in depth as indicated it is obvious that either the extent of the whole front must be considerably curtailed or the number of the troops employed greatly increased if an advance in a continuous line, as has hitherto been done, is to be attempted.

I think that under the conditions of the enemy's defences which obtain now, this is no longer necessary, and that considerable gaps might be left between divisions or corps. The enemy has deliberately substituted flexibility for rigidity in his defence, and I think the response should be a corresponding flexibility in our attack. Gaps left deliberately would naturally be localities which offered the least advantage to the enemy, and which could be adequately protected by artillery and machine-gun fire. The enemy would be confronted with the alternatives of attempting to interpose between our formations under unfavourable conditions, or of counter-attacking positions where we could be in considerable strength to meet them.

The foregoing remarks represent my personal views, but corps and divisional commanders have been consulted, and in view of their own recent experiences they are, I think, in general agreement with them.

HERBERT PLUMER,
General,
Commanding Second Army.

APPENDIX XXV

SECOND ARMY'S NOTES ON TRAINING AND PREPARATION FOR OFFENSIVE OPERATIONS
(DATED 31ST AUGUST, 1917)

The following notes are issued as a guide in training and preparation for future offensive operations.

1. The new system of defence adopted by the enemy, consisting of lines of shell holes in depth and a large proportion of his strength disposed in readiness for counter-attack, is liable to produce a condition of affairs by which

(a) the farther we penetrate his line, the stronger and more organized we find him;

(b) the farther we penetrate his line, the weaker and more disorganized we are liable to become.

2. There are no longer any definite lines of trenches to form objectives. Objectives must therefore be selected according to the lie of the ground which gives us the greatest advantages to defeat the enemy counter-attack, and must be so limited that the infantry will be in a condition to consolidate and hold the points gained.

3. The attack must be made in greater depth and the distance between the waves must be carefully regulated so that during any period in the advance there are several lines ready to support one another in case of a counter-attack.

4. The distance between objectives and consequently the areas to be cleared will decrease as the advance progresses on any one day. Further, the numbers of troops allotted to the final objective will be proportionately greater than those allotted to the first, so as to ensure that there are sufficient to hold on against counter-attacks and exploit success when the counter-attack is repulsed. The troops detailed to capture the first

objective should be lightly equipped. The advantages of covering the first portion of the attack quickly are obvious.

5. The ground must be divided up into areas, and each unit, battalion or company, will be responsible for clearing the enemy in that area. Any good defensible positions so cleared should be garrisoned by the " mopping-up " party.

6. The waves of attack, which have been hitherto used, do not give sufficient elasticity, nor are the platoons and sections sufficiently under the control of their leaders to deal with sudden opposition likely to be encountered under the new conditions.

The leading wave, in one or two lines, should be extended to force the enemy to disclose his positions, the remainder in small groups or in file ready to deal with unexpected machine guns or parties of the enemy. It must be impressed on all subordinate leaders that rapidity of action is of paramount importance, and that any delay in assaulting these points adds to the seriousness of the situation and increases the difficulties of dealing with it. *Known* machine-gun emplacements and defended points are dealt with by parties previously told off for the duty.

Careful study of the ground and aeroplane photographs will go a long way towards increasing the " *known* " and giving all leaders a clear idea of the points from which opposition may be expected.

The rear waves must keep closed up until across No Man's Land, and gradually gain their distance after this. Officers must be trained to ensure that this is done.

7. Every commander, down to the company commander, must have a small reserve in hand. Commanders of subordinate formations must also ensure that if groups or parties are drawn away to deal with unexpected enemy defences their places in the general alignment are at once filled in order to prevent gaps occurring.

8. As each successive area in the advance will be allotted to a definite unit, the leap-frog method becomes essential.

9. Very definite instructions must be given to commanders of units on the flanks of formations. In all orders a point of junction is given and the duty of securing it allotted to a unit. It is, of course, the duty of the commander of that unit to secure the point if he can, but if for any reason he fails to do so at the time appointed it is the duty of the commander of the other unit to endeavour to do so.

10. The ideas as regards the relative importance of the various weapons in the hands of platoon commanders require readjustment to meet present needs.

APPENDIX XXV

Rifle and Lewis-gun fire is becoming more and more important. The rifle grenade is most valuable for dealing with the enemy in shell holes. The hand grenade will only occasionally be required, and therefore the bombing squad should be trained primarily as riflemen.

It has been proved that smoke grenades (No. 27) and an improvised 3-inch Stokes mortar smoke bomb (The Varley Bomb) are of great value for blinding machine-gun emplacements and concrete dug-outs during the advance of the party detailed to attack them.

Arrangements should be made for a proportion of the above to be carried by rifle grenadiers and light trench mortar batteries respectively. It has been found by experience that when these points have been blinded better results are obtained if only a few men, working round the flanks, are detailed to deal with them.

11. It should always be assumed by every formation that they will have to meet a counter-attack, and the steps to be taken to defeat it should always be included in every plan, and all ranks should thoroughly understand that this is their real opportunity for inflicting loss on the enemy, who will expect them to be disorganized to some extent and an easy prey. His counter-attack must not only be repulsed, but it must be followed up within limits and the enemy routed and disorganized, and troops must be trained to reach their final objective in such a state that they will not be satisfied with merely repulsing a counter-attack. In addition to consolidating the objective gained they must be ready to receive, drive back and follow up the enemy counter-attack with rifle and bayonet and make the most of the opportunity which is sure to be afforded them.

12. During training, special attention must be paid to developing the initiative of junior commanders, creating unexpected situations, meeting and dealing with counter-attacks at all stages of the advance and reorganizing when they have been dealt with. These counter-attacks will be in the nature of immediate local counter-attacks during the earlier stages of the advance, with larger and better prepared counter-attacks during the later stages.

Artillery

The following are the chief points in connection with artillery :

The barrage must have much greater depth, and with the exception of the creeping barrage, the barrages must not move so regularly.

There will probably be several barrages of different natures of guns or a combination of natures.

The enemy must be driven to lie at the bottom of shell holes and be drilled to always expect another barrage to pass over. This can be done by making barrages irregular and unexpected.

His front system must be cut off and starved. All means of supply and reinforcement must be reduced and his morale lowered by every possible means.

His batteries must be located and destroyed.

This is the real road to the infantry success, and the enemy is well aware of it.

To avoid it, he draws back his guns to extreme range. Our reply must be to advance our counter-battery guns to positions from which his batteries can be effectively dealt with.

In the preliminary bombardment all known machine-gun emplacements, farms, dug-outs, etc., must be dealt with, and these must be kept under fire as long as possible during the attack.

Ground which is likely to contain machine-gun emplacements (especially that from which machine-gun fire may be expected through our creeping barrage) must be searched and swept continually, both during the attack and on the days prior thereto.

The pauses on each of the intermediate objectives must be longer, to ensure that the infantry have had sufficient time to clear the area, and to ensure a simultaneous advance to the next objective.

The rate of advance of the creeping barrage will probably have to be somewhat slower than heretofore, and slower still as the attack progresses and enemy resistance becomes stronger. It is more than ever essential that the barrage shall not get away from the infantry. In principle it may be said that the initial advance should be made as quickly as the state of the ground will permit, and will gradually slow down as the attack progresses.

Protective barrage

It is a point for consideration whether our protective barrage should not be put somewhat farther out, in order to give more freedom of movement to patrols, and also to permit of defeated counter-attacks being followed up.

Liaison

There should be a senior artillery officer at every divisional headquarters for liaison work. The value of such an arrangement has been constantly proved.

Machine Guns

1. All experience goes to show the increasing value of machine-gun fire, both for offensive and defensive purposes.

APPENDIX XXV

2. Special attention must be paid to bringing a harassing fire on the area likely to contain enemy machine guns which are endeavouring to put a barrage against our attacking infantry.

3. The greatest attention is required in the arrangement of machine-gun barrages, and the closest working with the artillery is necessary to ensure success.

4. Experience has shown that machine guns sent forward with the assaulting waves almost invariably get knocked out or suffer such losses of personnel as to be practically useless on arrival at the objective.

5. The best solution with regard to forward guns would seem to be for the sections to follow closely behind the battalion to which they are attached, and to attain their objective by a series of bounds previously reconnoitred in each case by the section commander.

6. Every preparation must be made for moving forward barrage guns by "bounds". It has been found that a bound of 800 yards can be accomplished, and the guns set up in their new positions and ready to fire, in one hour.

Pack Transport

Where the ground gives cover from observation during daylight, pack transport can be largely used for carrying rations, water, ammunition and R.E. material over ground which is impassable for wheeled vehicles.

Communications

The system of intercommunication is laid down in S.S. 148. The following extracts from reports may prove useful:

1. The power buzzer produced some excellent results and too much stress cannot be laid on the necessity for training personnel with this apparatus. Amplifiers should not be placed in cable heads or signal offices. Where this was done they were jammed.

2. *Visual.*—The Lucas lamp was used extensively and proved invaluable.

Shutters and flags were used by battalions and companies. They are not of much use to brigade forward stations.

3. Pigeons were not much used, but messages sent off generally arrived in good time. The supplies were good.

4. Sufficient stress is not yet laid on the necessity for dispatching an important message in duplicate, to increase the chance of its safe arrival. Where possible, such messages should be sent by alternative methods; when runners only are employed, they should be dispatched with the duplicated message at 100 yards interval.

Closer touch is desirable between battalions and the relay system of runner posts organized by brigades. The relay posts should be marked so as to be easily recognizable from a distance, e.g., with a large coloured flag by day and with a coloured lamp by night. In one instance it was found useful, also, to mark with small coloured flags the shortest route for runners from brigade headquarters to the brigade forward station. Alternative routes should not be marked.

C. H. HARINGTON,
Major-General,
General Staff, Second Army.

APPENDIX XXVI

G.H.Q. ORDER FOR THE ATTACK OF THE 26TH SEPTEMBER, 1917 (BATTLE OF POLYGON WOOD)

(DATED 21ST SEPTEMBER, 1917)
(Sketch 24)

1. The next general attack will be carried out on the 26th instant. This attack should be made by the Second and Fifth Armies on as wide a front as possible, both in order to obtain the tactical advantages of attacking on a wide front and to make the most of the present apparently settled condition of the weather.

Armies will submit to Advanced G.H.Q. their objective maps for this attack as early as possible.

2. In the event of the operations on the 26th being completely successful, it is probable that the II Anzac Corps (under the command of the Second Army) will relieve the V Corps with a view to attacking Broodseinde and the Gravenstafel Ridge and, subsequently, Passchendaele. This attack will be made simultaneously with an attack by the Fifth Army, which will include Poelcappelle.

The Second and Fifth Armies should make detailed arrangements so that the relief of the V Corps and the consequent extension of the Second Army boundary can be carried out, if required, with the least possible delay.

L. E. KIGGELL,
Lieut.-General,
Chief of the General Staff.

GENERAL INDEX

A

Addison, Dr. C. (Minister of Munitions), 239
Adlercron, Br.-Gen. R. L. (148th Bde.), 331, 395
Air Force: strength at Messines, 42, 46; (low-flying), 70; German strength, 93; strength at Third Ypres, 109; on the Flanders coast, 110, 118, 119; at Pilckem Ridge, 134–5, 149, 170, 172; at Langemarck, 193, 196, 200; at Lens, 221; at Menin Road, 248; (night bombing), 249–50; (anti-aircraft defence), 250, fn. 2; 260; (co-operation with artillery), 273; (summary of work), 319; at Poelcappelle, 331; at Passchendaele, 344, 347, 353
Albert, H.M., King of the Belgians, 27, 28, 109
Albrecht Line, 143
Alexander, Br.-Gen. H. L. (D.A. & Q.M.G., XIV Corps), 389
Alexandretta, proposed landing, 103
Allenby, General Sir Edmund (Third Army), 20, 107, 232
Allgood, Br.-Gen. W. H. L. (45th Bde.), 166
America, United States of, declares war, 22, 26
American Army, first arrival, 231
Ammunition: at Messines, 39, 42, 48, 49, 67, 76; at Pilckem Ridge, 132; (expenditure compared with other battles), 138; 209, 222; at Menin Road, 238; (expenditure), 270, 292; (supply), 283; at Poelcappelle, 238; at Passchendaele, 339, 346, 353; expenditure during Battles of Ypres 1917, 239–40
Andrew, Lce.-Corporal L. W., V.C., 150
Anderson, Br.-Gen. N. G. (D.A. & Q.M.G., I Corps), 388
Anthoine, Gen. (French First Army), 27, 28, 109, 110, 124; postponements, 132–3
Armin, Gen. Sixt v. (*Fourth Army*), 75, 86, 142

Army Commanders' conferences, 24, 46, 89–90, 132
Armytage, Br.-Gen. G. A. (117th Bde.), 159, 262
Artillery (*see also* Bombardments *and* Barrages). Ammunition railheads, 40; at Messines, 43, 46; (ammunition expenditure), 49; 76, 82–4; (casualties), 88; transfer to Fifth Army, 108; at Nieuport, 117–9, 120; at Pilckem Ridge, 128, 132, 135–6, 166, 173, 180, 184–5; at Langemarck, 186, 190, 191, 193, 200; (ammunition expenditure), 209; at Lens, 221–2; (casualties), 228; ammunition shortage, 232; at Menin Road, 238–9; (ammunition expenditure), 239, fn. 3, 270; (yards of front), 240; 244; (organization), 247, 264; (fatigue), 272; (casualties), 279; at Polygon Wood (advanced), 282; 286, 290; (ammunition expenditure), 292; (casualties), 293; at Broodseinde (gun casualties), 300; 305, 307; (casualties), 311, 315; 312; (field gun range), 317; at Poelcappelle (cannot advance), 328; (platforms), 328, fn. 2; at Passchendaele, 345, 346, 348; (ammunition expenditure), 352; general remarks, 374–5; Haig's demands never met, 386
Asquith, Rt. Hon. H. H. (Prime Minister until Dec. 1916), on importance of Flanders coast, 369
Atkinson, Br.-Gen. B. (D.A. & Q.M.G., XVIII Corps), 390
Atkinson, Br.-Gen. E. H. de V. (C.E., I Corps), 388
Attack tactics: British, 62, 67, 101, 102, 147; (changes), 206–7; (Plumer's), 240, 289–90, 304; German, 120 (fn. 3)
Attrition, 13, 21, 24, 25, 26, 27, 130
Austria, peace-inclined, 104

B

Babington, Major-Gen. J. M. (23rd Div.), 61, 207, 253, 392

GENERAL INDEX

Bacon, Vice-Admiral Sir Reginald (Dover Patrol), 2, 3, 117, 232
Bailey, Br.-Gen. V. T. (142nd Bde.), 61
Bainbridge, Major-Gen. E. G. T. (25th Div.), 57, 186, 392
Baird, Br.-Gen. A. W. F. (100th Bde.), 283
Baird, Br.-Gen. H. B. D. (75th Bde.), 68
Baker-Carr, Col. C. D'A. B. S. (I Tank Bde.), 148, 310
Balkans, proposed campaign, 103; held by Germany, 232
Balloons, 73, 74, 248
Banbury, Br.-Gen. W. E. (61st Bde.), 200, 270
Barnes, Major-Gen. R. W. R. (57th Div.), 351, 393
Barrages: at Messines, 47, 55, 66, 78; at Pilckem Ridge, 149, 150, 154 (fn. 1), 159; (box), 187; at Langemarck, 191; (box), 194; 195; at Lens, 222; at Menin Road, 240, 244, 247, 253, 254 (fns. 1 and 2), 259, 260, 262, 264, 269, 277 (fn.); at Polygon Wood, 282; at Broodseinde, 300-301; (wall of flame), 308; at Poelcappelle, 335 (fn. 3), 336; at Passchendaele, 341, 343, 349 (fn. 2), 355
Barron, Corporal C., V.C., 357
Battalion strength, 147
Beckwith, Br.-Gen. A. T. (153rd Bde.), 160
Belgian Army: *Division d'armée*, 27; at Third Ypres, 109; (strength), 130
Bellingham, Br.-Gen. E. H. C. P. (118th Bde.), 168, 287
Bennett, Br.-Gen. H. G. (3rd Aust. Bde.), 257
Benson, Br.-Gen. R. P. (B.G.R.A., V Corps), 388
Bent, Lieut.-Col. P. E., V.C., 302
Berners, Br.-Gen. R. A. (11th Bde.), 311
Best Dunkley, Lieut.-Col. B., V.C., 167
Bethell, Br.-Gen. H. K. (74th Bde.), 57, 188
Bethmann-Hollweg, Theobald v. (German Chancellor), 123
Birch, Lieut.-Gen. Sir Noel (R.A., G.H.Q.), 136, 374, 386

Birdwood, Lieut.-Gen. Sir William (I Anzac Corps), 237, 280, 285, 299, 317, 328, 390
Birks, 2nd Lieut. F., V.C., 257
Blackader, Major-Gen. C. G. (38th Div.), 160, 392
Blockhouse, 2-storey, 258 (fn.)
Bols, Major-Gen. L. J. (24th Div.), 78, 153, 392
Bombardments: at Messines, 41-2, 44, 47-8; (cost), 49; feint attacks in June, 113; at Nieuport, 117, 118, 119; at Pilckem Ridge, 135-6; (last great), 138-9; (too long), 179; 186; at Menin Road, 247-8; at Polygon Wood, 283; at Broodseinde, 298, 300, 303, 304; at Poelcappelle, 330; at Passchendaele, 341, 355
Bonar Law, Rt. Hon. A., 99
Bond, Br.-Gen. C. E. (51st Bde.), 344
Borrett, Br.-Gen. O. C. (197th Bde.), 332
Boyd, Br.-Gen. G. F. (B.G.G.S., V Corps), 388
Boyd-Moss, Br.-Gen. L. D. (165th Bde.), 158, 266
Braithwaite, Br.-Gen. W. G. (2nd N.Z. Bde.), 57, 341
Brake, Br.-Gen. H. E. J. (C.H.A., XVIII Corps), 390
Brand, Br.-Gen. C. H. (4th Aust. Bde.), 286
Bremner, Br.-Gen. A. G. (C.E., XIX Corps), 390
Briand, Aristide (French Premier, Oct. 1915-Mar. 1917), 12
Bridges, Major-Gen. G. T. M. (19th Div.), 262, 263, 392
Bridging, 192, 336, 340
British Army, health, 209, 329; distribution, 209; shortage of reinforcements, 234, 235, 266; strength, 386-7
Broodseinde, battle of, 296 *et seq.*; turning point, 303; result, 315
Brooke, Major A. F. (R.A., Cdn. Corps), 221
Brooker, Br.-Gen. E. P. (C.E., XIII Corps), 389
Brown, Br.-Gen. E. H. J. (1st N.Z. Bde.), 68, 395
Brown, Pte. H., V.C., 227
Bruchmüller, Col. Georg (German artillery expert), 12
Bruges, value of, 1

GENERAL INDEX 467

Buchanan, Lieut.-Col. K. J. (46th Bde.), 158
Buckle, Major-Gen. C. R. (G.O.C., R.A., Second Army), 247
Bugden, Pte. P., V.C., 285
Burman, Sergt. W. F., V.C., 262
Burn, Br.-Gen. H. P. (152nd Bde.), 159
Burstall, Major-Gen. H. E. (2nd Cdn. Div.), 223, 356, 393
Butler, Br.-Gen. Hon. L. J. P. (60th Bde.), 200
Bye, Sergt. R., V.C., 162
Byng, Gen. Hon. Sir Julian (Third Army), takes over Third Army, 107; proposes Cambrai 1917, 235; re Cambrai 1917, 345; (evacuation of Cambrai salient in March 1918), 383

C

Cabinet. *See* War Cabinet.
Cadorna, Marshal Luigi (Italian C.G.S.), fears enemy offensive, 99, 102; abandons offensive, 233; 372
Cameron, Br.-Gen. A. R. (B.G.G.S., X Corps), 389
Campbell, Major-Gen. D. G. M. (21st Div.), 313, 392
Campbell, Br.-Gen. H. M. (C.R.A., 46th Div.), 221
Cambrai, operations proposed at, 235, 345
Camouflage, 49, 137
Camouflet, 38, 57
Cannan, Br.-Gen. J. H. (11th Aust. Bde.), 308
Carruthers, Br.-Gen. R. A. (D.A. & Q.M.G., I Anzac Corps), 390
Carter-Campbell, Br.-Gen. G. T. C. (94th Bde.), 113
Carton de Wiart, Br.-Gen. A., V.C. (12th Bde.), 336, 344
Casualties, British, in raids in May-June, 34; gas-shell, 49; at Battle of Messines 1917, 87–88; at Nieuport, 10th/11th July, 122; in Fifth Army, 5th–13th June, 137–8; at Pilckem Ridge, 31st July–2nd Aug., 174, 177–8, 179; at Westhoek, 5th–11th Aug., 188, 189; at Langemarck, 16th–18th Aug., 194, 195, 197, 198, 199, 201, 203, 205; total 31st July–28th Aug., 208–9; at Lens, 15th–23rd Aug., 230; at Menin Road, 20th–25th Sept., 244, 249; (S. African Bde.), 267; 279; at Polygon Wood, 26th Sept., 293; at Broodseinde, 4th Oct. (Australian), 309; (Fifth Army), 311; (21st Div.), 314; (4th–8th Oct.), 315; at Poelcappelle (49th Div.), 331; (total on 9th Oct.), 334; at Passchendaele (N.Z. Div., 12th Oct.), 342; (Fifth Army), 345, 348, 351; (X Corps, 26th Oct.), 351; (Canadian Corps, 26th Oct.–11th Nov.), 359; total, Battles of Ypres 1917, Second and Fifth Armies, 31st July–10th Nov., 360–5
—, German, at Battle of Messines 1917, 87–8; in April–June, 95; British Intelligence estimate of, 96–7; total in Battles of Ypres 1917, 362–3
Caterpillar. The, tunnelling at, 60
Cator, Major-Gen. A. B. E. (58th Div.), 351, 393
Cavalry, Haig's faith in, 20; brought up, at Pilckem Ridge, 148, 163, 169; at Broodseinde, 298
Cavan, Lieut.-Gen. F. R. Earl of (XIV Corps), 33, 160, 200, 270, 352
Cayley, Br.-Gen. D. E. (88th Bde.), 201
Cecil, Lord Robert, 368
Challenor, Br.-Gen. E. L. (63rd Bde.), 315
Champ, Corporal W., V.C., 335
Champion de Crespigny, Br.-Gen. C. R. (1st Gds. Bde.), 337
Chantilly (Joffre's G.Q.G.), *see* Conferences
Charteris, Br.-Gen. J. (G.H.Q. I), 96, 316
Chavasse, Captain N. G., V.C., 177
Cheape, Br.-Gen. G. R. H. (86th Bde.), 336, 394
Chichester, Major-Gen. A. A. (D.A. & Q.M.G., Second Army), 388
Chinese Labour Companies, 112
Churchill, Rt. Hon. Winston S., suggests recovery of Flanders coast, 1; Minister of Munitions, 239
Clay, Br.-Gen. B. G. (34th Bde.), 310
Clemson, Br.-Gen. W. F. (124th Bde.), 60, 261, 394
Coastal operation (Flanders), 1, 2, 8, 9, 116; (tides), 124; 133
Cobham, Br.-Gen. H. W. (24th Bde.), 156

GENERAL INDEX

Coffin, Br.-Gen. C., V.C. (25th Bde.), 165, 394
Colville, Br.-Gen. G. N. (68th Bde.), 256
Colvin, 2nd Lieut. H., V.C., 263
Colyer-Ferguson, Captain T. R., V.C., 156
Coke, Br.-Gen. E. S. de E. (169th Bde.), 192
Collingwood, Br.-Gen. C. W. (B.G.R.A., XV Corps), 389
Compton, Br.-Gen. C. W. (111th Bde.), 314
Conferences (*see also* Army Commanders). Chantilly (Nov. 1916), 7; Paris (May 1917), 22; French-Belgian-British (13th June), 110; Lillers (14th June), 132; London (4th Sept.), 233
Cooke, Br.-Gen. B. H. H. (D.A. & Q.M.G., IX Corps), 389
Cooper, Sergt. E., V.C., 200
Cope, Br.-Gen. T. G. (176th Bde.), 288
Counter-attack (*see also* Defence tactics). Policy, 121; at Pilckem Ridge, 170, 196
Couper, Major-Gen. V. A. (14th Div.), 203, 204, 205, 391
Courage, Col. A. (II Tank Bde.), 67, 148
Coverdale, Sergt. H., V.C., 310
Coxen, Br.-Gen. W. A. (B.G.R.A., I Anzac Corps), 390
Craig-Brown, Br.-Gen. E. (56th Bde.), 59
Craven, Br.-Gen. A. J. (C.E., V Corps), 388
Croft, Br.-Gen. W. D. (27th Bde.), 394
Cubitt, Br.-Gen. T. A. (57th Bde.), 69, 263
Cunliffe-Owen, Br.-Gen. C. (54th Bde.), 187
Currie, Lieut.-Gen. Sir Arthur (Canadian Corps), 113, 219, 228, 346, 347, 390
Curzon, Rt. Hon. Marquess of, 99
Cuthbert, Major-Gen. C. J. (39th Div.), 159, 392

D

Daly, Br.-Gen. A. C. (33rd Bde.), 77
Dann, Lieut.-Col. W. R. H. (173rd Bde.), 395
Dauerstellung, 122 (fn.)

Davidson, Br.-Gen. J. H. (G.H.Q., O), 128, 129, 381
Davies, Major-Gen. H. R. (11th Div.), 77, 199, 310, 391
Davies, Corporal J. L., V.C., 161
Davies, Br.-Gen. P. M. (D.A. & Q.M.G., XVIII Corps), 390
Dawson, Br.-Gen. F. S. (S. African Bde.), 265
Debeney, Gen. (French G.Q.G.), 29, 370
Deception, 47, 113, 222, 226, 244 (fn.), 282, 301, 355
d'Esperey, Gen. Franchet (G.A.N.), 12
Defence tactics. German manual, 11; 21, 43-4; at Messines, 63, 72-5, 90-5; at "Third Ypres", 141-6, 179, 277-8, 289, 293; change, 294-5; failure, 316; change, 318, 348 (fn. 3)
Delavoye, Br.-Gen. A. E. (D.A. & Q.M.G., II Anzac Corps), 391
de Lisle, Major-Gen. Sir Beauvoir (29th Div.), 201, 311, 392
Derby, Rt. Hon. Earl of (Secretary of State for War), 98, 153
Deverell, Major-Gen. C. J. (3rd Div.), 391
Diversion attacks, 5, 112
Drafts, training required, 192 (fn.), 200
DuCane, Lieut.-Gen. Sir John (XV Corps), 116, 117, 121, 389
Duckwalks, 214-5
Dudgeon, Major-Gen. F. A. (56th Div.), 393
Dugan, Br.-Gen. W. J. (73rd Bde.), 81, 153
Dwyer, Sergt. J. J., V.C., 286
Dyer, Br.-Gen. H. M. (7th Cdn. Bde.), 354

E

East, Br.-Gen. L. W. P. (C.H.A., XIII Corps), 389
Edwards, Sergt. A., V.C., 160
Edwards, Pte. E., V.C., 200
Egerton, Corporal E. A., V.C., 262
Eingreif (super-counter-attack) divisions, 44, 74, 75, 94, 142, 143, 205, 225, 231, 241, 252, 276, 277, 292, 293, 295, 309, 318
Ellershaw, Br.-Gen. A. (C.H.A., I Corps), 388
Elles, Br.-Gen. H. J. (Tank Corps), 148, 183, 243, 379, 380

GENERAL INDEX

Elliott, Br.-Gen. H. E. (15th Aust. Bde.), 285, 291
Elmsley, Br.-Gen. J. H. (8th Cdn. Bde.), 350
Engineer work: at Messines, 35–41, 112; on Flemish coast, 117–8; at "Third Ypres", 137, 221, 245–6, 327–30, 340, 347
Erzberger, Matthias (German statesman), peace proposal, 104
Evans, Lieut.-Col. L. P., V.C., 313

F

Falkenhausen, Gen. v. (*Sixth Army*), 72
Fanshawe, Lieut.-Gen. Sir Edward (V Corps), 263, 388
Fanshawe, Major-Gen. H. D. (58th Div.), 268, 393
Fanshawe, Major-Gen. R. (48th Div.), 199, 310, 392
Farmar, Br.-Gen. G. J. (D.A. & Q.M.G., Cdn. Corps), 390
Fasson, Br.-Gen. D. J. M. (B.G.R.A., XVIII Corps), 390
Feetham, Major-Gen. E. (39th Div.), 261, 287, 392
Feilding, Major-Gen. G. P. T. (Guards Div.), 161, 336, 344, 391
Flamethrowers, 205, 301
Flanders campaign. First proposal for recovery of coast, 1; Haig's 1915 scheme, 2; Rawlinson's plan, 4; Plumer thinks July too late, 6; Fourth Army not available, 6; postponement in 1916, 7; to be main effort in 1917, 8; Plumer's plan, 9; the 1917 plan, 11; effect of Nivelle's plan, 13; Macmullen committee, 14, 18; its plan adopted, 19; German knowledge, 30; Haig advocates offensive, 100 (*see also* Messines *and* Ypres); nature of ground, 125; postponements, 132–3; difference between plans, 165; campaign to be pressed on, 232; revised plan, 236; advantage, 294; concentration of German army, 326; retrospect, 366; alternatives, 371; nature of country, 373; loss of time, 385
Flanders Positions, German, 143, 144, 152
Flying Corps, Royal, *see* Air
Foch, Gen. (in 1918, Maréchal) Ferdinand (French C.G.S.), on mud, 375; relations with generals, 384

Fowke, Br.-Gen. G. H. (Engineer-in-Chief), 35, 36, 37
Franks, Major-Gen. G. McK. (G.O.C., R.A., Second Army), 43, 388
Fraser, Br.-Gen. L. D. (C.H.A., I Anzac Corps), 390
Freeth, Br.-Gen. G. H. B. (167th Bde.), 192
French, Field-Marshal Sir John, 1
French Army. Effect of Verdun, 7, 21; mutinies, 26, 28–9, 231; at Third Ypres, 109; relieved on coast, 110; at Pilckem Ridge, 162; reported useless by Pétain, 235; wants rest, 236; recovery, 325; note on mutinies, 370
Freyberg, Br.-Gen. B. C., V.C. (173rd Bde.), 268, 395
Frickleton, Lce.-Corporal S., V.C., 63
Frith, Br.-Gen. G. R. (D.A. & Q.M.G., XV Corps), 389
Fuller, Lieut.-Col. J. F. C. (Tank Corps), 183
Fulton, Br.-Gen. H. T. (3rd N.Z. Bde.), 57
Füsslein, Lieut.-Col. (*Fourth Army*), in charge of German tunnelling at Messines, 91, 92

G

Gas, 46, 49, 56, 68; (first use of mustard gas), 119, 137–8; 139, 140, 180, 226, 228, 252, 269, 283, 291, 340, 341, 347, 353
Gater, Br.-Gen. G. H. (62nd Bde.), 394
Gathorne-Hardy, Br.-Gen. Hon. J. F. (B.G.G.S., XIV Corps), 389
German Army, artillery losses, 49, 93, 138; normal disposition, 63 (fn.); casualties and numbers, 95; Intelligence estimate, 96; moves East to West, 96 (fn.); the general reserve, 103, 234; Pilckem Ridge, artillery, 136; defences, 142–6; forces, 145–6; counter-attack, 170; artillery strength, 206; health, 209; drain on, 210; inferior artillery, 249; company strength, 270 (fn. 2); failure of counter-attack defence, 274, 275, 293, 295; concentration of artillery at Polygon Wood, 283; distribution and time of transit, 296 (fn.); Black Day, 316; wastage, 324; thin line except in Flanders, 326; machine guns, 335 (fn. 1); change

470 GENERAL INDEX

of tactics, 348 (fn. 3); total casualties, 362–3

Gheluvelt plateau, importance, 3, 5, 16, 17, 18, 124, 127, 129, 132, 152, 180, 181, 182, 184, 189, 206, 231, 236, 237, 239, 240, 249 (fn. 1); (German garrison), 255; 271, 273, 278, 283, 284, 293, 294, 299, 301, 312, 318, 382

Gilson, Br.-Gen. G. (B.G.R.A., X Corps), 389

Glasgow, Br.-Gen. A. E. (58th Bde.), 59, 262

Glasgow, Br.-Gen. T. W. (13th Aust. Bde.), 80, 286

Glubb, Major-Gen. F. M. (C.E., Second Army), 39, 245, 388

Godby, Br.-Gen. C. (C.E., II Corps), 388

Godley, Lieut.-Gen. Sir Alexander (II Anzac Corps), 32, 83, 150, 237, 299, 307, 317, 342, 391

Gold, Lieut.-Col. E. (Meteorological Section, G.H.Q.), 251

Goodman, Br.-Gen. G. D. (21st Bde.), 153

Gordon, Lieut.-Gen. Sir Alexander (IX Corps), 36, 78, 150, 237, 389

Gordon, Br.-Gen. A. T. (153rd Bde.), 160

Gordon, Br.-Gen. C. W. E. (123rd Bde.), 60, 394

Gordon, Br.-Gen. H. (70th Bde.), 61, 301

Gordon-Lennox, Br.-Gen. Lord E. C. (95th Bde.), 314

Goring-Jones, Br.-Gen. M. D. (146th Bde.), 331, 395

Gorringe, Major-Gen. Sir George (47th Div.), 61, 392

Gort, Major Viscount, 14

Gough, Gen. Sir Hubert (Fifth Army): selected to command Reserve Army in 1916, 6, 20; selected to command main operations Third Ypres, 19, 384; on exploitation of Messines, 88–89; takes over at Ypres, 107; at Third Ypres, 124; receives G.H.Q. plan, 126–7; makes changes, 128–9, 130; Haig's instructions, 131; agrees to postponement, 132; at Pilckem Ridge, 154, 165, 169, 383; prepares to renew attack, 180; at Langemarck, 190, 202; rôle reduced, 206; operations cancelled, 208, 244; on surprise, 248; at Menin Road (wants postponement), 250–51; at Broodseinde, (rôle) 296–7, 299, 317; at Poelcappelle, 323; on closing campaign, 325, 373; at Passchendaele (wants postponement), 340; selection of, 304, 384; order of Battle, 388, 389; memorandum of 28th June, 439

Grant, Major-Gen. P. G. (C.E., Fifth Army), 137, 388

Greaves, Corporal F., V.C., 310

Green, Br.-Gen. H. C. R. (20th Bde.), 312

Green-Wilkinson, Br.-Gen. L. F. (148th Bde.), 395

Griesbach, Br.-Gen. W. A. (1st Cdn. Bde.), 357

Grieve, Captain R. C., V.C., 29

Griffith, Br.-Gen. C. R. J. (108th Bde.), 196

Grimbaldston, Sergt. W. H., V.C., 201

Grogan, Br.-Gen. G. W. St. G. (23rd Bde.), 156

Guillaumat, Gen. (French Second Army), 231

Gwyn-Thomas, Br.-Gen. G. (115th Bde.), 161

Gwynn, Br.-Gen. C. W. (B.G.G.S., II Anzac Corps), 391

H

Haig, Field-Marshal Sir Douglas: anxious for coastal attack, 2, 4, 6, 7; doubts of Nivelle plan, 13; change of views, 14, 21, 24; proposes massed tank attack, 17–19, 25; on attrition, 26, 130; firm in dealing with French, 26; first meeting with Pétain, 27; informed of French mutinies, 29; decides on Messines, 30; re exploitation, 88–9, 131; re Summary of Intelligence, 96–9; outlines Flanders plan to Cabinet Committee, 100, 101; on Pétain tactics, 102; determines on Flanders, 104–5, 109, 123; opposes diversion of force to Italy, 105; limits diversion attacks towards Lille, 115; on Nieuport, 122; outlines Flanders campaign, 124; approves Gough's changes, 128–9; on postponement, 132, 133; visits corps, 147; advanced headquarters, 149; reports to War Cabinet, 177, 232; visits Gough, 180; gives Plumer principal rôle, 206; cancels Gough's operation,

GENERAL INDEX

208; alternative campaigns, 219; approves further action at Lens, 220, 230; relations with Pétain, 231, 235; advocates Flanders rather than Italy, 233; approves of Cambrai operations, 235; revised plan for Flanders, 236, 237, 238; stops minor attacks, 244; plans after success of 20th Sept., 278, 280–1; Broodseinde plans, 296; conference, 297, 299; on exploitation, 316; Poelcappelle date, 324–5; objects to taking over more front, 325; Germany can only be beaten on Western Front, 326; his requests not met, 327; optimism, 339; on winter position, 345; on closing the campaign, 346; no start till ready, 347; sends divisions to Italy, 352; decides to end campaign, 360; in favour of Flanders, 368, 370; on continuance of campaign, 378; liaison with front, 381; relations with generals, 383; requests for more guns not met, 386; memorandum of 12th June for War Cabinet, 422–6. 22, 46–47, 184, 234
Haking, Lieut.-Gen. Sir Richard (XI Corps), 352
Halton, Pte. A., V.C., 344
Hamilton, Lce.-Corporal J. B., V.C., 284
Hamilton, Br.-Gen. J. G. H. (154th Bde.), 269
Hancock, Pte. F. G., V.C., 336
Hanna, Coy.-Sergt.-Major R., V.C., 229
Hardress-Lloyd, Col. J. (III Tank Bde.), 148, 183
Harington, Major-Gen. C. H. (M.G.G.S., Second Army), 9, 35, 61, 294, 388
Harper, Major-Gen. G. M. (51st Div.), 159, 269, 393
Harrison, Br.-Gen. G. H. (Director of Light Railways), 244
Hart, Br.-Gen. H. E. (4th N.Z. Bde.), 309
Harvey, Col. R. N., R.E., 36
Headlam, Br.-Gen. H. R. (64th Bde.), 313
Health of troops, 209, 329, 361, 378
Heane, Br.-Gen. J. (2nd Aust Bde.), 256, 305
Heneker, Major-Gen. W. C. G. (8th Div.), 156, 165, 189, 192, 391

Heriot-Maitland, Br.-Gen. J. D. (98th Bde.), 283
Hertling, Count (German Chancellor), 123
Hewitt, 2nd Lieut. D. G. W., V.C., 159
Hewitt, Lce-Corporal W. H., V.C., 267
Hickie, Major-Gen. W. B. (16th Div.), 58, 195, 197, 391
Higgins, Br.-Gen. C. G. (174th Bde.), 268
Higginson, Br.-Gen. H. W. (53rd Bde.), 155, 189, 191, 193
Hill, Br.-Gen. F. W. (9th Cdn. Bde.), 349
Hill 60, tunnelling, 60
Hill 70, see Lens
Hilliam, Br.-Gen. E. (4th Cdn. Bde.), 229, 349
Hindenburg, Field-Marshal Paul v. Hindenburg and Beneckendorff (Chief of German General Staff), see Ludendorff
Hobbs, Major-Gen. J. Talbot (5th Aust. Div.), 285, 394
Hobkirk, Br.-Gen. C. J. (14th Aust. Bde.), 285
Hobson, Sergt. F., V.C., 223
Holland, Lieut.-Gen. Sir Arthur (I Corps), 113, 388
Holland, Germans expect violation of neutrality, 145
Hollond, Br.-Gen. S. E. (B.G.G.S., XVIII Corps), 390
Holmes, Br.-Gen. H. G. (8th Bde.), 288
Holmes, Pte. T. W., V.C., 350
Holmes, Major-Gen. W. (4th Aust. Div.), 77, 84, 394
Hordern, Br.-Gen. G. V. (B.G.G.S., I Corps), 388
Hornby, Br.-Gen. M. L. (116th Bde.), 159, 287
Horne, Gen. Sir Henry (First Army), plan for Lens action, 112, 114, 219; plan for further action, 230
Houthulst Forest, 337, 344, 347
Hudspeth, Major H. M., R.E., 58
Humphreys, Br.-Gen. G. (B.G.R.A., IX Corps), 389
Hunter, Br.-Gen. A. J. (198th Bde.), 332
Hunter-Weston, Lieut.-Gen. Sir Aylmer (VIII Corps), 3, 33, 237
Hutchinson, Br.-Gen. A. R. H. (190th Bde.), 354
Hutt, Pte. A., V.C., 310

Hyslop, Br.-Gen. H. H. G. (59th and 153rd Bdes.), 160, 270

I

Infantry, ratio of casualties against strength, 88 ; ammunition carried, 339 (fn. 2) ; Indian file, 340
Infiltration, 62, 203
Intelligence Section, G.H.Q., estimate of German losses and strength, 96–7 ; War Office disagrees, 98 ; appreciation at Broodseinde, 316 ; at Poelcappelle, 324
Inwood, Pte. R. R., V.C., 257
Italy, proposal to send help, 101–3 ; heavy artillery, 105 ; Ludendorff rejects invasion, 123 ; heavy howitzers sent, 219, 233 ; Eleventh Battle of the Isonzo, 232 ; short of guns, 233, 234 ; German plans, 324 ; cannot be helped, 326–7 ; despatch of divisions to, 352 ; Plumer goes there, 358 ; 5 divisions sent, 360 ; objection to sending, 372

J

Jacob, Lieut.-Gen. Sir Claud (II Corps), 33, 131, 152, 166, 189, 204, 205, 355, 388
Jackson, Br.-Gen. H. C. (175th Bde.), 289
Jeffreys, Major-Gen. G. D. (1st Gds. Bde. and 19th Div.), 162, 392
Jeffries, Captain C. S., V.C., 342
Jelf, Br.-Gen. R. G. (86th Bde.), 394
Jellicoe, Admiral Sir John (First Sea-Lord), wants Belgian coast occupied, 192–3, 371 ; 368
Jenour, Br.-Gen. A. S. (C.H.A., II Anzac Corps), 391
Jeudwine, Major-Gen. H. S. (55th Div.), 172, 266, 277, 393
Jobson, Br.-Gen. A. (9th Aust. Bde.), 56
Joffre, Gen. Joseph Jacques Césaire (French Commander-in-Chief until Dec. 1917) : plans for 1917, 1, 4, 8 ; superseded, 12 ; his plan scrapped, 13, 20, 139 ; on Pétain, 236
Johnston, Br.-Gen. G. N. (C.R.A., N.Z. Div.), 339
Joly de Lotbinière, Br.-Gen. A. C. (C.E., I Anzac Corps), 390

Joly de Lotbinière, Br.-Gen. H. G. (C.E., XVIII Corps), 390
Jones, Br.-Gen. L. O. W. (13th Bde.), 314

K

Kemp, Br.-Gen. C. G. (2nd Bde.), 119
Kennedy, Br.-Gen. H. B. P. L. (140th Bde.), 61
Kennedy, Br.-Gen. J. (26th Bde.), 343
Kerenski, Alexander F. (Russian War and Prime Minister) ; his offensive, 103, 123, 231
Ketchen, Br.-Gen. H. D. B. (6th Cdn. Bde.), 229, 356
King, H.M. The, 148
Kinross, Pte. C. J., V.C., 354
Kirby, Br.-Gen. A. D. (B.G.R.A., II Corps), 180, 388
Kirwan, Br.-Gen. B. R. (B.G.R.A., XV Corps), 389
Knight, Sergt. A. S., V.C., 269
Knox, Br.-Gen. H. H. S. (B.G.G.S., XV Corps), 389
Konowal, Corporal F., V.C., 229
Kuhl, Gen. v. (Chief of Staff of Rupprecht's Army Group), 90, 91, 94, 244 ; on losses, 362

L

Labour, 40, 112, 132, 246, 347
Laffargue, Captain André, 62
Laffert, Gen. v. (commanding Group Wytschaete), 72, 83, 92 ; removed from command, 94
Lambert, Br.-Gen. T. S. (69th Bde.), 61, 256, 302
Landing, projected, 116 ; apparatus, 117, 145 ; delayed, 190, 233, 281
Langemarck, battle of, 189–210 ; peters out, 202 ; operations stopped, 208
Lawford, Major-Gen. S. T. B. (41st Div.), 253, 392
Lawrence, Major-Gen. Hon. H. A. (66th Div.), 331, 393
Lawrie, Major-Gen. C. E. (63rd Div.), 351, 393
Learmonth, Major O. M., V.C., 228
Lee, Major-Gen. R. P. (18th Div.), 155, 186, 188, 343, 391
Legge, Br.-Gen. W. K. (D.A. & Q.M.G., X Corps), 389
Lens, feint at, 90 ; action at, 114, 219–30

GENERAL INDEX

Lesslie, Br.-Gen. W. B. (1st Aust. Bde.), 305
Lewis, Br.-Gen. F. G. (166th Bde.), 158, 267
Leveson-Gower, Br.-Gen. P. (49th Bde.), 58, 196
Liaison, 381, 461
Lille, feint at, 90 ; attack abandoned, 115 ; 145
Limited advances, 16
Lindsay, Br.-Gen. W. B. (C.E., Cdn. Corps), 390
Lipsett, Major-Gen. L. J. (3rd Cdn. Div.), 114, 349, 393
Lister, Sergt. J., V.C., 336
Lloyd, Br.-Gen. J. H. (90th Bde.), 154
Lloyd George, Rt. Hon D. (Prime Minister), urges attack, 23 ; does not want to know plans, 23 ; opposes attack without French, 26, 101 ; wants to attack Austria, 101, 102, 103 ; wants to sit still but to assist Italy, 233, 234 ; on state of Russia, 326 ; orders divisions to Italy, 352 ; exaggeration of casualties, 362 (fn. 3) ; in favour of offensive, 368 ; pamphlet on the campaign, 375 (fn. 4)
Loch, Br.-Gen. Lord (110th Bde.), 302
Logan, Br.-Gen. D. F. H. (C.H.A., II Corps), 388
Loomis, Br.-Gen. F. O. W. (2nd Cdn. Bde.), 224, 227
Lossberg, Col. v. (German defence expert), 92, 142, 145
Lucas, Br.-Gen. C. H. T. (87th Bde.), 201
Lucas lamp, 462
Ludendorff, Gen. Erich (Chief Quartermaster-General), 92, 121, 123 ; proposal withdrawal from Pilckem Ridge, 140, 144 ; 145 ; anxiety, 210, 294 ; on Broodseinde, 316 ; on wastage, 324 ; changes defence, 332 ; opposes retirement, 337 (fn. 3) ; impressed by severity of fighting, 359 ; interference with generals, 383-4
Lukin, Major-Gen. H. T. (9th Div.), 265, 343, 391
Lyon, Br.-Gen. F. (B.G.G.S., XIX Corps), 390

M

MacBrien, Br.-Gen. J. H. (12th Cdn. Bde.), 354

McCracken, Lieut.-Gen. Sir William (XIII Corps), 113, 389
Macdonell, Major-Gen. A. C. (1st Cdn. Div.), 223, 357, 393
Macdonogh, Br.-Gen. G. M. W. (Director of Mil. Intelligence), 98
McGee, Sergt. L., V.C., 308
Machine guns : barrages, at Messines, 47-8, 76 ; (casualties), 88 ; at Lens, 222 ; at Menin Road, 254 ; at Broodseinde (casualties), 315 ; in German divisions, 335 (fn. 1) ; principles in attack, 419-22
McIntosh, Pte. G., V.C., 160
Mackenzie, Major-Gen. C. J. (61st Div.), 203, 393
Mackenzie, Br.-Gen. G. B. (C.H.A., IX Corps), 389
Mackenzie, Lieut. H., V.C., 354
Maclaren, Br.-Gen. C. H. (C.R.A., 3rd Cdn. Div.), 221
Maclean, Lieut.-Col. H. D. N. (27th Bde.), 394
Macmullen, Br.-Gen. C. N. (Operations Section, G.H.Q. and D.A. & Q.M.G., XIX Corps), 14, 18, 126, 390
McNaughten, Lieut.-Col. A. G. L. (R.A., Cdn. Corps), 221
McNicoll, Br.-Gen. W. R. (10th Aust. Bde.), 56, 308, 342
Malcolm, Major-Gen. N. (M.G. G.S., Fifth Army), 107, 388
Malmaison, Battle of, 326
Marden, Br.-Gen. T. O. (114th Bde.), 161
Marshall, Br.-Gen. F. J. (44th Bde.), 157
Martel, Captain G. le Q. (Tank Corps), 25
Massie, Br.-Gen. R. H. (C.H.A., Cdn. Corps), 221, 390
Matheson, Major-Gen. T. G. (4th Div.), 311, 344, 391
Mats, 216
Maunsell, Br.-Gen. F. G. (C.H.A., XIV Corps), 389
Maurice, Major-Gen. F. (D.M.O.), 368
Maxse, Lieut.-Gen. Sir Ivor (XVIII Corps), 159, 199, 268, 355, 390
Maxwell, Br.-Gen. F. A. V.C. (27th Bde.), 121, 265, 394
May, Br.-Gen. R. S. (D.A. & Q.M.G., II Corps), 388
Mayson, Corporal T. F., V.C., 167
Mebus, 45 (fn.), 258 (fn.)
Melvill, Br.-Gen. C.W. (1st N.Z. Bde.) 309, 395

474 GENERAL INDEX

Menin Road Ridge, Battle of, 231–79
Messines Ridge, Tunnelling, 4; attack in 1916 postponed, 7, 9; Plumer's proposals, 15; his plan adopted, 19, 25, 30, 32; the battle, 54–85; German defences, 90–5; German tragedy, 94; delay after, 133
Michaelis, Dr. Georg (German Chancellor), 123
Micheler, Gen. (French G.A.R.), 12
Milner, Rt. Hon. Viscount, 99
Mining, at Messines, see Tunnelling
Mitchell, Lieut.-Col. C. H. (Intelligence, Second Army), 318
Mitchell, Br.-Gen. J. H. (C.R.A., 3rd Cdn. Div.), 221
Models of ground, 33, 34, 147, 221
Moeres, les, 125
Moir, Br.-Gen. A. J. G. (D.A. & Q.M.G., XIX Corps), 390
Molyneaux, Sergt. J., V.C., 336
Monash, Major-Gen. Sir John (3rd Aust. Div.), 56, 115, 150, 307, 341, 342, 394
Monkhouse, Br.-Gen. W. P. (C.R.A., 19th Div.), 263, 392
Montgomery, Br.-Gen. H. M. de F. (D.A. & Q.M.G., V Corps), 388
Moppers up, 149, 159, 257, 304, 309, 333
Morland, Lieut.-Gen. Sir Thomas (X Corps), 33, 59, 137, 150, 237, 299, 317, 389
Morrison, Br.-Gen. E. W. B. (B.G.R.A., Cdn. Corps), 221, 347, 390
Moser, Gen. Otto v. (German commander on Dutch frontier), 369
Mud, 173, 177, 179, 183, 190, 197, 199, 200, 207, 208; (disappears), 246; at Menin Road, 268, 269; at Polygon Wood, 287, 288; at Broodseinde, 300, 307, 313, 317; at Poelcappelle, 324, 327, 331, 332; at Passchendaele, 339, 344, 346, 349, 351, 355, 357; general remarks, 373–77
Mullin, Sergt. G. H., V.C., 354
Munitions, Ministry of, output in 1917, 239; does not meet Haig's demands, 386 (fn.)
Mustard gas, first use of by Germans, 119, 137–38
Mutinies. See French Army

N

Napier, Br.-Gen. W. J. (B.G.R.A., I. Anzac Corps), 390

Nash, Major-Gen. P. A. M. (D.G. Transportation), 298
Nelson, Br.-Gen. H. (88th Bde.), 336, 394
Nieuport, 27; German attack, 118–122; importance, 235
Night operations, 228
Nissen, Lieut.-Col. P., 375
Nivelle, Gen. Robert George (French C-in-C, 12th Dec., 1916–15th May, 1917); advent, 11, 12; plan, 12–14; its failure, 20; 22; effects, 21, 370; is superseded, 27
Norman, Br.-Gen. W. W. (89th Bde.), 155
Northern Operation, 25. See also Flanders Campaign
Norton-Griffiths, Major J., 36
Nugent, Major-Gen. O. S. W. (36th Div.), 57, 196, 197, 392

O

Ockenden, Sergt. T., V.C., 311
Odlum, Br.-Gen. N. W. (11th Cdn. Bde.), 226
O.H.L. (Oberste Heeresleitung, the German Supreme Command), 30
Oil drums, 46, 65, 222, 271
O'Kelly, Captain C. P. J., V.C., 350
Onslow, Br.-Gen. C. C. (7th Bde.), 57
Oppy, action at, 113
Order, capture of, 251
Orders, operation, 415, 417, 418, 430, 432, 444, 448, 463
O'Rourke, Pte. M. J., V.C., 227
Ostend, value, 1, 2; landing abandoned, 17

P

Pack animals, 67, 198, 218, 329, 352
Painlevé, Monsieur (French Minister of War), 145
Panet, Br.-Gen. A. E. (C.E., II Anzac Corps), 391
Panet, Br.-Gen. H. A. (C.R.A., 2nd Cdn. Div.), 221
Passchendaele, 5
Passchendaele, First Battle of, 338–45; situation, 341; Second Battle, 345–64
Paton, Br.-Gen. J. (6th Aust. Bde.), 306
Peace, 104; *Reichstag* resolution, 123; French longing for, 235

GENERAL INDEX 475

Peake, Br.-Gen. M. (B.G. R.A., I Corps), 388
Pearce Serocold, Br.-Gen. E. (123rd Bde.), 394
Pearkes, Major G. R., V.C., 354
Pedley, Br.-Gen. S. H. (34th Bde.), 199
Peeler, Lce.-Corporal W., V.C., 308
Pelly, Br.-Gen. R. T. (91st Bde.), 312
Perceval, Major-Gen. E. M. (49th Div.), 330, 393
Percy, Br.-Gen. J. S. J. (B.G. G.S., IX Corps), 389
Pereira, Br.-Gen. G. E. (47th Bde.), 58
Pétain, Gen. Henri Philippe (French Commander-in-Chief from 15th May, 1917): on Nivelle plan, 12; pessimistic, 22; cautious, 23; succeeds Nivelle, 27; objects to long distance objectives in Flanders, 27-28; waits for Americans, 29; unable to co-operate, 96; tactics, 101; handling of troops, 104, 109; still pessimistic, 231, 235, 236; Joffre's opinion of, 236 (fn. 2); wants front taken over, 325; wants British offensive continued, 326, 370
Phosphorus bombs, 254
Pigeons, 155 (fn. 1), 169 (fn. 2), 272 (fn. 1), 462
Pilckem Ridge, 3, 4, 5, 9, 15; bombardment, 133; German retirement, 140; German counterattack, 168; rain, 183
Pillboxes, 45, 62, 79, 147, 161, 164, 186, 191, 199; (how to tackle), 264
Plank roads, 245-6 (fn.), 300, 329
Plumer, Gen. Sir Herbert (Second Army): on Messines, 3, 7; on Gheluvelt plateau, 5; submits plan, 9, 11, 18; new instructions, 14-15; on mines, 35, 47; agrees to halt at Messines, 75-76; orders for further advance anticipated, 86-87; urges exploitation of Messines victory, 88-90; on diversion attacks, 115; Third Ypres, 124, 129; Haig's instructions, 131; given principal rôle, 206; asks for three weeks' delay, 207; submits plan, 237; request for guns, 238-39; new attack organization, 239-42, 271, 385; refuses postponement, 250-1; insists on increase of heavy howitzers, 253; plan after first success, 280 (fn.);

warning order for 21st Sept., 281, 284; Broodseinde instructions, 296-7, 299; considers exploitation, 316-7; Poelcappelle, 323-24; on closing campaign, 325; orders light railways, 328; Passchendaele plans, 338; against postponement, 340; takes over more front, 355; goes to Italy, 358; order of battle, 388
Poelcappelle, Battle of, 323-37; tanks not used, 323-4; bad ground conditions, 327-9; reasons for failure, 337 (fn. 3), 338-9
Polygon Wood, Battle of, 280-95; racecourse, 285
Ponsonby, Br.-Gen. J. (2nd Gds. Bde.), 162
Pope, His Holiness the, peace proposals, 104
Porter, Br.-Gen. C. L. (76th Bde.), 288
Powell, Br.-Gen. E. W. M. (B.G.R.A., II Anzac Corps), 307, 391
Price, Br.-Gen. G. D. (55th Bde.), 187, 343
Price-Davies, Br.-Gen. L. A. E., V.C. (113th Bde.), 161
Prisoners and Captures, in raids in May-June, 34; at Messines, 87; at Pilckem Ridge, 178; at Langemarck, 201; at Lens, 230; at Menin Road, 278; at Broodseinde, 309, 310, 315; at Passchendaele, 357, 363
Pritchard, Br.-Gen. A. G. (10th Bde.), 311
Pritchard, Br.-Gen. C. G. (C.H.A., XIX Corps), 390

Q

Quadrilateral, The, 287, 351

R

Radcliffe, Br.-Gen. P. P. de B. (B.G. G.S., Cdn. Corps), 390
Raids, 34, 43, 118, 140, 248
Railways, Ypres system, 39-40, 110; light, 244-45, 328; trains per day, 245
Rain, 176; (31st July), 183; (14th Aug.), 190; (23rd Aug.), 204; (27th Aug.), 207; (28th Aug.), 208; rainfall, 211-2; fine three weeks, 246; one hour's, 250; good weather, 21st Sept., 282; dust, 284; fine to end of Sept., 301;

476 GENERAL INDEX

rain, 4th Oct., 304 ; 8th Oct., 327 ; 12th Oct., winter rains begin, 340 ; improvement after 16th Oct., 347 ; heavy on 26th, 349 ; improves 27th, 352, 353 ; wet on 30th Oct., 353 ; fine 6th Nov., 356 ; 10th Nov., 359 ; Nivelle's view, 370 ; general remarks, 373-77
Ramsay, Br.-Gen. F. W. (48th Bde.), 195
Rawling, Br.-Gen. C. G. (62nd Bde.), 313, 394
Rawlins, Lieut.-Col. S. W. H. (R.A., G.H.Q.), 374, 381
Rawlinson, Gen. Sir Henry, Bt. (Fourth Army) : on coastal attack, 3, 4 ; comments on general plan, 17 ; takes over coastal sector, 109-110, 119 ; revised plan, 121-22 ; 128, 133 ; takes over Second Army, 358
Red Cross, German bombing of, 361
Reed, Br.-Gen. H. L., V.C. (B.G.R.A., X Corps), 312, 389
Rees, Sergt. I., V.C., 161
Rehearsals, *see* Models
Reinforcements, lack of, 234, 235, 266 (fn. 2)
Rennie, Br.-Gen. R. (4th Cdn. Bde.), 223, 395
Reynolds, Captain H., V.C., 266
Rhodes, Lce.-Sergt. J. H., V.C., 337
Ribot, Alexandre (French Prime Minister March-Nov. 1917), 23
Ricardo, Br.-Gen. A. St. Q. (109th Bde.), 57, 196
Rifle grenades, 62, 151, 160, 257, 278, 306, 308, 356, 460
Roads, 40, 176, 183, 185, 198 ; divisional system, 213-8 ; 245-6, 282, 327-9, 346-7
Robertson, Captain Clement, V.C., 313
Robertson, Br.-Gen. J. C. (12th Aust. Bde.), 79
Robertson, Pte. J. P., V.C., 356
Robertson, Major-Gen. P. R. (17th Div.), 344, 391
Robertson, General Sir William (C.I.G.S.), informs Joffre of London decision, 8 ; 22, 26 ; disagrees with Summary of Intelligence, 98 ; supports Haig, 104 ; reports lack of reinforcements, 234, 368 ; on sending troops to Italy, 372
Robinson, Br.-Gen. S. W. (D.A. & Q.M.G., XIII Corps), 389
Romer Major-Gen. C. F. (59th Div.), 288, 393.

Roon, Pte., F. E., V.C., 196
Rosenthal, Br.-Gen. C. (9th Aust. Bde.), 342, 394
Ross, Br.-Gen. J. M. (5th Cdn. Bde.), 223
Rupprecht, Crown Prince of Bavaria (Army Group Commander), 31, 86, 89, 90, 91, 92, 93, 94, 122, 141, 145, 181 ; (expects landing), 273 ; (on British attacks), 277 ; (Gheluvelt plateau), 283 ; (lack of men), 294 ; (considers withdrawal), 326, 337 (fn. 3) ; (welcomes rain), 341 (fn. 1), 374, 386
Russell, Major-Gen. Sir Arthur (New Zealand Div.), 56, 150, 341
Russia, revolutionary outbreaks, 98, 99, 101 ; Kerenski offensive, 103, 234 ; Bolshevist rising, 104 ; Armies disintegrating, 231 ; state in October, 236

S

Sage, Pte. T. H., V.C., 315
St. Eloi, tunnelling, 60
Salients, danger, 369
Salonika, 232
Sandys, Br.-Gen. W. B. R. (B.G.R.A., XIX Corps), 180, 390
Sargent, Major-Gen. H. N. (D.A. & Q.M.G., Fifth Army), 388
Sarrail, Gen., 232
Scholfield, Br.-Gen. C. P. (C.E., IX Corps), 389
Schuler Galleries, 267
Searchlights, 250
Sehnen Line, 91
Sergison-Brooke, Br.-Gen. B. N. (2nd Gds. Bde.), 337
Seymour, Br.-Gen. Lord Henry (3rd Gds. Bde.), 162, 345
Shankland, Lieut. R., V.C., 350
Sharpe, Captain G. M. (62nd Bde.), 394
Short shooting, 260, 283 (fn. 2)
Shoubridge, Major-Gen. T. H. (7th Div.), 312, 317, 391
Shute, Major-Gen. C. D. (19th Div.), 59, 78, 121, 392
Signals, at Messines, 43 ; at Pilckem Ridge, 155, 169, 170 ; at Menin Road, 248, 267, 271, 272 ; at Broodseinde, 300 ; at Passchendaele, 343, 462
Sinclair-Maclagan, Major-Gen. E. G. (4th Aust. Div.), 285, 343, 394

GENERAL INDEX 477

Singer, Br.-Gen. C. W. (C.H.A., XV Corps), 389
Skinner, Company-Sergt.-Major J., V.C., 201
Skinner, Br.-Gen. P. C. B. (41st Bde.), 207
Sladen, Br.-Gen. G. C. (143rd Bde.), 310
Smith, Br.-Gen. R. (5th Aust. Bde.), 258, 333
Smith, Major-Gen. W. Douglas (20th Div.), 200, 270, 271, 392
Smoke screen, 65, 161, 188, 193, 196, 200, 202, 207, 222, 258, 262 (fn. 3), 269, 271, 301, 306, 460
Smuts, Gen. Rt. Hon. J. C. (South African Premier), 102
Smyth, Major-Gen. N. M. (2nd Aust. Div.), 253, 306, 333, 394
S.O.S. rockets, 274 (fn. 2)
Sound Ranging, 247
Spanbroekmolen, 4, 19, 32 ; assault, 57
Spoil Bank, 69, 83
Spring, Br.-Gen. F. G. (33rd Bde.), 310
Stansfeld, Br.-Gen. T. W. (178th Bde.), 288
Steele, Br.-Gen. J. McC. (22nd Bde.), 302
Stephens, Major-Gen. R. B. (5th Div.), 314, 391
Stewart, Br.-Gen. A. E. (3rd N.Z. Bde.), 341
Stewart, Br.-Gen. I. (B.G.G.S., XIII Corps), 389
Stockwell, Br.-Gen. C. I. (164th Bde.), 167, 266
Stone, Br.-Gen. P. V. P. (17th Bde.), 81, 153
Strickland, Major-Gen. E. P. (1st Div.), 119, 391
Submarine danger, 2; losses, 22, 103 (fn.) ; Ludendorff relies on, 123 ; 337
Summer Time, xxii., 330 (fn.)
Sweny, Br.-Gen. W. F. (72nd Bde.), 153

T

Tactics. *See* Attack *and* Defence
Tanks, Ypres area unsuitable, 25 ; at Messines, 33 ; (organization and models), 50–1 ; 63, 67, 69, 70, 76, 79, 81; at Pilckem Ridge, 108, 109; (move to), 148 ; (formation of Tank Corps), 148, 151, 157, 158, 159, 160, 168; (gun carrier), 179 ; (halted by rain), 183 ; at Langemarck, 191, 199, 202, 203, 204, 207, 208; at Menin Road, 243, 256, 268 ; (wireless), 272, 278 ; at Polygon Wood, 287 ; at Broodseinde, 298, 310, 311, 313, 314 ; general instructions, 319–22; not used at Poelcappelle, 324 ; general remarks, 379–81 ; instructions for recovery, 441
Teacher, Lieut.-Col. N. McD. (2/Royal Scots), 288
Thacker, Br.-Gen. H. C. (C.R.A., 1st Cdn. Div.), 221
Thermit shells, 65
Thuillier, Major-Gen. H. F. (15th Div.), 157, 203, 391
Thwaites, Major-Gen. W. (46th Div.), 114
Tower Hamlets, 153, 261, 287
Towsey, Br.-Gen. F. W. (122nd Bde.), 69, 261
Tracks, 217, 246
Tramways, 216
Trench mortars, 45, 66, 139, 159, 256, 270, 278, 284, 357
Trenchard, Major-Gen. H. M. (R.F.C.), 134, 170, 371
Tulloch, Br.-Gen. J. A. S. (C.E., X Corps), 389
Tunnelling of Messines Ridge, 4, 7, 33 ; (safety distance), 34, 35–8 ; (table of mines), 52–3 ; (explosion). 54 ; (difficulties), 57 (fn.) ; (at St. Eloi and Hill 60), 60 (fn.) ; (effects), 61 ; (German views), 91–2
Turner, Br.-Gen. N. M. (15th Bde.), 113, 334
Tuxford, Br.-Gen. G. S. (3rd Cdn. Bde.), 224
Tyler, Br.-Gen. A. M. (C.H.A., V Corps), 388

U

Uniacke, Major-Gen. H. C. C. (G.O.C., R.A., Fifth Army), 135, 248, 388

V

Varley bomb, 461
Verdun, projected attack, 27, 29, 231, 235
Very lights, 171, 193
Vincent, Br.-Gen. H. O. (C.H.A., X Corps), 389

W

Walker, Major-Gen. H. B. (1st Aust. Div.), 253, 305, 394
War Cabinet: Flanders to be main effort, 8; French imitation of, 12; on offensive action, 26, 96; Committee on War Policy, 99; hesitates, 104; sanctions Flanders campaign, 105-6, 128; on Nieuport operations, 122; Haig's reports to, 232; sanctions continuance, 234
Wardrop, Br.-Gen. A. E. (B.G.R.A., XIV Corps), 389
Warneton Line, 124
Water supply, 40; table, 125, 198
Wateringues, 125
Watson, Major-Gen. D. (4th Cdn. Div.), 114, 226, 349, 393
Watt, Br.-Gen. D. M. (145th Bde.), 199
Watts, Lieut.-Gen. Sir Herbert (XIX Corps), 157, 194, 197, 390
Weather. *See* Mud *and* Rain
Webb-Bowen, Major-Gen. T. I. (R.F.C.), 42
Weldon, Lieut.-Col. K. C. (49th Bde.), 195
Wellesley, Br.-Gen. R. A. C. (B.G. R.A., XIII Corps), 389
Wenniger, Gen. (German commander at Messines), 77
Westhoek, captured, 188-9
Wetzell, Lieut.-Col. Georg (German Operations Section), 92, 123
White, Br.-Gen. C. B. B. (B.G.G.S., I. Anzac Corps), 390
White, Br.-Gen. Hon. R. (184th Bde.), 203
Whitham, Pte. T., V.C., 162

Wilhelm, Crown Prince of Germany, 30, 31
Wilhelm Line, 143
Wilkinson, Major-Gen. P. S. (50th Div.), 351, 393
Williams, Major-Gen. H. Bruce (37th Div.), 315, 392
Williams, Major-Gen. W. de L. (30th Div.), 153-5, 175, 392
Wilson, Br.-Gen. C. S. (C.E., XIV Corps), 374, 389
Wilson, Br.-Gen. S. H. (B.G.G.S., II Corps), 388
Wilson, Thomas Woodrow (American President), on peace offer, 104
Wireless. *See* Signals
Wisdom, Br.-Gen. E. A. (7th Aust. Bde.), 258, 306
Withycombe, Br.-Gen. W. M. (107th Bde.), 57
Wood, Major-Gen. P. R. (43rd Bde. and 33rd Div.), 204, 206, 283, 286, 392
Worgan, Br.-Gen. R. B. (173rd Bde.), 395
Wytschaete. *See* Messines

Y

Ypres Ridge: objective, 5; only partly suitable for tanks, 25; soil, 36; battles, 124 *et seq.* (*See* Pilckem Ridge, Langemarck, Menin Road, Polygon Wood, Broodseinde, Poelcappelle, Passchendaele); nature of ground, 125-6, 373-4; postponements, 132-3
Yser bridgehead, *see* Nieuport
Yukon packs, 67, 76, 422

INDEX TO ARMS, FORMATIONS, AND UNITS 479

Armies—
 First—troops and guns sent to other Armies, 41, 108, 110, 118, 338; operations towards Lille in June, 90, 112–16; composition, on 31st July, 111; at end of Aug., 209; operations against Lens, 15th–20th Aug., 219–30; suggested raid by tanks, 243.
 Second—For preliminary plans, etc., of Battle of Messines, 1917, and Battles of Ypres, 1917, see Flanders Campaign *and* Messines Ridge *in General Index*. Battle of Messines, 1917: final plan and disposition of troops, 82–3; allotment and employment of tanks, 67, 70, 76–7, 79, 81; orders for the assault, 33–4; tunnelling and mines, 35–9, 52–3, 54–61, 91–2; communications, 39–41; artillery (allotment and concentration), 41–2; (plan), 43–6; (bombardment and barrages), 46–9, 61–2, 63–4, 66–7, 76, 82; (ammunition expenditure), 49; air co-operation, 42–3. Operations on 7th June: II Anzac Corps, 55–7, 64, 68, 73–4, 77, 79–80, 82–3, 84; IX Corps, 57–9, 64–5, 68, 69, 77–8, 80, 82; X Corps, 59–61, 65–6, 69–70, 74–5, 78, 80, 81; German counter-attacks, 71–5. Operations, 8th–14th June, 84–7; prisoners and guns captured, 87; casualties, 87 (fn.); no exploitation of victory, 88–90; German defence, 91–5. Battles of Ypres, 1917. Battle of Pilckem: rôle of Army, 107, 108, 124; air co-operation, 109; communications, 110, 112, 114, 190; operations 31st July, 149–50, 175, 176; casualties 31st July–2nd Aug., 178 (fn.). Assumes principal rôle and takes over frontage from Fifth Army, 206, 207, 208. Battle of Menin Road: revised scheme of campaign, 236–9; artillery (instructions), 239–40;

Armies (*continued*)—
 Second (*continued*)—
 (concentration and bombardment), 247–8, 251, 253–4; new tactical scheme, 240–2; orders, 242–3; engineer preparations, 245–6; air co-operation, 248–50; casualties prior to attack (30th Aug.–19th Sept.), 249 (fn.); postponement of action suggested, 250–1; operations on 20th Sept., 253–63, 275–7; on subsequent days, 277–8; prisoners taken, 278; casualties, 20th–25th Sept., 279. Plans for future operations, 280–1. Battle of Polygon Wood: orders and preparations, 281–4; operations on 26th Sept., 284–8, 289–92; casualties, 26th Sept., 293 (fn.). Results of operations, 20th–26th Sept., 292–4. Battle of Broodseinde: preparations, 296–300; German counter-attacks prior to the assault, 301–2; operations on 4th Oct., 303–9, 312–5, 318; casualties, 4th Oct., 309 (fn.), 315 (fn.); prisoners taken on 4th Oct., 315 (fn.); no exploitation of victory, 315–17. Battle of Poelcappelle: plans and preparations, 323–5, 327–30; question raised of postponement and closing down of campaign, 325–7, 345–6, 360; operations on 9th Oct., 330–4; casualties on 9th Oct., 334 (fn.). Battles of Passchendaele: attack on 12th Oct., preparations, 338–41; operations, 341–3. Further attacks postponed, 345; German counter-attacks, 347. Attack on 26th Oct., preparations, 346–7; operations, 349–351; attack 30th/31st Oct., 353–5; attack on 6th Nov., 355–7; attack on 10th Nov., 358–9. Close of campaign, 360. Total casualties 31st July–10th Nov., 365. Second Army dissolved, 360. Order of Battle, 388.

480 INDEX TO ARMS, FORMATIONS, AND UNITS

Armies (*continued*)—
Third—troops and guns sent to other Armies, 41, 107, 108; General Sir J. Byng assumes command, 107; relieves Fourth Army, 110; composition end of July, 111; end of Aug., 209; plans for tank attack at Cambrai, 235, 243, 345.
Fourth—move to Flemish coast, 22nd May, 109; composition and armament, 110. German attack at Nieuport, 10th/11th July, 116–22; casualties, 122; concern of War Cabinet at German success, 122. Postponement of landing operations, 133; prospects on 26th Sept., 281. Divisions released, Oct., 323. Relieves Second Army, 14th Nov., 360.
Fifth—41. Battles of Ypres, 1917: concentration in Flanders, 107; composition (divisions, artillery, tanks, aircraft), 108–10; 112. Battle of Pilckem: rôle, 124; plans, 125–32; attack postponed, 132–3; artillery bombardment and barrages, 133–4, 135–9; air co-operation, 134–5; gas casualties in July, 137; Yser canal crossed 27th July, 139–41; operations on 31st July, 147–9, 150–63, 164–75; on 1st–2nd Aug., 176–7; casualties 31st July–3rd Aug., 178 (fn.). Plan remains unchanged, 180; further postponements, 183. Attack against Westhoek, 10th Aug., 183–9. Battle of Langemarck: operations on 16th Aug., 189–201; casualties, 194 (fn.), 195 (fn.), 197 (fn.), 198 (fn.), 199 (fn.), 201 (fn.). Operations 17th–28th Aug., 202–6, 207–8; casualties 17th–28th Aug., 203 (fn.), 205 (fn.). Principal rôle given to Second Army, 206. G.H.Q. cancels minor operations, 208. Results of operations 31st July–28th Aug., 209–10; casualties in Aug., 209 (fn.). Battle of Menin Road: rôle, 236–37, 237–8, 243; operations prior to main assault, 243–44; casualties sustained 29th Aug.–19th Sept., 249; postponement of attack mooted, 250–1; operations on 20th Sept.,

Armies (*continued*)—
Fifth (*continued*)—
250, 264–71, 275–7, 278; casualties, 20th–25th Sept., 279. Battle of Polygon Wood: rôle, 280, 281; operations on 26th Sept., 288–9. Battle of Broodseinde: reinforcement of Army, 297; rôle, 298, 299; operations on 4th Oct., 309–11, 317; casualties, 4th–6th Oct., 311 (fn.). Battle of Poelcappelle: rôle, 323–4; operations on 9th Oct., 334–7. Battles of Passchendaele. Attack on 12th Oct., 343–5; casualties, 9th–14th Oct., 345 (fn.). Co-operation in attack made by French First Army on 22nd Oct., 347, 348; casualties on 22nd Oct., 348 (fn.). Attack on 26th Oct., 351. Attack on 30th Oct., 354–5. Army withdrawn into G.H.Q. reserve, 360. Total casualties, 31st July–10th Nov., 364. Order of Battle, 386.
French First—move to Flanders to command of Sir Douglas Haig, 28; composition, 5th–10th July, 109; rôle on 31st July, 124; calls for postponement of attack, 132–3; 140; operations on 31st July, 149, 158–9; operations on 16th Aug., 201; operations, 9th Oct., 337; operations on 22nd Oct., 347, 348; operations on 26th Oct., 351–2.
Artillery—
Brigades, Field—
330th, 331st—328
Groups, Heavy Artillery—
XV—222; L—222; LXIII—222; LXIV—222; I Cdn.—222; II Cdn.—222
Cavalry—
Corps, move to Flanders, 131, 148; in action, 31st July, 163; in readiness, 4th Oct., 298, 9th Oct., 323
Divisions—
1st—298, 323
3rd—373
5th—298, 323
Regiment (Special Reserve)—
1/1st King Edward's Horse, 163
Corps—
I (First Army)—Operations, 24th–28th June, 113, 114; 15th–20th Aug. (Hill 70), 219, 222. 388

INDEX TO ARMS, FORMATIONS, AND UNITS 481

Corps (continued)—
II—In Second Army. Operation, 7th June, 33, 42; casualties, 1st-12th June, 87. Transferred to Fifth Army, 107. Battle of Pilckem Ridge: (composition), 108, 132; (objectives), 108, 128, 130; (artillery), 135-6; operations on 31st July, 150-7, 165-6, 168, 175, 177, 180, 181. Casualties, 31st July-3rd Aug., 178. Operations at Westhoek, 10th Aug., 184, 185, 186-9. Battle of Langemarck: operations 16th Aug., 190-4, 197. Operations 17th-27th Aug., 202, 203-6, 207. Transferred to Second Army, 206, 207. Composition at end of Aug., 209. Ammunition expenditure, 25th June-31st Aug., 209. Relieved, 5th Sept., 243. Relieves XVIII Corps, 2nd Nov., 355. Artillery co-operation, 6th Nov., 355, 356. Operations on 10th Nov., 358-9, 360. 388

V—In G.H.Q. reserve, 107, 108. Transferred to Fifth Army and relieves XIX Corps, 7th Sept., 243. Operations cancelled, 244. Battle of Menin Road, 20th Sept., 263-8, 278. Battle of Polygon Wood, 26th Sept., 288-9. Relieved by II Anzac Corps, 28th Sept., 280, 299. 389

VIII—In Second Army. Rôle at Battle of Messines, 7th June, 33; casualties, 1st/12th June, 87 (fn.) Transferred to Fifth Army in reserve, 107, 108. Transferred to Second Army in reserve, 237, 238. Takes over from II Anzac Corps, 243. Simulated attacks, 281, 282, 355. Relieves Canadian Corps, 358

IX (Second Army)—Battle of Messines, 1917: (rôle and objectives), 32, 34; (artillery), 42 (fn.), 43, 75; (machine guns), 48, 76; operations on 7th June, 57-9, 64-5, 67 (tanks), 68-70, 73, 77-8, 80, 82, 83, 85, 86; casualties, 1st-12th June, 87 (fn.). Operations on 31st July, 108, 150; casualties, 31st July-2nd Aug., 178 (fn.). Battle of Menin Road, 20th Sept. (rôle and

Corps (continued)—
IX (continued)—
objectives), 237, 238, 243. Simulated attacks, 281, 282, 285. Battle of Broodseinde, 4th Oct., 299, 300, 314-5; casualties, 315 (fn.). Operations on 12th Oct., 338. 389

X (Second Army)—Battle of Messines, 1917: (rôle and objectives), 32-3, 34; (artillery), 42, 43; (machine guns), 48, 76; (tanks), 67; operations, 7th-10th June, 59-61, 65-6, 69, 74-5, 78, 80-1, 86; casualties, 1st-12th June, 87 (fn.). Operations on 31st July, 108, 136-7, 150, 176. Casualties, 31st July-2nd Aug., 178 (fn.). Battle of Menin Road, 20th Sept.: (rôle and objectives), 237, 243; (artillery and machine guns), 238, 254, 292; (reserves), 242; (roads and communications), 245; operations, 253, 255-6, 260-1, 261-3, 273, 277-8. Battle of Polygon Wood, 26th Sept., 280, 281, 282, 283-4, 286-8, 290-2. Battle of Broodseinde, 30th Sept.-4th Oct., 299, 300, 301-2, 305, 312-314, 317. Casualties, 4th Oct., 315 (fn.). Battle of Poelcappelle, 9th Oct., 328, 334. Earmarked for relief, 338. Operations and casualties on 26th Oct., 351. Divisions sent to Italy, 352. 389

XI—Move to Italian front, 352
XIII (First Army)—Operations 26th-30th June, 112, 113-14. 389
XIV—In G.H.Q. reserve, 6. Action at Battle of Messines, 1917: 41, 71, 76. Transferred to Fifth Army, 107, 108. Battle of Pilckem Ridge: (preparations and plans), 112; (artillery), 135; operations 31st July, 150-1, 158-9, 160-2, 163, 168, 174-5, 181; casualties, 31st July-3rd Aug., 178 (fn.). Divisional reliefs, 185. Battle of Langemarck, 16th Aug., 197, 198-201. Casualties, 6th-19th Aug., 201. Operations, 27th/28th Aug., 207, 208, 254. Composition at end of Aug., 209. Operations cancelled, 244. Battle of Menin Road,

482 INDEX TO ARMS, FORMATIONS, AND UNITS

Corps (continued)—
XIV (continued)—
20th/21st Sept., 263, 270-1, 278. Battle of Broodseinde, 4th Oct., 311, 317. Battle of Poelcappelle, 9th Oct., 323, 324, 335-7. Battles of Passchendaele : operations on 12th Oct., 344-5 ; casualties, 9th-14th Oct., 345 ; operations on 22nd Oct., 348 ; on 26th Oct., 351-2 ; casualties, 26th Oct., 351 (fn.). Relieved, 352. Move to Italy, 352. 389

XV (Fourth Army)—on Flemish coast, 109, 110. Operations at Nieuport, 10th/11th July, 116-122 ; casualties, 122. 389

XVIII—To Fifth Army, 107, 108. Battle of Pilckem Ridge: (tanks), 109, 112, 168 ; (rôle and objectives), 128 ; (artillery), 135 ; (Yser canal crossed on 27th July) 140-1 ; operations on 31st July, 150-1, 158, 159-60, 163, 168, 171, 174, 177, 181. Casualties, 31st July-3rd Aug., 178 (fn.). Divisional reliefs, 185, 190. Battle of Langemarck : operations on 16th Aug., 197, 198-200. Operations, 17th-27th Aug., 202, 207, 208. Composition at end of Aug., 209. Operations cancelled, 244. Battle of Menin Road, 20th Sept., 263, 264, 268-71. Battle of Broodseinde, 4th Oct., 310-11, 317, 318. Battle of Poelcappelle, 9th Oct., 323, 324, 334-5, 336. Passchendaele : operations on 12th Oct., 343-4 ; casualties, 9th-12th Oct., 345 (fn.) ; operations on 22nd Oct., 348 ; operations and casualties on 26th Oct., 351 ; operations on 30th Oct., 354-5. Relieved by II Corps, 355. 390

XIX—To Fifth Army, 107, 108. Battle of Pilckem Ridge : (tanks) 109, 168 ; (rôle and objectives), 112, 128 ; (artillery), 135 ; operations, 31st July-1st Aug., 150-1, 157-8, 163, 165, 166-8, 169-74, 176-7, 180, 181 ; casualties, 31st July-3rd Aug., 178 (fn.) ; 184. Divisional reliefs, 185, 190. Battle of Langemarck, 16th Aug., 194-7. Operations, 22nd Aug., 202, 203, 207-8. Composition at end of Aug., 109. Opera-

Corps (continued)—
XIX (continued)—
tions on 6th Sept., 243-4. Relieved by V Corps, 7th Sept., 243, 307 ; relieves XIV Corps, 29th Oct., 351. 390

I Anzac—To Second Army, 108. Battle of Menin Road, 20th Sept., 237, 238, 242, 243, 245, 246, 251-3, 254, 255-60, 264, 273. Relief postponed, 278, 280. Battle of Polygon Wood, 26th Sept., 281, 282, 283-4, 284-6, 290-2· Battle of Broodseinde, 4th Oct., 298, 299, 300, 304, 304-7, 317 ; casualties on 4th Oct., 309 (fn.). Battle of Poelcappelle, 9th Oct., 323, 328, 333-4 ; casualties, 9th Oct., 334 (fn.) ; 355, 390

II Anzac (Second Army)—Battle of Messines, 1917 : (rôle and objectives), 32, 34 ; (artillery), 41, 43, 75 ; (machine guns), 48 ; (tanks), 67 ; operations on 7th June, 54, 55-7, 59 (fn.), 63-4, 68, 73-4, 77-80, 83-6 ; casualties, 1st-12th June, 87 (fn.), 108. Operations on 31st July, 150, 176 ; in reserve, 237, 242 ; withdrawn for training, 243 ; relieves V Corps, 280. Battle of Polygon Wood, 26th Sept., 285-6. Battle of Broodseinde, 4th Oct., 298, 299, 300, 305, 307-9, 317 ; casualties, 4th Oct., 309 (fn.). Battle of Poelcappelle, 9th Oct., 323, 328, 330-32 ; casualties, 9th Oct., 334 (fn.). Relieved by Canadian Corps, 338, 346. Operations on 12th Oct., 341-3. 391

Canadian—In First Army, 6 ; operations, 26th-28th June, 113, 114. Capture of Hill 70, 15th-20th Aug., 219-230 ; casualties, 15th-23rd Aug., 230 (fn.). Transferred to Second Army, 338, 346. Passchendaele : operations on 26th Oct., 349-51 ; 30th Oct., 353-4 ; 31st Oct., 355 ; 6th Nov., 355-7 ; 10th Nov., 358-9. Casualties, 26th Oct.-11th Nov., 359 (fn.). 390

Divisions—
Guards—(XIV Corps). Artillery support at Battle of Messines, 41, 75, 107, 108 ; crosses Yser canal,

INDEX TO ARMS, FORMATIONS, AND UNITS 483

Divisions (*continued*)—
Guards (XIV Corps) (*continued*)—
27th June, 140, 141 (fn.); operations 31st July, 161-2; casualties 31st July-2nd Aug., 178; relieved, 185, 209. Operations 9th Oct., 336-7, 12th Oct., 344-5. Fighting record 31st July-12th Oct., 345 (fn.). Casualties, 9th-14th Oct., 345 (fn.). 391

1st—(XIV Corps). Artillery support at Battle of Messines, 41, 75. Transferred to XV Corps on coast, 110. Operations at Nieuport, 10th/11th July, 116-22; casualties, 122, 209, 233. Transferred to II Corps, 358. Operations, 10th Nov., 358-9. 391

2nd—352, 373

3rd—(V Corps). Operations, 26th Sept., 288, 291-2; casualties, 293 (fn.). 391

4th—(XIV Corps). Operations 4th Oct., 311, 317; casualties 4th-6th Oct., 311 (fn.). Operations, 9th Oct., 336; 12th Oct., 344. Casualties, 9th-14th Oct., 345 (fn.). 391

5th—In XIII Corps. Operations 28th June, 113-14. Transferred to X Corps. Operations, 4th Oct., 314; (casualties), 315 (fn.). Operations, 26th Oct., 351. Move to Italy, 352. 391

7th—(X Corps). Operations, 1st Oct., 299, 302; 4th Oct., 312-13; casualties, 4th Oct., 315 (fn.), 317. Operations, 9th Oct., 334; 26th Oct., 351. Move to Italy, 352; 373, 391

8th—in XIV Corps, 107. Transferred to II Corps, 108. Operations, 31st July, 152, 156, 165-6, 175. Casualties, 31st July-3rd Aug., 178 (fn.). Relieved, 185. Operations, 16th Aug., 192-4; casualties, 194 (fn.), 209. Transferred to X Corps, 243. 391, 394

9th (Scottish)—In V Corps, 243. Operations, 20th Sept., 265-8. Casualties, 20th-25th Sept., 279. Transferred to XVIII Corps. Operations, 12th Oct., 343-4. Casualties, 9th-14th Oct., 345 (fn.). 391, 392

11th (Northern)—In IX Corps. Operations, 7th/8th June, 77-8,

Divisions (*continued*)—
11th (Northern) (*continued*)—
80, 85. Transferred to XVIII Corps in Flanders, 107, 108. Relieves 51st Div., 185. Operations 16th Aug., 199-200; 22nd Aug., 202, 203; 27th Aug., 208 209. Operations 4th Oct., 311-11; casualties, 4th-6th Oct., 311 (fn.). Operations, 9th Oct., 335; casualties, 9th-14th Oct., 345 (fn.); 391

14th (Light)—In II Corps, 108, 190. Relieves 56th Div., 194. Operations, 16th Aug., 203-6; 27th Aug., 207, 209. 391

15th (Scottish)—In XIX Corps, 107, 108. Operations, 31st July, 157-8, 166, 169, 170, 172-4; (casualties, 45th Bde.), 174. Operations, 1st Aug., 176-7. Casualties, 31st July-3rd Aug., 178 (fn.). Relieved, 185. Operations, 22nd Aug., 202-3; (casualties), 203 (fn.), 204. Operations, 27th Aug., 208, 209. 391

16th (South Irish)—In IX Corps. Operations, 7th June, 58, 65, 68-9, 77-8. Relieved, 85. Transferred to XIX Corps, 107, 108; relieves 15th Div., 185. Operations, 16th Aug., 194-7. Casualties, 1st-20th Aug., 197. Relieved, 203, 209. 391

17th (Northern)—In XIV Corps. Operations, 12th Oct., 344; casualties, 9th-14th Oct., 345 (fn.). 391

18th (Eastern)—In II Corps, 107, 108. Operations, 31st July, 153, 155, 175. Relieves 30th Div., 185. Operations, 10th Aug., 186-8; 16th Aug., 191, 209. Transferred to XVIII Corps, 343. Operations, 12th Oct., 343-4; casualties, 9th-14th Oct., 345. 391

19th (Western)—In IX Corps. Operations, 7th June, 59, 65, 67, 69, 80, 85. Operations, 20th Sept., 238, 261, 262-3; casualties, 20th-25th Sept., 279 (fn.). 392

20th (Light)—In XIV Corps, 107, 108. Relieves 38th Div., 185. Operations, 16th Aug., 200; casualties, 6th-19th Aug., 201; 209. Operations, 20th/21st

484 INDEX TO ARMS, FORMATIONS, AND UNITS

Divisions (*continued*)—
20th (Light) (*continued*)—
Sept., 270–1, 277–8; casualties, 20th–25th Sept., 279 (fn.), 392
21st—(X Corps). In reserve, 242. Operations, 4th Oct., 299, 302, 313–4, 317; (casualties), 315 (fn.). Relieved, 334. Move to Italy, 352. 392. 394
23rd—(X Corps). Operations, 7th June, 61, 66, 69, 190. Operations, 22nd–27th Aug., 205, 207, 209. Operations, 20th Sept., 253, 255–6, 258–9, 260, 261, 274; casualties, 20th–25th Sept., 279 (fn.). Relieved, 282. Operations, 20th Sept., 301, 302, 314. Move to Italy, 352, 392
24th—(X Corps). Operations, 7th June, 78, 80–1. Transferred to II Corps, 152. Operations, 31st July, 153, 165, 176. Casualties, 31st July–3rd Aug., 178. Operations in Aug., 185, 186, 209; 243. 392
25th—(II Anzac Corps). Operations, 7th June, 57, 67, 68, 73–4, 85. Transferred to II Corps, 107, 108. Operations, 10th Aug., 185, 186, 188–89; relieved, 192; 205, 209, 392.
29th—(XIV Corps), 107, 108. Relieves Guards Div., 185. Operations, 16th Aug., 201; casualties, 15th–18th Aug., 201 (fn.). Operations, 4th Oct., 311; casualties, 4th–6th Oct., 311 (fn.). Operations, 9th Oct., 336; casualties, 9th/14th Oct., 345 (fn.). 392, 394
30th—(II Corps), 107, 108. Operations, 31st July, 152, 153–6, 157, 165, 175. Casualties, 31st July–3rd Aug., 178 (fn.). Relieved, 185; 209, 243, 392
31st—(XIII Corps). Operations, 28th June, 113–14
32nd—(XIV Corps). Artillery support, 7th June, 41, 75. Transferred to XV Corps on coast, 110. Operations at Nieuport, 10th/11th July, 117, 121–2; casualties, 10th/11th July, 122; 209
33rd—To XV Corps on coast, 110, 209. Transferred to X Corps, 242. Operations, 26th Sept., 282, 283–4, 290–2. Casualties

Divisions (*continued*)—
33rd (*continued*)—
26th Sept., 293 (fn.); relieved, 301. 392
36th (Ulster)—In IX Corps. Operations, 7th June, 64, 68, 69, 73; relieved, 85. To XIX Corps, 107, 108; relieves 55th Div., 185. Operations, 26th Aug., 194–7; casualties, 2nd–18th Aug., 198; relieved, 203; 209, 392
37th—To IX Corps, 108. Operations, 4th Oct., 299, 314–15. Casualties, 4th Oct., 315 (fn.). 392
38th (Welsh)—To XIV Corps, 107, 108. Operations, 31st July, 160–1, 174. Casualties, 31st July–3rd Aug., 178 (fn.). Relieved, 185; 208, 209, 392
39th—To XVIII Corps, 107, 108. Operations, 31st July, 159, 168, 171–4; (casualties, 118th Bde.), 174 (fn.); 177. Casualties, 31st July–3rd Aug., 178 (fn.). Relieved, 185. Transferred to X Corps, 238. Operations, 20th Sept., 261–2, 263, 275; casualties, 20th–25th Sept., 279 (fn.). Operations, 26th Sept., 282, 287–8; (casualties), 293 (fn.). 392
41st—(X Corps). Operations, 7th June, 60, 65, 67, 69. Operations, 20th–21st Sept., 253, 255, 261, 277; casualties, 20th–25th Sept., 279. Relieved, 282. Move to Italy, 352. 392, 394
42nd (1st East Lancashire), 209. Operations, 25th Aug., 244
46th (1st North Midland). In I Corps. Operations, 26th–30th June, 114
47th (2nd London)—In X Corps. Operations, 7th June, 61, 65, 69, 82. Transferred to II Corps, 190; 194, 204, 209, 352, 392
48th (1st South Midland). To XVIII Corps in Flanders, 107, 108. Relieves 20th Div., 185. Operations, 16th–25th Aug., 199, 202, 203, 208, 209. Operations, 4th Oct., 310; casualties, 4th–6th Oct., 311 (fn.). Operations, 9th Oct., 335; casualties, 9th–14th Oct., 345. Move to Italy, 352; 392

INDEX TO ARMS, FORMATIONS, AND UNITS 485

Divisions (*continued*)—
49th (1st West Riding). To XV Corps on coast, 110. Transferred to II Anzac Corps, 323. Operations, 9th Oct., 328, 330-1, 332, 334; casualties, 9th Oct., 339. 393, 395
50th (Northumbrian)—In XIV Corps. Operations and casualties, 26th Oct., 351. 393
51st (Highland)—To XVIII Corps in Flanders, 107, 108. Operations, 31st July, 159-60, 163, 174. Casualties, 31st July-3rd Aug., 178. Relieved, 185, 204, 209. Operations, 20th Sept., 268, 269-70, 275-6. Casualties, 20th-25th Sept., 279. 393
55th (1st West Lancashire)—To XIX Corps in Flanders, 107, 108. Operations, 31st July, 158, 167, 169, 171-4. Casualties, 164th Bde., 174; 31st July-3rd Aug., 178 (fn.), 266 (fn.). Relieved, 185, 243. Operations (V Corps), 20th Sept., 266-8, 275-7; casualties, 20th-25th Sept., 279; 393
56th (1st London). In G.H.Q. Reserve, 107, 108. Transferred to II Corps. Operations, 16th Aug., 190-4; casualties, 16th Aug., 194 (fn.). Relieved, 194; 209, 393
57th (2nd West Lancashire)—In XIV Corps. Operations and casualties, 26th Oct., 351
58th (2/1st London)—In XVIII Corps. Operations, 20th Sept., 268-9, 275, 276. Casualties, 20th-25th Sept., 279; 26th Sept., 293 (fn.). Operations and casualties, 26th Oct., 351. Operations, 30th Oct., 354. 393, 395
59th (2nd North Midland)—In V Corps. Operations, 26th Sept., 288-9; casualties, 26th Sept., 293 (fn.), 293. 393
61st (2nd South Midland). In VIII Corps reserve, 107, 108. To XIX Corps. Operations, 22nd Aug., 203; 27th Aug., 208, 209; transferred to V Corps, 244. 393
63rd (Royal Naval)—In XVIII Corps. Operations and casualties, 26th Oct., 351; operations, 30th Oct., 354. 393

Divisions (*continued*)—
66th (2nd East Lancashire)—In XV Corps on coast, 110, 209. To II Anzac Corps, 323. Operations, 9th Oct., 328, 330, 331-2, 333-4; casualties, 9th Oct., 334 (fn.). Relieved, 339. 393
1st Australian—(I Anzac Corps). 108. Operations, 20th Sept., 251, 253, 255, 257-60, 274. Casualties, 20th-25th Sept., 279. Relieved, 280, 282. Operations, 4th Oct., 304-6; casualties, 309. Operations, 9th Oct., 323, 333. 394
2nd Australian—(I Anzac Corps). 108. Operations, 20th Sept., 251, 252, 253, 255, 256-60, 266, 275. Casualties, 20th-25th Sept., 279. Relieved, 280, 282. Operations, 4th Oct., 304-7; casualties, 4th Oct., 309. Operations, 9th Oct., 323, 333-4; casualties, 9th Oct., 334 (fn.). 394
3rd Australian—(II Anzac Corps). Operations, 7th June, 56, 64, 79, 80, 82, 83-6. Operations, 21st-26th June, 115. Operations, 31st July, 150, 280. Operations, 4th Oct., 300, 305, 307-309; casualties, 4th Oct., 309 (fn.). Operations, 9th Oct., 323, 332; operations, 12th Oct., 338, 339, 340, 341-3. 394
4th Australian—(II Anzac Corps). Operations, 7th June, 77, 83-4, 85. Transferred to I Anzac Corps, 242. Operations, 26th Sept., 282, 284, 285-6, 290, 291-2. Casualties, 26th Sept., 293. In reserve, 9th Oct., 323. Operations, 12th Oct., 343. 394
5th Australian (I Anzac Corps)— 108, 242. Operations, 26th Sept., 282, 284-5, 291, 92; casualties, 26th Sept., 293 (fn.), 305, 323. 394
1st Canadian—Operations in First Army, 15th-20th Aug., 219, 220, 222-5, 226-8. Casualties, 15th-22nd Aug., 230 (fn.). Transferred to Second Army. Operations, 30th Oct., 353, 355; operations, 6th Nov., 357-8; operations, 10th Nov., 359. Casualties, 26th Oct.-11th Nov., 359 (fn.). 393

486 INDEX TO ARMS, FORMATIONS, AND UNITS

Divisions (*continued*)—
  2nd Canadian—Operations in First Army, 15th–20th Aug., 219–20, 222, 228–9; casualties, 15th–23rd Aug., 230 (fn.). Transferred to Second Army. Operations, 6th Nov., 355, 356–7; operations, 10th Nov., 358–9. Casualties, 26th Oct.–11th Nov., 359 (fn.); 393
  3rd Canadian—Operations in Second Army. 30th Oct., 355; casualties, 26th Oct.–11th Nov., 359. 393
  4th Canadian—Operations in First Army, 26th–30th June, 113, 114; 15th–20th Aug., 220, 226, 228, 29; casualties, 15th–23rd Aug., 230 (fn.). Transferred to Second Army. Operations, 26th Oct., 349; 30th Oct., 353–4; relieved 355, 356. Casualties, 26th Oct.–11th Nov., 359. 393
  New Zealand—(II Anzac Corps). Operations, 7th June, 56–7, 63–4–67, 68, 73–4, 82, 86, 87. Operations, 26th–30th June, 115. Operations, 31st July, 150, 176. Operations and casualties, 4th Oct., 309. Operations, 9th Oct., 339–40, 341–3. Casualties, 12th Oct., 342. 394, 395
Engineers (R.E.)—
  Field Survey Company—
    No. 2, 247
  Special Brigade (Gas)—
    No. 4, Special Coy., 222
  Tunnelling Companies—
    171st—37, 58; 173rd—141; 175th—37, 60; 183rd—38; 257th—118
Engineers (Australian)—
  1st Tunnelling Company—38, 60;
  2nd Tunnelling Company—38, 118, 121
Engineers (Canadian)—
  1st Tunnelling Company—37;
  2nd Tunnelling Company—38;
  3rd Tunnelling Company, 37, 60
Engineers (New Zealand)—
  1st Field Company—340
Flying Corps (R.F.C.)—
  Brigades—
    II—42, 46, 48, 109;
    IV—109, 110;
    V—109
  Kite Balloon Section—2nd, 43, 73
  Squadron—43rd, 221

Flying Corps (R.F.C.) (*continued*)—
  Wing—Ninth, 109
Flying Corps (R.N.A.S.)—110
Infantry Brigades—
  1st Guards—162, 336, 391
  2nd Guards—161–2, 337, 391
  3rd Guards—162, 345, 391
  1st—391
  2nd—119–22, 391
  3rd—391
  7th—57, 392
  8th—288, 391
  9th—391
  10th—391
  11th—391
  12th—336, 344, 391
  13th—314, 351, 391
  15th—113, 114, 334, 391
  17th—80, 81, 153, 392
  19th—286–7, 392
  20th—312, 391
  21st—153, 154, 392
  22nd—302, 334, 391
  23rd—156, 165, 175, 192, 193, 194, 391
  24th—156, 165, 175, 391
  25th—165, 175, 192–4, 391, 394
  26th—343–4, 391
  27th—121, 265–6, 266–7, 391, 394
  32nd—335, 391
  33rd—77, 78, 80, 84, 310, 391
  34th—199, 310, 391
  41st—204–6, 207, 391
  42nd—391
  43rd—204–6, 391
  44th—157–8, 203, 391
  45th—166, 169, 170, 172–4; (casualties), 177; 203, 391
  46th—158, 391
  47th—58, 68, 391
  48th—195, 197, 391
  49th—58, 59, 68, 195, 197, 391
  50th—391
  51st—344, 391
  52nd—391
  53rd—155, 188, 189, 191, 193, 391
  54th—187, 391
  55th—187, 343–4, 391
  56th—59, 392
  57th—69, 78, 80, 263, 392
  58th—59, 262–3, 392
  59th—200, 270, 392
  60th—200, 392
  61st—200, 270, 392
  62nd—313, 314, 392, 394
  63rd—315, 392
  64th—313, 314, 392
  68th—256, 392

INDEX TO ARMS, FORMATIONS, AND UNITS 487

Infantry Brigades (*continued*)—
 69th—61, 256, 260, 302, 392
 70th—61, 301, 392
 72nd—153, 392
 73rd—80, 81, 153, 176, 392
 74th—57, 188-9, 392
 75th—68, 392
 76th—288, 391
 86th—336, 392, 394
 87th—201, 392
 88th—201, 336, 392
 89th—155, 392
 90th—154, 392
 91st—312, 391
 94th—113, 114
 95th—314, 334, 391
 98th—283, 284, 285, 286-7, 292, 392
 100th—283, 284, 287, 291, 392
 107th—57, 58, 392
 108th—196, 392
 109th—57, 58, 196, 392
 110th—302, 392
 111th—392
 112th—392
 113th—161, 392
 114th—161, 392
 115th—161, 392
 116th—159, 177, 287-8, 392
 117th—159, 262, 392
 118th—168, 170, 171, 174, 287-8, 392
 122nd—69, 261, 392
 123rd—60, 392, 394
 124th—60, 260, 262, 392, 394
 140th—61, 392
 141st—392
 142nd—61, 82, 392
 143rd—310, 392
 144th—335, 392
 145th—199, 392
 146th—330, 331, 393, 395
 147th—393
 148th—330, 331, 393, 395
 149th—393
 150th—393
 151st—393
 152nd—159, 174, 393
 153rd—160, 393
 154th—269, 393
 164th—167, 168, 169, 170, 171, 172, 174, 266-8, 393
 165th—158, 172, 266-8, 393
 166th—158, 172, 267, 393
 167th—191-2, 192-3, 194, 393
 168th—191-2, 393
 169th—191-2, 192-3, 194, 393
 170th—393

Infantry Brigades (*continued*)—
 171st—393
 172nd—393
 173rd—268-9, 393, 395
 174th—268-9, 393
 175th—289, 393
 176th—288, 393
 177th—393
 178th—288-9, 393
 182nd—393
 183rd—393
 184th—203, 393
 188th—393
 189th—393
 190th—354, 393
 197th—330, 332, 333, 393
 198th—330, 332, 333, 393
 199th—393
 1st Australian—305-6, 394
 2nd Australian—256, 305-6, 394
 3rd Australian—257, 394
 4th Australian—286, 394
 5th Australian—258, 333, 394
 6th Australian—306, 333, 394
 7th Australian—258, 306, 394
 8th Australian—394
 9th Australian—56, 340, 342, 343, 354, 394
 10th Australian—56, 307-9, 340, 342, 343, 394
 11th Australian—303, 307-9, 394
 12th Australian—79, 80, 82, 86, 343, 394
 13th Australian—80, 84, 85, 286, 394
 14th Australian—285, 394
 15th Australian—285, 291, 394
 1st Canadian—393
 2nd Canadian—224, 226-7, 358, 393
 3rd Canadian—224, 226-7, 393
 4th Canadian—223, 358, 393
 5th Canadian—223, 356-7, 393
 6th Canadian—228-9, 356, 393
 7th Canadian—354, 393
 8th Canadian—350, 354, 393
 9th Canadian—349-50, 354, 393
 10th Canadian—228-9, 349, 353, 393
 11th Canadian—226, 393
 12th Canadian—354, 393
 1st New Zealand—68, 309, 394, 395
 2nd New Zealand—57, 68, 340, 341-2, 394
 3rd New Zealand (Rifle)—57, 68, 340, 341-2, 394
 4th New Zealand—309, 394
 South African—265-6, 266-7, 267; (casualties) 391

488 INDEX TO ARMS, FORMATIONS, AND UNITS

Infantry Regiments—
  Coldstream Guards, 1st Bn., 162, 337
  —, 2nd Bn., 162
  Grenadier Guards, 2nd Bn., 162
  —, 3rd Bn., 337
  Welsh Guards, 1st Bn., 162
  Argyll & Sutherland Highlanders, 1st Bn., 283
  —, 1/8th Bn., 276
  Bedfordshire, 7th Bn., 187, 188, 191
  Berkshire, Royal, 6th Bn., 188
  Black Watch (Royal Highlanders,) 4th/5th Bn., 168, 171, 287
  —, 1/6th Bn., 160
  Border Regiment, 2nd Bn., 312
  —, 11th Bn., 121
  Cambridgeshire, 1/1st Bn., 287
  Cameron Highlanders, 6th Bn., 166
  Cheshire, 1/6th Bn., 168, 171
  —, 9th Bn., 263
  Cornwall L.I., 1st Bn., 314
  —, 6th Bn., 204–6
  Devonshire, 8th Bn., 312
  Dublin Fusiliers, Royal, 1st Bn., 311
  —, 9th Bn., 197
  Gordon Highlanders, 2nd Bn., 312
  —, 1/4th Bn., 276
  —, 1/6th Bn., 160
  Green Howards, 6th Bn., 335
  —, 9th Bn., 256, 302
  Hampshire, 14th Bn., 159
  Hertfordshire, 1/1st Bn., 168, 171
  Highland L.I., 1/9th Bn., 284
  —, 17th Bn., 121
  H.A.C., 1st Bn., 334
  Inniskilling Fusiliers, Royal, 8th Bn., 197
  Irish Rifles, Royal, 2nd Bn., 188–9
  —, 7th Bn., 197
  King's (Liverpool), 1/10th Bn., 177
  King's Own, 1st Bn., 344
  —, 1/4th Bn., 167
  King's Own Scottish Borderers, 1st Bn., 201, 314
  —, 6th Bn., 265
  King's Own Yorkshire L.I., 7th Bn., 200
  —, 8th Bn., 301
  —, 9th Bn., 313
  King's Royal Rifle Corps, 2nd Bn., 119–22
  —, 12th Bn., 200, 278
  —, 17th Bn., 262
  Lancashire Fusiliers, 1st Bn., 336
  —, 2/5th Bn., 167

Infantry Regiments (continued)—
  Lancashire Fusiliers (continued)—
  —, 2/8th Bn., 332
  Leicestershire, 9th Bn., 302
  Lincolnshire, 1st Bn., 313
  —, 8th Bn., 315
  London, 1/4th Bn. (Royal Fus.), 268
  —, 2/4th Bn. (Royal Fus.), 268
  —, 2/5th Bn. (London Rifle Brigade), 269
  —, 2/6th Bn. (Rifles), 269
  —, 2/8th (P.O. Rifles), 269
  —, 9th Bn. (Q.V.R.), 193
  —, 20th Bn. (Blackheath & Woolwich), 82
  —, 21st Bn. (1st Surrey R.), 69
  —, 23rd Bn., 69
  —, 28th Bn. (Artists Rifles), 355
  Loyal North Lancashire, 1/4th Bn., 167
  Manchester, 11th Bn., 310
  —, 21st Bn., 312
  Middlesex, 1st Bn., 283
  —, 2nd Bn., 194
  Munster Fusiliers, Royal, 1st Bn., 68
  —, 2nd Bn., 359
  Norfolk, 8th Bn., 188
  Northamptonshire, 1st Bn., 119-22
  Northumberland Fusiliers, 11th Bn., 256
  Queen's (R. West Surrey), 1st Bn., 283
  —, 3rd/4th Bn., 313
  —, 7th Bn., 187
  —, 10th Bn., 62
  Rifle Brigade, 1st Bn., 311
  —, 10th Bn., 278
  —, 11th Bn., 200
  —, 16th Bn., 262
  Royal Fusiliers, 2nd Bn., 336
  —, 11th Bn., 187, 188
  Royal Irish, 2nd Bn., 68, 196
  Royal Scots, 1/9th Bn., 269
  —, 12th Bn., 265, 266
  Scots Fusiliers, Royal, 6th/7th Bn., 166
  Scottish Rifles, 5th/6th Bn., 186
  Seaforth Highlanders, 2nd Bn., 311
  —, 1/4th Bn., 269
  —, 1/6th Bn., 160
  Sherwood Foresters, 9th Bn., 310
  —, 11th Bn., 70, 301
  —, 16th Bn., 262
  —, 17th Bn., 262
  Somerset L.I., 6th Bn., 204.
  —8th Bn., 315

INDEX TO ARMS, FORMATIONS, AND UNITS 489

Infantry Regiments (*continued*)—
South Staffordshire, 1st Bn., 312
South Wales Borderers, 1st Bn., 359
—, 11th Bn., 161, 174-5
Suffolk, 1/4th Bn., 286
Sussex, Royal, 13th Bn., 159
Warwickshire, Royal, 2nd Bn., 334
—, 1/7th Bn., 310
—, 15th Bn., 351
Welch Fusiliers, Royal, 1st Bn., 302
—, 2nd Bn., 286
—, 13th Bn., 161
—, 17th Bn., 161
West Kent, Royal, 1st Bn., 314
Wiltshire, 1st Bn., 68
Worcestershire, 4th Bn., 336
Australian, 5th Bn., 259
—, 6th Bn., 257
—, 7th Bn., 260
—, 8th Bn., 260
—, 10th Bn., 257
—, 11th Bn., 257
—, 17th Bn., 333
—, 18th Bn., 259
—, 19th Bn., 333
—, 20th Bn., 333
—, 31st Bn., 285
—, 34th Bn., 342
—, 37th Bn., 79, 82
—, 38th Bn., 64, 342
—, 40th Bn., 308, 343
—, 45th Bn., 79
—, 47th Bn., 79
—, 49th Bn., 80, 84
—, 52nd Bn., 80, 84
—, 58th Bn., 284
—, 60th Bn., 284
—, 3rd Pioneer Bn., 308
Canadian—
Princess Patricia's Canadian L.I., 354
—, 1st Bn., 357
—, 2nd Bn., 357
—, 3rd Bn., 357
—, 5th Bn., 224, 227
—, 7th Bn., 224, 225, 227, 358
—, 8th Bn., 224, 227, 358
—, 10th Bn., 224, 227
—, 13th Bn., 224

Infantry Regiments (*continued*)—
Canadian (*continued*)—
Princess Patricia's Canadian L.I. (*continued*)
—, 15th Bn., 224
—, 16th Bn., 224
—, 18th Bn., 223
—, 20th Bn., 223, 358
—, 21st Bn., 223
—, 22nd Bn., 223
—, 24th Bn., 223
—, 25th Bn., 223
—, 26th Bn., 223
—, 27th Bn., 229, 356
—, 28th Bn., 356
—, 29th Bn., 229
—, 31st Bn., 356
—, 43rd Bn., 350
—, 44th Bn., 349
—, 46th Bn., 349
—, 47th Bn., 229, 349
—, 49th Bn., 354
—, 50th Bn., 229, 348
—, 52nd Bn., 350
—, 58th Bn., 350
—, 72nd Bn., 354
—, 78th Bn., 354
—, 85th Bn., 354
Mounted Rifles, 4th Bn., 350
—, 5th Bn., 354
Newfoundland Battalion, Royal, 336
New Zealand—
—, 2nd Canterbury, 63
—, 2nd Wellington, 150
—, 4th Rifle Bn., 65
South African—
—, 1st Bn., 265
—, 2nd Bn., 267
—, 3rd Bn., 265
West Indies Regiment, British, 246
Tank Corps (*see also* General Index)—
Battalions—
D—268, 310 ; E—268
Brigades—
I—109, 148, 151, 202, 203, 248, 268, 310 ; II—67, 108, 148, 151, 157, 243, 256 ; III—109, 148, 151, 168
No. 5 Section, 5th Coy., 79

7498. Wt. 5210c. Ps. 14132. C. & Co. W. Ltd. 1948. Gp. 553.   S.O. Code No. 70-562*

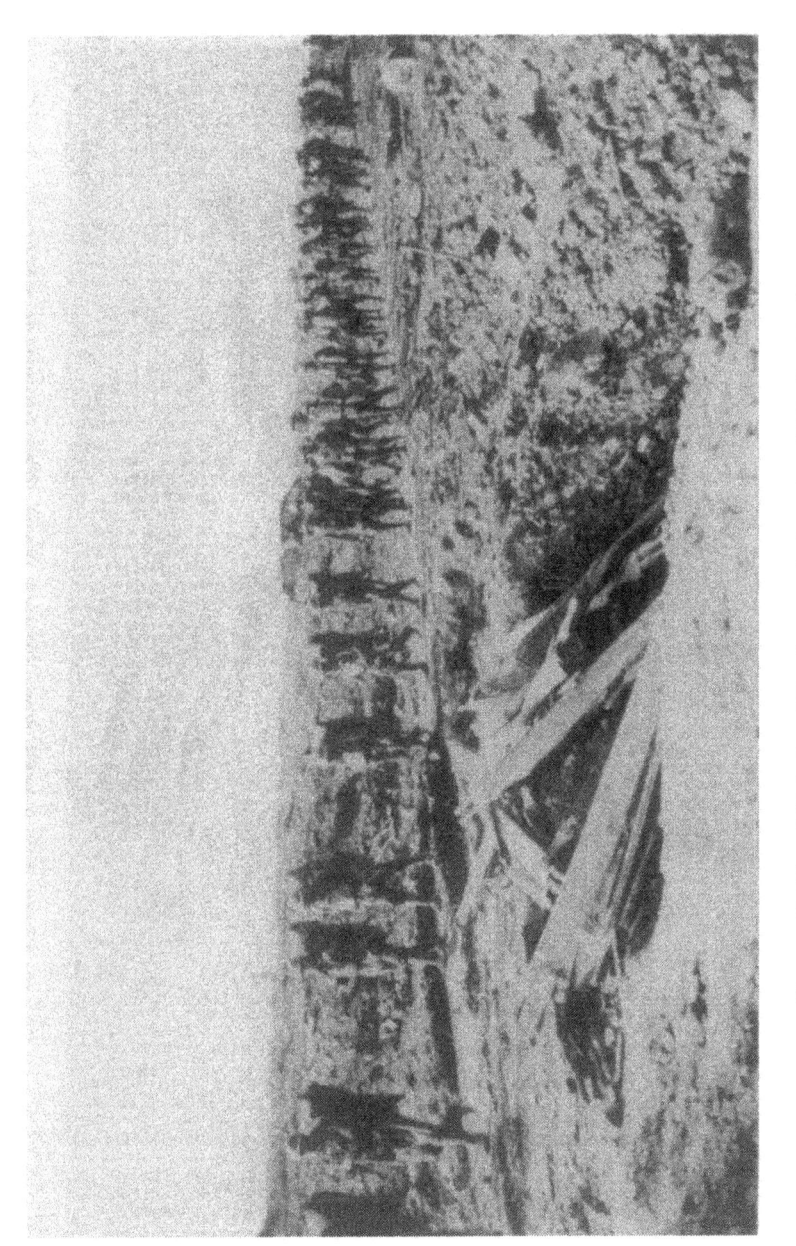

Fig. 1—Battle of Polygon Wood—carrying party, 27th September

Fig. 2 — Ypres-Menin road, near Polygon Wood, 30th September, 1917

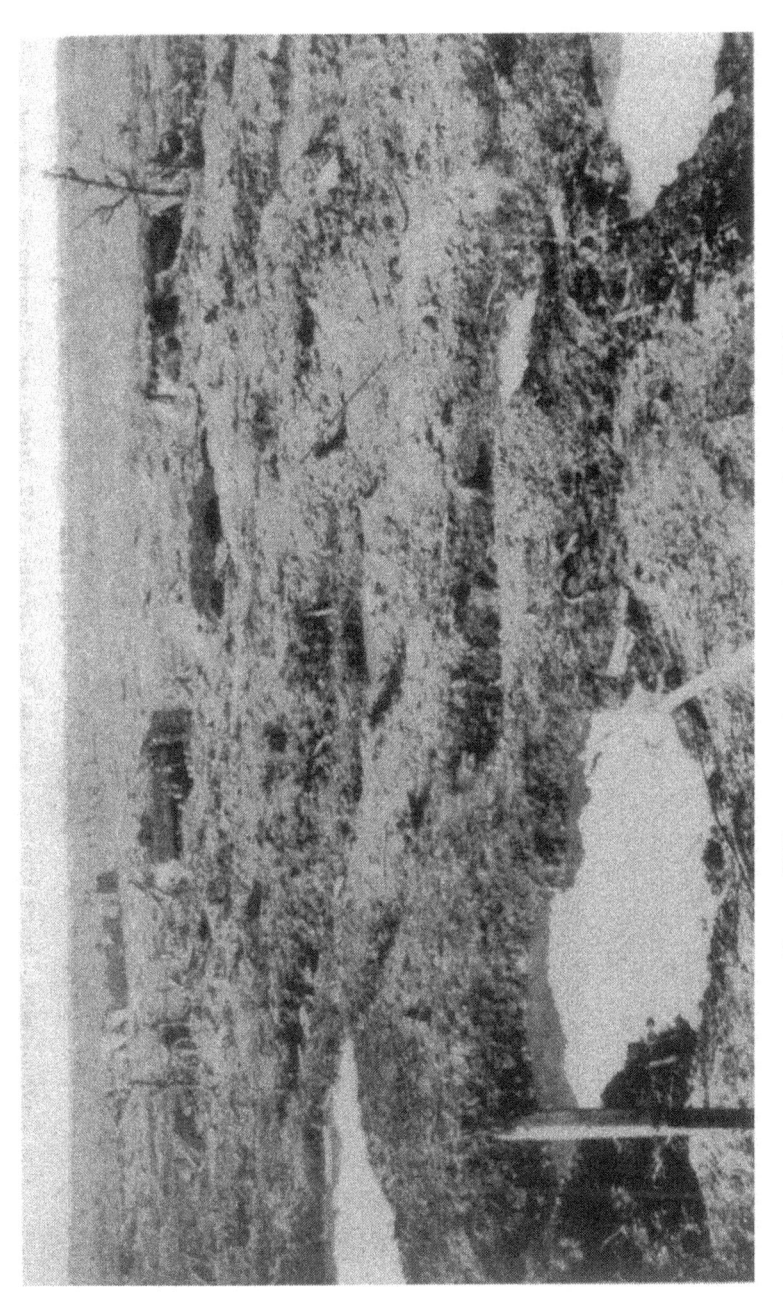

Fig. 3.—**Pillboxes at Nonne Bosschen, 1st October, 1917**

Fig. 4—Zonnebeke: brick kiln and church, 5th October, 1917, from near jumping-off place of previous day's attack

Fig. 5—Battle of Passchendaele, 6th October, 1917. Canadian Pioneers laying duckboard track

Fig. 6—Zonnebeke Valley on 15th October, 1917. Planked road on northern side of the Roulers railway

Fig. 7—Near Birr Crossroads, 25th October, 1917, from Menin road

Fig. 8.—Plank road at Idiot Corner (north-west corner of Bellewaarde Lake), 28th October, 1917

Sketch 1.

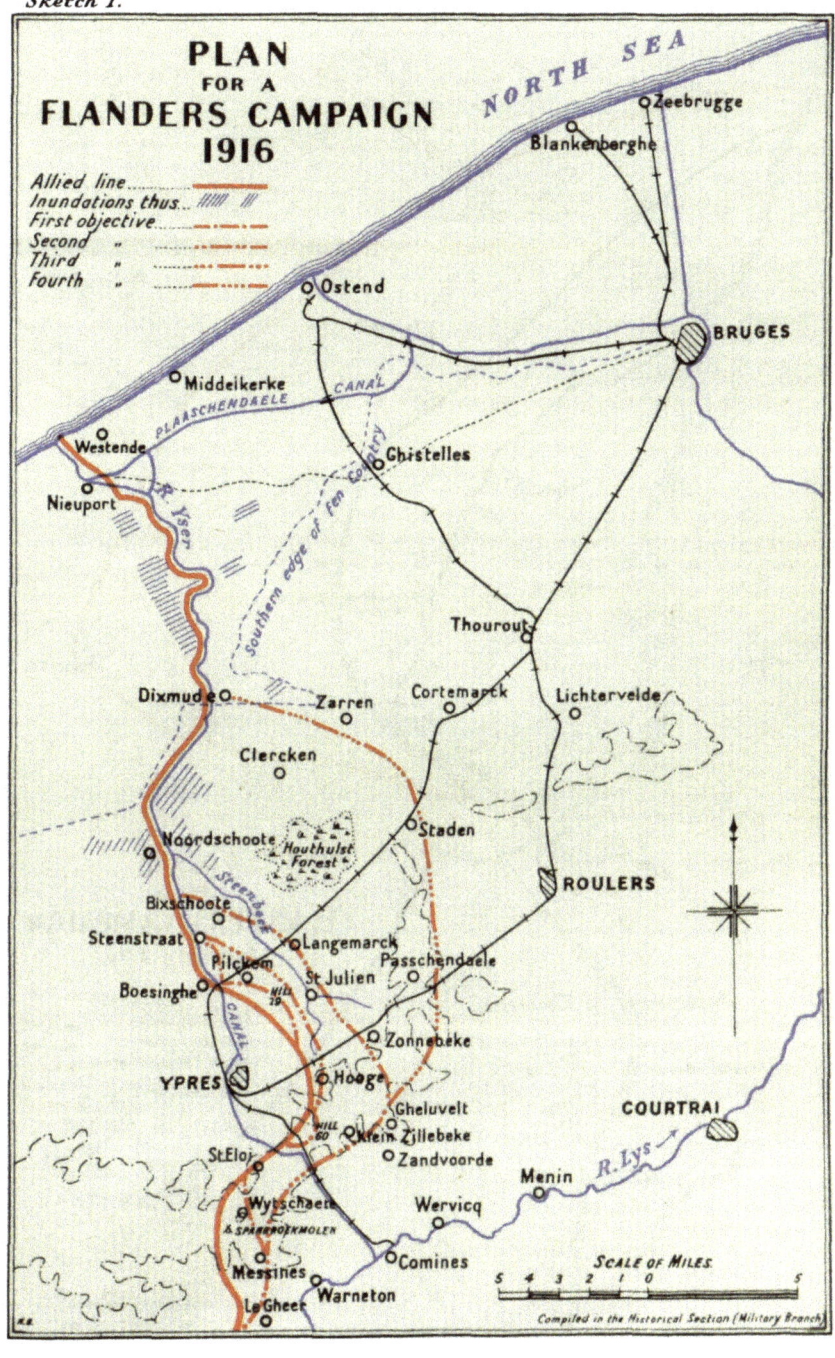

PLAN FOR A FLANDERS CAMPAIGN 1916

Sketch 2

PLAN FOR A FLANDERS CAMPAIGN
February 1917

REFERENCE
British front line
Zero day objective
Zero + 2 days objective
Tank attacks

Compiled in the Historical Section (Military Branch).

Sketch 3.

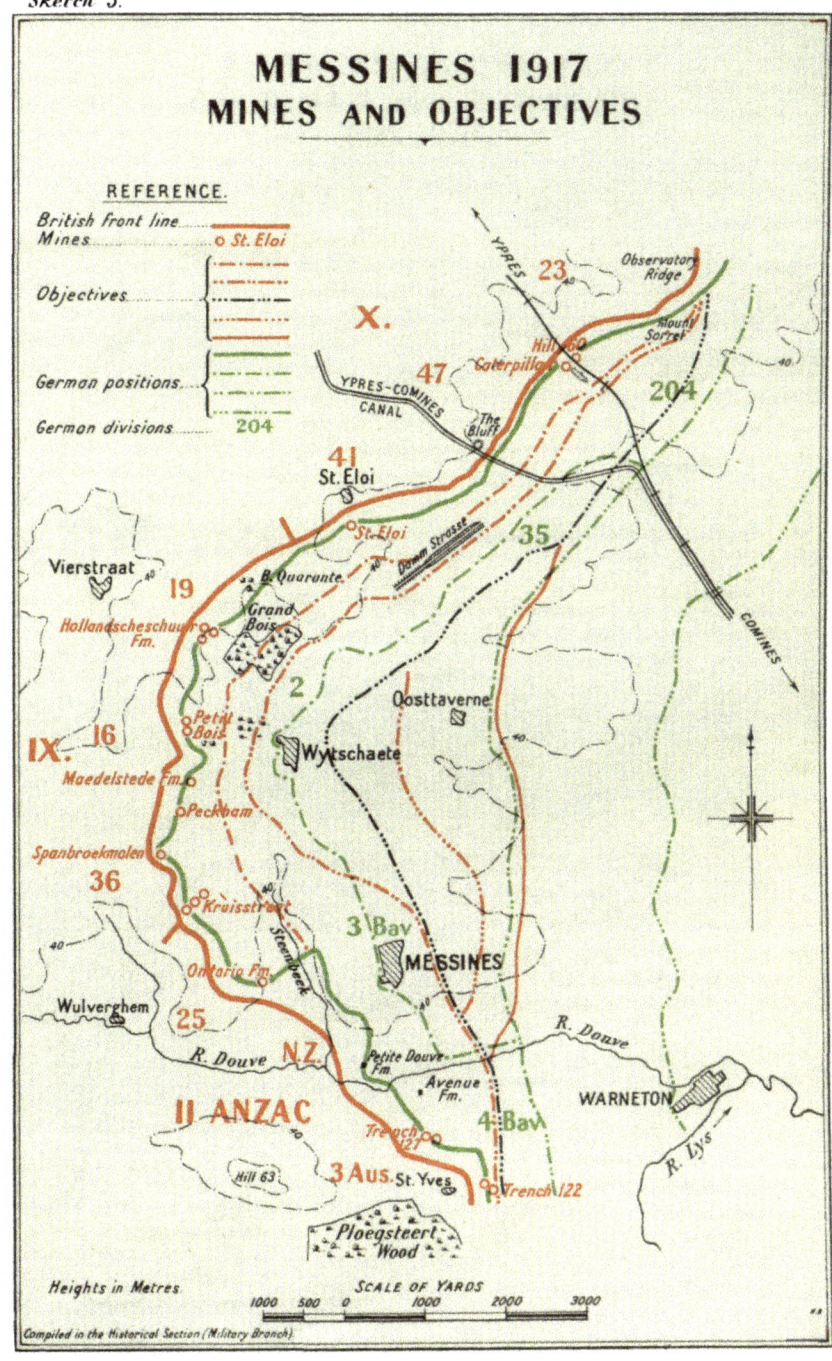

MESSINES 1917
MINES AND OBJECTIVES

Sketch 4.

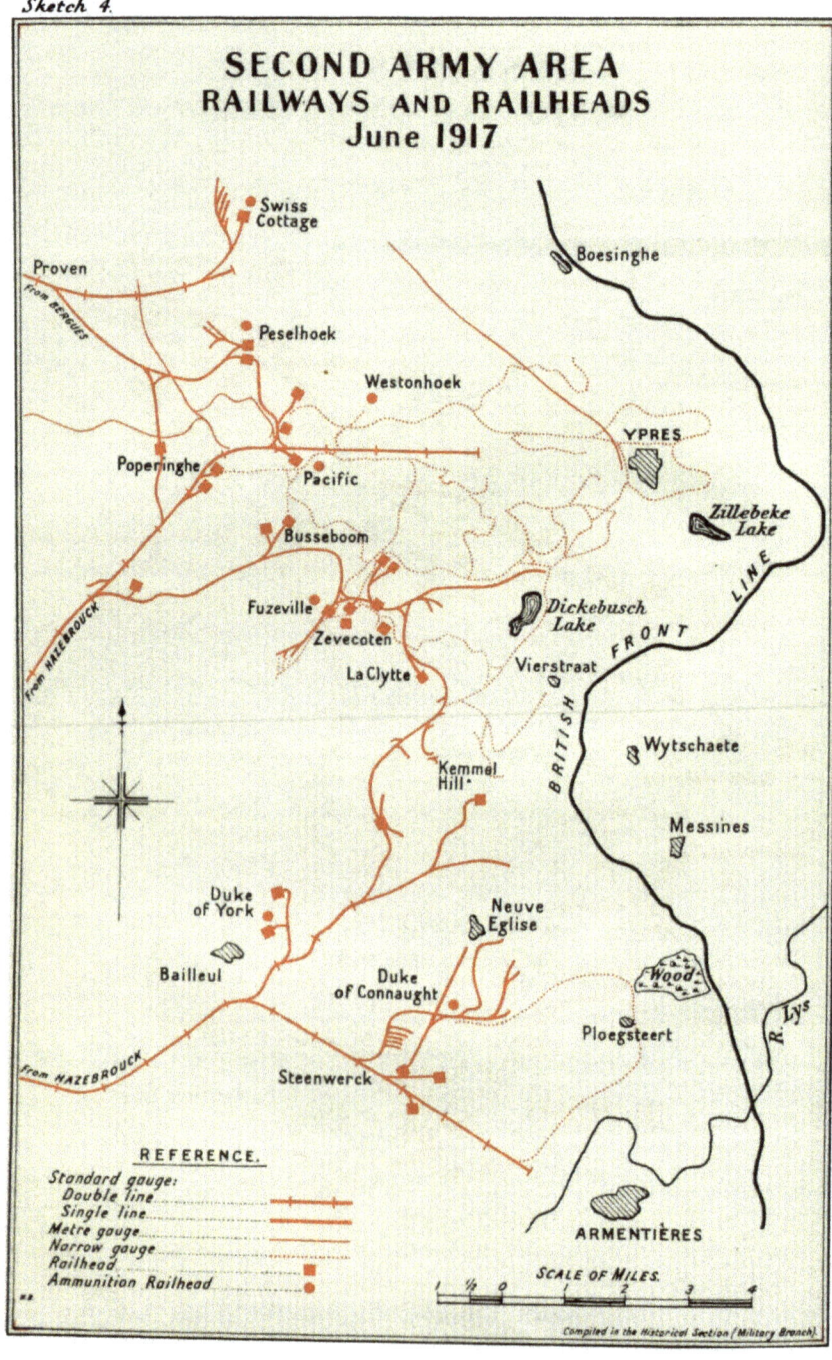

SECOND ARMY AREA
RAILWAYS AND RAILHEADS
June 1917

REFERENCE.
Standard gauge:
  Double line
  Single line
Metre gauge
Narrow gauge
Railhead
Ammunition Railhead

SCALE OF MILES.

Compiled in the Historical Section (Military Branch).

Sketch 5.

MESSINES 1917
THE END OF THE BATTLE
REFERENCE.
British Front line:
Zero 7th June
Nightfall 7th June
" 14th "
Objectives;
First
Second (observation line)
Third
Germans
23
X.
47
41
19
16
IX.
36
25
N.Z.
II ANZAC
3 Aus
YPRES 2 miles
YPRES
Mount Sorrel
Hill 60
Battle Wood
Spoil Bank
White Chateau
St. Eloi
Damm Strasse
Vierstraat
Hollebeke
Ravine Wood
Verhaest
Damm Wd.
Denys Wd.
Rose Wd.
Grand Bois
Marten's Fm.
Roozebeek
Kortewilde
Bug Wd.
Oosttaverne
Vandamme Fm.
Hospice
Leg Copse
Polka Est.
Van Hove Fm.
Houthem
Wytschaete
Torreken Fm.
Joye Fm.
Wambeek
Wambeke
Rommens Fm.
Lumm Fm.
Blauwepoortbeek
Oelporte Fm.
L' Enfer Wd.
4 Huns Fm.
Despagne Fm.
Garde Dieu
To WERVICQ
Deconinck Fm.
Blauwen Molen
Gapaard
MESSINES
Steingast Fm.
Bethleem Fm.
Fme de la Croix
R. Douve
WARNETON
LILLE 10 miles
R. Lys
Thatched Cottage
Hill 20
Hill 63
St. Yves
La Basse Ville
Trois Tilleuls Fm.
Ploegsteert Wood
SCALE OF YARDS
1000 500 0 1000 2000 3000
Compiled in the Historical Section (Military Branch)

Sketch 6.

PROJECTED ADVANCE THROUGH BELGIUM

REFERENCE.
Front line May 1917
First objective (54 mile line)
Second objective (62 mile line)

Sketch 7.

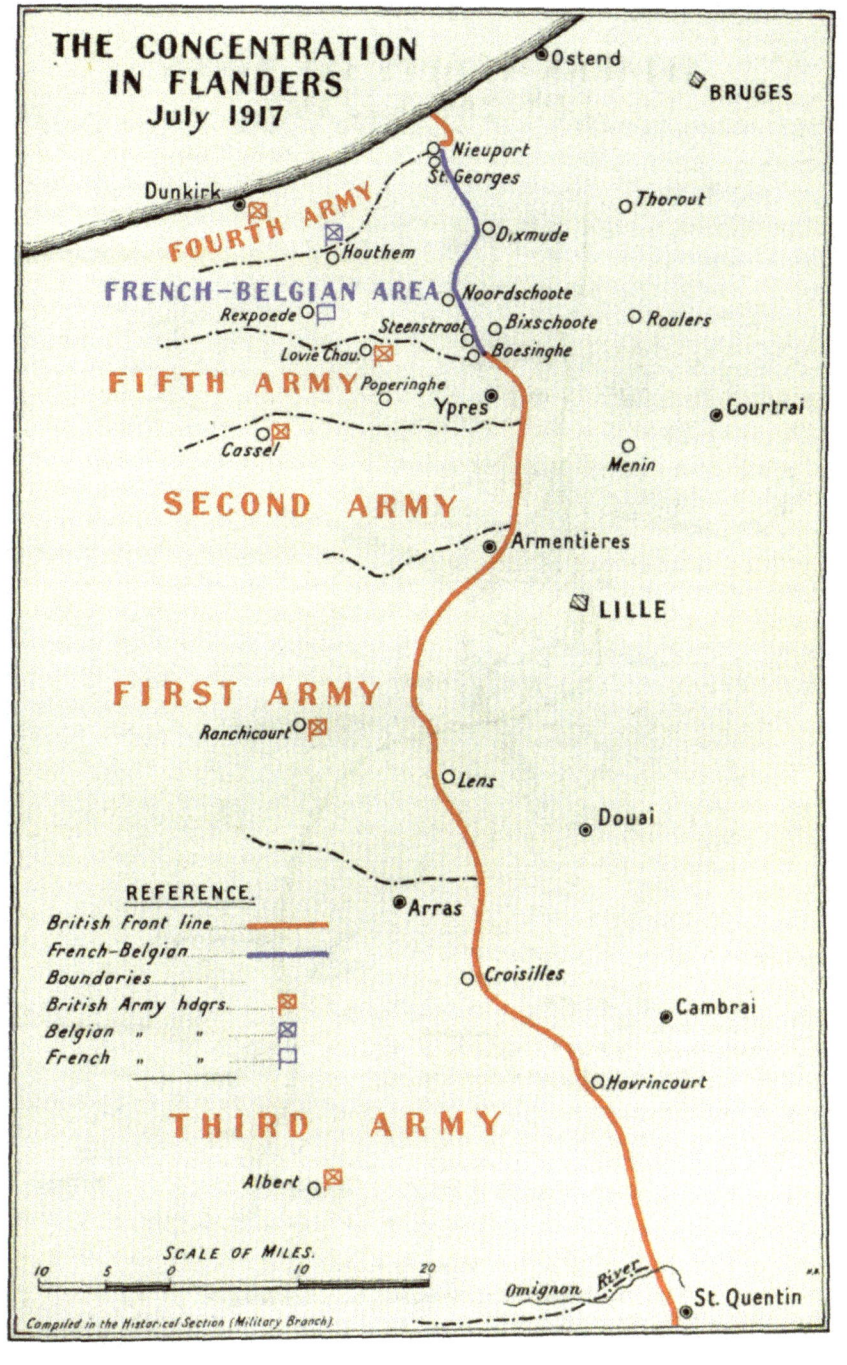

THE CONCENTRATION IN FLANDERS
July 1917

REFERENCE.
British Front line
French-Belgian
Boundaries
British Army hdqrs.
Belgian " "
French " "

SCALE OF MILES.
10 5 0 10 20

Compiled in the Historical Section (Military Branch).

FOURTH ARMY
FRENCH-BELGIAN AREA
FIFTH ARMY
SECOND ARMY
FIRST ARMY
THIRD ARMY

Ostend
BRUGES
Nieuport
St. Georges
Dunkirk
Thourot
Houthem
Dixmude
Noordschoote
Rexpoede
Steenstraat
Bixschoote
Roulers
Lovie Chau.
Boesinghe
Poperinghe
Ypres
Courtrai
Cassel
Menin
Armentières
LILLE
Ranchicourt
Lens
Douai
Arras
Croisilles
Cambrai
Havrincourt
Albert
Omignon River
St. Quentin

Sketch 8.

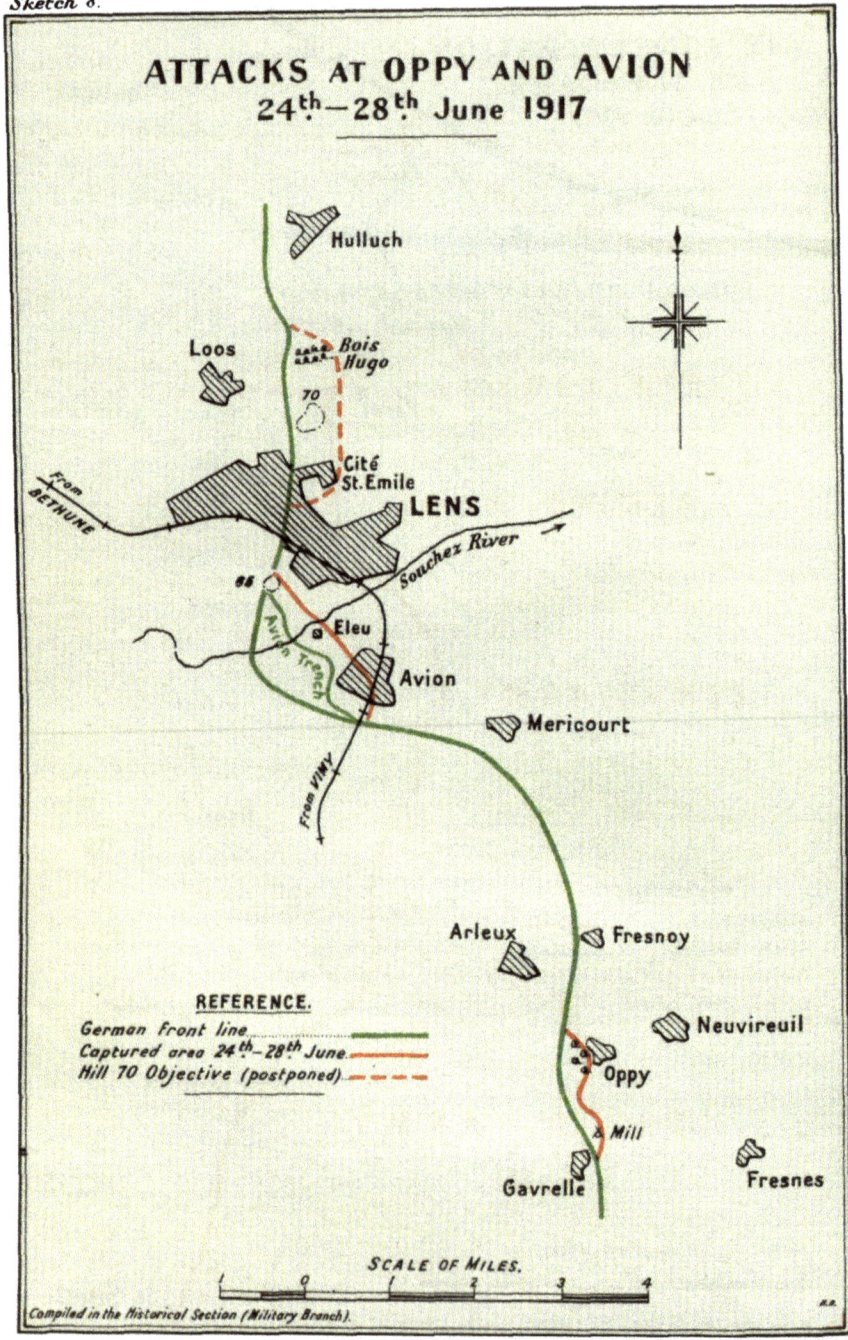

ATTACKS AT OPPY AND AVION
24th–28th June 1917

THE NIEUPORT BRIDGEHEAD
10th July 1917

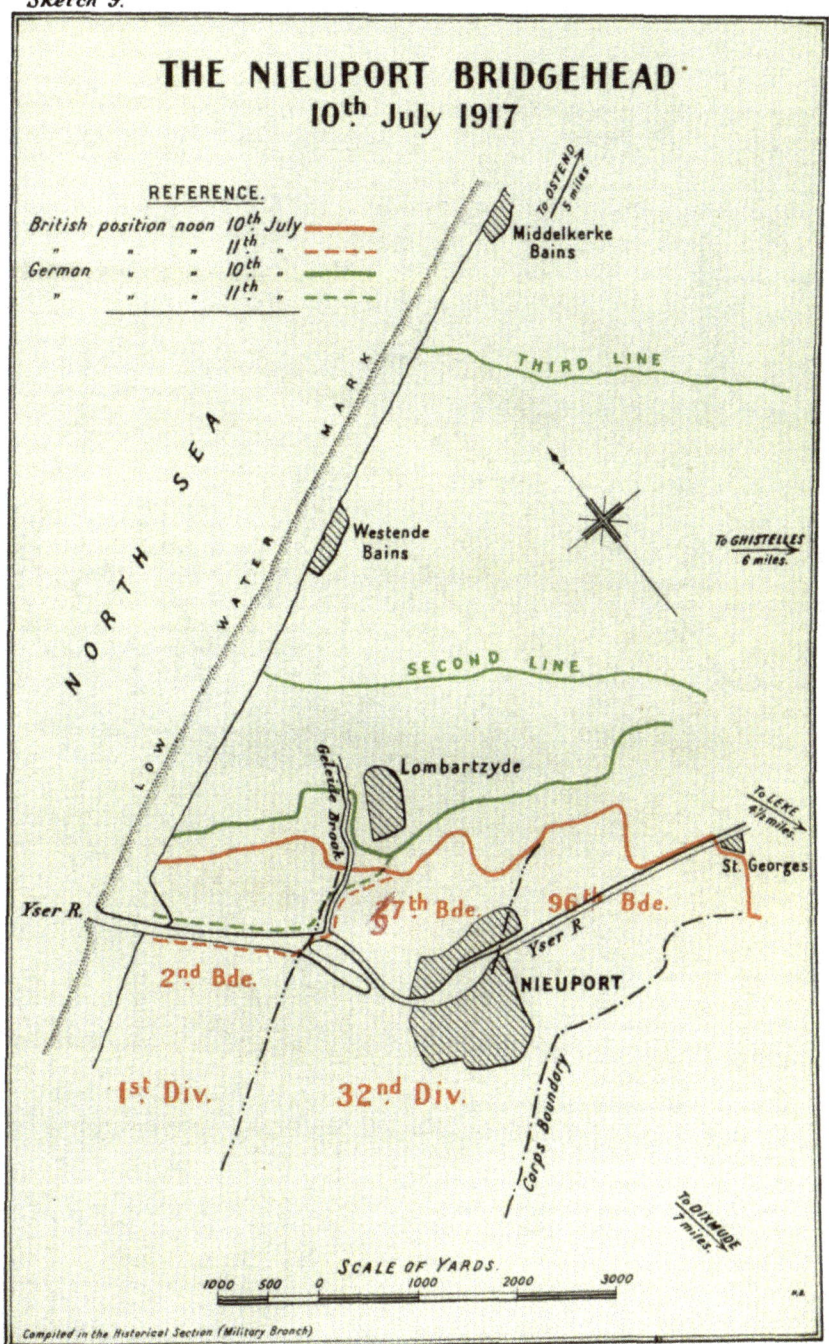

Sketch 10.

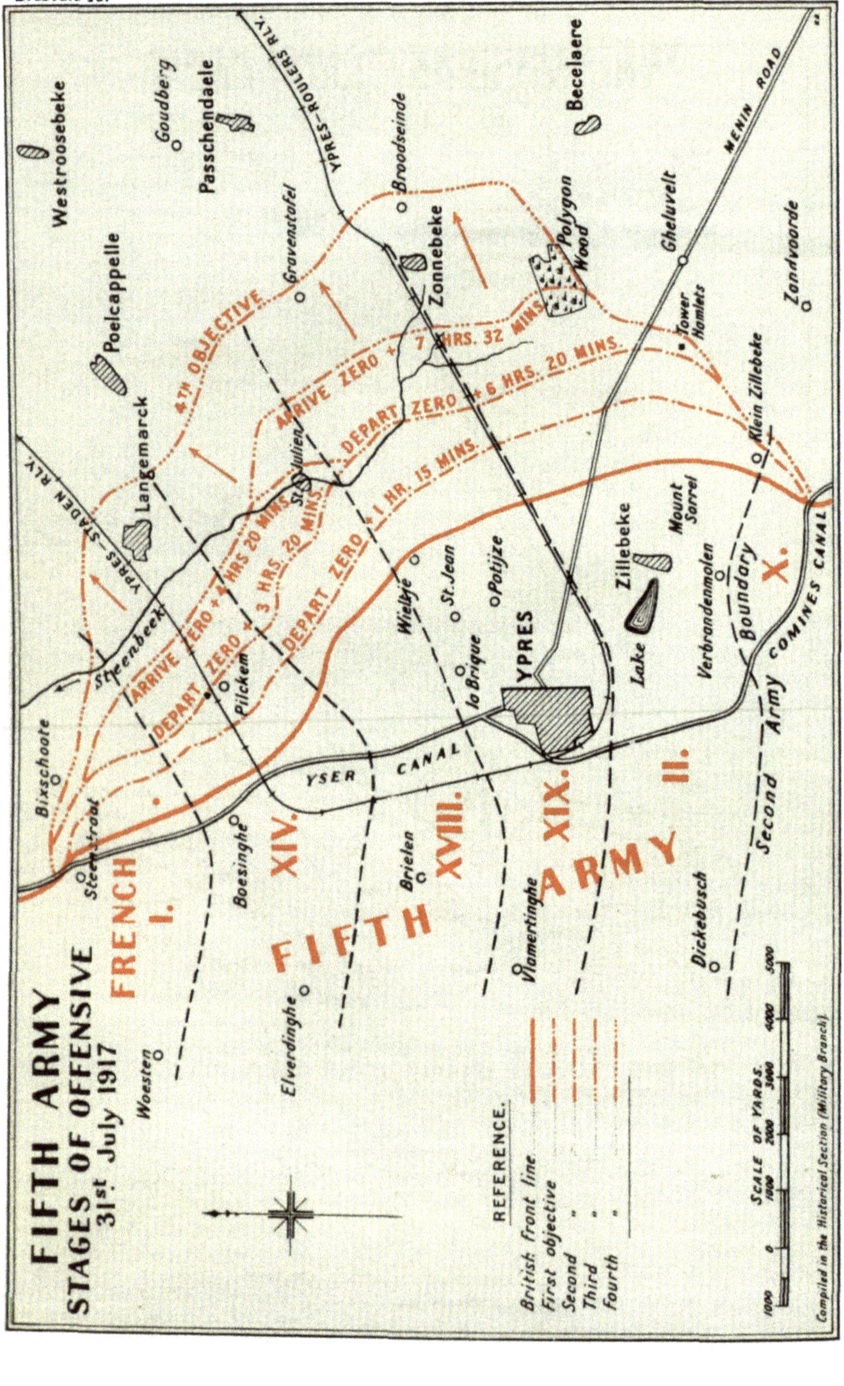
FIFTH ARMY
STAGES OF OFFENSIVE
31st. July 1917
REFERENCE.
British Front line
First objective
Second "
Third "
Fourth "
SCALE OF YARDS
1000 0 1000 2000 3000 4000 5000
Compiled in the Historical Section (Military Branch)
FRENCH
I.
XIV.
XVIII.
XIX.
II.
X.
FIFTH ARMY
Second Army Boundary
DEPART ZERO
DEPART ZERO + 3 HRS. 20 MINS.
ARRIVE ZERO + 4 HRS. 20 MINS.
DEPART ZERO + 1 HR. 15 MINS.
DEPART ZERO + 6 HRS. 20 MINS.
ARRIVE ZERO + 7 HRS. 32 MINS.
4TH OBJECTIVE
YPRES
YSER CANAL
COMINES CANAL
MENIN ROAD
YPRES-ROULERS RLY.
YPRES-STADEN RLY.
Steenbeek
Westroosebeke
Goudberg
Passchendaele
Becelaere
Poelcappelle
Gravenstafel
Broodseinde
Zonnebeke
Polygon Wood
Gheluvelt
Zandvoorde
Langemarck
St. Julien
Tower Hamlets
Klein Zillebeke
Bixschoote
Steenstraat
Pilckem
Wieltje
St. Jean
Potijze
la Brique
Zillebeke
Lake
Mount Sorrel
Verbrandenmolen
Boesinghe
Brielen
Vlamertinghe
Dickebusch
Woesten
Elverdinghe

Sketch II.

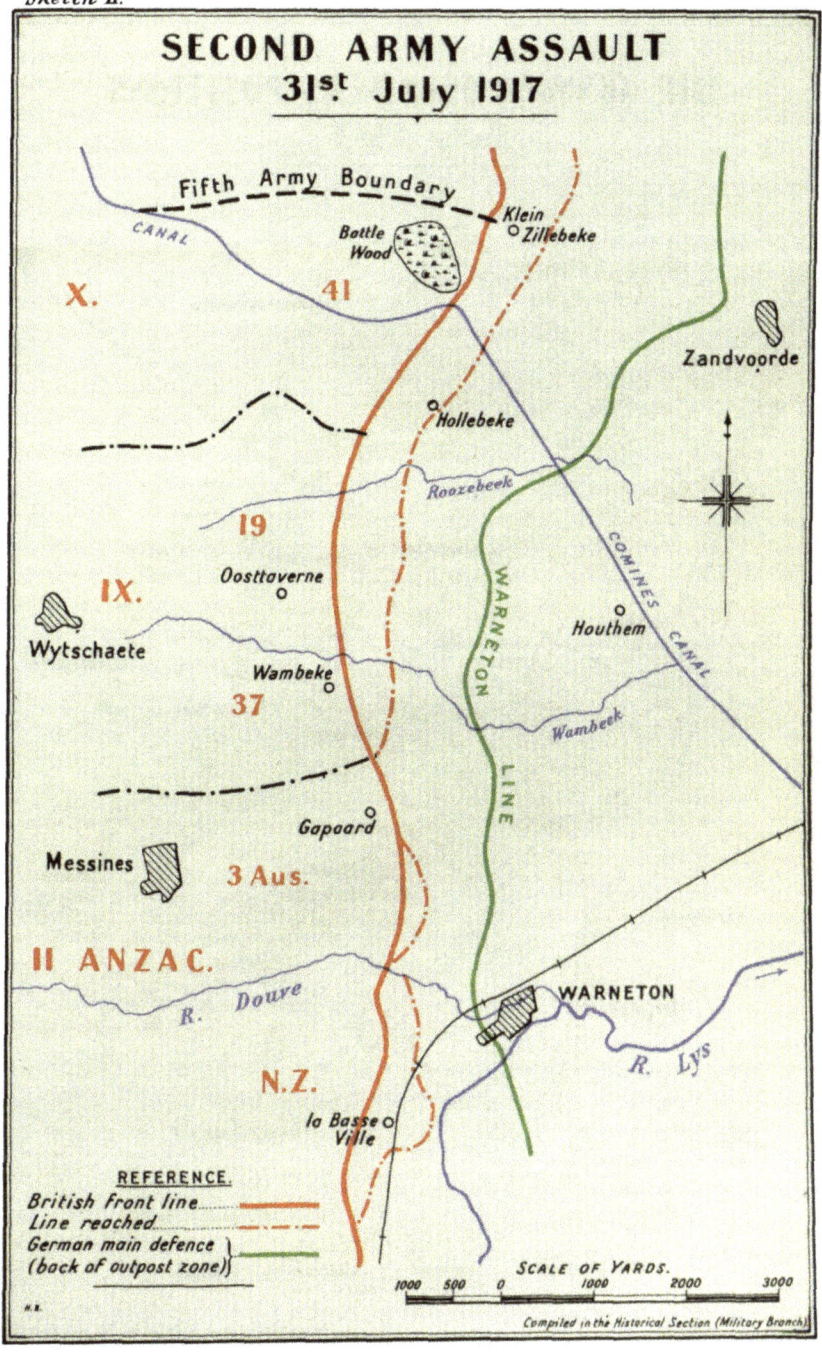

SECOND ARMY ASSAULT
31st July 1917

REFERENCE.
British front line ————
Line reached —·—·—·—
German main defence
(back of outpost zone) ————

SCALE OF YARDS.
1000 500 0 1000 2000 3000

Compiled in the Historical Section (Military Branch)

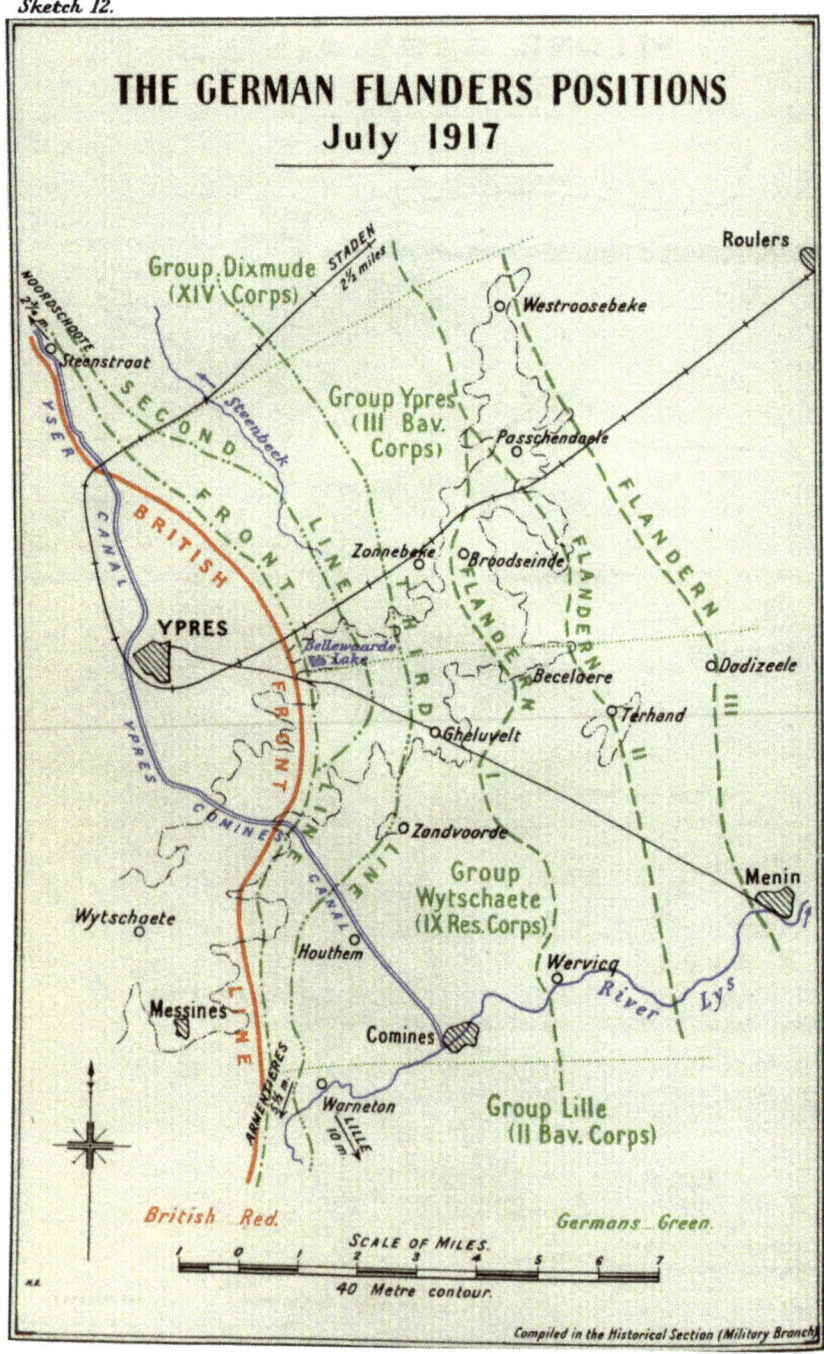

Sketch 12.

THE GERMAN FLANDERS POSITIONS
July 1917

British Red. Germans Green.

Sketch 13

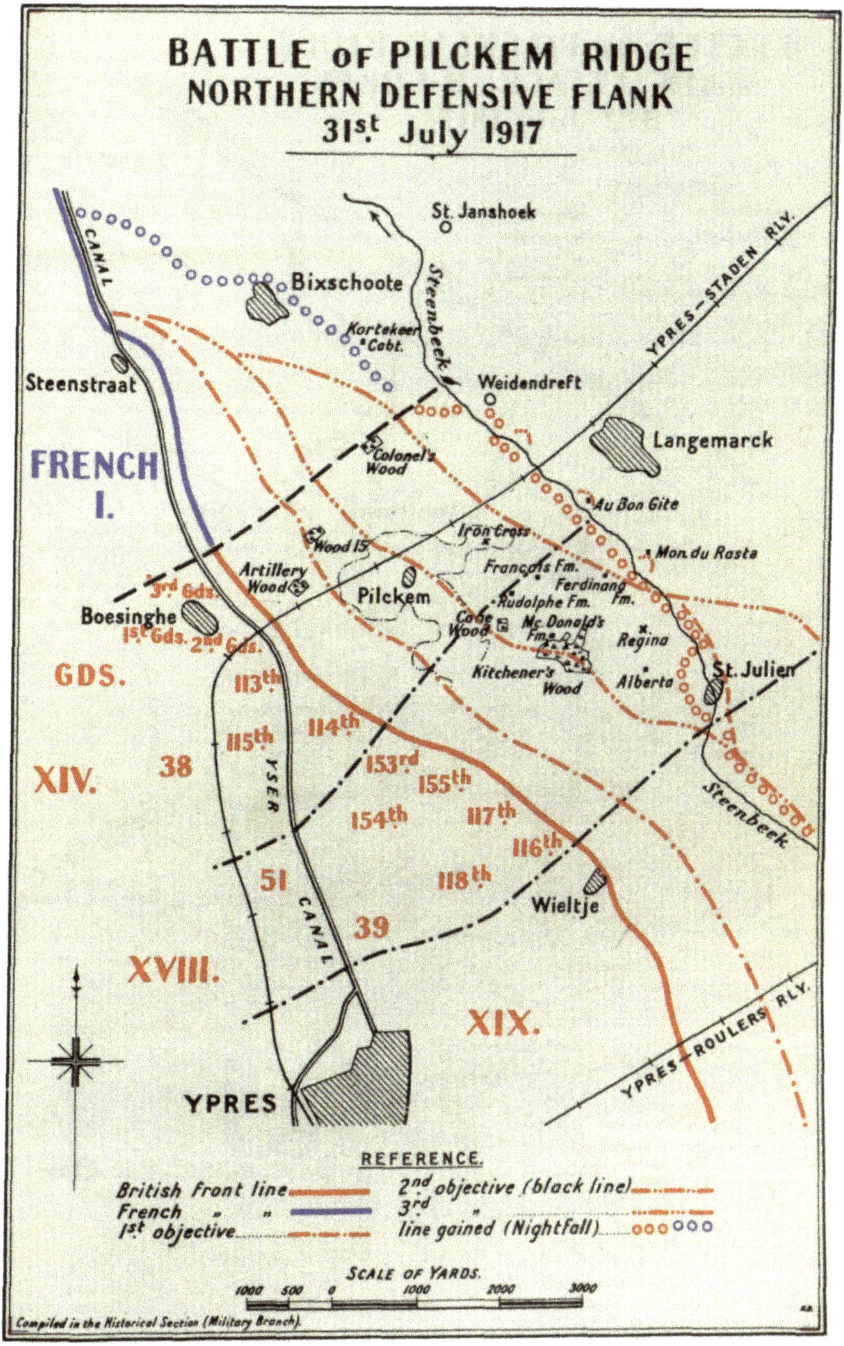
BATTLE OF PILCKEM RIDGE
NORTHERN DEFENSIVE FLANK
31st. July 1917
St. Janshoek
Bixschoote
Kortekeer Cabt.
Steenbeek
YPRES–STADEN RLY.
CANAL
Steenstraat
Weidendreft
Langemarck
FRENCH
I.
Colonel's Wood
Au Bon Gite
Iron Cross
Wood 15
Mon. du Rasta
Artillery Wood
Francois Fm.
Ferdinand Fm.
3rd Gds.
Pilckem
Rudolphe Fm.
Boesinghe
Caddie Wood
Mc. Donald's Fm.
Regina
1st Gds.
2nd Gds.
GDS.
113th
Kitchener's Wood
Alberta
St. Julien
114th
115th
XIV.
38
YSER
153rd
155th
154th
117th
Steenbeek
116th
51
118th
Wieltje
39
CANAL
XVIII.
XIX.
YPRES–ROULERS RLY.
YPRES
REFERENCE.
British front line
French " "
1st objective
2nd objective (black line)
3rd "
line gained (Nightfall)
SCALE OF YARDS.
1000 500 0 1000 2000 3000
Compiled in the Historical Section (Military Branch).

Sketch 14.

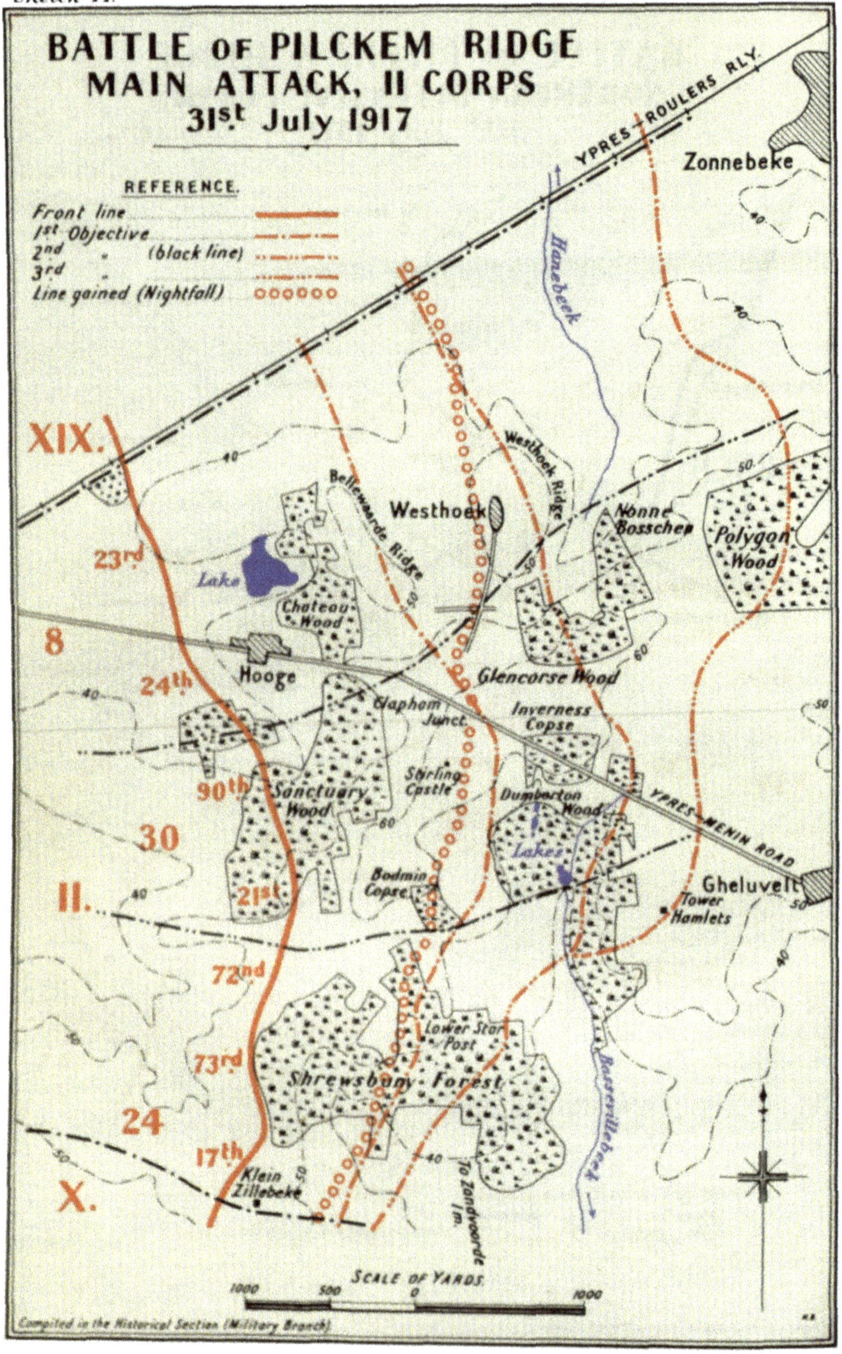

BATTLE OF PILCKEM RIDGE
MAIN ATTACK, II CORPS
31st. July 1917
REFERENCE.
Front line
1st Objective
2nd " (black line)
3rd "
Line gained (Nightfall)
YPRES-ROULERS RLY.
Zonnebeke
Hanebeek
XIX.
23rd
8
24th
90th
30
II.
21st
72nd
73rd
24
17th
X.
Bellewaarde Ridge
Westhoek
Westhoek Ridge
Nonne Bosschen
Polygon Wood
Lake
Chateau Wood
Hooge
Glencorse Wood
Clapham Junct.
Inverness Copse
Sanctuary Wood
Stirling Castle
Dumbarton Wood
YPRES-MENIN ROAD
Lakes
Gheluvelt
Tower Hamlets
Bodmin Copse
Lower Star Post
Shrewsbury Forest
Bassevillebeek
Klein Zillebeke
To Zandvoorde 1m.
SCALE OF YARDS
1000 500 0 1000
Compiled in the Historical Section (Military Branch)

Sketch 15.

BATTLE OF PILCKEM RIDGE
MAIN ATTACK, XIX CORPS
31st. July 1917
REFERENCE.
Front line
1st Objective
2nd " (black line)
3rd "
4th "
Line gained (Nightfall)
Langemarck
Poelcappelle
Passchendaele
Wallemolen
Wolf Farm
Keerselaarhoek
Broodseinde
Zonnebeke
Gravenstafel
Otto Fm.
Dochy Fm.
Aviatik Fm.
Stroombeek
Steenbeek
Triangle Fm.
Springfield Fm.
Winnipeg
Schuler Fm.
Kansas Cross
Hindu Cott.
Pond Fm.
Somme Fm.
Gallipoli
Hill 35
Hill 37
Border Ho.
Spree Fm.
Bank Fm.
Pommern Rdt.
Square Fm.
St. Julien
Zevenkote
Bremen Rdt.
Potsdam Ho.
Frezenberg
Verlorenhoek
Wieltje
Westhoek
Hanebeek
Glasgow Spur
Polygon Wood
YPRES—ROULERS RLY.
YSER—YPRES—COMINES CANAL
YPRES
XIV
XVIII
XIX.
II.
51
39
55
15
SCALE OF YARDS.
1000 500 0 1000 2000
Compiled in the Historical Section (Military Branch).

Sketch 16.

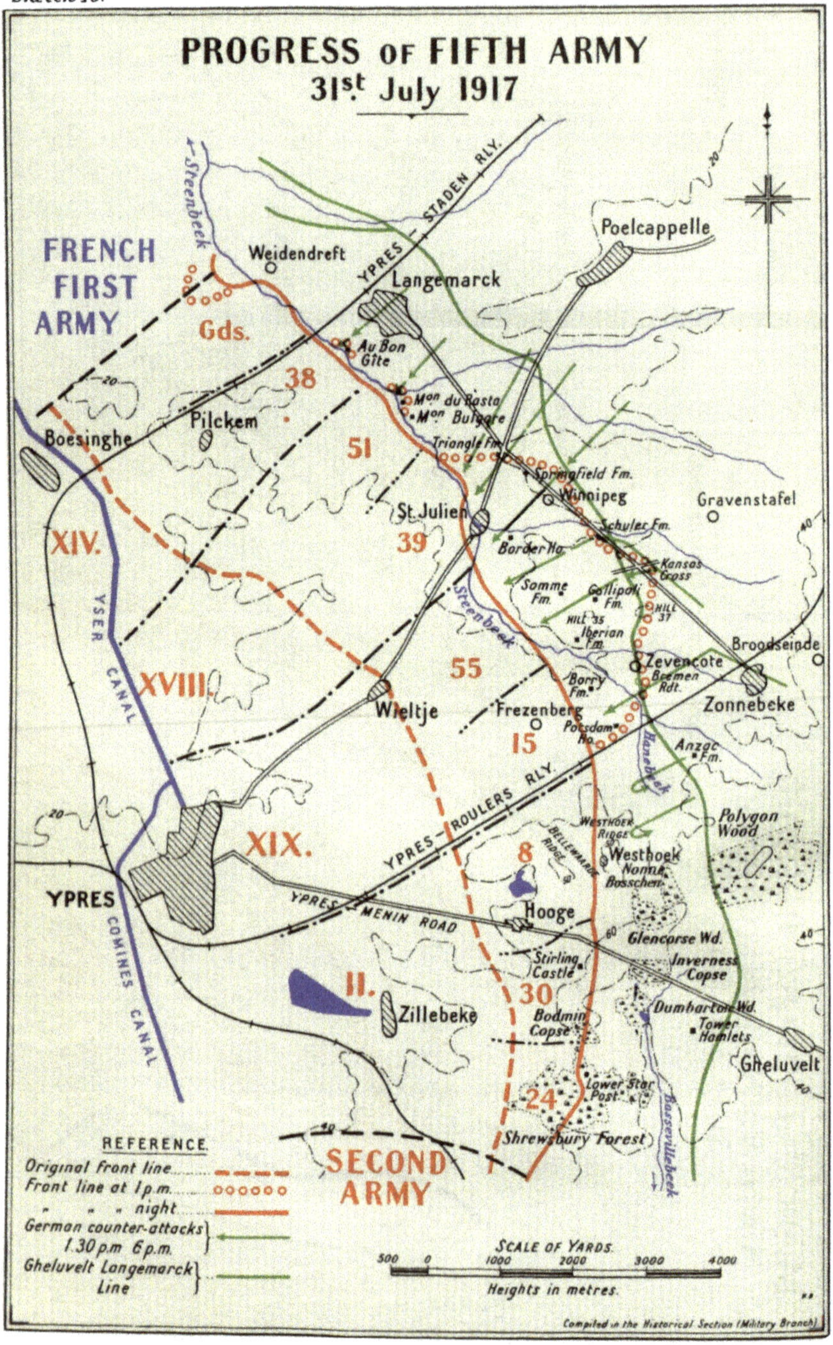
PROGRESS OF FIFTH ARMY
31st. July 1917
FRENCH FIRST ARMY
YPRES – STADEN RLY.
Steenbeek
Weidendreft
Langemarck
Poelcappelle
Gds.
Au Bon Gîte
38
Mon du Rasta
Mon Bulgare
Pilckem
Boesinghe
51
Triangle Fm.
Springfield Fm.
Winnipeg
Gravenstafel
St. Julien
39
Schuler Fm.
Border Ho.
Kansas Cross
XIV.
Somme Fm.
Gallipoli Fm.
HILL 35
Iberian Fm.
HILL 37
YSER CANAL
Broodseinde
Zevencote
Beemen Rdt.
55
Borry Fm.
XVIII.
Wieltje
Frezenberg
Zonnebeke
Potsdam Ho.
15
Anzac Fm.
Hanebeek
YPRES – ROULERS RLY.
Polygon Wood
XIX.
WESTHOEK RIDGE
BELLEWAARDE RIDGE
8
Westhoek
Nonne Bosschen
YPRES
YPRES – MENIN ROAD
Hooge
Glencorse Wd.
COMINES CANAL
Stirling Castle
Inverness Copse
II.
Zillebeke
30
Dumbarton Wd.
Bodmin Copse
Tower Hamlets
Gheluvelt
Lower Star Post
24
Bassevillebeek
Shrewsbury Forest
SECOND ARMY
REFERENCE.
Original front line
Front line at 1 p.m.
" " night
German counter-attacks 1.30 p.m 6 p.m.
Gheluvelt Langemarck Line
SCALE OF YARDS.
500 0 1000 2000 3000 4000
Heights in metres.
Compiled in the Historical Section (Military Branch)

CAPTURE OF WESTHOEK
10th August 1917

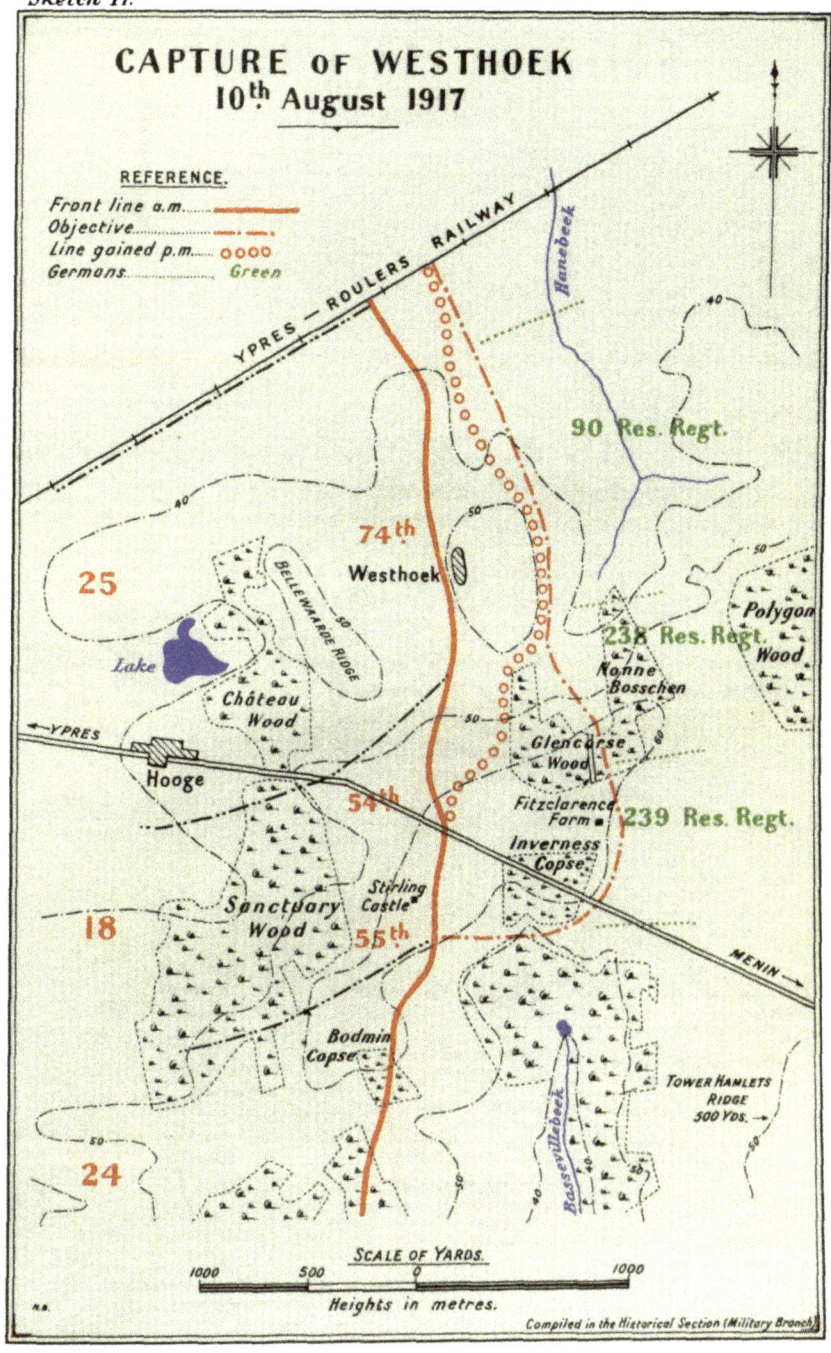

Sketch 17.

REFERENCE.
Front line a.m. ———
Objective — · — · —
Line gained p.m. ooooo
Germans .... Green

Sketch 18.

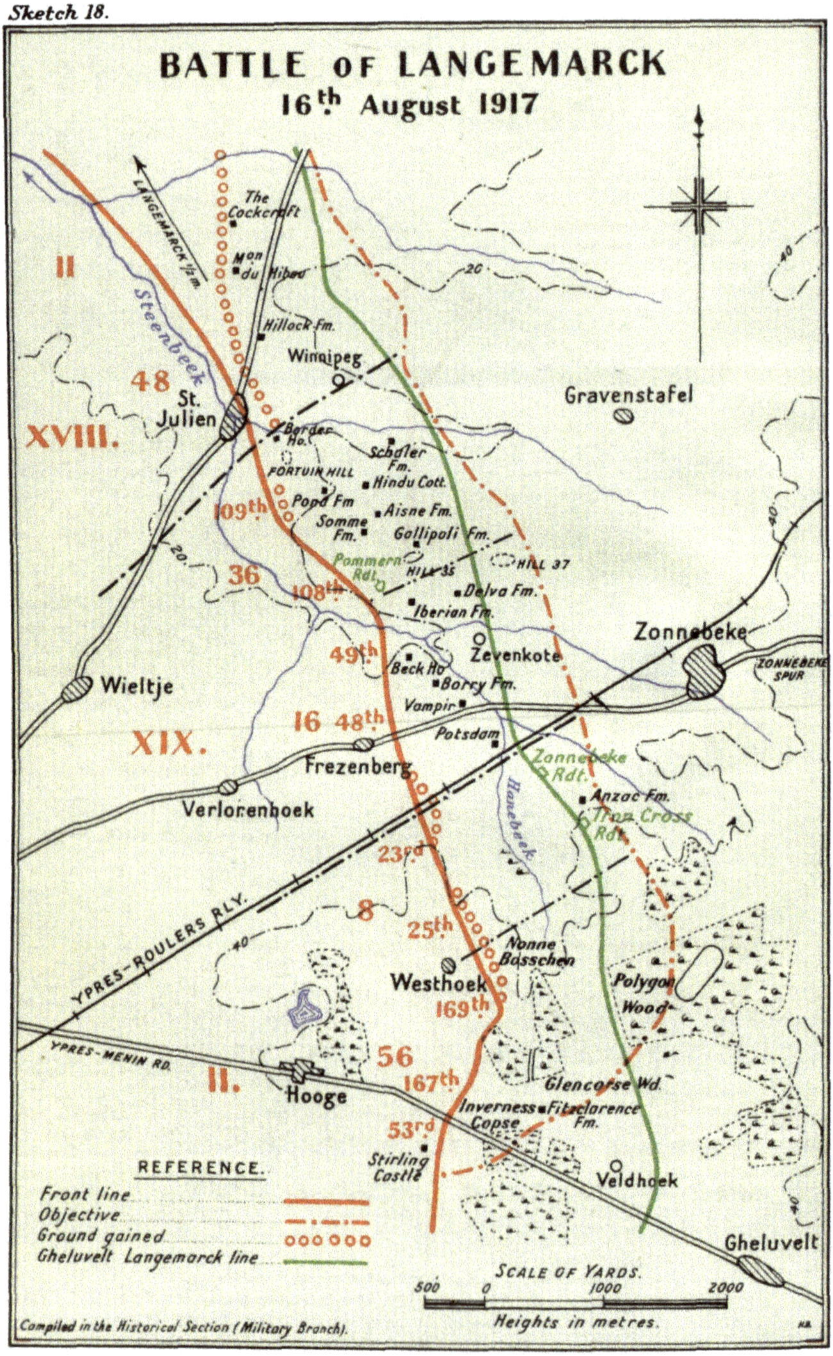
BATTLE OF LANGEMARCK
16th August 1917
LANGEMARCK ½ m.
The Cockcroft
Mon du Hibou
Hillock Fm.
Winnipeg
Steenbeek
II
48
XVIII.
St. Julien
Border Ho.
Schuler Fm.
FORTUIN HILL
Hindu Cott.
Pond Fm
Aisne Fm.
109th
Somme Fm.
Gallipoli Fm.
Gravenstafel
Pommern Rdt.
HILL 35
HILL 37
36
108th
Delva Fm.
Iberian Fm.
Zonnebeke
ZONNEBEKE SPUR
Zevenkote
49th
Beck Ho
Borry Fm.
Wieltje
Vampir
16
48th
Potsdam
XIX.
Frezenberg
Zonnebeke Rdt.
Verlorenhoek
Anzac Fm.
Iron Cross Rdt.
Hanebeek
23rd
YPRES-ROULERS RLY.
8
25th
Nonne Bosschen
Westhoek
Polygon Wood
169th
YPRES-MENIN RD.
56
II.
Hooge
167th
Glencorse Wd.
Inverness Copse
Fitzclarence Fm.
53rd
Stirling Castle
Veldhoek
Gheluvelt
REFERENCE.
Front line
Objective
Ground gained
Gheluvelt Langemarck line
SCALE OF YARDS.
500 0 1000 2000
Heights in metres.
Compiled in the Historical Section (Military Branch).

Sketch 19.

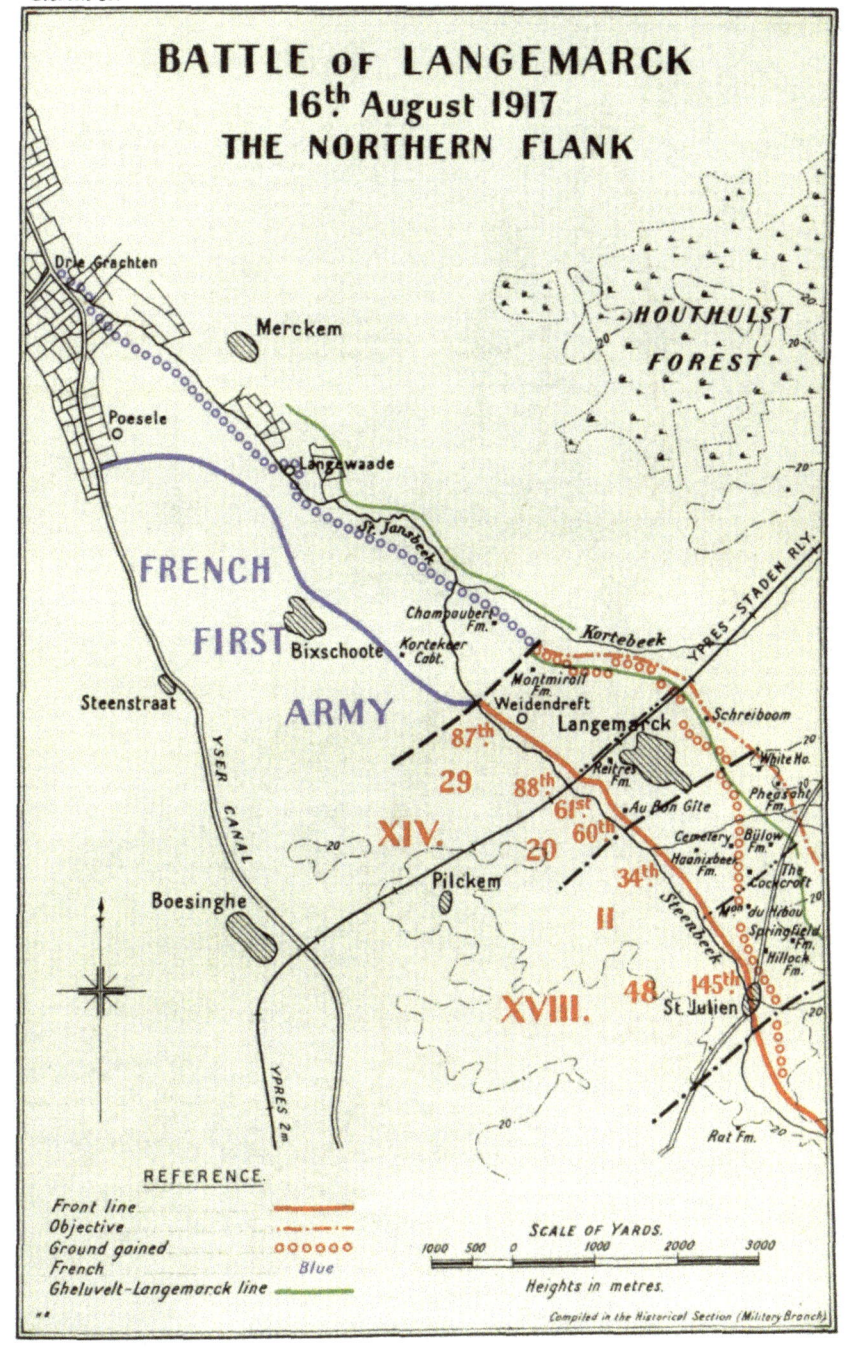

BATTLE OF LANGEMARCK
16th August 1917
THE NORTHERN FLANK

REFERENCE.
Front line — red
Objective — red dashed
Ground gained — red circles
French — Blue
Gheluvelt-Langemarck line — green

SCALE OF YARDS.
1000 500 0 1000 2000 3000

Heights in metres.

Compiled in the Historical Section (Military Branch).

Sketch 20.

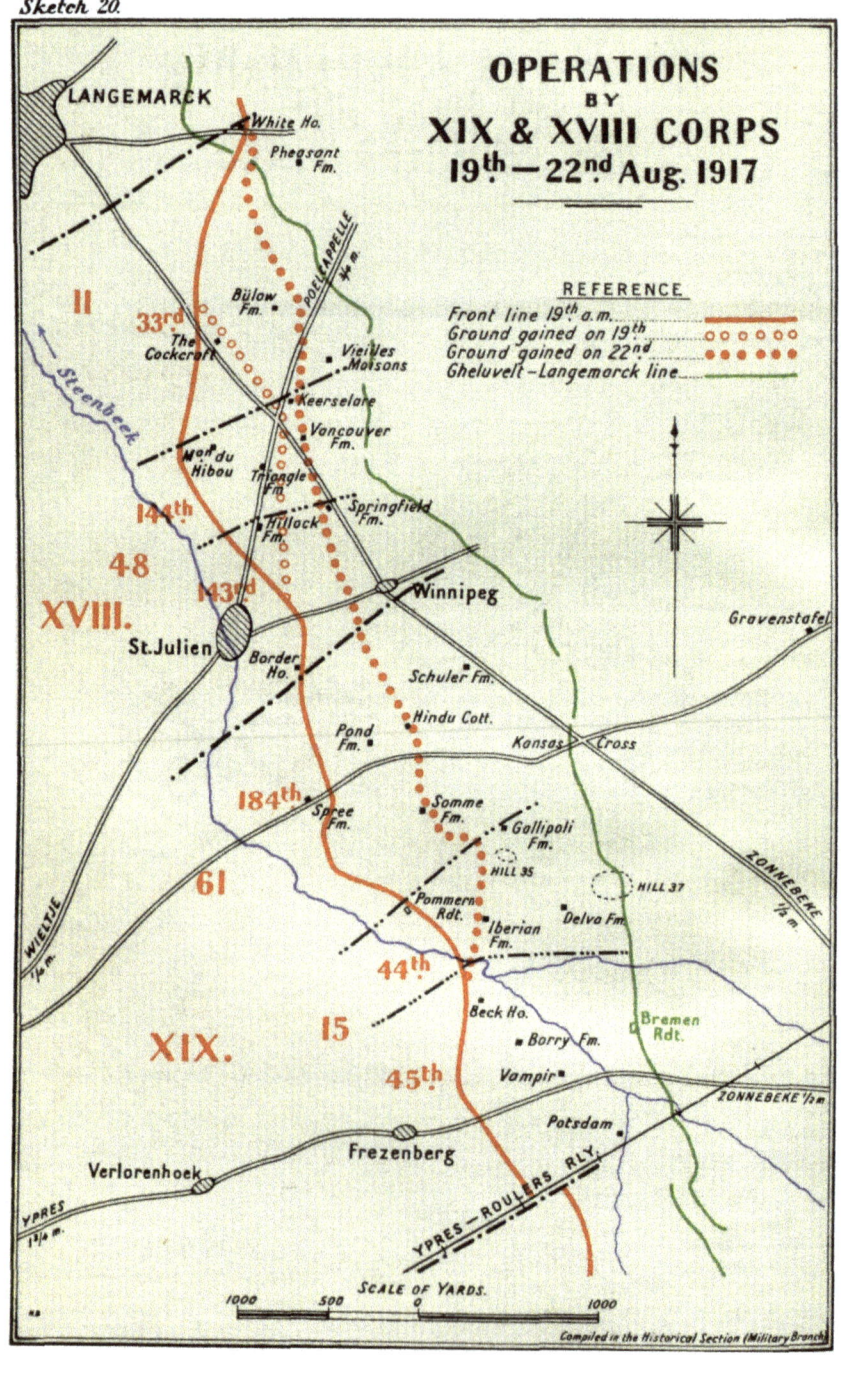

OPERATIONS
BY
XIX & XVIII CORPS
19th – 22nd Aug. 1917

REFERENCE
Front line 19th a.m.
Ground gained on 19th
Ground gained on 22nd
Gheluvelt–Langemarck line

Sketch 21.

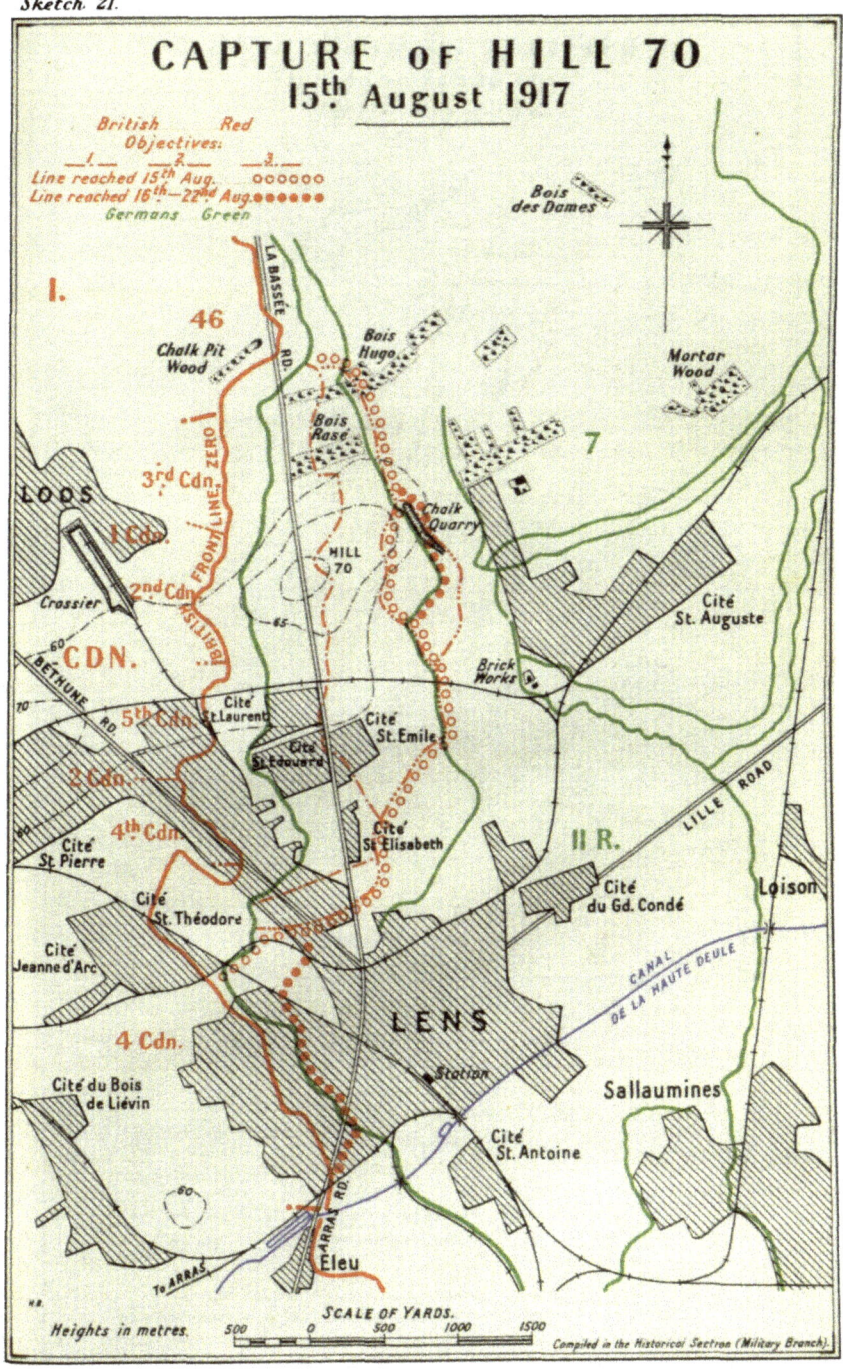

CAPTURE OF HILL 70
15th August 1917

Sketch 22

BATTLE OF THE MENIN ROAD
20TH SEPTEMBER 1917
SECOND ARMY

Sketch 23

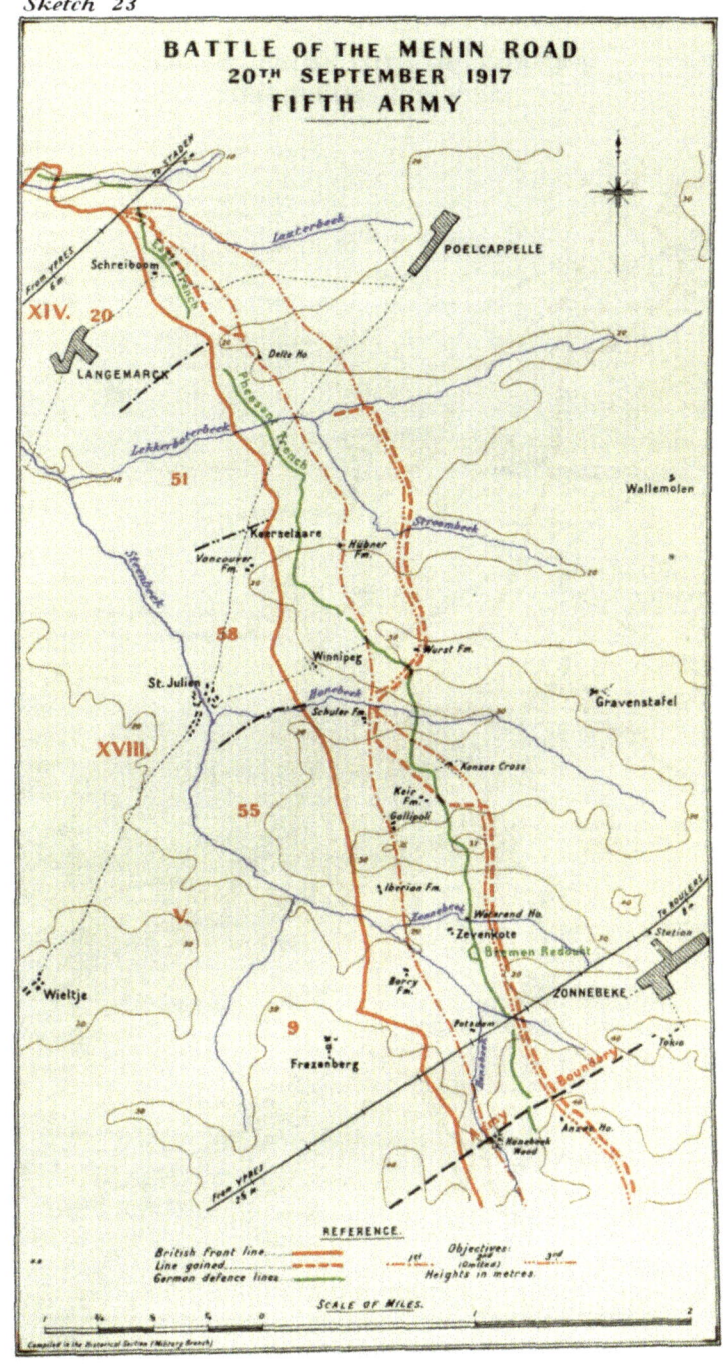

BATTLE OF THE MENIN ROAD
20TH SEPTEMBER 1917
FIFTH ARMY

Sketch 24.

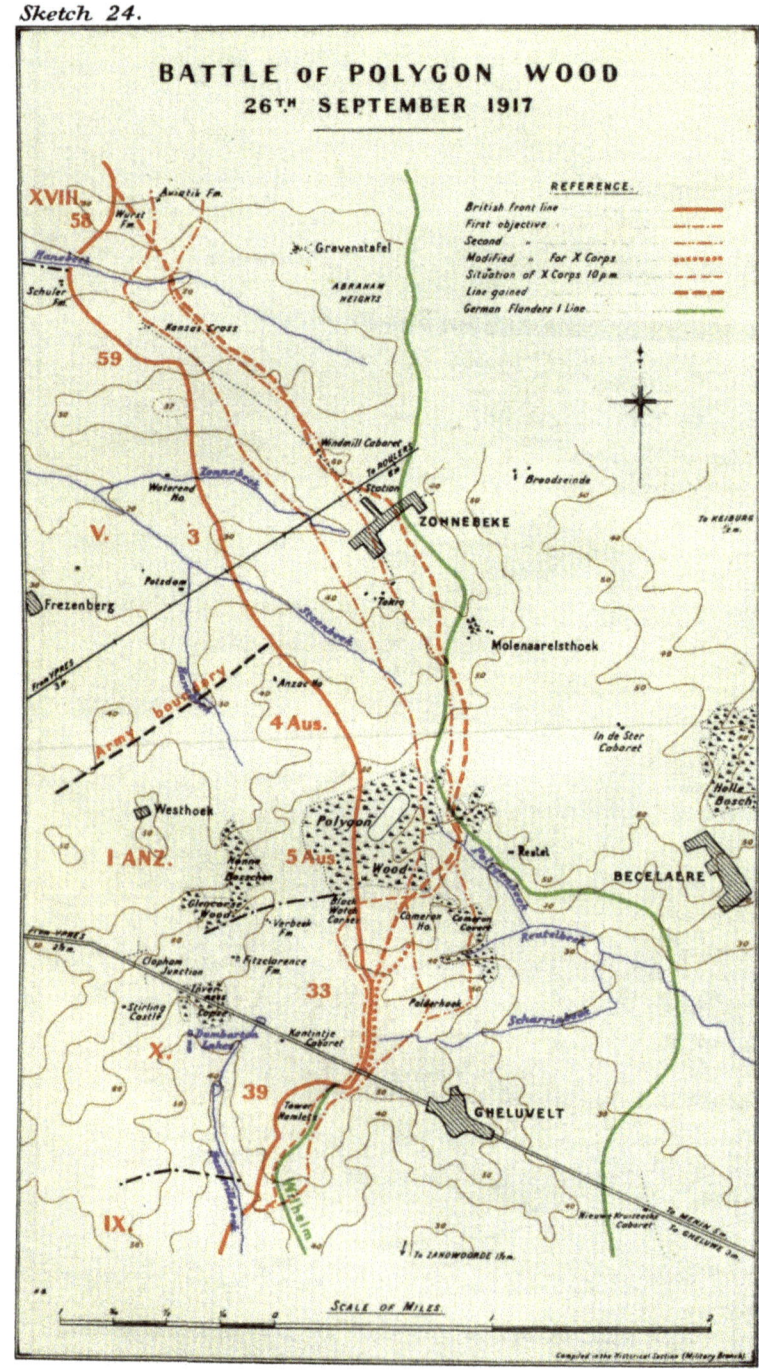

BATTLE OF POLYGON WOOD
26TH SEPTEMBER 1917

Sketch 25.

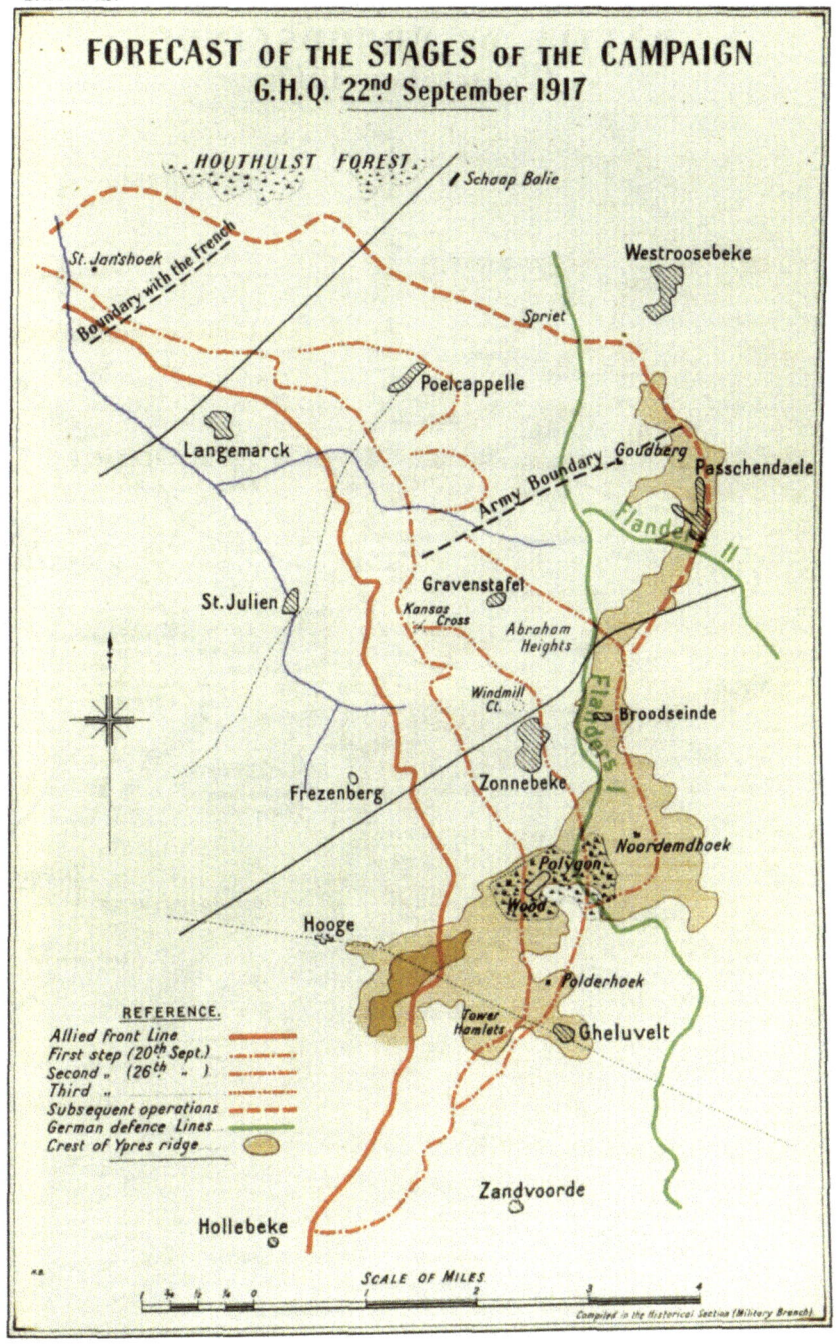

FORECAST OF THE STAGES OF THE CAMPAIGN
G.H.Q. 22nd September 1917

Sketch 26.

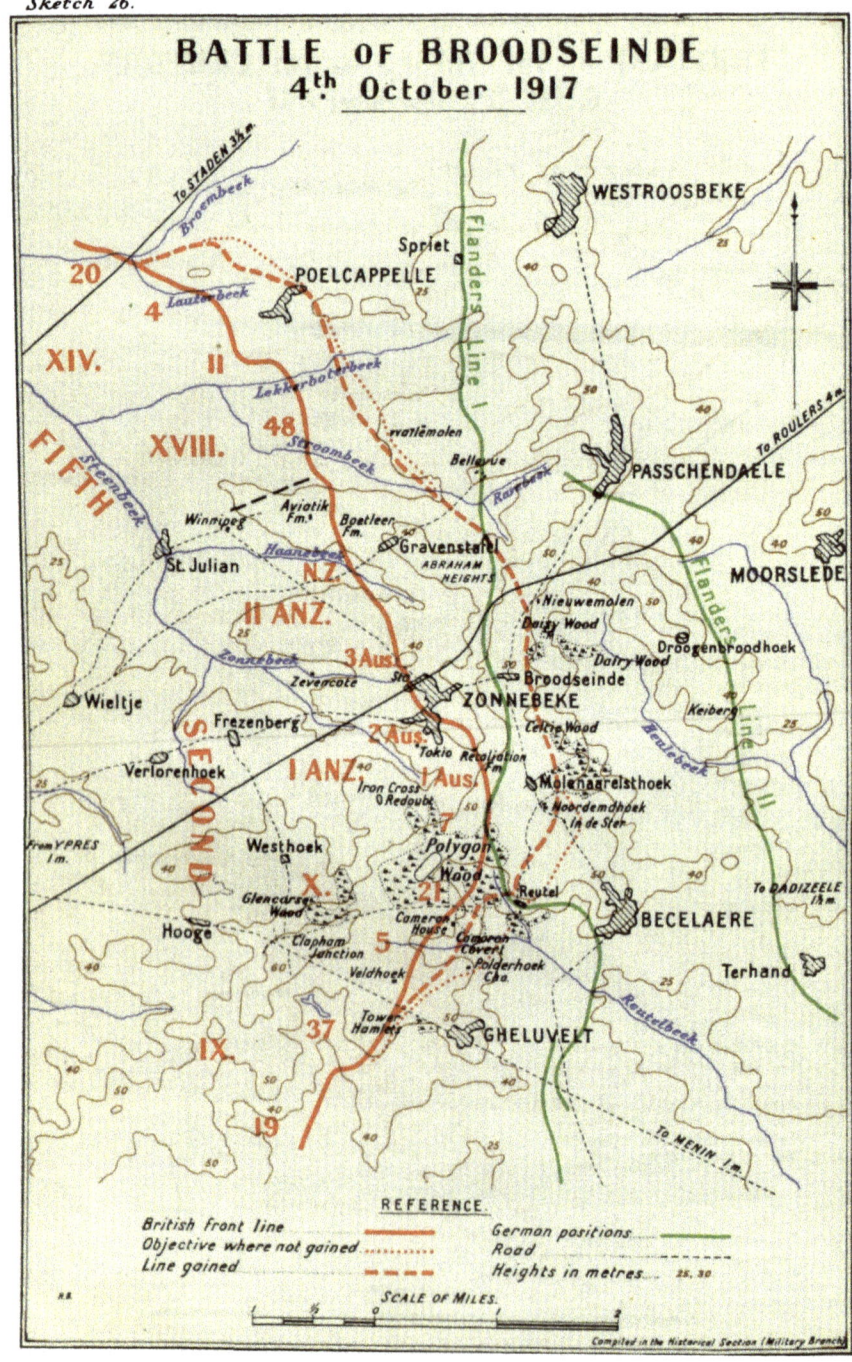

BATTLE OF BROODSEINDE
4th October 1917

Sketch 27.

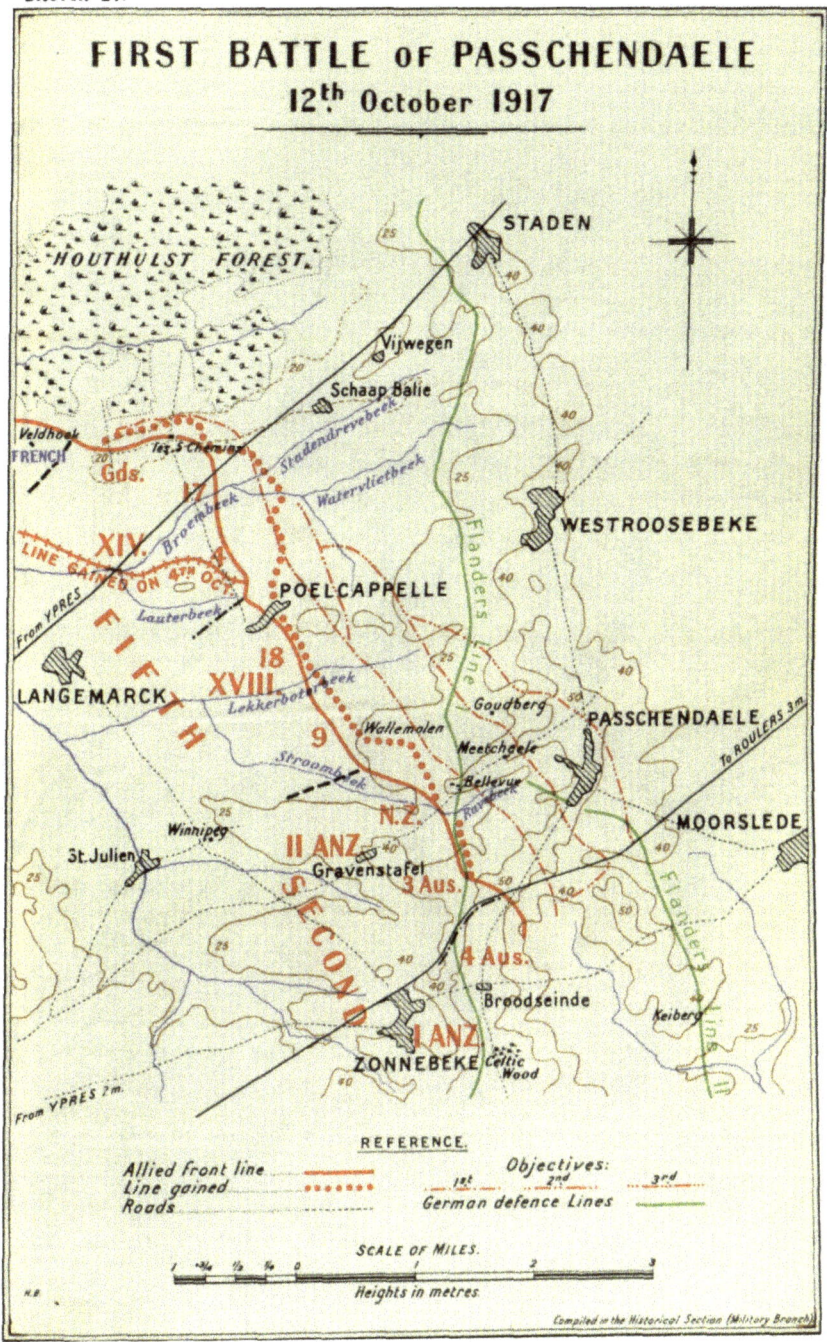

FIRST BATTLE of PASSCHENDAELE
12th October 1917

Sketch 28

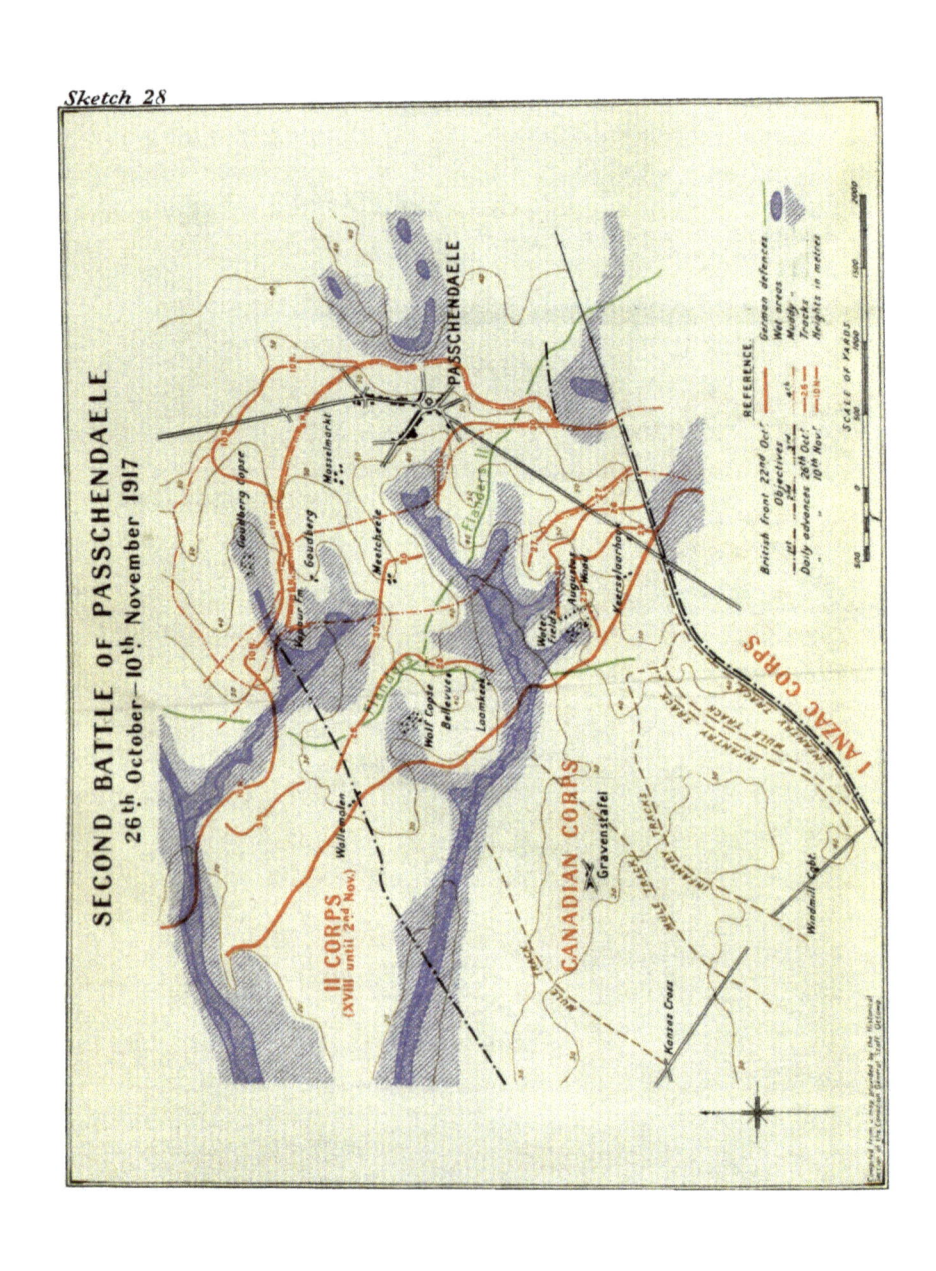

SECOND BATTLE OF PASSCHENDAELE
26th October – 10th November 1917

Lightning Source UK Ltd.
Milton Keynes UK
UKHW02f0003220918
329299UK00008B/189/P